THE INVISIBLE PRESIDENCY

Books by Louis W. Koenig

The Presidency Today (*with Edward S. Corwin*)

The Truman Administration (*editor*)

Public Administration (*with Marshall and Gladys Dimock*)

The Invisible Presidency

Louis W. Koenig

The Invisible Presidency

Holt, Rinehart and Winston
New York

Published, January, 1960
Second Printing, May, 1960

In Canada, Holt, Rinehart and
Winston of Canada, Limited

To Eleanor and Juliana

ACKNOWLEDGMENTS

THIS BOOK would scarcely have been possible without the kindness, encouragement and counsel of many people. I am grateful for the assistance given me by the two living figures treated in this book—Thomas G. Corcoran and Sherman Adams, who during his tenure in the White House facilitated my conduct of interviews there. The sons, daughters, sisters and wives of the central personalities of these pages and of the Presidents they served have been of inestimable assistance. I am particularly grateful to Mrs. Randolph Tucker, daughter of Colonel House; to Mrs. William Loeb, William Loeb, Jr., and the Misses Amelia and Lillian Loeb, wife, son and sisters respectively of William Loeb; to Archibald Roosevelt, son of Theodore Roosevelt; to Mrs. Franklin D. Roosevelt and James Roosevelt, who so graciously tolerated and helpfully answered my questions. In addition, I am indebted beyond expression to an exceptional number of United States Senators, cabinet secretaries, White House officials, stenographers, lawyers and businessmen who knew or worked with the presidential confidants of these pages and gave many hours from their busy lives to the interviews on which I have heavily relied. The more contemporaneous parts of this book were most helpfully discussed with Robert J. Donovan and Roscoe Drummond of the *New York Herald Tribune*, and Turner Catledge, Arthur Krock and James Reston of *The New York Times*.

I am also grateful for the many kindnesses rendered in response to my research needs by Herman Kahn and his excellent staff of the Franklin D. Roosevelt Library at Hyde Park; by Helen MacLachlan of the Theodore Roosevelt Memorial Association; by Howard B. Gotlieb, Librarian of the Edward M. House Collection at Yale University; and by the staffs of the New York University libraries, and the manuscript divisions of the Library of Congress and the New York Public Library.

Throughout the period during which this book has been in progress, I have often benefited from the counsel of my friend and former teacher, Arthur W. Macmahon. The substance of these pages has profited from the suggestions of Lawrence Chamberlain, L. Larry Leonard, Wallace Sayre and Donald Smithburg, and their form has been improved by George Genzmer and the late Glenn Mullin, who read portions of the manuscript. I have benefited from my privileged association with Edward S. Corwin in previous writing on the Presidency. Such scholars as John M. Blum, Hermann Hagedorn, Sidney Hyman and Charles Seymour have given generously of their counsel. Evelyn and Harold Lincoln patiently advised on my researches in the halls of Congress. My colleagues at New York University, Marshall E. Dimock, Ray F. Harvey, Thomas Hovet, Jr., Sterling Spero, Charles C. Thach, and Ellsworth Raymond and Joseph Tanenhaus who read chapters in draft, have provided invaluable encouragement and suggestions. My wife Eleanor and daughter Juliana have borne up heroically and compassionately under the impositions which a project of this nature makes upon family living. Chief among the constant friends of this book are my father, Casper Koenig, and mother, Pauline Graef Koenig.

Finally, it is a pleasure to acknowledge my gratitude for a grant from the Research Committee of the Graduate School of Arts and Science of New York University, without which much of the travel involved in the interviews could not have been undertaken. The Committee also facilitated the typing of the manuscript, which was expertly accomplished by Gloria Kersbergen, Sandra Cacaze, and Carol Tarzian.

July 11, 1959   Louis W. Koenig

CONTENTS

CONTENTS

PROLOGUE

PROLOGUE

AMERICAN HISTORY is customarily written as a saga of great men, especially great Presidents. It needs also to be written—or rewritten—in terms of "second men," the spectral figures who toil influentially in the shadows around the presidential throne. These little-hailed heroes are the President's favorite all-round advisers and assistants. Their invention, zest and talent for achievement have won fame for many a presidential administration and saved others from terrible failure.

Characteristically, favorites flourish with their chief in a relationship which is intensely personal. They are the men a President really trusts and confides in, among the hundreds, even thousands of men at hand who assist in affairs of state. To his favorites, he looks for counsel and inspiration on all sorts of official policy and on private decisions, ranging from whether he should run again to his choice of cigars and poker chips. Favorites do sundry important jobs which the President himself cannot do. Among other things, they function busily as ghost writers and administer programs on which the success of the Administration clearly hinges. They do leg work in far-off places, see people the President doesn't want to see, and make promises he'd like to make but can't. The President being a lonely man, his favorites serve invaluably as cronies. Some, in their fashion, are jesters whose wit and bursts of song relieve the tension and fatigue of the daily grind.

Sometimes these chosen few have been well known, like Harry Hopkins, confidant of Franklin D. Roosevelt, and Colonel Edward Mandell House, confidant of Woodrow Wilson. Others are little known, like William Loeb, Jr. and Henry A. Wise, of the administrations of Presidents Theodore Roosevelt and John Tyler respectively. In general, presidential favorites tend to have their greatest impact in the most critical periods of American history. Such advisers and assistants of yesteryear as Alexander Hamilton, Albert Gallatin and Martin Van Buren, and moderns like Loeb, House, Hopkins and Sherman Adams have played lead roles in practically all of the nation's principal crises. They launched the Republic in the rough waters of the eighteenth century. They were brilliant political strategists in the struggles for Jacksonian democracy and reform. They led in the transformation of the United States from a self-contained power to a world power in the Spanish-American War. They were the Brain Trusters of the ingenious humanitarianism of the New Deal. In the two World Wars, they were at the hub of the war effort and were premier architects of the "better" postwar world. Upon

3

their shoulders have fallen great responsibilities for fashioning America's response to the challenge of communism.

The man whose combined personal influence and formal power made him the principal presidential assistant of recent note—Sherman Adams—was seen by many men, including James Reston, the responsible analyst of *The New York Times*, as having a most extraordinary impact. As Reston envisaged him, Adams exercised more power in the Eisenhower Administration than two other distinguished Adamses, John and John Quincy, did as Presidents combined.

It is the purpose of this book to investigate the doings of the more important presidential favorites, to see what these privileged personalities were like, how they operated, and what they accomplished in their place beside the throne. Certain of these favorites came into their White House careers with a considerable political stature. Others were political nobodies, who emerged from more or less obscure origins and enjoyed the heady upward trajectory to fortune. To get where they did and stay there, favorites as a rule have had to cope with rivals in fierce and subtle struggles, and otherwise excel in the skills which bring success in the palace politics that dominates the invisible Presidency. Inevitably, although not by conscious design, this book is a "How-to-Do-It" book for the ambitious.

By no means are presidential favorites to be identified solely with high-minded effort and constructive achievement. They have on many an occasion been viewed and deplored as timid, mediocre and fawning. They, according to their critics, keep the President ignorant of developing problems by exuding flattery and cultivating atmospheres of spurious optimism. Although the country may be at war or caught up in other peril, the presidential favorite, thinking first and always of preserving the vested interest of his position, may wall off his chief from constructive sources of knowledge and counsel. Favorites have even been accused of playing a sizable part in at least several of the major tragedies which have befallen the Republic in the course of its history. Among these tragedies is the greatest, costliest and most agonizing one of all—the Civil War. Impressive evidence is at hand that in the days just prior to the outbreak of violence between the states, when wisdom could save much and a misstep could lose all, the trickery of an intimate presidential assistant pushed the country into disaster. In a series of ill-advised and ill-fated measures, conducted at the level of conspiracy, he strangled the last major effort of President Abraham Lincoln to avoid the conflict.

Part One

THE INVISIBLE PRESIDENCY

Intrigue, 1861

AT APPROXIMATELY midnight in Washington City, April 6, 1861, two men were hustling up Pennsylvania Avenue toward the Executive Mansion. One, the Secretary of State, William H. Seward, suited that dark and ominous night. Slender and slouching, his voice hoarse and his hair awry, he was completely unlovely. Dominating his rough-cut features and blanched complexion was a rampant beaked nose that Henry Adams said looked like a wise macaw's. Seward's companion, a solid, bearded man, could pass for some god of a murky mythological underworld. He was in actuality, Gideon Welles, the Secretary of the Navy, and an intensely virtuous New Englander.

Engaged avidly in conversation and unmindful of the unreasonableness of the hour, the secretaries passed beneath the Ionic columns of the covered carriageway into the Executive Mansion. An oil lamp flickered weakly in the hallway, bathing in funereal pallor the portraits of each of the past Presidents of the United States which adorned the walls. Edward McManus, the undersized Irish doorkeeper, who dressed in tight black clothes and who said he could "tell from a look" the business and the expectations of a caller, was off duty.

Fortunately for his midnight visitors, the President was still in his study on the second floor working over papers. Greetings were brief; the secretaries came right to the point. Mr. Welles drew from his pocket and in agitated tones read his order of yesterday, April fifth, to Captain Samuel Mercer to assume command of the frigate *Powhatan*, as the flagship of a squadron which was to proceed at once to the relief of Fort Sumter. The fort, as was widely known, was desperately low in munitions and supplies, faced as it was by threat of imminent attack. The *Powhatan* alone of the Navy's three available warships was sturdy enough to convey a relief flotilla of small boats and tugs safely past the batteries of the Confederacy which dominated the shore line of Sumter. Welles bluntly reminded the President that the order at hand had been issued with his approval, and then went to the heart of the matter. How could it be that the President, seemingly interested above all else in the relief of Fort Sumter, had issued orders that nullified those of the Secretary of the Navy, doing so with such secrecy that the Secretary was kept completely in the dark?

Welles, whose information had been telegraphed in by Captain Mercer from the Brooklyn Navy Yard where the *Powhatan* was stationed, recounted what had happened. Early this evening of April sixth, just as Mercer was to commence his critical mission, an officer inferior in rank, a Lieutenant David Porter, boarded the *Powhatan* and demanded that the ship be placed under his command. Porter (whom Welles privately analyzed as pro-Confederacy, "audacious," and "given to intrigues") flaunted an order to that effect signed "Lincoln" and bearing the extraordinary addendum, "Recommended, Wm. H. Seward." The new commander was enjoined to proceed at once with the *Powhatan* not to Fort Sumter, but to a wholly different destination, Fort Pickens, which guarded the Navy Yard at Pensacola, Florida. The order concluded with the emphatic and interesting direction: "Under no circumstance communicate to the Navy Department the fact that she [the *Powhatan*] is fitting out."

Lincoln, listening with his usual melancholic attentiveness, carefully assured the Secretary of the Navy that the policy of relief to Sumter still prevailed. The Mercer-Porter episode was all a mistake, said Lincoln, due to a personal lapse. ("He ought to have been more careful and attentive," Welles later set down his chief's words in his *Diary*.) The last presidential order was to be rescinded; the *Powhatan* was to set out for Sumter as before. When Seward started up in protest, Lincoln chopped him down with the imperiousness he could manage so well when he had to. This little byplay tickled the puritanical fancies of Welles. A New Englander of the old school, he had an established reputation for tracking down the failures of men, never being misdirected by their virtues. "I like to catch people in the suds," he once exuberantly explained his forte, "to fall upon them by surprise, when it is washing day, not only with their hands, but with their temper." Seward's present comeuppance was another titillating instance of iniquity brought to the block.

Although Lincoln offered no explanation at that moment, Welles learned subsequently that on the day the President approved the expedition to Fort Sumter, Seward and Lieutenant Porter had been at work in an office adjoining the President's, preparing a mass of papers for his signature. Carefully planted among these, according to Welles, and timed to reach the President's desk at the busiest part of a very hectic day, was Seward's draft of order to the *Powhatan*. Lincoln, as Seward must have hoped, proceeded to sign the order without reading it.

Seward's motivations in what Welles sized up as a major conspiratorial intrigue were easy to discern. The Secretary of State, as everyone knew, had carved out as his supreme mission in the Administration the prevention of the impending Civil War. Confident of the loyalty of the Southern states and of the fruitfulness of negotiation and compromise, Seward pursued various projects, some clandestinely, others open and aboveboard, to achieve his end. Lincoln, on the other hand, although giving Seward great latitude, and occasionally following his advice, by no means shared the optimism of his Secretary of State. The President was convinced that the Confederate states, already a going political concern of two months, constituted a perduring scheme for independence. It was a basic principle of Lincoln's policy that Sumter must be resupplied and held.

Yet, for all of his tenacity of policy and apologetics to Welles, Lincoln took one step at the extraordinary midnight meeting of April sixth which even to this day is extremely puzzling. He requested Seward to telegraph Porter at once and order him to turn over the *Powhatan* to Mercer. It is curious that the President did not himself issue this order, or, as is equally customary, that the Secretary of the Navy did not do so "at the direction of the President." Almost offhandedly, the President assigned the Secretary of State a function—the issuance of a military command—totally beyond the responsibilities of his office.

Probably the most useful clue to an understanding of Lincoln's peculiar tactics is the fact that William Henry Seward occupied a place in the Administration making him far more than a mere Secretary of State. Day in and day out, Lincoln had come to rely upon his counsel and assistance in an abundance of matters. This very ample influence thrived upon the circumstance that Lincoln's relations with Seward were more personal and satisfying than those prevailing with any other member of the cabinet. Although the Secretary of State had more than his share of bad moments—when he composed brazen memoranda and imperiously presented his resignation— "Seward," as Lincoln observed, "knows that I am his master." The passing skirmishes laid bare a residue of understanding on which both principals were pleased to build. Seward cultivated the habit of dropping in at the Executive Mansion. There was policy to discuss, the day's events to weigh, and it was convenient to read to the Chief Executive in draft the more important letters and messages of the Department of State. Before long, Seward was in the President's office far more frequently—from three to four times a day—than his cabinet colleagues.

Lincoln, for his part, was finding a much-desired respite from official travail by slipping across Lafayette Square to 15th Street in the late afternoon to Seward's hospitable abode. Unwinding his long legs before the gentle heat of the fireplace, Lincoln liked to ruminate on affairs of state, make small talk and swap anecdotes. The voluble Mr. Seward excelled at each turn of the conversation. For problems of the day, his practical imagination easily outreached his more mentally circumscribed colleagues, and his fund of anecdote was rich enough to match even Lincoln's. Seward's personal style was an intriguing blend of urbanity and vulgarity. His chic five-course dinners were the rave of smart capital society and his string of handsome Arabian horses rated a full-page picture in *Harper's Weekly*. But aesthetes like Henry Adams and George Bancroft were repelled by his manner. They found Seward "dirty," "rusty," "low," "profane," "loud" and "offhand." Yet in what other men saw as a studied coarseness was much that appealed to the earthy, log-cabin side of Lincoln. Before long, the President was dispensing with meetings of his cabinet for walks and drives and luncheon dates with his Secretary of State. Seward made the most of these tête-à-têtes by expertly insinuating his advice and by steering into his own hands scores of miscellaneous assignments of the genre of the new order to Lieutenant Porter.

The burgeoning Lincoln-Seward ties were by no means welcomed in every quarter. The cabinet, for understandable reasons, resented them. Senator Stephen A. Douglas complained openly of Lincoln that "Seward has too much influence with him." Horace Greeley's unremitting hostility in the *New York Tribune* was attributed to Lincoln's friendship for Seward. One of the favorite themes of Mrs. Lincoln's frequent didactic sermonettes was to the effect that "Seward draws you around his finger like a skein of thread." So intense was her dislike of the Secretary of State that she issued a standing instruction to her coachman never to enter the street where Seward lived.

In addition to uncommon expertise at ingratiation, Seward commanded a further specialty which Gideon Welles called—with marked restraint— "skill in oblique and indirect movements." Any doubts that one may have of the accuracy of Welles's findings are shattered by the sequel to the midnight meeting of April sixth.

Having the President's mandate to set matters aright between Mercer and Porter, Seward yet that night dispatched a new order to Porter as follows: "April 6, 1861. Give the *Powhatan* up to Captain Mercer. Seward." Although ostensibly in conformance with the President's wishes, this latest draft by Seward, as it appeared under the microscope of Welles's alert suspicions, was actually a clever machination. Lincoln doubtless had intended the order to issue in his name. But Seward, by affixing his own name instead, made the order a nullity. No naval officer *in compis mentis* would heed the instructions of anyone so alien as a Secretary of State in a matter of command. In point of fact, Porter, who was enjoying his faculties fully, did not. When a fast tug managed to overtake the *Powhatan* off Staten Island, Porter refused to accept the new order and steamed off to Pensacola. Even Seward's friendly biographer, George Bancroft, in an account authorized by the Seward family, concedes that he could not be certain that the Secretary's order "was not the result of subtle calculation."

The aftermath to these events is an epic of futility. Porter never did land at Fort Pickens because the local commandant believed that the fort's supplies and munitions were more than adequate, and that Porter, who had a reputation for flamboyance, was really bent on making a grand entrance. After a long fruitless wait in the harbor, Porter pulled anchor and returned to Brooklyn. In the meantime, Fort Sumter, after a heroic defense, fell. The Confederacy, heartened by this initial success, plunged into further violence and the Civil War commenced its terrible course. Seward's cabinet colleague, the shrewd Montgomery Blair, saw a direct incriminating connection between the events just reviewed and the war itself. Until his dying day, Blair contended that had the *Powhatan* not been removed from the Sumter fleet, the expedition would have succeeded "with incalculable effect upon history."

Seward's own motives and purposes, too, came in for analysis by his colleagues. For one thing, it was generally agreed, his "go-easy" policy with the South, despite occasional concessions by Lincoln, was in general eclipse. In one such concession, Lincoln did authorize the negotiations Seward was currently conducting with representatives of the Confederacy (the Crawford Commission) to resolve a number of differences between the North and South. According to both Welles and Blair, Seward was desperately trying to implement a pledge made to the Crawford Commission, in the course of their negotiations, to evacuate Fort Sumter. Getting nowhere in tête-à-têtes with Lincoln to secure his backing, Seward in desperation resorted to the techniques of conspiracy. He sidetracked the *Powhatan*, according to this theory, with the premeditated purpose of making the President's efforts to resupply Fort Sumter a failure. In essence, William H. Seward had used his personal and trusted standing with Lincoln to undermine and destroy the President's very own policy.

Wisdom of the Fathers

THE QUESTION raised by the indiscretions of Mr. Seward—the proper relationship of the President to his counselors—was considered long and hard by the Founding Fathers in creating the Presidency at the Constitutional Convention of 1787. Giving the efforts of the Fathers a special urgency was the haunting remembrance of the late tyrannous rule of George the Third. The Presidency, many a Father feared, might one day fall into evil hands and be perverted into a monarchy as personal and despotic and as easily the prey of dissolute counselors as the unfortunate Briton's.

If Britain bore testament to the monarchical danger in personal government, France warned even more eloquently of the havoc-potential of the other member of the arrangement, the court-favorite.

With the debacles of Europe so freshly in view, the American Founding Fathers pondered ways to preclude any similar misadventures under the new Constitution. Certain Fathers, after searching consideration, seemed to conclude that the most efficient safeguard against personal government was to annex to the Presidency some organ of collective advice. On the theory that many heads are better than just one or two, collective advice was envisioned as more competent and potentially less catastrophic than individual or personal advice. So fervent in their conviction were the espousers of this view, that they rejected the friendly Pinckney Plan which served as the discussion point of the Presidency in the first weeks of the Convention. This plan provided that the Chief Executive was to "have a Right to advise with the Heads of the different Departments as his Council." On the Convention floor, Oliver Ellsworth, one of those most fearful of personal government, proposed to enhance the force of the Council by adding to its membership the President of the Senate and the Chief Justice of the Supreme Court. Another spokesman contended that the Council would have real effect only if it derived from the chief sections of the country, the East, the Middle States and the South. James Madison, the most distinguished exponent of the Council idea, argued that the body should enjoy the initiative to advise the President and to record its feelings. Elbridge Gerry of Connecticut, seconding this view, felt that recorded opinions would make the Council "more responsible" and "enhance confidence" in the Chief Executive.

Yet for all of this respectable opinion, the Council idea was dropped once and for all in the Committee on Style, which developed the first complete draft of the Constitution. The prospect that the venerated Washington would serve as first President had rapidly dampened interest in the Council idea. Indeed, it was now believed that a council of some power might unduly harass the position of future President Washington. Even Pinckney, the original advocate of a council, was arguing that an able council might "thwart" the President. As finally drafted, the Constitution not only failed to provide a council, it did not even call for what is today known as "the cabinet." The document merely provided that the President could require the "opinions of the heads of his departments in writing." Even this sparse language the discerning Alexander Hamilton thought redundant as the right "would result of itself from the office." Other critics of the draft constitution were haunted to the very end by monarchical misgivings. George Mason, in a booming voice of doom, warned that a Presidency without a council was an "experiment" which even "the most despotic governments" had never undertaken. "The Grand Signor himself," he thundered in peroration, "had his Divan." Ben Franklin, Convention sage and ordinarily optimistic by nature, bespoke a melancholic augury for a council-less Chief Executive, seeing only "caprice, the intrigues of favorites & mistresses, etc."

The Legacy of George Washington

GEORGE WASHINGTON, in launching the Presidency under the new Constitution, strove with all his enormous prudence and dedication to disprove the prophets of doom. The great danger to be avoided, he perceived, was "seclusion from information, by too much reserve and too great a withdrawal." In making policy, he accordingly proceeded at the outset of his Administration to consult many and diverse sources in the conviction that the advice and information on which he relied should be broadly representative. Such advice, he believed, would more accurately reflect public sentiment, whose favorable disposition he considered the one true test of the success of his Administration. He therefore recruited his original cabinet from the three principal sections of the country, the North, the South and the Middle States. All through his tenure he was a close student of the grass roots. Inventor of the presidential grand tour, he traveled the length and breadth of the Republic by stage and horse over thousands of miles of crude roads and brambled paths. As a letter writer of uncommon industry, he maintained in the United States and on the continent a voluminous correspondence with private and public individuals remarkably well distributed as to occupation, geography and ideology. His correspondents he regarded as valued *rapporteurs* of local opinion, rumor and discontent, phenomena to which he was almost seismographically attuned. "Your communications without any reserve will be exceedingly grateful and pleasing to me," he wrote a favorite correspondent, David Stuart, brother of the celebrated portraitist, Gilbert Stuart. "I should like to be informed . . . of both men and measures . . . not so much of what may be thought commendable parts, if any, of my conduct, as of those which are conceived to be of a different complexion."

It was also Washington's theory that advice should be competitive. He seldom took one man's word unquestioningly, but checked it against other sources, especially those that were apt to be critical. Adhering to the letter of the Constitution, he very early in his Administration requested written opinions from all his department heads on decisions he was weighing. He skillfully exploited the opportunity of the cabinet, which he created in 1793, for the cross fire of debate. The separation of powers notwithstanding, he liked to check the favorite opinions of his executive subordinates against the judgment of the most distinguished members of Congress and the judiciary. Congressman James Madison was a favorite adviser on numerous matters of Anglo-American diplomacy, on executive appointments and on the President's reply to the formal addresses of the two houses of Congress. One of the busiest presidential consultants was the Chief Justice of the United States, John Jay. The Chief Justice's opinions were tapped on many a foreign policy matter, on troublous questions of constitutional law, and on the political aspects of a projected presidential tour of the New England states. When pulling together passages for an impending address to Congress, Washington requested from Jay, on a characteristically sweeping invitation, "ideas . . . not confined to matters judicial, but extended to all other topics which have occurred, or may occur to you, as fit subjects for general or private communications."

The Administration of Washington witnessed the elimination once and for all of two departments of government widely regarded as potential sources of counsel for the Chief Executive. These were the Senate and the United States Supreme Court. The limitations of the Senate were distressingly revealed one hot summer day in 1789. On that day Washington, accompanied by his portly Secretary of War, General Henry Knox, ventured personally onto the floor of the upper house. The purpose of their extraordinary visit was to secure the advice of the Senators on certain questions which had arisen in the course of negotiations of a treaty with the Southern Indian tribes. After a rather stiff introduction, Washington took over the Vice-President's chair, and to the Vice-President, Mr. Adams, fell the task of reading the executive papers on the matter at hand. He, unfortunately, had no great prowess at elocution. His reading was mumbled, rapid and interrupted by incessant clearings of his throat. In the streets outside, the passing carriages made such a clatter that one alert listener could not master a single sentence of the Vice-President's harassed presentation even after the doorkeeper had obligingly closed the sashes.

The first to break the rather awkward silence which followed this fruitless performance was Senator William Maclay, a brash spirit from Pennsylvania. "The business is new to the Senate," said the candid Maclay. "It is important. It is our duty to inform ourselves as well as possible on the subject." He proposed that discussion of the treaty be put over until another day. Robert Morris, also of Pennsylvania, and very much in agreement with his colleague, offered a resolution calling for reference of the papers to a committee of five Senators. Pierce Butler of South Carolina rose to object. The Senate, he said, was acting as a council, and it was unheard of for a council to refer to a committee. As debate ran on, Maclay became more and more convinced that the President's presence and authority were actually intimidating the Senate and that the treaty papers could be considered effectively only if the legislators discussed them in privacy. In a voice quivering with conviction, he reasserted Morris's resolution. "As I sat down," Maclay later reported the incident in his diary, "the President of the United States started up in a violent fret." With great emotion, he exclaimed, "This defeats every purpose of my coming here." But the Senate in good majority was more impressed with the Pennsylvanian's argument than with the display of presidential temper, and the resolution passed. The President, according to Maclay, withdrew "with sullen dignity." This bitter little scrimmage finished Washington, and for that matter all future Presidents, on such consultations with the Senate. For all of his chagrin, however, Washington evidenced no ill will to his obstructors; he was charity itself. A few days later, the dauntless Maclay had in hand an invitation for dinner at the President's House. He was, he said, "surprised."

The other rebuff, equally enduring in the history of the Presidency, was the refusal of the Supreme Court in 1793 to honor Washington's request for advice on certain complex legal questions arising under the prevailing Franco-American treaty of alliance and friendship. At the time, the French and the British were locked in an ever-spreading war, making the precise obligations of the United States under the treaty of more than passing interest. The cabinet pondered the matter with stormy inconclusiveness, and at the suggestion of the Secretary of State, Thomas Jefferson, Washington turned for counsel to the Supreme Court. In doing so, the President was following the practice of colonial executives who often consulted the judiciary. The United States Supreme Court, however, was not the colonial judiciary. It gelidly declined to co-operate with Washington. In language almost ungentle in abruptness, it ruled that the President's questions were "of national policy and international relations," whereas the judicial branch is limited under the Constitution "to matters arising in the administration of justice."

Washington's ill-starred experience with Court and Senate drove him into deeper reliance upon his executive associates and especially his personal counselors and assistants. But even his system of representative and competitive advice, which he carefully nurtured, was doomed to failure. When confronted with the major issues of his Administration, the cabinet turned into a nightmare of irreconcilable conflicts of principle and personality. In recoil from the tumult, and under the pressure of decision, Washington turned increasingly to a single confidential assistant, Alexander Hamilton. There thus commenced the practice which quickly became an enduring feature of the presidential office.

The Circles

ACTUALLY, most of Washington's successors in office have followed each of the several patterns he delineated in choosing and using advisers and assistants. Modern-day Presidents normally surround themselves with sizable numbers of people endowed with skills, information and convictions, which will give purpose and substance to their administrations. Through counsel and action, these people provide assistance in all realms of the presidential office: in party and legislative affairs, in public relations, in dealings with the executive departments, in every conceivable sort of policy-making. Some of these assistants operate as free-ranging individualities; others function under the aegis of bureaus or committees, or out of positions whose duties and authority are officially designated. It is useful to visualize these various assistants who grace the modern-day White House scene as a series of concentric circles rotating around the President. This bit of symbolism is as meaningful nowadays as in Washington's time, only there are more people and more circles.

At the center of the present-day circles is the White House staff, a modest corps of intimate personal assistants. Appointed without reference to the Senate, the staff are the President's own hired hands who help analyze and refine the problems injected unremittingly into the White House by the busy conveyor belts from the world outside. The staff also manage the considerable office routine of letter and memoranda writing, filing and record-keeping. Until the Administration of William McKinley, the White House organization was, in great degree, paid for by the President out of his own pocket. Those Presidents whose pockets were not so well lined managed to carry their assistants by digging up for them a salaried sinecure in some department. Being left so much upon their own, some Presidents have looked upon their administrative household as a fit place of employment for deserving members of their families. Actually, none other than Washington himself originated this practice and, true to his character, bolstered it with the most respectable standards. In a letter of April 8, 1792, the President invited his sister, Elizabeth Washington Lewis, to dispatch her son Howell to the capital to become a "writer in my Office . . . at the rate of three hundred dollars a year." In return for this princely stipend, which the letter of offer assured "will be punctually paid," Howell would have anything but a lark in the capital. The young man, stipulated the exigent President Washington, would have to be "diligent in discharging the duties . . . from breakfast until dinner, Sunday excepted."

Over the years, the White House staff, which was not officially designated as such until 1939, grew slowly. Even as late as Herbert Hoover's day, it numbered only three secretaries, a military and naval aide, and two-score clerks. F.D.R. added six administrative assistants and, chiefly because of the upsurge of White House mail to an average 3,000 letters a day from 400 in Hoover's time, considerably expanded the clerical force. President Truman superimposed another layer on the growing structure by creating "The Assistant to the President." In Eisenhower's day, Sherman Adams, who bore and fully lived up to this title, managed a White House staff of approximately 250 employees, including the traditional press and appointments secretaries, the clerical force—many of whom date from the somnolent days of paper cuffs and roll-top desks—and a small galaxy of specialists in atomic energy, disarmament, foreign trade and aid, national security and the like.

Another major circle comprises the top officials of the Bureau of the Budget, the National Security Council, the Council of Economic Advisers and the Office of Defense Mobilization. More specialized than the White House staff, all of these agencies have been created by act of Congress since

World War II, except the Budget Bureau which Congress set up in 1921 to prepare the executive budget. Over the years, the Bureau has taken on other duties, principally the clearance of legislation and management improvement in the Executive Branch. The National Security Council, consisting of the President, the Vice-President, the Secretary of State, the Secretary of Defense, the Defense Mobilization Director and anyone else the President chooses to invite, is a channel of collective advice on national security policy in all its aspects, from the military budget to tanks for the Pakistani. The Council of Economic Advisers watches the nation's economic pulse and prepares the President's economic report to Congress, and the Office of Defense Mobilization has bulging files of mobilization plans for the home front for every conceivable kind of war from the Korean "police action" to the dread all-out upheaval. Each of these presidential agencies is equipped with staffs of civil service experts who collectively constitute a sizable bureaucracy. The more than one thousand employees involved occupy 134,000 square feet of floor space in two buildings in addition to the east and west wings of the White House. Budget-wise, this organization represents an outlay of approximately five million dollars a year.

Another circle comprises the heads of the departments, who advise the President individually, and who collectively are the cabinet. Founded in 1793, when President Washington convened his department heads to consult on American neutrality in the Franco-British war, the cabinet has never developed as a source of advice upon which the President continuously relies. John Adams's cabinet was such a hotbed of conspiracy against his well-being that he regularly fled the capital for months on end for the sanctuary of Quincy, Massachusetts. Jefferson didn't consult the cabinet on the Louisiana Purchase, nor did Lincoln on the Emancipation Proclamation. Andrew Jackson hired and fired at least four cabinets in his remorseless quest for one that he could work with and ended up doing most of his consulting in other quarters. Woodrow Wilson and Franklin D. Roosevelt rarely met with their cabinets in the two World Wars. When F.D.R. did get around to convening his cabinet, he preferred to use it as a captive audience before which he rehearsed his favorite jokes and stories. Other Presidents have excelled equally in their strangulation of achievement in their cabinets. Calvin Coolidge, a master of brevity, whose talent was a contagious and effective form of social paralysis, specialized in cabinet sessions of a mere fifteen minutes duration. The significance amassed by Herbert Hoover's cabinet is gauged in the comment of one qualified observer that it constituted the most august body of "yes men" ever assembled in United States history.

The cabinet's influence has been minimal for various reasons. No President ever really picks his cabinet except in a relative sense. Impersonal factors such as geography, politics and aptitude operate in the selection of many, if not most, cabinet members. All such factors militate against a relationship of confidence and trust. Presidents like Jackson, Wilson and Franklin D. Roosevelt, it is clear, were temperamentally unattuned to group deliberation. Hard-driving, quick in creative instinct, they chafed under the aimlessness and feet-dragging of cabinet discussion. Lurking in not a few cabinets have been industrious would-be Presidents, whose self-ambition so transcends their loyalty to their incumbent chief, that their advice and assistance become highly suspect. President James K. Polk was so impressed with the enormity of this problem that he required from all his secretaries a pledge in writing that for the duration of their affiliation with his Administration, they would not advance their future presidential candidacies. Even this precaution did not prevent the ranking member of the cabinet, the Secretary of State, James Buchanan, from openly and flagrantly maneuvering for his party's designation in 1848.

In the world outside the Executive Branch lie numerous circles to which the President may resort for succor. He may consult members of Congress (as Lincoln occasionally did Senator Orville Browning, and William Howard Taft often did Senator Elihu Root); party leaders (especially national-committee chairmen like the ubiquitous Leonard Hall in the Eisenhower Administration and Mark Hanna, financial godfather and tactical mastermind of the extraordinary career of William McKinley); personal friends (Mr. Truman's former haberdashery partner, the adroit Eddie Jacobsen, played a significant backstage part in the making of American policy toward Palestine); and the leaders of industry, labor, agriculture and other major private interest groups. (It is a sacred principle of contemporary political etiquette that all such groups must be represented on the various presidential study committees whose impact in the twentieth century has been considerable. The report of one of these committees, for example, the President's Committee on Civil Rights, headed by Charles E. Wilson of General Electric, was a document of such eloquent rationality that it, as much as anything, prompted Truman to take a militant course.)

It is a matter of basic significance in the association of the President with his several circles of advisers and assistants that the White House is, as Benjamin Harrison once put it, "an office and a home combined." In Harrison's time, the whole executive staff was located in the White House proper on the second floor where the family bedrooms were situated. Five of these bedrooms were devoted to offices for the clerks and to a cabinet chamber. From these office-bedrooms, clerks would emerge into the corridors, where members of the President's family had to pass in going from their bedrooms to their baths. "It was all just like one family," one of Harrison's staff summed up the situation. Although an office wing was constructed in 1902, and another in 1939, in which many, but by no means all

White House employees are located, Benjamin Harrison's dictum is virtually as true today as it ever was. Day in and day out the White House is a commingling of cooks and clerks, butlers and secretaries, doormen and staff economists. In Woodrow Wilson's Administration, members of his domestic staff and even of his family almost invariably preferred to channel their household matters to the President through one of his leading policy advisers, Colonel E. M. House. This interlocking tenancy is productive of an informality which rubs off on to the business side of the White House. Advisers and assistants have, on the whole, easier access to the President and ordinarily work in a more flexible atmosphere than befalls the counselors of most chief executives the world has known.

The thrown-togetherness of the President and his subordinates does not always work to the advantage of both. The half-home, half-office aspect of the White House has resulted in administrative facilities that are grossly inadequate for the scale of present-day White House operations. Desks are jammed into rooms with a density that would drive an efficiency engineer mad, and hallways are lined with filing cabinets, tables and sundry officeware. George Allen, a leading adviser and assistant to President Truman, found that it was weeks before he acquired a desk all his own, and with telephones nearly as scarce just after World War II, it is not surprising that he forsook the White House, finding that he could work more efficiently out of the pay booths of drugstores and hotel lobbies.

The Inner Circle

THE SEVERAL circles revolving around the President do not, like the heavenly bodies, follow a fixed and settled course. If anything, their course is fluctuating and erratic. A given circle which today is remote from the President, later may come into closer, more influential proximity. The Bureau of the Budget, for instance, in the earlier years of the Administration of President Truman, had at best only a modest role in executive policy-making. Even this role was progressively shrinking at such a rate that by the middle of Truman's first term, some of the older and wiser heads among the Bureau's officialdom feared that the agency might soon reach a point where it would be little more than a compiler of data and a keeper of records, the more significant initiatives passing to other circles. But suddenly the clouds rolled back when Truman one day concluded that the Bureau's top officials were not ivory-towered budgeteers, as he seems to have suspected, but honest-to-goodness sophisticates of practicality. With this fortunate shift of presidential attitude, the Bureau was restored to something of the far-reaching influence it knew in its heyday under Franklin D. Roosevelt.

Now and then a President comes along who removes himself for lengthy interludes not only from one, but from all the circles of advice. His policy-making in such isolation is from beginning to end a perilous adventure in self-reliance. William Howard Taft, one of the most self-contained men ever to occupy the White House, is a case in point. According to his biographer, Taft consulted no one in approving the Payne-Aldrich bill, a major decision of his Administration. Payne-Aldrich was a super-protectionist law which withered the real incomes of the farmer, laborer and white-collar classes and did incalculable harm to Taft's later political fortunes. A competent adviser might have cautioned this normally judicious President on the pitfalls of the provisions which Taft himself confessed were "just like Choctaw to a man who is not an expert." Another phase of Taftian self-containment was his habit of writing his own speeches, spurning all assistance. As a result, he perpetrated in his time several terrible faux pas. In a campaign speech in Rhode Island, he called the senior United States Senator of the state, Nelson Aldrich, "the ablest statesman in financial matters in either House." These words were spoken just after Aldrich had conjured up sky-high schedules of imposts and excises that fell with crushing effect upon New England trade. Blundering on into Massachusetts, Taft hailed the Commonwealth's Senator Murray Crane as "a worthy representative" in Washington. What made these words singularly ill-chosen was the fact that Crane had fallen out with the regular party organization. The organization promptly retaliated by becoming conspicuously unenthusiastic for Mr. Taft. It has been estimated that these slips, as much as anything else, cost Taft New England in the election of 1912.

Most Presidents, however, do not indulge in Mr. Taft's catastrophic self-sufficiency. They not only utilize the various established circles of advisers, but see fit to develop a further circle—an inner circle—to assist in their most important and confidential decisions. This inner circle is more informal and less visible than all the others. Its "membership" derives from the various official circles and even from sources wholly outside the government. A listing of President Eisenhower's "inner circle," for example, would surely have included Sherman Adams from the White House orbit; George Humphrey, the Secretary of the Treasury, and the President's brother, Milton, whose occupational moorings have been at the Pennsylvania State and Johns Hopkins universities for the greater part of the Eisenhower Administration.

Admittance to the inner circle is strictly a matter of the President's own private and personal choice. The few who are called normally present an amalgam of personality and philosophy which stirs a special responsive chord in the President. Inner-circle members, unlike their remoter colleagues, have readier access to their Chief Executive, and are habitually looked to for advice not merely upon some special area of affairs but on all sorts of matters. To those who seek to enter it, the inner circle has strong allurements. The few who are chosen are most apt of all our citizenry to be on hand for those enthralling moments of presidential decision-making when history is really being made. A department administrator who gains entree to the cherished circle knows that his achievement numbers among its rewards the best protection that influence can buy not only for the security of his own career, but for that of his department, its policies and its programs, as well. For it is one of the uglier facts of official life that the business of most departments is coveted by alert, rapacious empire-builders who are to be found in any presidential administration.

It is not surprising that entree to the inner circle is a desideratum, an object of normal human appetite. The President's favor is unremittingly courted, positions are jockeyed for, ideas are pressed. The prizes sought and the ambitions at work, in their combined effect, make the environment of the Presidency something like that of a fortress under siege. The bewilderment and the strain which this ceaseless harassment can produce upon the Chief Executive was once revealed with clinical frankness by Grover Cleveland. Poor Cleveland had hardly taken office when he was beleaguered by hordes of politicos and plain citizens who, after wishing him well on his new job, invariably urged upon him some favorite policy or project. The behavior of even his oldest and most valued friends underwent a mystifying transformation. "It is hard to discover their springs of action," mused Cleveland at the close of an especially hard day, "and it seems so distressing to feel that in the question as to who shall be trusted, I should be so much at sea. I wonder if I must . . . face the difficulties of a new official almost alone."

Life in the inner circle is one of the riskier forms of political existence. The tides of preferment are constantly shifting. Some Presidents methodically limit the duration of membership by transferring their reliance from one adviser or chosen group to another, scrupulously preventing any one individual or combination from amassing too much power. Turnover in the presidential *haut monde* is likewise accelerated by the failures and fiascoes of policy. Those members of the inner circle whose misfortune it is to be identified with a policy which has gone awry, with no little embarrassment to the Administration, are usually among the first on the ensuing casualty list.

The workings of this grisly procedure can be detected in certain revisions which quietly occurred in President Truman's entourage following the Congressional elections of 1946. Of the inner circle as it was then constituted, the member who had perhaps the biggest stake in the outcome of these elections was George E. Allen. A jolly, elephantine man endowed with lots of horse sense, Allen was a major policy influence as well as social favorite. He moved freely in White House affairs and, as much as anyone, devised the campaign strategy for the 1946 Congressional elections. In top-level party powwows, he successfully carried his point that the President should play a minimum part in the campaigning. Mr. Truman accommodated by sequestering himself in the White House while the candidates battled. When on occasion the injection of the presidential voice into the clangor of the campaign seemed necessary, there were radio broadcasts of recordings not prepared by Truman, but selected from the oratorical archives of the late F.D.R. For Allen was convinced that the residue of pro-Democratic feeling developed by the late President among the voters, and the current economic prosperity the country was enjoying, made a Democratic victory a foregone conclusion. Mr. Truman's untried oratory was clearly superfluous, and "People just don't vote against prosperity," Allen kept chanting. Then came Election Day and the roof fell in. For the first time in sixteen years, the Democrats lost control of Congress. An immediate result of this calamity was that Mr. Allen was seen less and less at the White House. More and more of his time was put in at the World Bank on H Street, where he had a desk and an assignment which hitherto he had treated as altogether minor.

The Favorite

EVEN IN the inner circle, there are gradations and distinctions. Certain of its members from time to time become conspicuously closer to the President than all or most of their select colleagues. These favored members have freer access to the President. They see him more; their dealings have greater scope; on certain matters they alone may be consulted. A Harry Hopkins, for example, moves in an almost exclusive proximity to Franklin D. Roosevelt in World War II. Colonel E. M. House flourishes only less slightly with Woodrow Wilson; and Alexander Hamilton, in certain seasons, goes pretty far toward monopolizing his chief, George Washington.

The relationship of these privileged characters with their chief is intensely personal. They are his father-confessors and his rock of comfort. He harbors them in illness and is best man at their weddings. They reside in the White House or have an office there, or hover about the place so much that both these accommodations are eminently sensible. The range of business covered by these intimate advisers is virtually as broad as the Presidency itself. They are extensions of the President's personality, his eyes and ears. They keep his sights on the big objectives and delve brashly into all sorts of matters—foreign, domestic and military alike. To his most intimate advisers the President is especially prone to turn when he doesn't want to consult his cabinet or his party, but seeks to make major innovations of policy with a minimum of obstruction and a maximum of constructive assistance. Working ordinarily as "lone eagles," these advisers are free from the bane of cabinets and committees which, in their quest for the lowest common denominator of agreement, are apt to emerge with a pallid image of what the President needs and wants.

The President entrusts his most intimate advisers with missions of great moment to himself personally and to his Administration in general. They are his emissaries to the national nominating conventions of his party, where they are apt to convey the most significant of all political intelligence —whether he will run again and his preferences for a running mate. They venture abroad to take up affairs of state with foreign rulers. They are in the thick of rugged campaigns to get key Administration measures through Congress. They are ghost writers for the President's major addresses and other statements of high significance. Because they know his mind so well, they excel at putting the right words into his mouth.

Some presidential favorites go even further afield. The more acquisitive of these spirits strive mightily to annex operating authority unto themselves and to build up well-defined areas of policy responsibility. Merely pouring counsel into the ears of one's chief and doing chores around the White House, these careerists seem to find, is a pretty lonely business. It can even be downright futile if one must depend upon some fellow official or department to do the acting. Quite understandably then, an aggressive favorite such as Harry Hopkins lost no time in taking under wing the immense Lend Lease program in World War II. Amos Kendall, the trusted adviser of Andrew Jackson, personally conducted what in his time were the equally vital negotiations for the transfer of the government's deposits in 1832 from the Bank of the United States, against which he had warred so successfully, to selected private banks. Such proceedings, however, by no means meet with unanimous approval in the Executive Branch. Sooner or later our enterprising presidential favorite is found running across the field and around the ends of territory for which the members of the cabinet have specific statutory responsibility. There is a law of physics about the meeting of irresistible forces with immovable objects. The operation of this law has produced a fulsome charivari in more than one administration.

More than anyone, more than even the President's wife and other immediate family, the favorite lives with the mind and character of his chief. The favorite sees his hero at his very best, and certainly at his very worst, the latter being the one sure recompense of intimacy. Presidents, of course, differ infinitely in the virtues and vices that count most in a concentrated personal partnership—in their integrity, loyalty, charity, sentimentality, decisiveness, et cetera. Carl Sandburg, however, is convinced that all of the most successful Presidents, including "Washington, Jefferson, Jackson, Lincoln, Theodore Roosevelt, Woodrow Wilson, F.D.R." have had one important characteristic in common. It is, as Sandburg unsparingly put it, that they are "diabolically cunning, or they couldn't have lasted." Lest this pronunciamento excite unwarranted sympathy for the colleagues of these Presidents, one qualification, at least, is in order. Each of Sandburg's wicked Presidents was served by personal advisers whose talent for the diabolique was definitely major league.

The intimate adviser has to take in stride all sorts of presidential eccentricities. Many of these of which a record remains are models of individualism at its unbridled best. Calvin Coolidge, for example, never permitted anyone to ride in his automobile with him, except his immediate family, Mrs. Coolidge and his son John. While other Presidents have demonstrated at least normal generosity in sharing their vehicles with their aides, Frank Stearns, his one and only confidant, found that Coolidge was uncompromisingly different. Whenever Stearns was in town, Washington's curbstone onlookers knew they were in for a treat. At the appointed hour of the President's daily motor outing, they beheld the spectacle of Coolidge riding in solitary majesty down the avenue in his open touring car. Perched equally alone in a similar car close behind was the paunchy Stearns.

It was of the greatest significance that Andrew Jackson became President in a moment of bereavement and loneliness. He had just buried his wife, Rachel, and in his loss he eagerly reached out for the fellowship of his would-be confidant, Martin Van Buren, who also was a widower. Doubtless this mutuality of sorrow considerably speeded the New Yorker's subsequent palace career.

More than one White House favorite has had to cope with a President who has been caught in the coils of cupid. Grover Cleveland in 1886, at the age of forty-nine, became engaged to marry Frances Folsom, just out of Wells College, and only twenty-two. The country, of course, was agog from coast to coast. To relieve the situation, Miss Folsom and her mother devoted the engagement period to a tour of Europe, returning to the United States just before the wedding. It fell to Dan Lamont, Cleveland's personal secretary and confidant, to meet the future bride and her mother well out in New York Bay, whisk them aboard his waiting launch, and convey them into Gilsey House in the city without arousing the many reporters standing by, chafing at their professional bits. Lamont managed handsomely, and the wedding proceeded without untoward incident. For Lamont's tour de force, the President, from all appearances, was eternally grateful.

Presidential favorites, as a class, constantly secrete mystery. More than any other of the many men who function around the President, the favorite operates in the shadows of the palace. Those of his doings which count most are largely unseen. It is consequently no surprise that favorites, like the members of other secretive occupations, are a recurrent object of gossip and rumor in the modern-day syndicated column and the drawing room of yesteryear. Very judiciously and understandably, favorites abhor being photographed and breaking into newsprint. They have a talent for silence, or develop one on the job. Some, even, have taken obvious, almost indecent, delight in the secrecy of their work. They thus open themselves and their brethren to the charge that they are essentially undemocratic animals, dangerously aloof and remote from the American people. But even if this be granted, it is at most nothing more than a minor part of a major paradox. The paradox is that, although presidential favorites are seemingly remote from the common man, they time and again have struck some of the most telling blows to get him a better deal.

Cabinet Secretaries as Favorites

PRESIDENTS HAVE drawn their most intimate advisers, or favorites, in the inner circle from all points of our far-flung political structure. Cabinet secretaries and assistant secretaries, anonymous White House assistants and lowly departmental clerks, members of Congress, party professionals and plain private citizens—all have been appointed and anointed to the honor.

The cabinet secretary, uplifted to a place of special influence and trust, has been a highly recurrent phenomenon. Mostly these chosen secretaries have been secretaries of the Treasury and occasionally secretaries of State. Except for a rare Attorney General or Secretary of Commerce, the rest of the cabinet is confined to a remoter humdrum world.

Alexander Hamilton, the first Secretary of the Treasury, cut a great swath of influence, as personal adviser and executive assistant to President Washington. Although party control changed when Jefferson took over the Presidency in 1800, the precedent of a dominating secretary endured. Secretary of the Treasury Albert Gallatin, at least in that phase of his career passed in the Executive Mansion, was virtually a carbon-copy Hamilton. Gallatin, more than anyone, quelled Jefferson's doubts on the constitutionality of the Louisiana Purchase; he organized a big military expedition to occupy the new territory and impress the Europeans with American might. He did much to talk Jefferson out of going to war with Spain; he tried, but failed, to get Jefferson to go easy on the embargo and not to build the one hundred gunboats (to police the embargo) whose plans and specifications were founded on faulty engineering. These vessels performed exactly as Gallatin had warned. All but two sank on their first voyage.

Although Andrew Jackson was a precedent-breaker, he wholeheartedly perpetuated the emerging tradition of the cabinet favorite. He accorded the Secretary of State, Martin Van Buren, a lofty place in his Administration, even to the point of designating Van Buren as his successor to the Presidency. The man who most aided and abetted the imperialism of President James K. Polk, who went to war with Mexico, annexed California and stopped the British in the Oregon boundary dispute with the immortal war whoop, "54-40 or fight!" was Robert J. Walker, Secretary of the Treasury. A mere whiffet of a man, weighing less than one hundred pounds, stoop-shouldered, with a wheezy voice and vacuous face, Walker is also credited with inducing Polk to offer Spain one hundred million dollars for the purchase of Cuba. Attorney General Caleb Cushing in many ways duplicated, and even improved upon, the career and policies of Secretary Walker in the Administration of President Franklin Pierce.

The cabinet confidant has equally thrived in modern-day Presidencies. Grover Cleveland idolized his Secretary of State, the cultivated, intellectual and charming Thomas F. Bayard. Cleveland, in a moment of appraisal, said of him, "I think he is one of the most complete men, mentally, morally, and politically, I ever met." Although this opinion was by no means general, particularly in the Senate where Bayard's many enemies were wont to refer to him as "the pompous ass," he really counted with Cleveland. A constant visitor to the White House and favorite companion on the President's daily junkets, the Secretary of State was consulted on everything. More recently, Herbert Hoover as Secretary of Commerce in Harding's Administration, Henry Morgenthau as Secretary of the Treasury and Farm Credit Administrator under Franklin D. Roosevelt, and George Humphrey, Secretary of the Treasury in the Eisenhower Administration, have wielded an influence worthy of their illustrious predecessors.

Various circumstances may carry a given secretary into a more favored status with the President than his cabinet colleagues enjoy. It is a social commonplace that each member of a numerous group, such as a President and his cluster of department secretaries, is not on equal terms of sympathy and ease with all the members. Personality, the old school tie, remembrance of political things past, all help boost a secretary well above his fellows. The Franklin D. Roosevelt-Henry Morgenthau rapport, for example, was pre-destined to be unique because the two had been friends, Hudson Valley squires and political comrades-in-arms for twenty years prior to migrating to Washington. In F.D.R.'s ensuing presidential administrations, there were signs aplenty of the privileged status of "Henry the Morgue." He could poke freely into virtually any policy area he chose, foreign and domestic alike. He alone of all Washington had a standing luncheon date—Mondays—with Roosevelt, where anything and everything was discussed. He was in thirteen years the only member of Roosevelt cabinets who called the President "Franklin."

Morgenthau enjoys another extraordinary distinction. He is the only known mortal ever to defy F.D.R., who was sensitive about the proprieties, in refusing to close an interview. The particular occasion on which this reputation is based was a stormy conference on government spending one day in 1938 in Roosevelt's office. The President, after months of plaguing doubt, was veering toward a liberal spending policy. Morgenthau's approach was hardheaded conservative, for which he was making a last-ditch fight. In the mounting discomfiture, Roosevelt proposed to close the interview. "I've got Baruch waiting," he declared. "Let him wait," snapped Morgenthau. "This is more important." Baruch waited.

Some secretaries have not hesitated to step a little out of character or alter their *modus operandi* to progress in the graces of their chief. Although Herbert Hoover, at middle age, had achieved no great fame as a gregarious or accommodating man, he made unusual concessions to become and remain a personal favorite of Warren G. Harding. Mr. Harding, as history leaves no doubt, loved cards, especially poker. Hoover's staunch Quakerism prevented him from succumbing to the wicked game, but he permitted himself Harding's second love, bridge.

The particular occasion of this concession was Harding's famous last trip by rail through the West, which ended with his death in California. As the junket commenced, Teapot Dome and other scandals were beginning to break. Harding, to get away from it all, entrained with a small complement of friends, all untainted with criminality. Hoover was the one cabinet member invited to come along. Scandals kept breaking as the party sped west, and the dejected Harding sought relief in long outgiving conversations with a reliable counselor and by playing bridge. Mr. Hoover doubled in both capacities. The bridge began every day right after breakfast and continued, except for mealtime breaks, until well after midnight. Since there were only three other bridge players in the party, shifts could be set up to relieve one player at a time, but the pressure on Hoover was so terrific that he has never since sat down voluntarily at a bridge table. During pauses in the card spree, Hoover convinced Harding that he should come clean with the scandals to the public. From their confessional talks, conducted in the main parlor car sometimes until dawn, Hoover drew a store of precious intelligence which he handed over to Coolidge after Harding's death. The new President was thus enabled to move speedily and efficiently upon the malefactors.

A cabinet favorite may owe much of his rise to the circumstance that the President is having difficulties with one or more of the other secretaries.

The resulting embarrassment and remorse may drive the President into a compensating relationship with another colleague. Annoyances of many kinds and sizes bring on the malaise on which such transfers of favor seem to depend. President James K. Polk dimly viewed his Secretary of State, James Buchanan, as "not pleasant," "disposed to differ unnecessarily," "in small matters without judgment," and "sometimes acts like an old maid." Polk handled most of his foreign policy work with his affable Secretary of the Treasury, Robert Walker. Of all Presidents, probably James Monroe underwent the severest trials in his intercourse with his cabinet secretaries. One day, his Secretary of the Treasury, William H. Crawford, whose crusty manner was justly famous, stopped in at the Executive Mansion to launch a spirited discussion of how patronage should be handled in the customs offices of certain Northern port towns. Crawford made clear that he wanted several of his own most stellar henchmen appointed. To all of these worthies Monroe objected. The tension grew, and then soared, when Crawford roughly demanded to know whom Monroe intended to appoint. Monroe replied with some heat that it was none of the Secretary's business. Crawford hissed, raised his cane, and advanced on the President as if to strike him, exclaiming, "You damned infernal old scoundrel." By this time, Monroe had withdrawn to the fireplace where, to his good fortune, a pair of tongs were handy. With these appropriately poised, he let blast with a well-rounded curse and declared he would ring for the servants. Crawford quickly recovered himself, mumbled an apology, and left the house. The two men never met privately again, Monroe resorting elsewhere for his fiscal advice.

Being on the whole a rather brash breed of men, cabinet favorites have tended to entertain some rather grand ideas about the place they occupy in the administration. Some favorites see themselves as nothing less than "prime ministers," endowed with the power and the pre-eminence of the English model. Alexander Hamilton thought so strongly along these lines in the Washington Administration that many of his friends felt obliged to refer to him as "The Prime Minister." William H. Seward, whom Gideon Welles described as "anxious to direct, to be the Premier, the real Executive, and give away national rights as a favor," acted under a like compulsion. Although Caleb Cushing is not known to have styled himself as the prime minister of the Administration of President Franklin Pierce, he might just as well have. That his ambitions were at least in the neighborhood of that alluring apex is conveyed by his announced intention to make his post of Attorney General "the great, controlling, supervising office of the Administration." This was by no means idle bombast. Cushing proceeded to dominate foreign policy and administer most of the patronage, the anteroom to his office regularly having more office-seekers per square foot than the White House. On the big domestic issue of slavery vs. abolition, he drafted the presidential message endorsing the Kansas-Nebraska Act which admitted Nebraska to the Union without slavery and Kansas with it. This so enraged the prevailing antislavery opinion of the North, that it contributed as much as any single action to Pierce's failure to secure renomination in 1856. Historian George Bancroft's considered diagnosis of this political tragedy was that "Pierce died of . . . Cushing."

However much the secretary-favorite is prone to rate himself as prime minister, the stark truth of the matter is that he all too frequently is a destructive influence on the cabinet. He labors mightily at diverting its proceedings to advance his own ends, which may not always coincide with the President's or with the objective of a well-functioning cabinet. William H. Seward's talent at such subversion was impressive. If a matter on which he was working privately with Lincoln arose in the cabinet, Seward expertly parried questions and smothered discussion with extended, charming, highly irrelevant monologue. In periods when the cabinet loomed as a special threat, he would induce Lincoln not to have meetings at all. If the cabinet did meet, Seward would leave early before the matter he didn't want discussed came up. His absence might prevent it from ever coming up. Or he would send an assistant, usually his son Frederick, to the cabinet instead of attending himself. Frederick's powers to speak for his father were carefully circumscribed. Secretary of War Edwin M. Stanton expressed the feelings of many a colleague in confessing his reluctance to submit or discuss important business with a mere assistant present. This no doubt was precisely what father Seward wanted.

Cabinet favorites as a class are endowed with the frenetic industry, drive and sense of mission of the empire-builder. Caleb Cushing got along on four hours sleep, abhorred recreation, and was of such precise industry that he was always first on hand at the Athenaeum Library, during sojourns in his native Boston, when the doors opened. Herbert Hoover, in accepting the invitation of President Warren G. Harding to join the cabinet, took unusual pains to make clear that he would be no run-of-the-mill secretary. Mr. Hoover requested the President-elect to inform the other secretaries—in writing—that Herbert Hoover as Secretary of Commerce, in addition to managing the usual business of that department, would be in charge of all aspects of postwar reconstruction. Specifically, Harding was expected to point out, this meant that Hoover would handle the agriculture, labor, finance and foreign policy involved in reconstruction, as well as the regular business concerns of the Department of Commerce. Mr. Harding faithfully complied with Hoover's request in all particulars. Once installed as Secretary, Hoover repeatedly demonstrated that his extraordinary preparations were in deadly earnest. Within a matter of months, he called a major national conference to cope with postwar unemployment while the Labor

Department, which normally had jurisdiction of such problems, looked on. In subsequent coups, Hoover grabbed off the Bureau of Mines and the Patent Office from Interior, and annexed the important new government agencies in the housing, radio and aeronautics fields. When Attorney General Daugherty got an injunction against railway employees to forestall their big strike in 1921, Hoover, incensed at the arbitrariness of the action, marched straight to the White House and Daugherty backed down. "Harding," Hoover has said in retrospect, "encouraged me in everything I wanted to do."

Some cabinet favorites, who have lacked Mr. Hoover's capacity to take their objectives by main force, have made their way by other means. Not always, unfortunately, have these further means excited the admiration of colleagues and other sensitive onlookers. Thomas Hart Benton, the distinguished and forthright Senator from Missouri, once delineated Caleb Cushing's technique in such unflattering strokes as follows: "Cushing," said Benton, is "unscrupulous, double-sexed, double-gendered, and hermaphroditic in politics, with a hinge in his knee, which he often crooks that thrift may follow fawning." James Russell Lowell, the poet, who knew the New England politician all too well, was driven to commit his impression to verse:

> General C. is a dreffle smart man
>   He's ben on all sides that places or pelf;
> But consistence still wuz part of his plan,—
>   He's been true to one party—an' thet is himself.

Official Insiders

SOME PRESIDENTS resort for the principal members of their inner circle to the sequestered, reticent, guardedly anonymous figures who make up their official White House entourage. Of the numerous clerks and professional assistants there at hand, certain figures and the posts they occupy have been recurrently influential in presidential history. One, for example, is the aide who in bygone times bore the deceptively simple title, "The Secretary to the President." In the century or more between Andrew Jackson's Presidency and Franklin D. Roosevelt's, more than one of these secretaries has been both a favorite and something of a major-domo in the affairs of his Administration.

Andrew Jackson Donelson, who was President Andrew's nephew as well as his secretary, managed the White House as a family household, a center of social life and as a business enterprise. Donelson was also a stalwart of the "Kitchen Cabinet," and a skilled draftsman whose well-defined policy convictions seeped their way into leading presidential papers. President Grant's secretary, General O. F. Babcock, was a great personal favorite and man Friday. Working singlehandedly, Babcock almost brought off the annexation of Santo Domingo to the United States in 1869. While Grant was avowing to a hostile cabinet and the Senate Foreign Relations Committee that rumors of an annexation were wholly unfounded, Babcock was frantically negotiating with the Dominicans. He soon returned triumphantly to the United States with a draft treaty in his pocket. Grant blandly informed his cabinet of the *fait accompli*, and Hamilton Fish, one of the most illustrious of our secretaries of State and one of the few able men in the Grant Administration, promptly resigned. Overwhelmed by this wholly unanticipated step, Grant quickly dropped the project, Fish reconsidered, and Babcock turned his talents to another deserving enterprise—beating off an investigation of the Whisky Ring's evasion of the excise tax which threatened to blow the Administration sky-high with the scandal it exposed.

Of the modern-day secretaries, one of the most influential was George B. Cortelyou. Cortelyou succeeded to the post in the middle of the Spanish-American war when the incumbent secretary, John Addison Porter, broke under the strain of the White House phase of the conflict. The new secretary, at the time of his ascent, had just celebrated his thirty-third birthday and had to his credit three years of service as President McKinley's confidential stenographer.

Cortelyou flawlessly managed the growing White House clerical force, scheduled the President's appointments, did his drafting chores, organized his junkets about the country, and functioned as social secretary to Mrs. McKinley, a sniveling lady, whose bouts of melancholia were a difficult household problem. But it was in the major politics of the White House that Cortelyou's hand was most skilled. When Mark Hanna, for example, threatened to launch an all-out fight against the Teddy-Roosevelt-for-Vice President steamroller at the Republican Convention in 1900, Cortelyou, according to Charles G. Dawes, spurred McKinley, after considerable exhortation, into forbidding Hanna to interfere with the nomination. If Hanna had proceeded with his plans, McKinley, it is clear, would have suffered a dreadful loss of face.

Cortelyou's many talents were tried and proved under the most desperate of circumstances. When McKinley was assassinated at Buffalo, Cortelyou, who was by his side, became, at least in the week when death hovered by, virtually an acting President. After McKinley finally succumbed, Cortelyou, as much as anyone, eased the way into the new regime of Teddy Roosevelt. The latter was not long in showing his gratitude by appointing the erstwhile stenographer as the first Secretary of the newly created Department of Commerce and Labor.

William Loeb, Jr., who followed Cortelyou as Presidential Secretary, quickly became a favorite and a large influence on policy. T.R. himself has written that Loeb inspired the investigations which uncovered the frauds perpetrated by the American Sugar Trust at the New York Customs House. He masterminded the aligning of the party convention behind Roosevelt's anointed successor, William Howard Taft, in 1908. As secretary, Loeb was a shadowy presence at the leading meetings and conferences. When Roosevelt negotiated with management and labor in the big coal strike of 1902, Loeb sat by taking notes and whispering suggestions to his chief. In the Venezuela crisis, Loeb was the only witness present when T.R. expostulated the famous "hands-off" line to the German ambassador, Von Holleben. Loeb was widely suspected in his time of inspiring, or at least egging T.R. on, in the sundry fads and "horseback judgments" which he dangled before the country and which outraged many respectable quarters. Of these fads, Loeb's favorite was simplified spelling. Roosevelt proposed the revision of approximately three hundred words so that "chased" became "chast," "dropped" "dropt," and "thoroughly" "thoroly." In the blissful conservatism of the turn of the century, this was regarded as nothing less than a violent orthographical revolution and was summarily treated as such. Long after Roosevelt backed down before the shrill alarms, Loeb was doggedly pushing this favorite cause.

The Cortelyou-Loeb era is the high mark of influence of the President's secretary, though certain of the secretarial successors have been important. Joseph Tumulty was surely a confidant and a major influence in the Administration of Woodrow Wilson. Calvin Coolidge's secretary, Bascom Slemp, an ex-Virginia Congressman, was an important link between the President and Congress and with the Republican party organization. Louis McHenry Howe, the trusted secretary to F. D. Roosevelt, was an influential presence whose significance was limited by his peevishness toward the Brain Trust and by illness which resulted in his death in 1935. With Howe's passing, the post of Secretary to the President has been allowed to lapse, its functions being taken over by the appointments secretary, the press secretary, the speech writers and other specialists of the modern-day White House staff.

One of the most important of these "specialists" in the Roosevelt-Truman-Eisenhower era is the Counsel to the President. F.D.R. originally set up the office by executive order in 1941. The first incumbent was Judge Samuel Rosenman, bearer of the identical title in Roosevelt's New York Governorship. The justification for Rosenman's seeming duplication of the established function of the Attorney General was that a personally selected

White House counsel would be closer to the President than a politically appointed Attorney General ever could be, and could provide the legal advice best suited to the President's personal needs. As counsel, Rosenman, however, employed talents exceedingly more diverse than those of mere legal craftsmanship. Before very long, he was an overworked speech writer, idea man and trouble shooter par excellence, who probed some of the knottiest organizational problems of the squabbling executive agencies in World War II. When Truman took over as President, Rosenman stayed on temporarily. His eventual successors, Clark Clifford and Charles Murphy, reflected the original image of the office, Clifford particularly.

Clifford was the widest ranging of the Truman assistants. Presidential front man in dealing with the departments, Administration strategist in Congress, Clifford drafted the fighting speeches that played such a big part in Truman's spectacular victory over Dewey in 1948. Clifford was chief author of the message on aid to Greece and Turkey, which converted a moderate-toned State Department memorandum into a vigorous historic state paper. James V. Forrestal, the first Secretary of Defense, once said that with the exception of Mr. Truman, Clifford contributed more than anyone to bring about the "unification" of the armed forces in the National Security Act of 1947. Many months of Clifford's ingenuity, patience and drive went into negotiating the complicated differences on which Army, Navy and Marine die-hards had locked horns. By dint of this service, the increase of his friends were few, his critics great.

At least two Presidents, Andrew Jackson and Franklin D. Roosevelt, have used departmental subordinates on a personal and major scale for White House missions and assignments. A principal member of Jackson's Kitchen Cabinet was the Fourth Auditor of the Treasury, Amos Kendall, who passed most of his time not in the Treasury, but at the President's side, where he drafted messages to Congress and innumerable other state papers, and spearheaded the war on the Bank of the United States. Franklin D. Roosevelt's original Brain Trust held down departmental assignments while expending the better part of their energies on projects taken on at the White House. Chief Brain Truster Raymond Moley was Assistant Secretary of State; Professor Rexford Tugwell, who had specialized in agricultural problems in the 1932 presidential campaign, was an Assistant Secretary of Agriculture, and Professor Adolf A. Berle, whose forte was banking and credit, was counsel to the RFC. All through the New Deal, Roosevelt, when changing his favorites in the palace guard, was prone to solicit his fresh recruits from the departments, valuing that source for the flexibility and unobtrusiveness it permitted in hiring and especially in firing. For Roosevelt was not long in discovering that it was relatively easy to drop a departmental man from his presidential assignments simply by not inviting him around to the

White House any more, leaving him to his previous departmental chores. The bitter scene and the break with the Administration—complete and final and pitilessly publicized—were far less likely than when a member of the White House organization had to be induced to quit his job.

The administrations of Roosevelt, Harry S. Truman and Dwight D. Eisenhower will go down in the history of presidential advisers and assistants for their unprecedented efforts to entrust to a single figure of the White House entourage a general influence and co-ordinating authority in the affairs of the Executive Branch. This figure, who personally is very close to the President, has been called, significantly, "The Assistant to the President" and "Special Assistant to the President." In many respects he represents an adaptation and extension in the presidency of today of the former "Secretary to the President" as it flourished under McKinley and Theodore Roosevelt. The more recent "Assistant to the President" offers arresting possibilities for sparing the Chief Executive and lightening his burdens, objectives for which there is nowadays an almost universal sympathy. The assistant may, among other things, see people in the President's behalf, plan significant policy, and read and digest the sea of memoranda and reports up-churned by the departments. He may supervise the ever-growing personal presidential staff, take on party and legislative tasks, and impart order and quiet to the ferocious struggles always erupting between power-hungry departmental administrators.

In actuality, the Roosevelt, Truman and Eisenhower administrations have varied widely in their reliance upon the general presidential assistant. Although Harry Hopkins as "Special Assistant" to F.D.R. in World War II poked into every nook and cranny of the Presidency, he was at most only intermittently a unifying and co-ordinating influence in the sprawling Executive Branch. For one thing, Hopkins was engrossed with the overseas phases of the war, which took him out of the country for sizable interludes and tended to monopolize his energies. For another thing, his illness—he was never more than a few jumps ahead of death—frequently forced him to the side lines and prevented him from exercising any continuous direction of affairs. Yet, even if Hopkins had been lucky enough in the war to enjoy the swaggering good health of a prize fighter, it is doubtful that he would have aspired to the comprehensive and systematic power such as Sherman Adams one day was to wield. Neither by temperament or chosen method, was Hopkins an operator who worked within established lines and according to fixed patterns. In the belief that creativeness thrives upon one's freedom of action, he preferred to improvise and play by ear rather than work by routine and plan. It is not improbable that if Harry Hopkins had lived in the ordered world of Adams, he would promptly have gone mad from claustrophobia.

Harry Truman was not long in the presidential office when he sought to spare himself certain of its burdens by erecting a new post in the White House scheme,—"The Assistant to the President"—and into it he brought John R. Steelman. A onetime sociology professor, and for seven years the Director of the United States Conciliation Service, Steelman was a big man with a cherubic global face and a hearty backslapping, handshaking manner. It is widely agreed that in the matter of sparing the President, the post of "The Assistant to the President," as manned by Mr. Steelman, was not a tremendous success. Famous for his ability not to hurt anyone's feeling, even when under major provocation, Steelman meant to keep his record intact. He became, as a result, conservative and cautious in his tour of duty, qualities to be sure, which have their place, although they are hardly the most service-able in shielding the President from details and from the interdepartmental brawls which Truman thought his predecessor, F.D.R., got too much in-volved in. Steelman's limited effectiveness, however, was the President's own doing as well. Mr. Truman, who was alert to the importance of his own personal grasp of working details as the means of retaining effective control of his office, sat in with Steelman at staff meetings and conferences and in other respects was given to hovering by. Inevitably he became ensnarled in the very difficulties and commitments he had originally sought to avoid. No evidence has yet come to light that Truman ever particularly regretted this turn of events.

It is in the Administration of General Eisenhower, that the halting beginnings of a presidential chief of staff have come into a sudden and most complete evolution. The vehicle of this spectacular development is the personage of Sherman Adams, ex-Governor of New Hampshire and Eisen-hower's floor manager at the Republican National Convention of 1952. As "The Assistant to the President," Adams operated on all fronts of the Eisen-hower Presidency. He dealt with legislators and party chieftains on every conceivable matter, from pork barrel to vetoes, and with the envoys of powerful private groups in hot pursuit of some public benevolence. He at-tended meetings of the cabinet and the National Security Council, presided over the White House staff, and directed a subcabinet which does the very consequential spadework and follow-up on matters the cabinet proper con-siders. Adams largely determined who the President saw and what he read by controlling the admission of visitors and presiding over an elaborate staff system by which papers and reports channeled up from the departments to his desk. Few of these papers ever reached the President unless they bore the imprimatur, the open-sesame to the Chief Executive's attention, "O.K., S.A." In his conferences with the President, of which at least six occurred on a normal day, Adams expatiated on great numbers of matters. His power over the presidential agenda operated to the point where Senator John Sherman Cooper of Kentucky was prevented from seeing Eisenhower to warn against the Dixon-Yates contract, and where Assistant Air Force Secretary Trevor Gardner, resigning to protest against "the mismanaged guided missile program," wrote that "the President's chief advisers have left him, at best, incompletely informed."

Mr. Adams's sundry powers counted a great deal more in President Eisenhower's several illnesses. It was in the desperate interval of the heart attack that a careful observer of the firm and efficient grip which Adams lost no time in clamping on to the situation, wrote, "There is a growing feeling ... that Mr. Adams is now exercising more power than any other man in America."

The Outsider

SOME PRESIDENTS elevate to the most privileged positions in their inner circle men who are wholly outside the government, who hold no office, title, or place on the public payroll. However much these advisers flourish in influence, they doggedly cling to their status as private citizens. They have good reason to.

Presidents prefer "outsiders" because they have the perspective of detachment. They come without previous involvement in Administration policy, and are unencumbered by the vested interests a cabinet secretary has by virtue of his headship of a department, or a White House aide with established assignments. The detached outsider is a ready-made father-confessor for the President who is dubious of his policies, his subordinates, or both. By his very nature, the outsider can operate with a maximum of anonymity and freedom from the publicity which all too often destroys the usefulness of the official advisers. The outsider may never even come to the White House, but may do all his business by telephone or correspondence. Because of the distance he keeps from the official scene, he is the type of adviser who is most easily disposed of. He is, to be sure, an instantaneous object of jealousy, for his coming is a reflection on the insider and a potential threat to the advance, if not survival, of his pet ideas and projects.

The question which of the millions of American citizens are most likely to be tapped for duty as outsiders is primarily determined by two considerations: prestige and pocketbook. Outsiders tend to be wealthy men who can afford to work gratis for the government. They are apt to come into their White House duties after lush careers in such gilded callings as gunpowder merchants, insurance executives, stock-market manipulators and department-store entrepreneurs. Others are just plain dilettantes endowed by considerate forebears with generous trusts. There is a further major reservoir of talent in the various elder statesmen who are usually on hand—ex-Presidents, ex-cabinet secretaries and ex-Supreme Court justices, whose sheer prestige makes a subordinate executive post as a vehicle for their service unthinkable. They are forced by their importance to function as outsiders.

Presidents, both ancient and modern, have used outsiders on a major scale. Thomas Jefferson was incessantly communing with private citizen Pierre Samuel Du Pont de Nemours, the elder of the two brothers who founded the great industrial clan. Working chiefly by correspondence, Jefferson and Du Pont had what amounted to a pact of mutual assistance. Jefferson steered government contracts to Du Pont's struggling powder factory and wangled for the French émigré, whose intellectual aspirations were keen, a coveted membership in the American Philosophical Society. For his part, Du Pont was a valued father-confessor who bestowed his moral blessings on the President's ruthless patronage policy, and lighted with convincing rationalizations the shadows of Jefferson's many doubts on the legality of the Louisiana Purchase. As Jefferson's unofficial representative, Du Pont journeyed to France at his own expense to negotiate some of the knottier issues of the Purchase with his old friend Talleyrand.

A leading modern-day outsider is Frank Stearns, the man who discovered Calvin Coolidge. Prosperous Boston department-store owner, trustee of Amherst College, Coolidge's alma mater, Stearns had come upon his hero while negotiating a contract for the laying of a sewer by the Amherst township on the college campus. Stearns, who fancied himself as something of a kingmaker, was instantaneously impressed that Coolidge, the town attorney, was a political "comer." Coolidge's gaze, too, was fixed on higher things, and the ambitions of the two men fell in love at first sight. The faithful Stearns financed, toiled for and worried over Coolidge's subsequent rise in Massachusetts and national politics. By the time the Washington phase commenced, the politician and his benefactor were fast cronies on a simple, undemonstrative scale, for Stearns, like Coolidge, was a "solon of silence." The placid Bostonian, while surrounded by friends of at least average vivacity, was known to keep absolutely mum for twelve hours at a stretch. Because of this talent, Coolidge periodically would send for Stearns to come down from Boston, often on a "hurry-up" basis. When the going was bad, Coolidge liked nothing better than to have the merchant seated by his desk, smoking a big cigar in absolute silence. Coolidge would keep on working, worrying and puffing at his own cigar, while Stearns looked out the window. William Allen White was once reminded by this scene of impeccable quietude of two farm horses communing in a fence corner, haunch to neck.

This bucolic metaphor is actually a cover-all of several invaluable purposes which Stearns served and which Coolidge cherished. Stearns, in further metaphor, was a staff to lean on, a familiar figure in unfriendly surroundings. He was a refuge from the isolation of office, a man with whom Coolidge could chat for hours, as he was sometimes wont to do, about his official troubles. Suspicious of his fellow men to the point of neurosis, Coolidge took none of his cabinet secretaries or any lesser official figure into his confidence. Even Stearns functioned in an orbit that was severely circumscribed. His advice was seldom asked; he was sent on no errands and, for all of Coolidge's occasional volubility, he was told few secrets. For example, "I do not choose to run," Coolidge's classic declination of another term in the White House, broke upon the world without any foreknowledge on Stearn's part. To offer advice was hazardous indeed. Once, when a federal judgeship fell vacant, Stearns ventured to suggest a possible nominee. He broached the matter with gingerly casualness, without any intention of pushing it.

"What do you know about the qualifications a man should have to go on the bench?" snapped Coolidge.

"Nothing!"

"What do you know of this man's qualifications?"

"Nothing!"

"Well, then, I advise you in the future not to meddle in things you know nothing about."

Of the outsiders, the most influential has been Colonel Edward Mandell House, Woodrow Wilson's chief emissary, draftsman and idea man in World War I. For all of his considerable involvement as presidential right-hand man, House never came on the public payroll, never lived in Washington for any stretch of time, but in the main conducted his affairs by correspondence and telephone, and from a cubbyhole in his modest New York apartment to which very important persons steadily repaired.

A perennial citizen-adviser, whose influence has counted in every Presidency from Wilson's to Eisenhower's, is Bernard M. Baruch. In certain of these Presidencies, Baruch was a leading favorite. "Dr. Facts," as he was known in World War I, is credited with talking Wilson into accepting amendments to the Federal Reserve legislation in 1913, without which the whole project would doubtless have been lost. In 1917, Baruch temporarily dropped his outsider role by taking a high post on the Council of National Defense, and in the following year he became head of the War Industries Board, both top positions in the mobilization of the American economy. After the war, he tried to bring Presidents Harding and Coolidge to ease up on reparations and war debts and encouraged Hoover's pet anti-depression measure, the RFC. Franklin D. Roosevelt commandeered Baruch to draft his acceptance speech at the Chicago Democratic Convention in 1932. It happened that Brain Truster Raymond Moley also was assigned to prepare a draft. Roosevelt mastered the resulting diplomatic problem with a characteristic homespun compromise. He used half of Moley's draft and half of Baruch's. The latter's protégés manned many of the subsequent key New Deal posts: Hugh Johnson came in as Administrator of NRA, George M. Peek as Assistant Secretary of Agriculture and Herbert Bayard Swope, as an all-round assistant. Back home on Wall Street, Baruch excelled at the difficult job of convincing his fellow financiers of Roosevelt's intrinsic soundness on financial questions. In World War II, Baruch turned up with several what's-the-problem and what-to-do-about-it reports on the man-power and rubber shortages and demobilization. President Truman deputed him to prepare a plan for the international control of atomic energy, and Eisenhower consulted him on the issues of the 1952 campaign. Baruch is a bipartisan symbol of respectability, a speculator who has brought to the imponderables of politics a verve for the new approach, which has paid off handsomely in the stock market and in the administration of more than one beleaguered President.

On this note of well-being, ends our tour of the main haunts—the cabinet, the White House and the world outside—where the President is apt to find his ghosts and confidants, the men who constitute the principal advisers and assistants of his administration.

Myth of the Kitchen Cabinet

PRESIDENTIAL GHOSTS, like any other kind of ghosts, are a fertile source of myths. Probably the most persistent of these is one which treats of the relationships which obtain between the several members of the inner circle. The myth in question has it that the President's most intimate advisers have, time and again in history, worked in zealous close-knit co-operation toward a common purpose. They are exemplary of what in the parlance of today is called a "team."

Among the busiest and most resourceful propagators of this myth over the years has been the press. Whenever the most superficial evidences of solidarity appear within the President's circle, some enterprising journalist will rush the participants into baptism with such catchy epithets as "Kitchen Cabinet," "Brain Trust," "Tennis Cabinet," and the like. The names tend to stick, as an intriguing image is conjured up of a little band of unseen men striving jointly in the strictest secrecy. To the world outside is conveyed an air of conspiracy which never fails to excite interest in White House doings.

"Kitchen Cabinet," a term originally coined in the reign of Andrew Jackson, has become a permanent part of the American idiom. Jackson's Kitchen Cabinet normally constituted four or five personal advisers who achieved importance because they tended to supplant his regular cabinet with which he was chronically dissatisfied. Yet to conceive of these personal advisers as a "cabinet," as in "Kitchen Cabinet," does violence to the facts. Jackson's little band of gifted men had few characteristics of a cabinet. They had no regular time or place of meeting; indeed, it is doubtful if they ever gathered in plenary session. They never all worked simultaneously on the same policy problem. Their membership changed rather frequently. Historians estimate that close to a dozen men were identified with the Kitchen Cabinet at one time or another in Jackson's Administration. Probably the Kitchen Cabinet's strongest underlying characteristic was the closeness of all its members to Jackson. But that circumstance was as much a factor of disunity as of unity. Such Kitchen Cabinet stalwarts as Kendall, Blair, Van Buren, Duff Green, John H. Eaton and Isaac Hill, were split on key policies and their differences were exacerbated because each had ready access to Jackson and good prospects of swaying his decisions. The principal instances of peaceful collaboration transpired when several members—but by no means all—took on a common assignment, such as drafting a speech or an editorial, and lobbying Congress.

"Kitchen Cabinet," as a phrase, lay briefly in journalistic moth balls until the Administration of John Tyler, President from 1841 to 1845. Like Jackson, Tyler found his regular cabinet a chronic source of grief. Originally Vice-President, Tyler succeeded to the highest office when William Henry Harrison died after serving only one month of his term. At Tyler's very first cabinet meeting, the Secretary of State, Daniel Webster, announced, with characteristic pontification, that he hoped the new President would follow Harrison's policies, in particular his procedures in conducting the cabinet. The latter, elaborated Webster, involved bringing all measures of the Administration to the cabinet and deciding them by majority opinion. The President, needless to say, would have but one vote like any Secretary. Tyler, aghast at "this exhibition of adamantine cheek," recovered sufficiently to inform Secretary Webster and his colleagues in no uncertain terms that the new regime would be different.

Tyler took refuge in a coterie of personal and political friends from his native Virginia: Henry A. Wise, Thomas H. Gilmer and Francis Mallory, all of the House of Representatives; William Cabel Rives of the Senate; Judge Beverly Tucker of the State Supreme Court; and Thomas R. Dew, President of William and Mary College. The group was alternately called the "Kitchen Cabinet" and, because of Dr. Dew's background, somewhat derisively, the "Virginia Schoolmasters." There is no evidence that the Tyler aides ever met simultaneously. Judge Tucker was usually off on circuit and Dr. Dew's presence was so essential at William and Mary that he rarely got to Washington and did most of his advising by mail. The most influential

Schoolmaster by far was Henry A. Wise, of whom Tyler said, "He is truly a most extraordinary man. I have never known but one man more thoroughly at home upon all subjects and that is L. W. Tazewell." (Tazewell was another stellar Virginia politician of the day.) Wise, more than anyone, Tyler believed, was responsible for the Whig's victory in 1840. At one point, Judge Tucker was a top-notch idea man, right next to Wise in influence, but in 1842, Tucker-Tyler relations cooled and deteriorated into an open break. That fact was undeniably established when, through one of those mischievous tricks of fate, both men were passengers on an excursion steamer plying the St. James River one hot summer day in 1844. The inevitable face-to-face confrontation transpired and, according to several anxious onlookers, neither man spoke to the other, each riveting his gaze upon the scenery. Tucker's replacement was Duff Green, an editor and protégé of John C. Calhoun. He, too, passed into eclipse, and Congressmen Mallory and Cushing came in. The palace guard kept changing, chiefly because Tyler's contentiousness waxed as his Administration aged. In the unremitting upheaval, the cement of continuing personal relations, on which true cabinets are based, never had a chance to harden.

In modern times, Kitchen Cabinets have been said to exist on the basis of the flimsiest evidence. Grover Cleveland had what was hailed as a "Fishing Cabinet," consisting of Joseph Jefferson, the celebrated actor; E. C. Benedict, a wealthy New York friend; and Henry T. Thurber, a pleasant, well-heeled gentleman. The trio's chief apparent impact on the President was that they took him fishing. None of these august rodsmen was known to have significantly affected any public policy of importance.

In his day, Teddy Roosevelt had the "Tennis Cabinet," a motley corps which counted thirty-one members at its farewell luncheon at the close of the Administration. The Tennis Cabinet was truly cosmopolitan. It included the French ambassador, Jusserand; the German ambassador, von Sternberg; Robert Bacon and George von L. Meyer of the State Department; Archie Butt, the President's military aide; Gifford Pinchot, the conservationist; and the secretaries of the Interior and Navy. Occasional members were Senator Elihu Root, the United States Marshal of Oklahoma; Seth Bullock; and Jack Abernathy, a man who impressed Roosevelt by catching wolves with his bare hands. According to Ike Hoover, the observant chief usher at the White House, one's game of tennis was the chief criterion of membership in T.R.'s special cabinet. "No poor player was invited a second time," Hoover put it trenchantly. The favorites were those whose game was just slightly below T.R.'s. Anyone gauche enough to beat the President was apt not to be reinvited for some little while. T.R. himself has written that "Tennis Cabinet," as a term, was used "laughingly," at the White House, that the main idea was several hours of vigorous play to counterbalance hard work, and that important advisers like Senator Henry Cabot Lodge and presidential secretary William Loeb were not included simply because they did not play the game.

Recreational activity, although distinctly of an indoor type, was also the *raison d'être* of the infamous "Poker Cabinet" of Warren G. Harding. Its most stellar members included Senator Albert Fall, the later culprit of Teapot Dome; Attorney General Harry Daugherty, of nearly equal rascality; and Jesse Smith, his side-kick, a highly accomplished embezzler, who eluded his considerable debt to society by blowing his brains out. The more respectable membership comprised the millionaire Washingtonian E. B. McLean, Senators Cummings and Hale, and Secretary Weeks; also Henry Fletcher, the rising Florida Congressman; and Albert Lasker, the philanthropist. Certain out-of-towners were privileged to participate upon turning up in Washington. The Poker Cabinet industriously averaged two meetings a week at the White House and one outside, and kept the chips falling from right after an early dinner to one o'clock in the morning.

President Herbert Hoover instituted the more salubrious "Medicine Ball Cabinet." Its members—department secretaries and assistant secretaries, Justice Harlan F. Stone, White House aides Richey and Newton, and newsmen Will Hard and Mark Sullivan, among others—undertook a brisk twenty minutes of medicine ball commencing at eight A.M. All who survived were regaled with toast and coffee and, on occasion, oatmeal, in the White House kitchen, and were expected to be at their offices at nine A.M. sharp. Hoover often invited Sullivan to stay on for a full-course breakfast, topped with a news story as yet denied to his fellow professionals. The brief, tightly scheduled existence of the Medicine Ball Cabinet afforded it little influence on policy. In his memoirs, Mr. Hoover sizes up the institution's significance wholly in terms of its contribution in keeping down the waistlines of his colleagues.

"Brain Trust," like "Kitchen Cabinet," has become part of the language. As piquant nomenclature, its invention has been attributed to the journalist, John Kieran. As a going enterprise of influence, it was founded by Samuel I. Rosenman a few months before Franklin D. Roosevelt received the presidential nomination in 1932. The Brain Trust consisted chiefly of Columbia University professors (Rosenman is a staunch alumnus of that institution) who did research and spun out ideas and paragraphs for Roosevelt's subsequent campaign speeches. Each Brain Truster was assigned to a policy field such as agriculture, banking, or tariffs. Raymond Moley, professor of government at Columbia, helped Rosenman recruit the group and handed out assignments. Late Friday afternoons, after his university classes were out, Moley would board the New York Central for Albany with one or two of his specialists. They would dine and spend the night in the Governor's mansion, all the while stimulating Roosevelt's thinking in some field of policy.

After the inauguration on March 4, 1933, the paths of the Brain Trusters parted when each of the major members took on responsible administrative posts. The appointments, which entailed heavy involvement in day-to-day executive activities, signified the abandonment of Rosenman's original conception of the Brain Trust as a consultative group of experts assisting the President in an anonymous advisory capacity. The term, "Brain Trust," however, endured, being applied indiscriminately to practically anyone in Washington upon whom the President seemed to rely for advice or assistance. But at no point did the collective pattern by which the original Brain Trust functioned reappear. Roosevelt's advisers, like those of many another President, worked on a highly individualistic basis.

Palace Politics

INSTEAD OF the blissful solidarity of the mythical Kitchen Cabinet, the environment in which presidential advisers ply their trade is the highly competitive one of palace politics. To make their way into the inner circle and to remain and progress there, they must fend off the challenges of ambitious would-be successors. The competition takes on a multitude of forms. It may simply be a race to serve the master best, wholly without evidence of friction, a gentlemanly decorum being impeccably preserved. In more intensive stages, the competition may variously be a contest of pinpricks, an occasional battle, even a war to the death, such as Alexander Hamilton and Thomas Jefferson waged during the Presidency of George Washington. As the struggle proceeds, issues are scrupulously chosen, positions are maneuvered for; intrigues of the most elaborate sort have been perpetrated. Advisers cultivate one another's favor, enter into alliances, and often formulate advice on the theory that it must appeal not only to the President, but to one's strategically influential colleagues as well.

The palace competition centers upon the giving of advice. Success in this fine and subtle art captures assignments and missions for the advice-giver and pulls the administration into the policy and ideological directions he wishes it to follow. The production and consumption of advice represents the intellectual substance of the Presidency and involves the Chief Executive as reader, listener, deliberator and decision-maker.

It is important from the standpoint of the advisers' competition to understand the circumstances under which the President performs his several roles. Since time immemorial, the reading phase of the Presidency has been something of an ocular endurance contest. George Washington had hardly settled down in the office when he was lamenting the inordinate number of man-hours he had to put in studying official papers, which left him little time for anything else, least of all reflection. Harry S. Truman, by his own testimony, spent a major part of his regular seventeen-hour workday perusing staff memoranda. Something of the burden involved in this epistolary challenge is conveyed by his diary entry for June 1, 1945: "Eyes troubling me somewhat. Too much reading 'fine print.' Nearly every memorandum has a catch in it, and it has been necessary to read at least a thousand of them and as many reports."

Most of the advice the President receives, however, is rendered by ear. This by no means is a phenomenon of the modern tempo, but was equally true of older times. The cabinet secretaries of James K. Polk, President from 1845 to 1849, as a matter of daily routine, drove up to the Executive Mansion, hitched their horses to the posts with knobs of laughing lions, and dropped in on their chief without prearranged appointment. A modern-day President sees more people for briefer intervals. Harry Truman, on a typical day in 1950, absorbed a fifteen-minute briefing from the executive secretary of the National Security Council and met for an hour each with his personal staff and the advisory committee to the National Security Resources Board. He allotted twenty minutes to General Omar Bradley to review the current status of the fighting in Korea, eleven minutes to Secretary of State Dean Acheson for a sudden foreign policy problem and an hour to J. Frederick Lawton, the Budget Director, to tidy up the preliminary ceilings for next year's budget. Two hours were distributed among Senator Brien McMahon on atomic-energy matters, Congressman Mike Mansfield on new power facilities for Montana, and Congressman Frank L. Chelf of Kentucky and his reapportionment bill.

"Advice" passes through many stages from raw material to finished product. Problems fitting for the President are discovered, described and defined, and even redefined. Research methods are chosen; sources are consulted. Alternative courses of action or "solutions" are framed, consequences predicted, and choices are recommended. Not only in the final stages, but in every step along the way, the adviser may advocate a viewpoint or an interest, if not openly, then by subtle indirection. The priority he gives the matters he sets before his chief, his verbal colorations, his inflections and gestures, his omissions and elaborations are standard tactical weapons in the drive to get what he wants. Some advisers never really cease being advocates. Even in the face of a presidential "no," they can play a waiting game, regrinding their axes at propitious moments, and waging undercover campaigns of attrition on the policies they don't like.

The competition of the palace is fostered by various circumstances of the President. The problems he has to cope with are big, unobvious as to solution, and above all controversial. The ultimate condition of security of status in the palace—the possession of the President's complete and abiding confidence—is unattainable. No President can afford to give his confidence wholly to one man, for to do so would be to hostage himself to that man. Presidents keep their faith and dependence moving around, distribute their candor mostly in little pieces, and sparingly in big chunks. The fact that the President's confidence is normally divided begets continual struggle among his personal associates for bigger and better shares of it. Nor does the struggle lend itself to the stabilizing influence of a formal investiture of power. An adviser's status is not something that can be settled and defined by resonant titles, explicit conferrals of authority, or the organization chart. Status is the subtle, changeable, but unmistakable florescence of the President's mind.

Some Presidents, taking the lesson of George Washington to heart, deliberately cultivate the competition of their advisers. Competition, these Presidents seem to find, gives zest and energy to their administrations. Franklin D. Roosevelt thought it made his associates behave better. Both Roosevelt and his ideological forebear, Andrew Jackson, who on occasion were highly uncertain of the course their administrations should pursue, took pains to keep on hand a corps of advisers whose assorted political faiths traversed a broad spectrum. Each President enjoyed the self-created comfort of having, outstretched from many sides, eager hands pointing the way to the sunlight of decision. In 1938, when Roosevelt was mulling over a spending policy appropriate for the economic recession of that year, he looked to the left, to the Keynesians in his Administration; to Tom Corcoran, the RFC counsel and White House favorite; Secretary of the Interior Harold Ickes; and WPA Administrator Harry Hopkins; and on the other hand to the right, to conservatives like secretaries Morgenthau and Hull, and Vice-President Garner. For weeks, Roosevelt cogitated and made soundings until finally he threw in with the Keynesians. Having consulted the conservatives fully, he could do so with a minimum of mental anguish.

To maintain his advisers' competition at just the right pitch requires no little finesse on the part of the President. When problems arise, he must avoid identifying himself too early with a specific course of action. If he does, he discourages his advisers from plunging into their creative cerebrations and coming up with alternatives. He must expect, in fixing his course, that even his most tentative association with a problem will unleash ambitions and channel thinking, because the dispenser of prestige is at hand and practically everyone will strive to please him. But the President must also steer clear of the opposite and equal danger. If he stays aloof from his problem too long, he may end up at the mercy of his advisers. For when time is running out and action becomes inexorable, he can do little more than work within the range of choices they set before him.

The palace competition has its own system of penalties and rewards. In making decisions of policy, the President is not merely choosing between conflicting advice, he is also choosing between advisers. His decisions are simultaneously conferrals of recognition and rebuff; they are major occasions for defining and redefining status. The President also may scatter the pearls of status simply by being cordial, expansive and confiding. He has choice assignments and missions to dispense; he can make temporary aggrandizements of jurisdiction permanent. A President such as Harry Truman quite systematically ran his inner circle on a career basis, with promotion the reward for those discharging their established assignments with special merit. Clark Clifford, of the White House staff, after a stint as assistant to Judge Samuel Rosenman, succeeded Rosenman, when the latter retired from government service. Charles Murphy, President's Counsel from 1949 to 1951, put in a lively apprenticeship under Clifford and took the big step upward when Clifford went into private law practice.

Presidential favorites also live in a world abounding in pitfalls and penalties. If their conduct displeases their chief, he can mete out a plethora of social sanctions. His jollity wanes; he becomes matter-of-fact, distant, frosty, et cetera. At the very worst, an adviser may lose the President's confidence and be unceremoniously ejected from the throne room into the outer darkness. This dread catastrophe seldom comes to pass, however, via a full-scale blowup. Andrew Johnson, however, speaking from his own tumultuous experience, has asserted that the mutual confidence which obtains between a President and his adviser, is rarely obliterated by a single act, but "may be just as effectually destroyed by a series of causes too subtle for demonstration. As it is a plant of slow growth, so, too, it may be slow in decay."

Outside the White House lurk equally horrendous perils against which the adviser is well-nigh defenseless. He is a favorite object of abuse which the President's foes really intend for him, but can't level at him directly because it's bad politics to do so. It's safer to attack those most intimately identified with his works, the toilers in the shadows, the ready objects of suspicion, his confidants. Likewise, ambitious private interests, meeting rebuff to their policy aspirations in the White House, may conclude that they'll never get anywhere until a particular adviser or confidant, the attributed source of obstruction, is removed from the scene. Inevitably, therefore, the adviser and his advice become a stake in the power game. He is apt to be a matter of contention in general politics as in office politics, and the object of all the means of political struggle, fair and foul.

Part Two

———

EMINENT FAVORITES

———

Operation Genius

ALEXANDER HAMILTON

"I CONSIDER Napoleon, Pitt, and Hamilton as the three greatest men of our age," wrote Talleyrand in the autumn of his career, "and if I had to choose between the three, I would unhesitatingly give the first place to Hamilton." Talleyrand, for all of his wisdom, did not go far enough. He might quite legitimately have contended that what Hamilton did in just five lively years as Secretary of the Treasury in the Presidency of George Washington, was enough to match, if not surpass, what his formidable contemporaries required a lifetime to accomplish. As Washington's aide, Hamilton dealt brilliantly with nothing less than the founding of a government, the remaking of an economy, organizing an army and conducting diplomacy where the price of a misstep was war or ruin.

He established himself as the original planner of the Great American Miracle: the transformation of the United States, over the course of a century and a half, from a simple countryside of small farms and indifferent towns into the industrial colossus of the universe.

In applying the new, untried plan of government—the Constitution drafted at Philadelphia in 1787—he discovered how to make the document function like a rubber suit instead of a strait jacket, and enabled it to adjust successfully not only to the exigencies of his own time, but equally well for those of years later. While building with such distinction for the future, Hamilton faced and conquered every one of the many difficult problems which bedeviled the first Presidency. He rescued the country from incipient insolvency by ordering its tangled finances, installing a currency, building up its manufactures and quadrupling its trade. When all was going well, and a strong undertow of popular clamors threatened to drag the Republic into what would surely have been a ruinous war with Britain in 1793, he was the rescuer in that thankless situation, too.

Hamilton carved out his achievements in a capacity that far exceeded in function and power the post of Secretary of the Treasury which he nominally occupied. He operated as chief adviser and confidential assistant to President Washington, and in that creative, free and conveniently obscure status, he came to dominate the Executive Branch as no one has

49

dominated it since. Time and again, he literally snatched the State Department right out of the extraordinarily competent hands of the Secretary of State, Thomas Jefferson. He had immensely more to say about the conduct of the militia of the United States, even on the field of battle, than did the Secretary of War, General Henry Knox, or any of his professional commanders. The principal legal opinions in the Presidency were drafted not by the Attorney General, Edmund Randolph, but by Alexander Hamilton. Into every corner of the Executive Branch he penetrated with tumultuous force and whenever, as rarely happened, opposition dared appear, he would efficiently and unmercifully overwhelm it.

The very special talent on which Hamilton relied and thrived in these vigorous enterprises, had been amply developed long before the Presidency of Washington. In the middle of the Revolution, a sharp-eyed colleague, General Charles Lee, clearly exposed this key to Hamilton and his comrade-in-arms, the Marquis de Lafayette, by describing those gentlemen, not altogether graciously, as "dirty-ear-wigs who will forever insinuate themselves near persons high in office."*

Technically, dour John Adams was also correct when he called Hamilton "the bastard brat of a Scotch pedlar." Behind this epithet, however, lies an involved and troubled tale. Rachel, the mother of Hamilton and the daughter of the Doctor John Fawcetts, Huguenot refugees residing in the island of St. Kitts in the British West Indies, was placed by her parents into an arranged and wholly unhappy marriage with a wealthy middle-aged local merchant, when she was barely sixteen. Apparently, there were months of unmitigated grief, and when a new lover, handsome copper-haired James Hamilton, came upon the horizon, there was more grief. Rachel, consulting with attorneys, discovered that divorce could be granted only by Act of Parliament which required money and influence, which she didn't have. Remarriage, under the law, was therefore impossible. The unfortunate girl did what seemed to her the only thing to do in such circumstances. She repaired to the neighboring island of Nevis, and there lived, without benefit of clergy, with Hamilton, a Scottish émigré and island merchant of slender means.

After two sons were born (Alexander, it is believed from uncertain records, came on January 11, 1757), father Hamilton's business crashed; other noble efforts failed and, in his discouragement, he abandoned his growing brood by taking off one moonless night in a borrowed rowboat for the freedom of other islands. (Island-hopping seemed to be the favorite solvent

---

* The earwig is an insect which, according to legend, searches out the ear of a sleeping person, crawls into it and nests there.

in those days for the troubled less well to do.) Rachel, who under calmer circumstances revealed unmistakable signs of a first-rate intellect, died heart-broken from her marital tribulations, penniless and overworked, when Alexander was only eleven. Her son, save for fitful help from relatives, inherited the immediate problem of making his way alone and the embarrassment of dubious lineage that was to bedevil his proudest hours the rest of his life. Years later, Gouverneur Morris, confronted by the unseemly immutable fact in his sad duty of composing a funeral oration, congratulated himself for contriving a mode "to pass over this handsomely."

In his twelfth year, Hamilton was taken as a clerk in the house of Nicholas Cruger, a local merchant prince. The youngster's quick intelligence easily mastered the routines of keeping accounts; his verbal fluency put him to writing commercial letters; at fourteen he even managed the business with great skill and judgment during Cruger's long absences, building up clientele in that island area. But it was the off hours from his work that Hamilton really lived for, the sessions with Dr. Hugh Knox, a Presbyterian minister and family friend, who had sized up the lad as nothing less than a prodigy and therefore worthy of tutoring in all the learning within the grasp of the Biblical scholar that Knox was. Under the Reverend's direction and in tireless study—beginning beneath the oil lamp and regularly trailing into early morning hours—Hamilton executed a series of rigorous intellectual projects at a pace that was amazing. A natural linguist, he learned to speak and write French, a rarity in the islands. He read Latin and also acquired a smattering of Hebrew in the classes of a Jewish schoolmistress. (He was the only Founding Father acquainted with that language.) He tackled ancient history, mathematics and art with equal success, and turned out some lively, graceful verse. After three years of facing his scholar's merciless application, Dr. Knox found his intellectual reserves just about used up.

Hamilton's exploits, which up to then were a private matter between himself and his tutor, were literally swept into public view by a hurricane which ravaged St. Croix and flattened Christiansted, the capital. The devastation and human grief sparked the young man and his facile pen into a descriptive essay of compassionate eloquence. The essay was printed in the *Royal Danish Gazette*, chief English newspaper of the islands, and the impression it made exceeded the storm itself. Governor Walsterstorff asked for the author and summoned a conference of Dr. Knox, other wards of culture in the islands, and the prodigy's relatives. Such rare talents, all agreed, must be encouraged and trained. Before he knew it, Hamilton was on the seas bound for a brief interlude of grammar school at Elizabethtown, New Jersey, and a rewarding excursion into higher learning at King's College (later Columbia) in New York.

In the classroom, Hamilton dazzled his professors and fellow students by the zest of his intellectual curiosity, his agility under the fire of debate, and a versatile literary output, which included three sonnets, an elegy on the death of a lady and the prologue and epilogue of a play. He mastered the curriculum of literature, philosophy and science with record speed, excelling equally with the "Iliad," Plutarch, Rousseau, or anatomy—at one time, apparently, he planned to follow in his grandfather's footsteps and study medicine. His favorite working place was a nearby cemetery, where he repaired at dawn and, ordinarily, on return trips to the college at twilight, puzzled and amused his fellow pedestrians by proceeding through the streets, engrossed in some intellectual problem, talking and gesturing earnestly to himself.

But if there was anything in which Hamilton wished above all else to excel, it was not scholarship, or business management, or belles-lettres; it was the military art. There was no finer glory. At the height of his success in the house of Cruger, he had written to Ned Stevens, his cousin, his preference for the excitement of the battlefield to his current lot, closing with an emphatic, "I wish there was a war." Midway in his studies, the gunfire at Lexington and Concord answered his prayer, and shortly thereafter the New York legislature further obliged by commissioning him captain of artillery. Hamilton formed his own company, and established a wide reputation as a pitiless drillmaster. "A soldier," he lectured a homesick rank-and-filer, "should have no other wife than the service." By drilling his unruly squads of tattered farmers and awkward mechanics from early morning until dusk, Hamilton converted them into that rarity of the Revolutionary Army, an able, orderly force. Their leader, a mere boy, with cocked hat pulled down over his eyes, would march behind his cannon and, apparently lost in thought, pat it every now and then as if it were a favorite horse or plaything. On the battlefield, his mastery of fundamentals paid off handsomely. At Princeton, his coolness and resource and the accuracy of his cannon saved two desperate situations and won the notice of General Washington himself. Hamilton was summoned to commanding headquarters.

In the youth standing before him, Washington, who was known to be withdrawn at first meetings, took immediate interest. This mere lad of twenty, barely five feet seven in height, had perfect military presence. Straight as a battle spear, his uniform immaculate, his face handsome in an imperial way, he was made to command. His features, uniformly prominent but balanced, were dominated by deep-set eyes; he had a long, perfect aquiline nose; reddish fair hair, powdered, turned back over a high forehead, and collected in a queue; a broad mouth and full lips; a deep jaw, majestically tilted a little high and rising higher in moments of emphasis.

Washington's purpose in the interview was to size up Hamilton for an unusual and difficult capacity. For some time the General had needed an all-round aide to care for duties behind the battle lines that had become increasingly irksome and demanding. Supplies had to be managed; correspondence with the Continental Congress and the state governors, and negotiations with the French allies had to be handled; his own generals, several of whom were bent on undercutting him, had to be instructed and watched. "It is absolutely necessary," Washington stated his requirements, "for me to have persons that can think for me, as well as execute orders."

On March 1, 1777, in his twentieth year, Hamilton accepted appointment as aide-de-camp to the Commanding General. As was his habit, Washington had tapped the right man. Overnight, the newcomer converted headquarters into a throbbing hive of plans, reorganizations and special missions. He revised the inspector general's office, drafted a comprehensive set of military regulations and provided the blueprints for the reorganization of the entire army. With the French Admirals Ternay and Rochambeau, both bent on cutting broad swaths in history, Hamilton negotiated plans for joint campaigns which pleased Washington and the eager French alike. Hamilton, clearly, was far more than a mere literary assistant or conventional aide-de-camp. He was a general administrative deputy and trusted adviser.

Meanwhile, Hamilton had taken a wife. If ever he came close to writing off his lowly origins, he did so in his marriage to Elizabeth Schuyler, second daughter of General Philip Schuyler, scion of one of the richest and most influential families in the State of New York. The Schuylers, who dazzled with social eminence, were that rarity, a fourth-generation family in a brand-new country. They had connections, prestige and wealth; union with a Schuyler could demolish the most formidable barrier that propriety might raise to the misbegotten in any drawing room in America.

Elizabeth Schuyler was skilled at domestic management, and deserved the kudos a friend once passed along to Hamilton: "She has as much merit as your Treasurer as you have as Treasurer of the wealth of the United States." Over long years of her husband's impecunious devotion to public service, she successfully reared a brood of eight children and functioned as his literary critic, listening as he wrote, to see how his phrases fell upon the ear. Her courage was infinite. She weathered the shock of losing both her husband and eldest son in duels; one daughter went insane; Hamilton himself lapsed into an extra-marital venture with a boardinghouse proprietress which resulted in some ungrammatically rendered blackmail and painful publicity. But Elizabeth's loyalty never wavered. Even in her ninety-fourth year, after a whole half century of widowhood, it was still undimmed. When James Monroe came to apologize for slanders he had cast upon Hamilton for his romantic backslide decades earlier, she proudly turned him away, declaring that "no lapse of time, no nearness to the grave, make any difference."

Neither a devoted wife nor distinguished success in his duties under Washington could offset Hamilton's rising dissatisfaction with his lot less than one year after his assignment to commanding headquarters. The boyhood fantasy of the military hero had reclaimed its dominion; the powder smoke, shrieking fifes and foaming horses, the distant adventure and glory of the battlefield beckoned. Paper work at headquarters was a pallid substitute. Friends abroad teased with insinuations that his office tasks were beneath the honor of a gentleman. Finally, sick of it all, Hamilton decided to request a corps command, gathered supporting letters from General Nathanael Greene and Lafayette, but Washington adamantly refused to part with his aide-de-camp. Hamilton brooded and grew irritable on petty things. Washington, a proud nature and absolute disciplinarian, was never one to tolerate meddling with proprieties, and on February 16, 1778, the break so long threatened, came. Washington had summoned Hamilton to his quarters. On the way, Hamilton was stopped by Lafayette for several minutes of conversation; he then abruptly excused himself and hurried to Washington. The General was awaiting him at the top of the headquarters stairway. His face was dark as a thundercloud and his hand clenched the balustrade. "Colonel Hamilton," he exploded, "you have kept me waiting at the head of the stairs these ten minutes. I must tell you, sir, you treat me with disrespect." Hamilton drew up his full middling height and his wrath shot to the stars. "I am not conscious of it, sir." he flared back, "but since you have thought it necessary to tell me so, we part." Washington stared at him. "Very well, sir," he said coldly, "if it be your choice." A few hours later, with a great man's humility, Washington sent the olive branch. The General had enormous confidence in Hamilton's abilities, his integrity and usefulness, declared an intermediary. He must remain as aide-de-camp. But Hamilton was firm, and in letters to friends that evening, announced that he had quit his office and the society of the man for whom "I have felt no friendship and have professed none." He set out for the battlefield, praying righteously, "May the time come when characters may be known in their true light."

But time speedily reduced the quarrel of Hamilton and Washington to what it really was: a passing bit of pyrotechnics on the part of two proud men who at heart were friends and truly admired each other's good works. When demands began, in 1789, for the General to abandon the peace of Mount Vernon and provide, as only he could, the leadership which the Republic required, the voice of Hamilton rang out clearly above all the rest. "Without him," he proclaimed, "the ship was sunk before it had even quit port."

On April 30, 1789, the President-elect took the oath at the new Federal Hall on Wall Street in New York and the new ship—Washington solemnly christened it "the last great experiment for promoting human happiness by reasonable compact in civil society"—was launched under skies that were brightly favorable. Prosperity was high everywhere, for farmer, mechanic and merchant alike. Lucrative old markets in England and the West Indies, lost in the Revolution, had firmly revived, and trade with the French and the Dutch climbed so fast that many a merchant in Boston fell behind with his ledgers. Manufacture, that odd new form of enterprise, had caught hold in several Eastern towns, and factories were already turning out limited and exceedingly expensive quantities of wrought iron, woolens, sailcloth and glass. The West, (i.e., the territory between the Appalachians and the Ohio River) and the vast unsettled forest lands of the East called with seductive promises of wealth and adventure.

There were also fears abroad in the land; none, indeed, so hardy as the general prosperity and optimism, but substantial enough to trouble thoughtful men. Only four years before, in 1785, a commercial letdown had seized the country: prices of staples toppled, shops closed their doors, many a farmer went under, and idle laborers wandered menacingly over the countryside. A few mistakes in the inexperienced Treasury, and the tragedy might strike again. Even worse was the debt inherited from the Revolution, a thoroughly dismal proposition—more than forty million dollars owed by the central government to its citizens, another twenty-five million owed by the states and nearly twelve million owed to foreign investors. How could a new government, with untried powers of taxation and of borrowing, flourish under that crushing heritage?

"There is but one man in the United States who can tell you," said Robert Morris when President Washington put this vexing question to him. "That is Alexander Hamilton." Intrigued by the wizardry of Hamilton's financial reports in the Revolution, Morris had long held the younger man as his number-one protégé. On September 2, 1789, when Congress established the Treasury Department, Washington first offered the post of Secretary to Morris out of respect to his status as elder financial statesman, but because of ailing health, and wholly as Washington expected, Morris declined. Then, in line with his previous conversation with the financier, Washington offered the appointment to Hamilton, now aged thirty-two, and furiously engaged, after a mere five months of reading law, in establishing himself as the leading barrister in the courts of all New York. Hamilton accepted at once, notwithstanding the alarms of friends who hated to see a brilliant legal career sacrificed for the futile horrors of a fundless, debt-ridden

Treasury office, whose meager salary of three thousand dollars per annum offered certain impoverishment to its young incumbent, his wife and his children who already numbered five and would increase to eight.

What enabled Hamilton to take office so serenely was his discovery, in two secret conversations at the President's house during the preceding summer, that Washington saw eye to eye with him on the first big steps to be taken by the new Administration. The Republic, the General believed, must establish confidence in its own solvency and stability, encourage trade and manufacture, and throw open the vast Western territories. But his ideas in all these matters, at best, were vague and hopeful. His Inaugural Address, which reflected the extent of his thinking, was a brief prayerful expression of general sentiments on the country's future. He had no program and few policies. But from Hamilton's power-conscious standpoint the situation was perfect. The sound fundamentals and general vagueness provided an infinite opportunity for a talented executive assistant to transmute the President's several ideas into scores of concrete measures, join them into a consistent program and endow them with a militant philosophy to win Congressional and public support—all to the end of starting the young, promising land down the surest and most direct road to power and greatness. What, indeed, the first Presidency plainly called for was the resourceful vigorous aide-de-camp of the Revolution, the general deputy and trusted adviser who would be nothing less than the main source of inspiritation and action for the whole Administration.

But how far Washington would go in seeking out collective advice, with all the secretaries full and free participants, was not at all clear. As the Administration got under way, the secretaries were not on equal footing. Of them all, Washington knew only Hamilton well. The Secretary of the Treasury was the first to be offered appointment, and an air of special confidence prevailed as the further appointments developed. Washington sent Hamilton a list of the names under consideration, seeking his advice, and kept him current with the negotiations which brought Thomas Jefferson into the Administration as Secretary of State, Edmund Randolph as Attorney General and General Henry Knox as Secretary of War.

Jefferson was an enigma who looked the part. Hamilton knew him only by reputation; they had never met before taking up their duties under Washington, but in the record of the new Secretary of State, Hamilton perceived several disturbing ambiguities. Jefferson, abroad when the Constitution was framed, had remained conspicuously silent toward the new government when one in his place should have promptly and forthrightly praised it. At first, he had refused the foreign-affairs post, claiming—and one might question his sincerity—that he might serve his country better at the French court. His general bearing seemed always to mask the real person.

Known for his learning, wizardry at architecture and invention, and cosmopolitan tastes, his appearance strangely contradicted his reputation. He dressed like a beggar, even for affairs of state, in worn-out clothes and carpet slippers, whose effects were exaggerated by his slouch and outrageous manner of sitting. At the most formal occasion he would quickly and unceremoniously retreat to a divan, slip into a lounging manner on his hip, with one shoulder pushed high above the other, and survey the room with the distant majesty of a misplaced gargolye. Mrs. Bayard Smith, leading matron of capital society, was pleased to discover that beneath a carrot complexion lived a meek and mild, though ordered, spirit, a voice low and soft in resonance and a benign intelligence. Unfriendly critics thought his glance shifty, revealing a lack of candor, and Senator Maclay saw nothing of that "firm collective deportment which I expected would dignify the presence of a Secretary or Minister."

Randolph, the Attorney General, belonged to the planter aristocracy and the little coterie of Virginians who led their countrymen through the tempestuous events from the twilight of colonialism to the new day of the Constitution. He had the ineffable charm and dignity of the South, but was plagued, like many of his class, with heavy debts from land speculation and general mismanagement of his affairs. Several times he borrowed substantial sums from Hamilton. Gossips at the capital made sport over Randolph's debts to grocers, costumers and wine sellers. Yet his gifts at the law were considerable, although an irresistible urge toward perfectionism pulled him so deep into technicalities that means often triumphed over ends.

The final member of the presidential family, General Henry Knox, Secretary of War, was a ponderous New Englander of two hundred and eighty pounds, carried gracefully on a tall, straight superstructure, though seemingly overtaxing a pair of spindly legs, bowed from a lifetime in the saddle. Ordinarily the General would have tucked under his arm a cane which, in conversation, he drew and flourished like a sword. His left hand, mutilated in a childhood accident, was always wrapped in a black silk handkerchief. He was kindly, sincere and generous, but there his virtues ran out. Appointed to the War Department mainly to bolster the sectional representation of the Administration, he quickly showed himself to be beyond his depth, and settled down to his main and innocuous function of shattering the tedium of stiffly formal capital parties with his hearty laughter and off-color wit.

During the summer preceding his appointment, Hamilton, with usual foresight, had fashioned a neat little mechanism to transport himself straightway to the loftiest place of influence in the Administration. Congress, at the time, was on the verge of founding a Treasury Department, and Hamilton somehow arranged to have the task of drafting the necessary legislation diverted to his law office. "Neglecting his practice terribly," according to his son John, Hamilton spent days drafting, tearing up and redrafting until he came up with a document that was foolproof. The magic language in the bill of seven sections and eight subsections, which Congress enacted exactly as Hamilton prepared it, was as follows: The Secretary of the Treasury shall "make report and give information to either branch of the legislature, in person or in writing (as he may be required), respecting all matters referred to him by the House of Representatives, or which shall pertain to his office." This sweeping mandate was wholly without limitation. The Reports of the Secretary would apply not merely to "Treasury" matters, but to all matters, and potentially under Hamilton's brisk direction, the influence of the department might fasten onto every conceivable activity of the Administration.

Hardly had the new Secretary and his staff of thirty-nine officers, clerks and messengers established themselves, when the wondrous capacities of the new Treasury Act began to be demonstrated. Hamilton composed a resolution which his college-days friend, Congressman Elias Boudinot, introduced in the House of Representatives, requesting what came to be the First Report on the Public Credit. Days before the Resolution passed, Hamilton was deep in work on the Report. In rapid succession, and by the same slick process, came calls for reports on a National Bank, on Manufactures, on the establishment of a Mint, and later, a further report on the Public Credit. It was nothing for Hamilton to draft several documents simultaneously, work intensively first on one, then drop it, shut the door of his mind to it, and plunge into a fresh subject. His mind, like the inside of a mansion, was an elaborate layout of perfectly walled compartments.

His capacity for work was unbelievable. Talleyrand, who, during a spell of social gadabouting in New York, observed him toiling at any and all hours in his law office, called it "a wonder of the world." Hamilton seemed "to depend on industry," said Fisher Ames of his hero, "as if nature had done nothing for him." Upon his ordinary workday, which commenced at six o'clock in the morning and closed at ten o'clock at night, and proceeded with an intensity that would crush a galley slave, Hamilton thought nothing of superimposing a further rigorous schedule for major enterprises, such as the Reports. Seized with inspiration, no matter what the time of night might be, he would rise from his bed, gulp down several cups of strong coffee, and seat himself at a table for an eight-hour stretch of rapid uninterrupted writing, which required amazingly little correction. Such stints, which continued for months on end, never exacted from the tough Hamilton the weary letdowns and nervous eclipses of the ordinary executive. The one trifling price the Secretary paid for his overindulgence was duly reported by Angelica

Church, his sister-in-law and ardent admirer, "Hamilton writes too much and takes no exercise, and grows too fat."

The yield of this demonic industry was an output of documents which in word count and the expanse of policies proposed has never been exceeded by even the most kinetic teams of modern-day Brain Trusters. "The Great Reports," as they quickly became known, provided the basis of every important domestic decision for Washington's first term of office and for a good part of the second, and served ingeniously and simultaneously to strengthen the central government, develop the country's resources and stimulate trade and capitalistic enterprises. The First Report on Public Credit tackled the most formidable problem facing the Administration by proposing that the entire debt of the Continental Congress be refunded at face value and the Revolutionary debts of the states be taken over by the central government, as the one sure way to build up confidence and attract investment capital at home and abroad. In further reports, Hamilton called for the establishment of a mint and a decimal currency founded on the dollar to replace the motley system of coins—English guineas, crowns and shillings, French pistoles, Spanish milled dollars, and Portuguese joannes which drove merchants and travelers wild by fluctuating unpredictably in value from town to town, and required laborious translations into accounts kept entirely in terms of English currency. The final unit of Hamilton's fiscal structure was the Bank of the United States, a semi-public institution, with authority to receive deposits, make loans to private individuals, the states and the federal government, and issue instruments of credit. The Bank would become the principal source of active and productive capital in the country.

But the document of the most enduring influence was the *Report on the Subject of Manufactures*, the uncanny master plan of America's future greatness. Impressed that simple agricultural countries produced the least wealth, that in the Revolution the lack of manufacture had gravely handicapped the American forces, and that all history taught that prosperity is greatest where the objects of enterprise engaging the human mind are the most numerous, Hamilton urged that the predominately agricultural society of his time be replaced with a balanced economy of manufacture, trade and agriculture. Specifically, he proposed that government protect infant manufactures against European competition, grant patents to encourage invention, prohibit the export of raw materials required by domestic industry, and improve the labor force by fostering the immigration of foreign artisans. The Report on Manufactures provided a store of stimulus and argument not only for all good Federalists of the day, but for such latter-day Hamiltonians as Henry Clay and his American system, William McKinley and the young Arthur Vandenberg.

In further writings, Hamilton sketched out plans for a national system of highways, bridges and canals to open new markets and bind together the remotest portions of the Union. For military defense, he urged the immediate creation of a navy, the erection of arsenals, foundries, dockyards and fortifications. He drew the plans for what was later the Military Academy at West Point, and for years he advocated the establishment of a national university, commanding the "ablest professors" and open to every qualified youth of the country.

Hamilton's program joined the most powerful and seemingly everlasting forces of society into a firm partnership with government. He made it the interest of persons of capacity—the wealthy and the talented—to support the central government, since that government's primary interest would be to guard their property and multiply opportunities for the exercise of their talents. His plans drew further strength from the fact that they possessed a unity which has never been matched since his time in the output of any presidential administration. There have been New Deals, Square Deals and Fair Deals, and other valiant programs of many parts, but each bears scars of hasty improvisation, internal contradiction and weakening compromise. Hamilton's production was all of a piece. Nothing was omitted, no elements clashed, the thread of a common philosophy runs unbroken throughout it. It was a flawless monument of his belief that every activity of government—finance, the regulation of commerce, public works, education, agriculture, foreign affairs and national defense—related intimately to one another, and that the good executive marshaled each of these many potent parts to contribute to the success of the whole.

Hamilton secured his unified effects by a simple expedient: he established himself as the solitary creator of the Great Reports. He, and he alone, conceived the ideas, grubbed out the research facts in notes that would fill a ten-foot shelf, and wrote every word of his documents. While toiling furiously away in his Treasury office, he allowed none of his fellow secretaries so much as a glimpse of, or let fall a single revealing word about, his pages. Secretary of War Knox, who showed unmistakable signs of admiration and devotion, was firmly held at the same arm's length as every other member of the Administration. Even Hamilton's most trusted subordinates in the Treasury Department were elaborately and exclusively occupied with other duties. But one figure loomed who could not be avoided: the President.

It was not too much to say that General Washington envisaged for himself a sharply circumscribed role in the new government—one of dignified power, far and above the rough-and-tumble phases of policy-making. Such bruising, though influential, activity of necessity would fall to one or more of his subordinates. With deep reluctance, he had embarked again, in his revealing phrase, "on the tempestuous ocean of public life." A sensitive spirit, who faltered under criticism, he brooded over his conviction that his countrymen expected too much of him. His health had badly gone back on him. Headaches, influenza attacks, rheumatic pains seized him in a constant cycle; soon after he took office a large and painful tumor appeared upon his thigh, making walking or sitting almost impossible, and forced him to take exercise in a coach altered to permit him to stretch out the full length of it. These everlasting trials of Job, he was reported to believe, had enfeebling effects upon his intellect.

The President, then, was a man who needed his confidence bolstered, his weary hours lightened, and his talents, where they fell short of the problems before him, extended by the ministrations of an efficient intellect. So, at least, Hamilton fixed his course to Washington. Two or even three times a day, he would hustle up the winding brick steps of the President's House on Cherry Street,* stride past the household slave posted at the door, and proceed unannounced into the moderate-sized drawing room where visitors were received. It was a comfortable room, with a giant sofa sloping halfway across it, a floor-to-ceiling Normandy stone fireplace, and a claw-footed desk where Washington sat engrossed in his papers.

Removing his spectacles with a slow, composed gesture (he seemed utterly incapable of rapid movement), the President would rise to his full erect stature of well over six feet. His austerity struck the atmosphere like a whipcrack. Prompting this effect were a strong face with gray-blue lack-luster eyes set wide apart in deep orbits, a square jaw and tight-clamped mouth, and a manner that was invariably calm, stately, sober, almost sad, but never dull. He addressed Hamilton always as "Sir" or "Mr. Hamilton."

Beneath this glazed exterior, Hamilton discovered, as did nearly every-one associated with the President in any degree, lay springs of melancholia that were forever bubbling to the surface. Overconscientious, seething with worry and gloom, Washington seldom laughed and then only for purposes of sarcasm. His customary approach to the most festive and what the ordinary run of men would consider the most joyous occasions was downright woeful. The men's dinners of the President of the United States were, at least by present-day standards, a dietetic orgy, and if anything can gladden humankind, they surely could. The dining table, managed by five servants, would be loaded with roast beef, veal, turkey, ducks, fowl, ham, fish (roasted and boiled), jellies, pies, puddings, iced creams, oranges, apples, nuts, almonds, figs, raisins and a titillating assortment of fine wines and punch.

* Twice the President changed residences. He moved to the McComb house on lower Broadway, one of the largest in New York, and when the capital was transferred to Philadelphia in the fall of 1790, he rented the mansion of Robert Morris.

But, according to Senator Maclay, the President's "settled aspect of melancholy" fixed the temper of these proceedings. "No cheering ray of convivial sunshine broke through the cloudy gloom of settled seriousness," complained the Senator. "At every interval of eating and drinking he [the President] played on the table with a fork and knife like a drumstick."

Hamilton was the one member of officialdom who could shatter the gloom with any consistency. With bursts of a repartee second to none in the capital's *haut monde*, he could touch off rounds of laughter, to which even Washington had to capitulate with a quiet chuckle, not a muscle of his face moving. Later, in the passage of cordials and coffee, Hamilton would unloose one final assault on the rigid decorum, by rendering in his rich, untrained voice, his favorite, "The Drum," a rafter-shaking, somewhat irreverent ditty, in which a sergeant coaxes a clergyman to follow along to battle— "When we die, we'll want a man of God near by." In private moments with the President, Hamilton tried to keep his best foot forward. This, in light of his history, was no mean accomplishment. Unfortunately, Hamilton was eaten with vanity, a failing which commonly befalls men of his attainments. He became intolerant of anyone who even slightly questioned his actions or opinions and openly insulting to those poor souls who could not keep up with his galloping pace. Inevitably he offended and fought with all manner of men—even the clergy would drop their sacred toil and take up cudgels against him. The Reverend Doctor William Gordon, chaplain to the legislature of Massachusetts, became locked with Hamilton in a ridiculous little quarrel, involving gossip and sensitive honor, reams of correspondence, and trying moments for anxious friends who feared that it all might end up in lawsuits or violence. In the city of New York, a group of respectable and peaceful gentlemen were goaded by Hamilton's insufferable manner into concluding that everything considered, Hamilton was best dead and out of the way. Solemnly the gentlemen resolved that each one in turn should challenge their hated foe to a duel until, no matter the cost in lives, one of their numbers accomplished the objective. Fortunately, the project never advanced, and fortunately President Washington was always spared his Secretary's bitter ways. This calculated act of grace, be it noted, Hamilton bestowed exclusively upon Washington. With the two other leading figures of the Administration, the Vice-President and the Secretary of State, Hamilton ripped into quarrels that had the proportions of a triple-headed cyclone.

Resuming where he had left off as aide-de-camp in the Revolution, Hamilton promptly took over as the President's general literary draftsman and Jack-of-all-assignments. As draftsman, he converted Washington's roughly sketched ideas into finished, sometimes classic, and always diverse, state papers: messages to Congress, letters to its committees, directives to department secretaries and diplomatic representatives, proclamations ranging from duties on cotton imports to the establishment of Thanksgiving as a public holiday, and even the President's personal and intimate letters. Though these documents issued under Washington's responsibility and name (and not infrequently proceeded through as many as six agonized drafts with repeated Presidential importunities for "a plain style," relieved of all "tautology" and "verbosity," and copy "as perfect as the formation is susceptible of"), the influence of Hamilton was as plain as the Presidential seal upon the face of the papers he prepared. Treasury matters were more prominently placed and were accorded more verbal yardage in messages to Congress than the matters of other departments. Easily two thirds of the President's proclamations were devoted to the Treasury, and directives calling upon the several departments to render fact-gathering, enforcement and sundry other services to the Treasury were more readily and more numerously forthcoming than in cases where some other department stood to gain.

The Great Reports? Between assignments at the President's house, Hamilton trundled in his documents one by one, as they were completed. The matter was a delicate one. Hamilton wanted only general approval, not a page-by-page, proposal-by-proposal scrutiny which might mar the perfect labor. He got what he wanted. The President assented to each and every document, with never the least resistance even on his most fretful days. He disturbed not a single phrase, contributed not a single idea, yet the Reports emerged with his unqualified approval and support. As a matter of fact, the tête-à-têtes rarely dealt with the Reports. Partly, this most welcomed neglect was owed to Hamilton's talent at wheeling his business so unobtrusively on stage that it was hardly noticed, let alone discussed; but even more important was the attitude of Washington, certainly much too alert an executive to be hoodwinked for each of five Reports. There was no discussion, simply because that was his wish. The President was captive to a reticence in these matters which he once put: "I was so little acquainted with commerical affairs that I should very much distrust my own judgment, even in the opinions which I might be obliged to hazard in treating casually of them." Military and foreign affairs, he knew from the Revolution and took the lead in dealing with them as President, but when faced with the intellectual complexities of major financial and commerical policy, fields in which he lacked experience (as did Hamilton), he fell back with sensations of inadequacy, underrating his own really good capacities, and developed the painless habit of leaving all economic policy to his masterful Secretary of the Treasury.

The daily meetings, dealing so little with the Great Reports, went on to scores of troubling questions and semi-crises that were not by any stretch of the imagination Treasury business, but from which Washington found surcease by turning his ingenious friend, who was always seated at just the right time on the great sofa across from his desk. A Post Office had to be created. Ministers had to be appointed to the principal diplomatic posts and the sensitivities involved were frightful. For a meager five posts there were no less than twenty men whose prestige and accomplishment entitled them to expect appointment. All through the second year of the Administration, reports were at hand of rising dissatisfaction in the Southern states—should the President drop his duties for a tour to see things for himself? And again, a scheme of etiquette had to be established for the President's numerous social functions. Upon brief reflection, Hamilton could spin out answers that were thoroughgoing, politically wise and, in every respect, perfectly aimed at the hard-to-hit target of Washington's fastidiousness.

Take the question of Presidential etiquette. Washington wished to end once and for all the distressingly common charges that he was too standoffish from the generality of men and really an old-style monarch in republican disguise. Yet, on the other hand, he keenly desired his great office to be clothed with the dignity it deserved. (On this latter point, he was so insistent that he never shook hands with anyone during his two terms of office, but made his greeting with a stately bow from the waist.) Hamilton proceeded to clear a convincing way out of the dilemma, eluding several further perils the harassed President had missed. He suggested that there be a levee once each week, open to all the citizenry, the President mingling with the assemblage and "conversing cursorily on indifferent subjects." For the more intimate functions, the President would satisfy his obligations and avoid embarrassment by observing several basic rules. Give formal entertainments only twice or four times a year on the anniversaries of leading events of the Revolution and thereby minimize any inference concerning the real purpose of the gatherings. Never linger at table with guests, to avoid "dissatisfaction and cabal" and, for equal reason, return no visit to anyone. Nearly all Presidents to this day have followed at least the latter part of this advice and every element of it was followed in the first Presidency.

As Hamilton was quick to realize, his rising status with the President was a perfect vantage point from which to lay his hands on the affairs of the other departments and shape them according to his own incomparable inspiration and direction. Henry Knox, befuddled manager of the War Department, is one sad example of a secretary who saw substantial portions of his business grabbed up by the Secretary of the Treasury operating from the President's house. One particularly devastating snatch occurred in the wake of the crushing and humiliating defeat of General St. Clair's forces by the western Indian tribes in 1792. Contributing heavily to the fiasco, was the poor management of supply services in the rear. Congress howled with criticism; Secretary Knox howled back. In the tumult, Hamilton galloped off simultaneously in several directions to intervene in an affair that was in no way his responsibility, but plainly required his talents and beckoned with opportunities for extending his power. A friend in the Senate introduced legislation directing the Treasury to take over army supply. This threat planted, Hamilton moved upon Knox with blueprints of reform that had the same effect as the legislation. Knox dug in his toes; he would do nothing. Thereupon, Hamilton proceeded to the *coup de grâce*. He spread his plans before the President, secured his approval of them, and that spelled finis for the balky Mr. Knox. St. Clair was replaced, the Treasury took over the purchasing accounts of the army and indirectly the supply system.

However, life was by no means one unbroken course of conquest for the President's friend. Washington, while leaning upon Hamilton, was following increasingly the practice of seeking out the advice of various quarters in matters of importance. On questions of foreign policy and his relations with Congress, he was regularly consulting Jay and Madison. His correspondence with private citizens at home and abroad was at a new high. He was regularly following the procedure suggested by the language of the Constitution, of posing some question or proposition which required his decision and inviting all his department secretaries to communicate their recommendations individually in writing. On the basis of the replies and his own reflection, Washington made his decision.

As Hamilton uneasily recognized, the presidential habit of multiple consultation threatened his own position of rising influence. Even worse, the sacred Reports might be caught up and hamstrung in the unenlightened review of all the secretaries. But by some adroit, intense maneuvering in the President's study, Hamilton somehow managed to elude this latter menace and keep his projects safely beyond the reach of his colleagues—with one exception. In February, 1791, when legislation authorizing his pet venture, the Bank of the United States, passed Congress by a close vote after fierce debate over its constitutionality, and came to the President for signature, Washington, perplexed by all the argument, sought the advice of Jefferson and Randolph. "Is the Bank constitutional?" he asked, and in elaborate written opinions, both answered in the negative. The Bank was not among the enumerated powers of Congress, and to step beyond them, warned Jefferson, "is to take possession of a boundless field of power."

This opinion, delivered in the afternoon of February fifteenth, haunted Washington all through dinner and a quiet social evening with the Robert Morrises. At ten o'clock, his guests gone, and unable to fight off his anxieties any longer, he ordered out his magnificent cream-colored coach, ornamented with cupids and festoons and drawn by six white horses of the finest Virginia breed, and sped down Broadway, the hoofbeats on the frozen street ruts breaking the silence of the night. Washington turned into Wall Street and proceeded to the bend, where Hamilton's rather ungainly red-brick house stood within sight of the bay. Washington went straight to the living room;

Hamilton was still laboring over papers at his ponderous rosewood worktable with Venuslike faces carved upon its legs. The President poured out an agitated summary of Jefferson's opinion. Was an answer to it possible? Hamilton, as though he had rehearsed for this moment a thousand times, gave a rapid incisive rebuttal, which calmed the President and soon had him nodding in agreement. Would Hamilton be good enough to draft a statement of his views? He would yet that night. By daybreak, the Secretary finished his opinion proving the constitutionality of the Bank by advancing the sweeping doctrine that the Bank rested on implied powers which are delegated as much as the express powers of the Constitution, "that every power includes a right to employ all the means requisite to attain the ends of such power, which are not precluded by the Constitution, or are not immoral, or not contrary to the essential ends of political society." In several scores of elaborating pages, Hamilton provided the main legal, philosophical and inspirational text and vindication of the whole Federalist movement.

Concurrently with his attentions to the President, Hamilton was deep in projects building up his dominion in Congress. Combining his passion for new fields to conquer with the convenient theory that the mainspring of leadership in legislation should be the Executive, Hamilton found the first Congress, which straggled into Wall Street in 1789, ideal for his purposes. Loosely organized, confused by the semicrisis of launching the Republic, it was haunted by the failures of the Confederation. "We are in a wilderness," Representative James Madison summed up the situation. But what of the President? Was not the role which Hamilton eyed properly his? If it was, Washington was indisposed to claim it. Scrupulously aloof and deferential toward Congress, he suggested in only the broadest terms subjects for legislative consideration, and left the heat and dust of battle to his secretaries.

Hamilton brought in his Reports and field-marshaled the whole, frequently stormy, campaign to convert them into legislation: steered them into favorable committees, watched over the hearings, got bills on the floor at the right time for debate and vote, wrote speeches for his lieutenants, and spent endless hours "running from place to place among the members" organizing caucuses—"the rendezvousing of the crew of the Hamilton galley," Senator Maclay described it—to keep his ranks solid and convert the fence sitters. In a day when party machinery and discipline were nonexistent, and men yielded easily to passing sentiment, such tasks severely challenged Hamilton's energies and magnetism. Seemingly hopeless situations, and even defeat itself, he could turn into victory. When assumption of state debts was first voted down in the House, he set up the immortal logrolling deal with Jefferson whereby the latter brought the Virginia delegation to vote for assumption, and Hamilton, the Northern Congressmen to support the location of the permanent capital at Georgetown. Assumption then passed the House.

In the Senate, nothing was left undone to get assumption through. One evening in the week before the vote, Maclay was confronted with two unexpected callers at his lodgings: the Reverend Doctor Rodgers—Hamilton had a flair for using the clergy—and the Speaker of the House, Frederick Augustus Muhlenberg. The visitors came right to the point—a barefaced request for the Senator's vote. The further backing that Hamilton brought up sliced across nearly every influential political element in the country. The Order of Cincinnati, a body of upper-strata Revolutionary heroes, sent in petitions. Government officials, including a nucleus of Washington's own private secretaries and nephews, waited outside the Senate door to besiege the legislators. Squads of citizens descended on the capital in such numbers that Maclay concluded: ". . . the whole city of New York is a machine." Rumors about bribes being used flew thick and fast, but nothing in the way of concrete proof was ever uncovered. With such thorough groundwork, assumption inevitably passed.

The backbone of Hamilton's organization and support was a corps of able Congressional lieutenants who shared the burdens of debate and party management. In the Senate, his chief aide was Rufus King, opulent New York merchant, oracle on commerical affairs and consummate orator. King was a master at whipping the Federalists into line in the Senate. Assisting in this mission was a forceful clique, "the Senatorial Gladiators," Maclay called them. Oliver Ellsworth, the future Chief Justice, was the most formidable, tall, dignified, imperial, who in intense moments of debate would pull out his snuffbox, go through the motions of taking a pinch, and then drop most of it on the carpet near him in little piles. Ellsworth pushed Hamilton's programs through tempestuous interludes in Senate committees with a fidelity that bordered on obstinacy, concerning which Aaron Burr once made the informative comment: "If Ellsworth had happened to spell the name of the Deity with two d's, it would have taken the Senate three weeks to expunge the superfluous letter." Completing the Senate phalanx were Hamilton's father-in-law, Philip Schuyler; Caleb Strong, the sober trustworthy Calvinist and chief pleader for the Bank; and Ralph Izard, the South Carolina planter, president pro tempore of the Senate, confidant of Washington, father of fourteen children and a man of notorious irascibility in his frequent painful sieges of gout.

In the House, the most dedicated Hamiltonians were William Smith of South Carolina and Theodore Sedgwick of Massachusetts, but the most brilliant and the most effective was Fisher Ames. Totally lacking in vanity, suave and pleasing in appearance, Ames was an orator without equal in the span between Patrick Henry and Henry Clay. Colleagues admired his candor, depth of knowledge, oratorical grace and racy metaphors. His defenses of Hamilton's measures, founded on the conviction that an energetic executive should lead Congress, are classics of argumentation. He rose from his sickbed, tottered to the floor of the House, and in a voice that was faint and cold in diction, he rendered in the judgment of an English visitor and connoisseur of parliaments, "the most bewitching piece of parliamentary oratory I have ever listened to." His opponents frantically rushed through adjournments to break the spell. Never an intimate of Hamilton, but unfaltering in support, Ames was driven by his affliction to leave the House in 1796, decline the Presidency of Harvard at the "advancing age" of forty-seven and retire to the life of a cheerful country squire in his birthplace, Dedham, Massachusetts. Clearer in reasoning than Madison—his chief rival in the House—cleverer, more forceful and more courageous, failing health denied him the lofty place in history which rightfully was his.

Hamilton's superb organization had but one defect, an unforgivable one in legislative politics: it was too perfect. Its triumphs were too assured; it dominated too obviously and too completely the affairs of Congress. An opposition began to form from the inevitable human impatience with another man's unbroken success, and from the emerging suspicion of Executive power. "Have we in truth, originated this money bill?" cried Mercer of Maryland. "Do we ever originate any money bill?" The Secretary of the Treasury and his Reports had usurped the essential authority of the House. "The whole business of Legislation may as well be submitted to him," declared Congressman Jackson of Georgia, "so in fact the House would not be Representatives of their constituents, but of the Secretary." The real, although prudently anonymous, leader of this opposition was Thomas Jefferson, working out of the back door of the State Department. His position on government finances reconsidered, Jefferson had come to regret his deal with Hamilton on assumption, which policy he now saw as amounting to legalized looting of the people by hordes of greedy speculators. Jefferson's floor captain was Congressman James Madison, generally considered the first intellect of the House, whose sentiments toward the Administration, too, were changing. Short, pious-faced, bald, potbellied, with a hankering for black clothes which made him look like a friar, Madison dominated the debates with tactical finesse and a cool, monotoned analysis that was devastating. Allied with these two, The Brains of the opposition, was its Hatchet Man, William Branch Giles of Amelia County, Virginia. Squat, untidy, equipped with animal vitality, leather lungs and shrewd instinct in a fight, Giles badgered Hamilton with earsplitting requests for information on the conduct of the Treasury, broadly implying that the department's finances were by no means in the shape that they should be. As the attack wore on, Giles left less and less to innuendo and on February 27, 1793, with only the flimsiest indirection, accused Hamilton in a wild speech of malversation of funds. Roaring his way into a perfectly contrived climax, he flung on the Speaker's table a handful of resolutions to the same effect drafted by The Brains. Not altogether unrelated was the coincidence that the session of Congress was nearing its end, leaving Hamilton with inadequate time to prepare his answer. His silence would condemn him with the public, and possibly the President. But the wily trio had underestimated their victim. Instructing his followers in the House to join with the enemy and request a complete accounting of the Treasury's finances, Hamilton rallied his departmental staff, put aside the gaieties of the social season and the comforts of his hearth, and plunged into three full weeks of what were little short of round-the-clock labors. The deadline was beaten to the surprise of everyone except the Secretary of the Treasury; Giles, for once, was speechless when the report appeared explaining every disbursement and receipt since the beginning of the government. To the judicious observer, Hamilton disproved, without a doubt, the charges of irregularity. "Wonderful reports," glowed the *Columbian Centinel* of Boston. "He will come forth pure gold."

On a bitter March afternoon, the curtain ran up on the climax of the struggle, the floor debate on Hamilton's answer. The battle posts were fully manned. Sedgwick and Smith led off for Hamilton, followed by Giles with all his cannon roaring. Madison rose to make what, for sheer cogency, was the most telling argument for the Jeffersonians; but Ames, who had been held in reserve, outdid him with a reply that dazzled with wit and reason. By now, the day had worn on, darkness had fallen, and candles were lighted in the House. Seven o'clock found the galleries packed, Senators on the floor, and privileged spectators jamming the rear of the Chamber. Dinners went neglected, dances were canceled, the whole city was absorbed in the struggle. A little before midnight the resolutions were finally taken up, and overwhelmingly, one by one, they were voted down. Before the end, many members, exhausted and confident of the outcome, had wandered out into the night, into the light snow that was falling, snow as shining and pure as Hamilton's vindication.

On July 14, 1789, the other great Revolution of the eighteenth century had exploded in Paris into its glittering idealism and horrendous spectacles of human butchery and plunder. "Liberty, Equality, Fraternity"—the People had come into their own: the Bastile stormed and burned; ex-King Louis XVI so hurried to the guillotine that the axe fell before his neck was properly placed and he was mangled; purges and counterpurges proceeding at such a pace that Gouverneur Morris, United States Minister to Paris, reported to

Hamilton, eager to keep up with the situation: "It is not worthwhile to detail the characters of those now on the stage, because they must soon give place to others." Then the wild men who survived the ordeal of power led their muddled countrymen into war with Prussia, Austria and Spain, and in 1793, with England.

America, from all the signs, was next on the list of doom. On April 12, 1793, the British man-o'-war, *Grange*, chased the French frigate *L'Embuscade* into Delaware Bay and forced her into submission with cannon fire that could be heard from the shore. Never a week passed without a report that the British navy had stopped an American trader on the high seas and seized a few crewmen who, though frantically demonstrating the unmistakable accent of an American state, were pronounced subjects of His Majesty and eligible to serve in the royal Navy. The French were equally bad. Their frigates would land at Baltimore, New York, Charleston, and even at the capital, to be fitted out with cannon and then put to sea to plunder not only ships under the Union Jack, but American ships as well, bound for English ports. Hanging like a Damoclean sword was the Franco-American treaty concluded at the high mark of amity in the War of Independence, the provisions of which contained a pledge of mutual aid, including resort to force, if either power should ever engage in the future in war in the Western Hemisphere. Technically, such a war then existed.

For Hamilton, the necessities of policy were plain. The country and his own good works must be shepherded safely through the crisis. The United States, having nothing to fight with—a few patched-up frigates and ill-assorted regiments—must keep out of war. Of the alternative tragedies, war with France or war with Britain, the latter would be by far the more catastrophic. France, having no navy, could not reach the American Continent, but the British, apart from overwhelming sea might, were the main prop of the American economy: chief customers in trade and underwriters of nine tenths of the public debt, stock company investment and land speculation. War with Britain meant the instantaneous economic collapse of the United States and ruin for everything that Hamilton had built and planned for. The statesmanlike thing to do, he was convinced, was to keep America's other cheek turned to British affronts. With the French, however, we could be firm, and had better be, for they, playing wild and free with American rights, might embroil us with the British, and disaster.

The most formidable obstacle to these policies was the enigmatic Secretary of State, Thomas Jefferson. Abiding friend of France, its enchanted resident for nine years, his most cherished purpose as Secretary, he once declared to his admirer, the Duchess of D'Auville, would be to strengthen ties between their countries. The slaughter of Revolution Jefferson shrugged off with a comment that never was the prize of liberty won with so little innocent blood. He spurned Hamilton's conciliatory approach to the British as a cowardly exposure of "our breech to every kick" and proposed to take a strong line against the bullying British Navy. But, in true paradoxical fashion, he did not want war. Hamilton, however, was convinced that Jefferson longed to bring the country into the fight on the side of France, and so far as future events are concerned, what Hamilton thought, and not what Jefferson intended, is what really counted. It is a moot point whether the bitterest and most lacerating combat of the war occurred on the Continent of Europe or in the Administration of President Washington.

Now, more than ever, Washington was fearful that a single misjudgment might wreck his statesmanship, and in his anxiety, he began calling his department secretaries into weekly, and in more urgent periods, even daily meetings to tap their joint advice on questions which required his decision. Out of this practice emerged the new institution, the cabinet. After the image of his military staff conferences in the Revolution, Washington presided as moderator, drew out opinions, guided debate, and reserved decision for himself.

A two-edged sword from Hamilton's standpoint, the cabinet meant that no longer, on top policy matters, might his views prevail simply by ardent private recitals of them to Washington, but henceforth they must withstand the scrutiny of all the secretaries. Yet the cabinet might also have its usefulness in providing a broad illumined stage where the dangerous Mr. Jefferson and his fatuous notions might conveniently be exposed once and for all. Opportunity for this latter purpose promptly offered itself when Citizen Genêt, the twenty-nine-year-old, dashing, brilliant, uninhibited Minister-designate of the French Republic, arrived at Charleston on March 16, 1793. Deliberately taking a long route to the capital, he was greeted at every stop by great cheering throngs wearing liberty caps, waving French flags and thus obliquely criticizing the Administration for its coolness toward his government. Genêt's crude diplomacy constituted a perfect occasion for a strong presidential reprimand and some plain talk on American neutrality, the privateers and the French treaty on the tough-minded basis that Hamilton advocated. Accordingly, on the evening of April eighteenth, alone in his Treasury office, Hamilton framed his thoughts into several artfully slanted propositions on the Genêt problem for discussion in the cabinet. Washington, from general nervousness, was instantly agreeable. Copying off Hamilton's statements, he circulated them under his own name that same evening to the secretaries, calling a meeting of the cabinet for nine o'clock the following morning.

Punctually, the secretaries gathered around the heavy long mahogany council table in the dining room of the President's house. Washington took up the first question. Should Genêt be received? Yes, said Hamilton, with qualifications. Yes, said Jefferson, unqualifiedly. Knox bellowed agreement with Hamilton, "acknowledging at the same time," noticed Jefferson, "like the fool that he is that he knew nothing about it." Randolph agreed with the Secretary of State. The chief protagonists took over the debate. Hamilton sketched out a clear-cut plan—receive Genêt, administer a full official spanking, and declare that the treaty's status is reserved for future consideration—and covered each proposition with fusillades of fact and telling analysis. Then Jefferson, in halting terms—although brilliant in friendly controversy, he was never effective when under excitement, and at that moment he was shaking with it—expounded his opinions. It was a sad performance, disconnected, confused as to fact, blinded by cobwebs of sophistry; Hamilton drove him into corners and easily polished him off with quick thrusts of his invincible logic. The ordeal, which made minutes seem like hours, ended only when Jefferson, his glance rolling wildly everywhere, let his remarks trail off into incoherent gasps. Randolph, surrendering to the obvious, announced that he had changed his mind and agreed with Hamilton. Before tension slackened, Hamilton blithely skipping over the proprieties due Washington as moderator, summoned the cabinet to consider his second big proposal: that the President issue a proclamation of neutrality. Jefferson, in his trembling voice, opposed it on five different grounds and each time he went down in defeat. Only on some minor matters of phrasing—which Hamilton perhaps tactically conceded out of Washington's noticeable dismay at the fracas —did he finally prevail.

The meeting of April nineteenth amply foreshadowed the course of future sessions in those desperate months of 1793. Randolph, who held the balance of power and was regularly dazzled by Hamilton's harrowing blend of arrogance and talent, tipped the scales to the Secretary of the Treasury. "R. half for it, half against it, according to custom," Jefferson snorted, "a man totally without spirit or principle, the poorest cameleon I ever saw having no color of his own, & reflecting that nearest him." Only Jefferson provided consistent opposition, but the poor man had little chance. His chief tactic, which occasionally paid off, was to carry the debate into a roaring deadlock by jumping to his feet, with Hamilton following, each baying at the other for all he was worth. Quiet was restored only when Washington extended his long arms out on the conference table and, clasping his hands in a gesture of finality, snuffed out the rage.

In this steady caloric atmosphere, hatred inevitably consumed the two battlers. Officially and personally, without pity or remorse, the secretaries became enemies. "A man of sublimated and paradoxical imagination," "tinctured with fanaticism," "a mischievous enemy," "a contemptible hypocrite,"

Hamilton sonorously denounced the Secretary of State. Upon his rival, Jefferson passed the harshest verdict that can fall on any man. The Secretary of the Treasury was a coward. True to the facile imagination with which Hamilton accredited him, Jefferson waxed as follows: "A man as timid as he is on the water, as timid on horseback, as timid in sickness, would be a phaenomenon if his courage, of which he has the reputation in military occasions, were genuine."

Victory in the cabinet carried Hamilton far, but by no means all the way to his goal: control of the country's foreign policy. Numerous policy matters never came to the cabinet, and even when that agitated body functioned, Thomas Jefferson and his State Department might slyly undo its decisions in the course of executing them. The necessities of Hamilton were plain. He must control nothing less than the whole machinery of diplomacy, our ministers overseas and every phase of affairs with Britain, on the peacefulness of which the success of his policy turned. Accordingly, both Major George Beckwith, the unofficial British representative to the former colonies and his successor, George Hammond, the first accredited Minister, who took over his duties in midsummer 1791, were showered with Hamilton's attentions. Upon Minister Hammond, Hamilton lavished rounds of sumptuous dinners overflowing with the cream of society, wangled him lodgings at the best boardinghouse in town, and introduced him to the wealthy Philadelphia merchant, Andrew Allen, whose daughter Margaret later became the bride of the young but hardened twenty-seven-year-old diplomatist. For his part, Hammond, carefully instructed to deal wherever possible with Hamilton as the officer "of distinction and weight in the American Government," was delightfully impressed with "that gentleman's just and liberal way of thinking." Simultaneously as the British Navy stepped up its havoc on American cargoes and seamen, and public resentment soared, the intimacy of the two men deepened and sweetened. When Secretary Jefferson presented tart memorials of American grievances and hinted broadly at drastic countermeasures, the Minister would race to the Treasury for a more authoritative and always more cheerful summary of affairs. "I prefer," Hammond informed his superiors, "to make most of my communications privately to Hamilton and to have relations with Jefferson only when absolutely necessary."

The seething Jefferson hit upon a plan to crack this little ring of subterfuge once and for all. He composed a list of fiercely worded grievances against Britain and, with malice aforethought, took his document to Hamilton, and invited his comments. Hamilton swallowed the bait—back came a memorandum with a score of suggestions for watering down the draft. Then, according to plan, Jefferson marched to the President with his own draft and Hamilton's reply. It was a showdown, flawlessly timed and staged. Forced to choose between the rivals, the President would render a clear unimpeachle pronouncement of United States policy which could be laid on the line to Mr. Hammond. To Jefferson's huge delight, Washington chose not Hamilton's views, but the Secretary of State's, and the latter, triumphantly, and with a few good anti-British kicks of his own, delivered the presidentially blessed text to the Minister. Instinctively, Hammond repaired in his anguish to Hamilton. There ensued a smooth bit of dramaturgy, which utterly undid every part of Jefferson's manipulative masterpiece. Hamilton could not believe it. How, in the name of reason, could the "intemperate violence of his colleague" be taken as the true position of the United States Government? Indeed, declared Hamilton, with a knowing, confiding gleam, and doling out every word, the President had had no opportunity of reading Jefferson's paper and had approved it, relying on the Secretary's assurances that it represented the opinion of the cabinet. In point of fact it did not. The clouds rolled back, and in the hard, clear light of day, Hammond saw this whole little episode as a characteristic invention of an incurably duplicitous man.

Thereafter, with his friend in the Treasury egging him on, Hammond took a consistently arrogant line toward Jefferson. "Whenever Mr. Hammond applies to our government on any matter whatever," complained the Secretary, "be it ever so new or difficult, if he does not receive his answer in two or three days or a week, we are goaded with new letters on the subject." But when Jefferson approached the British Foreign Office, on even the most urgent matters, he would have to cool his heels six months or more before being favored with a reply. "Due to the war," Hammond would airily excuse his government, "the Foreign Office was under great pressure of business."

Also well under way was Hamilton's companion project aimed at swinging every United States diplomatic representative overseas into the circle of his influence. The most violent portion of this enterprise settled upon the sturdy frame of William Short, Minister to The Hague. If there was anyone whose loyalty Jefferson could count on, it was Short's. An old ally in Virginia politics, Short, a well-to-do, charming, needle-witted planter of Surry County, had clambered up a diplomatic career as Jefferson's protégé, first as his private secretary in Paris, then as secretary of the legation, and when Jefferson returned to the United States to take over as Secretary of State, he set Short up as the chargé d'affaires and logical choice as the next Minister. On diplomatic questions and the French Revolution, the protégé echoed his master.

Then came Hamilton. With much ado, he settled upon Short his flattering choice for a mission far loftier than any yet tackled by the budding eager diplomat, negotiation of the great loans at Amsterdam for the funding of the debt, and followed up quickly with potions of the most infallible brew of human subversion: the kindly man in the Treasury personally looked after Short's investments in Western lands, with results that were stupendous.

What Jefferson secretly dreaded finally happened. Midway in the toil at Amsterdam, the roof fell in, in the manner of some nippy public expressions by Short of disillusionment over affairs in France. Working frantically to check the vanishing loyalties of his friend, Jefferson tried bare-knuckled rebukes, then planted seeds of doubt, reporting in elaborate detail how Hamilton, in order to stave off criticism, had deceitfully spread before the Senate batches of Short's confidential letters, bristling with indiscreet anti-French statements. "I have done what I could do to lessen the injury this did you," Jefferson purred, but it was all in vain. Though Short lost the French post to the eminent Gouverneur Morris, he settled down happily as Minister to The Hague, grateful that his new friend Hamilton had pulled the wires, and the Secretary of State sadly wrote off his erstwhile protégé as a casualty of battle.

In Paris, Minister Gouverneur Morris was a consecrated Hamiltonian and a total loss to Jefferson. There was never doubt of that. He was brilliant, erratic, an aristocrat to the very tip of his wooden leg, an industrious ladies' man and gourmet. When an excited courier broke in one evening while he was at dinner to gasp that there were riots at the Tuileries and a mob had stormed its way to the King, Morris never yielded to the excitement a single precious moment from his favorite repast of frogs' legs.

Everyone knew that Hamilton had engineered Morris's appointment and that Jefferson had resisted it desperately. In the race to draft for the President the new Minister's instructions, Jefferson won out and stopped at nothing in exploiting his triumph. In the middle of the draft instructions, he planted the admonition that, in France, Morris was considered "a favorer of the aristocracy and unfriendly to its Revolution," followed by a passage which for its personal and censorious nature is virtually unheard of in a document of this type which, if anything, is ordinarily well padded with the amenities. In direct unabashed prose, Morris was informed that he suffered from a "hauteur, disgusting to those who happen to differ from you in sentiment." Washington signed the draft.

But it was all in vain. Morris ran the Paris outpost with unremitting fidelity to Hamilton's interests. At the high mark of the Jacobin blood bath, when every foreign diplomat had fled his post, Morris stayed on, gathering data for Hamilton that clinched many a cabinet debate, and offering the asylum of his house to refugees from the guillotine in general and to his favorite ladies of the aristocracy in particular. Meanwhile, if Jefferson succeeded in committing a despatch that was friendly to the Jacobin government, Morris, in delivering it orally to the Foreign Ministry, would surely rework it beyond recognition in Hamilton's interest. Though the wide Atlantic lay between them, the teamwork was perfect; each partner knew the other's mind through free-speaking communications that employed code names like Scipio, Paulus, Scaevola and Tarquin for the leading American political figures of the day. Tarquin, the most hateful creation of the lot, was the unmistakable symbol of Thomas Jefferson.

Fighting back, Jefferson communicated only driblets of information on department policy—"Our Secretary of State seems much attach'd to brevity," Morris would complain—and ignored the Minister's letters though they were laboriously prepared in duplicate, triplicate and, in final desperation, quadruplicate, and sent in separate packets. But Morris, never one to be denied, cracked the wall of silence by directing communications to Hamilton, who personally bore them to the Secretary of State. There was one thing left to do: blast Morris out of his post. Armed with a fat portfolio of French complaints, Jefferson begged the President to answer the appeals from Paris to send over "a good Minister." But Hamilton, learning of the move, put up such a rousing defense that Washington declined to act, and Morris toiled faithfully on at Paris for the man he revered.

In London, Minister Timothy Pinckney, hand-picked by Hamilton, seemed made for the post. Mild, urbane, dignified, educated at Oxford, admitted to the bar at Middle Temple, he could be counted, as one Londoner put it, "among the party of the British interest." But what Hamilton and his English partners unfortunately overlooked was that Pinckney was a self-assertive patriot with the mild-mannered man's inner toughness and fight. In the Revolution, he broke up a mutiny of his troops by cutting down its leader with his sword. In 1793, angered by British arrogance upon the seas, he bombarded the Foreign Office with finger-wagging protests. But the Foreign Office, gently and effectively brushed the wayward Mr. Pinckney to one side. Lord Grenville, the Minister in charge, simply shunted all Pinckney matters back across the Atlantic for settlement in the kindlier councils of Hamilton and George Hammond. Meanwhile, the assignments directed from home to Pinckney dwindled like water in a leaky barrel. At the peak of the crisis, in an audience with George III, the conversation, ruefully notes the neglected diplomat, dwelt exclusively "on the weather or other topics equally important."

Jefferson saw but one way to halt the juggernaut—put Hamilton's own citadel, the Treasury, under siege. The Act of Congress establishing the Mint in keeping with Hamilton's Report on that subject gave Jefferson his chance. Although the statute was silent on the point, by every indication of departmental logic, the Mint would go to the Treasury, if it would go anywhere. Jefferson, however, set up a spry little interlude with the President and, perhaps to the amazement of all concerned, emerged with the exotic decision which gave the Mint to the Department of State. For every such defeat, Hamilton came thrashing back with double the devastation. In one mighty snatch, the Treasury took over the enforcement of the Neutrality

Proclamation when Hamilton simply, on his own authority, tossed off a circular to his collectors of customs, instructing them to "superintend their neighborhood, watch for all acts of our citizens contrary to laws of neutrality." Jefferson protested frantically to the President this larceny of a function which on any view belonged to his department. Washington stroked back the ruffled feathers; he would personally look into the whole matter. Next day, Hamilton was summoned with his circular. There ensued a fast-talking little sequence, which terminated in agreement on the rather inconclusive procedure of referring the document to Jefferson and Randolph "for further consideration."

Far too explosive to simmer along as a quiet family quarrel, the Jefferson-Hamilton fracas burst upon the public with all the force of a no-holds-barred verbal war in the press. *The Gazette of the United States*, founded by Hamilton in 1790 to function as a court journal (and whose prodigal editor, John Fenno, required considerable personal financing) began showering adulation on anything and everything that unraveled from the master's genius, took an unctuously pro-British line, and pounced on even the mildest opposition as tantamount to criminal incitement. In his countermove, Jefferson brought in Philip Freneau, a stoop-shouldered little man who could make words sing with excitement, to edit the new *National Gazette*, also published in the capital. Writing in details that could only have been leaked by someone in high place—who else but Jefferson?—Freneau excoriated the Administration as a giant conspiracy to restore the monarchy, and in a supreme moment unfurled a puckish verse to the effect that for the best interests of the country Washington should resign. The editor personally sent two copies of his masterpiece to the President himself. Forever after Washington could refer to him, only with great detriment to his blood pressure, as "that rascal Freneau."

Convinced that the fight was out of hand, Hamilton joined in, and under his favorite noms des plume, "Publicola" and "Pacifius," contributed free-swinging letters and editorials for Fenno's paper, on the theme that if Jefferson wished to attack the government, he should resign, as any honorable man would do. Jefferson brought up the extremely verbal James Madison and the angry dialectic, with its new and more expert gladiators, raged furiously on. The affair, an inevitable topic on street corners, in taverns and at dinner tables, had blossomed into the first big scandal of the new Republic.

The President, sick with embarrassment, took refuge in the role which had always proven itself in personal and political crisis. He proposed to stay neutral, ride safely above the storm, his coveted prestige unsullied and intact. In the most violent cabinet upheavals, he avoided taking sides, and bent over backward with attentions to Jefferson, wined and dined him *en famille* and consulted him with nervous regularity on policy. The President neglected no opportunity to act as peacemaker. Time and again, he contrived pleasant little social occasions to throw his secretaries together worlds away from controversy, praying that fellowship might work its healing magic. Just after the blowup over Neutrality, he arranged an outing for Hamilton and his wife, Jefferson and Mrs. Washington, and early one sunny afternoon they rolled amiably off in the President's coach for a visit to Mr. Pearce's newly opened cotton manufactory. After trooping through the shop, chattering gaily and inspecting the curious machines, the party returned at sundown for a mellowing feast of partridge and grouse. But it was all in vain. Next day, the fight roared on, unimpaired.

Thus defeated, and fed up with the scandalous journals, Washington stepped up his pressures to end the quarrel. Without mincing matters in the slightest, he addressed practically identical letters to Hamilton and Jefferson deploring the dissensions "harrowing and tearing our vitals," and offered a solution wholly in keeping with his role of neutral: "I ardently wish," wrote Washington, "that some line may be marked by which both of you could walk," and henceforth when opinions differed, in place of "irritable suspicions and charges," he proposed "liberal allowances, mutual forbearances, and temporizing yieldings on *all sides*." The President got nowhere.

But he remained neutral. On the matter which had touched off the whole controversy, the Revolution in France, he was cautious, hopeful and temperate. "Let us wait and see," was his unwavering attitude. But the blood flowed on; credible travelers returned from France with gruesome tales; friends in Paris wrote despairing letters. Slowly, doubts began seeping through the barricaded neutrality of his mind. Not in his official actions, but in private correspondence with friends and intimates was the hand of change first evident—expressions of horror at the busy guillotine, open anger at the murder of the royal family, and then a final virulent denunciation of "the designing men" manipulating the city masses for their own wicked ends. In the United States, the antics of Citizen Genêt were enough to unnerve any man, even the President, for all of his lofty purpose and force of character. Genêt's months on American soil were an unbroken round of affronts, from his rudely managed journey from Charleston and weekly violations of American neutrality in fitting out privateers, to his *pièce de résistance* of July 4, 1793: the conversion of the brig *Little Sarah*, a French prize, in the harbor of Philadelphia, right under the government's nose. When the United States authorities requested that the vessel be stripped of its guns, Genêt defiantly ordered it out to sea and shouted strange things about going over the head of the President to the people. Even Jefferson had to give up on what probably was the most undiplomatic diplomat of all time. "Hot-headed, all imagination, no judgment, disrespectful & even indecent towards the President," cried the Secretary in despair. "His conduct is indefensible by the most frivolous Jacobin."

If his private opinions were changing, the President was determined that his official conduct should not. He redoubled his attentions to Jefferson, consulting him elaborately in the cabinet, by correspondence and in conference. Toward Hamilton, on the other hand, Washington tightened with caution, as he was wont to do when his feelings were engaged, and repeatedly put his friend through moral wringers that he would never think of applying to Jefferson. When at the peak of the war crisis, Edmund Pendleton, a professed Jeffersonian, wrote to Washington confidentially what his party was claiming openly, that a giant conspiracy of the "moneyed interest" was being masterminded from the Treasury, the President uttered not one word in defense of his Secretary, but replied in simple candor, "No one, I will venture to say, wishes more devoutly than I do that they [the charges] may be probed to the bottom, be the result what it may." When the mischievous Giles resolutions passed the House of Representatives, charging malversation of funds in the Treasury, Washington repaired forthwith to his Olympian mount, making plain to Hamilton that a public explanation was in order. Furious not to be backed up unequivocally in an obvious political maneuver when nothing less than the honor of the whole Administration was at stake, Hamilton was saved by his own valiant efforts, as he was in at least a half dozen other like ordeals from which his chief remained circumspectly aloof.

Yet for all of his vigilance and fine intentions, the President was tending strongly in his major policies in a pro-British, anti-French direction. Inevitably his private convictions were seeping into his public actions, and aiding and abetting the process was, of course, the indefatigable Hamilton. Although Jefferson in cabinet might argue cogently the case for summoning a special session of Congress to deal with the crisis—to Washington in private afterthought, and with Hamilton by his side—the step seemed utterly unwise. To the French went stiffly worded protests on each of their leading privateers—The Swallow, The Little Democrat, The William, The Little Sarah—but to the British, whose offenses were just as bad or even worse, there was relative silence in 1793. Indeed, notwithstanding Jefferson's frantic resistance, Hamilton, by elaborate citations of international law, was able to convince Washington that the United States should even make financial restitution to the British for losses suffered from French privateers launched from American shores. The President's positive frame of mind opened up wide Hamilton's latitude as draftsman. The first communication of the United States to the National Assembly of France, the governing body emerging from the Revolution, drafted not in the State Department but by Hamilton, was a stern tract on the virtues of public order. This particular choice of theme amounted to a slap at the Revolutionaries, but Washington readily approved the paper.

Sometimes Hamilton's literary enterprise plainly got out of hand. In one presidential State of the Union message, he inserted a politically fatuous recommendation that the pro-Jefferson, pro-French Democratic Societies, organized in many of the towns of the country, be outlawed as insurrectionary bodies. To the President's friends, this strange dictatorial step, one wholly alien to his character, came as a terrible shock and its reverberations in editorials, in Congress, and in mass meetings around the country, not unlikely had an identical effect upon Washington himself.

Not in these particulars only, but in the whole conduct of his office, Washington was extending both the growing pro-British, anti-French policy and the opportunities for Hamilton's influence. Spurred by the urgency of crisis, Washington had tightened his grip on the reins of power. Into his own hands he gathered the making of every important decision of the Administration and trained a watchful eye on the progress of work everywhere. He called for files, made regular early-afternoon visits to the departments, especially the State Department, settling his large frame into a high-backed office chair for hour and more talks with the secretaries and clerks and for perusals of papers, all to ready himself for matters which would come to him for decision. Every item of correspondence of the departments, incoming and outgoing, passed across his desk. "By this means," noticed Jefferson, "he was in accurate possession of all facts and proceedings in every part of the Union, and to whatsoever department they related; he formed a central point for the different branches; preserved an unity of object and action among them . . ." Washington's management was a priceless stroke of fortune for Hamilton. With all matters centered in the President, Hamilton, by the simple fact of his rapport with his chief, was able to fasten on to nothing less than every decision and every piece of information in the Executive Branch that counted in foreign policy.

What this meant, as of July 15, 1793, only three months after the crisis had begun, was that Thomas Jefferson could nourish not the slightest hope of getting a document or a policy past the Hamiltonian barricade at the President's house. The Secretary of State could perceive the handwriting on the wall without his customary spectacles. Little was to be gained by his continued presence in the Administration. If the fight was worth continuing at all, it must be done from the outside, free of the embarrassment and restraint of his official post. On July 31, 1793, Jefferson submitted his resignation. Washington drove out to the Secretary's country place and, seated on the lawn under the plane tree, tried to dissuade him from the step, but Jefferson was adamant. As a friendly gesture, Washington brought up the choice of a successor. What about Madison, Jefferson's chief lieutenant? It was agreed he would not accept. Then Washington mentioned John Jay and William Smith, the most fanatical Hamiltonians extant. Jefferson countered by advancing the name of Chancellor Livingston, the man who could never forgive and forget that Hamilton years ago had blocked him from a sure place in the Senate. Washington dismissed the idea at once; Hamilton being from New York, two Yorkers would be in the cabinet. The effusions of fairness and good will persisted right down to the closing curtain. What did Jefferson know about Wolcott, Hamilton's chief lieutenant in the Treasury? "I have heard him characterized as a very cunning man," Jefferson replied dryly.

On December thirty-first, the resignation of the Secretary of State became effective. A week later he set out for home, to the thousand neglected acres and the house he had planned on the hill, to his daughters and grandchildren, to his books and the view of the valley that glistened like a bowlful of diamonds at sunrise.

The triumph of Hamilton was complete.

Enthroned on the loftiest pinnacle of his career, Hamilton beheld his own scene with perfect satisfaction. He was master of all the eye surveyed. The cabinet was prone before him. Randolph, who moved up as Secretary of State, sometimes friendly and sometimes indifferent, was utterly incapable of making any real trouble; William Bradford, the new Attorney General, was a man whose purity of life and purpose would never let him descend into the grubby world of power-snatching. And there was Knox. The cabinet, to put it bluntly, was a collection of amiable mediocrities whose main function was to provide background and stimulus for Hamilton's brilliance and drive. His presence flashed through the whole government. Washington solicited his advice on all matters; and foreign policy, which stumbled along in crisis, remained his pet concern. Randolph, in a naïve moment, wrote something about wishing to be consulted on everything having to do with diplomacy, but it was like shouting against the wind. The British Minister, save for routine calls, dealt exclusively with Hamilton; and the Department of State, hastening to repent the heresies of its late chief, dropped its Francophile course, and avidly took up whatever policies Hamilton laid down.

Riding high, wide and handsome, above and beyond all mortal criticism, exposed Hamilton to the particularly grave danger that his natural conceit might drive him into taking measures which, unchecked by opposition, might prove intemperate, inept and unpopular in the country. Twice, as a matter of fact, Hamilton fell hard on his face and dragged the Administration down with him, with much harm to both. The first time, it was the 1794 Whisky Rebellion of the frontiersmen of Western Pennsylvania, who wore coonskin, kept their muskets handy, and who, using liquor for currency, were hard hit by the tax on alcohol, which Hamilton had devised and Congress had recently adopted. Accustomed to taking matters into their own hands, the frontiersmen stoned and chased U.S. revenue officers and burned the barns of those farmers who informed on the whereabouts of tax-eligible stills. Hamilton, incensed by the disrespect for federal authority and particularly for a measure wrought by his own genius, induced Washington to send out a punitive force of nine thousand foot soldiers and three thousand horses to the rebel area, with the Secretary in charge. Outnumbering the frontiersmen fifty to one, perched in full battle dress and diminutive pomposity on a pure white charger, Hamilton led the way over the cavernous muddy roads only to discover that the lawbreakers had completely vanished. Wherever, according to his earlier advice to the President, there was rioting and pillage, calm now reigned. "Not many fugitives from justice as yet," he wrote glumly to Washington from Cherry's Mill, and not until a long fortnight later could he report his first and only triumph, the capture of John Holcroff, alias Tom the Tinker, a minor rebel leader. Hamilton frantically combed the wilderness some more, but the best he could emerge with was a mere handful of rumpled, unseditious-looking fugitives.

The overwhelmingly one-sided aspect of Hamilton's undertaking did not pass unnoticed. To the lawabiding, economically embattled farmer, the invading constabulary was a terrible apparition of tyranny. Anti-Administration journals pounced joyfully on the affair and poor Washington was variously compared with Tiberius, Satan and George III at his worst. Thomas Jefferson, too, detected an opportunity in the debacle, and promptly moved in to recruit the discontented frontiersmen to the swelling crowds gathering under his agrarian flag.

The companion piece to this Pennsylvania misadventure was the Jay Treaty, bedeviled from beginning to end by Hamilton's free-ranging ego. Alarmed by the rising clamors for war, which kept pace with Britain's steadily rising depredations on the seas, Hamilton and his Senate friends proposed, and Washington readily approved, the appointment of Chief Justice John Jay as a special envoy to London to compose the differences troubling the two nations. Brainy, simple in integrity, but a total egoist ("Mr. Jay's weak side is Mr. Jay," an intimate put it), the envoy's resolution crumbled the moment he set foot in London where the Foreign Office regaled and touted him, and the Queen, in a rare act of generosity, extended her hand to the American ex-colonial. His instructions, which Hamilton drafted, provided no stiffening agent to rally his bargaining instincts and win the main objects of negotiation: indemnification for British depredations on American commerce, a guarantee not to seize future articles except contraband, and trading privileges in the West Indies. Jay's bargaining power, which never was particularly good, vanished completely when Hamilton got tangled up in the complicated mechanism of his personal power. In the course of a routine conversation with British Minister Hammond, he accidentally revealed that the United States had no intentions of entering the "Armed Neutrality," a union of the navies of Denmark, Austria and Sweden to protect their trade from the belligerents. London, nervous that the United States would join the continental nations, and deflect sorely needed British naval strength to the Western Hemisphere, evidently was prepared to buy Jay off with substantial concessions. Hammond joyfully made his report, and poor Jay, although he never knew it, had the ground cut out from under him by the faux pas of his manager in the Treasury.

The treaty, in final form, was the toughest conceivable bargain the British could drive. Nothing was said of ship seizures or impressments, or of indemnification. The few commercial privileges quickly proved illusory. Hamilton, in his power-paradise, indulged in a passage of self-congratulation over Jay's good works, or more accurately, his own. But when the frail provisions were publicly announced, the uproar was so terrible that even Hamilton couldn't miss it. In towns and villages everywhere, flaming effigies of "that damned arch-traitor, Sir John Jay," lighted the night. Public meetings passed hateful resolutions, the British Minister was jeered by Philadelphia crowds, and Hamilton, in a valiant effort to explain the treaty in New York, was stoned and driven from the platform, his eyes bruised, and bleeding from his mouth. In the House of Representatives, the Jeffersonians confidently rallied to oppose the appropriations necessary to carry out the treaty. But Hamilton put his organization to work, Fisher Ames tottered in for his superlative effort, and the appropriations barely passed. Hamilton was vindicated not only in the judgment of his peers, but eventually in the more considered and more penetrating judgment of history. As years passed, the Jay Treaty took on increasingly the proportions of first-rate statesmanship. Whatever its imperfections, the fact remained that Hamilton had established a firm area of agreement and reinforced the habit of negotiation sufficiently to put off what surely would have been a disastrous war, and gave the country a precious eighteen years of peace in which to develop its trade, manufacture, population and natural wealth—the basic sources of national power.

The hopeful aftermath of the Jay Treaty fight seemed to Hamilton the ideal time to take the step which had seemed more and more attractive in recent months: retirement from the Administration. He was, for good reason, "heartily tired of office." The Jeffersonian party, which was now firmly in control of the House of Representatives, was systematically defeating every legislative project he proposed. Equally disconcerting was the genteel poverty of five long years of officeholding which required a family of ten to get along on a sparse three thousand dollars a year. His ties with official affairs need not be severed; his intimacy with Washington and his influence in the Administration would continue. On January 31, 1795, Hamilton resigned his post, with Washington's understanding but reluctant permission, and installed his protégé, Oliver Wolcott, as Secretary of the Treasury. It was immediately apparent that only the official toga had been dropped. Hamilton continued to thrust the long arm of his confidential and unofficial influence into every section of affairs. He edited the President's Farewell Address, whose guarded isolationist emphasis became a favorite and often misinterpreted oracle of American foreign policy for the next century and a half. He provided inspiration and organizing genius to followers in Congress. Wolcott consulted him on every important decision of the Treasury, and even President John Adams, midway in his own Administration, rated Hamilton as "commander-in-chief of the House of Representatives, of the Senate, of the heads of department, of General Washington, and last and least if you will, of the President of the United States."

As was appropriate, the departure and the magnificent accomplishments of this rare public servant were extravagantly celebrated during his last days at the Treasury. Though premature, as such occasions always are in honoring figures having both official power and unofficial influence, the commemorations were full of aristocratic trappings which Hamilton loved so dearly. Eminent merchants and social leaders of Philadelphia, Supreme Court justices and Congressional dignitaries gave lavish farewell dinners and eloquent testimonials in his honor. The Lancaster Troop of Horse saluted him, prancing by in the glory of scarlet and gold, and striking sparks from the cobbles. And his journalist protégé, John Fenno, who had announced Jefferson's retirement in two meager lines, splashed the departure of his benefactor across a whole page of *The National Gazette* in double space, and the heaviest type available, recounting in copious detail the noble work of one who had accomplished all that he had sought and who had given unstintingly to his country his incomparable talent to make "two blades of grass to grow where none grew before."

The Little Magician

MARTIN VAN BUREN

EARLY ON a spring evening in 1829, a brougham, handsomely carved and immaculately kept, jogged down Pennsylvania Avenue toward the White House at a dignified pace. Within was a solitary figure, seated with the pompous grace of a Hindu rajah. He was the new Secretary of State, Martin Van Buren, only an hour in Washington after a hard journey from Albany through the wilderness and cities along the seaboard. Recollections of that journey made his solitude welcome. He had much to think about. For the step he was this evening to take, in committing his services to the new President, Andrew Jackson, defied the urgent warnings of many friends whose judgment he had leaned upon from the day he had become a figure in national politics. They considered him foolhardy to join this Administration, and the force of their reasons had haunted his mind throughout the wearing journey.

Everywhere along the way people insistently reminded him of his mistake. When he reached New York, Levi Woodbury, the shrewd, skillfully noncommittal Senator from New Hampshire, was there to open his carriage door and rage against that man in the White House. Woodbury had wanted a place in the cabinet, but not only was he rejected, but New England itself was left totally unrepresented. That outrageous slight had encouraged a "federal phalanx" among the Democratic-Republican party's New Englanders, who busied themselves with storming against the Administration's seeming surrender to the "people," or more accurately, the "mob." The pattern was plainly evident at the inaugural, which the people, so ran the unbelievable story, had turned into a first-rate Saturnalia. By the President's own invitation, the mob had rushed into the White House by the thousands, and poured everywhere through the halls and chambers, a ceaseless torrent of mud, grime and humanity, screaming, scrambling, fighting, romping. Did you hear of one incredible report of a stout wench sitting astride a table in the President's House eating jelly with a golden spoon? Her more proper countrymen were aghast at the price of the frolic, its quantities of spirits and cakes, bleeding noses, and thousands of dollars in broken china and glassware, torn carpets and damask chairs hopelessly beyond repair.

Far more disconcerting was Van Buren's stopover at New Castle, Delaware, where Louis McLane, at rest from the House of Representatives, poured out a mournful tirade. The new cabinet, he said, was hopelessly weak, and within a month would become the laughingstock of the nation. Saddled with Ingham, Branch and Berrien, all mediocrities, the cabinet was intellectually and administratively inadequate. The plot, said McLane, was clear. Quite obviously this sad collection of men Van Buren was about to join betokened the fiendish intention of Vice-President John C. Calhoun to pack the Administration with satellites and direct it ruthlessly to further his own political advancement. As forcefully, but as politely as he could, McLane informed Van Buren that it was idiotic to work under such terrific odds and risk his own political future in Calhoun's headlong rush to his long-cherished goal, the Presidency itself.

Then there had been that angry letter from James Hamilton, Jr., of South Carolina. At face value he had accepted President Jackson's announced willingness to discuss the formation of the cabinet. Armed with the names of candidates, he had gone to Jackson's temporary quarters at the Hotel Gadsby. Two men he suggested for the Treasury, Langdon Cheves and Louis McLane, were vigorously rejected, indicating unmistakably that everything was arranged, and the cabinet was a closed question. Dazed and indignant, Hamilton hurriedly departed. Invited to give advice, he merely had heard an edict. "I assure you," his letter had bitterly closed, "in the words of Sir Anthony Absolute, 'I am perfectly cool—damn cool—never half so cool in my life.'"

To such grievous reports Martin Van Buren had turned his back and accepted the President's invitation to become Secretary of State. His close friends were not altogther surprised. He was a gambler; he always bet on his own elections, and this time the odds seemed well worth the taking. One potent consideration guided his decision: if he remained out of the cabinet, he would be forfeiting the predominant influence in the Administration to Calhoun without a struggle. This would be tantamount to political cowardice, for Van Buren was not without friends in the cabinet, and thus he would not fight alone. Neither was the low caliber of the cabinet altogether a bad thing.

By now his carriage had entered the White House grounds, and approached the front portico, where a lackey was on hand to open the door and help him alight. The figure that emerged was in dress and form most outstanding—scarcely more than five feet and a half, and free of the corpulence that afflicts middle age. It was a pleasantry among Washington society that he wore a corset. Everything about his features seemed exaggerated: his hair was emphatically yellow and curly, parted over the right temple, and combed back in wavy masses, hiding his ears and crowning a forehead of great proportions. Red sideburns came to the point of his jaw. His long and aggressive Roman nose suggested the fox, and his guileless, deep-set blue eyes seemed to promise, as the mood required, easy laughter or prodigious determination. His clothes were a cartoonist's delight. For years his dandy-like dress had been the butt of political broadsides, and on this fair evening he equalled his reputation, attired in a snuff-colored coat, mauve trousers, a lace-tipped cravat, yellow gloves and morocco shoes.

Into the White House this impeccable little creature marched with tiny, light steps, but within the President's office was disappointment, darkness, cold and uncordiality. A single candle lit that enormous room, and for a moment Martin Van Buren was transfixed not alone because of the quiet gloom, but because it encased so well the face which looked up near the candle—a face on which bereavement had left its harsh stamp and drained all spirit. For Andrew Jackson had just buried his beloved wife and that event and the torment of ceaseless physical illness had left him with the counte- nance of Job; cadaverous eyes were burned sharply by pain and anguished lines were cut beneath them. Withered white hair crowned this misery. Then Andrew Jackson rose, and there occurred a miraculous transformation from despair and exhaustion to an affectionate and eager greeting which devoured every anxiety in Van Buren's mind. Leaving his own misfortunes unmen- tioned, Jackson inquired anxiously about Van Buren's recent illness and, noticing his weariness, insisted that all business be postponed until the next day. Paternally, he ordered Van Buren to bed. In that short interlude, from those few gestures, Van Buren considered his choice vindicated, certain that he did well in joining this Administration so peculiarly formed. Years later, in writing his recollections, his faith, built as it was upon such fragile evi- dence, he found altogether justified. From that first evening on until Andrew Jackson's death, relations between that noble old man and himself always were, he wrote, "of a cordial and confidential character never surpassed among public men."

The appreciative Mr. Van Buren was born December 5, 1782, in a long low one-and-a-half story clapboard farmhouse in Kinderhook, New York. His parents were second-generation Dutch-Americans, who preferred the original spelling "Van Beuren" to the Anglicized Van Buren, and regularly spoke the ancestral language at the dinner table. The father, Abraham, a farmer and tavern operator, was one of the few local residents well enough to do to meet the stiff suffrage requirement of land owned and valued at a hundred pounds over and above encumbrances. Martin was one of seven children; his mother had two children by a previous marriage, and five more by Abraham. Situated on the post road and within easy reach of the Hudson

River, Kinderhook was the main stopover on the busy route between Pough-keepsie and Albany, and the Van Buren tavern was decidedly the better of the two hostelries in town. Its guests of distinction numbered Alexander Hamilton, Aaron Burr and John Jay, and high-ranking colonial officers of His Majesty, George II. The tavern was the local polling place, which, with Abraham's fund of genial hospitality, made it the favorite resort of partisans the year round. Young Martin, hovering by, all ears in the shadows, discovered his taste for politics in the brisk conversation that drifted in with the sundry alcoholic aromas from nearby tables.

The chief constructive influence on young Van Buren was his mother, Maria. Bearing the brunt of the tavern work, she comprehended enough of the world from her oven and kettles to conclude that the surest course to a better life for her sons was education. At least Martin, easily her brightest child, she resolved, should have the opportunity. Her husband, who was something of a spendthrift—he once came home with six slaves, purchased on impulse with the year's seed money—was amenable, and Martin was enrolled in the Kinderhook Academy. This institution, although far from the best of that day, gave adequate grounding in the pedagogical staples, Latin, rhetoric and mathematics. Academy instructors long remembered Van Buren as a good student in the main, who excelled in composition and just got by in mathematics. Most gratifying of all, he was fired with zest for further learning.

Van Buren set his heart on entering Columbia College, alma mater of several of the most distinguished Founding Fathers. Just as he was completing his application, his own father's finances went into an unexpected tail spin, and the boy was forced to go to work. The change of plan left its scar. Forever after, Van Buren venerated the learning that had been denied him to the point that he developed a conspicuous sense of intellectual inferiority. "Whatever weaknesses I may be subject to—and doubtless they are numerous," he once said in a moment of introspection, "dogmatism, I am very sure, is not one of them." If anything, his writings on political questions show lack of assurance and originality, and were customarily predicated on elaborate consultations with associates and friends. In later years, he aggressively cultivated such intellectuals and men of letters as Washington Irving, William Cullen Bryant, Frances Wright and Robert Dale Owen. As President he conferred official appointments upon Nathaniel Hawthorne, George Bancroft, J. K. Paulding and William Leggett.

With his schooling ended, Van Buren, thanks to the intercession of family friends, commenced a clerkship in the office of Francis Silvester, first lawyer of Kinderhook. Martin did the usual serving of papers and copying of pleadings in chancery plus certain custodial duties—tending fires, sweeping out the office, and sleeping in the general store of Silvester's brother, Cornelius, when the latter's clerk was away for the night. In his first days on the job, Van Buren showed up in coarse linens and woolens homespun by his industrious, economy-minded mother. His employer, appalled by the daily ungainly apparition, finally took his clerk aside and ardently lectured on the importance of dress to the would-be barrister. Next day Van Buren arrived in a sartorial transformation which left his employer gasping. Young Martin was decked out in a complete gentleman's outfit consisting of a black broad-brimmed cocked hat, a waistcoat with layers of frilly lace, silken hose and huge flashing silver buckles. Forever after, Van Buren lavished unstinting attention and expense upon the principle that clothes make the man.

Silvester's protégé showed great professional promise. He excelled in minor cases argued in taverns where court was held, where judge and jury guzzled drinks while deliberating and spectators noisily sympathized with the litigants. A telling wit and a capacity for presenting the essence of complicated matters in rapid-fire expostulation during the brief moments his listeners were attentive, marked Van Buren as a comer. In 1803, at the age of twenty-one, he opened his own office in Kinderhook, after a brief try in New York City, the chief consequence of which was that he struck up a lifelong friendship with Aaron Burr. Van Buren's country practice thrived, and it thrived even more when he moved to nearby Hudson, then a booming whaling port. Increasingly, Van Buren took on appellate cases tried in the highest state tribunal, the Court for the Correction of Errors, in Albany. Van Buren's painstaking preparation of briefs, mastery of detail, and quiet persuasive manner of pleading, made him an ideal appellate lawyer. His reputation quickly snowballed over the next five years, during which he moved to Albany and formed a lucrative partnership with the brilliant Benjamin F. Butler. Well before his fortieth year, he had amassed a small fortune. So impressive was his professional skill, that one day President John Quincy Adams, who detested Van Buren as a politician, but venerated him as a lawyer, considered him the best qualified man in the country to serve as Chief Justice of the United States Supreme Court.

Like his father's, Van Buren's politics were Jeffersonian, and like many a young lawyer, he went into politics at a tender age. At eighteen, he campaigned so zealously for Thomas Jefferson that he was elected a delegate to the Republican caucus in Troy to which he forthwith journeyed on a borrowed horse. Politics was his consuming passion. He unflinchingly took on a pitched political argument with his employer, Silvester, who was an ardent Federalist. The young man's reward for this act of courage was the loss of his job. In Kinderhook, Van Buren presided at the local caucus where his tact, which he could turn on expertly when he wanted to, so excelled at composing differences, that he was rewarded with a major local plum. At twenty-six, he was elected surrogate of Columbia County. He cut short his honeymoon with Hannah Hoes a year later to go off into the deep snows for the hustings, and innumerable rounds of speeches at taverns and to rowdy throngs at fire-lit crossroads.

While completing a term as surrogate, Van Buren was elected State Senator. Upon commencing his first legislative session in Albany, he was prepared to settle down to the freshman Senator's traditional unobtrusiveness. Instead, he was immediately summoned into the presence of his party leader, the Lieutenant Governor, the great De Witt Clinton, who had heard of his forte at peacemaking. Clinton gave Van Buren one important assignment after another, aimed at healing the breaches between the several factions of the Democratic-Republican party, predecessor of the modern-day Democratic party.

For a time, all went swimmingly between the mighty leader and the fast-blooming novice. This state of comradely partnership suddenly terminated, however, when the Lieutenant Governor, in a bargain which was by no means unheard of in those days, threw the election for United States Senator in 1813 to the candidate of the rival Federalist party, Rufus King. As quid pro quo, the New York Federalists pledged support of Clinton in the next presidential election. Van Buren, who was never one to be caught napping, sensed what was afoot quite early in this chain of events, and went to Clinton. The Lieutenant Governor made a complete denial that anything irregular was transpiring. When the vote was in, however, and King was elected, Clinton, in a suave effort, said to Van Buren, "I hope you no longer entertain the suspicions you spoke of." Van Buren answered that he didn't. As Clinton turned to go, Van Buren stopped him and said firmly, "Mr. Clinton, you must not misunderstand me. My suspicions have become convictions." This was the opening gun of a conflict that kept New York politics in a state of general upheaval in the coming decade.

When he was not fighting with Clinton, Van Buren followed a Jeffersonian line. He advocated strict construction of the federal power under the Constitution, holding that internal improvements—the vast canal- and road-building projects getting under way—were legally the province of the states and not the nation. Van Buren struck several lusty blows for the common man. He successfully introduced legislation abolishing imprisonment for debt, making his state one of the leaders in the emancipation of humanity who suffered long and hard in an age when installment credit was not yet recognized as a legitimate technique of commerce. In 1817, he proposed to repeal the system of special banking charters in order to open up the field to general competition. He later pushed through legislation admitting Negroes with freeholds of the value of $250 or more to the suffrage, and exempting from taxation all Negroes denied the vote. His liberal policy pattern was broken only once when, in 1820, he opposed the popular choice of presidential electors. He did so purely on grounds of expediency because a popular vote would surely have rejected his party's candidate of that year.

Van Buren put in two terms as Senator, served as Attorney General, and steadily occupied a leading place in party councils. His striking rise in politics was owed not so much to his devotion to policy as to his gifts at political management. He presided over an enormously successful organization known both popularly and in professional circles as the "Albany Regency." In certain respects, the Regency was a forerunner of the modern political machine. Its most pertinacious enemy, the political wizard, Thurlow Weed, described the Regency as "a body of men who possessed so much power and used it so well . . . who had great ability, great industry, indomitable courage, and strict personal integrity." The Regency consisted of a handful of state officials who dominated the party caucus which they adroitly employed as an instrument of discipline. Putting it bluntly, they traded jobs in the executive branch for votes in the legislature, and made their bargains stick. As the Regency's leader, Van Buren ran a tight ship and was bold in innovation. In 1820, for example, at his initiative a floundering newspaper, the *Albany Argus*, was acquired to operate as an adjunct to the party organization. Under the aggressive editorship of Edwin Croswell, a Regency Member, the paper quickly achieved a circulation of four thousand, largest of any newspaper in the state. The *Argus* served as the Regency's chief propaganda organ, and its lead was followed by Democrat-Republican journals throughout New York.

In 1821, Van Buren first emerged onto the national political scene when the Regency boosted him into the United States Senate. By every appearance, his coming made no great splash. Though Van Buren toiled with exemplary diligence on the finance and judiciary committees, he became identified with no measure of significance. He spoke infrequently on the floor and seldom with much impact. His pianissimo style of debate was hopelessly lost in the oratorical din of such titans as Henry Clay, Daniel Webster, Robert Hayne and John C. Calhoun. Another freshman Senator shining with the same indifferent luster was the future President of the United States, Andrew Jackson.

In Washington, as in Albany, Van Buren achieved his chief distinction in the occult groves of party management. As head of the prevailing party in New York, he became a leading influence in the Congressional caucus and in the wide-open presidential race of 1824, the first in the country's history. After twenty-four years of uninterrupted dominance of the presidential office, the Virginia Dynasty, contributor of Jefferson, Madison and Monroe, at last had petered out. The horizon was totally bereft of available Virginians;

the next President clearly would have to derive from a state other than the Old Dominion. In choosing among the many candidates entreating his support, Van Buren, in the manner of his hero, Jefferson, aimed to link the power of New York with that of the South. The Magician accordingly came out for William H. Crawford, a Georgian, the Secretary of the Treasury in the Monroe cabinet, and the leading Southern candidate. Jefferson, now an old man, likewise supported Crawford.

Van Buren's first venture in the "art and business of President-making," as he called it, was totally disastrous. Hardly had Crawford announced his candidacy when he was felled by a general paralytic stroke. His nervous system was shattered; he permanently lost the use of his lower limbs and temporarily his sight and speech. The tragedy notwithstanding, Crawford, pressed by his anguished managers, stayed in the race. Van Buren, by general consensus the mastermind of the campaign, had already set up headquarters in Bradley's boardinghouse in Washington with a sizable corps of lieutenants. But the standard accouterments of campaigning—speeches, pamphlets, parades and rallies—went forgotten while Crawford's distraught promoters labored overtime at hiding the distress of their candidate from the public. He made no speeches; a tightly covered coach carried him about when travel was unavoidable. Whenever a meeting with impressionable visitors was necessary, they were ushered into his room so darkened by heavy curtains and dimmed lights that the pitiful Crawford, propped between several devoted associates, was scarcely visible. Hardly had a visitor settled in his chair when he was, for some reason or other, whisked out. Notwithstanding these precautions, rumors got around that Crawford was "sick . . . very sick"; Daniel Webster confided to his brother that the Georgian's death was imminent. Support for his candidature began slipping badly. In desperation, Van Buren attempted a bold eleventh-hour deal, by offering Henry Clay of Kentucky the Vice-Presidency if he supported Crawford. Clay turned it down cold. Being nevertheless impressed with Van Buren's inspiration, Clay hastily negotiated a comparable pact with the other major candidate, John Quincy Adams, which was enough to elect the latter when the presidential election of 1824 was thrown into the House of Representatives.

The sly maneuver and the ruthless machination provide the basis of much of Martin Van Buren's lasting political reputation. All his nicknames —and no other public figure in his time, and probably since then, has had so many—have a common censorious note. "The Magician," and "The Red Fox of Kinderhook," by which he was first known in New York politics, and the later "American Talleyrand" betoken the tricky, unprincipled operator. Each of his several chief competitors for the great prizes of politics remarked on this characteristic. De Witt Clinton spoke of Van Buren as "the prince of villains" and " a confirmed knave." A later foe, John C. Calhoun, said: "He is not . . . of the race of the lion or of the tiger; he belonged to a lower order —the fox." And John Quincy Adams, in the same vein: "His principles are all subordinate to his ambition."

A kindred characteristic for which Van Buren was equally famous was his noncommittalism. A favorite story of the day was that Van Buren, after laboring at length over the writing of a letter, asked his clerk to read it and tell him what he thought of it. The clerk read carefully and then said, "I will tell you what I think, Mr. Van Buren, if you will tell me what it is about." Van Buren smiled, evidently pleased. "Then it will do; it will answer," he said, folding the letter for the mail. Such stories multiplied with the years; little wonder that a new word, "Vanburenish," became part of the language. In the United States Senate, Andrew Jackson's curiosity was piqued about his New York colleague's reputed noncommittalism. Seeing the Magician eagerly taking notes one day as another Senator spoke, apparently intending to reply, Jackson waited. Van Buren, according to Jackson, soon rose to make "a clear straight-forward argument" disposing of the whole subject. Pleased, Jackson turned to a colleague, Major Seaton, listening nearby. "Major," asked Jackson, "is there anything non-committal about that?" The Major agreed there wasn't.

The elections of 1824 were nothing less than a double calamity for Van Buren and the Regency. Not only was their national nominee, Crawford, defeated, but their gubernatorial candidate, Samuel Young, had lost to Van Buren's archrival, Clinton. Deliberating amidst the ruins of his fortunes, Van Buren decided to reverse his strategy and make peace with Clinton. Several deals appropriate to the situation were consummated and, happily, all became well. One major motivation of Van Buren's burying the hatchet was that it opened an avenue to Andrew Jackson. Clinton was a staunch ally of Jackson and the presidential election of 1824 proved impressively that the hero of New Orleans was a comer. He had, after all, garnered the largest popular vote cast, including that of the victorious John Quincy Adams, who was elected by the House of Representatives. Peace with Clinton would assure New York for Jackson in 1828, and if the old Crawford organization of the South could be brought into the fold, Jackson was certain to be elected. For the next several years, Van Buren quietly and painstakingly built up a pro-Jackson sentiment in the pivotal Richmond Junto. In 1827, he cast his bread more widely when he made an intensive tour of Virginia, the Carolinas and Georgia. At its close, he concluded, altogether reasonably, that he could take the Crawford Radicals into the Jackson camp en bloc. At least several close observers of Van Buren and his enterprises hold that at this juncture the Magician was really working to absorb the Jackson camp into his own. Jackson was to be the candidate, the popular façade, with Van Buren pulling the wires. A more likely theory, considering all the circumstances, is that a genuine mutuality of interest actuated the two men. Jackson's election depended in no small degree upon New York, and Van Buren, his acquisitive gaze fixed upon the gubernatorial elections, likewise depended upon Jackson. In any case, Van Buren worked zealously for Jackson's candidacy. In September of 1827, at the Magician's signal, the New York party adopted a Jackson-for-President resolution at a monstrous meeting at Tammany Hall. The *Argus* pulled out all the stops and the state's Democratic editors joined the chorus. At the climax of this noisy dedication, Van Buren boldly declared himself to be "the Jackson candidate" for Governor.

In the ensuing campaign, Jackson and Van Buren never met face to face and, at most, exchanged only several letters. The chief of these Van Buren wrote at the height of the considerable personal abuse Jackson suffered in the campaign, variously depicting him as a murderer, adulterer, thief, liar, cockfighter, drunkard and schemer of shady land deals. He was accused of bigamy on the ground that he married his wife, Rachel, before she was legally divorced from her first husband. "Ought a convicted adultress and her paramour husband," asked a partisan pamphleteer, "to be placed in the highest offices of this free and Christian land?" Van Buren counseled the General to endure these indignities in silence, arguing that the public thought the "calumnies" overdone and were seldom impressed with "personal explanations." Jackson consistently followed this suggested course.

Of the 178 electoral votes carrying Jackson to victory in 1828, 107 votes constituted those of the six states of the Van Buren-Crawford empire. The Magician's not inconsiderable part in this achievement was sure to be rewarded with a top post in the new Administration. It was not altogether clear what that post would be. The choicest spot would, of course, be appointment as Secretary of State, the traditional steppingstone to the Presidency. But Van Buren by no means had that field to himself. Rumors were afoot that Jackson was veering toward his old and valued ally, De Witt Clinton, but fate intervened when Clinton died unexpectedly on February 11, 1828. Shortly after this occurrence, Jackson wrote the Magician, offering him the Secretaryship. Implanted in the President's letter was an irresistible extra inducement. "It would afford me great pleasure," declared Jackson, "to have you here early as possible that I may consult with you on many and various things pertaining to the general interest of the country."

By every indication, Van Buren proposed to be far more than a mere presidential counselor. His eyes were fastened on bigger game. He intended to do nothing less than succeed General Jackson in the Presidency itself and, everything considered, this ambition was altogether reasonable. It was widely believed that Jackson did not have long to live. The creeping dropsy, the

racking cough and the wizened frame signified a man whose days were numbered. There was, further, the enthralling statistic that in the twenty-eight
years subsequent to 1800, every President except John Quincy Adams had
been succeeded by a member of his Administration, and three of the Presidents of that period—Jefferson, Madison and Monroe—had previously served
as Secretary of State. As befitted his situation, Van Buren busily denied to
one and all any interest whatever in the highest office. For posterity, too,
which he courted as assiduously as any constituency, he provides in his
memoirs the pious testamentary, "When I went to Washington the idea of
becoming General Jackson's successor had never acquired the slightest lodg-
ment in mind." It is often the case in politics that actions tell us more than
words. They usually did in the extraordinary career of Martin Van Buren.

The Magician was not the only party of interest hungering for the succession. His most formidable competitor was another member of the Administration, the Vice-President of the United States, John C. Calhoun, a
man of consuming drive, maturer national political experience and wider
public fame. Everything about Calhoun was formidable. His appearance was
menacing to the point of fascination. His clipped shock of stiff dark hair
bristled with ferocity. Indented in deep sockets, under bushy eyebrows,
yellow-brown eyes burned, piercing all that they beheld. His manner exuded
confidence. In interviews and conferences, he made short shrift of the social
graces, coming right to the point. His mind was penetrating and quick, his
conversation animated and convincing. At mid-passage in a career marked
by large successes and costly failures, Calhoun had contributed valuable
support to Jackson in the 1828 campaign. As Vice-President in the preceding
regime of John Quincy Adams, Calhoun had broken with the New Englander and was read out of the Administration. Almost simultaneously, he
engaged in a titanic struggle with Henry Clay whose American system of
high tariffs and intensive internal improvements was anathema to Calhoun's
own state of South Carolina and the South in general. Faced with the choice
of going it alone—his popularity was almost as great as Jackson's—or joining
the opposition, Calhoun chose the latter course. With Jackson good for but
one term or less, it seemed the more likely route to the Presidency, an office
he craved with dogged intensity.

The Van Buren-Calhoun competition was hardly a matter of conjecture;
it was starkly manifested even before the inauguration when both camps
launched a series of maneuvers designed to control the selection of the
cabinet. Both seemingly proceeded on the assumption that whoever controlled that body would control Jackson and therefore the succession. Van
Buren, who could not be in Washington when the cabinet was formed,
being occupied in Albany with his duties as Governor, dispatched his trusty
deputy James A. Hamilton to represent his interests. Hamilton conferred at

length with Jackson and the personal entourage he had brought from Tennessee on the composition of the cabinet. Calhoun apparently did not approach Jackson directly on the subject, but the Vice-President's wishes seem to have been fully known by the President. Van Buren, through Hamilton, trained his guns on the two most patronage-rich departments, the Treasury and the Post Office. To his great chagrin, the Magician lost out on both. His candidate for the Treasury, Louis McLane, was rejected in favor of a loyal Calhounite, Samuel D. Ingham of Pennsylvania; and the Post Office went to a staunch Calhoun man, John McLean. As Secretary of War, Jackson chose his long-time friend from Tennessee, John H. Eaton, whose preference between Van Buren and Calhoun was not at all clear. The other two members of the cabinet would not count for much. The Attorney General, John M. Berrien, was a foppish nonentity addicted to waistcoats loaded with trinkets. Probably his most important characteristic was his distrust of Van Buren. The Secretary of the Navy, John Branch, was an advanced hypochondriac; "a miserable old woman," Louis McLane called him. When the cards were down, Branch was expected to throw in with Calhoun. The cabinet slate was duly announced and the Van Buren camp was duly stupefied by the revelation. The general neglect of their leader was utterly incomprehensible.

Of equal moment to the Van Buren-Calhoun competition was the disposition of the several Westerners constituting the personal entourage of General Jackson. The members of this little coterie of personal and family friends had either taken up residence in the White House or enjoyed the freest access to it. Outstanding among the figures involved was William B. Lewis, Jackson's quartermaster in the Creek and Natchez campaigns, and a founder of the Nashville Junto which in 1821 commenced the earliest promotion of Jackson's candidacy for the Presidency. Lewis's estate, Fairfield, was situated across from The Hermitage. For years, Lewis, who had inherited wealth, saw Jackson daily, and their families were close. Lewis had accompanied Jackson to Washington, expecting to stay only briefly to see the General settled. But Jackson prevailed upon his friend to continue on indefinitely, appointed him to the nominal post of second auditor of the Treasury, and provided him living accommodations in the White House. It wasn't long before Lewis was pursuing confidential assignments of high importance for the President. For the better part of two terms, Lewis's gifts at cold analysis and subtle maneuver enabled him to function in the thankless but essential job of Jackson's political bodyguard. Some years later, when James K. Polk was inaugurated as President, Jackson felt constrained to offer one bit of constructive advice. "Keep Wm. B. Lewis to ferret out and make known to you all the plots and intrigues hatching against your Administration," wrote the ex-President, "and you are safe." In 1828, Martin Van

Buren was not long in knowing the force of Lewis's presence. Hardly had the Magician taken the oath as Secretary of State, when Lewis was pressuring to install his friend, Major Henry Lee, as chief clerk in the Department of State, then the number-two post of the department.

A second Tennessean also residing at the White House was the President's confidential secretary, Andrew Jackson Donelson. A nephew of Rachel Jackson reared in The Hermitage as Jackson's ward, Donelson attended West Point, graduating second in his class, and later studied law at Transylvania College in Lexington, Kentucky. He was Jackson's aide-de-camp in the Seminole Indian War and private secretary in the presidential campaigns of 1824 and 1828. Donelson's estate, Tulip Grove, supported by a healthy law practice in Nashville, was adjacent to The Hermitage. As presidential secretary, Donelson was displaying his well-known capacity for responsibility and discreet anonymity. His wife Emily, a spare, aristocratic, titian-haired beauty, presided expertly as the official White House hostess. As was widely known in the Executive Mansion and the world outside, the Donelsons had little regard for their fellow resident, Lewis. Emily contemptuously referred to Lewis as "that sycophant" and Donelson was patently annoyed by his insatiable jealousy and lust for privilege.

The most politically experienced of the Tennesseans in the personal circle was the Secretary of War, John H. Eaton, a long-time fixture of Jackson's career. His marriage to Myra Lewis, a ward of Jackson and a sister of Mrs. William B. Lewis, had originally provided entree. Eaton's services rendered included the authorship of an idolatrous biography of the General in 1816, and upon his own election to the United States Senate shortly thereafter, Eaton was the General's chief defender as a member of the committee appointed in 1819 to investigate his alleged insubordination in the Seminole Indian War. In the decade or more when Jackson was actively seeking the Presidency, Eaton was a leading promoter of the cause in the Nashville group and as Senator was its chief emissary in eliciting support in other states.

However influential were the men who had Jackson's ear, none excelled in importance the man to whom the ear belonged, the President himself. What kind of man was Andrew Jackson? For all of his wide acclaim, he had a large reputation for ferocity. Thomas Jefferson, who had shuddered at the thought of the General taking over the Presidency, spoke of him as a "madman." In New England, a Sunday-school teacher asked her class, "Who killed Abel?" "General Jackson," a pupil replied. Even Van Buren, for all his discernment, seems to have been taken in by the reputation and the evidence at hand. Time and again he saw his chief break up conferences with terrible rages. Actually, such demonstrations were shrewdly calculated and rendered with such gusto that visitors in their alarm, forgot what they had come for. This state of abject confusion Jackson seemed to prefer to the inconclusiveness of long futile argument. As the curtain rang down upon one masterfully uproarious exhibition, Jackson said to his colleague, "I saw that my remarks disturbed you." Van Buren acknowledged that they had. "No, my friend," replied Jackson. "I have great respect for your judgment, but you do not understand these gentlemen as well as I do." Subsequent events vindicated Jackson. "This was but one of numerous instances," wrote Van Buren, "in which I observed a similar contradiction between his apparent undue excitement and his real coolness and self-possession in which, I may say with truth, he was seldom if ever wanting."

Van Buren's own relations with Jackson were flawlessly untempestuous. In fact, the Magician's companionship was much welcomed, both during business hours and after, by a President who was just emerging from the pit of terrible tragedy. Jackson had buried his beloved wife, Rachel, the previous winter, and in the loneliness of his loss he found in Van Buren, also a widower, the solace of shared experience. Van Buren was a constant visitor at the Executive Mansion. Unconstrained by the demands of family, he could respond to every beck and call. By all odds, he was the favorite dinner guest and on those evenings when he was not at the President's table, he would drop in at the White House at about seven o'clock for a visit of an hour or so. Jackson and Van Buren communed with perfect ease. Both were devotees of gracious living, cherishing the best in foods, wines and accouterments, and the finest in thoroughbreds. Both conversed readily on the topics of the day, although neither was learned, profound, or introspective. Jackson had the fragmentary book knowledge of the self-made frontier lawyer, and Van Buren was little better off. His close associate and fellow boardinghouse resident, James A. Hamilton, observed of the Magician that "in conversation about the historical events of this and other countries, I was amazed to learn how uninformed he was."

Van Buren moved easily in the considerable circle of personalities residing in the White House. In its size and essential informality the circle was unprecedented. Besides the President, Lewis and the Donelsons, the inmates included Mrs. Donelson's attractive cousin, Mary Eastin (Van Buren's eldest son, Abraham, was courting her), and the President's adopted son, Andrew, and his family who subsequently moved into the Mansion. Together, the resident families contributed four children to the White House population. These were considerably supplemented by other juveniles of the far-flung Jackson clan, who constantly visited the President. Long an intense family man, Jackson was intimately involved in the routines and crises of this considerable humanity. A nightly scene in the Executive Mansion was the President of the United States tripping sprightly down the hall in his baggy sleeping gown and tassled nightcap to comfort a crying child or summon a needed parent.

Evening callers, such as Van Buren, ordinarily found Jackson well attended in the family sitting room. Reposing in his easy chair, puffing gently on a great Powhatan pipe whose bowl rested upon his knees, Jackson was an island of composure in a sea of chaos. Children would be romping around the room, rolling, climbing, falling and brawling, while the adults would bravely try reading, sewing, or conversing only to be lurched into a sudden crisis. Entering unannounced, Van Buren would retire to a corner with Jackson for conversation that was incessantly interrupted. After finishing with the President, Van Buren paid heed to the ladies, with whom he got on famously. A suave charmer, he fared equally well with the ingénue and the grande dame. His reputation in this art, as a matter of fact, was well established before his advent to the Washington scene. In New York, observers marveled at how he delighted sophisticated Mrs. Edward Livingston, première femme of the city's social world, with repartee and anecdote. With Mrs. Livingston's teen-age daughter, Cora, he was also markedly successful, thanks to his knack for juvenile levity and for treating younger folk always as equals. Everybody in the family circle liked Van Buren.

Jackson and his friend transacted most of their business not in their evening encounter, but in a reserved hour during the day. Every afternoon, at about three thirty, they would meet at the White House, slip out the back door, and dash off with their horses for a canter. Although by preference a coach rider, Van Buren, in order to be at the President's side, threw desire and comfort to the winds and acquired a trusty charger. The outings at first were modest, extending merely to the forested outer limits of Georgetown. Soon there were lengthier sorties down the Warrentown Road or along the Potomac toward Alexandria, several hours at least being invested in these junkets. Free from the press of business and visitors, the President and his friend conferred in the luxury of unhurried quietude.

It was in such outings that the seed of Jackson's earlier invitation for Van Buren to function as general adviser and confidant was coming into real fruition. Anything and everything was discussed. Legislation, appointments to office, correspondence, messages to Congress—on such instruments of policy Van Buren constantly impressed his influence. He easily brought forward the business of his own Department of State, and used his opportunity to full advantage. Probably his major achievement in the Administration's first months lay in bringing Jackson to reverse himself in choosing L. W. Tazewell and Edward Livingston for the principal diplomatic posts at London and Paris. Sometime before the Magician had come to Washington, Jackson evidently had settled on these men. Preliminary feelers had even gone out to both prospective diplomats and the responses were encouraging.

With his own necessities and deserving protégés very much in mind, Van Buren, by some skillful exhortation, managed to bring Jackson to abandon his selections and nominate Louis McLane for London and W. C. Rives of the Virginia dynasty for Paris. A singular attraction of both appointees was their loyalty to Martin Van Buren.

Together with Lewis and Donelson, Van Buren was functioning as a presidential drafting assistant. Jackson, from all indications, required considerable help with his compositions. His prose tended to be abrupt and disconnected, his intelligence expressing itself in judgment rather than in analysis. He had, as Benton put it, "a rapid and almost intuitive perception, followed by an instant and decisive action." Van Buren noticed a lack of regard for "precise terms," and Roger B. Taney, who in his time toiled over many a speech, allowed: "He had never studied the niceties of language." Both as military chieftain and as statesman, Jackson depended upon others to impart logic to his thoughts and polish to his papers.

Although Van Buren performed heroically as an expositor in Jackson's service, he was by no means the best verbal craftsman in the White House. Addicted to long and complicated sentences, obscure phrasing and gross lapses in spelling, Van Buren needed considerable help himself. His intimate, J. A. Hamilton, has testified that the Magician moved heaven and earth to bring his law partner, the brilliant and cultured Benjamin F. Butler, into the State Department. And for good reason. There Mr. Butler was given very special employment. He busied himself not so much with foreign policy as with brushing up Van Buren's many literary productions, especially those taken on assignment from the White House.

Van Buren's particular forte, on which Jackson relied most, whether in speech-drafting or on other occasions of decision, was his skill in the subtleties of political tactics and in discerning the motives of men. Jackson's respect for Van Buren's capacity in these basic arts was not a sudden development. Sometime before, in the Senate, Jackson had marked Van Buren's savoir-faire and cool composure in explosive party situations. After one such convincing demonstration, Jackson was heard to exclaim to several fellow Senators, "I am no politician; but if I were a politician, I would be a New York politician." Everyone knew that he had Martin Van Buren in mind.

The extent to which Jackson as President relied upon the Magician's political judgment is suggested by a project conceived early in the Administration and centering upon ex-President John Quincy Adams. After yielding the Presidency to Jackson, Adams had been elected to the House of Representatives. Jackson had broken with his predecessor during the late campaign, holding him responsible for a heavy diatribe against Mrs. Jackson contained in a series of articles Adams had permitted to run in the *Washington Journal*. Members of the incoming Jackson Administration joined with their chief in meting out punishment of unprecedented severity by banishing Mr. Adams from official social circles. Cabinet secretaries who previously had shared the ex-President's hospitality, conspicuously stayed away from his new abode, Commodore Porter's comfortable mansion, on the top of Meridian Hill.

Van Buren, whose constant principle was never to make a political enemy a personal enemy, could not abide this state of affairs. One afternoon during his regular outing with the President, Van Buren stated flatly that he was planning to call on Adams. To the Magician's astonishment, Jackson expressed approval. Van Buren went ahead with his plan and Adams was completely delighted. This initial success encouraged Van Buren to go on to the further and ultimate step of bringing Jackson and the old President together to bury their differences. Van Buren again put the matter up to Jackson, who, trusting the Magician's judgment, acquiesced. A careful search ensued for a suitable occasion on which the President and the ex-President might meet. At last one was found that seemed completely satisfactory—the funeral of Congressman Doddridge of Virginia. The solemnity of the locale, Van Buren was hoping, would emit an aura of brotherhood affecting all concerned. Van Buren himself could not attend the funeral, but having made certain that Adams would be there, he got Jackson to promise to go. Several days later, during a canter, Jackson reported what had transpired. He did so with a half-suppressed smile. He had approached "the old gentleman," after the ceremony, he said, intending to offer his hand. Adams, however, misread the oncoming smiling visage as masking a pugnacious intent. Fearing that Jackson would strike him, Adams hastily withdrew into the depths of the crowd. Van Buren, who knew futility when he saw it, dropped his project.

Van Buren's thriving rapport with Jackson was at most only erratically reflected in presidential policy. Jackson was his own master. He made his own decisions and never hesitated to act even where Van Buren's personal and political interests were bound to suffer. In handing out patronage, for example, Jackson, on at least several occasions, trod hard on the Magician's toes. The juiciest plum in all New York State, the Collectorship of the Port of New York, Jackson unhesitatingly awarded to Samuel Swartwout, an old and faithful supporter who was decidingly *persona non grata* with the Van Buren organization. The Magician, knowing the appointment was pending, had spoken strongly against it, but to no avail. When the news of Jackson's decision broke upon the political world, Van Buren spent the night walking the streets of Washington in sleepless anguish. He had ample cause for his distress. Not only did the appointment badly damage his prestige in his own organization, there was the ugly fact that Swartwout had a wide reputation of dubious honesty. C. C. Cambreleng, the New York Congressman, upon hearing of the appointment, snorted, "if our Collector is not a defaulter in four years, I'll swallow the Treasury if it was all coined in coppers." Cambreleng's prophesy matured in half that time when Swartwout absconded with a million and a quarter dollars in Collector's fees. By the time the police caught up with him in far off Algiers, he had squandered every penny of his loot in the games of the local bazaars.

The saga of Swartwout tells much of Jackson's nature and *modus operandi*. The President, beyond a doubt, had certain blind spots. Loyalty was one, as Swartwout proved; honor and courage were others. Let these be the factors of a situation, and the President was beyond all counsel. In other respects, however, he displayed exceptional liberality of thought and openness to recommendation. "I never knew a man," Van Buren once evaluated Jackson, "more free from conceit or one to whom it was to a greater extent a pleasure, as well as a recognized duty, to listen patiently to what might be said to him upon any subject. . . . Akin to his disposition in this regard was his readiness to acknowledge error." Several of Jackson's colleagues even thought him overtolerant. Amos Kendall, of subsequent Kitchen Cabinet fame, believed, "If he be censurable on this score it is for too much forbearance." But once his mind was made up, he made short shrift of opposition. "Jackson," Benton put it, "went for the clean victory or clean defeat always. Every step he took was a contest." Which of these elements of Jackson's nature would hold sway in the emerging contest between Van Buren and Calhoun?

To the casual observer, Washington, in the crisp autumn of 1829, glowed with a high gloss of serenity. This was a condition sedulously cultivated by the two contenders. Duff Green, editor of the Administration organ, the *United States Telegraph*, appears to have been instructed by his *de facto* chief, Calhoun, to scotch all rumors of disharmony and to chant in his columns a steady song of bliss. Van Buren reciprocated in turn, by endorsing Green's appointment to the lush post of public printer. Toward Calhoun personally, Van Buren was sweetness itself. He wined and dined the Vice-President and his family regularly, and in all other respects their dealings persisted, in Van Buren's phrase, on "a friendly and familiar footing." This, it should be noted, was a typical Van Buren tactic. A critic, perceiving this same phenomenon in other situations, said somewhat unkindly, "Van Buren pursues enmity as if he thought it might be one day his interest to seek friendship."

Behind the façade of official beatific calm, Van Buren was advancing his fortunes with ruthless vigor. In private sessions with Jackson, the Magician was quietly but effectively taking over a principal source of power in the new Administration, the patronage. Jackson had commenced wholesale removals from the government offices shortly after his inaugural. Clerks employed in the service since the days of John Adams were routed out to be replaced by men less sympathetic to the old Federalism and more democratic in their thinking. Faced with such encouragement, good Democrats descended on Washington in droves. Kentucky backwoodsmen, pioneers from western Ohio, immigrants from the coastal cities, war veterans, politicians and journalists poured into Washington "like the inundation of northern barbarians into Rome." Cabinet secretaries were followed by imploring humanity from their offices to their homes and, to accomplish anything during business hours, were forced to bolt their doors.

When Van Buren indicated willingness to take on the patronage problem, Jackson, confident of the Secretary's talents in the arts of political management, eagerly handed over the entire debacle. The Magician's touch was not long in becoming evident. To Jackson's great relief, applicants no longer jammed his office; they now went straight to Van Buren. There they were apprised of a complete reversal of policy. Applicants would get no jobs, the Magician blandly announced, until they returned to their homes and awaited a summons for a definite appointment. Washington gradually quieted down; the ranks of job seekers thinned as Van Buren's advice, thoroughly backed by the White House, was heeded. In the months which followed, he resolutely pursued the policy of holding the dismissals to moderate numbers, successfully beating off the proposals of the Calhoun camp and the Westerners in the President's entourage for turnover on a vaster scale. Apart from the wear and tear which his policy saved the Administration, Van Buren stood to gain more personally by adhering to the *status quo*. With many of the incumbent clerks sympathetic to his cause, he would suffer considerably if great numbers of appointments ensued, many of which would have to be shared with Calhoun and the Westerners.

Van Buren's success in quelling the bedlam received quick presidential recognition. Jackson established the Magician as curator of another rich vineyard of plums, the letting of printing contracts. Although Duff Green, a Calhoun man, was the officially designated public printer and was frothing with expectation of magnificent profits, Van Buren was not in the least deterred. He neatly steered the fattest contracts of all, those of the Post Office, into the hands of several of his own most tried and true followers. This was but the first of a series of assaults upon the privileges of Duff Green.

Van Buren was also launching his moves against the Calhoun camp in another locale. Being an intense social animal, the Magician had become a major figure in Washington society, a tireless party-giver and party-goer, and it was in his social enterprises that he found his finest opportunities to advance his long-range purposes. The situation which worked to his greatest profit was the marriage of widower John H. Eaton to Mrs. Margaret "Peggy"

O'Neale Timberlake, which occurred on January 1, 1829, and rocked Washington society to its heels. Peggy was the daughter of a Washington tavern keeper and the widow of a Navy purser who allegedly had committed suicide because of Peggy's extra-marital flirtations. It should be established at once that Peggy was uncommonly beautiful. "She is very handsome," society matron Margaret Bayard Smith expressed the wide consensus of her set. Fair, azure-eyed and graceful, with red-brown hair piled back in ringlets, Peggy never failed to command attention. Prior to marrying Eaton, she ran the flourishing ancestral tavern while her purser husband was at sea. Responsible observers of this interval, including a member of the clergy, held that Peggy was overfriendly with one of her guests, John H. Eaton. When she finally married, indignant capital ladies stayed away en masse from what should have been an all-out social event.

Peggy Eaton's troubles indeed were only beginning. At the inaugural dinner, she was not spoken to by her feminine peers. Mrs. Calhoun established the precedent, which others quickly followed, of refusing to call on her. The President, gallant and sensitive to suffering femininity, became concerned. The lady in question meanwhile was facing up to the situation, not like a frail violet, but with the ferocity of a tigress. Given Mrs. Eaton's gameness, the President's interest and the unyielding opposition of the proper Calhouns, Van Buren had all the ingredients of a highly profitable situation. He lost no time in exploiting its potential.

He proceeded to pay, as Jackson was to term it, "the most devoted and assiduous attention to Mrs. Eaton." While other cabinet members were bulldozed by incensed wives and squeamish daughters into slighting the wife of the Secretary of War and the President's well-known wishes, Van Buren, widower and daughterless, could maneuver as he pleased. He called on Mrs. Eaton. He gave parties in her honor. He prodded his friends, the British and the Russian Ministers, who both were bachelors, to give dances at which Mrs. Eaton was treated with pointed distinction. No little finesse went into these calculated endeavors. Consider, for example, the first cabinet dinner which Van Buren as Secretary of State was required under the inexorable rules of protocol to give. He, of course, invited Mrs. Eaton and all the other ladies of the cabinet. All the other ladies promptly declined; only their husbands promised to attend. At first appalled by the unanimity of the feminine abstentions, the Magician made a magnificent counterthrust. As his most honored guest, he brought in Mrs. Thomas Mann Randolph, the only living daughter of Thomas Jefferson and the acknowledged *grande dame* of Washington society. To supplement this eminent lady, whose prestige exceeded that of all the cabinet ladies combined, Van Buren dragooned military men and their lovely wives into adorning the festivities with their presence. "The party being free from any kind of embarrassment," he later wrote triumph-antly of the event, "their joy was unconfined."

Mrs. Eaton was not one to lighten her mentor's burdens. Her tactless-ness, which to many who encountered her was her most unbearable offense, often got in the way. At one large evening party arranged by Van Buren and attended by the cabinet, members of Congress and the diplomatic corps, Mrs. Eaton was suddenly the center of an explosive situation. Up to this unhappy point, the party had been going tolerably well. The dancing, which was in full swing, seemed all-engrossing. Van Buren, who was not feeling well, but was sustained by a sense of accomplishment, had retired to a sofa in a lower room. Scarcely had he settled down when a friend rushed in, ex-claiming, "You ought to be above if you wish to prevent a fight." Now more alarmed than ill, the Magician dashed to the floor where he readily learned from a colleague that in the dancing Mrs. Eaton and a hostile cabinet lady had jostled each other—"doubtless accidentally"—his informant added wryly. The collision had touched off some expressions of resentment, rendered with sufficient vigor to attract the attention of everyone in the room. Fortunately, by the time Van Buren reached the floor the ladies had parted, although the company still was buzzing. To relieve the situation, the anxious host induced his orchestra to abandon the intermission they were enjoying, and break into a spirited number.

L'affaire Eaton, strenuously fanned by the busy Magician, was becom-ing a roaring holocaust. It was gutting the cabinet. The President, who was choleric on the subject, convened his Secretaries into special meeting and sternly ordered them to order their wives to be hospitable to Mrs. Eaton. At another point, he proposed to fire Ingham, whose wife was one of the shriller buglers of the crusade against Mrs. Eaton. But Van Buren managed to pull the President off; there was bigger game to bag. In the White House, the ranks were bitterly divided. Although Jackson was pure loyalty to Mrs. Eaton, the Donelsons, with equal conviction, deemed her a terrible blot on the social horizon. Not only that, Mrs. Donelson was blaming Van Buren and Van Buren alone for keeping her there. The intensity of the good lady's feelings was becoming increasingly apparent to the Magician. Until these recent rending events, Emily Donelson had been his favorite companion at the dances and dinners. Of late, however, she was noticeably distant, even frosty.

One evening when l'affaire was spiraling into a new crescendo, Van Buren dropped in at the White House, as was his habit, for a chat with any-one happening to be about the sitting room. Jackson, he was disappointed to find, was not there. But Emily and several of her friends were. After some small talk, she drew Van Buren aside and with deadly candor told the Magician that she was puzzled about his disposition toward Mrs. Eaton and would appreciate having the point cleared up. The trapped Mr. Van Buren squirmed awkwardly and ingloriously out of the situation by declaring that he had an engagement for which he had to leave at once. Under Emily's exacting gaze, he felt compelled to add that he would be glad to discuss the subject further at their earliest mutual convenience. Emily insisted on a definite date.

At the appointed time, Van Buren and the piquant Mrs. Donelson commenced a long lively discussion in the sitting room. Also on hand and quite alert was Emily's like-minded cousin, Mary Eastin. The discussion quickly became heated. Greatly affected, Miss Eastin withdrew to the embrasure of a nearby window and emitted some heavy sobs. Alarmed by the deterioration of the situation, and even more alarmed that Jackson might at any moment enter upon the awful scene, Van Buren worked desperately to set things aright. He rendered up a long consoling monologue, a masterpiece of inspired suavity. The upshot was that Miss Eastin's tears were checked and, perhaps more important, Emily Donelson agreed that they should never discuss the subject again. In the weeks which followed, Van Buren zealously plied the ruffled lady with attentions. The Donelsons, after all, were much too close to Jackson to be alienated. The Magician's sure touch is demonstrated by the thoroughgoing nature of his success. When Emily Donelson's first-born daughter was christened in an elaborate ceremony at the White House, the mother had the pick of Washington's man power in selecting godfathers for her child. The two godfathers she unhesitatingly chose were the President and her recent antagonist, Van Buren.

The dangling state of Martin Van Buren's agitated fortunes was suddenly transformed by a momentous development. While the Eaton affair was running its merry pace, the country's attention was turning to the infinitely more complex and menacing issue of nullification. Nothing less than the safety and future of the Union turned on the outcome. Some months earlier, the igniting spark had been provided by the Tariff Act of 1828, or "the tariff of abominations" as it was designated in the South. The Act's rate structure discriminated strongly, as the structures of that era were wont to do, against the Southern states and in behalf of the more populous North, whose industrial awakening was sharply quickening in tempo. Coming in the wake of several earlier discriminatory tariff acts, the legislation of 1828 provided release for the long-accumulated resentment of the South. In Vice-President Calhoun's own state, South Carolina, men spoke openly of declaring the Act to be null and void, and Charleston, the state's leading port, a free port. In Congress, the South Carolina delegation was seriously considering resigning as a body to give force to their protest.

The discerning Calhoun saw that the tariff was simply the occasion of the "present unhappy state of things." The real cause, as he put it with customary perception, was "that the peculiar domestic institution of the Southern states [slavery], and the consequent direction, which that and her soil and climate have given to her industry, has placed them, in regard to taxation and appropriations in opposite relation to the majority of the union." The nullification doctrine was the political shield of the embattled economic position of the Southern slavocracy. Although others had first formulated the doctrine, Calhoun provided its most eloquent and completely reasoned statement in his famous pamphlet, *Exposition*. In this remarkable essay, of which the South Carolina legislature ordered five thousand copies printed, Calhoun advanced the principle that a state might annul any law of Congress which, in its considered judgment, was unconstitutional. Further, the general government, Calhoun argued, was a mere agent of the states, indeed the agent of any particular state, so far as the will of that state was concerned. The issue was not long in being drawn when the Webster-Hayne debate spectacularly put the rival theories of the union before the country.

In the bewilderment of the continuing controversy, the eyes of the country turned inevitably to Jackson. There was little to be seen. As yet the President had taken no definitive public position on either the tariff or nullification. But within the inner circle, strong surmises were afoot as to what that position eventually would be. With his emotions so entangled in the Eaton affair, the President would hardly be endeared to the nullification doctrine, knowing that its leading advocate was also Mrs. Eaton's principal persecutor, Vice-President Calhoun.

Nullification first squarely confronted Jackson on no less an occasion than Thomas Jefferson's birthday. On that day, too, nullification injected itself as a shaping factor in the Calhoun-Van Buren struggle. Hitherto in the Republic's history, the late President's birthday had never been the object of any special celebration, however much Jefferson was venerated by his countrymen and by the party he founded. This year, however, would be different. Thanks to a watchful informant, Van Buren got word that a corps of self-interested party men planned to honor the father of all Democrats with a gala dinner at a leading Washington hotel. The President, the Vice-President, the cabinet, the state delegations in Congress, all would be invited to attend. There would, of course, be toasts and speeches intermixed with a hearty repast and booming brass bands. Van Buren's suspicions, always trigger-alert, were instantly aroused by the unprecedented nature of the projected conviviality. The plot was clear, and he rushed to the White House to put the President on guard. The dinner, Van Buren described the impending maneuver to his chief, would be used as "a stalking horse" for linking Jefferson's prestige and congenial philosophy in the Alien and Sedition Acts to the current doctrines expounded by Calhoun and Hayne. Jackson needed no convincing. At once he considered the action to be taken. Donelson joined the discussion and it was agreed that all three should go to the dinner collectively, after meeting beforehand on the appointed day at the White House. Jackson would surely be called upon to make a toast. What should he say? In a voice choked with defiance, the President declared that he would make a fighting anti-nullification pronouncement that would not soon be forgotten. Van Buren was highly delighted. For the very first time, the President's displeasure with the Vice-President would be brought into public view.

On April fifteenth, shortly before five o'clock, Jackson, Donelson and Van Buren left the White House for Jesse Brown's Indian Queen Hotel where nearly one hundred guests had gathered. The mood of the President and his comrades as they sloughed grimly along that humid spring evening, was more akin to the battlefield than the festive board. As they entered the dining hall of the hotel, the atmosphere decidedly chilled. Van Buren quickly discovered the cause by picking up from one of the tables a card on which had been printed the formal toasts to be offered in the course of the evening. It was clear at a glance that the impending proceedings would resound with sentiment dear to the nullifiers. Only a few minutes before the arrival of the presidential party, the Pennsylvania delegation, taking one look at the toast cards, had walked out in a pique. Several other delegations were feverishly conferring on the same decision. The Marine band, meanwhile, was blaring away with extra vigor to drown out the rising tension. Somehow the meal began and passed without incident. Then, after what seemed interminable preliminaries, the toast of the President of the United States was called for. The room crackled with expectation. Van Buren, his modest stature hopelessly lost in the crowd, climbed up on a chair to observe the full effect. Jackson at last rose. In a voice rough with defiance, he declared, "Our Union: It must and shall be preserved." Without a word more, he lifted his glass as a sign that the toast was to be drunk standing. Chairs scraped and there was a hum of excited whispering as the company rose. Calhoun stood with them. "His glass," noticed a nearby participant, "trembled in his hand and a little of the amber fluid trickled down the side."

The fight was now in the open, and the prey was badly gored. A visitor to the Senate gallery found the Vice-President "more wrinkled and careworn than I had expected from his reputed age. His voice is shrill. . . . His manners have in them an uneasiness, a hurried, incoherent air." With the stealth and evil grace of the fox, Van Buren came in for the kill. His route was typically circuitous, and the weapon he used to carry out his homicidal intentions was a letter. It was a very special letter, solicited by his trusted aide, James A. Hamilton, and written long ago by his old mentor, William H. Crawford, in his term as Secretary of the Treasury in the cabinet of President Monroe. Secretary Crawford's letter centered upon a climactic episode of the Seminole Indian War in 1818 when Jackson, as commanding general in the field, invaded Florida without consulting President Monroe, and seized the Spanish forts of Saint Marks and Pensacola. To the nation, Jackson was instantaneously a hero; to the President he was a case of arrant insubordination. Monroe took up the problem with his cabinet. There, according to the Crawford letter, John Calhoun, who was Secretary of War in the Monroe Administration, forthrightly recommended that General Jackson be arrested and punished.

The Crawford letter, which had been retrieved from an old trunk in the Georgian's manse, reached Jackson via a number of trusted hands, including the Magician's faithful White House ally, W. B. Lewis. Through Lewis, the letter finally came to Donelson, who made the presentation to the President. Jackson, to whom the disclosures were not altogether a surprise—only recently he had discussed the entire incident with ex-President Monroe—was still seething from the Jefferson Day Dinner. The evidence is impressive that he desired to strike further at Calhoun, and Van Buren's conveniently timed skulduggery gave pretense for doing so. The President, accordingly, lost no time in dispatching a peremptory request to Calhoun to explain his conduct in the Monroe cabinet. In a painstaking answer of some fifty-two pages, the Vice-President freely admitted the charges, defended his own conduct and condemned Crawford for betraying the secrets of the cabinet. Evidently eager to keep the fight going, Jackson tartly informed Calhoun that his reply was unsatisfactory. Simultaneously, Jackson dispatched a messenger with Calhoun's answer to Van Buren's abode just across from the White House. But the wily Magician, in a characteristic gesture, refused to read it. He would be accused, he told the waiting messenger, of fomenting trouble; he much preferred to know nothing about it. When these sentiments were relayed to the White House, Jackson was heard to remark, "I reckon Van is right. I dare say they will try to throw the blame on him."

Calhoun and his followers indeed tried, but Van Buren nimbly stayed untouchable. Scrupulously keeping a safe distance from the affair, he left the real dagger work to a network of friends in Congress, to Lewis in the White House, and to such organization men as Crawford, Forsyth and James A. Hamilton. All over town, the Van Buren camp worked overtime at keeping the dispute simmering with, as Calhoun himself expressed it, "whispers, wise looks, & shrugging of shoulders."

Meanwhile the screws were steadily tightening. Sometime ago, in arrangements for the distribution of several highly cherished items of patronage, it had been decided in party circles that the clerkship of the House of Representatives, a major plum, would go to Calhoun man Virgil Maxcy. Lo, now some months later, when the House came to vote on the appointment, Maxcy was thoroughly beaten by a solid phalanx of pro-Jackson and pro-Van Buren Congressmen. Simultaneously, former Senator Henry Baldwin of Pennsylvania, whose high-tariff views were anathema to Calhoun, was nominated by the President to the Supreme Court. In New York, J. Watson Webb, editor of the New York *Courier and Enquirer* who was very close to the Magician, devoted his editorial page to the proposition that Jackson run for a second term, with Van Buren the Vice-presidential candidate and ultimate successor. Other journals quickly took up the chant.

Utterly routed in the Administration infighting, the desperate Calhoun decided to go to the people. He composed a long, reasoned, carefully documented pamphlet to "the people of the United States," disclosing that the real instigator of his growing differences with the President was Martin Van Buren. The Magician was mercilessly depicted as an unscrupulous schemer who placed his own rise to the Presidency above the Administration's welfare, who crushed anything blocking his way, including the comity which once existed and should exist between the President and Vice-President. Before publishing his expertly contrived epistle, Calhoun, who no longer went to the White House, asked Eaton to clear it with the President. The choice of Eaton for so delicate an undertaking seems strange, to say the least. Yet it must be remembered that Calhoun had not only alienated Jackson; equally important, his pariahlike status had frightened off the entire White House entourage. John Eaton accepted the assignment with unexpected grace and secret relish. Inwardly, he must have been recalling the instrumentality of the Calhouns in heaping humiliation and grief upon his wife. Here was an opportunity for revenge, handed on a platter. Eaton simply decided not to show the document to the President. Calhoun, however, was led to believe that Jackson had seen and approved it. At any rate, the Vice-President proceeded to publish his masterpiece upon that unfortunate assumption. When a copy of the *Daily Telegraph*, which carried Calhoun's effort in full, arrived at the White House, Jackson howled with rage at what he deemed a traitorous attack upon his whole Administration. Van Buren's response was to deny all charges airily and categorically in a letter to the *Globe*. Duff Green, the Calhoun editor, retorted crudely that Van Buren was a liar. Rumors briefly circulated that a challenge had passed between the Vice-President and the Secretary of State.

His break with Jackson irreparable, Calhoun retreated temporarily to the happier climate of South Carolina. There, at his ample estate with its gentle hills, soft-hued magnolias and spacious cotton fields, he found the serenity he could never find in the capital. Word drifted back to Washington that at one of the several public dinners tendered by proud Carolinians to honor their spokesman's homecoming, the customary toast to the President was pointedly omitted. Mr. Van Buren however, was toasted. With considerable feeling, the assemblage responded to the following: "Ah, that deceit should steal such gentle shapes, and with a virtuous visor hide deep vices."

Van Buren's triumphs up to this point were those of personal careerism fashioned in the murky recesses of palace politics. They were not triumphs achieved on the open field of policy, a lacking which suggested some over-concern on the part of the Magician with personal self-advancement and dereliction in representing the established attitudes of his following on the issues of the day.

If the Northern and Southern wings of Van Buren's organization were united on anything, it was in their opposition to internal improvements financed and constructed by the federal government. The era of the turn-pike was still in flower and the era of the steamboat and the canal had barely begun. States east and west, avid for commercial advantage, were pressing for gigantic programs of federally constructed roads and canals. Van Buren's own New York State was not among those crying for federal action. In respect to canals and roadways, the state was handsomely situated. The great Erie Canal, stretching 363 miles from Albany to Buffalo, had been completed in 1825. Through the Erie, the regions of the Northwest were brought for the first time into direct touch with the Atlantic seaboard. New York City's spectacular commercial destiny was clearly portended. Federal money, if available, would surely concentrate on canal-building in the "have-not" states, enabling them to compete with New York for the rising and potentially enormous Western trade. New York's natural interest, therefore, was to oppose federal improvements. The view of the Southern party wing, of which the sagacious Nathaniel Macon was representative, was that federal outlays would be concentrated in the Middle and Western states, and negligible in the South. Southerners would be immeasurably better off if the expenditure proposed for improvements were applied to the national debt. A high tariff, under whose yoke the South so badly suffered, would be less justifiable if federally administered improvements were held to a modest level. For most of the revenue yielded by the tariff was used to finance federal outlays, of which internal improvements already formed a substantial part.

By reflecting his party following and coming out against federal improvements, Van Buren would be challenging three main centers of power in the political firmament. His constant foe, Calhoun, had long been an exponent of federal action. Henry Clay, perhaps Van Buren's most dangerous competitor for the Presidency, was father of the American system, calling for lavish federal activity in the development of a national transportation system. Finally, the Westerners, Eaton, Lewis and others, who had Jackson's ear, were unalterably aligned on the issue of improvements with the thinking of Calhoun and Clay.

Andrew Jackson's opinions on the subject of internal improvements were a mystery to one and all. As Senator, he had voted for federal road constructions, impressed by his military experience that a national road system was indispensable to sound national defense. The expressions of his inaugural address, as they bore upon improvements, were a masterpiece of ambiguity. The President endorsed "constitutional" improvements. Van Buren hopefully interpreted this language as revealing a certain bias against federally constructed improvements.

On his rides with Jackson, the Magician tactfully probed his chief, and finding the President more receptive than he had expected, drilled away with arguments in behalf of the New York view. Knowing Jackson's aversion to debt in any form, Van Buren worked the theme that improvements would drain the Treasury. Spendthrifts in Congress, he pointed out, would have an orgy of logrolling producing a "torrent of reckless legislation." After several such stagings of argumentation by Van Buren, Jackson told his friend that he had decided that the public debt should be liquidated and any civil construction program developing in Congress should be stopped. He instructed Van Buren to keep watch for a bill whose veto would most pointedly convey the new Administration policy. Van Buren, who preferred to work by stealth and surprise, requested his more open-dealing President to keep their discussion secret.

One fine day, during their customary canter, Van Buren announced that he had found his bill. It called for a turnpike to be constructed from Maysville to Lexington, Ky., a distance of some seventy miles. The modesty of the mileage was hardly indicative of the importance of the road. Its real significance was its location in the home state of that zealot of federal improvements, Henry Clay. Jackson seemed immensely pleased with the choice, and Van Buren toiled far into the night, preparing a brief expounding the argument on which the veto might be based. Next morning, the brief was dispatched by messenger to the President. For five long days there was no response, only a void of silence which, as it persisted, became creepingly alarming.

Van Buren had nearly lost hope when, one morning during breakfast, there was a knock on his door. It was a messenger with the eagerly awaited note from Jackson. All was well. "As far as I have been able to decipher," wrote Jackson in his own frantic scrawl, "I think it is one of the most lucid expositions of the Constitution I have ever met with." Thus spurred on, Van Buren speedily drafted the veto from the brief, and took the finished document to his chief. Reading in his rapid manner, Jackson unhesitatingly approved Van Buren's effort, and the Magician, exercising usual caution, asked that the veto be kept secret until the very moment of its release. Jackson's penchant for undervaluing even the most rudimentary secrecy drove the Magician mad. On more than one occasion, he pointedly lectured his chief on the dangers of leaving important papers strewn about his table exposed to the gaze of interested visitors. As a matter of fact, it was probably just such a lapse that caused the Westerners to get wind of the veto a few days before its issuance. Losing no time, they dispatched their most persuasive emissary, Colonel R. M. Johnson, an old frontier friend of Jackson and the reputed slayer of Tecumseh. "General," cried the Colonel, a man of ready flamboyance, "if this hand were an anvil on which the sledge hammer of a smith were descending and a fly were to light upon it that fly would not be more surely crushed than you will crush your friends in Kentucky if you veto that bill."

Jackson sprang up and in a strong theatrical counterthrust, exclaimed, "There is no money to be expended as my friends desire. I stand committed before the Country to pay off the National Debt. This pledge I am determined to redeem." Johnson hastily withdrew. The Westerners, however, were only beginning to fight. On the morning the veto was due, Van Buren made his usual reconnaissance visit to the White House. To his immense distress, he found Jackson breakfasting with the Westerners—Barry, Eaton, Lewis and Grundy—no one was missing. The meal was just concluding and Jackson, still weak from his recent illness, started up the stairs. Van Buren outrushed the others to assist him. While holding the General's arm and ascending slowly, the Magician remarked that his company seemed distressed. "Yes," acknowledged Jackson, "but don't mind that." And touching his breast pocket with an air of finality, "The thing is here and shall be sent up as soon as Congress convenes."

The veto appeared on schedule, exactly as Van Buren had drafted it. A masterly appeal to general opinion over the heads of entrenched interests —contractors, merchants, bankers and the like—the veto played upon patriotism, cited the sacred Jeffersonian texts extolling local action, and convincingly admonished the common man that payment of the debt would reduce taxes, while a federal program of improvements would inordinately increase them. The veto was readily sustained in Congress.

From the standpoint of Van Buren's ambitions, the Maysville veto was pure gold. It was a major setback for Calhoun, who had gone on record in the course of the debate, emphatically favoring federal improvements, to placate his Northern supporters. Henry Clay, too, had suffered. In the White House itself, the veto signified a major redistribution of influence among the occupants of the treadmill of high policy. The stalwarts of the Nashville Junto—Lewis and Eaton—had suffered a jarring rebuff. For the first time, the long-standing intimacy with Jackson, on which they so boldly traded, was shown to be vulnerable. They had plainly been outflanked and out-ranked in the President's counsels by the wily Magician.

Although Calhoun was in full eclipse, Van Buren's own situation was not without peril. For one thing, Duff Green and other articulate like-minded journalists were working overtime detailing Van Buren as a monstrous Machiavellian. The cabinet was still strongly pro-Calhoun. Being a genius at co-ordinating seemingly disparate forces, Van Buren fell to work to bring order out of chaos, and in no time at all, he concocted a masterpiece of creative manipulation. Consulting no one, he hit upon a plan which would simultaneously solve the Eaton affair, reconstitute the cabinet, and project himself to the public in a bit of vivid dramaturgy as a selfless magistrate dedicated to the commonweal.

The crux of the plan entailed nothing less than his resigning as Secretary of State, ostensibly for so noble a purpose as the peace and welfare of the Administration. His real object was to compel by his own resignation the resignation of Eaton and the rest of the predominately pro-Calhoun cabinet. The cabinet could then be reconstituted with a membership denoted by its loyalty to the Magician's interests. With Calhoun, his only real rival for the succession out of the way, the Magician need no longer be on hand at the White House to protect his interests and could afford at least a brief absence from that arena of destiny.

Whither would he go upon leaving the Secretaryship? His enterprising gaze was fixed upon a post outside the country, the Ministership to Great Britain. Rich in prestige and far from the tumult of Washington, the post was ideal in every way. The current Minister could easily be displaced. He was, fortunately, the Magician's protégé, Louis McLane, an ambitious man chafing to return to his native shores and partake of its superior political opportunities. In a reconstituted cabinet, McLane would doubtless be delighted to become the new Secretary of the Treasury.

With his bag of tricks now packed, the Magician was ready to launch his complex sleight of hand. He told his son, Abraham, of his intention to resign. But although it was easy to tell Abraham, it was painfully difficult to tell the President. Weeks passed with Van Buren seeking unavailingly to muster courage to break the shattering news, so fearful was he of the General's reaction. Time and again opportunities would arise for the revelation, only to be lost because Van Buren turned speechless in his anxiety. One day, for example, a heavy thunderstorm overtook the two on their customary canter, forcing them to take shelter in a nearby tavern for several hours. Now was the time. But Van Buren, try as he might, was tongue-tied. As one abortive day after another passed, young Abraham Van Buren began teasing his father for his lack of nerve. Goaded by Abraham and the abhorrent spectacle of fumbled opportunity, the Magician finally came to grips with fate one afternoon while riding with the President through Georgetown and down the Tenallytown road. The subjects under discussion were the Eatons and the disintegration of the cabinet. Van Buren somehow managed to seize the gaping opening and blurted out in a nervous exhalation, "No, General, there is but one thing that will give you peace."

"What is that sir?"

"My resignation."

The President, in Van Buren's word, "blanched." "Never, sir," replied Jackson with peremptory vigor. "Even you know little of Andrew Jackson if you suppose him capable of consenting to such humiliation of his friends by his enemies."

For the next four hours, Van Buren sought to justify his course and beat off frequent pointed interrogations from Jackson. So engrossed were the riders that they passed the Tenallytown gate, their customary turning point, and not until long past the dinner hour did they finally reach Washington. Jackson requested his friend to stay on for dinner and talk further, but Van Buren pleaded another engagement. He promised, however, to return the next morning. Meantime, he requested the General to mention their conversation to no one, not even to Lewis or Eaton.

The next morning's meeting Van Buren said he could remember the rest of his life.

Without preliminaries, Jackson opened the conversation. "Mr. Van Buren, I have made it a rule through life never to throw obstacles in the way of any man who, for reasons satisfactory to himself, desires to leave me, and I shall not make your case an exception."

The icy candor momentarily terrified Van Buren. Had he gone too far? Was he out of favor? He quickly recovered for a bold counterthrust. With all the fervor at his command, the Magician said he wished that he had a window in his breast through which might be read his inmost thoughts. "Now, sir!" he exclaimed. "Come what may, I shall not leave your Cabinet until you shall say, of your own motion, and without reference to any supposed interests or feelings of mine, that you are satisfied that it is best for us to part."

Taken aback by such unusual force of statement, considering the nature of its source, Jackson seized the Magician's hand. "You must forgive me, my friend," he said with imploring warmth. "I have been too hasty in my conclusions—I know I have—say no more about it now, but come back at one o'clock—we will take another long ride and talk again in a better and calmer state of mind." This was done, with the desired effect. Then at Jackson's suggestion, the Western circle, Barry, Lewis and Eaton, were called in. The discussion was long, intense, but inconclusive, whereupon Van Buren invited the three assistants to his home for dinner.

Toward nightfall, the party commenced their fateful march. Along the way, Eaton suddenly stopped as though transfixed by supernal inspiration. It was wrong for Van Buren, "the most valuable member of the cabinet," to resign, he exclaimed. Then, after a breath, tumbled out the statement the Magician had so expertly and painstakingly built up to in the discussions through the long afternoon. It was he, Eaton, who should resign. He, not Van Buren, had brought the Administration its woe. For a long moment, no one spoke, a hiatus that must have seemed like ages to Eaton if he waited for someone to say that he was mistaken, that he, too, was indispensable. No one, as a matter of fact, ever did, and Van Buren, after a decent interval, swooped in with the clinching blow. "What about Mrs. Eaton?" he asked with quiet finality. The Secretary of War managed to mumble that he was sure she would not object. At dinner, Eaton appeared deeply hurt at being taken up so quickly.

The next several days the Magician's plans moved along with inexorable smoothness. First, Eaton resigned, and then Van Buren. The sequence was important. Van Buren, after all, did not want to depart from the cabinet only to have the Secretary of War renege. The latter was a distinct possibility, for in the cold clear light of reality, leaving the cabinet had a pallid allure to the Eatons, husband and wife alike. This was apparent when Jackson and Van Buren went around to the Eatons one day, after the Secretary of War had resigned, to pay their respects. Peggy was decidedly chilly toward her fearless champion.

When the first official news of Van Buren's conjurations broke upon the world, the reactions of his friends were deeply divided. Several loyal associates frankly lamented that he was taking excessive risks in leaving the seat of power. Most of his friends, however, hailed his action as a splendid coup. "Nothing is more noble or in itself more gratifying to a free people," exulted the canny Benjamin F. Butler, "than the voluntary relinquishment of high station, extensive power and commanding influence, especially when dictated by an enlarged and patriotic devotion to the general good." Van Buren's many critics had no difficulty seeing through the façade. "Did you ever read such a letter as Mr. Van Buren's?" asked Henry Clay. "It is perfectly characteristic of the man—a labored effort to conceal the true motives, and to assign assumed ones. . . ." In the quiet of his plantation in far-off

South Carolina, John Calhoun confidently analyzed the situation in Washington. "It is a Van Buren move," he said, "and has for its object the increase of his control in the movements of the government and at the same time to diminish his responsibility."

"The increase" of Van Buren's "control" was first manifested in the new cabinet. After Eaton and Van Buren had resigned, the rest of the cabinet, as the Magician hoped and calculated, had done likewise. Upon communing with Jackson concerning the resulting vacancies, Van Buren emerged with control of the two principal posts of the reconstituted cabinet. The State and Treasury departments were stocked with his own hand-picked men. Edward Livingston, whiling away the hot summer at his country place on the Hudson River, was peremptorily summoned by the Magician to come on the first stage to Washington, letting no one know his destination. An aristocrat by ancestry, Livingston by conviction was a democrat. Jefferson had appointed him federal district attorney, Alexander Hamilton had campaigned against him, and the people had elected him mayor of New York. Louis McLane, as Van Buren planned, resigned his London post for the seat in the Treasury. Inducing McLane to take the step had not been easy. His overriding ambition, much to Van Buren's surprise, was a place on the high court, and only after considerable negotiation did he settle for the Treasury. The incoming Secretary of the Navy, Levi Woodbury, was also close to Van Buren. The new Secretary of War, Lewis Cass, ex-Governor of the Michigan territory, a massive man of stolid intellect, was Jackson's own choice, as was the new Attorney General, Roger B. Taney of Maryland, a former Federalist. Both were unknown quantities. When the new cabinet was announced, John Calhoun was heard to comment on the Magician's latest sleight of hand: "He has so surrounded the President with his creatures that his affairs can be safely administered in his absence."

The absence was further speeded when Van Buren was designated Minister to England via a presidential recess appointment. The Magician lost no time in packing his bags and quitting the country. On a blistering August day in 1831, he settled down in sweet contentment into his deck chair on the packet ship, *President*, for "the first relief in twenty-five years from partisan agitation." After a voyage of unimpaired serenity, he reached London and fell avidly to work at once, having exceptionally long and cordial audiences with the King and the Royal Ministers. With customary parsimony, he defrayed his sizable personal expenses, above and beyond his impossible salary, by taking into his home as a paying guest the First Secretary of the legation, Washington Irving. Secretary Irving was more than Van Buren's tenant and chief of staff; they became fast friends. Both being confirmed travelers, they ranged far and wide over the countryside on weekends and holidays. Christmas season, for instance, they spent in a gay excursion by carriage to Oxford and Blenheim, and on to Warwick Castle and Newstead Abbey. The quaint pageantry of the many ancient towns they passed through was completely enthralling. They saw mummers and morris dancers cavorting in graceful steps, and glee singers celebrating with merry song. Irving, like Van Buren, a gourmet, they feasted at the famous Red Horse Tavern at Stratford with all the trimmings: boar's head crowned with holly, the tangy wassail bowl, and the sweet scent and mingled pastels of boughs of snapdragon piled high as a tablepiece.

Amid his festive junketing, Van Buren was still functioning, even at long distance, as Jackson's personal counselor. "Any suggestions which your leisure will permit," Jackson graciously extended a broad invitation, "and you may choose to make on any subject will be kindly received." Van Buren responded with customary zeal. He poured over the advance copy of the annual address to Congress, which came by special packet, and by return mail he was suggesting several significant revisions. He advised on department imbroglios, situations in Congress and the never-failing vexations of patronage. But Van Buren at long distance was far less satisfactory to Jackson than Van Buren close by. "You know Mr. Livingston is anxious to go abroad," wrote the President after a season of transatlantic counseling, "and I am as anxious again to have you near me, and it would afford me pleasure to gratify both." While conceding that Livingston was a man of talent, "he knows," continued Jackson, "nothing of mankind—he lacks in this respect, that judgment that you possess, in so eminent a degree."

Jackson's prayer for the Magician's home-coming was suddenly, and not altogether unexpectedly, answered by no less an agency than the United States Senate. Van Buren's being a recess appointment, Jackson passed along his name to the Senate when the regular legislative session commenced in December. The titans of Capitol Hill, Webster, Calhoun and Clay, smarting under Van Buren's unchecked rise, were sharpening their claws for vengeance. Burying momentarily their own past differences, these doughty individualists united to put the nomination to slow death. Three months dragged by even before Van Buren's name was referred to the Foreign Relations Committee, a step which under normal circumstances was instantaneous. Senator John Homes of Maine, who detested Van Buren, introduced a resolution instructing the Committee to investigate the late cabinet upheaval and the wicked Van Buren's part in it. In the subsequent debate on the resolution, the opposition presented its case linking the Magician with every known evil of the day. This effort was considerably simplified by the fact that the anti-Van Buren forces constituted a majority of the Senate, insolubly united by common hate. With homicidal glee, they concocted a strategy to subject the Magician to the most excruciating humiliation. As the cards were played, his nomination was reported out favorably by the Foreign Relations Committee, and another mudslinging floor debate ensued (including a full account of Van Buren's alleged attentions to a half-dozen Washington ladies). Finally, the vote was taken, and by careful prearrangement, it resulted in a tie. The situation called for Calhoun, presiding officer of the Senate, who had returned to the Washington wars, to cast the deciding vote. Preening himself with the clamorous encouragement of the onlooking Senators, Calhoun committed his long-awaited act of sweet revenge. He voted against Van Buren. The Senate rang with cheers, as the crowd does when the matador makes his death thrust at the fallen bull. In the exhilaration of accomplishment, the Vice-President was heard to declare, "It will kill him, sir, kill him dead. He will never kick, sir, never kick."

Van Buren's friends, however, took a rather different view of the gory situation. "Some of your best friends," the faithful Cambreleng had written, weeks before the issue was settled, "hope the Senate will reject you." The stab in the back, Cambreleng figured, would make Van Buren a national martyr. The local party organizations and the rank and file would well up with resentment at the gross personal injustice and the travesty on party integrity. Cambreleng was not disappointed. After Calhoun cast his vote, protest meetings broke out around the countryside; and the democratic press bayed with indignation. "There is such a thing in politics," observed Cambreleng with insight, "as killing a man too dead." Calhoun's spiteful act and the revulsion it engendered had all but clinched the vice-presidential nomination for Van Buren.

On May 21 and 22, 1832, while the Magician was inspecting cathedrals and sampling the cuisine of the most distinguished hostelries of the continent, delegates gathered in Baltimore for the first national convention of the Democratic party. Jackson, of course, was quickly renominated. As attention turned to the Vice-Presidency, Administration men circulating among the delegates were emphatically quoting a declaration of the President to the effect that a vote for Van Buren was a vote for Jackson. The first ballot gave Van Buren 260 votes; Philip Barbour of Virginia, the Calhoun candidate, 40 votes, and R. M. Johnson of Kentucky, 26. The Magician, spurned in Washington, was now redeemed in Baltimore.

With characteristic foresight, Van Buren long had in readiness a central issue for the ensuing electoral campaign. Perfect in every way, the issue would spark the contest, divide the parties and rally men. Best of all, it promised to redress a major weakness in the Magician's onrushing career— his tenuous association with the Western faction.

Early in the Administration, the Magician's circling eye alighted on the mighty financial fortress of the Second Bank of the United States. Chartered in 1816 for a period of twenty years, the Second Bank was an extension of Alexander Hamilton's monumental creation, the First Bank of the United States. The present Bank did not altogether use its enormous power with the gentle grace portended by the elegant Greek temple in which it reposed on Chestnut Street in Philadelphia. Predominately private in character, with but one fifth of its capital subscribed by the federal government, the Bank's control resided in a board of twenty-five directors, five appointed by the President, and the remainder elected by the stockholders. The Bank was the depository of governments funds; its currency circulated more widely and with less depreciation than the notes of the state banks. By demanding or threatening to demand specie for the state bank notes it took in, or by refusing to take them altogether, the great Bank exercised a powerful check upon state banking activity. Although the Bank's charter had some years to run, rumors were afoot that Congress would soon be requested to grant a renewal.

In terms of the political necessities of Martin Van Buren, a fight with the Bank of the United States had great allure. His popularity in New York, where local banking interests bitterly opposed the Bank, would surely rise. Operating free from the safety-fund requirements imposed by state law upon New York banks, and having its headquarters in Philadelphia, the Bank of the United States made that city the financial capital of the country. New York, its manufacture, trade and population soaring, was chafing to wrest supremacy from Philadelphia. It would undoubtedly do so, if the Bank toppled. In the South, Van Buren's supporters, too, were anti-Bank. Stirred by the oppression of the tariff and the beckoning call of nullification, they could be counted on to jump at the opportunity to avenge their states rights principles by exterminating a major national institution like the Bank. But the most valuable feature of the Bank was its unpopularity in the West. The frontier lands, booming with migrant farmers and rising towns, were desperate for credit. To the unremitting inflationary demand, the Bank's response was a doggedly conservative credit policy. The vast debtor population in the West and in other sections reacted, in turn, with fierce resentment. As an organ of concentrated economic power, the single national establishment of its kind, the Bank was also feared as well as hated. "All the flourishing cities of the West are mortgaged to this money power," cried Senator Thomas Hart Benton. "They may be devoured by it at any moment. They are in the jaws of the Monster! A lump of butter in the mouth of a dog! One gulp, one swallow, and all is gone."

What of the President? Would he be receptive to an anti-Bank policy? To numerous visitors at The Hermitage just previous to the election of

1828, Jackson had made plain his hostility to the Bank, and the fact that he was turning over in his mind a plan for a new banking system to replace the existing Second Bank. Would Jackson, now buffeted by the pressures of office-holding, pursue the sentiments uttered in the freedom of his pre-inaugural days?

One of the most significant pressures to which the President was exposed was Nicholas Biddle, the suave, scholarly, dictatorial manager of the Bank. Biddle counted on his own considerable charm to lull Jackson into approving recharter. In his first move, Biddle dispatched several formidable emissaries of good will on the payroll of the Bank to the White House. After sufficient softening up, Biddle himself descended upon Jackson. The results of the banker's suave ministrations were decidedly encouraging. The President seemed by no means incorrigibly hostile to the Bank and there was strong support in several of the higher echelons of the Administration. A solid majority of the cabinet favored renewal, as did the President's influential secretary, Donelson. In his good friend Major William B. Lewis, Biddle had an untrammeled pipeline to the inner councils of the White House. Over the months, Lewis provided a continuous flow of highly optimistic intelligence to the effect that Jackson was rapidly coming to tolerate the Bank. "I think you will find," reported Lewis in his rosy way, "that the old fellow will do justice to the Bank."

The President's first annual message to Congress of December 8, 1829, must have jolted Mr. Biddle clear out of his massive executive chair. The message was vigorously anti-Bank, bearing not even a trace of the magnanimity Biddle had counted on on the basis of his own and Lewis's observations of the White House scene. The presidential opposition rested upon two grounds. One, constitutional, asserted the Jeffersonian states rights position. The other, an argument of efficiency, contended that the Bank had failed "in the great end of establishing a sound and uniform currency." Jackson proposed that Congress consider the wisdom of establishing a new bank founded wholly upon the credit of the United States government and its revenues.

The Biddle camp convulsed with speculation over the source of this unnerving and unpredicted catastrophe. Several discerning observers were convinced that a single machinator was at the bottom of it all. His name: Martin Van Buren. Soon after the President's message blasted the serenity of the Bank men, Roswell Colt, a leading spokesman for the bank, dispatched a friend to reconnoiter any further doings of the Magician, who was then billeted in a New York hotel. The friend, received with suffocating courtesy, managed to blurt out that the message was a shocker. With an air of great injury, Van Buren answered that he knew nothing about it; he had not been consulted; and he disapproved everything Jackson said. The wary Bank men were not particularly impressed by such abject innocence. Alexander Hamilton the Second, loyal to the institution his father had begotten, voiced the prevailing suspicion. "Have no confidence in Van Buren," he warned Biddle. "As an aspirant for the Chief Magistracy, he is without principle, and totally destitute of sincerity."

Meanwhile Van Buren was assaulting the Bank with his polished but deadly indirection. Although he never discussed the Bank publicly or even in his most confidential letters, his trusted lieutenant, James A. Hamilton, another son of Alexander the First, who was decidedly not proud of his father's handiwork, busied himself for weeks at Jackson's side arranging the details of a new banking structure. Van Buren himself was quietly working with two leading Westerners whose influence in the Administration was rocketing, Amos Kendall and Francis Preston Blair, both Kentuckians. Gaunt, funereal in expression and totally gray at forty-five; Kendall, the older of the two, was affectionately called "the Deacon." After graduation from Dartmouth and a brief spell of schoolteaching, Kendall had emigrated from New England to Kentucky. There he found his way into journalism, a demanding profession in frontier days, calling for readiness with the fist and the pistol as well as the pen. Kendall's gift for piercing invective earned a quick rise up the local journalistic ladder, eventuating in his editorship of the Argus of Western America, published at Frankfort, the Kentucky capital. In 1829, an impressed Jackson brought Kendall on to Washington as Fourth Auditor of the Treasury. Martin Van Buren, uncanny at spotting a comer, quickly fastened onto the journalist. "Kendall," prophesied the Magician, "is to be an influential man." The duties of his Treasury post being almost nominal, Kendall was soon helping with major drafting chores around the White House. In 1830, he was largely instrumental in establishing the Globe to replace Duff Green's Telegraph as the official organ of the Administration. To edit the new journal, the President brought up Frank Blair, Kendall's successor on the Argus and a master of slashing journalism. A corpselike man, six feet tall and weighing less than one hundred pounds, Blair arrived in Washington with a great gash in his head and his coat in shreds, suffered when his coach, en route from Kentucky, had overset in the mud.

Not all the maneuvering concerning the Second Bank of the United States was going on at the White House. Henry Clay, after a siege of illness at Ashland, had returned, restored, to Washington. His spirits high, his old charm exuding from every pore, his ambitions were charged with a new intensity for his constant goal, the Presidency. Beholding his situation, he concluded that he, too, needed an issue. What could be better than the Bank? In all other fields of policy—the tariff, internal improvements and nullification—the President had so consolidated his position that he was hardly vulnerable. Only the Bank offered sizable opportunities for profitable maneuver. Clay began pressing Nicholas Biddle to move for recharter, and the latter, thoroughly disillusioned with Jackson, needed little encouragement to take the plunge. At Biddle's instruction, legislation was introduced in the House of Representatives on January 6, 1832, providing for recharter. C. C. Cambreleng reflected the jubilation of the Van Buren camp when he wrote exultantly to his chief, "Your cause and the President's are now blended."

The bill for recharter was referred to committee, and a mammoth propaganda drive commenced. Petitions, patently inspired by a common source, poured in by the hundreds in the Bank's behalf. In Pennsylvania, the legislature passed a resolution endorsing recharter, setting an example which other states quickly followed. The great Bank, meanwhile, was unstintingly dispatching its shrewdest lobbyists to Washington under the direction of Horace Binney, one of the most distinguished lawyers of the day. When, after long debate, Congress prepared to vote, Biddle personally appeared on the scene to direct his forces. He was joined by as distinguished a triumvirate as the Congress of the United States has ever known. Allied with Clay were Daniel Webster, a hireling of the Bank who received a regular cash stipend, and John C. Calhoun, whose appetite for vengeance was insatiable since his ejectment from the Administration. Borne by the mighty triumvirate, recharter passed in both houses of Congress by comfortable margins in the summer of 1832.

At about this time, Martin Van Buren was on the high seas bound for the United States. Thanks to his alert organization, he was fully informed on the Bank war. As a matter of fact, he knew so much of the goings on, that after landing in New York and briefly tarrying there, he managed to reach Washington by stage on Sunday, July eighth, just as the presidential veto was being put into final shape. Upon receiving the Bank bill, Jackson had ordered a veto prepared. Roger B. Taney, the Attorney General, a brilliant, cigar-chewing man, who spoke in a low monotone, had done the major share of the work, assisted by Kendall and Donelson, and possibly Woodbury, in four days of round-the-clock sessions. The little band still were hard at it when Van Buren rolled up to the portico in his brougham. Scarcely had the Magician set foot in the foyer when the President, who normally greeted his friends only in his parlor or study, rushed up, his face screwed with agitation. "Holding my hand in one of his own," reported the anxious Van Buren, "and passing the other thro' his long white locks, he said, with the clearest indications of a mind composed, and in a tone entirely devoid of passion or bluster—'the bank, Mr. Van Buren, is trying to kill me, but I will kill it!'" After fittingly acknowledging his agreement, Van Buren was installed as a guest in the bedroom recently vacated by Sarah Yorke Jackson, the President's favorite daughter-in-law.

Nicholas Biddle and others of his school contended that Van Buren—"before he could unpack his bags"—was put to work polishing up the veto for transmittal to Congress early Monday morning. Plainly bearing the touch of a practical political hand, the veto was a shrewd campaign document expertly angled to a broad cut of the electorate. Challenging the constitutionality of the Bank and the expediency of concentrating vast power in the hands of an irresponsible few, the message fervently expounded a social philosophy envisioning a better life for the common man. For all of the veto's excellence and wide acclaim, Van Buren persisted in his studied course of avoiding any public identification with the Bank struggle. To questioners, one and all, he stoutly maintained—choosing his words carefully—that in respect to the veto, he had no "direct agency in its construction." The outcome of the struggle, after all, was still unclear, and the Magician, under no circumstances, wished to be identified with failure.

Yet for all of Van Buren's caution, the veto ultimately prevailed in Congress. The Bank, as he had hoped, became the central issue in the subsequent presidential campaign, and the Jackson-Van Buren ticket won easily by 219 electoral votes to Henry Clay's 49.

On the morning of September 11, 1832, Secretary of the Navy Levi Woodbury, was faced with an alarming communication from the President of the United States. "*Confidential*," it read. "*Efforts have been made, and perhaps not without success . . . to disaffect the Officer of the Navy in command at Charlston. . . . The idea is . . . to prevent a blockade. This must be guarded against.*" All through the past summer, events in South Carolina had bounced madly from crisis to crisis. John C. Calhoun, having broken with the Administration, was busily stirring the ferment by providing inflammatory restatements of the nullification doctrine in *An Address to the People of South Carolina* and his *Fort Hill Letter*. Although Congress had recently enacted a new tariff law, removing certain inequities of previous legislation, the reaction of the nullifiers was more drastic than ever. They maneuvered the calling of a special convention in South Carolina and swiftly passed a nullification ordinance holding the tariff law of 1828 and the current law of 1832 unconstitutional and not binding upon the state. The nullifiers boldly threatened that any attempt by the federal government to oppose enforcement of the ordinance would absolve South Carolina from allegiance to the Union and leave it a separate sovereign state.

"The duty of the Executive is a plain one," Andrew Jackson had responded. "The laws will be executed and the Union preserved by all the constitutional and legal means he is invested with. . . ." At the President's order, seven revenue cutters and the *Natchez*, a ship of war, had been dispatched to reinforce Charleston. Joel Poinsett, and later George Breathit, were posted as special presidential agents in South Carolina to report on local occurrences. In the face of Jackson's actions, the more rabid nullifiers cried out for troops to be raised to "defend" the state against federal aggression. Jackson countered by ordering the Charleston garrison alerted against incipient attack and dispatched General Winfield Scott to take command.

In the onrushing deterioration, Martin Van Buren was caught in the vise of a dilemma. At opposite and seemingly irreconcilable extremes of the nullification issue were the two principal constituencies claiming his loyalty, his party following and Andrew Jackson. If he pleased Jackson, he would displease the Southern element of his party, and vice versa. Letters from numerous Crawfordites dwelt upon the necessity of genuine tariff revision.

The line Van Buren proceeded to follow was more attuned to the necessities of his party following than to the policies of Andrew Jackson. The essence of the Magician's approach was the substance of the toast he offered at the famous Jefferson Day Dinner. After Jackson had made his famous pronouncement on that occasion and Calhoun a spirited reply, Van Buren offered a toast which in the general melee largely passed unnoticed. "Mutual forbearance and reciprocal concessions," he had said, "thro' their agency the Union was established—the patriotic spirit from which they emanated will forever sustain it." Van Buren's even-tenored endorsement of the golden mean was more than an opportunistic concession to his party. It was an effusion of temperament and of his conviction that the craft of politics, which he so deftly practiced, was essentially a process of compromise.

Van Buren toiled busily applying his formula for peace. In private letters to his Southern friends, he forthrightly disapproved the nullification doctrine. In counsel to Jackson, he tirelessly sought to reduce the intensity of the conflict, or at least head off measures threatening to aggravate it. For example, soon after Calhoun had rendered his famous Address with its philosophical dynamite on secession, Jackson began planning his annual message to Congress, scheduled for December 4, 1832. To forestall any oratorical intemperance which might be regretted later, the Magician proposed "great moderation and entirely exempt from any thing that could be construed into personal allusion of a hostile character. . . ." The message which finally went to Congress must have enormously pleased Van Buren. Conciliatory throughout, it said nothing of meeting nullification with force and recommended tariff reductions which Van Buren had long been urging.

Even while Van Buren was rejoicing over his success, his policy on nullification suddenly and unexpectedly went into relapse. The source of this painful upheaval was a letter to the President dispatched by special agent Poinsett from his observation post in South Carolina. In anguished prose, Poinsett related how some sixteen thousand citizens had been deprived of their rights by the nullification position of the South Carolina legislature and despairing unionists were leaving the state in droves. Poinsett painted the situation in the gory terms of the chroniclers of the French Revolution. If he was bent on arousing Jackson's fighting instincts, he surely succeeded. The President promptly directed Secretary of State Edward Livingston to draft the famous fighting nullification proclamation. Although the phrasing was largely Livingston's, the spirit and many ideas of this classic of militancy were Jackson's. Van Buren, who as Vice-President-elect had repaired to Albany to await the coming March inaugural, was not consulted. Jackson merely forwarded a copy of the proclamation after its issuance and invited his counsel on further moves.

The horrified Van Buren immediately composed a forceful restatement of his approach of moderation, begging Jackson to show the nullifiers the "toleration and magnanimity, which you have never failed to exhibit in all honest differences of opinion. . . ." The Magician proposed that Congress be consulted on every move and that such "doctrinal points," as the right to secede, "should not be discussed" in future presidential pronouncements as they had been in the proclamation. It was Van Buren's own workaday principle never to allow controversies to be sublimated into slogans and high-minded debate. Reason then lost its force and compromise was immensely more difficult to establish. "You will say," concluded the Magician, that "I am on my old track—caution, caution." Such a theme, Van Buren believed, was warranted "considering our respective temperaments." In his substantive solution, the Magician contended that the only way out was genuine tariff revision.

"No, my friend," Jackson answered, your policy "would destroy all confidence in our government both at home and abroad. . . . I expect soon to hear that a civil war has commenced. . . ." But Jackson's actions were different from his words. Although seemingly rejecting Van Buren's advice, he adhered to its major points. His statements no longer considered the niceties of "treason" or other "doctrinal points." His fulminations against the nullifiers were henceforth expressed in private, save for one exception. This transpired when he announced to a delegation of visitors his desire to hang Calhoun and any other nullifiers who were handy in the trees of Pennsylvania Avenue. There were no further proclamations or messages. Congress was consulted on every major move. In his famous "force bill," or "bloody bill," as the nullifiers derisively called it, Jackson sought Congressional authorization of force to execute the revenue law, should the need arise. Van Buren was having his impact.

While flagging down the President, Van Buren was also busy with positive measures to quell the crisis. Directing his Washington lieutenants from his Albany lair, he was eying the tariff laws for possible reforms as the most promising solution to the nullification crisis. But he was blocked by the old dilemma: how could he please his Southern and New York followers simultaneously? How, too, could he win the necessary support of the Calhounites, whose natural interests favored tariff reduction, but whose zest for vengeance might tempt them to reject anything identified with the Magician? To diminish possible antagonism, Van Buren worked through his shrewd associate, Secretary of the Treasury Louis McLane. The Secretary bravely invaded the political morass by turning out a draft of proposed tariff reductions. But these the Southerners of both the Van Buren and Calhoun camps summarily dismissed as too minor to consider. Then, with Van Buren's secret encouragement, Congressman Gulian Crommelin Verplanck of New York took a try. Verplanck, chairman of the House Ways and Means Committee, seemed ideal for the assignment. An independent not previously identified with Van Buren, the Congressman was not apt to inspire any venom. After weeks of intensive work, Verplanck emerged with a bill containing reductions substantially exceeding those proposed by McLane. Southerners of all camps so warmed to the new tariff bill that the Magician was now openly and confidently identifying himself as its real instigator. He stood at the brink of new fame. If the bill passed—and according to every indication it would—the Magician would surely be hailed as "the Great Compromiser" and gain for the first time in his career a genuine national popularity among a people who desperately did not want a civil war.

The serene progress of Van Buren's plans was unexpectedly throttled with the sudden finality of which political maneuver is capable. The Magician's mighty rivals—Clay and Calhoun—meeting together, decided that the indomitable palace politician must not at any cost become a popular hero. So anxious was Henry Clay to block Van Buren, that he put aside his famous long-standing tariff convictions and introduced his own reform bill. His object, plainly, was to snatch away the accolade of "Compromiser" from the grasping hands of the Magician. Although Clay's tariff bill made only a portion of the cuts of Verplanck's, militant Southerners, led in both houses of Congress by John Calhoun, rallied around Clay. (Calhoun was by this time United States Senator from South Carolina, having stepped into the vacancy created when Senator Robert Hayne resigned to become Governor of South Carolina. As Senator, Calhoun enjoyed considerably greater freedom for parliamentary maneuver than he had as Vice-President.)

The wheels of collusion started turning. By some adroit parliamentary sleight of hand, Clay's bill was substituted for Verplanck's in the House and easily passed. Late in the afternoon of the very same day, it whisked through the Senate, being debated and voted during the dinner hour, as Benton put it, "before the hot dinners of the legislators became cold." The Van Buren camp was petrified and impotent before the Clay-Calhoun juggernaut. "New York," Cambreleng ruefully explained the nightmare, "had no friends." Henry Clay, whose long devotion to high-tariff policy had done more than any other man to bring on the crisis, was now hailed and chronicled as "The Great Pacificator," "The Great Compromiser." Van Buren's Vice-Presidential inaugural, some days after the congressional disaster, was an understandably limp affair.

While events were concluding their mad dance in Washington, state legislatures in both the North and South were passing resolutions assuring the President of their support and disavowing the nullifiers. Two states remaining conspicuously silent on the subject were New York and Virginia, Van Buren's strongholds. Fearing that a New York resolution might offend Virginia and jeopardize their hero's political future, Van Buren's state organization was discreetly tight-lipped in Albany, while other states were rushing to Jackson's banner. With the situation so laden with potential calamity, the harassed Van Buren, following the inaugural, arranged to spend much time in the state capital to see that nothing went amiss. When a trusted colleague wrote, urging passage of a resolution condemning the President's policy, the letter was returned "opened, but unanswered." Meantime, the New York Whigs, led by two wily rising politicos, William H. Seward and Thurlow Weed, had fathomed Van Buren's game. To put the Magician squarely on the spot, they concocted a special brew of mischief. They introduced their own resolution into the state legislature, approving Jackson's proclamation in lavish terms. Seward, in a word, was doing what Van Buren should have done. With Van Buren and his party in the majority in both houses of the legislature, the situation was perfect. The Red Fox of Kinderhook was trapped; the kill was near. Van Buren couldn't avoid taking a stand, and whatever he did would be ruinous. If he supported the resolution, he would break up his party and lose his status as Jackson's most likely eventual successor. If he opposed, he risked breaking with Jackson. There was no escape; Van Buren proceeded to choose between his party and his President. Be it said for the Magician that he did not long keep his tormenters in suspense. He acted quickly and, as always in such dilemmas, he chose his party. He prepared a resolution forthrightly taking issue with "the history given by the President on the formation of our Government." Accompanying the resolution was a labored report expounding a states rights position which would hardly fail to please Van Buren's most fastidious Virginia supporters.

As for Jackson, the Magician forwarded him the resolution, the report, and a letter of explanation. The letter, unfortunately, is lost and its contents unknown. Its precise effect upon the President also is obscure. According to one eyewitness account, Jackson, upon receiving the documents, perused them thoroughly, drawing all the while hard on his Powhatan pipe. Then, without comment, he handed them over to his secretary, Donelson, in whose presence they had been received. The President directed that the papers be filed. According to Van Buren, the entire incident was never mentioned by the President.

It was Van Buren's expectation and hope that the veto would bring down the curtain on the drama of the United States Bank. The mighty institution, the Magician believed, should be permitted to linger on undisturbed until 1836, when its charter was scheduled to expire. Further warfare upon the Bank would clearly invite serious dislocation of the economy, involving political implications of the utmost gravity. Not the least of these was that Martin Van Buren's interest in capturing the Presidency could be weakened or totally wrecked.

The Magician's policy of passivity quickly ran into an unyielding wall of opposition from certain of the most influential members of the Administration, Amos Kendall and his Kitchen Cabinet confreres, Taney and Blair. It was folly to assume, they argued, that Nicholas Biddle, with his love of power, was incapable of further trouble. The Bank, with huge assets and farflung branches, was a central factor in the economy capable of enormous self-interested maneuver. The necessary strategy was a bold follow-up blow to weaken the Bank's formidable striking power. Specifically, Kendall proposed that the government remove its enormous deposits of funds, which under law it made in the Bank, and cease the paradoxical absurdity of "buffeting the bank with our left hand" while "we feed it with our right." By placing its deposits in a number of carefully selected state banks, the national government would enable the latter institutions to resist the intimidation to which the United States Bank intermittently subjected them in wielding its power to honor or reject their drafts. State banks, squeezed mercilessly by Biddle, might withdraw their hitherto firm support of Administration policy even to the point of enabling Biddle again to push recharter through Congress.

Kendall was so convincing that Jackson instructed his aide to draft a letter to the Secretary of the Treasury, Louis McLane, requesting that the deposits be removed from the Bank of the United States. (Under statute, only the Secretary could effect the removal.) McLane, protégé of Martin Van Buren and conservative in orientation, went straight to his benefactor. With the Magician's assistance, the aggressive Secretary of the Treasury prepared a report to the President of ninety pages skillfully opposing the removal of the government's deposits.

Van Buren himself met Kendall head on at a White House "family dinner." During the meal, Van Buren protested with hearty candor that the removal plans framed by the Kentuckian would start a needless fight entailing grave risks for the Administration and the party. Kendall, who ordinarily exuded the mildness of a limpid pool, rose from the table in great excitement. In a voice taut with anger, he said that under Van Buren's policy, the Bank would surely win, and that faced with the certainty of that dismal prospect he and the other Administration journalists might as well lay down their pens. "I can live under a corrupt despotism as well as any other man by keeping out of its way," exclaimed Kendall, resuming his seat. Jackson, who gave his obligations as host priority over the claims of politics, expertly poured oil on the troubled waters, and the meal resumed a tranquil course. As the evening wore on, however, Van Buren concluded that Jackson was unmistakably veering toward Kendall's plan. The Vice-President of the United States found it politic to apologize fully to the Fourth Auditor of the Treasury for the unfortunate incident, taking the entire blame upon himself.

To relieve his friend, Louis McLane, of possible embarrassment, Van Buren engineered a minor reorganization of the cabinet, with McLane stepping up as Secretary of State and Edward Livingston proceeding to his beloved France as the American Minister. The incoming Secretary of the Treasury was the little-known William J. Duane, whose appointment stands as one of the more intriguing mysteries of the Jackson Administration. Chosen under circumstances where clearly his main job would be to extract the fangs of the United States Bank by removing the government's deposits, Duane proved a more dedicated champion of the Bank than McLane ever was in his most shining hour.

Duane dallied two months in accepting the appointment. In that interlude Jackson apparently never probed the candidate's convictions, for everything known of Duane pointed to a staunch anti-Bank man. He was a proven Republican workhorse in the trying politics of Pennsylvania, and his father before him had been a distinguished Republican editor and ancient enemy of such leading protagonists of the Bank of the United States as Albert Gallatin and Alexander James Dallas. Duane's appointment, it is clear, was originally inspired by Martin Van Buren, who somehow snatched up the mission of finding a new Secretary of the Treasury. The cautious Magician had Louis McLane check the Philadelphian's qualifications. A glittering report ensued. "Duane," wrote McLane to Van Buren, "is a warm and active friend of yours, was among the earliest to espouse your cause, and has been sincere and efficient in his endeavors to divert the electoral vote of Penn. to your support. . . ." On this testimonial, Van Buren, while strolling with Jackson on the White House terrace one night, broached the name of Duane for the vacancy.

W. J. Duane beautifully lived up to expectations in advancing the inter-

ests of Martin Van Buren. These, to be sure, had been undergoing redefini-
tion. Convinced that Jackson was unalterably pro-removal, the Magician
was now arguing that removal should not take place until after Congress reconvened, for the statute governing removal seemed to require Congressional
approval before the action could be taken. Amos Kendall, however, in a
counterthrust proposed that removal be done by executive fiat before Congress met in lieu of facing the risk and embarrassment of legislative defeat.
As the debate raged on, Duane began performing as hatchet man for Van
Buren. The President again sided with Kendall and ordered Duane to begin
the transfer of the government's deposits at once. For weeks, the Secretary
ingeniously demurred by lapsing into exaggerated illness, by staging artfully
fruitless discussions with the President, and sending up rambling, inconclusive memoranda. At last, Jackson blew up. He dragooned the reluctant
Secretary, whose delaying tactics had consumed precious months, into agreeing to co-operate or resign. Martin Van Buren maneuvered desperately to
keep the indispensable Duane in office.

While their chief was thus engaged, certain members of the Magician's
camp were further scrutinizing the lively career of Amos Kendall. They beheld, they were convinced, a highly dangerous man. Beneath the heroic
exterior of selfless dedication, a pitiless Machiavellian mentality was at work.
According to this theory, Kendall's frenetic devotion to removal was really
designed to kill two mighty birds with but one stone: the Bank, which was
obvious, and Van Buren, which was less obvious. James Gordon Bennett,
editor of the New York Enquirer and a seasoned observer of political manipulation, was convinced that Kendall's most rankling ambition was to prevent
the Magician from capturing the presidential nomination. Kendall, Bennett
believed, considered the Magician too conservatively disposed toward the
Westerners' most cherished policies, free banking and liberal credit. On
September 25, 1833, just after Kendall had toured New York, ostensibly to
line up state banks as future government depositories, Bennett wrote to the
Magician in panic. Kendall, according to the editor, had devoted most of his
peregrinations not to banking, but to spadework for the presidential candidacy of Richard M. Johnson, the Kentucky Congressman. During his two
days in New York City, Kendall and a dozen Tammany sachems had sat in
the wigwam of that formidable organization arranging a plan committing
the Tammany leadership to come out publicly for Johnson and launch un-
limited war upon the Regency. Johnson, Bennett believed, had already consented to becoming a candidate; the Argus, Kendall's old paper, was sounding the tocsins for the Kentuckian, with Blair chiming in in the Globe.
Kendall himself was mercilessly diverting the customs and Post Office patronage in New York to those who demonstrated by positive deed their conviction that Van Buren was "to be abandoned as soon as possible." James

Gordon Bennett was not alone in his suspicions. Similar warnings arrived by post from Washington Irving, now in New York, and Irving was no alarmist.

Van Buren's innermost reactions to this shattering intelligence cannot be deduced with any precision. His response to informants Bennett and Irving was a courteous nothing—admiring comment on Kendall's prowess and not the least encouragement to his loyal friends to burrow further into the doings of the mysterious Kendall. Van Buren was plainly working on the plausible assumption that he could not afford open warfare with the Westerners.

By late summer, Jackson had come around fully to the position of Kendall, Blair and Taney. The government's deposits were to be removed from the great Bank before Congress reconvened. With policy settled and ready for launching, the support of Van Buren and his party following was imperative. It was high time to crack down on Van Buren, which Jackson proceeded to do by directing a strong letter to the Magician, then sojourning in Albany. "It is already hinted," wrote the President bluntly, "that you are opposed to the removal of the Deposits, and of course privately a friend to the Bank. *This must be removed* or it will do us both much harm." A full and forthright expression of Mr. Van Buren's views was requested. In a response of the most mellifluous flattery that Talleyrand would have been proud of, the Magician pleaded for delay in order to consult Silas Wright, a Regency colleague and Senator from New York. After several long weeks of preparation, the Magician finally produced his answer. When the President wrote back sternly that Van Buren was simply rearguing an old proposal which had long ago been rejected, the New Yorker pointed out, by some highly involved verbal gymnastics, that he had been terribly misunderstood.

Convinced that the Magician could not be cornered by correspondence, Jackson requested that he return to Washington at once. An interview would straighten things out. Van Buren, at this moment, was conducting a month's tour with Washington Irving of the old Dutch settlements on the North River and Long Island. The junket was partly archaeological, partly political fence mending; primarily it was to keep the Magician out of the Washington maelstrom. In an elaborately constructed letter, Van Buren told Jackson that although he would be governed by his wishes, he was convinced that his presence in the capital would make the removal attributed to himself and the wicked New York monied Junto and make Congress's already considerable opposition even worse. Everything considered, he had better remain in New York.

While Van Buren poured over Long Island antiquity, the bank crisis rushed into climax. Duane, resisting valiantly to the very end, was fired, and Attorney General Roger Taney took over the Treasury via a recess appointment. He promptly announced that the government's deposits would no longer be made in the Bank of the United States after September thirtieth. When Congress finally reconvened, the pro-Bank Senate retaliated by refusing to approve Taney's appointment to the Treasury.

Van Buren quickly adjusted his own line to the changing situation by writing to the President, lavishing praise upon his course of action. "I now invite you here," Jackson magnanimously responded. "I have my dear Sarah's room prepared for you, until your own House can be put in order." Van Buren did not exactly rush to Washington, although once on the scene, he was the good soldier. Taney, who was nearing the end of his brief term in the Treasury, was preparing the special report, required under statute, to Congress justifying the removal and the annual message which inevitably dealt with the Bank. Van Buren combed over both documents, making numerous changes in substance and phrasing. He was later said to have characterized the report on removal as the greatest state paper to be fashioned since the founding of the Republic. To which John Quincy Adams snorted that, if Van Buren made such a statement, it was only because he wrote most of the report himself.

As Vice-President and presiding officer of the Senate, Van Buren bore the brunt of the pro-Bank onslaught. Unlike the lower house, the upper chamber was dominated by the anti-Administration party, now functioning as a vociferous adjunct of the Bank. There was much to shout about. Across the country, the Bank was tightening credit by calling in loans and by refusing to honor the paper of numerous state banks which hitherto it had never questioned. The Bank was seemingly bent on bringing about economic dislocations all to the end of turning public opinion against the Administration. The Senate became the chief mounting platform for fierce critical bombardments of the Administration, belaboring the theme that because of Jackson's war on the Bank, the country was going to the dogs economically. In general, there was little relation between the actuality of the distress, which proved to be mild, and the savagery of the oratory. On one occasion, Henry Clay, who was having a forensic field day, addressed an elaborately pathetic appeal, bordering on the ludicrous, imploring Van Buren to inform the President of the spreading unemployment and numbing hardship his Bank policy was inflicting upon the country. Senator Benton, an onlooker, said that Van Buren maintained "the utmost decorum of countenance, looking respectfully and even innocently at the speaker all the while as if treasuring up every word he said to be repeated to the President." After Clay had finished his theatrical masterpiece and fittingly heaved himself into his chair, Van Buren called over a nearby Senator to preside in his place and serenely descended to the floor. Casually, as though unwatched, when actually all eyes were fixed upon his portly frame, he ambled over to Clay's seat.

With a low exaggerated bow, and in the most courtly manner, he asked for a pinch of snuff. The startled Clay dangled his snuffbox with the grace of a scarecrow. Taking a pinch, Van Buren delicately applied it to his ample nostrils, returned the box with a flourish, bowed low again, and resumed his chair as though nothing had happened. The Senate guffawed.

For all of his tempestuous interludes and narrow squeaks, the Magician emerged with the hard core of his fortunes intact. His New York following was rent by no unmendable schisms. He had more than held his own at the White House. Jackson still counted him as the heir apparent, and consulted him more than ever on speeches, appointments and policy. The new Attorney General was no one other than the Magician's old law partner, Benjamin F. Butler. With the several characters of the Kitchen Cabinet, the Magician's relations were in a state of abiding peace. Frank Blair solicited his support in pressing for a much-needed assistant for his paper. Kendall was friendly. Roger B. Taney, who emerged from the Bank War with the greatest prestige, Van Buren was playing as a top influence. The going was noticeably easier with the President if a project bore Taney's endorsement. Deference to Taney paid off in other respects. The Magician had stepped on many toes in his rise to power, and when protestations against his presidential candidacy became embarrassingly shrill in various state organizations, Taney sprang valiantly to his defense. Repeatedly, he praised Van Buren's soundness on policy and the breadth of his popularity. "He was well received by our friends," Taney informed the President of a meeting of political chieftains with Van Buren at Harpers Ferry, "I am satisfied he will gain more and more favour as he mixes more and more with the people."

But the swelling bitterness against Van Buren was far too much for the agile Taney to keep bottled up. Its greatest force was achieved in the West. The Congressional delegation of Jackson's own state of Tennessee openly endorsed the candidacy of Hugh Lawson White. Other states rumbled with protests. Jackson, unwaveringly loyal, angrily refused to confer with a delegation of party insurgents waiting upon him at the Executive Mansion. With usual impulsive finality, he dismissed the widening revolt as a machination of Henry Clay. The President nevertheless saw fit to direct Taney to give his undivided attention to tying up the convention for Van Buren. The job was masterfully done, and Jackson's hand-picked ticket of Martin Van Buren for President and Colonel Richard M. Johnson of Kentucky for Vice-President, easily prevailed in the Democratic convention at Baltimore. The ensuing campaign was a mild race between Van Buren, his chief competitor, William Henry Harrison of Indiana, and several minor candidates. With 148 electoral votes necessary to elect, Van Buren carried

170 votes, of which 110 were contributed by New York, Pennsylvania, Virginia and North Carolina, strongholds of the old Crawford organization. The long ordeal was over; the grail was won. Van Buren's success was by no means owed altogether to the unstinting endorsement of his chief. The Magician's inviolable principle of keeping his own party organization intact, even at the expense of his loyalty to the President, was an indispensable element of victory.

On March 4, 1837, the scepter passed. The day was bright, glistening with the exhilaration of spring and the sense of renewal implicit in the inauguration. Seated side by side in the carriage, Constitution, drawn by the famous grays, were the outgoing President and his confidential adviser and chosen successor. After a dignified passage down Pennsylvania Avenue, the two men on whom all interest centered, appeared on the east portico of the capitol. Below on the grounds was a vast crowd wedged breathlessly together, faces upturned—"a field," said one observer, "paved with human faces." The crowd was silent, still and reverent. The inaugural proceeded. The newly appointed Chief Justice of the United States, Roger B. Taney, whose nomination for the Treasury had been spurned by a vengeful Senate, stepped forward to administer the oath to the President-elect. He, too, had experienced the humiliation of Senatorial disavowal. Retribution briefly seized the moment. The new President began delivering his message, but its urbane substance was lost in the droning monotone of his speaking style. Platitudinous, inoffensive, the message was politically proper throughout. No applause interrupted it; that at the end was polite but unenthusiastic.

The old General, now divested of power, rose to descend the broad steps of the portico to take his seat in the carriage. The feelings of the crowd, so long restrained, rolled forth like a giant thunderclap. The cheers rolled and rerolled from three thousand hearts. The new President descended, too. However he was all but unnoticed and forgotten. All eyes were on General Jackson as he uncovered and bowed, the wind stirring his silver locks. A part, indeed a substantial part, of the tribute being paid the General and his outgoing Administration belonged to the unnoticed man behind him. Jackson, more than anyone, knew it did. But the crowd did not know, and never would know. Martin Van Buren, on his most glorious day, the day for which he had plotted and gambled, and maneuvered and flattered, for eight anxious years, was paying the price for the secrecy of his success in the palace shadows. "For once," Thomas Hart Benton expressed the significance of the moment, "the rising was eclipsed by the setting sun."

The Perfect Stenographer

———

WILLIAM LOEB, JR.

ALTHOUGH THE cherry tree which symbolizes George Washington's probity was the invention of Parson Weems, the cherry tree in the life of the youthful William Loeb, Jr., is both authentic and symbolic. In the eighteen seventies on the grounds of the Governor's Mansion in Albany, New York, stood a large heavy-bearing oxheart cherry tree. Boys of the neighborhood loved to steal into the Mansion grounds and scurry up the tree to cram their mouths, pockets and caps with luscious fruit. The Governor, Samuel J. Tilden, a nervous little man, quickly grew tired of the cherry thieves, an attitude he conveyed by charging upon them, his cane raised, screeching imprecations in his asthmatic voice. But the culprits invariably escaped, compounding his exasperation. One day, to his enormous delight, he managed to tiptoe to the tree and catch three young boys in the act. With a triumphant squeal, he summoned them down. After rendering a lengthy monologue on honesty and the sanctity of property, he paused, as would a judge before pronouncing sentence. Did the boys have anything to say? A big-eyed lad of seven did. It was all his fault, he said; he had proposed the larceny of the others. The candor, the selflessness, the rugged assurance impressed the Governor. The boy was William Loeb, Jr., who was to make a career of martyrdom, of taking blame and shouldering burdens for others to whom he was dedicated, including a future Governor of New York State and President of the United States, Theodore Roosevelt. As Roosevelt's office secretary for one gubernatorial term and two presidential terms, Loeb bore many crosses.

This capacity for unquailing sacrifice, Loeb first manifested in the home. To his parents and three younger brothers and three sisters, he was a rock of assurance, a provider in adversity. His father, William Loeb, and mother, Louisa Myer Loeb, were industrious German emigrees, from the Black Forest and Alsace-Lorraine respectively, who never mastered the indigenous American art of making money. They were, in the full sense of that graphic term, "dirt poor." Billy, their eldest child, was born October 9, 1866, in their tiny home in Albany. Billy applied himself to his schooling, making serene progress until his second year of high school. Then the economic cycle took a dip, and the family finances shrank so alarmingly that Billy had to go to work. He took on as messenger boy for one of the first telephone companies, the Commercial Telephone Company of Albany, which, shortly after hiring Billy, was absorbed by Western Union. Billy, who also was involved in the intercorporate consolidation, was assigned to run the dispatches of the Associated and United presses to the local Albany newspapers. His daily route entailed stops at the *Evening Journal*, the *Press and Knickerbocker*, the *Times Union*, the *Morning Express* and finally the *Argus*, Martin Van Buren's trusty paper. The twelve-year-old messenger was a favorite of the *Argus*'s night editor, Dan Lamont, the future secretary to Grover Cleveland, both as Governor of New York and as President of the United States. Billy loved to sit beside Lamont's desk, where together they read the day's dispatches and engaged in idle chatter. Three decades later, history brought about an interesting transposition of the boy and the man when Loeb was ensconced in Washington as secretary to Theodore Roosevelt. One day the White House usher led into Loeb's office Dan Lamont, old friend and a visitor in town. Settling down in the chair beside Loeb's desk, Lamont laughingly pointed out how the pattern of the former newspaper days had been exactly reversed.

No one could have been less surprised by this little quirk of history than Dan Lamont. Back in the Albany days, he had been highly impressed by young Loeb's intelligence and industry. "You like to read," Lamont observed one night. "You ought to be in school." To Billy's amazement, Lamont proposed to advance a loan enabling him to go to law school. Just as this stroke of generosity fell upon Billy, the fortunes of Loeb senior began improving and the offer of the benevolent Lamont was declined with fitting expressions of gratitude. The Loebs, although better off, were not so handsomely situated that Billy could take on the extended curriculum of law school. He turned instead to a subject less expensive to master—stenography—and enrolled in Miss Walters Secretarial School, which is today the Albany Business College. Graduating at the top of his class, he took as his first job an assistantship to a court reporter, bearing a stipend of eight dollars per week. To increase his earnings, Loeb worked after hours for various lawyers and doctors of Albany. After exploratory pokings into the possibilities of the stenographic field, Loeb concluded that a career as a court reporter offered the best future. But to qualify for the choice prizes of the calling, he discovered, he had to satisfy several prerequisites. He needed political approval, and it was toward that end that he proceeded to join the Republican party organization of his ward, the thirteenth, in Albany. Court reporting also had complex technical facets in which he steeped himself. To master the ample jargon and patterned ways of the legal craft, he studied law in snatches taken from his regular employment. Law cases also abound in medical technicalities, and to prepare himself, Loeb attended several classes in the Albany Medical College at night. In those days he was no homebody.

While girding for the long future, Loeb had his ear to the ground for immediate opportunities for more profitable employment. His soundings, which he made constantly, brought him to the doorstep of William Doane, Bishop of the Episcopal Diocese of Albany. August personality and meticulous judge of character, the Bishop took Loeb on as his private secretary. Billy's duties included keeping up with Bishop Doane's staccatoed dictation of his sermons, handling the voluminous details of the many social affairs in which the Bishop engaged, and keeping out of the way of an enormous St. Bernard dog, Cluny, who ambled imperiously around the office. A flamboyant dynamic man, the Bishop provided an admirable apprenticeship for Loeb and his future service under the volcanic T.R. Bishop Doane ran his diocese as a local social force in the image of an English cathedral town. He preferred everything English. His dress was that of a high English prelate, complete with pancake hat and gaiters. Ardently High Church, the Bishop took his convictions and position with the utmost seriousness. When attending conferences of the church, for example, he would register at his hotel by signing himself not as William Doane, but as William of Albany. On one occasion, at a convention of Episcopal prelates of New York State, just after Doane had affixed "William of Albany" to the hotel blotter, a low churchman from the city of Buffalo, another William, who was next in line and who had noticed this brazen High Church gesture, stepped up to register. With inspiration in his eye and a flourish of his pen, he wrote, "Buffalo Bill."

After some years of diocesan labor, Loeb trailed off into more remunerative stenographic jobs in insurance and banking, and in the railroad and express offices of Albany, each change of employment lifting his pay slightly. He next shifted to journalism, when he was taken on as stenographer to William Duffy, reporter of the *New York World*, who covered the Cleveland-Blaine campaign. Loeb traveled around the country with Duffy, meeting many newspapermen, of whom the most famous and influential was Frank W. Mack of the Associated Press. In 1888, when the post of official stenographer of the New York State Assembly fell vacant, Mack proposed the twenty-two-year-old Loeb for the post, and with unstinting help from various other newsmen friends of his travels, Loeb was elected. His victory had the aspect of the miraculous, for he triumphed over the candidate advanced by the mighty Boss Platt and his ubiquitous machine. Loeb squeezed through with four votes to spare.

Despite his youth, Loeb was no newcomer to politics. He was an assiduous and respected member of several leading Republican clubs of Albany. There was scarcely an evening when he was not on hand at the headquarters of his ward club situated in a loftlike room above Dorsey's saloon on James Street. He also joined a Repulican marching club, the Capitol City Club, an organization of nearly two hundred members, and later made the right connections which brought him into the most select marching club of Albany, the Unconditionals. They occupied a sedate four-story building on Columbia and Chappel streets; when they marched, their garb was a pure silk plug hat, black clothes and cane—a dandy's delight. Loeb, however, didn't march with the Unconditionals, and in the meetings he so assiduously attended, he seldom spoke. No hand-pumping, backslapping artist merrily circulating among his fellows, he was, nevertheless, one of the most popular of the membership. A quiet-spoken man of judgment, with good sense oozing from every pore, he excelled at the tête-à-tête in the back of the room or off to the side, away from the crowd on the floor. His patience inexhaustible, he could listen to trivia with implacable dignity and work with the most obtuse of his brethren with tireless serenity. Since trivia and obtuseness abound in politics, these capacities counted for much. But the virtue which sparkled like a diadem was one which politicians treasure above all else. William Loeb was a man who could be trusted. Any confidence imparted to him was deposited in the vault of a memory closed with an unbreakable seal. Indeed, Loeb was an engine of discretion from the moment the conveyor of the confidence opened his mouth. Instinctively, the young stenographer's large rotund brown eyes would shift about without waiting for his head to turn to ascertain if some interloper was hovering by to catch up the information about to be communicated. Loeb was also respected as a man of courage. He was one of the few men in Albany politics who talked with uninhibited directness to the local Republican boss, William Barnes, Jr. This feat was impressive because Barnes was a two-hundred-pound authoritarian juggernaut and an implacable taskmaster who was unaccustomed to being questioned.

Loeb's steady ascendance in Albany politics was evidenced by the sizable prizes falling into his lap. In 1890, he became secretary to Senator J. Sloat Fassett, president pro tempore of the New York Senate; and in the following year moved on in a similar capacity with the Lieutenant Governor Charles T. Saxton. Fassett, while Senator, was also Collector of the Port of New York, an undertaking which was particularly demanding upon his secretary. By looking after "details," Loeb developed an encyclopedic acquaintance with port business and the organization of the work force of 1,900 employees. This knowledge did much to enable Loeb to perform with such imposing effectiveness some two decades later, when, after appointment as Collector of the Port of New York by President William Howard Taft, he turned the port inside out in a prodigious effort to cleanse it of corruption and inefficiency.

In 1894, the enterprising Loeb snatched up another large plum when he was appointed official stenographer for the ample proceedings of the New York State Constitutional Convention. What made his reporting especially worth while was a contract he concluded with an Albany newspaper to supply its pages with the Convention debates. Since constitutional revision was a big state issue in 1894, Loeb was well rewarded. When the Convention finished, Loeb became secretary to Eugene Burlingame, District Attorney of Albany and an influential participant in the councils of the state Republican organization. While ministering to Burlingame, Loeb was simultaneously the official stenographer for the Grand Jury of Albany County. Being one who loved work, and to supplement his earnings, now approximately five thousand dollars a year, Loeb sought out a third job. Governor Levi P. Morton duly appointed him part-time stenographer in the Executive Chamber, as the Governor's office was called. His new duties tended to be intertwined with his court reporting. He wasn't long on the job when the Governor dispatched him to nearby Troy, where a tumultuous local election had been marked by violence and murder. Loeb's assignment was to take down the confession of John Gough, who with "Bat" Shea, was indicted for the slaying of Robert Ross. Loeb's report of the confession permitted the case to be taken into the courts and enabled the grateful Governor to side-step any further investigation of the messy local political situation.

The excitement of high drama rolled in upon Albany with the chill new year of 1899. As that year began, Theodore Roosevelt, dashing Rough Rider, hero of the splendid little war just ended with Spain, was inaugurated as Governor of the state of New York. No newcomer to politics, a former Assemblyman, New York mayorality candidate, United States Civil Service Commissioner and Assistant Secretary of the Navy, T.R. first thrust himself solidly upon the national consciousness by the bravura of his charge up San Juan Hill. Albany was agog over the war hero and intrepid crusader against public corruption. Inaugural week had commenced with a ball for Roosevelt's valorous Squadron A of the National Guard, but the high light of the event was the Governor-elect's own arrival. Attired in a sombrero and topcoat, with the famous blue silk handkerchief knotted about his brawny neck, he was greeted with a rending ovation, as the band struck up "Hail to the Chief." In the round of receptions which followed, Albany was in no way disappointed by its hero. The forty-year-old Governor-elect conveyed an air of infinite energy and cheery cordiality. His disdain for precedent and zest for innovation imparted unfailing interest in his activities. After taking the oath shortly after noon on New Year's Day in an informal ceremony in the

Governor's office, he startled the onlooking assemblage by inviting all officers-elect and heads of departments on hand to call at the Executive Mansion during the afternoon to discuss the official business for which they were responsible in order that the new Administration might commence without delay. His formal inauguration in the Assembly Chamber was the briefest on record. In a mere twenty minutes, the Governor presented his address, the band played, and the benediction was pronounced by Bishop Doane.

Intermixed in the events of these crowded days of homage to the Governor-hero is an occurrence which constitutes a turning point in the life of William Loeb. Although seemingly minor, the event was a kind of trick that fate sometimes loves to play, for it shaped and directed the rest of Loeb's existence. After the inaugural ceremony, Governor Roosevelt had returned to his office, raring to begin his tour of duty. He had dictation to give and, with a view to getting the work under way, he flung open the door of his chamber which led into a large adjoining room occupied by the four stenographers assigned under law to the Governor, and three Negro messengers, one of whom, Henry Pinckney, would one day accompany T.R. to Washington as a steward in the White House. Without addressing anyone in particular, T.R. requested in his commanding falsetto, that someone "send me in a good stenographer." The assembled stenographers sat numb at their respective desks, not from thrill over the awaiting honor, but from fear. Each of the four had learned with trepidation from Cal MacKnight, a shorthand expert who had accompanied the Governor on the electoral campaign, that "Teddy" was a "terror to take." The stenographers were still immobile when the part-time Loeb, pricked by his usual supervening sense of duty, trudged into the Governor's office. By every indication, the several hours of unbroken dictation which followed went swimmingly. For next day, when the Governor again flung open the doors of his chamber, his request was for "that same stenographer I had yesterday."

One evening, after a wearing session of T.R.'s galloping dictation, when Loeb planned to relax by going ice skating, he was called in by the Governor's secretary, William J. Youngs. It was the Governor's wish, declared Mr. Youngs, that Loeb should be not a part-time, but a full-time executive stenographer. "I said I meant to return to court work," Loeb afterward reported of the interview, an attitude that was quite understandable, for by giving up court work for full-time executive duties, Loeb would sustain a sizable cut in income. So anxious, however, was the Governor to have his favorite stenographer always at his beck and call that he proceeded to demolish the obstacle. "Mr. Roosevelt induced me to stay," Loeb revealed, "by increasing my pay out of his own pocket." Loeb went skating that evening as planned and next morning resigned from his other jobs.

T.R., to be sure, needed help. His office was a chain explosion of activity. To establish his Administration as a vessel of reform, he dispatched message after message of pointed recommendation to the legislature. His reception room teemed with visitors, arriving and departing in batches at closely scheduled intervals. Several hours were reserved for public audiences, and somehow in between the allotted calling hours, T.R. sandwiched in the office routine. He by no means limited his endeavors to New York affairs. Few national issues arose which did not elicit his comment or proposal. "Mr. Roosevelt," an opposition paper noticed with equal parts of accuracy and scorn, "is in training for national office."

Loeb's duties in the unrelenting bustle do not admit of precise definition. They mounted steadily as T.R., a shrewd and exacting judge of human character, was increasingly impressed with Loeb's "excellent judgment," "alertness," "industry" and "loyalty to his former employers." In addition to taking dictation, Loeb took up slack from the chief secretary, Mr. Youngs, a former district attorney of Queens. At times, the slack was considerable. Once Youngs was bedridden for weeks with typhoid fever, from which he never fully recovered, and Loeb expertly assumed his full duties. At other times Youngs was diverted by political missions entrusted him by the Governor, and his social engagements were numerous. When Youngs was captive to his obligations in Albany, and T.R. was passing the summer at Oyster Bay, Loeb went along as secretary. There, one of his heavier duties was to receive telephone calls at his headquarters in the village and relay the messages involved to T.R. by a fast horseback ride to Sagamore Hill. The Governor at the time wouldn't tolerate a telephone in his house. When substituting for Youngs in Albany, Loeb arranged the Governor's appointments, made visitations to local political leaders and handled the enormous office correspondence. Neither Loeb nor Youngs had much to do with T.R.'s social calendar, which was the domain of his military secretary, Colonel George Curtis Treadwell. The Colonel, who took his position seriously, went about attired in a flamboyant uniform like that of a fairy-tale coachman.

T.R. himself has averred that Loeb was a positive influence on policy. Of the imposing program of economic regulation and reform expostulated by the Governor, a central feature was the proposal to control the abuses of the insurance business, an enterprise hitherto free of public regulation. Although the legislature rejected Roosevelt's plan, it endured as a model for future action. Under its terms, ambiguous and misleading policies, exorbitant agent's fees, officers' misuse of company funds for personal gain, and the investment of policy premiums in bogus securities were all to be outlawed. "In reaching this determination," T.R. has declared in his *Autobiography*, "I was helped by Mr. Loeb." Drawing from his own observant employment experience in the insurance field, Loeb authoritatively briefed his chief on the abuses of the business. This was by no means the last time when Loeb's acquaintanceship with the wiles and guiles of commerce would shape the policies of Theodore Roosevelt.

The signal accomplishment of the well-ordered, routine Republican National Convention of 1900 was the nomination of Theodore Roosevelt for the Vice-Presidency, the office John Adams once styled "the most insignificant . . . ever the invention of man contrived or his imagination conceived." The selection of Roosevelt was governed by several considerations neither consistent nor altogether honorable. The national ticket, weakened by the death of the popular incumbent Vice-President, Garrett A. Hobart, required strengthening, and the war hero, T.R., ideally constituted the infusion needed. In New York, the cultivated but heartless Boss Thomas Collier Platt, who was sick and tired of T.R., the obstreperous gubernatorial reformer, longed to eject him from the local scene and substitute a more pliable figure. Elsewhere, the Old Guard of the national party organization viewed T.R.'s formidable presidential ambitions as a menace which could be neatly controlled by a ball-and-chaining the dynamic Governor to the leaden innocuousness of the Vice-Presidency. Dutifully, but reluctantly, T.R. accepted the nomination.

President McKinley campaigned for re-election in his proven front-porch style, and T.R. made a fighting tour across the country. Loeb was by his side throughout the expedition, performing with impeccable efficiency as a political man Friday. When the victorious McKinley-Roosevelt team was inaugurated on March 4, 1901, Loeb witnessed the ceremony as the newly appointed stenographer to the incoming Vice-President. (No provision was made in law for the loftier position of secretary.) In accepting the post, Loeb suffered a 50 per cent pay cut. He was cheered in his loss, however, by the prospect that his duties like T.R.'s as Vice-President, would be utterly inconsequential. Indeed, in talking the situation over with Loeb some weeks before the inauguration, T.R. seemed to feel that he had reached the end of the road politically in the Vice-Presidency and that the next step, for which he had better prepare himself, would be into private life. In fact, T.R. already had evolved several quite definite ideas as to the future. He proposed to Loeb that they both employ their impending quadrennium of enforced leisure by enrolling in one of the better of the Washington law schools. Upon completing their studies and their hibernation in the Vice-Presidency, they would confidently withdraw to New York and there hang out the shingle of the metropolis's newest law firm—"Roosevelt and Loeb."

The law studies, it was agreed, should commence in the fall semester.

In the spring and summer following the inaugural, on March fourth, Loeb and T.R. were so often out of Washington, that the latter presided over the Senate only once. T.R. passed the time by taking his family to the Pan-American Exposition at Buffalo, returning by way of Geneseo, to visit an old friend, Austin Wadsworth. There the youngest Roosevelt son, Quentin, became quite ill, preventing further travel. After some days, Quentin was sufficiently restored to enable his family to venture to the Tahawus Club in the interior of the Adirondack Mountains, in the interests of a family vacation and the child's further recovery. The unpacking was hardly done when a messenger, disheveled and exhausted from an all-night hike, stumbled into camp with stupefying news. An anarchist had shot President McKinley at a public reception at the Buffalo Exposition. T.R. forthwith emerged from the Adirondacks and rushed to Buffalo, but as the President steadily improved, he returned to Tahawus. So confident of McKinley's recovery were the doctors and friends attending him, that Loeb, who was vacationing in the vicinity of T.R. at Rogers Rock in the Lake George country, never budged from his lair.

But McKinley's condition suddenly and irreversibly worsened and on September 14, 1901, he died. As the President's condition began deteriorating at a perilous rate, messengers with communiqués of the crisis rushed to the Loeb home in Albany, only to be routed to Lake George. Facing Loeb was the problem of fetching T.R. out of the Adirondack wilderness. Loeb did not venture onto the dense and winding trail, which would have put Daniel Boone on his mettle, but dispatched an experienced local guide. After many hard miles, the guide spotted T.R., who was climbing the lofty mountain, resting well up on its side, on a tiny ledge. By an all-night ride of fifty miles requiring three changes of horses, T.R. and the guide reached the nearest railroad station at North Creek early the following morning. Loeb, waiting with a special train he had commandeered, informed his chief that the President was dead.

The special train raced on to Buffalo where Roosevelt paid final homage to McKinley and took the oath of office in the home of Ansley Wilcox. In one of his first official acts, the new President directed several reassuring announcements to the country at large. He informed the press that the McKinley policies "for the honor and prosperity of the country" would continue "unchanged." In the same vein, he invited the entire membership of the late President's cabinet and other high officers to remain in their posts. In New York, the stock market, which had been doing a St. Vitus dance reflecting worry in high financial circles over the bellicose reformer, T.R., noticeably quieted. One most convincing indication of Roosevelt's adherence to the policies of McKinley was the retention of George Bruce Cortelyou in his confidential position of Secretary to the President. Urbane, ambitious, reliable, Cortelyou had been devoted to McKinley and close to the late President's intimate counselor, Mark Hanna. Both Cortelyou and Hanna were on hand in Buffalo, co-operating in the crisis. The wealthy, swaggering Hanna, who had once warned McKinley against "that damned cowboy," T.R., was to become Roosevelt's most formidable competitor for the real leadership of the Republican party and therefore of the Administration itself.

With Cortelyou staying on, Loeb was allotted the innocuously titled number-two post in the White House staff hierarchy, "the assistant secretary to the President." T. R.'s political friends and counselors were widely horrified at the announced disposition of the secretaryships. To continue Cortelyou, a McKinley holdover, in a capacity entailing the closest personal working relationships with the President was deemed fool-hardy at the very least, and the bypassing of Loeb, an act of callous ingratitude. "Fortunately," Loeb, as T.R. put it, "never took this view," and Cortelyou discharged his duties with such skill and trust that he was subsequently rewarded with appointment to even higher posts in the Administration and the party.

No precise division of duties existed between Cortelyou and Loeb. Although the former had the higher responsibility, the partnership was close, flexible and friendly. Loeb sometimes acted when Cortelyou faltered. Convinced that problems if left alone long enough will often solve themselves, Cortelyou was given to tucking troublesome letters and memoranda into his desk drawer and leaving them unanswered while the problems from which they had derived eventually evaporated. Sometimes Cortelyou was given to overstretching his conviction, but the meticulous Loeb, who checked the files regularly, would pull out the papers which seemed unduly neglected and quietly press for the attention they deserved. On at least one occasion in their joint tour of duty, Loeb had to come to Cortelyou's physical rescue. One day, in Pittsfield, Massachusetts, where the President had just completed a speaking appearance, a trolley car crashed into the presidential carriage containing T.R., Cortelyou, Governor Crane of Massachusetts, and a Secret Service man. The Secret Service man was killed, Cortelyou was cut and bruised, and T.R. was thrown thirty feet to the pavement, although he was quickly on his feet, exclaiming "I am not hurt," and inquiring anxiously for the safety of his colleagues. He rushed to the fallen Cortelyou, applying his handkerchief to stanch the blood flowing from the Secretary's neck. When Cortelyou was sufficiently re-established, T.R. went up to the unscathed trolley motorman. "Who has charge of this car?" the President asked commandingly. "I have," the motorman replied. Shaking his first, the President exclaimed, "This is the most damnable outrage I ever knew!" Reports of the accident, filtering back to Sagamore Hill, where the family and Loeb happened to be at the time, were fragmentary and most alarming. Frantic with fear, Mrs. Roosevelt, Aunt Lizzie, and the older children, Kermit and Ethel, proposed to go by boat from Long Island to Bridgeport to meet the President. The official yacht, *Sylph*, was anchored in Oyster Bay, and Loeb, once the family decision had been made, competently handled the several details of the sudden expedition. The assistant secretary accompanied the family on the voyage across Long Island Sound, sat up most of the night by the pilot's side, and once ashore guided the family to the shaken President and his maimed assistant, Cortelyou.

Loeb, in contradistinction to Cortelyou, acted as private secretary to T.R., and was therefore more involved in the President's personal and political affairs. Loeb handled such impedimenta of daily living as depositing the President's checks and paying his lodge dues. In the realm of politics, the assistant secretary's chief preoccupation was putting his hand to the spadework necessary to assure the presidential nomination for T.R. in 1904. Loeb's diggings, which were considerable, owing to fears that Mark Hanna might capture the great prize, entailed interviews and correspondence with party leaders everywhere and attention to hundreds of details, major and minor. The assistant secretary was alert to the distribution of proxy votes in the Republican National Committee, of the problems and progress of T.R. supporters in Texas, of the asseveration of Senator Mat Quay of New York that, in devotion to Roosevelt and in the interests of Republican unity in the Empire State, he would break with his "old time friend" (Boss Platt), "if need be." Loeb kept abreast of the brief but ferocious struggle in the Alabama State Convention of 1902 over the seating of Negro delegates and explored a proposal for the re-creation of the nearly twenty thousand Republican Leagues of Clubs, used in the 1892 campaign to attract younger speakers and workers and to broaden the base of financial contributions, thus making the party less dependent on big contributors who, as one advocate of the idea put it, "expected too much in return."

Loeb's busy junior status in the White House firmament abruptly terminated on February 21, 1903, when Cortelyou was appointed Secretary of the newly created Department of Commerce and Labor. Loeb was immediately designated Cortelyou's successor as "Secretary to the President" at a salary of five thousand dollars a year. The shift of title gave Loeb no new office space, for he and Cortelyou had shared the same room. Loeb simply moved across to the desk of the secretary, situated parallel to, and several steps from, his former situs. In this new location, Loeb faced the door through which all visitors had to pass to see the President. Occupying Loeb's former desk was his temporary successor as assistant secretary, Rudolph Forster. On the other side of Loeb was a large room jammed with clerks and stenographers. All these people of quiet industry were under the super-

THE PERFECT STENOGRAPHER: William Loeb, Jr.   147

vision of the Secretary to the President. Loeb's own office was a spacious square-built room, the chief of whose meager decorations were the Great Seal, framed on the wall, and a stuffed armadillo, looking morosely at its feet in a corner. The desk of the Secretary to the President, a standard mahogany affair, was occupied by a long quill pen, a dozen or so reference books lining the outer edge, and piles of papers which vanished into file boxes at night. Loeb himself contributed to the scenery with a trim handle-bar mustache he had lately cultivated, and the formal business attire of the day—gray trousers, a heavy blue morning coat extending below the knees, winged collar, cuff links, and a cravat and stickpin. For the times, his wardrobe was average in taste and quality.

Loeb's advancing career emboldened him to take as his wife Katherine Dorr of Albany, his skating companion on that epochal evening when T.R. as Governor offered him full-time appointment as executive stenographer. The Loebs moved into a house on Riggs Place, only to remove shortly to a larger abode on Q Street. Both residences were located in northwest Washington, a few blocks from the White House. In the back of the Q Street house was a flower garden which Loeb loved to care for, and a barn for a horse or two. A dog fancier, he lost little time in acquiring a hound-dog and an Airedale. The latter, on the basis of its character, was fittingly called "Pepper." Loeb also brought into his homes the sizable library he had long been accumulating. An omnivorous reader, he had turned, after completing his several courses in law and medicine, to the literary masters. Shakespeare, Carlyle, Scott and Dickens were among his favorites. A nearly complete collection of Masonic Manuals also occupied his shelves, for Loeb was an enthusiastic brother of the Order. Master of the Wadsworth Lodge in Albany, he was, for the duration of his Washington career, a member of local chapter number two of the Royal Arch Masons and seldom missed a meeting. A man of unremitting modesty and loyalty, Loeb left a bequest to the Masons when he died in 1937, the nature of which, in compliance with a directive in his will, has always remained secret.

As Secretary to the President, William Loeb was major-domo of the most tumultuous establishment on the face of the earth. "It is no place for nervous people," it was truly said of the White House. The unchallenged monopolizer of the scene was, of course, the incomparable cyclonic T.R.; wherever he was, energy infused the atmosphere; neutrons and protons crackled and jumped. A perpetual-motion machine, the President spoke and acted with tempestuous animation. In conversation, his close-clipped brachycephalous head would shake until his pince-nez threatened to pop from his nose. His whole being was committed unstintingly to the effort—

he bared his cuspids, flung his hands, extruded his mouth and eyes, while his crinkly forehead, puffy cheeks and thickset neck played their mobile parts. In the upsurge of emphasis, his voice cracked in a weird falsetto.

No modern President has brought to the office a more enterprising or cosmopolitan intelligence. In all the fields of learning no subject failed to elicit his probing curiosity—approaches to the study of crustaceans, the incidence of tropical diseases, the migrating habits of the white-throated warbler —everything interested him. At the age of forty-three, when he assumed the Presidency, T.R. was already an established naturalist, a discoverer of rivers and author of books and articles produced in a quantity, with a craftsmanship that would make a full-time professional writer envious. Cowboys, scientists, fakirs, corporation executives, authors and trainmen numbered among his friends, and for them—as, indeed, for any man of distinction or of promise in virtually any endeavor—the welcome mat was always out. The White House calling lists in T.R.'s day read like an occupational encyclopedia. T.R.'s venturesome intelligence was also spurred by the times. His adult years encompassed a span of enthralling challenge and change on many fronts—the quickening industrialization and urbanization of the country, the unsettling theses of Darwinism, the dawn of scientific scholarship and critical realism. The American nation and all humanity seemed at a turning point.

The principal constructive outlet for Roosevelt's energy and zealous reflex to the times was "The Square Deal," a moralistic semi-crusade, constrained by its leader's innate conservatism and shrewd political instinct, to promote social justice and curb economic evil. By busting trusts, curtailing the more arrant abuses of banks and railroads, by a bold program of conservation, irrigation and reclamation, by launching pioneering regulation in the labor field (workman's compensation, child labor, factory inspection and safety controls), by extending governmental supervision over foods and drugs, the Square Deal provided succor for the downtrodden in society—the farmer, the workingman and the consumer. In foreign affairs, T.R. capitalized on America's sudden thrust upon the world stage following the war with Spain. Although he carried, and on occasion, flourished "the big stick," he made singular contributions to world peace. He gave the Hague Tribunal its first case, smoothed over a dangerous controversy with Japan, stemmed the fast-deteriorating Franco-German situation by boldly prodding the Europeans into staging the the Algeciras Conference, and won the Nobel Peace Prize for successfully mediating the Russo-Japanese war. He expedited a new solidification of Anglo-American ties, a first fruit of which was his proudest achievement as President, the building of the Panama Canal. Above all, Theodore Roosevelt loved power, and with extraordinary insight, he comprehended, cherished and used the Presidency as a matchless instrument for self-assertion.

For six years in his capacity as Secretary to the President, William Loeb hewed to the sprightly assignment of keeping up with his indefatigable chief. As secretary, Loeb occupied an office which, in the decade preceding his incumbency, had exerted a rising and imposing influence in the business of the Presidency. In the Cleveland Administration, his old mentor, Secretary Dan Lamont, and in the McKinley and Roosevelt Administration, his immediate predecessor, George B. Cortelyou, were in the forefront of the Chief Executive's assistants and counselors. By dint of his special status as a friend and confidant of Theodore Roosevelt, Loeb was enabled to extend and deepen the tradition his predecessor-secretaries had so expertly commenced. Indeed, his scope of function in the Roosevelt Administration establishes his office of Secretary to the President as a direct lineal precursor of the later and more powerful office of "the Assistant to the President," occupied by Sherman Adams in the Administration of Dwight D. Eisenhower. Loeb in his time discharged many of the duties subsequently entrusted to Adams on a larger scale.

In his attitude on the policy issues of the day, Loeb was a replica of T.R., a foe of privilege, friend of the underdog, a good Square Dealer. He accepted the several planks of economic regulation and social improvement of the Square Deal with equal and sometimes greater enthusiasm than T.R. himself. Loeb's faculties, like T.R.'s, were concentrated upon the means rather than the ends of government. He was no philosopher, and measures and detail counted more with him than program and purpose. Although impressed with the large capacity of the business community for wrongdoing, he was not anti-wealth. He aspired in his own life plans to an eventual business career, the accumulation of property and the enjoyment of its comforts, all of which pleasingly materialized after he left public office. Although Loeb lacked the broad-roaming intelligence of T.R., a university education and the assurance of the patrician background, his value as an assistant nevertheless was high. His competent knowledge and shrewd insight into the seamier side of business practice filled many a gap in T.R.'s preparations of policy and on occasion provided the impetus of Administration reforms.

Loeb never sat down and outpoured advice to his chief. One couldn't do that with T.R. Instead, Loeb dropped comments and threw out opinions, often in a casual way, at any point in the many times he saw the President each day. The utterances made might jolt T.R. partly or completely from his determined course. The secretary's most opportune interludes for this kind of assertion came when he was taking dictation. The dictation was voluminous, usually several hours in duration, but filled with pauses when, at the spur of a Loeb comment or jab, a phase of policy might be discussed. Even as T.R. was dictating, Loeb would interject remarks, which might be incorporated in their precise form, in the letter or memorandum being prepared, often with direct attribution to the secretary.

In his moments with T.R., Loeb covered the gamut of domestic affairs and, to a degree, foreign policy. He was repeatedly involved in the unfolding anti-trust program. According to the evidence, he counseled the President on several of the more important moves of the government's negotiations with the Standard Oil empire, and prepared statements for the press whose phrasing, worked out with the President and the Justice Department, constituted authoritative pronouncements of Administration policy. Loeb was at the President's side when T.R. intervened between labor and management in the great bituminous coal strike of 1902. Technically, Loeb was a stenographer transcribing the proceedings around the conference table; in fact, he was a general aide whose whisperings to his chief had visible effects upon the negotiations. In political matters, Loeb was one of the President's most trusted counselors. As a prognosticator of political trends and the moves of the opposition party, Loeb had a gift of prophesy which T.R. respected. In the presidential elections of 1908, for example, William Jennings Bryan was making hay in his campaign oratory from a proposal, with which he had for some time been identified, calling for governmental guarantee of bank deposits. Well before the campaign, the Roosevelt Administration, after long consideration, had decided not to espouse the measure. At the time, Loeb had warned that the decision would be costly politically. His forecast unfortunately materialized. "Loeb was entirely right in prophesying last winter," T.R. wrote to William Howard Taft, the Republican presidential candidate, "the trouble we should have over this guaranty of bank deposits business."

Loeb's advice prevailed on occasion against seemingly insuperable odds, when pitted against an imposing array of colleagues enjoying great influence with the President. The secretary faced such a challenge in the brief but bitter tempest which raged over the content of whiskey labels in 1906. Various blends of whiskey then on the market provided little information on the label of the several ingredients of the blend. The existing Pure Food and Drug Act called for information of this nature, and the provisions of the act seemed applicable to whiskey and other spirits. T.R. himself has said that it was Loeb who first directed attention to this seeming violation of the pure-food law. It was Loeb also who spurred T.R. into summoning the leading whiskey companies to a hearing at the White House. The session, unfortunately, was fruitless, the whiskey barons adamantly taking the position that the Pure-Food law did not apply to their industry. The undaunted Loeb persisted in his minority counsel until, eventually, T.R. accepted his position. At the President's order, prosecutions were brought against the whiskey companies, and the government, to T.R.'s great joy, triumphed in the courts.

It was Loeb's "truculent attitude," as T.R. termed it, which prevailed against the imposing odds, and resulted in "one of the most righteous decisions rendered during my variegated term of office."

Loeb's chief official responsibility as Secretary to the President was that of office manager of the White House. He supervised the force of approximately fifty stenographers, typists, ushers, messengers and clerks employed in the Executive Mansion, and kept up with the colossal correspondence of the Presidency. T.R.'s outgoing letters, which might number several hundred a day, were handled by a squad of three stenographers and three typists, headed by Loeb. The teamwork of this group was rather exceptional for an office force due to the special necessities of T.R. Under Loeb's patient direction, the three stenographers were trained to record their shorthand symbols in impeccable clarity and accuracy, and the three typists to read and transcribe the notes of each of the stenographers. The beauty of this system was that it permitted the President to dictate a letter and have it typed for signature while his dictation to the same stenographer continued uninterrupted. "It makes the office force work at high pressure," said an observer who knew the system well, "but it gets results." Normally, T.R. persisted with a given stenographer until, because of writer's cramp or general fatigue, the substitution of another stenographer was necessary. On the basis of ample daily experience, it was found that T.R.'s staccato-type dictation could reduce to trembling exhaustion at least a trio of stenographers, each scrupulously chosen for his or her high endurance potential. Loeb, who took the more important and confidential dictation, was the unchallenged champion of the office force, in word rate and lasting power. It was not uncommon for the Secretary to the President, after a full day's work, to endure several hours of dictation in the evening. This marathon was especially apt to transpire when T.R., contemplating a speaking tour, liked to dictate well in advance his addresses for each of his many stops.

T.R.'s multifarious activities required that his time on the job be organized in the most efficient and economical fashion possible. Loeb, therefore, as a continuing assignment, administered various gadgetry to hasten the march of business across the President's desk. The longer letters and documents received from the departments or from the world outside, the secretary summarized with covering memoranda consisting of a brief paragraph. His flair for pithy statement was severely put to test in his reporting of the many telephone conversations he conducted in the President's behalf. The telephone was first introduced into the White House in T.R.'s Administration, and this marvelous, although as yet imperfect device—the instrument was small and not too reliable, and extensions did not exist—was installed not upon T.R.'s desk, but upon Loeb's. Calls directed to the President were customarily handled by the Secretary, who then relayed the gist of the conversation to his chief. Seldom did T.R. venture to the telephone. By keeping his distance from the instrument, T.R. in effect, passed to Loeb the vital and not infrequent task of conducting unpleasant conversations with important people and conveying decisions of the President which were bound to be disappointing. When for example, Mr. E. H. Harriman, imperious overlord of the Union Pacific Railroad, telephoned the White House one day and vehemently expressed his dismay over reports circulating in the industry that the forthcoming State of the Union Message would recommend increased regulation of the railroads, he did not talk to the President. That was out of the question; the President was busy. The man at the other end of the line was the dutiful Mr. Loeb, who assumed the exasperating position of neither affirming or denying the reports. So vexed was Mr. Harriman by the impregnable evasiveness of the secretary, that he launched into a jeremiad against each and every railroad policy hitherto adopted by the Administration. Since the policies were numerous and rather complicated, Harriman had a lot of ground to cover, but Loeb, as Harriman himself would have agreed, listened with impeccable courtesy and patience throughout.

Secretary Loeb was keeper of the President's engagement list, the arranger of his appointments. Somehow the Senators, fakirs, scientists, bishops, cowboys, educators and ward heelers who appeared had to be scheduled according to the quantity of time T.R. might be expected to want to pass with each caller. Although the system the secretary used could never be satisfactorily explained, Loeb built up an enviable record of divination. Sometimes he even had to go out of his way to induce people to come on the particular day and hour the President wished them to appear. This was especially apt to be the case with the lunches T.R. loved to stage, consisting of several guests, the decided disparity of whose backgrounds and interests made any previous association on their part quite unlikely. Loeb's job as the negotiator and arranger of these occupational Smörgasbords wasn't made any easier by the fact that T.R., being a creature of impulse, was often seized with a notion about his guest list hours or even minutes before lunchtime. The secretary was expected to corral a cowboy, who was somewhere in town, a Methodist clergyman and a foreign diplomat for lunch at T.R.'s board one day, and Mark Twain and the Attorney General the next. Loeb, too, negotiated the several visits of the eminent Negro educator and scientist, Booker T. Washington, to the White House. One of these occasions included the entertainment of Mr. Washington as luncheon guest. This in its day constituted one of the boldest strokes of social policy imaginable. The occurrence thoroughly discomfited the exponents of prejudice, for the educator was the first member of his race in the history of the Republic to sit thus at the President's table.

Loeb was responsible for policing the daily crush, known formally as "visitors' hours," a high point in the White House routine. Six days a week, Monday through Saturday, from ten A.M. to one thirty P.M., T.R. received all visitors from cabinet secretaries and Supreme Court justices to office seekers. On a given day, fully two hundred assorted individuals might be on hand. Legislators and cabinet secretaries enjoyed privileged entree between ten o'clock and noon; everybody else secured a special appointment card from Loeb and took their luck on hours. All card bearers were herded into several anterooms by the venerable doorkeeper, Major Loeffler, a fixture in the Executive Mansion since the Administration of Ulysses S. Grant. At strictly regulated intervals, Loeffler, upon a signal from Loeb, would lead visitors from the anterooms in packs of twenty into the cabinet room. T.R. would promptly come bouncing in from his office which adjoined, step up to a visitor, hail him with some personal reference extracted from the President's marvelous encyclopedic knowledge of people and politics of the local countryside, get at the business involved, briskly dispose of it, say good-bye, and pass on to the next in line. Occasionally T.R. would direct a visitor into his office for further private conference. Most callers, however, had to state their business in public, within earshot of their fellow visitors, and with T.R. who spoke emphatically and in loud tones, it was very public. There were no secrets in the cabinet room.

While Loeb let people in, he had an equal and more drastic duty to keep some of the citizenry out. Time wasters and the occasional cranks who came along, had to be rebuffed. Although basically courteous and even-tempered, the Secretary to the President could when necessary be crushingly opinionated in demonstrating the unworthiness of the cherished business which a caller wished to press upon the Chief Executive. Loeb would thoroughly dissolve the confidence of the most self-assured individual. One day a crusader called upon Loeb, seeking to interest the President in a method of forest culture which, the man was convinced, would go far to assure the retention of the most favorable features of American climate. The connection between forests and climate is not readily apparent to the layman, and the crusader experienced some difficulty in getting his theories across to Loeb who was totally unschooled in the subject. "The rebuff I met with," declared the visitor afterward, "was such as to discourage me from further interesting myself in the procedure of the Washington government in attempting to rectify the errors, not to say crimes, which are committed upon posterity by the present generation."

The several ground rules, governing one's conduct around the White

House, Loeb applied uncompromisingly even to notables who appeared upon the premises. In 1908, a famous American chanteuse, the Ethel Merman of her day, was entertained at the White House for several hours. By pre-arrangement, the chanteuse brought her mother to share in the privileged occasion. The ladies lunched with the President, after which they were taken by an usher on a special tour through the public part of the White House. The mother, who was curious about the President's family, had expressed several times in the course of her visit a desire to meet some of its members. Knowing how adamant the President was in maintaining a wall of privacy between his family and his official duties, Loeb sought to dissuade the good lady of the whole idea, but she managed to escape from the usher and maneuver herself into the presence of the President's eldest son, Ted. Boldly introducing herself, she engaged the bewildered Ted in some minutes of conversation. This was too much for Loeb. He tracked the mother down and firmly interposed himself as her personal guide for the remainder of her stay at the White House. All further perambulation, as the lady ruefully noted, was confined to the several rooms of the executive office wing.

At times, Secretary Loeb endured substantial risks to the safety of his own life and limb in shielding the President from trifling interruptions. The most harrowing incident ever experienced by the secretary in his line of duty began under circumstances of the most deceptive innocence. One day in 1905, the doorman announced to Loeb that a lady outside, obviously of considerable social background, wished to see the President. Her calling card, which Loeb scrutinized, was expensively engraved. The lady, handsome of dress and mien, was shown in, and Loeb pleasantly put to her the routine question, "What can I do for you?" Rather positively she declared that she must see the President at once. Only he could help her. Loeb offered that he, too, would like to help, and in any case he must know her business. Reluctantly, the lady proceeded to explain that the postmaster at Pittsburgh had taken to opening her mail of late and, to put a stop to this outrage, she wished him removed at once. "Ah," said Loeb, "that is a matter you should take up with the Postmaster General." This to the lady, who was quietly becoming more and more excited, was just too much. She hadn't come all the way from Pittsburgh merely to experience a polite bureaucratic run-around. At the height of her excitement—which in her state was quickly reached—she opened a large handbag she was carrying and there, nestled on the top of its contents, was a pearl-handled revolver. Loeb grabbed the revolver just a whisker before his visitor could reach it. In the next instant, he was cooly summoning the Secret Service, and the screaming pistol-carrying lady was hustled from the premises.

Loeb's most worrisome concern as secretary was the protection of the life and safety of the President. It wasn't a part of the established duties of his job for Loeb to thus exert himself, but was evoked by his friendship with the President and by his standing as an intimate of the Roosevelt family. The Secret Service, whose main preoccupation in T.R.'s day was the apprehension of counterfeiters, maintained a twenty-four-hour watch at the White House, posted one of its force outside the President's office when he was at his desk, followed him on his Sunday-morning walks up 16th Street to the Dutch Reformed Church, on his hikes through Rock Creek Park, and on any other excursion he might choose to take. From Loeb, the Secret Service learned of the President's plans sufficiently in advance so that a detail could be on hand wherever he decided to be. A fearless, free-ranging spirit, Roosevelt chafed bitterly at the interminable dogging of his steps, but his secretary, grimly mindful of the assassinations of Presidents McKinley and Garfield, and with that of Abraham Lincoln still hovering in the mists of memory, persisted in his co-ordinations with the Secret Service. For his pains, Loeb was rewarded with the ever-mounting fretting of the President and the invention of little schemes to dodge the Secret Service men responsible for his safety. So frequent became T.R.'s objections and so successful in time became his evasions that Loeb was driven to a showdown. He issued an ultimatum. Either the President would put up with the Secret Service or do without the services of William Loeb, Jr. An addendum to this ultimatum provided that henceforward Loeb would be the sole and undisputed judge of the precautions necessary. From T.R. there was instantaneous and total surrender. "Billy," said the President, "you are perfectly right, and you will not hear another word of complaint from me."

Loeb functioned as the President's social secretary, the counterpart to Isabel Hagner, who performed in a similar capacity for Mrs. Roosevelt. Although the State Department handled certain questions of protocol for official dinners, receptions and other formal occasions, Loeb ranged over a vast and treacherous moorland of situations and details which the department did not provide for. When his Serene Highness, Prince Louis Battenberg, and his staff were in town, under a tight schedule permitting a small reception of only fifty minutes at the White House, it was Loeb who wrestled with such knotty questions as the hour to be chosen and who of the Washington hierarchy should be invited to attend.

The secretary was chief engineer of such massive affairs as the President's New Year's reception, when the Executive was at home both to high officialdom and the general public for a strictly defined interval of three hours. For the President to meet the thousand and more people involved and to give due time to each of his several categories of visitors, required the observance of a master plan, or order of the day, which Loeb arranged and promulgated.

A representative sample of his toil is the order of the day for the New Year's reception of 1909, printed and issued over Loeb's signature as Secretary to the President:

11 A.M. the Vice President, the cabinet, the diplomatic corps.
11:20 the Supreme Court, the lesser federal courts, former members of the cabinets; the ambassadors, and ministers of the United States.
11:30 Senators and members of the House of Representatives.
12:15 The Director of the Smithsonian Institution, the Civil Service Commission, the Isthmian Canal Commission, the Commissioners of the District of Columbia, the Assistant Secretaries of Departments, the Solicitor General, the Assistant Attorneys General, the Assistant Postmaster General, the Treasurer of the United States, the Librarian of Congress, the Public Printer, the Bureau heads of departments, the President of the Columbia Institution for the Deaf and Dumb.
12:30 Society of the Cincinnati, the Aztec Club, various veteran organizations, including the Sons of the American Revolution, the Oldest Inhabitants Association of the District of Columbia.
1:00 Reception of citizens.

Loeb's most important and difficult task was to make certain that one battalion of guests did not interlock with another. Arriving guests had to be steered to the proper anterooms, and guests in the grand ballroom, whose time was running out, had to be discreetly encouraged into the routes of departure. Thanks to Loeb's skill, there never was a breakdown.

Much the same problems of scheduling and controlling the progress of the manswarm was involved in his encounters with another social endeaver —parades—in an era when that form of display was popular in the capital. The secretary, as a standard matter, represented the interests of the White House in the marches organized for inaugurals, holidays and other special occasions. The tendency of each marching group was to pause for as long an interval as possible before the Presidential reviewing stand, the prized place of honor toward which the hundreds of shuffling tired feet had been patiently directed for hours. But Loeb, who thought only in terms of his duty to the President, was fertile in discovering or developing little expedients to keep the dawdling paraders manageable. He took pains to check with the several bands in the line of march the pieces they planned to play upon arrival at the President's reviewing stand. In consulting with the bands, the secretary was invariably known to encourage the rendition of short snappy numbers. Long slow pieces, he simply wouldn't tolerate. Loeb kept the show moving.

Now and then, the rather hectic extravaganza of which William Loeb was impresario took to the road, for T.R. was one of the more peripatetic Presidents, and wherever his restless spirit turned in its erratic fashion, Loeb was sure to follow. Summers at Oyster Bay, hunting trips in spring and fall, grueling transcontinental political campaigns and the inevitable parks and bridges to be dedicated in remote hinterlands took Loeb and Roosevelt out of Washington for months at a time.

During Roosevelt's lengthier sojourns at Sagamore Hill, Loeb transferred a good deal of his operation from his White House offices to a set of rooms over the Morris Grocery Store in Oyster Bay. Loeb did not install his typewriter at Sagamore Hill, which is located several miles outside the village, due to T.R.'s insistence that his family and business domains be separated. Although typing, telephoning and composing the President's appointment list were handled in Oyster Bay, the President's dictation was taken by Loeb at Sagamore Hill in the library off the front hall. In summertime, Loeb was a familiar sight riding on horseback or driving his covered surrey on the road between Oyster Bay village and the President's residence. At about ten o'clock each morning, the secretary would reach Sagamore Hill to find the President racing through a huge pile of magazines and newspapers or vigorously rocking and talking with his family on the porch. Promptly upon arrival, Loeb would hustle off with T.R. to the library, where they worked until lunch. The door was always open, and anyone passing by could see T.R. pacing to and fro, dictating in his strenuous style.

The customary indicia of confusion which prevailed in Washington also abounded at the summer White House. There were droves of callers—Senators, cabinet secretaries and distinguished private figures. Newsmen were encamped in the village, and any one of three government vessels—the Mayflower, the Dolphin, the Sylph—rode at anchor off Sagamore Hill. Some crisis seemed always to be swirling across the landscape. One day the press was agog with rumors that the President was lost deep in the woods adjoining his home. Loeb had to convince the clamoring reporters that T.R., although undeniably in the woods, knew where he was and where he was going. At the twilight of an August day, at the outer limits of Sagamore Hill, a reasonably well-dressed man approached a guard in measured strides bespeaking a determined purpose. Quivering with excitement, the man announced that he had just invented a new type of gun which would revolutionize the art of warfare and which therefore he wished to show to the President. As a matter of fact, he was ready to see the President at once. The man was by every indication a "nut," or at least the guard, who was under hire to detect such species, so concluded. "See Mr. Loeb in the village in the morning and secure an appointment," quietly proposed the guard. This advice, or passing of the buck, was accepted and heeded. Early next morning, the perturbed inventor with his formidable device confronted Loeb. Mustering his courage, the secretary somehow convinced the man that he really didn't need to see the President, but could do better by dealing directly with the War Department. Most important of all, Loeb induced the inventor to be on his way, without in the process offending his sensitivities and creating a terrible and dangerous uproar. Due to the skillful Loeb, the inventor departed without so much as firing a single shot.

Loeb handled the details of T.R.'s many travels, ranging from simple junkets to cross-country journeys and hunting expeditions into regions remote and wild. If the President and his party ventured to the commencement exercises of Georgetown University, or to Cleveland for the funeral services of Secretary of State John Hay, it was Loeb who made plans, issued instructions, and generally saw that things went smoothly. That was not always easy. In the case of the Hay funeral, for instance, Loeb had to cope with some confusion over the course of the President's special train, which had been organized to transport the entire cabinet as honorary pallbearers from the East to distant Cleveland. The trouble originated from the fact that Philadelphia, where the train was to be boarded, had several railroad stations. To set the potential confusion into motion, the Pennsylvania Railroad, which planned the route to be traveled, stipulated that the presidential train upon arriving in Philadelphia from Oyster Bay, would stop for ten minutes, and for ten minutes only, at the West Philadelphia station to pick up the cabinet members. Just before the due day, the railroad switched the stop to another of its stations in Philadelphia, the Broad Street station. Of this change of plan Loeb had to notify the cabinet, many of whom—because these events were transpiring in the summer months—were traveling or vacationing in distant parts of the country. By dint of his crystal-clear directives and several additional precautions, no member of the cabinet was lost in the ten minute stopover in Philadelphia.

All sorts of embarrassments were apt to plague T.R.'s excursions, even in the seemingly most innocent circumstances. Once, through the intercession of Vice-President Fairbanks, T.R. agreed to journey to Indianapolis to participate in the 1907 Memorial Day exercises of that city. A parade, of course, was on the schedule, and as a special event, a statue of General Henry Ware Lawton was to be dedicated, with the President making the address as the high light of the ceremonies. What should have been a routine and joyous function turned in its planning stage into a wrangle between the veterans of the Spanish-American War and the Grand Army of the Republic respectively. The veterans of each war demanded to be first in the order of parade. Neither would give way after some days of argument, and word of the deadlock filtered back to the White House. Loeb hurriedly investigated the situation, and on the basis of his findings and recommendations, the President ventured to propose a solution for the impasse. General Lawton, to whom honor was to be rendered, he pointed out, was a Grand Army man. Accordingly, declared the President, emphasising that he was speaking as "a Spanish war veteran," the Grand Army should be given "the right of line." Accompanying this counsel of undeniable good sense was a prayerful admonition. "I feel that it would be a most unforunate thing," wrote T.R., "reflecting honor upon no one, to have an undignified squabble mar the solemnity of the Memorial Day exercises." Henceforth the Indianians were on their good behavior.

For T.R.'s longer journeys—the bear hunts in Louisiana, lion hunts in the Rockies and the hunts for votes on the transcontinental political tours, Loeb organized the itinerary, arranged the stopovers, and determined whom T.R. was to see and for how long. At times, these chores involved political problems of great moment. On the lengthy Western trip undertaken by T.R. in 1903, for example, a question of seemingly small detail arose, although, as such questions sometimes do, it quickly puffed into an issue of exceptional magnitude. T.R., at the time the difficulty began, was in Montana and was scheduled shortly to travel by rail to the West Coast. In anticipation of the impending journey, the Utah Federation of Labor, through its secretary, Daniel I. Elton, requested the President to avoid as far as possible utilizing the facilities of the Union Pacific Railroad in proceeding to his destination. The Labor Federation made this unusual request, Mr. Elton explained, because the Union Pacific was "radically unjust to its employees in the various shops and the result is that their rolling stock is in very bad repair." Having made this somewhat ominous observation, Mr. Elton next rose to a moral plane—"Hoping this will appeal to your sense of justice," he wrote to the President in closing. The Elton letter derived additional force by being duly leaked to the press. When this skillfully contrived test of the President's friendliness to American labor broke upon the country, T.R. had progressed in his travels to the point where he was hunting mountain lion in the far recesses of Yellowstone Park. Indeed, T.R. was so deep in the woods that he was beyond reach for effective consultation, and Loeb therefore had to face the problem alone. In anticipating what T.R. would say, were he there to say it, Loeb knew that his chief was a stickler for holding to his plans once they were made, and that he wasn't in the habit of truckling to any group in the body politic, including organized labor. The President, of course, would want his position stated in a manner which would avoid any unnecessary offense, an attitude with which Loeb strove to comply. The President's itinerary could not be changed, the secretary forthrightly but politely informed Mr. Elton, as it "would cause serious disappointment to thousands of people, many of whom have been to considerable expense in preparing for the visit." The blow of the refusal was cushioned by several complimentary allusions to organized labor. All this, of course, did not satisfy the exacting Mr. Elton, but it served to put the Administration in a sufficiently favorable light when the episode was again taken up in the press.

When T.R. was off in the wilds hunting or fishing, Loeb would be shut in a hotel room in the nearest town, discharging the business of the Presidency. Scores of telegrams arrived from the departments, many in code, presenting matters for the President's attention or decision. Loeb himself disposed of a good percentage of the messages received, and where the President had to be consulted, the secretary organized the matters in a fashion permitting a quantity of them to be disposed of in a single conferral. Although Loeb was pretty much buried in his papers, while T.R. was out warring on the animals, now and then the secretary partook of the pleasures of the expedition. Once in a junket to Florida with two Rough Rider friends and the presidential physician, Dr. Rixey, T.R. induced Loeb to drop all business one afternoon to embark in a naphtha launch for an island off St. Augustine, which, according to the local pilot, was ideal for swimming. Although the day was chilly and overcast, Loeb gamely but briefly immersed himself, freezing to his very marrow, for what the wildly splashing T.R. termed "a splendid surf bath."

Loeb on occasion was also invited to the gastronomic interludes which were part and parcel of T.R.'s junkets. At the conclusion of one very successful hunt in the lower Mississippi valley, T.R. and his comrades decided to commemorate their happy adventure with a dinner utilizing the bag of the final day. The take, as it developed, consisted of two huge grizzly bears. Loeb was invited, although like many other of his countrymen, he did not particularly care for bear meat. Not wishing to offend his proud and jubilant hosts, he grimly chewed away in polite appreciation.

Loeb also assisted in the crises which sometimes arose and seriously threatened the prolongation of these gatherings. On one hunting trip, for instance, a pistol-carrying cowboy, who was a member of the party and a good friend of the President, showed incontrovertible signs of having drunk too much. As a responsible host, T.R. moved to cope with the situation by urging the cowboy to return to the presidential train and go to bed. The man refused to budge; T.R. talked further, but in vain. All the prestige and authority of the President of the United States could not induce the cowboy to take what to him seemed such an abysmally ignominious course. Indeed, he had sufficient control of his faculties to suggest an alternative. He had a gun, he pointed out, a long forty-four, a circumstance of which the assembled guests had long been painfully aware. He would, he said, gladly hand over the gun to Mr. Loeb, the most responsible man in the party, for safekeeping, and favor the gathering with his continued presence. Loeb nervously spent the rest of the evening toting about his cumbrous trust.

Loeb was a balance wheel to the thundering, on-rushing, fire-belching T.R., a man who cherished balance wheels. For all of the fury of his ranting at deviltry in the business community, T.R. was intrinsically conservative. Although he warred upon the trusts, disciplined the railroads, and stomped out malpractices by the score, T.R. stopped well short of fundamental change. He and the melange of measures known as the Square Deal hadn't traveled very far down the road of reform before the conservative elements of his nature exerted their sway. Victorian, property-minded and Harvard-devoted, T.R.'s compassion for the common man was limited by the credo and pride of his patrician background. But the President wasn't content merely to rely upon his own better impulses and ingrained values to stay on the track. He liked to have Loeb on hand as a check where his own personal resources faltered. The secretary was an admirably constituted balance wheel —"a hardened skeptic and cynic," the President once put it. By self-admission, T.R. was neither. He went overboard with his enthusiasms, was careless about details whose neglect meant trouble, and was prone to plunge into minor crusades hardly worth the cost of the struggle. Loeb, in contrast, was a practical, show-me-minded assistant. By some fifth sense, he could spot any enemy of equanimity—the snake in the grass, the wolf in sheep's clothing, and other such ominous species—miles away, and what is more he could make his chief take heed.

One of the many incalculable disasters from which Loeb saved T.R. materialized from the President's warm friendship with several leading prel-ates of the Roman Catholic Church in the United States. Over the years, T.R. developed an especial fondness and admiration for Archbishop Ireland of St. Paul and for Cardinal Gibbons of Baltimore. So impressed, as a matter of fact, was T.R. with the intellectual and administrative prowess of Cardinal Gibbons, that at one juncture he proposed to communicate directly with the Pope and frankly point out to His Holiness the dreadful mistake the Church would be making if it failed to give the Cardinal a special and important assignment then impending in the United States. Fearing that some other less qualified Cardinal might receive this assignment, T.R. had trained his thoughts to the Vatican. One morning just after dictation was finished, T.R. informed Loeb of what he proposed to do in behalf of Cardinal Gibbons. The secretary, who thought first and foremost in political terms, was aghast at the disclosed plans, a discomfiture he took no trouble to hide. He bluntly pointed out to T.R. that the whole project was impossible for two incontrovertible reasons. For one thing, it would antagonize the Pope, since the President of the United States would in effect be presuming to tell the Pontiff how to run his own organization. Even worse were its domestic political implications: it would touch off a cacophonous explosion of Protestant outcry and remonstrance. The press would surely get hold of the story, the doctrine of separation of church and state would be thunderously reasserted, and mad rumors of Vatican spies hiding and operating in the White House would fill the air. Overpowered by Loeb's objections, the President, without argument, dropped his plans.

Sometimes, for all of Loeb's watchfulness and counsel, T.R. toppled off the deep end. In the inevitable upheaval, Loeb customarily took the blame, a function he uncomplainingly fulfilled. Thanks to his efficient martyrdom, the national image of the President as a right-thinking, right-acting hero remained undefiled. Indeed, in the course of time, Loeb bore so many of T.R.'s eccentricities, that he became known, unofficially and irreverently, in capital circles as T.R.'s "goat." If things went wrong, the trusty formula was applied, "blame it on Loeb." When T.R. failed to invite Sir Thomas Lipton, the eminent British merchant and yachtsman to dinner at the White House, the omission provoked an international storm. It was all my fault, said Loeb, and he gamely suffered the resulting Anglo-American deluge of criticism, even though T.R. was known to be something less than enthusiastic in his regard for Sir Thomas. Again, when the President concluded, as the result of one his wilder brain storms, that it would be nice to put the attachés of the White House into livery like that of the better royal households of Europe, Loeb bravely confronted the shrieks of indignant egalitarians. Another time, Congress rose in wrath when, in a budget transmitted by the President, sixty thousand dollars was requested for the maintenance of the White House edifice and ninety thousand dollars for the maintenance and improvement of the nearby stables in which reposed the President's favorite horses. By some roundabout and not altogether convincing explanations seeking to prove he was to blame, Loeb took the lashes involved for this gaudy fiscal expression of equine love.

In various ways, Loeb's personality was well attuned to the necessities of T.R. An actor who hogged the stage, the President didn't tolerate competition from his colleagues for public attention. With one or two exceptions, his cabinet was a pack of drab personalities utterly incapable of evoking a flicker of popular enthusiasm. Loeb's personality coloration, too, blended nicely with the shadows. He was totally unspectacular, and he easily accepted the necessity of his complete self-subordination as a condition of employment. Serving T.R. was the central event, the final ambition, the crowning achievement of William Loeb's life.

On the job and off, his style was unremittingly unobtrusive. Quiet, courteous and imperturbable, mild in humor and free from airs, his inner nature matched his outer self. Modest himself, he could not bear pretense in others. One day, an English earl of the school of insufferable pomposity arrived at the White House and informed Loeb that he had made his ocean trip something of a lark by traveling incognito and rubbing shoulders with the common man. "I always travel incognito," sniffed Loeb, repelled by the snobbery, "I meet nicer people that way."

Loeb's innate modesty completely directed his private life. He was no blazing star in the firmament of Washington society as other presidential secretaries, before and after his time, have been. His vacations were spent not at distinguished social resorts, but at ranches in Wyoming, Montana and Colorado, where he loved such solitary pursuits as riding and trout fishing. Off the job, Loeb was a homebody whose social interests were few. Only on occasion did he emerge from his lair for an evening of cards, or to partake of some function at the White House. The social intercourse Loeb liked best was actually semi-business in character. After the model of T.R.'s famous luncheons, Loeb liked to bring guests home for the noonday meal. Politicians, cowboys and businessmen who were in town, Loeb would load into his carriage at the White House and gallop off to his home a few blocks away. His luncheons were devoted largely to discussions of political conditions in his guests' home towns and states, and were arranged with the same spur-of-the-moment inspiration as T.R.'s, and precipitated the same upheaval for Mrs. Loeb as T.R.'s did for Mrs. Roosevelt and her kitchen staff. But on the whole, in lieu of consorting extensively with his fellow men, Loeb was most contented caring for his flower garden, his horses and dogs, and a pet bird.

As the only man who ever became really close to T.R., Loeb was unswerving in loyalty and dedication, but he was no "yes man." Such a species T.R. could never tolerate with the responsibilities he entrusted his secretary. Loeb's loyalty was devotion tempered by candor. A lover of work, uncomplaining under the duress of long hours and the piling on of duties, Loeb was all square with T.R.'s personal credo that hard work was in itself a good thing and that what such work did was right. The secretary had boundless courage, fearing neither bear nor mountain lion, outraged Senator, or shrill femininity. No man could have evoked T.R.'s regard as Loeb did without being valorous, for in the spirit of King Arthur's Round Table, the President cherished courage as a manly, ennobling symbol of moral vigor.

The ties extending between the President and his secretary produced a web of friendship that was never broken, that withstood crisis and accident, and every assault of human frailty. Near the close of his Presidency, T.R., who was not given to gratuitous praise, termed Loeb one of his "best friends," and "the man who has been closest to me politically." To Loeb, T.R. was "the best friend I have or ever expect to have." Supplementing the affinities of the partners was the sturdy closeness of their families. Mrs. Loeb was often a guest at the White House and a favorite of the President. Indeed, her acquaintance with the Roosevelts antedated her marriage to Loeb. In 1905, a son, William, was born to the Loebs, and the President subsequently stood up as godfather for the child in the christening ceremonies at Christ Episcopal Church in Oyster Bay.

In the Roosevelt household, Secretary Loeb was part of the family. "Uncle Bill," the children called him, and he was the one adult, apart from the parents and Aunt Lizzie, whose presence was permitted at the younger folks' birthday parties. For years, long after Roosevelt's presidency had terminated, the Loebs presented Christmas gifts to the children. Even in 1918, when an older son, Kermit, was an American soldier stationed in far-off Baghdad, the Loebs did not fail to dispatch to the young man something for his Christmas stocking.

Any intimate aide such as Loeb had to be fully accepted in familia to achieve his extraordinary status, for the President's first allegiance was not to his work, but to his wife and children. They were a family of enormous vitality, zest for living and capacity for mutual enjoyment. Of the children, Alice, Ted and Kermit were away at school, while Ethel, Quentin and Archie were at home in the early Presidential years. The latter two children were infants.

Like T.R., the children were devoted to "exercise," as it was called. Each youngster became in time an expert horseback rider, an activity customarily pursued in the afternoons. Evenings were given to the family passion—reading. It was nothing for T.R. to race through three or four books in a sitting, with an acuteness of comprehension that enabled him to recall any fine detail. For the children, who burst with vigor, verve and a wondrous capacity for mischief, the White House was a vast and splendid playground. "From the basement to the flagpole on the roof," Ike Hoover, the late chief usher at the White House has written, "every channel and cubbyhole was thoroughly investigated." The acres of smooth hardwood floor presented an irresistible invitation for roller skating and bicycling. Each child owned a pair of wooden stilts which were employed with such dexterity that no stairs were too steep or thickly carpeted to represent a mountain to be climbed, the crest of no stuffed chair too remote to represent a fortress to be taken. There were pranks galore. The children had a little pony, Algonquin, which one day they led right into the White House. Algonquin was put on the elevator and transported upstairs to Archie's room. For the better part of an afternoon, according to Ike Hoover, the youngster's bedroom served as an equine promenade. T.R.'s own favorite game with the children was called "pillow," a simulation of football. The President would get down on his haunches on the floor, clasping a pillow, and scamper madly about, trying for a goal, with all the children pouncing, clinging and rolling on top of him.

Loeb, who loved children, participated in the less violent games, although his significance was more than that of extra playmate. Mrs. Roosevelt, who was very fond of her husband's secretary, considered him a decidedly wholesome influence on the younger generation. Even T.R. was constantly holding Loeb up to the children as a man of character and industry supremely worthy of emulation. Children normally resent those they are bidden to respect, but this, it appears, was never the case with Loeb. For the older boys, he was a sought-after companion. If Kermit, newly arrived at Harvard, proposed to make a walking tour of the historic sites of Boston, he unhesitatingly chose Loeb as a guide. The expedition was something of a test for the secretary, for Kermit, a lanky lad, traveled in long fast strides, but somehow the moderate-sized, puffing Loeb gamely shuffled along with the pace. In various ways, Loeb ministered to the needs of daily living of Kermit and Ted when the lads were at Groton and later at Harvard by arranging for the forwarding of the daily New York Tribune to the boys at school and by supplying material to Kermit as an industrious member of his prep school's debating team. When the lad was involved in an interschool debate concerning the Panama Canal, in which he had to argue the case for the lock canal as against the sea-level canal, Loeb helped out magnificently by supplying instructive papers on the subject that were handy around the office. The secretary was also the watchdog of the exchequer, who oversaw the boys' bank accounts and replenished them periodically with fresh deposits. When Ted, in his first blaze of financial freedom, overdrew his account, it was Loeb who, through the President, set the young man aright. "Mr. Loeb suggests," the President wrote Ted, "that I add the information that a bank account is not elastic and only good for the amount deposited—which means you have overdrawn your fourteen dollars."

The secretary was a fount of wisdom which the President tapped and appealed to in solemn parental discussions with his children. When Kermit reported to his family the courses he had chosen to study at Harvard, it was not enough that his father, the President of the United States, approved the selection. The President was delighted to inform the young man that the courses were exactly those which Mr. Loeb would have chosen were he at Harvard. The year Kermit entered college, upon graduating from Groton, was one of crisis in his educational career. As his prep-school days were coming to an end, the lad was betwixt and between whether to take a job— to which he was decidedly inclined—or go on to Harvard. The latter choice was being strongly but tactfully urged by the President, who acutely appreciated the limitations of parental power under the circumstances. In dealing with Kermit in this hour of crisis, the President turned to Loeb for the confirmation of respected authority. "Mr. Loeb agrees with me," the President took pains to inform Kermit of the judgment of the oracle. According to Mr. Loeb, T.R. related, a lad should wait at least until his twenty-first year before going to work. One's earlier years are better spent at education, for in employment, as Loeb was said to have put it, "up to twenty one, he cannot do very much good work of the kind that will tell most afterwards."

Loeb's status as family intimate was also advanced by another branch of endeavor, his responsibilities as manager of T.R.'s private business affairs. As a regular duty, Loeb supervised a clerk, a Mr. T. H. Netherland, employed by the President out of his own pocket, to maintain his personal accounts. Although Mr. Netherland handled his task with model efficiency, Loeb had to make many a knotty decision as to whether given bills incurred by T.R. were to be charged against the Executive Office or the President's own private account. The discretion Loeb exercised in the President's business decisions was extraordinary because T.R. was never particularly interested in his personal estate, either in keeping what he had, or least of all in increasing its substance. Only by the most vigorous insistence, could Loeb bring T.R. on occasion to audit his own and Mr. Netherland's stewardship. "In a fit of spurious conscientiousness, instigated by Mr. Loeb," T.R. wrote candidly of one such session, "I tried to go over the accounts in detail."

Loeb was much involved in the business aspects of the two principal enterprises of T.R.'s private world—the marketing of his literary output, and the care of his estate at Sagamore Hill. For T.R.'s books and articles, Loeb handled the fine details of contracts, watched over royalty accounts, and secured permissions from authors to be quoted in his chief's writings. Editors and publishers grew accustomed to dealing with Loeb. When Edward Bok, the famous Philadelphia editor, proposed to carry an authorized article in the Ladies' Home Journal on a typical day of Mrs. Roosevelt in the White House, Mr. Bok submitted an outline of the projected article he had prepared not to the President, but to Loeb, "putting it into your hands, to give to him when it seems wise to you." Now and then Loeb had to step into nasty literary situations and say harsh things which clearly needed to be said, but were inappropriate for the President to utter. One of these occasions arose when Rasmus B. Anderson, editor of a modern edition of Norroena, an ancient Anglo-Saxon classic, had incorporated as the frontispiece of his book a facsimile of a personal congratulatory letter which the President had written him a few days prior to publication. The presidential letter, which employed language of generous praise, was being energetically exploited by Mr. Anderson's publishers to promote the sale of Norroena. In the exuberance of his commercial success, Mr. Anderson committed the error of sending several copies of his book with the facsimile to the White House. The President, upon looking into the volumes, exploded with rage at the publication and exploitation of his letter, which was intended to be strictly private. Some portion of the Chief Executive's prolix wrath had to be conveyed to the author, a task which fell to Loeb. For the President to engage in a public altercation with Mr. Anderson would be in poor taste, and it might well have the unwanted effect of stimulating the author's sales. Loeb accordingly dispatched a letter, pointing out to Anderson in no uncertain terms that a breach of faith had been committed. But mere protest was not enough; as Loeb and the President jointly appreciated, the situation called for positive threat. "Unless these facsimile letters are recalled at once," warned Loeb, with careful clarity, "and the President's letter kept private by you, the volumes will be returned and a statement published setting forth the reasons for their return." The author quickly complied with this ultimatum.

Sagamore Hill was operated under Loeb's alert and constant scrutiny. He examined all bills incurred by the Oyster Bay estate prior to their payment—a responsibility he administered with remorseless exactitude. Under Loeb, the principle of receiving full value for every dollar spent was unqualifiedly observed. In making payment to the grocer in Oyster Bay, for example, Loeb on one occasion deducted from the bill rendered the sum of twenty-five cents, the price of a bottle of vinegar, for which Mrs. Roosevelt had been charged, but which she had never received. In auditing a bill approved by the caretaker of the estate, Noah Seaman, representing the cost of treating a polar-bear rug, Loeb pointedly inquired of Mr. Seaman whether the taxidermist had relined the rug with cloth or canvas. Presumably the price was different, depending on the material used. Mr. Seaman, looking again at the rug, wasn't quite sure, and payment was withheld until the taxidermist himself could satisfactorily explain which of the linings had been applied.

Loeb frequently placed orders for the needs of the household, acting not so much for his chief as for Mrs. Roosevelt. On her authorization, for example, he would order from Bloomingdale Brothers in New York City such household appurtenances as five gallons of cooking wine, three dozen bottles of Gosman's sarsaparilla and a shade for a pyramid night light. Loeb was concerned not only with the comfort and nourishment of the President's family, but with providing the means of enjoyment for its hours of recreation. With Steinway and Sons, he arranged the rental of an upright piano, at fifteen dollars per month, plus cartage. A more complex transaction entailed the transporting of one of the Roosevelt children's favorite ponies from Oyster Bay to the stables in Washington. So eagerly was the pony awaited by the children, that Loeb took pains to track down the precise officials of the Pennsylvania Railroad who could most expedite the progress of the creature at two crucial points—Jersey City, to which it would be brought by boat for transfer to the railroad, and at the Washington depot, to assure that after it was received there, it would be promptly forwarded to the White House. The children's outcries of delight as the pony, a shaggy dapple-gray, arrived on the precise day it had been promised, was the reward of Loeb's vigilance.

William Loeb, Jr., was by T.R.'s own avowal his leading political counselor and number-one legman in matters of party politics. The magnitude of Loeb's responsibilities derived not from his secretaryship, but from T.R.'s abiding respect for his political acumen. "Loeb's judgment in politics," T.R. once stated to William Howard Taft, "is that of an expert." In political crisis, the secretary was T.R.'s favorite emissary to local trouble spots, to glean facts, weigh imponderables and muster solutions. In 1908, for example, the New York Senatorial situation erupted into such alarming chaos, that in T.R.'s eyes it patently required the expert applications of Loeb. A United States Senator was to be elected, but none of the several aspirants scrambling for the Republican nomination had boosted himself to a position of dominance. The as yet unexpressed White House sentiment strongly favored Elihu Root of New York City, but Mr. Root, unfortunately, had been so convincingly negative toward the nomination that sufficient support from the local party organization had failed to materialize. Meanwhile, time, in the form of the approaching state convention, was running out. In the vagaries of the situation, it was not impossible that an aspirant lukewarm or even hostile toward the Administration ultimately might capture the nomination. At this desperate juncture, T.R. dispatched Loeb to the Empire State. There the secretary conferred with Root and conveyed pointed words from the President concerning one's duty to one's party and Administration, with heartening results. The former Secretary of War shed his murky indifference and began to appear eager for the nomination. The grateful Loeb hustled through a series of conferences with local leaders. He was still frantically negotiating when the New York County delegation took the gratifying and way-pointing step of voting to support Root. Other delegations quickly fell into line like boxcars set into motion. At the close of his sojourn, Loeb was jubilantly reporting back to T.R., "I am now safe in saying that Root will be elected without any difficulty."

Loeb's political maneuvers, launched with T.R.'s full authorization and often his initiative, sometimes brought the secretary into head-on conflict with members of the cabinet. In his set-to's with the Administration's upper crust, Loeb, or in reality the President, never came off second best. One of the presidential secretary's livelier jousts transpired with Secretary of the

Treasury Leslie Mortier Shaw in 1906. Time and again, as the electoral campaign of that year had proceeded, Secretary Shaw had embarrassed the Administration by his free-speaking zeal for a high protective tariff. Where protection was concerned, Shaw believed in piling Ossa on Pelion. The sky was the limit. He indulged his convictions to the point of taking leave of his duties in the Treasury Department and making a brisk speaking tour of Iowa to prevent the renomination of Governor Albert B. Cummins, who was both a Republican and a distinguished low-tariff advocate. An extremist in his own right, Cummins endorsed free steel, free lumber, free hides, virtually free anything, and full reciprocity with Canada. Hopping from stump to stump in an unstinting oratorial war on Cummins, Shaw cleverly cultivated the impression that he was representing the sentiment of the Roosevelt Administration. In time, Shaw's Iowa campaign began having so much impact that friends of Governor Cummins feared he would be defeated. Among these friends was the President, who valued the Governor as a salutary pressure for a sensible Republican middle-of-the-road position on the tariff. As the situation in Iowa mounted to the peril point, Loeb stepped in by releasing to the press a letter he was sending to Charles Grilk of the Iowa Republican Central Committee. In this letter, Loeb declared quite pointedly that Secretary Shaw spoke only for himself and in no respect whatever for the Administration, according to the Washington *Post*. Meanwhile, the President privately made known to Shaw his annoyance with the Secretary's frolic in Iowa. This double-barreled White House maneuver sufficed to muzzle Shaw and thrust Cummins on to victory.

Loeb was the President's deputy in the big business of handing out patronage. Although the Second Assistant Postmaster General, in keeping with tradition, oversaw the distribution of the great volume of jobs, he was in some respects Loeb's junior partner. As a matter of routine, Loeb was consulted in matters involving the interests of the President. All jobs entailing presidential nomination were handled through the White House. For each of these jobs, Loeb maintained a file card on every candidate proposed for the President's consideration. Notations on the cards summarized the candidate's qualifications and everything said for and against him by the party sources consulted. Since Loeb had the skill of a high-grade sleuth in flushing out backgrounds, the card inscriptions were usually extensive. In co-operation with state leaders and the Second Assistant Postmaster General, Loeb sometimes helped work out the general pattern or formula to be followed in allocating patronage among party elements or factions in given states. When jobs were finally handed out, Loeb was also busy applying soothing syrup to the disappointed and the crushed. Sometimes the President conveyed the decisions, but the authority of his word did not always make things easier for Loeb. The President's pronouncements ranged widely between gentle tact and lacerating insult. "I doubt, Sir," he would, on his better behavior, inform a Senator, "whether your friend is *quite* the best man for the place, from the information which reaches me." At his worst, T.R. might declare, also to a Senator, "They tell me he is a crook."

Patronage is a hard business, abounding in bleak moments for its trans-actors. Loeb's most harassed interlude of the many he experienced was pro-vided, not by the enemies he inevitably created, but by an article entitled "Spirit of Graft," which appeared in the respected and influential *Outlook* magazine. The general import of the article was: ". . . the spirit of graft finds universal expression throughout the government service." In support of so sweeping and distressing a thesis, the author related how a widow had been appointed to a position in a government department in Washington as a reward for returning a valuable gold watch lost by an "influential official." "Is there any authority of law for handing out a Government appointment in payment for a personal obligation?" the author asked rhetorically. The official guilty of this moral relapse, the article made unmistakably clear, was one William Loeb, Jr. The secretary's troubles, however, were only be-ginning. When the article appeared, *The New York Times* quickly snatched up the story as the basis of a vigorous editorial condemning graft in high places. Thereupon the wheels of rebuttal began to turn in behalf of the assailed secretary. A full statement of the facts completely exonerating Loeb was released by the White House to the press. The President himself wrote to *Outlook* terming its published story "a wicked lie." Meanwhile, *The New York Times* had been so impressed with the validity of the counterattack that it retracted its condemnation of Loeb and candidly acknowledged that the story reported in *Outlook* and the judgment passed in its own editorial were wholly unfounded and unmerited.

Loeb's familiarity with Republican politicians in Congress and in states and localities across the nation was truly encyclopedic. He knew intimately the chairmen of potent legislative committees and freshmen Congressmen, the stalwarts of Republican conservatism and the most resolute of the party's insurgents. He was at equal ease with the urbane, wealthy, Harvard-bred Eastern Senator and the champion spitoon marksman of the hinterlands. His two closest Congressional friends were poles apart in philosophy and mien. One, Uncle Joe Cannon, was the most autocratic and the most powerful Speaker in the history of the House of Representatives. "Foul-mouthed Joe," "Hayseed from Illinois," Cannon was also called due to the coarseness of his speech and his uncouth manners. Loeb passed many a pleasurable hour in the company of this man of raw power. But the secretary's closest legis-lative friend was Senator Albert J. Beveridge of Indiana, distinguished biog-rapher of John Marshall, and an eloquent, courageous, trail-blazing Republi-can Insurgent. To Beveridge, Loeb was an "Old Peach" and a favorite vacation companion, hunting and fishing "in the deep, deep woods—twenty-five miles from everywhere and everything." "I would like to deliver an oration on you some time," Beveridge once declared to Loeb in an outburst of admiration, "for you are the real thing and then some."

Among local political leaders, Loeb's acquaintanceship was wider even than the President's, which in its own right was phenomenal. Politicians visiting in Washington made almost as much a point of talking to Loeb as to the President. The secretary's list of correspondents was prodigious—the United States Bankruptcy referee in Montgomery, Alabama, the Governor of West Virginia, the United States District Attorney of North Carolina, the Auditor of Delaware, the Collector of the Port of Baltimore, the President of the Hungarian Republican Club of New York City—are typical. Politicians liked to correspond with and talk to Loeb because he gave a sympathetic ear, provided a ready channel to the President, and he got things done. Loeb's thriving personal contacts provided himself and his chief a vast and sensitive network of political intelligence.

Loeb, accordingly, was steeped in the minutiae of detail which has to be mastered if state and national conventions are to run smoothly and elections are to be won. He kept books on the income and outgo of the President's campaign finances, right down to the very last postage stamp. "It is ridiculous small matters like this," T.R. once said apropos of postage stamps, "that sometimes make the most trouble." As for income, Loeb received scores of financial contributions, usually of small amounts, toward the expenses of the President's campaigning. The secretary equally had at his finger tips the record of performance of specific election-district captains in given cities across the nation. He knew who the feet-draggers were and their precise tactics in delaying the badly needed reorganization of the New York County committee in 1904. From memory, he could recite the time schedule for distributing campaign literature from various state headquarters in that year. He had a play-by-play familiarity with the maneuvers undertaken to speed up the naturalization process in 1904 on the theory that the new citizenry thus created would substantially increase the Republican vote. His interest in political detail, indeed, was boundless. In 1904, for example, he was, as a matter of course, even sent a copy of a new musical march, composed especially for that year's campaign, which was tried for the first time at a mass rally at Madison Square Garden. According to intelligence trickling back to Loeb, the tune was a huge success, transporting the crowd into the gay prancing enthusiasm "of a nominating convention." So pleased were Loeb and the President with the march when it was played on the White House piano, that they ordered copies of the music to be rushed at once to the "doubtful" states. There commenced a frenzy of symphonic serenading that has never since been exceeded, even in the heyday of John Philip Sousa.

Loeb was intricately involved in T.R.'s sizable dealings with national, racial and economic groups. Viewing sympathetically the aspirations and necessities of Irish, German, Jewish, Catholic, Negro, Labor and other groups, the President placed great store upon securing their favor at the polls. Loeb, it is clear, encouraged and at times even led the President in his course of alert attentiveness to the special groups. The Secretary to the President, who well perceived that the task of winning their support is never done, watched over detail and protocol and the shifting currents of group opinion. He encouraged the President to do obeisance to the courted groups by making speeches before them, consulting their leaders, sending congratulatory and inspirational messages on their anniversaries, and by pushing hard for the right planks in the party platform.

Of all groups, Loeb was most sensitive to the changing political situation of the Negro. Alarmed at the drift of the race to Democratic ranks in the larger Northern cities at the turn of the century, he incessantly encouraged the invigoration of existing Republican Colored Clubs, as they were known, as a step toward reversing the trend. In New York City, for example, when Charles Anderson, loyal Republican and head of a local club which had been allowed to languish in neglect, sought to revive his organization by luring back its former members who had drifted to the rival Democratic club, the Secretary to the President rushed to his assistance. He prevailed upon the national party chairman to supply funds to Mr. Anderson sufficient to provide the rental for an adequate clubhouse with furnishings, including a plentiful supply of pool and billiard tables, and food and drink for an ample program of socials. It was largely at Loeb's initiative that the Negro achieved significant recognition in the Republican National Convention at Chicago in 1908. After long months of quiet agitation, on the part of Loeb, a Negro was placed on the executive committee of the national party organization. It was the first step of its kind in the party's history.

Loeb was in all but name the President's press secretary. He was kept busy in his quasi-official capacity because T.R. was a genius in publicly dramatizing the issues of the day and in resourcefully inventing them when they were in short supply. To Loeb's press work, an extra zest was imparted by the President's constant embroilments with reporters. A stickler for the proprieties, whose lofty standards were not easily lived up to, the President summarily banished any and all violators to the famous "Ananias Club." This was a spacious journalistic doghouse that T.R. built where the membership was always full and the dues exorbitant. "T.R.," observed Oscar King Davis, Washington correspondent of The New York Times, "ceased entirely to give his confidence to the man who had not respected it. It was all or nothing with him."

To the press, Loeb was a sympathetic collaborator and gentle pacificator of ruffled feelings. The kindly secretary issued statements to reporters and conducted press conferences in which he was customarily helpful, although, when necessary, he could be as bland and discreet as a polished diplomat. When, early in the Administration, T.R. was quietly contending with Mark Hanna for the leadership of the Republican party, a meeting eventually ensued between the mighty Senator from Ohio and the Chief Executive. Loeb fittingly informed the awaiting press that "a most pleasant interview" had transpired. But Loeb could also deliver the bold and forceful statement. He could, if necessary, in a pronouncement to the press, do nothing less than question the integrity and efficiency of the Federal judiciary. Yet he was skillful enough to stop a step or two short of contempt of court. One of his more drastic expressions was instigated by the famous suit brought by the United States Government against the Standard Oil Company, a critical piece of litigation in T.R.'s trust-busting program. After triumphing in federal district court, the administration encountered a devastating reversal in the Circuit Court of Appeals in consequence of which the lower court decision fining Standard Oil $29,240,000 for violating the Elkins Act was set aside. Since the defeat, if the Circuit Court decision should stand on appeal, threatened to reduce much of the trust-busting program to a shambles, a rallying cry was called for to encourage the sagging Administration forces. Loeb moved to provide it by declaring to the press that the Circuit Court had not touched on the merits of the case, and that of course there was no question concerning the guilt of Standard Oil.

Since the country took lively interest in the activities of the entire Roosevelt family, Loeb's communications to the press sometimes dealt with the more private happenings of the White House. Here the secretary faced innumerable situations requiring special skill and care. One of these occasions arose from seemingly innocent circumstances—the traditional Thanksgiving Day commemorations at the White House. After this particular Thanksgiving day of 1904 had ended, the Boston Herald, a paper which long had been unfriendly to the Administration, attracted nation-wide attention with a news story and an editorial devoted to the abuses suffered by a turkey given by a Bostonian, a Mr. Vose, to the White House for the holiday festivities. Mr. Vose, a turkey-grower, had for a number of years presented a prize fowl to the Roosevelt family for the holiday. A few days before the Thanksgiving in question, according to the Herald, the bird had been terribly mistreated. The Roosevelt children, said the news story, had released the turkey from its cage and chased it around the White House grounds, screaming, teasing and plucking at it, until the bird fell exhausted to the ground.

The President, it was also said, stood by, witnessing the entire cruel performance and laughing uproariously. In the face of the story and an editorial of strong moral condemnation of the President and his family, a counter-attack was called for, and Loeb, his verbal saber poised, led the charge.

"There is not one word of truth in these statements," he declared categorically in proceeding to set the record straight. Mr. Vose's bird, in point of fact, was dressed when it arrived at the White House, and was consumed at the family dinner. There had been a live turkey, to be sure, supplied, not by Mr. Vose of Boston, but by Messrs. J. Bach and Company of Milwaukee, Wisconsin. This turkey, however, had never been taken out of its box, but "because of its beauty," had been shipped to Oyster Bay, where it was reported to be "living peaceably with the rest of the inhabitants of the barnyard." Having repaired the record, Loeb proceeded to pass judgment upon the transgressor, the *Boston Herald*. The story just disproved, he coldly declared, "marks the culmination of a long series of similar falsehoods, usually malicious and always deliberate, which have appeared in the news columns of the *Boston Herald*." So sweeping a condemnation foreshadowed a penalty of merciless severity. "Until further notice," Secretary Loeb passed sentence in a statement that was circulated the length and breadth of the Executive Branch, "the departments will exclude the individuals responsible for this series of misstatements from all facilities for information." An immediate consequence of this edict was that the *Boston Herald* was cut off from all forecasts of the Weather Bureau. A strict order to this effect had gone out to the weather forecaster in Boston, the chief of the Bureau acknowledged. In making his disclosure, the chief, *The New York Times* reported, "laughed heartily."

Loeb was also involved in several private controversies of the President that were conducted at least partially in the press. In the most spectacular of these episodes, President Roosevelt was pitted against a most formidable adversary, the President of Harvard University, Charles W. Eliot. The trouble began when two members of the Harvard varsity crew, Fish and Morgan, deviously and illegally took out several books from the college library in order to expedite the progress of their Senior theses. President Eliot, a rigorous disciplinarian, hit the wrongdoers with a drastic penalty. He took the boys off the crew. Under ordinary circumstances, Dr. Eliot's course might have been commendable, or at least tolerable, but the circumstances were hardly ordinary. The Harvard crew was facing a difficult schedule, including a race with Yale. Among the staunch athletic-minded alumni who were most distressed by the severity of Dr. Eliot's action were President Roosevelt and the Assistant Secretary of State, Robert Low Bacon. The President and Bacon pooled their consternation in a joint telegram to Eliot, requesting that some other punishment be substituted to avoid the injustice of the present penalty in making the great body of the University's alumni suffer. In plain language, the boys should be put back on the crew. Replying by return telegram, President Eliot refused to budge from his decision. His adamancy was made all too discouragingly clear when, in referring to the conduct of the boys, he employed such invective as "dishonorable," "crooked" and "scurvy."

The battle between the Presidents passed into a new and more sensational phase when the exchange of telegrams was published verbatim in a New York newspaper. Hereupon, Dr. Eliot's assistant, Mr. J. D. Greene, in the manner of a second arranging a duel, wired to Loeb at Oyster Bay, "President Eliot is much concerned at publication of telegrams in New York paper with Boston date. Careful inquiry has excluded possibility of their having come from this office." Faced with this accusing innuendo, Loeb rose to the challenge. "The telegrams were certainly not published from this office," he fired, or wired, back to Mr. Greene. "As a matter of fact we have no copy of message sent by the President and Mr. Bacon, which was sent by Mr. Bacon from Washington after having been submitted to the President and approved by him. In view of their publication the President is making certain inquiries and will write President Eliot himself." Meanwhile, as T.R. frantically inquired and corresponded, the days and weeks flew by with inconclusive result. The boys remained off the crew, and Harvard, as the President had originally feared and dreaded, put in a dismal season.

Loeb's relations with individual reporters covered the gamut from intimate friendship to utter rejection. One of his closest friends was Bob Davis, whose popular column of homely philosophising appeared in the New York Sun. Some reporters knew Loeb so well that they took liberties with him in doing their day's job that they would not take with their bosses. It was nothing for Loeb to be awakened at one o'clock in the morning by his ringing telephone, and on the line would be a young Associated Press reporter inquiring after some detail he needed in order to complete a story given him in outline by his boss, the head of the local AP bureau. Loeb obligingly supplied the missing detail by repeating substantially what he had said earlier in the day to the bureau head. Why didn't the young man call his boss and obtain the information from him? Loeb was asked. "He wouldn't dare call his chief at one o'clock in the morning," muttered Loeb with sleepy equanimity.

The Secretary to the President was constantly alert in guarding reporters against the perils and pitfalls of their trade. When Oscar King Davis of The New York Times, a favorite at the White House, received from Loeb an "exclusive" consisting of the substance of a special message of the utmost significance T.R. was planning for Congress, Davis exultantly proposed to exploit the possibilities of this treasured strike to the full. Although the message had not yet been written, Davis planned to score a "beat" on all other papers with an immediate story in the *Times*. Mindful of the applicable rules of the Associated Press, to which the *Times* was subject, "Loeb warned me, earnestly," Davis has written, "to look out, or the Associated Press would fine the *Times* heavily for premature publication of a document delivered in advance, and under confidence until released." At Loeb's suggestion, he, Davis, and Davis's editor, Carr V. Van Anda, met to grapple with the problem. After some hard mulling over, they concocted a subtle and delicate formula for the news story, enabling Davis to get his "beat" without incurring a fine for premature publication.

In certain respects, Loeb was the equivalent of press secretary for the entire Executive Branch. He dealt extensively with the departments in press matters. As daily routine, he collected editorials from the nation's press dealing with various aspects of Administration policy. Sometimes, he, with the President, would draft a reply, to be issued as a White House statement, and circulate both the editorial and draft of reply to the departments for their comments. From the responses received, Loeb and his chief could improve the White House statement or commence a rethinking of departmental policy if such seemed called for. Loeb also worked closely with the departments in keeping within bounds those reporters who stood in official disfavor. A frequent practice of journalists who had become *persona non grata* at the White House was to resort to the departments for new terrain to exploit. With the alacrity of a jungle cat, Loeb throttled these switches of operation. "Let me talk to you about this man," he would admonish Secretary of War William Howard Taft concerning a reporter who had requested an interview after banishment from the White House because of repeated improprieties, "I wouldn't have anything to do with him." Taft didn't have anything to do with him. The departments, for their part, reciprocated by occasionally saving Loeb from disaster. Once, for example, the President wrote a letter to the Pope, in which several candid allusions were made to public affairs. After the letter was dispatched and was beyond recall, T.R. and Loeb fell by chance to talking about its contents. The more they talked the more clearly they saw that if the Papacy were to release the letter for publication, as well might occur, powerful and sensitive Protestant quarters would howl with criticism. The letter had to be kept from the press, but how? A further letter from the President to the Vatican, making such a request, would be terribly misunderstood and even more damaging than the first, were it to get into the press, an eventuality which had to be anticipated. After some moments of anxious exploration, Loeb hit upon a solution that proved acceptable to the President. Under its terms, Loeb wrote to the Secretary of State, John Hay, asking that he intimate as tactfully as possible to the Apostolic Delegate in Washington that, everything considered, the letter dispatched earlier to the Pope should not be published. Secretary Hay met with the Apostolic Delegate, applied his bountiful diplomatic skill, and happily saved the Administration from costly embarrrassment.

But the departments also created problems as well as solved them, and the worst of these, which drove T.R. into states of gnashing fury, was the leaking of confidential information to the press. "The President says it looks as if there is a leak in the Department," Loeb was habitually writing to the cabinet secretaries, "and he would like to be advised if you know how the information got out." Usually, Loeb didn't get very far, for the departments were as open as the breaks in a worn-out hose. The leaks which maddened T.R. most were the disclosures of happenings in meetings of the cabinet. He, like other Presidents, felt that, if there was anything which should be kept confidential, it was his consultations on the intimate business of his office with his top-ranking counselors. Despite pointed Presidential admonitions and tireless vigilance on the part of Loeb, the leaks continued until the distraught T.R. devoted a cabinet meeting to the problem. After this meeting, Loeb communicated to each cabinet secretary a rather detailed reminder of the President's expectations for the future guidance of all concerned. The President was especially distressed, Loeb pointed out, by reporters' unabashed buttonholing of department secretaries as they were leaving the cabinet room after a meeting concluded. "Reputable reporters" had been driven into this unseemly practice, said Loeb, mincing no words, because some cabinet secretaries were regularly giving out confidential information in their offices to favored correspondents. The indulgent cabinet secretary, observed Loeb somewhat clinically, was led not by malice or conspiratorial intent, but "by weakness or good nature into giving . . . information to some newspaperman whom he wishes to befriend or for whom he feels sorry." As a further precaution, Loeb notified the several press associations that henceforth no information would be given anyone by any executive source concerning the proceedings of the cabinet. This directive quickly collapsed in melancholy futility. Before many a day, leaks were merrily spouting forth again from innumerable executive apertures, with Loeb rushing hither and yon, desperately mending and plugging in his impossible assignment.

Loeb's most formidable diplomatic problems arose not in the tempestuous public relations he conducted with irate ladies, eager reporters and pompous politicos, but in preserving peace and good will between the White House and the executive departments. A conflagration was invariably smoldering in the departmental hinterlands due to T.R.'s predisposition to run the Executive Branch, from top to bottom, himself. Meddling constantly in the business of his department chiefs, going freely over their heads to deal directly with their subordinates, he blithely disregarded human feelings and the necessities of departmental authority. Loeb was at once the agent of T.R.'s mischief, carrying out the diabolical assignments involved, and the source of redress—a stroker of ruffled egos, a giver of hope, a channel to the President. For all of the awkwardness of his position, the secretary maintained a rapport of unbroken friendliness with all the membership of the cabinet. He was the good fellow everybody liked and understood. He was especially close to James R. Garfield, Elihu Root and John Hay, and closest of all to Oscar Straus, Secretary of Commerce and Labor. Loeb, as a matter of fact, journeyed up to New York in 1906 to offer the cabinet post to Straus.

No President of the United States tinkered more with departmental minutiae than T.R. Loeb worked overtime in couching T.R.'s projects of outrageous intervention in language of minimum offensiveness. As a former United States Civil Service Commissioner, Theodore Roosevelt was, more than most Presidents, interested and involved in the everyday personnel problems of the executive departments. Through Loeb, he kept abreast of scores of details that most executives would do without and was a force to be reckoned with in the promotions and assignments of civil service employees. If, for example, a Civil War veteran was long languishing in his departmental job without a promotion or salary increment and he complained of his lot to the President, most likely he'd strike a sympathetic response. In behalf of such forgotten men, Loeb customarily looked into the situation on the assumption, articulated to department heads in clear and persuasive English, that if a promotion could be made, "we would like this done." T.R. and Loeb, in their ministrations, dealt not only with the employees, but even with their wives. When a vacancy arose in the upper echelons of one department, for example, the spouse of a man who was serving in a somewhat lower rank and conceivably might be considered for the vacancy, boldly wrote to the President, in terms of glowing uxorial praise, proposing her husband for the post. Loeb, as he was apt to do, looked into the matter, and on the basis of his findings, T.R. replied to the anxiously waiting wife. The President was candid. The position under consideration, "the most important in the Bureau," he pointed out, could not be held by any man "who is not on hand always and able to devote his sole attention to it." Unfortunately, he fearlessly went on to state, spurred by Loeb's report, her husband failed on both counts.

Where White House interests were at stake, Loeb was frequently involved in departmental dealings with Congress. His most trying duty was to watch over the progress of bills on Capitol Hill and the conduct of the departments which might help or interfere with the President's objectives.

Committees of Congress, for example, would request a given department to express its views on pending legislation. Loeb's concern, or big headache, was to see that the President's interests were adequately reflected in the department's response. "If the anti-trust bill is sent to you," Loeb would write to the Attorney General, "the President wishes you to talk to him about it before making your report thereon to the committee of Congress." If the President was puzzled whether to sign or veto a bill, Loeb might solicit the recommendations of the departments most concerned to assist in the ultimate decision or to provide the substance of the veto should one be issued. Department heads, for their part, prized Loeb as a counselor on the tactics they might employ in bringing their views on legislation before the President. When an immigration bill was developing in Congress, for example, Oscar Straus, the Secretary of Commerce and Labor, was convinced that a substantial educational test should be incorporated into the bill as part of the immigration procedures. He vaguely recalled that the President was opposed to such a step. Was T.R.'s position, if he had one, tentative or absolute? Should Straus see the President and press his views? Loeb frankly advised the Secretary of Commerce that T.R.'s mind was unalterably made up against the test. Straus thus was spared the embarrassment of imposing a futile conference upon a busy President.

Loeb was especially apt to be involved with Congress in departmental dealings which bore tangibly upon party matters. This kind of situation could sometimes be quite difficult, as the one which transpired in Loeb's office one summer morning in 1908 proved. On hand was a crabbed aggressive citizen, a thoroughly unendearing type of mankind, with both Senators of his native state of South Dakota. The mean citizen was an Indian trader whose license had been suspended by the Commissioner of Indian Affairs, F. E. Leupp, for ample cause. After numerous complaints, each of which was thoroughly investigated by his staff, Commissioner Leupp had concluded that the trader had been mercilessly hornswoggling countless Indians, practicing a business morality nearly on a par with that of a storied predecessor who acquired fifty thousand mineral-rich acres for a pint of watered whiskey. Following his suspension, the South Dakotan trader had made a large cash contribution to the Republican presidential campaign of 1904. On this particular morning in Loeb's office, the trader blusteringly made clear that as quid pro quo for his sacrificial act he deserved reinstatement so that he could continue his business career among the Indians. The South Dakota Senators limply accepted this point of view, but Loeb did not. In plain talk of which he was capable he informed the trader that a campaign contribution provided no basis whatsoever for his reinstatement. Furthermore, said Loeb, with a dire air, any such suggestion would surely anger the President. For his own sake, therefore, the trader had better forget about accosting the Chief

Executive with his brazen appeal. So forceful and so convincing was Loeb that his unscrupulous listener withdrew, together with his Senatorial entourage, who wore noticeable expressions of relief and satisfaction upon their faces. Thanks to Loeb, they had been spared an uproarious interview with the President.

Loeb also had to relate himself to his several fellow members of the presidential inner circle. Theodore Roosevelt, although seemingly impulsive (an impression he liked to cultivate) and self-reliant, valued counsel. He sought out and listened to what others had to say, and then acted according to his own judgment. To this end, he drew around himself a substantial and often changing circle of friends of varying talents, opinions and interests. His favorite counselors, in addition to James R. Garfield, the Secretary of the Interior; Elihu Root, Secretary of War and State; William Howard Taft, Secretary of War; Gifford Pinchot, chief of the Forest Service; and Loeb, were drawn from outside the Executive Branch. Senators, financiers, industrialists, educators, and even foreign ambassadors, most persistently populated his inner circle. The most important and the most enduring of the nonexecutive membership was Henry Cabot Lodge. Wealthy and patrician, cold and distant, the Senator from Massachusetts enjoyed enormous prestige on both sides of the aisle in the upper house. A prolific writer, even while in public life, he was known widely and admiringly as the "scholar in politics." "Father looked up to him and considered him something rather special," the President's daughter, Alice Roosevelt Longworth, has written of Lodge. One day, when a foreign diplomat was quizzing T.R., seeking to determine his position on a matter, the President admonished, "Go to Senator Lodge and talk with him. There is no one who knows my mind better and whom I trust more." Lodge was in and out of the White House nearly as often as he was in and out of his palatial home on Massachusetts Avenue. Yet, although T.R. consulted Lodge on multitudinous problems, the nexus was an uneasy one. Early in the presidency, Henry Adams had predicted that the two would not be long in falling out. "The most dangerous rock on Theodore's coast is Cabot," Adams had said. "We all look for the inevitable shipwreck there." After two years had passed without fatal incident, Adams was pleased to acknowledge his error. But a barrier always remained. Originally Lodge had been mentor of Roosevelt's political career, securing his appointment as Civil Service Commissioner, and smoothing the way to the Assistant Secretaryship of the Navy. But with T.R.'s assumption of the Presidency, the positions of the partners became transposed. T.R. for the first time was in ascendance. The ambitious, aggressive, willful Lodge doubtless contributed much less to the ensuing adjustment than the generous openhearted Roosevelt. As for Loeb, he always was on good footing with the difficult Senator. It was Lodge who, subsequent to William Howard Taft's election to the Presidency in 1908, journeyed to Augusta, Georgia, to propose to the President-elect the inclusion of Loeb in a key place in the future Administration.

Among those closest to Roosevelt, was Jules Jusserand, the French Ambassador to the United States, dean of the diplomatic corps and T.R.'s favorite tennis partner. Bearded, delicate in complexion, short in stature, charming and vivacious, Jusserand exuded learning. Like Lodge and T.R., he combined successful literary and political careers. Evenly matched at tennis, the President and Jusserand would devote the better part of an afternoon to the game, or walk about T.R.'s favorite haunt, Rock Creek Park, consulting on policy or losing themselves in some frivolity, such as seeing who could recall the most passages from *Alice in Wonderland.*

Of the businessmen intimates, perhaps the one of longest standing was George W. Perkins, partner of J. P. Morgan and architect of the labyrinthian corporate structure establishing United States Steel. Perkins's "straightforwardness and intelligence will commend to you whatever he has to say," wrote Speaker Tom Reed in introducing the business magnate to Roosevelt. Indeed they did, for T.R. persistently consulted Perkins in matters of business regulation. T.R. also turned to the universities, and especially to Nicholas Murray Butler, President of Columbia. They corresponded on a broad miscellany of affairs, and were companions on the President's long Western tour in the summer of 1903. Because Perkins and Butler were in Washington only occasionally, their relations with Loeb were casual but pleasant. Others penetrated the inner circle from time to time, of whom Speck von Sternberg, the German Ambassador; Leonard Wood, the physician-general; and Benjamin Jones, the Pittsburgh industrialist, are representative.

The inner circle must be viewed in conjunction with the famous "Tennis Cabinet." Some, but not all, of the inner circle membership belonged to the "Tennis Cabinet." Likewise, some but not all of the Tennis Cabinet enjoyed admittance to the inner circle. And, to compound the confusion, not everyone in the Tennis Cabinet played tennis, a circumstance which periodically evoked the guffaws of the President and his aides. The "membership" of this phantasmagorial institution comprised T.R.'s companions in his several favorite branches of applied athletics, whether tennis, hiking, or hunting. At least several of these playtime companions were clearly neither qualified nor inclined to advise on official problems. Jack Abernathy, for example, was an Oklahoma cowboy who wrestled wolves and provided T.R. with many a happy hour by boxing with him in the White House. "Jack, are you doing your best?" the President would ask as they poked and puffed their way around the library. Loeb first met Abernathy when the Oklahoman barged into the secretary's office wearing cowboy pants and a six-shooter, the carrying of which into the Executive Mansion violated a cardinal rule of the Secret Service. To forestall this onrushing menace, an usher had asked for his card. "I don't carry cards," snorted Abernathy. The usher futilely followed him into Loeb's office. "I know you Mr. Abernathy," Loeb said amiably, overlooking the several infractions, "the President told me so much about you that I know you without an introduction."

The President's favorite tennis companions were Jusserand, Lodge, Garfield and William Phillips of the State Department. Captain McCoy of the Secret Service and Archie Butt, his military aide, played occasionally, and Loeb rarely. Tennis occupied the better part of an afternoon following a late lunch, a period T.R. always reserved for exercise. Seven sets were the rule, after which T.R. and his guests would stomp into the White House for his favorite repast of orangeade and gingersnaps. The single-known exception to this simple observance, which endured until Loeb broke upon the scene with urgent business, was the farewell luncheon held by the Tennis Cabinet in the closing days of the Administration. Fully thirty-one "members" of that amorphous body were on hand, including Loeb. The luncheon table was bedecked with tennis emblems and "Teddy bears." Earlier in the day, T.R. had presented each of the assembled guests with his personal memento—a make-believe commission of appointment to the Tennis Cabinet, with the full-fashioned phrase and ample ornamentation of a solemn state document. Sentiment overlay the gathering in bulging clouds, and a rain of tears almost fell as Jusserand rose to present the gift of the Tennis Cabinet to the President. The ambassador spoke sincerely and beautifully, except for occasional difficulty with his English pronunciation. Although a man of distinguished literary attainment, Jusserand never did master the phonetical eccentricities of the language. Near the close of his remarks, he held out the group gift, and said, climactically, "and I have the honor to beg your acceptance of this silver bowl" (pronouncing "bowl" to rhyme with "howl"). Everyone indeed howled, and the sadness of the moment was forgotten.

William Loeb's proudest accomplishment in his tour of duty transpired not in his lively office in the national capital, but in the desolation of the river front of Brooklyn. There nestled in the infinite acres of shabby buildings, littered weedy expanses and weathered docks, was the Havemeyer and Elder refinery of the American Sugar Company of New York, a constituent company of the famous Sugar Trust. It was here that a colossal and unremitting fraud was perpetrated against the government of the United States until it was discovered and exposed through the courage and pertinacity of William Loeb and several executive colleagues.

Under federal law, a customs duty of one and a half cents per pound was levied on every bag of sugar entering the United States. Customs officers determined the tax by weighing the sugar coming off a ship on giant Fairbanks scales, placed at intervals along the docks. All seventeen of the scales employed at the Havemeyer plant belonged to the company. Each scale was flush with the surface of the dock, while the brass bar, by which the weight was read, was inside a little house fronted with glass, which enabled the weigher to see the platform and its load as he adjusted the poise. Also inside the house, behind the registering bar, were two men, each with a small blank book reposing on a ledge or desk. One man was the government weigher, the other the company checker. In their respective books, they recorded the agreed weight of each bag of sugar as it emerged from shipboard and was placed upon the scales.

As early as 1904, T.R. himself has written, Loeb began expressing his suspicions that the Sugar Trust was defrauding the government in its importations through the New York Customs House. The suspicions were stoked to a flaming pitch near the close of that year when Richard Parr, a sampler at the New York Appraisers' Stores, whose duties took him upon the Brooklyn docks, called at Loeb's office with fresh and impressive evidence that the Elder refinery was cheating the government by manipulating the dock scales. The excited Parr volunteered to become a Treasury Department investigator at once, in order to acquire necessary additional evidence to establish the crime of fraud in a court of law. A solid man, whose inveterate bowler crowned piercing eyes and a long sharp nose, which seemed instinctively to sniff for trouble, Parr had been an old schoolmate of Loeb's in Albany. Convinced that Parr was "efficient, honest, and loyal," Loeb was determined that this new information shoud be acted upon. He lost no time in urging upon the President Parr's appointment as a special investigator. Roosevelt approved, but the Treasury Department reported that it had no vacancy, although it did agree to appoint Parr at the very first opportunity.

In the spring of 1905, Parr, still awaiting a vacancy, again came to the White House with even more imposing information, which sent Loeb scurrying to his chief. T.R. was impressed that further delay was intolerable and he ordered the Treasury to appoint Parr to its force at once. After tours of duty in Boston and Portland, Parr was convinced that his Treasury superiors had all along meant to keep him out of New York. In desperation, he appealed to Loeb to pull wires for a transfer to that city so that the sugar frauds, which were rolling lustily onward, could be investigated. Loeb importuned the President, who ordered the Secretary of the Treasury to transfer Parr to New York and to keep watch that officials of the departmental

Customs Service did not sabotage the investigation. By now it was all too clear to Loeb, T.R. and the Secretary of the Treasury that Customs was honeycombed with corruption. Another agent, James O. Brzezinski, was detailed to assist Parr on the case, and it was arranged that the investigators would report their progress periodically to Loeb, who, in turn, would keep the President posted.

Parr and Brzezinski took up their vigil in New York and, one day in November, a break finally came. Another Treasury agent, a Richard Whalley, informed Parr that he had noticed lately how, whenever a draft of sugar was placed upon the scales, the company checker in the weighing house dropped his left hand to his side in a peculiar way. A plan was arranged, calling for Parr and Brzezinski to come to the dock on the morning of November twentieth, at ten o'clock. Whalley, in the normal course of things, was due to weigh in the sugar with the company checker in the scale-house. It was agreed that if on that morning the checker should engage in any suspicious gestures, Whalley would raise his hat, whereupon Parr and Brzezinski would come rushing in.

On the appointed day, Parr and his aide appeared on the dock as drafts of sugar were being weighed. Whalley was in the scale-house and another government inspector was outside, directing the sugar to the scales. Upon a motion from Parr, the inspector outside stopped the last three drafts of sugar which had just been weighed on the company scale. The drafts were now reweighed with most significant results. The draft last removed from the scales registered exactly the same the second time. But of the two other drafts, one weighed fourteen pounds more than it had when it was first weighed three minutes before, and the other eighteen pounds more. As the reweighing was proceeding, Whalley's hat went up. Parr slipped into the scale-house unnoticed by the company checker, who was crouching in a curious fashion, his back turned to the door, and his left arm thrust down in a corner under the ledge behind which he sat.

Moving swiftly upon the company checker, Parr sat down in the checker's place. A moment's groping revealed that under the ledge by his left knee was a spring with a curved handle. In further pokings, Parr saw how the spring of the steel exerted force upon the levers and made the registering beam drop. By careful testing, Parr found that a pressure of one ounce on the spring produced a loss of forty-eight ounces on the platform outside. As the vindicated investigator prepared to report his triumphant discoveries to Loeb, he had to surmount a further obstacle—a bribe of one thousand dollars which the dock superintendent of Havemeyer and Elder kept thrusting frantically into his face. In return for his generosity, the superintendent was later subjected to criminal indictment and imprisonment.

After a briefing from Loeb on Parr's stupendous findings, President

Roosevelt ordered prosecutions to be begun at once and put Henry L. Stimson, United States District Attorney for Eastern New York, in charge of the case. Stimson had previously distinguished himself in sugar trust litigation, and in his new assignment he was assisted by the cream of the Justice Department legal corps, which then included the youthful Felix Frankfurter. This was fortunate, for the government was opposed by a task force of juridical Goliaths corralled from the best Manhattan law firms, and headed by John E. Parsons, general counsel of the American Sugar Refining Company, and John B. Stanchfield, the eminent trial attorney. The trial against the Sugar Trust lasted an entire month, although the jury was out for only an hour. The verdict returned was for the government, which recovered some four million dollars in customs duties of which it had been defrauded. Judgment was entered on March 5, 1909, the day Roosevelt left office. Subsequent civil and criminal proceedings meted out punishment to irresponsible company officers and bribers, and Inspector Brzezinski, who had nearly wrecked the government's case by committing perjury, was hustled off to jail. For his arduous and distinguished investigation, Parr was awarded one hundred thousand dollars by the top command of the Treasury Department, a rare expression of governmental gratitude. As for Loeb, he basked contentedly in his own satisfaction and the radiant approval of the President.

Next to the mighty T.R., William Howard Taft owed his nomination for the Presidency in 1908 to William Loeb, Jr., more than to any other man. T.R.'s decision not to run for a "third" term was taken with insoluble doubt and gnawing reluctance. Still a young man, only fifty years of age, he would gladly have persisted in his office, rather than fall into a limbo of anticlimax for the remainder of his years. Throughout the autumn of his second presidential term, he was running on a mental treadmill, making and unmaking his decision not to run. Finally, one January morning in 1908, Loeb, who appreciated the political importance of settling the matter, emphatically pointed out to his chief the necessity for a firm decision to avoid the risk of a party draft for the nomination. It wasn't renomination that troubled T.R., but the fear that the electorate, offended by his violation of the time-honored tradition against a third term for any President, would reject his candidacy at the polls. If T.R. decided not to run, Loeb pointed out in his entreaties, sufficient time had to be allowed to build up Taft, his chosen successor. After some further discussion on that January morning, T.R. surrendered totally and unconditionally by expressing complete agreement with Loeb's position. The President immediately dispatched his secretary to Taft to convey the final momentous intelligence that the Secretary of War was the appointed and anointed successor. Several days after his conference with Taft, Loeb provided the necessary public disclosure of the great decision when the press brought to his attention the prediction of a leading Minnesota Republican that Roosevelt would be renominated. This forecast Loeb dismissed as "ridiculous" and confidently declared that Taft would be nominated on the first ballot.

Loeb worked overtime at converting his prophesy into reality. He tackled the mountainous task of lining up state delegations for Taft and, utilizing his encyclopedic knowledge of local Republican personalities, he counseled the presidential aspirant on the selection of state managers for the campaign. Where local or state organizations resisted the gaining movement for Taft, Loeb plotted strategy with the local leaders sympathetic to Taft for starting "back fires" in the regular organizations. In Taft's behalf, he likewise made soundings of party sentiment concerning the several contenders for the Vice-presidential nomination. Meanwhile, T.R. was moving to assure Loeb's presence at the convention, as one of two delegates from the Queens-Nassau Congressional district to which Oyster Bay belonged. The President especially wanted Loeb at the convention "because when he speaks for me we get all the effect of an authoritative statement on my part with none of the attendant disagreeable features." But alas for T.R. and Loeb, the Queens-Nassau Republican organization was bitterly disgruntled, to the point of revolt, over the distribution of patronage in T.R.'s administration. For eight full years, the organization felt, it had been insultingly slighted. The opportunity for retaliation was at hand. With quiet dispatch, the Nassau organization rejected the Secretary to the President as a delegate. Loeb, who quickly surmounted the disappointment, cheerily sent Taft off to the convention with a ringing cliché, "May the steamroller smother all our foes!"

Taft was nominated, and Loeb, although rejected as a delegate, was widely talked of as the next chairman of the Republican National Committee. "You are absolutely the best man in the country to be Chairman of the National Committee, and I hope the Committee will unanimously tender you the position and that you will accept," one state leader expressed the widely entertained sentiment. So persistent became the rumors of Loeb as National Chairman-to-be, that Taft felt driven to issue a statement denying that the secretary had been or would in future be offered the post. Loeb, Taft declared to the press, planned to go into business at the close of the Roosevelt Administration. Whether this statement was cleared beforehand with the secretary is uncertain. As the campaign proceeded, Loeb neither went into business nor became party chairman, but oversaw the New York state political situation and arranged local speaking engagements for the presidential nominee.

The Republican triumph in November raised even more sharply the question of Loeb's future. Would he move into business as Taft had disclosed in June? A business career, indeed, had been long impending. A year before the President-elect's pronouncement, *The New York Times* had reported that Loeb, upon conclusion of the Roosevelt Administration, might become President of the Washington Railway and Electric Company, or possibly of other mentioned enterprises, but this did not materialize. In the final year of the Administration, Loeb indeed was probing several opportunities in the insurance and railroad industries, and his friend, Secretary of Commerce and Labor Straus (in private life President of the American Smelting and Refining Company), was also watching for a suitable niche in the business world in Loeb's behalf. On the basis of his several explorations, Loeb seems to have concluded that he would do better to continue in the Taft Administration. The correspondence of President Taft suggests that Loeb may have been briefly interested in a cabinet appointment, but the latter's friends hold that he never suffered any illusions over his availability for a place in the Taft cabinet, for he assumed, quite realistically, that he could not be an intimate in the new Administration after having been one in the old. The most suitable post would be one situated an ample distance from the capital. The Collectorship of the Port of New York, to which Loeb was eventually appointed, admirably satisfied his necessities. Even more important, Theodore Roosevelt, who proposed the appointment to the President-elect, was delighted. "The collectorship of the port of New York is a very important office which he can fill with the utmost credit to himself and the utmost advantage to the public and to your administration," T.R. wrote to Taft. The President-elect acquiesced to the appointment with genuine good feeling. "It will give me the greatest pleasure to carry it out," he wrote to Loeb on January 7, 1909. "There is not any man in the United States to whom I feel more grateful and for whom I have more pleasure in doing the right thing than you."

While preparing for the transition to the collectorship of the New York port, Loeb was assisting the exodus of the beloved T.R. from Washington. After the inaugural proceedings were concluded, Roosevelt retreated briefly into the halls of Congress and, to facilitate his get-away, emerged a few minutes later from a little door under the steps of the main entrance to the Senate wing. An awaiting throng of New York Republicans rushed forward to pick up T.R. and, holding him aloft, toted him to his carriage. Several thousand onlookers laughed affectionately. "Good-bye, Mr. President," came the cries from the crowd. "You're all right," "Good luck"; hundreds of hand flags waved. The double surrey, with the ex-President and Mrs. Roosevelt in the back seat and Loeb opposite them, drove off to Union Station. Nearly one thousand members of the New York County Republican Club formed and marched as a hollow square around the onrolling carriage. A large brass band headed the procession, and trailing behind came long lines of spectators on each side of the street. T.R., although not an emotional man, evidently felt keenly the tribute being paid him, and Loeb, eying his chief quizzically, wore a suspicion of a smile. The procession bore the departing T.R. right to the President's waiting room in the big new railroad station. There, until his train pulled out, T.R. received admirers and well-wishers, Loeb taking his place by the door, out of habit, to regulate the human traffic.

T.R. went on to his beloved Sagamore Hill and Loeb took up his duties as Collector in New York. His service, extending from 1909 to 1913, was, by general agreement, distinguished. He gave the Customs House the thoroughgoing shaking up so long overdue. The corruption and bumbling inefficiency, which for years had cost the government millions of dollars, were replaced by administration immeasurably more honest and alert. While cleaning up the port, Loeb also functioned as occasional political adviser and assistant to his former chief. When T.R. was in Africa on his famous hunting trip, Loeb, in his cabled wisdom, exhorted T.R. not to give out anything on politics, but to tend strictly to his business in the jungle. This advice T.R. heeded. Loeb made the arrangements for T.R.'s triumphal return to New York, faithfully meeting the former President's specifications that any commemorations be on a "big scale" or not at all, and that no one speak "but myself, save the Mayor or whoever introduces me." The result was a grand jamboree in Madison Square Garden exactly as Roosevelt had stipulated. When President Taft showed interest in coming up to New York to share in the homecoming, it was Loeb who faced up to the task of dissuading the President by admonishing, "It will be a T.R. day and there will be no other note sounded."

In the tragic break between Roosevelt and Taft, Loeb walked the impossible tightrope of remaining loyal to both. He begged Roosevelt not to bolt the party in 1912, but to sit out the election, and allow Taft to be nominated and defeated. In 1916, Loeb argued, Roosevelt would be the inevitable Republican nominee. T.R. nevertheless bolted in 1912; Loeb stayed with the regulars and proceeded to the Republican convention in Chicago chiefly to work with his old friend Cortelyou to build support for Roosevelt's nomination in 1916.

With the advent of the presidential administration of Woodrow Wilson in 1913, Loeb resigned his collectorship to commence his long-pending business career as manager of the Guggenheim properties. After several years, Oscar Straus, now full-time President of the American Smelting and Refining Company, brought Loeb into the enterprise as vice-president. Loeb's tenure in the post extended until 1934, when he retired. Along the way, he assumed the directorships in a number of concerns, including the Connecticut Light and Power Company and the Angola Company. When he died in 1937, he left a modest fortune. The earlier portion of his business career Loeb passed as the next-door neighbor of T.R. In 1914, after resigning the collectorship, Loeb purchased a five-acre shore-front estate, "Westerleigh," adjoining Sagamore Hill. For five idyllic years, until T.R. died in 1919, the constant friends reminisced and communed on the domestic political scene and the cataclysm of World War I.

Although T.R., the central event of Loeb's life, had departed, the remainder of the perfect stenographer's days were devoted in no little way to the honor of his old and revered chief. Loeb was a founder and president of the Roosevelt Memorial Association and, each year, as long as he lived, he accompanied a little band of former associates who, on the anniversary of T.R.'s birth, made a pilgrimage to the hilltop grave in Oyster Bay. After laying a wreath, the following, which regularly included James R. Garfield, Gifford Pinchot, William Allen White and Herbert Knox Smith, would adjourn to Sagamore Hill and there, in the paneled grace of the North Room, surrounded by mounted moose heads, ivory tusks, bearskin rugs and other proud mementos of the Strenuous Life, they read aloud from T.R.'s works, told stories and recollected experiences of the incomparable old days. No one was more committed in heart and mind in these simple devotions than William Loeb.

Sphinx in a Soft Hat

EDWARD M. HOUSE

IN THE autumn of 1912, just after the presidential election, there was published what was undoubtedly one of the worst novels of the year, *Philip Dru, Administrator*. A hybrid romantic novel and utopian political tract, *Philip Dru*'s clumsiness of form repelled most reviewers, although the daring of its ideas fascinated some. The first draft of the book was dashed off in a mere thirty days during the better part of which the author was sick in bed with influenza. There wasn't much time for polishing after that, because the author, who remained anonymous, had been deeply involved in the presidential campaign of 1912. He was in actuality Edward Mandell House, then a Texan of modest fame.

Viewed in the light of the subsequent history of Mr. House, however, every page of *Philip Dru* ought to have been read and pondered by every American of the day as an obligation of citizenship comparable to that of paying taxes. For *Philip Dru*, in at least one respect, is a most extraordinary volume. It is nothing less than a coolly delineated master plan, a prolegomenon, of House's considerable future activities in the presidential Administration of Woodrow Wilson.

Philip Dru centers upon two principal characters, a fictional President of the United States and his chief counselor and assistant. The President, who was Dru, was the symbolic equivalent of George Washington and Abraham Lincoln rolled into one in the hearts of his countrymen. Dru soared to his haloed heights by virtue of being the force of a great social regeneration. His Administration, as he declared in his inaugural, was dedicated to "the unhappy many who have lived and died lacking opportunity, because, in the starting, the world-wide social structure was wrongly begun." Reformer Dru instituted measures placing corporations under stringent national control, abolishing holding companies and socializing the telephone and telegraph. The worker was protected against his most dreaded hazards by a full-employment law and old age and unemployment insurance, and represented on the boards of corporations under equitable profit-sharing arrangements. The farmer entered a new dawn of prosperous self-esteem by conducting his production and marketing through fair-dealing co-operatives.

190

Dru's beneficence was by no means confined to the American homeland. He was by all odds the mightiest and most constructive force of his time in world affairs. Crusader against tyranny in any guise, he smote down history's worst autocracies in a terrible war. The new order he raised out of the ruins of the old was a structure of lasting peace, founded on the prevalence of democracy everywhere, general disarmament and the clear demarcation of zones of influence for all the great powers.

Despite his considerable achievements, Dru in actuality was little more than the ornamental exterior of his Administration's greatness. Its real shaping and energizing spirit was his unseen assistant, the trusted, all-wise Selwyn. Originator of ideas, architect of plans, dauntless trouble shooter, Selwyn was the dominant force of the Administration. Responsible only to Dru, he was virtually unknown to the public. His comings and goings were shrouded in absolute secrecy. He was never photographed, his name rarely appeared in the press, and he never submitted to interviews, laughingly ridding himself of reporters by saying always that he knew nothing of importance. None of his colleagues partook of his confidence, and thereby he avoided the most forbidding hazard of his occupation, betrayal. As a matter of fact, Selwyn dealt with but few public men. For politicians, such as legislators and party workers, he had only contempt. Early in his career, Selwyn had observed that public affairs in the United States, as elsewhere, are really run by a handful of men behind a façade of democratic politics. Outside the little circle of the influential, no one counts. Selwyn deliberately dominated that circle, systematically building up his role, and dwarfing all others by his influence.

Why did the mighty Selwyn hide his true greatness? The considerations were largely practical. It was a way of avoiding any personal responsibility for the results of his influence. If things went wrong, if policies misfired, another took the blame; public opinion could never reach him. Secrecy, too, was a shield against the crush and ennui of hundreds of personal contacts. Although dedicated to the welfare of man in the mass, Selwyn regarded man in particular as a fool and a bore. But Selwyn, for all of his pragmatism, satisfied a certain aesthetic appetite in his *modus operandi*. It was intellectually challenging, requiring considerable agility in design and movement, to manipulate a nation's affairs as he did without exposing one's true role. There was an even greater delight. It tickled a puerile streak in his fancy to cheat History itself of all knowledge of his deeds. Being a presidential counselor was a kind of prank. But the most intriguing thing about Selwyn is that in writing of him, Edward M. House was in actuality writing about himself.

Colonel House in the flesh was a fitting replica of Selwyn. To the American public, House exuded a cultivated air of quiet inscrutability. Beneath the bold arc of his mauve fedora was a spare impeccable figure with catlike eyes, Mongolian cheekbones, and a short, flawlessly clipped mustache. His manner was one of disciplined gentility, unmistakably suggesting that his most natural habitat was a Louis XIV drawing room where, surrounded by his books and teacups, he could watch mankind stumbling by, chasing after folly. If, as often happened, the chaos became unbearable, he could reach out, flick a knob and set the world aright. His hands were small and soft like those of a woman. Should speech be necessary, his vocal delivery had a controlled huskiness such as one uses in cathedrals. The most he allowed for emphasis or excitement was to enunciate slowly, making protracted pauses between each syllable. His most extravagant exuberance was a brief smile, or, in a rare explosion, a half chuckle. In conversation, he exercised that complete control of facial expression that is so often the proud professional accomplishment of the vice-president of a bank.

The only blemish upon House's imposing gentility was his birth in 1858 in Texas, shaggy land of cactus, longhorns and bad men. Billy the Kid was at the height of his outlawry, and Sam Houston, the state's own facsimile of George Washington, was rounding out his Governorship. Duels were commonplace, and House felt it wise to pass many an hour before his mirror practicing the quick draw. He was deft with his hands. For years, even after becoming a national figure, he could throw eight pebbles, carried in his pocket, into the air and catch them all. Except for one or two minor skirmishes, his shooting skill was never tested. If anything, House's boyhood surroundings were secure, comfortable, even plushy. His father was a wealthy entrepreneur with many irons in the fire. Banker, fleet operator in the coastal trade, cotton and sugar planter, his holdings covered the better part of Fort Bend and Brazoria counties. The elder House derived his initial capital from highly successful blockade-running operations in the Civil War. Many a night, father and small son would clamber onto the rooftop of their home, which covered an entire block in Galveston, and scan the horizon to determine the positions of the Union gunboats. The reward of this circumspection was an accumulation of a tidy three hundred thousand dollars by the end of the war. The Houses wisely built their hoard not out of Confederate money, but of gold securely deposited with Baring Brothers in London.

After the war, the Houses, who had a knack for outriding disaster, withdrew from the collapsing Southland, and crossed the seas to peaceful England. Although proudly English in orientation, the House family goes back to Holland, where the name was Huis. Some ancestor at some time migrated to England, where the family lingered three hundred years before the Colonel's father ran off to Texas.

In England, Edward Mandell—the "Mandell" derived from a Jewish Houston merchant and intimate family friend—was enrolled in a first-rate public school, which by all accounts did him little good. After two years of abortive education, the family—consisting of seven children, of which Edward was the youngest—returned to the United States.

There shortly ensued an occurrence of enormous significance to House. At the age of twelve, he suffered a high fall from a swing. Although he miraculously avoided death, brain fever set in, and permanently bedeviled him as an incurable affliction. A few years later, his health was further battered when he succumbed first to malaria and then a sunstroke. The resulting enfeeblement shaped his entire future career. For years he had to shepherd his fragile health by never holding down a regular job, by sleeping in a bed whose head was raised five inches by blocks to facilitate his breathing, by taking protracted vacations in New England and abroad, and by shunning humid places like Washington, D.C., in the summertime. By faithfully adhering to this regimen and spurning all blandishments to depart it, including those extended by the President of the United States, House lived to the ripe old age of eighty.

The death of his mother when he was but fourteen shunted House off to more private schools, including Hopkins Grammar in New Haven, a preparatory school for Yale. Finishing at Hopkins, House's hopes were set on Yale, but deficiencies in certain subjects kept him out. He went instead to Cornell, although his heart belonged to Yale. It was with the latter university that he deposited his voluminous personal papers at the close of his public career. At Cornell, House achieved something of a reputation as a campus diplomat, his skillful peacemaking settling many a dormitory row. "He had an exceptionally sweet disposition," a fellow student put it, "he got on with everyone." As a scholar, House was undistinguished. By his own confession, he neglected his courses until the very last minute and by concentrated boning barely passed his examinations. "I didn't give a hang for my studies," House frankly evaluated his encounter with higher education. "There were just two subjects that did interest me from my childhood— politics and history—and I read everything on those subjects that I could get my hands on. But I cared about nothing else." Thanks to a classmate at Hopkins Grammar, Oliver T. Morton, son of the Indiana Senator, House could traverse from his books on occasion to the working world of politics. The high point of his several peregrinations into reality was a visit to the White House with personal introductions to President and Mrs. Grant and the entire cabinet.

House's political reconnoitering and academic studies were abruptly terminated in his second year at Cornell by the death of his father in 1880. The resulting multifarious heritage was divided among the seven sons, House acquiring the cotton plantations and a sizable treasure of choice stocks and bonds. Altogether, the young man's inherited properties were expected to yield and did yield, an income in the neighborhood of twenty-five thousand dollars a year the rest of his life. While in the midst of rearranging his affairs, House took a bride, the beautiful, charming Loulie Hunter of Hunter, Texas. After a year of European travel, the newlyweds settled briefly in Houston and then moved to Austin, where the climate was better suited to House's health and where also the seat of the Public Land Office was located, through which House might more conveniently develop his holdings. Most important of all, given House's appetite for politics, Austin was the capital of Texas.

High Mongolian cheekbones were not House's only Oriental character-istic. He had the Asiatic's large capacity for planning and conceptualizing his life and adhering vigorously to the design he evolved. Cushioned by indestructable income, he decided while in his twenties that he could devote his terrestrial years to no higher purpose than influencing the progress of public affairs. He never faltered in that decision until the day of his death in 1938. In launching his new career, the youthful House first hired a pro-fessional agriculturalist to whose management he entrusted his plantations. His own released time House devoted to electing to public office, as he put it, "men of integrity and intelligence." House himself never sought public office, lacking stamina for the daily grind and the personal force customarily requisite for the winning of elections. By influencing the deserving men who could win, House hoped to root out evil and institute progressive legislation in the image of *Philip Dru* to improve the lot of the common man. For the next few years, House proceeded to beat the political brush for his candidate. Renting a tiny office near the capitol, and pasting his calling card on its door, the eager tyro operated out of it, building up his contacts.

After careful seeking, House concluded that he could do no better than support the re-election of Governor James S. Hogg in 1892. Fearless and blustery as a tornado, Hogg in his first term had battled for regulatory legis-lation for the railroads against the vested interests led by Collis P. Hunting-ton and the horrendous financial might of the Southern Pacific. Hogg not only lost his fight, but went into the electoral campaign solidly opposed by the business community. "We had no money," observed House, "and every daily paper in Texas was against us." To offset the tremendous odds, House, then thirty-four, advanced upon the Governor, offering help provided it was kept anonymous. An unofficial campaign committee was quietly organized, with House as chairman. Working independently of the regular party organ-izations, House painstakingly set up volunteer committees of energetic and dedicated citizens in precincts and election districts throughout the state.

After a hard campaign, or "battle royal," as House called it, in which the volunteer committees played a central part, Hogg was re-elected. At the ensuing victory dinners, House himself took no stage calls; the single ac-knowledgment he tolerated was an honorary Texas colonelcy conferred by the grateful Hogg. House first knew of the honor when a suit box arrived one morning containing the commission and a dress uniform complete with aiguillettes, epaulettes and gold braid. House is not known ever to have worn the uniform.

From 1894 to 1902, House did for three other Texas governors what he had done for Hogg. In the successive victories of Charles A. Culberson and Joseph D. Sayers, each for one term, and Thomas W. Gregory for two terms, House was the unofficial campaign manager, expertly and anonymously heading the march to victory. In the decade and more of his electoral invincibility, House was titillated that the public, ignorant of his contribution, gave all credit to the official party chairman. "The public," he was bemused to find, "is almost childish in its acceptance of the shadow for the substance."

Colonel House's succor to his governors by no means terminated on election night. All sought his counsel and assistance for the duration of their terms of office. Of the governors, he was probably closest to Culberson. "You must take charge of things here and organize the work," Culberson wrote following his inauguration. "My room will be open to you at all hours." House went there nearly every day, and his assistance did not stop at the boundaries of official business. His encyclopedic familiarity with party organization in every Texan town and hamlet made his advice on knotty patronage questions an item that was highly prized. One day Governor Sayers, baffled by the inundation of ten thousand letters from avid job seekers, for whom less than two hundred jobs were available, fled to House in desperation. How could he match man and job when most of the glut of names to him were meaningless? The Governor arrived in a highly anguished state at two thirty in the afternoon and by six in the evening his slate was completely filled. Throughout the interval, House lay under an afghan upon a large lounge in his sitting room—his health was in one of its declines—ticking off his opinion of the best man for each office as Sayers called it from his list. The Governor accepted House's suggestions in every instance but one, and left in a noticeably better frame of mind than when he came.

As a five-time kingmaker in Texas, House began craving the bigger prizes of national politics. At the turn of the century, the national Democratic organization, when House's acquisitive gaze came upon it, was dominated by the leonine personality of William Jennings Bryan. In general, House liked The Commoner's social policies, although he considered his oratorical plumping for a currency based upon silver in a ratio of 16 to 1 to gold dangerous nonsense, and he was not altogether sure of Bryan as a person. In the year before the campaign of 1896 got under way, House was suddenly presented with an opportunity for sizing up Bryan when The Commoner moved into the house right next door to the Colonel's in Austin. Bryan's daughter, Grace, was ill at that time, and the aridity of Texas seemed better suited to the young lady's recovery than the chill gusts of Nebraska. In their ensuing neighborly association, Bryan and House saw much of each other. Although the atmosphere connecting their adjoining abodes radiated with constant good will, House soon was regretfully concluding that The Commoner was not his man. When the Bryans completed their sojourn and were heading back to Nebraska, House wrote dejectedly of their trial association, "I was amazed to see how lacking he was in political sagacity and common sense. Mrs. Bryan was much more practical than he. She was open to advice and suggestion."

House settled down for a dreary decade of watchful waiting. Bryan had to be thrice defeated before his grip on the Democratic nomination loosened, and his successor, the conservative Judge Alton B. Parker, was, if anything, even more unsatisfactory. Suddenly the star of Mayor William J. Gaynor pierced the gloom, and House promptly volunteered to promote his claim upon the presidential nomination. But the Mayor spurned this offer, causing House to observe with some acerbity, "I wiped Gaynor from my political slate, for I saw he was impossible."

House had little time to mourn over Gaynor, thanks to the rhapsodic reports coming in concerning another exciting new personality, the Governor of New Jersey, Woodrow Wilson. Victor in a great industrial state that normally went Republican, the Governor was enjoying astonishing success in pushing a liberal program of some magnitude through the legislature. House kept abreast of Wilson's achievements through the press and through politicos peregrinating between Texas and the Eastern seaboard. The other favorable things he heard about Wilson issued from local academic circles with which he was in touch. House's brother-in-law, Sidney Mezes, president of the University of Texas, and several deans and professors of the university, who had known Wilson professionally, spoke admiringly of his qualities. So impressed was House that he decided to hold in abeyance a project he was readying to steer his protégé, Culberson, now a United States Senator, into the presidential sweepstakes of 1912. With Culberson appearing more and more a long shot—his health was poor and "he is too entirely Southern to win"—House decided to switch to Wilson, and in the summer of 1911 began working to line up Texas for the former president of Princeton University in the future national nominating convention. Wilson was not long in writing House expressing his appreciation and his hope for an early meeting.

House promptly dispatched a personal emissary, another gubernatorial protégé, T. W. Gregory, to New Jersey, bearing an invitation for Wilson to address the Dallas fair. Wilson followed through magnificently in a speech which constituted his first bid for support outside his state. House unfortunately did not meet Wilson on this occasion. As the latter was speaking, the

Colonel was miles away in Austin, tied to his bed by a bout of illness. The image of the future was previsioned in these circumstances.

But the first meeting of Wilson and House was not long in coming. The momentous day was November 24, 1911, and the place the Gotham Hotel in New York, where House was staying. The intermediary this time was William F. McCombs, general manager of the Wilson-for-President campaign. McCombs appeared with a message from the Governor inquiring if he might come up from Trenton to consult on several aspects of the campaign. House's response was fittingly enthusiastic, and on the scheduled day Wilson appeared. They talked at the Gotham for an hour, when Wilson had to leave for another scheduled appointment with Senator Phelan of California.

As for the tête-à-tête, it had all the makings of rapturous fascination. "We knew each other for congenial souls at the very beginning," House wrote ecstatically afterward. "We agreed about everything." When the meeting ended, each asked simultaneously when the other would be free again, laughing over their mutual enthusiasm. Several days later they met for dinner in House's suite. The conversation, which was sprightly, waxed on for hours and covered "everything." "We found ourselves in such complete sympathy, in so many ways," recounted House, "that we soon learned to know what each was thinking without either having expressed himself."

Wilson fully shared the enchantment. One evening, several weeks later, after a characteristically engrossing conversation, House said, "Governor, isn't it strange that two men, who never knew each other before, should think so much alike?"

"My dear fellow," Wilson answered, "we have known each other all our lives."

Would Wilson, for all of his captivation, take counsel and guidance as the Texas governors had done? House was certain that he would. "I think," the Colonel reported to Culberson, that "he is going to be a man one can advise with some degree of satisfaction."

In the pre-convention build-up of Governor Wilson, House's chief mission was the crucial one of wooing the support of William Jennings Bryan. The race for the Democratic nomination presented a crowded field, with none of the principal contestants—Wilson, who appealed to the progressives; House Speaker Champ Clark, candidate of the party regulars; and Oscar Underwood, of the Southern Bourbon Democracy—able to command the lead. A nod from Bryan would go far to clinch the nomination.

Bryan was biding his counsel; his disposition toward the candidates was a matter of complete obscurity. Boldly trading on their previous neighborly association in Texas, House arranged a breakfast meeting with the Bryans, where with quiet eloquence he put the case for Woodrow Wilson. When House was finished, Bryan was garrulously noncommital, although Mrs. Bryan emitted a few flickers of encouragement. House nevertheless was overjoyed by this seemingly meager development, for he counted on the lady's considerable influence with her husband. In succeeding weeks, House painstakingly "nursed" Bryan, as he put it, showering him with little notes and visiting him in New York and at his farm deep in the Rio Grande country. The reward for this rather considerable investment of effort was a few glimmerings of preference for Wilson.

Just as House was daring to hope for an expression of outright commitment from The Commoner, there occurred an unimaginable disaster which seemed to blow Wilson's entire chances for the nomination to smithereens. A trustee of Princeton University, a Mr. Adrian H. Joline, smarting from several lacerating encounters with Wilson when the latter was university president, released for publication a letter written by Wilson nearly four years before on April 29, 1907. This letter, although clearly private and confidential, was indiscretion at its very worst. Wilson had permitted himself to write to Mr. Joline, "Would that we could do something, at once dignified and effective, to knock Mr. Bryan once and for all into a cocked hat."

The Wilson camp convulsed with despair, not only because of the letter, but also because Bryan and Wilson would shortly be meeting face to face at the Jackson Day Dinner in Washington. In fact, at the very moment the letter was published, Bryan was proceeding from Key West, Florida, where he had been vacationing, northward to the capital for the celebration. From every side, anguished Wilsonians implored House to intercept Bryan on his journey and apply all the diplomatic salve available in his ample kit to avoid the impending debacle. House, unfortunately, was bedridden with fever in Austin. Travel was out of the question, although the Colonel rallied himself sufficiently to press into service another accomplished diplomatist who spoke The Commoner's own homely language, Josephus Daniels, editor of the Raleigh, N. C., *News and Observer* and a devout Democrat. Daniels masterfully applied his art with thankful results. The Wilsonians gave a nationwide sigh of relief when Bryan, upon reaching Washington, declared that he had nothing to say about the letter. Joyous bedlam ensued when at the dinner Bryan went out of his way to show cordiality for Wilson. He spoke warmly of the Governor in his prepared address and while the two were standing on the rostrum, put his arm around his shoulder and kept it there while the photographers snapped the happy scene.

If Bryan was a source of anxiety for House, he also had his moments of consummate usefulness. It was Bryan, for example, who was instrumental in eliminating House's chief competitor at this interval for the prized position of Wilson's premier counselor. The gentleman in question was Colonel George Harvey, editor of *Harper's Weekly*, whose association with the Governor antedated House's. Harvey had originally encouraged Wilson to drop his academic career and take up politics. When Wilson was responsive, Harvey skillfully cut through the brambly thickets of New Jersey machine politics to clinch the gubernatorial nomination for his protégé. Thereafter he was a frequent counselor to the Governor and articulately supported his presidential aspirations in his influential magazine. For all of the worthiness of his contribution, Harvey had an Achilles' heel. He was firmly linked with the most unseemly symbol extant in American politics, Wall Street, and with the symbol's symbol, Mr. J. P. Morgan. It was this side of Harvey that Bryan objected to in conversations with House. Biding his time, the Colonel carefully chose his opportunity to pass along these distasteful impressions to Wilson. The response was gratifying. Moving remorselessly on, House prevailed upon a friend, another editor, E. S. Martin, of *Life*, to point out to Harvey the desirability, indeed the necessity, of his playing a less conspicuous part in the Wilson campaign. Harvey evidently took this counsel very much to heart. Encountering Wilson a few days later at the Manhattan Club in New York, Harvey, his morale thoroughly dehydrated, asked if his support was harmful. Wilson, never one to shrink from directness, said that it was. Harvey dejectedly withdrew into the background, first of the clubroom and then of the Wilson movement. Thereafter things were never quite the same between Harvey and House.

As the Convention drew near, House's health went back on him, forcing him first to repair to his summer home at Beverly, Massachusetts, and then to take off for Europe. He was on the high seas when the Democratic convention assembled at Baltimore; and when, on the forty-sixth ballot, Wilson finally captured the nomination with the indispensable support of William Jennings Bryan, House was one day out of Liverpool. In August, he returned to American soil in time for the campaign. In the following tumultuous months, House counseled Wilson on the issues and took on the difficult assignment of mediating the churlish warfare raging between the National Democratic Chairman, the ailing hyper-suspicious, William F. McCombs, and the Vice-Chairman, William Gibbs McAdoo, a man of brute ambition. The out-of-the-ordinary three-cornered race between Wilson, the Republican nominee William Howard Taft, and the insurgent Bull Mooser Teddy Roosevelt, called for a fresh approach to party management, and House supplied it. He saw to it that a Taft Republican was placed on every Democratic precinct committee to convince the outraged Republican regulars that Woodrow Wilson was the best bet to stop the treasonous T.R.

Wilson swept on to victory, and one of his first acts in the exuberant afterglow was to invite House into his cabinet, but the Colonel declined for his usual reasons of health, which Wilson readily understood. Although he did not join the cabinet, House was influential in its construction. Having little familiarity with the party personalities who counted and even less with the winding currents of loyalty and commitment subsuming party affairs, Wilson turned the task of preparing a preliminary cabinet slate over to the more knowledgeable House and went off to the sands of Bermuda to recuperate from the rigors of the campaign. The Colonel settled down to the grind of interviewing and corresponding with innumerable aspirants and their sponsors. When at last the completed cabinet was unveiled, most of its members owed their presence in no small way to House's initiative and support. Among the membership were two of House's old friends and fellow-Texans, Albert S. Burleson as Postmaster General and David F. Houston as Secretary of Agriculture.

House was equally responsible for the appointment of Franklin K. Lane as Secretary of the Interior and William Jennings Bryan as Secretary of State. Bryan, House contended, would be less troublesome in the Administration than out, and would command broad support in Congress which the Administration would sorely need. House was mainly, but not solely, responsible for the assignment of his friend, Josephus Daniels, to the Navy Department and James C. McReynolds to the Justice Department. As regards the other members of the cabinet, House had little part. William Gibbs McAdoo in the Treasury was Wilson's own choice; Lindley M. Garrison, the Secretary of War, was advanced by Wilson's confidential secretary, Joe Tumulty; and the appointments of W. C. Redfield as Secretary of Commerce and W. B. Wilson as Secretary of Labor resulted from a broad canvass.

In various ways, House was functioning as a general assistant to Wilson. Patronage was a taxing responsibility, House devoting whole days to "dictating letters to office seekers." He was telephoning and lunching with Tumulty, and even Mrs. Wilson was seeking his counsel. A silk manufacturer of Paterson, New Jersey, offered to present the incoming First Lady with his choicest material for her inaugural dress. Sensing, perhaps, Mrs. Wilson's real desires, House advised her to accept the proffered gift. Another act of generosity transpired when William Loeb, Jr., Collector of the New York Port and a Republican, graciously offered a revenue cutter to pick up the President-elect upon his return from Bermuda and with blaring horns and festive bunting, convey him onto American shores. Should the offer of the Collector be accepted, Tumulty inquired of House? House unhesitatingly recommended that disembarking at the dock in the ordinary way would be preferable, which is what Wilson did.

One of the President-elect's first acts upon returning was to invite the Houses to Princeton for a weekend combining business and relaxation. House was particularly struck on this occasion by Wilson's extreme courtesy.

He refused either to enter or leave a room before his guest and, as House observed, in a diary notation for his first evening at Princeton, "He was particularly solicitous as to my comfort and got up during the dinner to regulate the air."

Wilson needed little urging to make several visits to House's New York apartment between the election and the inaugural, each admixing business and pleasure. On the first occasion, the Colonel dispatched Mrs. House uptown to his daughter Janet's apartment, ahead of Wilson's arrival from Princeton about dinnertime. The meal being already prepared, they fell to it at once, and then were off to the Cort Theater to see Laurette Taylor in *Peg O' My Heart*. Wilson was an avid devotee of the stage play and of vaudeville. On this particular evening, he, House, and the two Secret Service men posted in their box enjoyed Miss Taylor's performance vastly. After the theater, House returned with his guest to the apartment for sandwiches and talk until midnight on almost any subject under the stars. Next morning, when Wilson rose at eight, House personally served up a breakfast, flawlessly catering to the President-elect's well-defined tastes, consisting of cereal and two raw eggs into which lemon or orange juice was squeezed. Since Wilson took neither coffee nor tea, neither was on the table. The morning the two friends gave to a carefree excursion to Ellis Island by boat from the Battery and taxied to the Metropolitan Museum, Wilson being an avid sight-seer. On another visit, when Wilson expressed eagerness to see the prized Morgan collection at the Metropolitan, House, the dutiful host, induced the Museum's officials to open the collection at nine o'clock, rather than the regular ten o'clock hour.

Wilson's reciprocity consisted not only of entertaining House at Princeton but at his very first social function at the White House, the inaugural luncheon. To be invited was, of course, a signal honor. Since the guest list was limited to the incoming and outgoing Presidents and their cabinets, and the professional military, House, as the only one present without official connection with public office, was something of an interloper. The luncheon, however, was both the beginning and the end of House's participation in the ritual of the inaugural. He did not attend the official ceremonies at the capitol. Nor did he partake of the gaiety of the presidential ball that evening at the Shoreham. He brought Mrs. House around and looked in, but not finding the crush and the din to his liking, he retreated to the staid quietude of the Metropolitan Club. There he spent the evening, he said, "loafing around."

House's chief working place in the new Administration was not the White House or the Metropolitan Club, but his own apartment at 145 East

35th Street in New York, situated in an unpretentious building in an un-fashionable block between Lexington and Third avenues. His study, a room of moderate size, furnished with a Queen Anne desk, a convertible chaise longue, two giant, leather-covered Cogswell chairs, and a wall lined with books, was the chief scene of his toil for the next three years, until 1916, when he moved to 115 East 53rd Street. Most of House's day was passed seeing visitors. These came not as single spies but in battalions. Once his influence with the President was bruited about, everybody clamored to see him—office seekers ("I am overwhelmed with them"), businessmen, journalists, ambassadors, machine politicians, cabinet members and crackpots, all beat a path to his door.

One saw House only by appointment. Any visitor brash enough to appear on the premises unscheduled was almost sure to be turned away. Even celebrities were subjected to this summary humiliation. To be late was an unpardonable crime. The Colonel rigidly deducted the minutes lost in tardiness from the total time which he budgeted beforehand for each appointment. The penalty was unmercifully applied regardless of the distinction of the visitor, his intimacy with House, or the significance of his business. Certain intervals in House's crowded day were considered the choicest for seeing him. One was his daily half-hour walk after breakfast and a similarly allotted excursion in the afternoon—his only exercise—when he could be talked to away from his busy telephone and the tumultuous ingress and egress of other visitors. The other choice interlude was after lunch when, to conserve his strength, he would recline on the sofa in his study, tucked under an afghan. Instead of sleeping, the outstretched House normally dictated his voluminous correspondence, or if there was a visitor of importance on hand he would confer with this individual, unhurried by other visitors awaiting their scheduled turn.

House's considerable correspondence was handled by but one secretary, called "Miss Fanny" by her boss, and known more formally as Miss Frances Denton. A fellow Texan who had migrated northward with House, Miss Denton was the daughter of an old physician-friend of the Colonel's. At first his protégé, she quickly became invaluable, and dedicated her life unremittingly to House until his death, and then to Mrs. House until her death. Although her system of shorthand was somewhat antiquated and her typing would never win prizes at Katharine Gibbs, Miss Fanny's discretion, in any test of responsibility, was absolute, and her courage illimitable. House could with complete equanimity entrust the most confidential papers to her care for carrying by hand to ambassadors and foreign ministers or to specially chosen mailboxes. As House well knew, the world's most dastardly and proficient spies would stop at nothing to snatch Miss Fanny's papers from her. But she would bravely take up her treasure, tuck a revolver in her muff, and march off to her destination. The revolver was no meaningless gesture. Miss Fanny was an excellent shot.

The chief correspondent of House's voluminous letter writing was the President, who rarely dictated his letters for House, but, in the interests of secrecy, typed them himself on his small Corona. If the matter couldn't wait, it was handled by telephone over the direct wire between House's apartment and the White House. To some degree, the conversations were conducted by special code. House's telephone would ring. "This is Ajax," came the familiar voice of the President over the wire. House was variously known as "Beverly," "Bush" and "Roland," and the individual cabinet secretaries as "Priam," "Pythias," "Neptune" and other ancient names of like distinction ransacked from mythologies and dictionaries. In the Administration's first years, House's and Wilson's telephoning and letter writing mainly focused upon implementing the New Freedom, which consisted of a cluster of domestic reforms expounded in the campaign speeches and the inaugural address. In its ideals and working measures, the New Freedom proposed to rescue the embattled common man from the oppressions of corporate bigness, the sweatshop, the chilling fear of unemployment and the irresponsible manipulation of credit. Of the several elements of Wilson's program, the one House was most involved in was the reform of the banking structure embodied in the Act of Congress of December 23, 1913, establishing the Federal Reserve System. Being one who liked to steep himself in facts before sliding into the abyss of action, House, preparatory to the President's recommendations to Congress, methodically collected the banking laws of Europe and a wealth of reports and abstracts from American professors of economics. He conferred at length with both friend and foe of banking reform. His appointment lists in those formative days of modern banking history glitter with the titans of finance—Paul Warburg, Otto Kahn, Henry Frick, Major Henry Higginson. "Mr. J. P. Morgan, Jr., and Mr. Denny of his firm came promptly at five," states a characteristic diary entry of March 27, 1913. After Congress passed the necessary legislation, and the new Federal Reserve System had to be launched as a going concern, House had a large hand in the exacting job of sifting out scores of prospective appointees to the system's Board of Governors; the better part of the membership of the first Board appear on House's list.

Although the Administration's energies were deeply committed on the battlegrounds of domestic politics, House's own interests in 1913 were drawn increasingly into foreign affairs. The rough road of patronage originally provided his entree to this mysterious field, which hitherto had at most only fleeting importance in the nation's history. As a dispenser of offices, House had a big influence in selecting practically all the major ambassadors, including the choicest assignment of the day, the post in London. After Wilson himself had failed by his best exertions to induce President Charles Eliot of Harvard and Richard Olney, Secretary of State in the Cleveland Administration, to take on the British ambassadorship, House proposed the name of Walter Hines Page, former editor of the *Atlantic Monthly* and partner of the publishing firm of Doubleday, Page. The President, after some hesitation, acquiesced to Page's appointment. The ambassador-select first learned of the Colonel's success when the latter telephoned one morning with the greetings, "Good morning, Your Excellency." Most of the other principal appointments eventuated when House conferred one night with the President in his study. "We went over the entire list from top to bottom," said House, "and almost every post was decided upon."

House dealt not only in ambassadors, but in the lesser lights of the diplomatic service as well, consuls, first secretaries and plain junior officers. A secretary of the American legation in Japan, learning by the grapevine in that far-off place of House's rising influence, beseeched the Colonel to bring about a transfer to France. House, whose desire to do things for his friends, was often overpowering, intervened at one point for a capable young Houstoner he had known since boyhood. The lad had just taken his Ph.D. in a respectable university and had qualified for the foreign service on both the written and oral examinations. He was anxious to commence his breadwinning career, and House felt justified in hastening the usual recruiting procedures, which were hardly noted for their speed, by speaking in the Ph.D.'s behalf to the Third Assistant Secretary of State. In general, however, House fought heroically for the integrity of the merit principle. Time and again, he bucked up Wilson's resistance to the importunities of Secretary of State, who as an old political pro, was ready to toss the foreign service to the hungry spoilsmen as a matter of course.

House was more than a job broker in diplomacy; he was articulate and resourceful in the field of policy. Critical of the long drifting of our Latin-American policy, for example, House proposed the establishment of a league of all the American states, equipped to settle disputes between the members peacefully and empowered to use force against aggression if necessary. House's proposal was a forerunner of the League of Nations and the future Rio pact concluded a quarter of a century later in 1939. In 1914, House, unfortunately, got nowhere. Wilson was only superficially sympathetic, and the State Department indifferent.

House was more successful in tackling two major problems besetting America's pre-World War I diplomacy. The country's relations with Great Britain were being vexed by the tolls imposed upon foreign vessels using the facilities of the Panama Canal. The issue had its smoldering start in legislation in the Taft Administration exempting United States coastwise vessels from the tolls of the canal. This act of national self-interest might have been perfectly understandable were it not that the Hay-Pauncefote Treaty, concluded between the United States and Britain prior to the Taft Administration, provided that the canal should be kept open to the ships of all nations on "terms of entire equality." The treaty-breaking act of Congress made the British lion groan with steady detestation. Colonel House worked hard to restore the happier *status quo ante* in Anglo-American relations. He encouraged the President's inclination to champion legislation repealing the American exemption, and when Congress got around to considering the delicate issue, he peppered the British ambassador in Washington and the Foreign Office in London with admonitions to keep British official expressions within discrete confines. After some anxious interludes, the repealing legislation pulled through.

House also toiled with success in the tri-part jungle of Anglo-American-Mexican relations. In 1913, the Mexican Madero regime toppled from power; various local leaders scrambled to fill the vacuum, but none could dominate the situation. Wilson's chosen policy of "watchful waiting," or withholding recognition until a constitutional regime emerged, was jeopardized by the blatant support given Huerta by Sir Lionel Carden, British Ambassador to Mexico, in return for lavish promised concessions to British oil interests. Wilson was greatly distressed by the undercutting of his policy. House managed to convince his embittered chief that it was worth trying to bring the British around to a genuine "hands-off" policy. With Wilson's approval, House negotiated with the British leadership in Washington and in London, to which he ventured on a special mission with happy results. The British began talking and practicing "hands off" and pesky Sir Lionel was taken out of the way via a reassignment to Brazil.

House's more intricate dealings with the President, such as those involving Mexico and Panama, to a large degree, were conducted at the White House. Although House never stayed in Washington for more than a few days at a time, he traveled frequently to the capital. The midday train, taken from Pennsylvania Station in New York, got him into Washington by late afternoon. A little reception committee would be on hand—the President and Mrs. Wilson, or their daughter Eleanor and her beau, Secretary McAdoo. Once at the White House, the Colonel dropped his bags in the Yellow Room, his favorite because it was the smallest of the bedrooms, and rushed off to the President's study to talk business, or present his "budget," as he called it, of matters he wished to place before Wilson. The talks went on until dinner time which was at seven sharp. Dinner customarily was family only, the fare simple and the conversation easy. After dinner, the President and his friend retired to the library for more business. This room, situated on the second floor, was reached by a hand-operated elevator, which Wilson took boyish delight in running. Some evenings business went begging while they looked at pictures or discussed the plentiful historical bric-a-brac which crammed the library. Or, the President, an entertainer of no mean talent, might delight his little family with several *divertissements*—convincing pantomime of bowlegged cowboys and tippling beggars, recitals of exuberant verse like James Whitcomb Riley's "The Man in the Moon," or readings in his finely modulated voice from Pope and Wordsworth and the sketches of A. G. Gardiner, the English historian-biographer. When House stayed over several days, the President and his counselor sometimes cut off work in midafternoon to go for a drive, resorting to any one of several points of interest, including a cemetery near the Soldiers' Home. Much taken with a statue in the cemetery by Saint Gaudens depicting Grief, the President spent the better part of an hour one afternoon exclaiming to House over the exquisitely outlined figure and the heroic resolution of the face. The retreat most preferred was the golf course. His own game being poor, House consistently turned down the President's many invitations to play his favorite game. House's contribution was limited to lining up partners for the President and trailing the players around the links as the game progressed.

House was a migratory counselor, whose comings and goings followed a certain pattern. Like barn swallows and other feather-folk, his habitat changed with the seasons. Approximately from May until September, House would escape the heat of New York and Washington by taking off for the gentler climate of his summer home at Beverly, Massachusetts. His absences are not to be interpreted as signifying any faltering in zeal and application. He was just as industrious in the cool hinterlands as in the big cities. But no matter how much they telephoned and corresponded, House's absence from the Washington scene meant that he might not see the President for months on end, and inevitably the press would simmer with speculation as to whether things were right between the partners. These dire anticipations, which raised up annually, were known inside the Administration as "the September breaks." House and Wilson had fun thinking up cute little ways to enlighten the press.

In actuality, the relationship of the President and his confidant was one of continuously progressive closeness. Informing signs of this happy phenomenon are the several changes in form of the salutations and closings of their correspondence. Wilson, starting out with "Dear Colonel House," soon switched to the more familiar "My dear Friend," ultimately to "Dearest Friend" and the closing "Affectionately yours." House progressed from "My dear Governor Wilson" to "My dear Governor," and the same fond closing as Wilson's once the President commenced the pattern. Here and there other signs of the growing bond between them were observable. One night, for example, as a large White House social of several hundred guests was coming to a close, House, who was New York bound, went up to his host to do the customary amenities. The President grasped his friend's hand and, pressing it hard, said in a voice vibrant with sincerity, "My only regret was that you were so far from me."

House was also much occupied with the several members of Wilson's immediate circle. With Mrs. Wilson, the President's compassionate influential helpmate, the Colonel's relations were close and cordial. From that discerning lady, House obtained a running commentary of her husband's preoccupations and telling vignettes of the several major personalities dominating the White House scene. The Colonel, in turn, was useful to Mrs. Wilson. Respected by both Wilsons for his sophistication in the field of financial management, House was Mrs. Wilson's favorite consultant on the crucial subject of ways and means to improve the family purse. In his underpaid career as scholar and teacher, Wilson had amassed precious little capital for the future rainy days of old age, and the relatively mammoth salary he received as President offered arresting possibilities. House was duly commissioned by Mrs. Wilson to work on plans to exploit the windfall. After some careful computations, the Colonel came up with a plan whose provisions of stringently controlled expenditure would enable the Wilsons to save in the course of a presidential quadrennium somewhere between thirty-five and forty thousand dollars. As a next step, House appended a carefully selected list of stocks and bonds in which the hoard might be safely and profitably invested.

Apart from contributing to her sense of financial well-being, House also pleased Mrs. Wilson with his talent for fitting in as a co-operative and congenial member of the family circle. To the Wilson daughters, Margaret and Eleanor, House was a kind of benevolent uncle. Time and again he interceded in their behalf with their father, by whom they were somewhat awestruck, and provided counsel on their knottiest problems. When, in 1914, Eleanor and her bridegroom, Secretary of the Treasury McAdoo, proposed to live in the White House while her parents were away for the summer at their rented home at Portsmouth, New Hampshire, the Colonel argued against the plan. It "would cause comments," he said. All present were gratified by his forthrightness, and the McAdoos took up residence elsewhere. With Mrs. Wilson's sister and brother and other relatives and friends who occasionally numbered among his fellow guests, House got on handsomely. He particularly endeared himself as a loyal and constructive supporter of the little parlor socials the First Lady loved to organize. This extended to sharing in a demonstration of the wonders of the Ouija Board, meticulously staged by Mrs. Wilson and her brother, Dr. Axson, one evening. Although House gamely co-operated in evoking the outer spirits, and acknowledged afterwards that the performance was "rather remarkable," he was, he said, "still unconvinced."

Being absent from the White House scene so much, the Colonel necessarily attached the highest value to any resident of that edifice willing and able to serve as his informant on local happenings. Probably his most rewarding source for this supremely important intelligence was the President's personal physician, Admiral Cary T. Grayson, whose status with the President was more than professional. An expert golfer, superb anecdotist, and convivial all-round companion, he was a great favorite. The physician's accord with House was equally special. "Your devoted friend," Grayson signed his letters to the Colonel, who characterized the doctor as one who "tells me everything concerning the President in the most minute detail in order to get my advice." Actually, in return for his services as a sort of oral gazetteer, Grayson demanded more than advice. At the good doctor's request, House took on a variety of missions, indispensable to the health of the President. When, for example, Grayson was convinced that the recurrent attacks of indigestion the President was suffering at one juncture were brought on by McAdoo's and Tumulty's habit of talking business during meals with their chief, House agreed to provide the necessary corrective by speaking frankly to the transgressors. Grayson himself shrank from the possibility of incurring their disfavor. But House's expert intramural diplomacy rose to the occasion and the President's health was saved.

With the most important member of the official White House circle, Joseph Patrick Tumulty, Secretary to the President, House's dealings were more complicated. Gregarious, capricious, humane, Tumulty had served as secretary during Wilson's Governorship, rising to the post from Jersey City ward politics. In his comparable post in the White House, Tumulty fearlessly guarded the President's door, supervised the clerical routine, handled patronage and watched over local politics in Massachusetts, New Jersey, New York and Illinois. He was the Administration's chief link with the press and the President's favorite consultant on speeches. "When it is especially important that I be understood," Wilson once told Ida M. Tarbell, "I try . . . [a speech] on Tumulty, who has a very extraordinary appreciation of how a thing will 'get over the footlights.' He is the most valuable audience I have." With an office next to his chief's on the ground floor of the west wing of the White House, Tumulty was the only man in the world enjoying free access to the President of the United States.

At first, House and Tumulty fared tolerably well. House had backed Tumulty for the secretaryship in the crucial moments when Wilson was wrestling with doubts over the appointment. Tumulty had duly acknowledged his gratitude to House and invited his benefactor "to call on him at any time." "I hope," thought House, the tough realist, "he is sincere." But, in the course of time, House's motives, too, became suspect. From all the evidence, he seems to have resented Tumulty's steadily increasing closeness to the President. In fact, the Colonel launched a considerable campaign to keep Joe Tumulty in his place. On one occasion, for example, several patronage appointments, actively promoted by Tumulty, to the offices of the United States Minister and Receiver of Customs in Santo Domingo, backfired terribly when the appointees used their posts for some messy financial manipulations bringing on a first-class scandal. Colonel House reported on the situation to Wilson, painting Tumulty in colors substantially more hideous than those warranted by the facts. While remaining outwardly cordial, House busily berated the Secretary to others in the White House circle and eventually to the President himself. In his pointings and whisperings, House variously represented the garrulous Tumulty as leaking valuable state secrets, as lacking in appreciation for the New Freedom and grossly mismanaging the seriously deteriorating political situation in New York. Adding fuel to these more serious charges were innumerable petty incidents the Colonel was alert to magnify to his own advantage. The substance of one of these occasions, for example, was provided by an outing to the theater one night whose membership included the President, Colonel House, House's friend, Dudley Field Malone, and Dr. Grayson. The shrapnel of the delayed reaction to the event began flying wildly about the premises the following morning. Tumulty had been left out and in House's biased eyes, at least, he was in a terrible humor over it. This was nothing less than unforgivable. The culprit had to be brought to justice. House duly went to the President and reported the incident, expertly building up to the damning observation that Tumulty was jealous. Alas, to the Colonel's consternation, Wilson did not agree. The confidant gracefully steered the conversation into other subjects and bided his time.

The purpose of Colonel House's considerable and somewhat hazardous campaign was nothing less than the removal of Tumulty from the presidential scene. At one point House sought to speed up the process by interesting Tumulty in succeeding McCombs, who seemed destined to resign as National Democratic Chairman. McCombs, unfortunately for House's purposes, did not resign. But another opportunity was soon in coming. One day, Tumulty, who seems never to have suspected House's well-concealed backbiting and remorseless maneuvering, told the Colonel, confidentially, that he had thought of resigning because of the hardship his meager salary was inflicting upon his family. House knew that this was idle talk, that wild horses couldn't drag Tumulty from his beloved job. But to test Wilson's disposition toward Tumulty, the wily Colonel reported the confidential conversation in full to his chief. Wilson was openly upset at the thought of losing his secretary, thus demonstrating a loyalty that was hardly appreciated by his disgruntled audience. Once again House retreated to await a more propitious occasion for demolishing Joe Tumulty.

Beyond the White House, the Colonel was busily tilling more constructive enterprises in the vineyards of the cabinet departments. House's considerable association with the cabinet was spurred, at least in part, by the special focus of his ambition. He proposed to be more than a mere presidential adviser; he sought to influence nothing less than the whole apparatus of government, of which the great departments constituted the most substantial part. In pursuing his long-entertained ambition by building up contacts with the departments, House was also building up his value to his chief. By cultivating the secretaries, assistant secretaries and lesser departmental personalities, House learned of impending problems and policy alternatives long before they reached the President through the regular channels. The peculiar talent upon which success in such undertakings most depends, House had in abundance—he excelled as a brain picker. Not having an original mind, he depended upon extracting ideas from the more creative and insightful minds of others. In general, the departments welcomed House's subcranial explorations; his victims, for all of the hardship involved, were rewarded with invaluable access to the President.

House did his brain-picking in various ways. On days the cabinet met, he stationed himself just outside the cabinet room and buttonholed the secretaries as they arrived and departed. When the cabinet did not meet, the Colonel's usual procedure was to seek out the secretaries after breakfasting with Wilson. Having finished the meal, the President would go to his office and commence the day's dictation, leaving House to his own devices. The Colonel might devote his morning at the White House exclusively to telephoning the cabinet. Or he might make the rounds, visiting the secretaries personally. The first stop was the William Jennings Bryan residence on 16th Street. Since the Bryans rose later than Wilson, House, in order to mingle with them, usually had to consume a second breakfast. This gastronomical hardship House willingly endured, for he preferred to deal with the Secretary of State with Mrs. Bryan present—"She usually agrees with me." After the Bryans, House was whisked by the official car at his disposal for the day to the offices of the three secretaries he dealt with most, Burleson in the Post Office, McReynolds at the Justice Department and McAdoo at the Treasury, the departments where practically all the patronage was concentrated. Of all the secretaries, House was closest to McAdoo. This observant confiding Secretary provided the fullest summaries extant of goings on in cabinet meetings and in Washington in general. "I saw much of House," McAdoo has written. "We became good friends." McAdoo, for his part, valued the

Colonel's "extraordinary political clairvoyance" and "subtle feeling for the inwardness of events." House's subtlety was put to an acid test when the Secretary of the Treasury married the President's daughter Eleanor, in 1914. This momentous event, in its administrative implications, called for careful adjustments in McAdoo's relations with the President, the cabinet and in furthering his urgent ambition to succeed Wilson as President. In the bewildering process of refinding himself, McAdoo often consulted House with, the Secretary felt, invariably happy results.

Like his fellow countrymen, Woodrow Wilson was engrossed in the domestic politics of the day and oblivious to happenings in the world at large. In Europe, these were assuming formidable shape. Local wars were raging in the Balkans; a network of alliances stretching from Moscow to London and from Berlin to Rome was hardening into a steely structure of might, fixed to spring at the least touch of events. Here and there a Nicholas Murray Butler or an Elihu Root discerned the rising shadows of general war. Edward House belongs to the little band of clairvoyants.

Well before the inaugural, House foresaw the possibility of a European war that would become a world war with the United States an inevitable participant. Could the holocaust be prevented? It could, House was convinced, if the frantic rivalry and suspicion festering between Germany and Britain could somehow be tamed. In the conviction that face-to-face negotiation might have the same efficacy in obliterating differences and distrust in international relations as in private business affairs, House conceived the idea of going to Europe to induce the rulers of Germany, France and Britain to meet in general conference for basic discussions. Wilson's approval of the project was instantaneous. "I might almost say," declared the jubilant House, "he was enthusiastic."

Plunging into characteristically elaborate preparations for his mission, or "The Great Adventure," as he called it, House sought out Benjamin Ide Wheeler, long-time American professor at the University of Berlin, who knew the Kaiser intimately, and Irwin Laughlin, a veteran American diplomat with service in both London and Berlin. There was much checking with a score of ambassadors, journalists and sundry ladies and gentlemen of affairs. On the voyage over, House's fellow passengers included Count von Moltke, cousin of the German Chief of Staff, whom the Colonel rewardingly cultivated.

On May 16, 1914, House slipped into Berlin and immediately began conferring with German officialdom—Grand Admiral Tirpitz, Minister of Marine; Jagow, the Foreign Secretary; and Zimmermann, the under secretary.

Although the men of the Foreign Office seemed tolerable, House was alarmed by the intensity of Tirpitz's detestation of the British, his commanding position in the government and the dizzy pace he was plotting for German armament. "It is militarism run stark mad," House reported to Wilson.

The confidant's dour impressions were somewhat brightened in an interview he had with the Kaiser at the Imperial palace at Potsdam. The interview, which had been arranged with great difficulty, was worked in during the "Schrippenfest," the event of the day at the Imperial Palace. In the Schrippenfest, or "White Roll Feast," the Kaiser entertained the common soldiers of the regiment achieving the best record of the year, regaling them with white bread, instead of their usual black bread, and such further luxuries as meat courses, stewed prunes and wine. As an integral part of the ceremony, the Kaiser sat in the midst of his troops, sharing their repast and eating with their utensils. The Empress, the princes and their wives, sundry German cabinet ministers, the American ambassador, Gerard, and House similarly dispersed themselves after witnessing a morning-long pageantry consisting of religious exercises, a parade and the conferral of decorations. The symbol-laden luncheon took place in the famous Shell Hall, whose walls consisted of sea shells encrusted on the plaster. House, seated opposite the Imperial party and next to the Minister of War, spent considerable time explaining that his title, "Colonel," was not that of a professional soldier, but a sort of political honorarium, a concept that his militaristic audience had great difficulty in grasping.

After luncheon, House was granted the privilege of a private fast-moving conversation of a half hour with the Kaiser. The Kaiser was, as B. I. Wheeler had painted him, a man of peaceable instincts for all of the militaristic frippery of his surroundings. In midafternoon, House left Potsdam convinced that Germany had no plan to go to war, but faced the world with such thyroid nervousness that she might easily be triggered into reckless attack.

Embarking for Paris, House was convinced more than ever that negotiation was the key to preventing war. His sense of high purpose was spurred on by Wilson, who wrote of "the thrill of pleasure" his emissary's reports were providing and his conviction that House's undertaking was "a great thing" and he was "doing it right." In Paris, unfortunately, House's spiraling hopes were abruptly dashed by the indifference of the French, who were wallowing in a cabinet crisis precipitated when Madame Caillaux shot Calmette. As the dust of scandal was settling, House lost a week groping through government offices, getting nowhere.

Moving dispiritedly on to London, House encountered another impenetrable wall of indifference. The British social season was in full swing and everybody who was anybody in politics was doing the garden parties, Ascot and the teas at Claridge's. Public business slowed down to a crawl. No amount of anguished exposition, demonstrating that the world was sitting on a powder keg, could step up the languid official pace. Fully a week elapsed before House was granted an audience with the Foreign Minister, Edward Grey. House whiled away the plentiful time on his hands in dinner parties and interviews, which were cordial but not immediately productive, with the cream of British *Who's Who*—Lord Curzon, the Conservative leader; Lloyd George, the future Prime Minister; James Bryce, the historian; Henry James, the American expatriate novelist; and the Bishop of London. When at last he was allowed to lunch with Grey, House thoroughly reviewed the European situation as he had found it in his travels, and exhorted the Foreign Minister to meet with the Kaiser at the earliest opportunity. Although House found Grey "a willing listener and very frank and sympathetic," try as he might, he could elicit no positive commitment for the meeting with the Kaiser. Two weeks elapsed and a third began with no final answer forthcoming. Nothing could be done until the cabinet endorsed the venture, Grey explained the delay, and the cabinet was so engrossed in the Irish crisis then raging that it could not possibly consider the international situation serious enough to warrant immediate attention. A well-nigh insuperable obstacle to an Anglo-German meeting, Grey pointed out, was the deleterious effect such a step would have upon Britain's alliances with France and Russia.

As House was talking and waiting, with still no definitive word from Grey, the first of a fatal train of events occurred at Sarajevo, in the province of Bosnia. Archduke Franz Ferdinand, heir to the Austro-Hungarian throne, was murdered by a Serbian nationalist. Austria marched against Serbia. The wheels of the alliances began grinding; the European checkerboard blazed with drastic moves. Germany, with little aforethought of the possibility of war, sanctioned Austria's undertaking any retaliation against Serbia that was necessary. House, meanwhile, had written to the Kaiser summarizing the progress of his talks in Paris and London. But it was much too late. Russia, as leader of the Slavic world, mobilized in behalf of Serbia. Germany, fearful of being crushed between two enemies, declared war on Russia and then on France, which was bound to support Russia. Germany struck at France through Belgium, and Britain declared war on Germany. The First World War was at hand.

Colonel House's Great Adventure thus expired under the boots of marching soldiery. Critics of House's career are disposed to write off the whole project as foredoomed by its visionary design and amateurish execution. One dissenter to this proposed historical judgment is the Kaiser himself. After the war was over, the Kaiser, exiled at Doorn, with plenty of time to reflect on the past, remarked to G. S. Viereck, the author, "The visit of Colonel House to Berlin and London in the spring of 1914 almost prevented the World War."

"President Wilson," House used to say, "was like my oldest brother, Tom. My approach to them both was very much the same." Those journey-man years with brother Tom were undoubtedly a priceless investment, for House is the only man Woodrow Wilson ever worked with on intimate terms over a long period. Aloof from his cabinet, forbidding to his colleagues, President Wilson was not easy to get on with. Yet, paradoxically, he had an almost insatiable thirst for affection and approval. "My salvation is in being loved," he once said. "There surely never lived a man with whom love was a more critical matter than it is with me." To Fred Yates, a British friend, he wrote in 1906, "It is always affection that heals me, and the dear friend-ships I made were my real tonic and restorative."*

Apart from House and Professor Hibben of Princeton, with whom he broke in 1916, the President's close friends all were women. When House arrived upon the scene, Mrs. Wilson was ministering expertly to her hus-band's psychic cravings, as were Mrs. Hulbert, Mrs. Hibben and Miss Rickets of Princeton; Mrs. Toy of Harvard, and Mrs. Reid of Johns Hopkins. Wilson deluged each of these ladies with letters, conveying a running account of his tasks, successes and disappointments, sparing no detail and laying open his innermost thoughts. The ladies, for their part, exuded a continuous flow of sympathy and reassurance, seldom obtruding upon their troubled correspond-ent with the problems and cares of their own immediate worlds. Those who so nobly sacrificed their self-concern, Wilson rewarded with projection to the loftiest pedestals attainable in his estimation. These rarest of friends were "cultivated and conversable," and of a "deeper sensibility" and "finer under-standing" than the ordinary mankind always at hand pressing for his dis-pensations. It was Colonel House's rare achievement, and one indispensable to his assumption of the status of confidant, that he penetrated onto the President's lofty phantasmal sphere. Like all other Wilson intimates, House was a fountainhead of approval, the receptacle of worriment; his reward was the President's unquestioning esteem.

It is essential to an understanding of their relationship to note that House and Wilson judged each other by totally different standards. Wilson idealized House as a paragon who transcended all criticism, the "friend who so thoroughly understands me." He was "my second personality . . . my independent self. His thoughts and mine are one." House toiled in "selfless service," noblest calling of man. "What I like about House," said Wilson, "is

* Alexander and Juliette George have made a skillful psychological analysis of the Wilson-House relationship in *Woodrow Wilson and Colonel House: A Personality Study.*

that he is the most self-effacing man that ever lived. All he wants to do is serve the common cause and to help me and others."

Colonel House, the tough realist, on the other hand, judged Wilson with cool and calculated detachment. Unlike any other intimate of Wilson's lifetime, House aimed to use Wilson much as the fictional Selwyn had used Philip Dru. Various qualities of the extraordinarily talented President, House, of course, admired—his intellect and superb articulateness, his innate refinement and implacable correctness. But House, who, as Wilson himself said, "had a wonderful gift for fixing on the really important issues," clearly perceived the debit side of Wilson's character—his surfeit of pride and narrowness of outlook, his capacity for hating, his chariness of decision, his overweening self-righteousness, product of a rigorous Scotch Presbyterian upbringing. "Talking to Wilson," said Clemenceau on the basis of first-hand experience, "is something like talking to Jesus Christ."

Yet for all of Wilson's stern requirements and heavy faults, House endured through eight years of the closest association, steering the President into many a decision while eluding the gaping traps of his personality. In bringing off his singular accomplishment, House skillfully contrived a pattern of conduct which both protected and steadily extended his privileged rapport with Wilson. House, for example, ministered tirelessly to the President's need of approval. If Wilson asked for suggestions on a draft he had prepared of a speech or message, "I nearly always praise at first," House described his routine, "in order to strengthen the President's confidence in himself which, strangely enough, is often lacking . . ." In the course of his career with Wilson, House pealed the most sonorous platitudes imaginable. The part "you are destined to play in this world tragedy," he once opined, pulling out all the stops, "is the noblest part that has ever come to a son of man." Again, "You are so much more efficient than any public man with whom I have heretofore been in touch that the others seem mere tyros." And again, "No man has ever deserved better of his country." And again, "I do not put it too strongly when I say you are the one hope left to this torn and distracted world. Without your leadership God alone knows how long we will wander in the darkness." House wasn't content simply to brew his own platitudes; he was alert to pass along the frothiest praises which other men bestowed upon Wilson. When the great Paderewski says the world has never seen Wilson's equal, House loses no time in hustling the dictum of the pianist-statesman on to his chief. After Wilson has made a major speech, and William Wiseman, the respected British emissary, proclaims that it couldn't have been more perfect "if Shakespeare himself had written it," House sees to it that the heady pronouncement is handed on in all its ample form.

Quite apart from his contrivances, House had a considerable natural capacity to impart confidence and give a lift to the man he was talking to.

It was this quality of House that Wilson valued most in his thirst for appro-bation. In a tête-à-tête, Colonel House was anything but a sphinx, as journal-ists for good reason described him in the press. He was not the clammy, stringently discreet humanity so deliberately cultivated in the public image. The Sphinx was merely a pose. House in private was a voluble companion, whose talk was full of life and interest. Wilson would be in his study, his spirits sagging beneath the overhanging clouds of his duties, and House could enter upon the scene and in a matter of minutes the magical chemistry of his nature would dominate and brighten the atmosphere. This, above all, is why Woodrow Wilson liked to have Colonel House around him.

House never argued with the President. He rigorously observed the admonition inscribed in *Philip Dru*, "If we would convince and convert, we must veil our thoughts and curb our enthusiasm, so that those we would influence will think us reasonable." House stated the various aspects of a problem, the several possible solutions, and his choice of the one which seemed best. If Wilson opposed his recommendation, House would drop the subject for a time and reassert it when circumstances permitted, although only in terms which did not invite argument. His approach throughout was one of seeming objectivity. So, at least, Wilson was impressed. "House," said the President, "can hold a subject away from him and examine it and analyse it as if he had nothing to do with it, better than any man I ever knew."

On the assumption that "no man honestly likes to have other men steer his conclusions," House rendered his counsel as unobtrusively as possible. "It was invariably my intention with the President," he explained, "as with all other men I sought to influence, to make them think that ideas he derived from me were his own." Viewing his position as one which easily aroused envy and distrust, House clung to the background, yielding all acclaim to his chief. He avoided photographers, or, if there was no way out of it and he was snapped with the President, he presented a sphinxlike immobility while Wilson beamed or waved. Journalists found House an elusive subject who discouraged interviews, or, if by some miracle he was cornered, he said astonishingly little. Nothing raised more goose-pimples on House's sense of propriety than the references which kept popping up in the press to "Assist-ant President House." Once upon seeing that grandiosity spilled all over an article in *Harper's Weekly*, House observed with understandable feeling, "I think it is time for me to go to Europe or take to the woods." He was nothing less than frantic when on one occasion he attended church with Wilson and the dutiful vicar proceeded to pray comprehensively for "the President and his counselor." Pondering the experience, House wondered how many more such instances could be tolerated "without causing trouble."

House was careful not to impose upon Wilson in any way. Knowing that the President's time was a precious commodity, House's presentation of matters was well considered and to the point. He never intruded with his presence at the White House, except at the President's specific invitation. Even then, the Colonel carefully limited his visits to several days at the very most. On one occasion, he became frantic when he fell ill with a cold while at the White House and had to stay on for the duration of his convalescence which, because of the general weakness of his condition, required the better part of three weeks. Although House was desperately ill at the time, it took some lengthy exhortation by the President and a firm order from Dr. Grayson to deter him from rising from his sickbed and hopping a train for New York. It cheered House little when the President stole in repeatedly to sit by his bedside or forewent the theater, which he normally visited three times a week, for the entire period of the recovery so that he might watch over his impatient guest. The sun did not break through until the final stages of House's convalescence, when the President, who was working on a speech, came in each evening to discuss it. House, at long last, was earning his keep.

House never presumed that the President was obligated to him in any way because of their intimate working association. If, as occasionally happened, a considerable interlude elapsed when the two did not meet and Wilson, immersed in daily business, failed to write, House did not complain or show annoyance. He likewise suffered without reproach several Wilsonian malpractices which at times put the severest strain upon their mutual endeavors. On many an occasion, House had to take in stride Wilson's obdurate disinclination to issue even the most elementary instructions in behalf of assignments that were both momentous and complex. House's mission to Europe in 1914, for example, whose object was nothing less than saving the peace of the world, was settled by the President and his confidant in a conversation of not more than twelve minutes. There were no instructions, oral or written. "You need no instructions," Wilson said when House lightly suggested their desirability, given the magnitude of his responsibility. "Your mind echoes mine." House never asked for instructions again. Once when Wilson was conferring a large and troublous assignment upon him, an aide, aware of what was going on, exhorted the Colonel to secure written instructions. The aide knew something of Wilson's large reputation for forgetting the substance of oral commitments, and was therefore shocked at the enormous risks that House seemed unnecessarily to be taking. "Of course I would like to have specific instructions in writing," retorted House, "but as the 'Governor' never gives them we can dismiss that idea."

As the Germans crashed through Belgium and into the northern provinces, and the French dug in at the Marne, much of the adjustment in

American diplomacy fell upon the fragile shoulders of Colonel House. Wilson's preference for solitary endeavor sharply circumscribed his personal role in foreign politics. His contribution centered upon such solo acts as the speech and the note, leaving the hard toil of the conference table to House. Unbending and aloof toward the major diplomats in Washington, the President refused to see at all the British ambassador, Sir Cecil Spring-Rice, whom he considered impossible, and he rarely received the German ambassador, von Bernstorff. When, on occasion, they did meet, a futile procedure was invariably followed. Bernstorff, ushered into the presence of the Chief Executive, would recite his business, whereupon the President would answer, quickly reaching the climactic recommendation that the visitor see Colonel House.

House's chief impulse in tackling the challenge of diplomacy was to end the war at the earliest possible moment. Victory was an illusion; the price if the conflict continued, would be prohibitive regardless of the outcome. An allied victory, House wrote to Wilson on August 22, 1914, would mean "largely the domination of Russia on the Continent of Europe, and if Germany wins, it means the unspeakable tyranny of militarism for generations to come." Wilson's sturdy religious pacifism produced a ready sympathy for House's objective, and on August 5, 1914, the President dispatched a note to the belligerents, declaring that the United States would "welcome an opportunity to act in the interest of European peace." House rolled up his sleeves to give the President's general and impersonal offer concrete effect. He conferred unremittingly with the Washington ambassadors—Spring-Rice, Bernstorff, Jusserand of France, Dumba of Austria, Bakhmetieff of Russia, and conducted an enterprising correspondence with Edward Grey, the British Foreign Minister.

After some weeks of such activity, House concluded that he was "travelling in a circle" in Washington and that his attentions to the dove of peace might be better served if he were on the scene in Europe. With Wilson's eager blessing, he sailed off on a new peacemaking mission on the *Lusitania* on January 30, 1915. He traveled without official diplomatic rank, although in his pocket was a letter by the President identifying him simply as an informal emissary, empowered to facilitate the contribution of his government to peace. At the President's insistence, all of House's expenses and those of Miss Denton were paid out of the contingency fund of the State Department. The four thousand dollars budgeted for this purpose, House confidently estimated, "would last for six months." Expenses of the other two members of his party—Mrs. House and her maid—were footed by House himself. The special allowance for his own expenses House accepted most reluctantly. Hitherto in his long career he had never taken a single penny's reimbursement for his expenses which cumulatively amounted to a tidy sum.

House reached London on February eighth. The great city was muffled and dark, its gay West End deserted and street lights dimmed, the upper halves of their globes painted black to foil the dreaded Zeppelins. House promptly launched into talks with Edward Grey, "the one sane, big figure here." Although Grey spoke vaguely of a future convention of the nations of the world, he gave little encouragement of early peace. The British cabinet, House discovered, was hostile to talk of peace, doubtless reflecting opinion at large. King George V, in an audience at Buckingham Palace, impressed House as "the most pugnacious monarch loose in these parts," His Majesty spending the better part of a luncheon blaspheming the likes of his cousin, Kaiser Wilhelm. After finishing with the King, House conferred with Prime Minister Asquith and other ministers of the cabinet, and with representatives of the opposition. He dined assiduously with the lords and ladies of the upper social strata, with business executives and the intelligentsia, including his favorites, Lord Bryce and Henry James. The latter author he found "very interesting." Critics of House's diplomatic technique hold that he wasted much precious time on social trivialities with little positive result. Charles Seymour, the historian, however, contends that House's hurrying and scurrying between dining tables and conference chambers constructed a sturdy cordiality with British leaders capable of cushioning the several disputes which were to bedevil Anglo-American relations in future months. House, Seymour holds, won the confidence of the British Government when British public opinion was turning anti-American and Wilson was bitterly envisaged as an isolated ill-informed executive, whose ignorance was fortunately penetrated by House's knowledge of the inner currents of European politics.

House, as a matter of fact, was so close to the British that he discussed with utter frankness with Grey and Asquith the significant question of the timing of his departure for the European mainland. Fearful that the Germans might endorse the call of a peace conference, the Britishers, to forestall the materializing of what would surely be a grave diplomatic embarrassment, invariably advised House to stay in London a little longer, as time was hardly ripe for the journey to Berlin. After a full month of British-encouraged procrastination, House was suddenly confronted with a blunt cable from Wilson pointing out the danger of overyielding to the British in deferring the move to Berlin. But among the Germans, House found an equal indifference to peace. "Some serious reverse will have to be encountered," he reported the failure of his mission to his chief, "by one or other of the belligerents before any Government will dare propose parleys."

In the months which followed, House was engrossed in the difficult business of maintaining American rights and interests against the rising encroachments of the belligerents. As the world's foremost naval power, the British had clamped a tight blockade on Germany, aimed at starving its foe, a heavy importer of war materials and foodstuffs, into submission. Like other neutrals, the United States suffered under the broad definition of "contraband" which the British vigorously asserted. American vessels were searched and interminably delayed, their cargoes confiscated, and mail censored. Anguished protestations welled up from embattled business interests, articulately supported by sympathetic Congressmen. Even the President, for all of his predilection for the British, was embittered by the heavyhandedness of the blockade, and openly spoke to House of the possibility of war.

Colonel House was convinced not only that an Anglo-American war must be prevented, but that the United States and "civilization itself" could not afford to see the British "go down in the war." He proceeded to use to the full the extraordinary flexibility of action which the unofficial character and informality of his position permitted. At times, his play of method was productive of diplomacy that was unorthodox in the extreme. When, for example, after some weeks of British affronts upon the seas, the State Department drafted a vituperative note on the subject, House, alert to the shaping events, intercepted the note in the President's office. Upon reading the document, the Colonel was convinced its publication would precipitate a major crisis in Anglo-American relations. To nip such a disaster in the bud, House had Ike Hoover, the chief usher at the White House, commandeer the home of William Phillips, the Third Assistant Secretary of State, for a meeting rapidly being blueprinted in the Colonel's busy imagination. Then he put in a call to the British ambassador, Spring-Rice, to meet him there. On the appointed hour in the library of the Phillips home, House showed the State Department draft to the ambassador, who, upon reading it, cried out that it amounted to a declaration of war. Extraordinary happenings ensued. House and Spring-Rice sat down together and outlined a despatch for the United States to send its ambassador in London, and a second despatch for the ambassador to hand to the British Foreign Minister, Sir Edward Grey. The resulting despatches, needless to say, constituted an innocuous discussion of an issue which the State Department regarded with the utmost solemnity. By force of the Colonel's presence at the White House, his drafts were substituted for the original State Department draft. In effect, a British ambassador, thanks to the latitudinarian agency of House, was writing United States foreign policy.

On some occasions, House even coached the British on how to operate the blockade with minimum offense to American sensitivities. Once, when feelings were especially high, House suggested that some of the onus for enforcing the blockade—that is, halting and inspecting ships, and impounding cargoes—might well be transferred to the French. If the French held up our vessels, House pointed out to Sir Edward Grey, American domestic opinion would not react so violently as when the British did it. "You will understand, of course," added House judiciously, "how confidential this is and that it is merely my personal view for your information alone."

House was also at the center of the diplomatic swirl raised by Germany's naval retaliation against the British. Counting heavily on her U-boat fleet, Germany, on February 4, 1915, decreed the establishment of a war zone around the British isles into which neutral shipping henceforth entered at its peril. The terrible grimness of this policy broke upon the world on the evening of May 7, 1915, when House was dining at the American embassy in London. Just as he was completing his dessert, a despatch came in revealing that the *Lusitania* had been sunk off the southern coast of Ireland, with a loss of 1,198 lives, including 128 Americans. House cabled Wilson at once, proposing the substance of a strong line to be taken toward the Germans. Wilson was so impressed that he read House's proposal in its entirety to the cabinet. The note finally despatched to Germany incorporated House's recommendations, although it lacked the ringing tone of an ultimatum which the Colonel clearly hoped for. Proceeding nevertheless on the assumption that "war with Germany is inevitable," House began discussing with Lord Kitchener, the British commander, how American armed intervention in the war might best help the Allies. Almost as the conversation was proceeding, the President unexpectedly dashed House's rising hopes. Rightly interpreting American opinion as opposed to war, the President included in a speech in Philadelphia an idealistic paragraph on the U-boat crisis, crowned with the memorable sentence, "there is such a thing as a man being too proud to fight." This righteous withdrawal transfixed House momentarily with despair and dreadfully embarrassed his relations with his British friends.

In the weeks and months ahead, there were more sinkings and more notes, followed by pacifistic speeches. "I am surprised at the attitude he takes," said House in private resignation upon completing one of his many swings through the dreary cycle. "He evidently will go to great lengths to avoid war."

But one evening in the autumn of 1915, House was jolted out of his funk when the President, in the White House library, told him "he had never been sure that we ought not to take part in the conflict and if it seemed evident that German militarism were to win, the obligation upon us was greater than ever." The tide, at the moment, unquestionably was running in Germany's favor. The Russians had suffered disastrous defeats; Bulgaria was joining the Germans; Serbia was nearly overrun; the Turks were repelling the daring Allied assault at Gallipoli; Rumania was veering away from the Allies and negotiating with the Central Powers. Allied progress on the Western Front was measurable in yards and the losses in thousands. The general deterioration and the President's casual comment sparked House into evolving a most extraordinary plan which he shortly laid before Wilson when the latter was visiting the Colonel's New York apartment. The plan, to which the President immediately acquiesced, called for House, in his unofficial capacity, to propose to the British government that the United States, in pre-agreement with Britain and the Allies, invite the belligerents to a peace conference under American mediation, aimed at securing peace terms strongly favorable to the Allies. If Germany refused to participate in the conference or concur in its results, the United States "probably"—Wilson insisted on this word—would join the war on the side of the Allies. House's proposal was conveyed in a "split message," consisting of two letters plus a letter of explanation on how to put them together. The reliable Miss Denton mailed each letter from a different post office. To give his bold project every opportunity of realization, House took off for Europe. The Germans, heady with victory, rejected the plan, as he had expected and, indeed, hoped. But he was crushed with disappointment by the intractable negativism of the British. Although Grey was sympathetic, the cabinet was not, counting, as it did, on the U-boats to drive the United States into war wholly irrespective of the Colonel's plan. House returned to the United States fulminating against British conservatism. History promptly began repeating itself: the ship sinkings with their toll of American lives, the harassments of the blockade, the notes of protest. "Shall we ever get out of this labyrinth?" asked the despairing Wilson. "Only by adopting a positive policy," replied House. This entailed nothing less than America's entry into the war.

House was operating a mechanism of influence which in its scope and effect has never been paralleled in the history of American diplomacy. Its success required the deliberate curtailment of duly appointed cabinet officers and their established departments. It wrought drastic change in the normal modus operandi of the governments of the major belligerent powers. The essence of House's system was the personal contact which he cultivated with an efficiency that would make a ward heeler gasp. House excelled at flattery and favors; he knew the magic of little attentions. He used power and influence with exceptional insight. He knew when to coax and wheedle, when to be heavy-handed, and when to be merciful. Being human, and therefore susceptible to fault, House also had his moments of naïveté and arrogance which led him into error. When on occasion a mountain could not be moved by his limited artistry, the necessary extra force was provided by the President. What Colonel House was, he was by approval of, and at times by direct connivance of, Woodrow Wilson.

Colonel House's role necessitated the continual subordination of the Secretary of State. House undercut the Secretary, William Jennings Bryan, by dealing directly with the department hierarchy, the American ambassadors, the career foreign service and the spokesmen of foreign governments. Bryan, whose vision in the jungle of palace politics was decidedly on the dim side of 20/20, evidently never saw through House's game. Although Bryan, a pacifist, eventually broke with Wilson over the *Lusitania* issue, the Secretary, to the end of his days, steadily regarded House with sunny friendliness.

Bryan's successor, Robert Lansing, a handsome diminutive man and brilliant lawyer, was ardently pro-Ally in policy orientation and his natural capacity for self-subordination enabled him to fit easily into the Colonel's scheme of things. That he was expected to do so was made abundantly clear from the very start. His induction into his new capacity was largely managed, not by the President, but by Colonel House. After receiving only the most cursory briefing on the nature of his duties in a hurried conference with the President, Lansing was summoned to House's summer abode at Beverly, Massachusetts. The arrangement, which required the new Secretary of State to drop all work and journey 350 miles from the capital to an out-of-the-way resort town, was devised not by House but by the President himself. "Should I," asked House, looking to Wilson for his cues, tell Lansing "the whole story" of "my European work?" "No, not fully," replied the President, "but enough to get him to work in harmony with us." Considerable leeway was permitted by these instructions because the President, House discovered, had told the Secretary virtually nothing.

House was not long in reaching the satisfying conclusion that Lansing, "not a great man," was hardly a threat to his position. To a degree, House even proceeded to take his associate under his wing. Time and again he protected the Secretary of State against the bruising inattentiveness of the President. To bolster the neglected Secretary's morale, which badly dwindled on occasion, House would induce Wilson to call the uneasy triumvirate into conference, not because it was necessary but, as House put it, to make Lansing "feel his is being consulted." Paradoxically, the Secretary of State seemed to enjoy the greatest sense of security, not when his competitor was far away, but when he was on hand in Washington. One day House remarked to Wilson how Lansing was constantly urging him to come to the capital, and that if he actually came as often as the Secretary wished, he would be there all the time. Smiling, Wilson observed, "I suppose he has found out that the only time he knows anything of what is going on is when you are here." But Lansing, it should be noted, also had his moments of reciprocal usefulness to Colonel House. Once, for example, Wilson was urging House, with much force, to embark on a European mission at a date considerably earlier than the one the Colonel believed desirable. In desperation, House turned to Lansing, asking that he discreetly employ his influence to bring about a postponement of the venture. The Colonel's own lips were sealed; if he spoke out frankly, the President, under the circumstances, might misinterpret his position as indicative of a lack of enthusiasm, if not an unwillingness to go. Lansing, however, intervened magnificently, and the mission was postponed to House's complete satisfaction.

The American ambassadors and ministers at each of the key posts abroad owed their appointment primarily to House, and what is more important, they acted accordingly. Walter Hines Page at London, James G. Gerard at Berlin, William G. Sharp at Paris, Brand Whitlock at Brussels, Thomas Nelson Page at Rome, all were originally recommended by House. They and other similarly indebted diplomats kept their benefactor abreast of happenings and portents all over the world. To his loyal friends, House was a spur line running straight and true to the President. One could expatiate one's ideas more frankly and fully to the unofficial House than to the austere Wilson, and with perfect confidence that they would arrive unimpaired at the seat of power. "The President seems to like our way of doing things," reported House to Walter Hines Page, heaviest user of the Colonel's unofficial trackage.

With Page, incumbent of the premier diplomatic post of the day, the ambassadorship to the court of St. James's, House enjoyed relations of confidence and trust such as exists between parent and child and priest and penitent. House was a wailing post for outpouring his dissatisfaction with policy, with the President, and with the harrowing inefficiencies of the State Department. The latter constituted the ambassador's chief complaint. Time and again, he would howl with anguish when confidences entrusted him by the British Foreign Office, and duly reported to his department, were leaked to the press in Washington. At other times, the department, although confronted by his most urgent dispatches, would lapse into maddening silence. Days would pass with the international situation erupting in every direction and the only communication arriving from Secretary of State Bryan would be one requesting that certain ladies from Texas and Oklahoma, whose spouses were meritorious Democratic politicians, be honored by presentation to their Majesties' court. Quite understandably, Page in his tribulation preferred to do business with Colonel House.

Page's most useful feature was not his trustworthiness, but the President's dissatisfaction with him as an ambassador. Little similarity existed between Page's ambassadorial policy and his government's policy. An ardent Anglophile, Page, in 1914 and 1915, openly flaunted, in public speeches and in conspiratorial audiences with the British Foreign Minister, the President's neutralism toward the British. Although House warned Page time and again not to express "unneutral feeling either by word of mouth or by letter" and to cease conduct that "would materially lessen your influence," the ambassador was not to be budged. His deficiencies required that House be on hand for weeks on end in London mopping up blunders and dealing with the Britishers directly in lieu of the unreliable hands of Page. In such missions, the increase of House's role was greatly spurred. In essence, what was bad for American diplomacy was good for Colonel House.

In addition to the friendly ambassadors, House was served by informants abroad who reported to him directly. In London, William H. Buckler, an archaeologist and special attaché to the embassy, cultivated significant circles of opinion which Ambassador Page distrusted. A man of broad friendships, Buckler was in touch with the Liberal Socialist pacifist wing and such figures as Ramsay MacDonald, Norman Angell, Philip Snowden and Charles Trevelyan. By means of Buckler's reports, House, and thus Wilson, kept abreast of opposition attitudes concerning American policy. House had a comparable pipeline to the domestic German scene through Bernard Ritter, the prominent German-American journalist, and Carl W. Ackerman, a roving journalist in western Europe. Acting as middleman, House correlated Ridder's and Ackerman's reports with those of the friendly William Bullitt, an expert on Germany, whose employment in the State Department in Washington was owed to the Colonel. Thanks to House and his confreres, Wilson was able to couch his several appeals to German forces of unrest in the very phrases which local leaders were employing. Another of House's major correspondents abroad was Arthur Bullard, a free-lance writer, who, after service in England, went to Russia in 1917 and became the Colonel's chief informant on the course of the Revolution.

House also busily cultivated the Washington ambassadors of the major belligerent powers, seeing them constantly in Washington and New York, and enjoying an assurance of approach permitting discussions of exceptional breadth. Of the ambassadors, House probably was closest to the British envoy, the garrulous, cantankerous Sir Cecil Spring-Rice. Corroded by vanity and given to frequent slashing rages, Sir Cecil was as disliked as his prede-cessor, James Bryce, was beloved. Negotiating with Spring-Rice, a State De-partment official (whose devotion to the Allies was beyond question) once said, left him "feeling a sympathy for the Germans." Despite occasional set-to's, House managed to keep his dealings with Sir Cecil on a steady foot-ing. This exceptional achievement came to pass thanks to House's enduring tact and the enchantment of both men with the trappings of secret diplo-macy. They communicated by an elaborate private code, which each fore-swore never to reveal even to his government. To elude prowling newspaper-men and lurking spies, they made a habit of transacting business in such out-of-the-way places as House's limousine, parked in an obscure corner of Pennsylvania Station in New York, with the shades drawn and a chauffeur standing guard. House was also close to Bernstorff, the German ambassador, the ablest, the Colonel believed, on the Washington scene. Although others might reject the ambassador as slippery and unreliable, "I think better of Bernstorff than most people who know him," said House, "and if he is not sincere, he is the most consummate actor I have ever met." House would one day have cause to reconsider his words.

Recognizing the dependence of the foreign ambassadors upon his favor as a sort of ticket of admission to the President's attention, House was not above exploiting his strength on occasion. If Spring-Rice, for instance, telephones to make an appointment for tomorrow, the day House planned to return from Washington to New York, the ambassador had jolly well better come over to the White House tonight to see the Colonel if he wants to get the appointment in and avoid a long trip to New York. Change of House's plans was utterly out of the question. If Bernstorff wishes to have House to luncheon downtown in New York, he is informed that the invitation is declined. Mr. House never takes luncheon downtown. It has to be uptown, and preferably at Delmonico's. When Spring-Rice, on a day his goiter is acting up, dares to speak a trifle severely of the policy of the United States, the Colonel's own unofficial status does not deter him from administering to the official ambassador a thorough dressing down, culminating in the proclamation, "I knew of no official anywhere who was serving his country so badly as himself."

Probably House's most extraordinary relationship with foreign dignitaries was that with Edward Grey, the British Foreign Secretary. Colonel House, the tough realist, a master at disassociating sentiment from hard judgment, displayed for Grey an admiration bordering on infatuation. Grey could do no wrong. His government might dawdle and fumble, but Grey was an unremitting hero, a man of superhuman understanding, battling impossible odds—his own incipient blindness and the political myopia of his colleagues of the cabinet. Handsome and inspiring, with a classically ascetic head and large, well-proportioned frame, Grey radiated sincerity, fairness and truthfulness. House and Grey quickly discovered a community of tastes. Both were consecrated to duty and indifferent to conventional honors; both were artists at conversation and philosophical musers over the meanings of events. Breaking off work at seven o'clock each evening, Grey would hold the hour before dinner for intimate chats with House on official business intermixed with such subjects as poetry, the Greek tragedians and the songbirds of the Fallodin ponds. The Colonel was completely enraptured. "We sat by the fire in his library," wrote House of one of these experiences, "discussing every phase of the situation with a single mind and purpose." This blissful accord triggered House into pursuing a brand of diplomacy that was informal in the extreme. House freely showed official and confidential papers of his government to Grey, seldom made a move in European diplomacy without consulting his British friend, and almost invariably abided by his wishes. The available evidence does not suggest that Grey, although fair and trustworthy, reciprocated with equal candor and accommodation toward House. Not that Grey was not appreciative of his friend. "It was not necessary to spend much time in putting our case to him," Grey has written in tribute to Colonel House. "He had a way of saying 'I know it' in a tone and manner that carried conviction both of his sympathy with, and understanding of, what was said to him."

Like Jack the candlestick jumper of nursery-rhyme fame, House had to be both nimble and quick to avoid entanglement in the many wires on which he was constantly performing. When on one occasion, House arrived in England eager to meet with Sir Edward Grey at the earliest possible moment, Ambassador Page exultantly announced, with a sense of major achievement, that he had arranged a luncheon date for House and himself with Grey on Wednesday of the coming week. Outwardly manifesting polite pleasure, the Colonel inwardly was disturbed. As it happened, House wanted to see Grey without Page present and, furthermore, he had already arranged through the good offices of the British ambassador at Washington to meet Sir Edward on the day following Page's announcement of his glorious news.

House's earlier and private meeting with Grey came off as scheduled. Page was neatly taken care of when House frankly informed the ambassador that a conference had taken place, giving as an excuse the necessity for preparing for the future more formal conference on Wednesday. The Wednesday meeting, as it turned out, was fairly innocuous.

Nineteen sixteen contained a threat more ominous to the future of the Wilson Administration than the continued harassments of the U-boats and the British blockade. It was a presidential election year, and the prospects were decidedly unencouraging. Wilson, after all, had won in 1912 because the Republicans were rent by the Taft-Roosevelt clash, and even then he had secured only a plurality—not a majority—of the popular vote. Should the Republican voting strength, previously dissipated, become reunited in 1916, as it surely promised to, Wilson's chances would be dim indeed.

They seemed even dimmer when the President announced in the spring of that year his engagement to marry Mrs. Norman Galt, widow of a leading Washington jeweler. Across the nation, the President's followers were instantaneously panic-struck by the political implications of the step. Remarriage, they feared, transpiring within less than a year after the first Mrs. Wilson's death, would be widely resented in the country as an insufficient and disrespectful interlude, costing dearly in votes among millions of proper constituents. Colonel House was not on the scene when this hysteria broke out, being overseas on a mission at the time. He had known something of the romance through the faithful Grayson, but had never expected that marriage would result. In any case, the inaccessible House was spared the approaches of a corps of anguished high-placed Democrats who were seeking an emissary to go to Wilson and by some plain talk about the political situation induce him to call off the marriage. In the lamented absence of Colonel House, the Secretary of the Navy, Josephus Daniels, was summoned on the strength of his "tact to do it in the best way." But Daniels, who was wise as well as tactful, begged off, refusing to trade the "tranquility of the Navy," as he put it, for the "dangerous high and exalted position of Minister Plenipotentiary and Envoy Extraordinary to the Court of Cupid."

House, while sharing the concern of his worried fellow Democrats, was even more impressed with his friend's "pathetic" loneliness since Ellen Wilson's passing. "If he does not marry, and marry quickly, I believe he will go into a decline," concluded House. "Dr. Grayson shares this belief." Spurred by such alarming convictions, House hastened to lend a helping hand with the President's matrimonial plans. He advised on a wedding date, and took on the intimate assignment of securing from Tiffany's in New York models of engagement and wedding rings, from which the President might make his selections. House was also attentive to the myriad problems of Mrs. Galt. He explored the possibility of having an eminent artist do her portrait for presentation as a wedding gift to the President. In addition, House counseled the future bride with a kind of avuncular benevolence on how she might best assist the President to face the cares of office. Colonel House was being more than kind. In actuality, he was setting up a future competitor.

While grappling with the matrimonial venture, House was puzzling over a formula for winning the election. Like many another leading Democratic strategist, he concluded that the party might find victory by uniting the Solid South with the pacifistic and progressive vote of the West. House's calculations also included deposing the ailing, waspish William F. McCombs as Chairman of the Democratic National Committee. McCombs's unseating necessitated some brisk maneuvers generaled by House with the co-operation of Bernard M. Baruch. By skillful entreaty, Mr. Baruch brought McCombs to the point where he agreed to write to the President, declining to serve again as chairman. House, in a corollary phase of the arrangement, promised that if McCombs would write the letter, he, House, would undertake to obtain from Wilson a courteous and complimentary letter, or return McCombs's to him. At first, McCombs was somewhat distrustful of the proposition, but Baruch wrestled with him for several days and finally extracted the letter. House, fortunately for all concerned, managed to follow through with his end of the bargain.

With McCombs out of the way, Wilson telegraphed House urging him to take on the national chairmanship, and dispatched Dudley Field Malone, a magnetic advocate, to subdue any doubts the Colonel might be entertaining. But House declined for his usual reasons, and as a substitute, brought on Vance C. McCormick of Pennsylvania after regaling him with luncheon and dinner on a single day "to get a thorough view of him." House was immensely satisfied, and duly reported to Wilson. The President, after some hesitation, bestowed his approval. In the ensuing campaign, House was a ubiquitous influence, conversant with all that was going on. His son-in-law, Gordon Auchincloss, was installed as party treasurer, and House himself was not long in supplying the receptive Mr. McCormick with a campaign plan whose thematic bugle cry came to be, "He kept us out of war." (This accomplishment House privately, of course, found quite repelling.) In addition, House developed a plan for distributing the campaign effort which is a worthy forerunner of the system applied by James A. Farley with such spectacular success in 1932 and 1936. House divided the states into several groups and to one of these, whose electoral outcome seemed fixed and immutable—the "safe" and the hopelessly lost states—the campaign gave little heed. House's other major category was the doubtful states, which he divided into several subgroups, each representing, on the basis of careful calculation, a different probability of success. The campaign effort allocated to each subgroup was more or less correlated with the varying degrees of confidence in ultimate victory.

On Election Day, House, rechecking his prognostications of the electoral-college vote, on the basis of his schematic analysis of the campaign, confidently announced "the fight is won." His optimism was not shared by Democratic leaders in general, and the returns that evening disputed him. Hughes was overrunning the East with great majorities, and by midnight, after the South and Middle West reported, the searchlight on The New York Times tower was beaming a Republican victory. At the nearby Biltmore Hotel, a throng of Democratic leaders and workers, gathered in the feeble hope of celebrating a possible victory, were reluctantly settling down to mourn the passing of the Administration. House was not among the shrouded watchers at the Biltmore. Still exuding confidence, he had begged off attending the macabre festivities and spent the early part of the evening with Attorney General Gregory, and then gone on to his apartment where his daughter Janet and her husband, Gordon Auchincloss, were following the returns. House stood by until eleven, when he retired, since the Far West would not be heard from until well into the morning. At daybreak, House checked the reports and saw, with the thrill of redemption, how close the race had become. At five in the morning he called party headquarters urging vigilance and the issuance of a strongly worded disavowal of the prevalent press reports that Charles Evans Hughes was elected. Mindful of the Hayes-Tilden impasse of his youth, House was wary of allowing the election to go by default. By further telephoning, he induced Attorney General Gregory to stand by with measures to protect the ballot boxes in states where ballots were still to be counted and the outcome was doubtful. A telegram from the pixyish E. S. Martin of *Life* spurred House onward: "Mr. Martin," it read, "is holding up the funeral wreath he ordered for Colonel H. till he knows the result of the current proceedings to reanimate the corpse."

The harrowing hours passed, beating with excitement until, at last, the California vote was in, and Hughes conceded to Wilson. The election followed almost to the letter the prognosis of victory made by House in midsummer. His campaign strategy had contributed not a little to winning the election. So too had the slogan, "He kept us out of war." The country clearly wanted peace, but as the second term commenced, House hoped that the President would not take this sentiment over seriously.

On the day after Election Day, House was summoned to Washington with a peremptoriness suggesting crisis. Hardly had he settled down in the presidential study, when Wilson was announcing his readiness to make a move House had been urging fully a year before. The President proposed to direct a note to all the belligerents, demanding the immediate termination of the war and the convoking of a peace conference. While a year earlier House would have turned cartwheels of joy over the President's announced position, he now opposed it. Events had completely outmoded its feasibility. With the U-boats devouring ever more American lives, a peace proposal now, House believed, would be interpreted by the Allies as an act of cowardice taken to avoid conflict with the Germans. The discussion in the little study went on inconclusively into the night. Next morning, House breakfasted alone, Wilson appearing unusually late. This, to the confidant, was the infallible indication of a "bad night." The spectacle of a disquieted President twitched the Colonel's conscience. "I dislike coming to the White House as his guest," he lamented, "and upsetting him to the extent I often do."

Wilson nevertheless went ahead with his plan, meeting, as House expected, rebuff from each belligerent camp, their respective positions on peace terms being poles apart. Impressed with the President's tenacity for peace, House moved to steer his purpose into more practical channels. Apparently with Wilson's approval, the Colonel, in January of 1917, approached the sympathetic Bernstorff, urging the ambassador to seek assurances from his government that it would rely upon Wilson's befriending Germany and co-operate in a new presidential effort to gain acceptable peace terms. The President, House confided to Bernstorff, was willing to propose "peace without victory" and "freedom of the seas." Bernstorff proceeded to contact his government through special arrangements made by Colonel House permitting the ambassador to use the State Department wires, instead of his embassy's facilities, in an effort to thwart the astonishingly effective British intelligence. Bernstorff's message was relayed via the special German code without revelation of the code to the State Department. In a notable speech in the Senate on January 22, 1917, sketching the future League of Nations, Wilson introduced the conception House had previewed with Bernstorff, "peace without victory." The President's prophetic phrase sent chills down the spines of many a nationalistic leader in the Allied camp who considered it an act of betrayal. For at least a fortnight, House was busy silencing the raucous indignation of his Allied friends at home and abroad.

Meanwhile, he and Bernstorff were co-operating closely. Just as they dared to begin thinking of success, the Berlin government blasted their efforts to smithereens by announcing a few days after Wilson's address the levying of unrestricted submarine warfare, effective February 1, 1917. As the momentous news, accompanied by a summons to Washington, was handed to House, he was giving a small dinner party at the Plaza. Making discreet apologies, he withdrew from his guests and hustled down to Pennsylvania Station. Reaching the White House in time for breakfast, the Colonel spent the morning with the President, although the two quickly agreed that relations with Germany should be broken off. Sad and depressed, Wilson defied all efforts to uplift his spirits. The suddenness of Germany's action, he said, made him feel as if the world had reversed itself and he couldn't get his balance. With policy settled, the President and his friend—awaiting Lansing's appearance with the necessary papers—had time to kill and the morning seemed endless. Walking up and down the floor, the President would pause now and then and nervously rearrange his books. Mrs. Wilson spoke of golf. Would it look bad, she asked House, if the President went to the links? Rather tartly, the Colonel answered that the American people would feel that the President "should not do anything so trivial at such a time." Wilson suggested pool, and led his confidant off to the basement where a table had been installed. During the second game, Lansing arrived with his draft of a message to Germany, which was quickly approved. House went on to press the point that Bernstorff should be handed his passports at once. On February sixteenth, the staff of the German embassy sailed from New York, the departing Bernstorff leaving a last message for the Colonel: "Give him my love and tell him he is the best friend I have in America."

An eerie sequel of eight full days of unbroken calm ensued. The President was still hoping and working for peace. No U-boat sinking involving the loss of American lives transpired. Finally on February twenty-fourth, the quiet was shattered by the transmission to Washington of a sensational telegram intercepted by the British, and sent by Zimmermann, German

Minister of Foreign Affairs, to Bernstorff while still in the U.S. to relay to
the German Minister in Mexico. The intercepted message instructed the
German Minister, in the event the United States should enter the war, to
propose to Mexico an alliance designed to reconquer the "lost territory,"
constituting parts of Texas, New Mexico and Arizona. Mexico, it was further
proposed, might also invite Japan into the alliance. President Wilson released the Zimmermann note to the press on March first and American
opinion was galvanized against Germany instantaneously. Among the ires
most lividly aroused was that of Colonel House. The Zimmermann note had
come in over the State Department wire in German code, under the privileged arrangements the Colonel himself had provided for the convenience
of the departed Bernstorff. After intercepting the note, the British by some
wizardry had decoded it, and sent it to the President. House, needless to say,
felt terribly put upon; in plain language, he had been duped.

On February twenty-sixth, the Cunard liner, *Laconia*, was sunk with
two American lives lost, followed several days later by other American ships.
On the basis of the cumulative provocation, Wilson finally decided to peck
out on his typewriter the draft of a message requesting Congress to declare
the existence of a state of war. House, who was on hand, offered a few suggestions, and on April second, at eight o'clock in the evening, the President
delivered the message in person to a joint sitting of Congress. House, in an
unprecedented exception, allowed himself to attend this singular proceeding.
Afterwards, he returned to the White House with the President, Mrs. Wilson and Wilson's younger daughter Margaret in the official car. We "fore-
gathered in the Oval Room," House remembered that evening, "and talked
it over as families are prone to do after some eventful occasion."

The United States now at war, House's little study on 53rd Street
throbbed with brisk activity. Interviews, telephone calls, telegrams and
letters flooded his waking hours. Ambassadors hustled up from Washington.
Foreign Ministers and Finance Ministers, Defense Ministers and commissioners of war production raced across the Atlantic, choosing for their first
stop not Washington, but House's apartment. Sometimes this invading
officialdom came organized as teams or missions—the British Balfour and
Northcliffe missions, the French Joffre mission and a comparable Italian
mission. The visitors engaged in a kind of cutthroat competition with one
another to annex to their respective national efforts a maximum share of
America's expanded productivity as a belligerent. Ignace Paderewski, for-
saking his music, aimed, with the aid of House and U.S. generals, to establish a Polish army. Bergson, the eminent French philosopher, and T. P.
O'Connor, the articulate Irish nationalist, came entreating succor for their

countrymen. Letters poured in by the hundreds from American professors, corporation executives, artists and journalists, seeking jobs in the new war government. All manner of complainants turned hopefully to House as a dispenser of beneficence: industrialists shackled by a fuel or a transportation problem, financiers shrieking in mortal pain over the announced tax plans of the Treasury, journalists distraught by the Administration's standoffishness with the press.

To most of his callers and correspondents, House offered encouragement and advice and put them in touch with the proper official authority. The foreign missions found it wise to bring their requisitions to House, especially if Wilson's notice were necessary, to avoid the slow-moving regular channels. "I am doing everything through House," declared the head of one mission, "who acts remarkably quickly." So appreciated was House by his numerous foreign clientele that when summer came and he embarked for his customary vacation at Magnolia, near Beverly, his following, like the Pied Piper's, took out solidly after him. Lord Northcliffe, a man of succinct comment, observed, "All the roads lead ultimately to Magnolia."

House left his summer home periodically for meetings with the President in Washington. More than ever, Wilson was urging his confidant to remain by his side in the capital. The situation, the President argued, surely warranted it, and the Colonel's comings and goings created so much comment that it would be better if he came more often and stayed longer instead of coming infrequently and provoking a sensation each time. But House was not to be budged; it was the President who did the adjusting by making increasing visits to House's New York apartment for discussion of urgent business.

Next to the President, House's most significant dealings in these busy war days transpired with the Chief of British Intelligence in the United States, William Wiseman, who thoroughly lived up to the flattering connotation of his surname. The House-Wiseman nexus, which has few parallels in history, was not limited to intelligence in the traditional sense but covered every conceivable problem affecting Anglo-American co-operation. It was productive of results far exceeding those of any committee, mission, or other species of negotiation. Gassed at Ypres and temporarily blinded, assigned to the United States for lighter duty, Wiseman first met House one autumn day in 1916 when he showed up in the Colonel's study with a confidential dispatch from the British ambassador. The attraction was mutual and instantaneous. A friendship quickly flourished, House soon professing his preference for doing business with Wiseman "because of his ability, loyalty, and trustworthiness. He has qualities which are rarely met with in one man." Alert to please House, the British catered to his obvious preference to work through Wiseman instead of the regular diplomatic machinery.

House and Wiseman established a direct method of informal constant communication between their governments. Delays were obviated and the most delicate negotiations facilitated. To make things easier, Wiseman rented quarters in House's apartment building and arranged a private telephone connection to the British Embassy in Washington. The two emissaries met each morning at ten o'clock and at innumerable other times during the day. Thanks to House's intervention, Wiseman could see the President freely, with minimum prearrangement. Lord Northcliffe, who observed the workings of the wartime Anglo-American governments at first hand, declared, "Wiseman is the only person, English or American, who has access to the President and Colonel House at all times." House likewise gave Wiseman entree to British leadership, a privilege the latter wouldn't enjoy relying simply upon his own modest official position. The intelligence job was advantageous, however, in affording Wiseman facilities for communicating directly and secretly with Grey and his successor, Balfour, in the Foreign Office and with their private secretary, Sir Eric Drummond. In minutes or hours, knotty matters were disposed of, which through regular channels would take days. The volume of business in the irregular channels must have been terrific because Wiseman, as he put it, tended to discuss matters "frankly" with House and "cautiously" with the State Department.

Now and then the British Foreign Office muttered that the whole arrangement was "most unorthodox," but in general knuckled down to it. On several occasions at least the House-Wiseman alliance teetered on the brink of disaster. Once a sizable crisis was precipitated when influential officials of the Foreign Office began speaking ominously of their Washington ambassador, Spring-Rice, as "nervously unfit for his duties" and seriously in need of returning to Britain "for a rest." Both House and Wiseman were greatly disturbed by these reports. The success of their collaboration clearly depended upon the inadequacies of the official ambassador. His illness simultaneously created a vacuum of need and an atmosphere of tolerance for their large-scale enterprise. The replacement of the ailing, failing Spring-Rice with a zestful new ambassador would gravely imperil the entire unofficial structure. Drastic measures were called for and the Colonel lost no time in taking them. For several weeks he plied various high-placed officials in the Foreign Office with messages laden with the most complimentary references to the talent and worth of Sir Cecil Spring-Rice. The Foreign Office duly saw the light, Spring-Rice stayed on in his post, and the prodigious co-operation of House-Wiseman tandem continued measurably to shorten what the latter called, "The greatest asset Germany has today—the 3,000 miles that separates London from Washington."

House was drawn into another sector of the wartime administrative apparatus in the autumn of 1917. Lloyd George, now the British Prime

Minister, was pressing for an American War Mission to be dispatched at once to Europe. The Mission's objective would be a smoother dovetailing of the Allied and American production and military efforts. House was enthusiastic; Wilson at first resisted, but finally came around on condition that House would head up the Mission. Hereupon the Colonel resisted. He was much too busy, he said, and suggested instead the dispatching of the administrators most concerned, Secretary of the Treasury McAdoo and Secretary of War Newton D. Baker. House abhorred getting bogged down in the operational detail the Mission would surely involve or entering into technical discussions of finance and supply far beyond his competence. But Wilson continued to insist and House reluctantly agreed to take on the Mission. In late October, he embarked with a delegation extracted from the chief war-making agencies: the military, the Treasury, the shipping board, the food administration, and the industries board. In addition, House was accompanied by his customary personal entourage, consisting of Mrs. House, Miss Denton, his son-in-law, Gordon Auchincloss, the latter's secretary, and a maid, Mary Flattery. The Mission arrived in London in November at a critical juncture in Allied fortunes. The Italian Army had just collapsed at Caporetto; mutiny was brewing among the French; the Bolsheviks had wrested power in Russia and were commencing peace negotiations with the Germans. The spectacle of House moving into this milieu of desperate failure prompted the local New York Times correspondent to observe, "Never in history has any foreigner come to Europe and found greater acceptance or wielded more power. Behind this super-Ambassador, whose authority and activities are unique, stands the President."

In London, the War Mission held long, intensive and productive meetings with Lloyd George and his ministers. House maintained careful oversight of the multiple negotiations in progress by holding frequent briefing and planning sessions, and by requesting from the members of his flock memoranda summarizing their activities each day and copies of every cable they sent to and received from their departments in Washington. With characteristic caution, he regularly admonished his colleagues against the machinations of spies, who, he said, were infesting the Claridge Hotel where the mission was housed. While thus controlling the London situation, House kept abreast of happenings in Washington chiefly through the ample cables not of an American official, but of his British friend, Wiseman.

After London, House and his colleagues went on to Paris for further conferences in which all the Allies were represented. The proceedings, known officially as the Inter-Allied Conference, were designed to achieve a massive co-ordination of all phases of the war efforts. The participants consisted of a vast galaxy of prime ministers, foreign secretaries, chiefs of staff, admirals, ambassadors, shipping and finance experts, and food controllers meeting in the ornate Salon de L'Horloge of the French Foreign Ministry on the Quai d'Orsay. The plenary sessions, like the hall they were held in, were largely decorative. The real work was accomplished in a series of small committees of experts set up at House's initiative and insistence. The informal, down-to-earth discussions of these committees paved the way for the principal accomplishment of the conference: the establishment of a series of permanent inter-allied administrative committees on munitions, petroleum, food, maritime transport and the like. The conference got these committees off to a good start by reaching general agreements on issues deriving from the blockade, naval co-operation, man power, tonnage and other thorns in the side of inter-Allied relations.

House had more than his share of troubles at Paris. He had to beat off Anglo-French insistence that the battle-green American troops just arriving on the European mainland be merged with experienced Allied units. House staunchly represented the determination of the President and General Pershing to keep American batallions intact. The Colonel also struggled valiantly, but with less success, to reform the recently established Supreme War Council, consisting of the French and British premiers and their deputies, with House sitting in with his deputies. The Council, House found, had a farcical talent for accomplishing nothing. House's proposal to stiffen the Council by infusing it with real power, ran into a hard wall of British resistance. Although he got nowhere, House did build up, in the cloakroom buttonholing he carried on for a better Council, a succession of useful personal contacts with the new premiers of Britain and France, Lloyd George and Clemenceau, and with the leaders of the lesser Allies. Clemenceau, who presided at the Inter-Allied Conference, he sized up as "one of the ablest men I have met in Europe."

However absorbed House was in war-making, he was applying himself with even greater ardor for the future peace of a better world. As far back as 1915, he had engaged in thoughtful correspondence with Edward Grey on the outline of a permanent organization for maintaining peace. Wilson had encouraged his confidant's interest, and in a major address on May 27, 1916, announced his adherence, in general terms, to the establishment of a league of nations. Fifteen months later, with the war going decidedly against the Germans, and aware that the several Allied governments were "getting their pipes laid" for the impending peace conference, Wilson turned to House. "What would you think," asked the President, "of quietly getting about you a group of men to assist you to do this? Under your guidance these assistants could collate all definite material available and you could make up the memorandum by which we should be guided."

Naturally, House was enthusiastic. In fact, Sir William Wiseman contends that the Colonel planted the germ of the whole arrangement in Wilson's mind in the first place. House set about organizing his study group or the "Inquiry," as it quickly became known. He named his brother-in-law—the Colonel was a trifle inclined to nepotism—Dr. Sidney Mezes, then president of the City College of New York, as Director of the Inquiry, and Walter Lippmann, then of the *New Republic* as secretary. House recruited a small expert staff from academic circles, and divided the vast domain of the Inquiry into several fields of responsibility. Headquarters for House's enterprise were established in the American Geographical Society in New York, which offered its offices, library and invaluable map facilities. The Inquiry rapidly compiled a vast store of fact and opinion, stayed out of the press and avoided any major discord with the Department of State.

House's own energies, supplemented by David Hunter Miller's, the legal expert of the Inquiry, were concentrated on working out a draft constitution for a league of nations. The draft House finally came up with consisted of twenty-three articles, of which all but five were approved and adopted by Wilson for subsequent use. House's plan called for a permanent association of nations, served by a secretariat, a permanent international court and an assembly of delegates. The league would guarantee the political independence and territorial integrity of its members, enforce disarmament and bring about the abolition of munitions-making by private enterprise. Wilson, in revising House's draft, dropped the international court and expanded the league's sanctions to include the use of military force, which House had not provided for, against its members. While poring over the draft with his chief, House was simultaneously pressuring Wilson to strive mightily to bring the Allies around to establishing a league of nations as a going concern well before the peace conference met. The confidant figured that American leverage for winning Allied acceptance was greater the more the Allies depended upon us, and that such dependence would decline the closer the war advanced to its final stages. Wilson, unfortunately, was slow to act, and the opportunity was lost.

House's second major architectonical contribution to the postwar world is represented by the famous fourteen points. In the winter of 1917–18, House told the President of difficulties being encountered in bringing the Allies to agree on war aims, and pressed for a speech setting forth the American position on the subject. Wilson was readily amenable and directed House to organize the preliminary material. The speech was to serve a threefold aim: to hold the Bolsheviks with the Allies, to encourage German liberals' suspicion of their government, and to serve notice to stodgy Allied thinking that the traditional ways of conducting international affairs no longer would do. The Colonel put the Inquiry to work and was soon descending upon

Wilson with a wealth of proposals. In the President's study, the two hammered out the draft of the famous Fourteen Points. First, they outlined a series of general terms or points on open diplomacy, freedom of the seas, disarmament, equality of trade, a league of nations, and the like. As further points, they worked out the details of territorial adjustments with certain necessary concessions to the Allied secret treaties. (House and Wilson reviewed the more important of these treaties in a conference at the White House with Balfour earlier in 1917.) After the draft was tidied up, House checked its provisions with several of the foreign ambassadors in Washington, and dashed off a cable to the British Foreign Secretary, forewarning that the President's pronouncements were imminent and expressing hope that "no utterance is in contemplation on your side which is likely to sound a different note or suggestion." The cable was a mite too late. Lloyd George was delivering a comprehensive speech on war aims to the Trades Union Congress. Thereupon Wilson was all for throwing away his draft, but House successfully pointed out that the speech was more necessary than ever, particularly since it placed considerably more emphasis on the league than Lloyd George's. On January 8, 1918, Wilson delivered his memorable address giving the Fourteen Points to the world.

The war, meanwhile, was racing to a climax. The failure of the final German offensive in the west in the summer of 1918 was followed by the cracking of her allies, the routing of her troops and the dissolution of her war government. The new cabinet, formed under Prince Max of Baden, lost no time in communicating through the Swiss government with Wilson, urging immediate conclusion of an armistice and the initiation of peace negotiations based on the Fourteen Points. House assisted the President in drafting a conditional reply to Prince Max.

A full, seemingly interminable, week passed before the Germans responded. Finally, one evening, when House was dining at the Waldorf, Tumulty broke into the festivities with the thrilling word that the Germans had accepted Wilson's terms. Before he knew it, House was on the high seas, Paris-bound, bearing a commission as "Special Representative of the U.S. government" and a letter designating him as "personal representative of the President." In his several capacities, House was to sit on the Supreme War Council with the prime ministers of Britain, France and Italy to work out the provisions of an armistice. In reality, House was sitting on the horns of a dilemma. He was duty bound to keep Wilson's moral and altruistic principles intact without disrupting Allied unanimity, which at best was a fragile grouping of nations whose self-interest was sharply defined and fiercely asserted.

House, upon reaching Paris, had to face the customary avalanche of visitors and conferences. "I do not know," he gasped after his first twenty-four hours, "how I have lived through the day." Plenary meetings of the Allied Council were held in the vast, elegant, rococo ballroom of the Trianon Palace Hotel at Versailles. The real work, however, was not done in the ballroom but in informal sessions in several hideouts. House and the prime ministers, buttressed by their foreign ministers, met variously at Quai d'Orsay in French Foreign Minister Pichon's study, in Clemenceau's room at the War Office, and most often in House's private apartment at 78 rue de l'Université. House's abode was most preferred because of its superior privacy, and its underscoring of the informality of the talks, making it easier to invite or exclude others as circumstances warranted.

Leaving the military and naval aspects of the armistice terms to the experts, House concentrated on the Fourteen Points, and the task of securing their acceptance. In the face of repeated bruising objections to their vagueness from his Allied colleagues, House had Walter Lippmann and Frank Cobb, editor of the New York World, work out an interpretive commentary. As sections were completed, they were telegraphed to Wilson for his comment and approval. House was applying himself to the arduous job of selling the Fourteen Points to the Allies. The British in general were friendly except for the provision dealing with freedom of the seas. Fearful of its effect upon the blockade, their principal offensive weapon, they objected strenuously. Clemenceau and Sonnino, the Italian representative, similarly raged over affronts to their respective national interests. Days and weeks were consumed in heated inconclusive discussion. Finally, unable to stand the futility any longer, House decided to resort to drastic measures. One day, when the meeting room was clogged with incendiary bombast, the Colonel calmly announced that if the Allies did not accept the Fourteen Points, on which Germany had based her request for an armistice, the question would then arise whether the United States would not have to negotiate directly with Germany and Austria. "That would amount," said Clemenceau, his beady eyes twinkling with incredulity, "to a separate peace between the United States and the Central Powers." "It might," replied House, in his husky tone. Count Luigi Aldrovandi-Marescotti, secretary to the Italian premier, who witnessed the scene, said afterwards, "Colonel House was perfectly calm as he made this declaration. He seems to be a man without nerves." House himself, in reporting the incident to the President observed, "My statement had a very exciting effect on those present."

However much he threatened and maneuvered, House, in the end, had to be satisfied with something less than a full loaf. In the hope of defining and narrowing the disagreement, he acquiesced to the British proposal that reservations be prepared to the several points in issue. Even then no agreement as to the nature of the disagreement could be worked out on the freedom of the seas and reparations, and it was decided that these issues should be held over to the forthcoming peace conference. The league, envisaged by the Wilson Administration as the keystone of the future peace, was accepted in principle. The remainder of the Fourteen Points, to House's great pride and delight, were accepted in their entirety. This in itself, representing the concensus of many nations, on a broad canvass of action, was nothing less than a major diplomatic achievement. "I am proud of the way you are handling the situation," Wilson cabled when the results were distinguishable in the clearing diplomatic smoke. Walter Lippmann, whose endurance and skill had been so fully tested, declared, "Frankly, I did not believe it was humanly feasible, under conditions as they seemed to be in Europe, to win so glorious a victory."

Suddenly, House was jolted by a most unexpected development. The President wrote announcing that he would head the American Commission to the Peace Conference. The sparse little message touched off an explosion of disappointment because House had counted on occupying the premier position himself. Several days later, the cables spewed out more bad news: "I assume also," wired Wilson, "that I shall be selected to preside." House shuddered, knowing the objections of the Allied leaders to his chief's mere presence, to say nothing of his presiding. The Colonel, who was sympathetic to the leaders' views, took on the ticklish job of convincing Wilson that he should not come to Paris. It was like walking on eggshells with hobnailed boots. To discourage his chief's attending exposed House to the interpretation that he was engaging in a passage of shabby self-seeking by grabbing up the delegation's leadership for himself. Although House duly wrote in frank and measured words, it was all in vain. Wilson's instantaneous reaction was to dismiss the several objections as "a way of pocketing me."

While grappling with Wilson, House also was up to his head in the local preparations. He carried off the by no means easy coup of establishing English on a par with French as the official language of the conference. With Lloyd George and Clemenceau, he negotiated the hotly disputable question of where the conference should be held. Clemenceau insisted on Versailles, Lloyd George held out for Geneva, and though House himself preferred a neutral country for the conference site, he faithfully represented Wilson, who sided with Clemenceau. Apart from negotiating with the premiers, House spent long hours interviewing the representatives of innumerable countries and would-be countries beseeching American succor for their causes at the approaching conference. The premier of the new Poland and the president of the new Czechoslovakia were constant visitors; Felix Frankfurter eloquently related the plight of the Jews in Palestine; Alexander Kerensky, the deposed head of the provisional Russian government, was clamoring for arms and money to resuscitate his cause. The King of Montenegro urgently requested House's presence at the royal suite for discussions of the highest importance. On the appointed day, a squad of Montenegrin attachés in gorgeous uniforms of gold and aquamarine gathered up House at his apartment and marched him off to His Highness at the Hotel Meurice. "I found the King," wrote House, who was titillated by the experience, "a pleasant old gentleman who told his story with much dignity."

By December 13, 1918, President Wilson was taking the road to Paris in a state of triumphant acclaim. All along the way, great throngs hysterically cheered the President as the protector of the oppressed, the dispenser of justice, the architect of the future. But there were other indications abroad, far less assuring in nature. Lloyd George had just achieved a brilliant victory in the British elections, campaigning on such vengeful slogans as "Hang the Kaiser" and "Make the Germans pay to the last pfennig." This hardly portended a peace of reason. In the same vein, Clemenceau survived a test of confidence in the Chamber of Deputies by asserting that France would find security in the traditional balance of power and system of alliances and not in the *noble candeur* of President Wilson. The flood of ill luck even swallowed up House, who was incapacitated by a severe attack of influenza which prevented his attendance at the important preliminary meetings of the conference. His friend, Wiseman, was among the first to discover the misfortune when, stopping by one morning, as he was wont to do, he found House lying in bed pallid and unshaven, his voice barely audible. Abed nearly a fortnight, House was sufficiently incommunicado that rumors of his death began circulating. Matters even reached a point where the Colonel had the ghoulish pleasure of reading his own obituaries served up with the incomparable extravagance of the French press.

Once back on his feet, House plunged into the center of the conference. He moved from the rue de l' Université to larger quarters in the Hotel Crillon, where Wilson worked and where his American Peace Commission, of which House was a member, had its official headquarters. To facilitate his enormous business with the President, House had a phone installed connecting directly with Wilson's apartment and ordered the wire constantly covered to prevent tapping. In his sundry activities, House was aided and abetted by a small secretariat comprising Miss Denton, several military and naval aides, Gordon Auchincloss, who acted as a sort of aide-de-camp, and a confidential interpreter, Colonel Stephen Bonsal. The latter was much called upon because House's linguistic mastery was limited to English.

House played a major part in bringing to pass Wilson's foremost achievement at the conference: winning the adherence of the Allies to the incorporation of the League of Nations Covenant into the peace treaty. While Wilson was battling for his ideals in the Supreme Council, House was hacking out progress in the byways of behind-the-scenes negotiation. He got on so handsomely with David Cecil, who supervised the British draft of the League Covenant, as to produce drafts for their respective countries which were pretty much identical. House pressed forward by proposing that a resolution be prepared by which the Council would approve the League in principle and entrust the drafting of the covenant to a committee instructed to begin work at once. House developed the text of the resolution, and the Council quickly passed it. This enactment constituted the President's first, and many believe his greatest, victory at the peace conference.

The resulting committee or "Commission" as it was officially known, was the scene of miraculous labors. Within a mere ten days, it reported out an intricate mechanism for the maintenance of world peace. The President and House represented the United States on the committee, whose regular meeting place was House's office on the third floor of the Crillon. Wilson presided at the head of the table, with Orlando, the Italian Foreign Minister, on his right, and House on his left, bright-eyed, watchful, rising intermittently to whisper with a colleague, otherwise silent. Of the nineteen members of the committee, House was heard from least in open discussion. He spoke at only one meeting and on an occasion when Wilson was away and a few words from an American representative were imperative. Yet for all of the Colonel's unobtrusiveness at the conference table, Ray Stannard Baker, who observed the sessions closely, considered House the dominating personality. His real contribution, according to Baker, was made behind the scenes. "Cecil and I," House himself explained, "do nearly all the difficult work between the meetings of the committee and try to have as little friction at the meetings as possible." The searching analysis and hard debate were done by the expert staffs and by ad hoc conferences of selected delegates in House's study, or "cloakroom," as he liked to call it.

House also fostered the harmony and progress of the conference by continuously wining and dining the delegates in his apartment. His culinary projects, which made his headquarters virtually the local social center, were of two main types. One was the highly successful dinner or luncheon for eight to ten delegates. In these rather intimate sessions, where the best in food and wines was unstintingly provided, productive discussion was given the right of way. When he aimed to promote general good will rather than specific understandings, House relied upon a formal, rather massive, affair, taking on as many as eighty guests. While these, too, enjoyed much success, they were not without their problems. One evening, for example, a small crisis was precipitated when Ali-Kuli Kahn, reconnoitering among the place cards before the repast, discovered to his consternation that his colleague, the Prince of Tabriz, was farther removed in the seating from Mrs. House at the head of the table than M. Benes of Czechoslovakia. Since the Prince represented a going political organization well over six thousand years in age, while M. Benes's recently created republic was not yet six weeks old, this was, indeed, an unbearable outrage. It took some careful explaining by House and his harassed assistants to convince Ali and the Prince that the affair was really taking place in honor of the new republic, thus entitling the Czechoslovaks to their privileged proximity to Mrs. House.

It was while the conference was going so swimmingly that Wilson decided to return to the United States. There things were not going swimmingly at all. The Senate was threatening to wreck the League by subjecting its powers to impossible exceptions. Wilson, House and others in the American entourage were confident that the Senate had acted out of ignorance, and that if the President discussed the situation with high-placed Senators, the damage could be rectified. During the President's absence, House acted as head of the American delegation, superseding Secretary of State Lansing, who was one of its members.

With Wilson on the high seas, House plunged into intensive negotiations with the British, the French, the Italians and the Japanese, putting a premium on speedy agreement. House was spurred on by the chaos of the war-battered countries, the popular eagerness for peace, and by the hunger, fear and uncertainty upon which revolution and bolshevism thrived. "We are sitting upon an open powder magazine," House expressed the danger of the moment. His negotiations encompassed the tough territorial and economic questions previously set aside while the League Covenant was being considered. House's assiduity and skill produced a number of understandings which awaited the President's approval when he returned to Paris on March fourteenth.

The oncoming Wilson's spirits were low; he had had a bad time of it in the United States, getting nowhere with the recalcitrant Senators. Mrs. Wilson holds, however, that the President's distress was due not so much to occurrences in Washington as to occurrences in Paris during his absence. The President, Mrs. Wilson has asserted, "aged ten years" when he learned how House had conducted his stewardship. "House has given away everything I had won before we left Paris," the President is said to have exclaimed. "He has compromised on every side, and so I have to start all over again." As for House's account of it all, he acknowledged that the President's mood was "hostile to compromise" and especially to the Colonel's contention that broad concessions would have to be made to French fears of a German resurgence.

Instead of consummating the compromises which House had laboriously prepared, Wilson plunged into protracted wrangles with Lloyd George and Clemenceau. House, seeing Clemenceau after "the Tiger" had finished an all-afternoon session with Wilson and Lloyd George, asked how they had gotten on. "Splendidly," Clemenceau replied. "We disagreed about everything." Yet, when all seemed darkest, the President, exercising his ready capacity for changing his mind, lurched the conference back onto the track of agreement by making large concessions to the French and the British. Wilson had come to identical conclusions which House had reached some time before, that the Fourteen Points were inapplicable in their entirety, and that the League Covenant could not be placed in the treaty without substantial concessions to the special demands of the great Allies. In a series of reluctantly executed turnabouts, the President consented to detaching the Saar from Germany for at least fifteen years. He dropped his opposition to the occupation of the Rhine and his purpose to write into the peace treaty a definite sum of reparations based on the pre-Armistice agreement. He acquiesced to a mandate system which worked excessively to the advantage of the conquering powers, and embarked upon other compromises which House had once proposed.

With this rush of agreement, the peace conference moved into its climactic stages. On June twenty-eighth, the German treaty was signed in the Hall of Mirrors in the historic palace of Versailles. Wilson promptly started for home, and House began sitting for a portrait Sir William Orpen was painting under commission from the British government. The Germans were crying betrayal, that the promise of peace based on the Fourteen Points had not been lived up to. In the Senate, Henry Cabot Lodge was mounting his attack. Even House was privately and ruefully observing, "How splendid it would have been had we blazed a new and better trail."

As the President took leave of Paris, House was among the few granted the privilege of a final conversation. He devoted himself largely to urging his chief to approach the Senate in a conciliatory spirit in seeking its approval of the peace treaty. Wilson manifestly soured at this advice. "House," he replied, "I have found one can never get anything in this life that is worthwhile without fighting for it." House, in his own account of the conversation, says that he disputed this and reminded the President that "Anglo-Saxon civilization was built upon compromise." The conversation ended amiably and they parted.

They were never to see each other again.

House went on to London to launch the League as a going concern, and Wilson, after reaching the United States, embarked upon a frantic tour of the West, scheduling thirty speeches in twelve days to rally support for the peace treaty. On September twenty-fifth, with his tour only partially completed, he collapsed at Pueblo, Colorado, from physical and nervous exhaustion and was rushed back to the capital. On October third, he suffered a stroke which paralysed his left side, an arm and a leg, and invalided him for the remainder of his presidential term and until his death in 1924. By interesting coincidence, House, at the very time of Wilson's seizure, was boarding ship in Britain and falling dreadfully ill from renal colic. During the voyage, his condition grew steadily worse, and he landed in a state of almost complete collapse. The fates were having their joke. Both partners were immobilized, Wilson in Washington and House in New York, while their great project for world peace, to which they had so fully given themselves, lay upon the scales.

With Wilson incapacitated, the conduct of the Presidency passed into the hands of a Regency, entrenched on the White House premises, consisting of Mrs. Wilson, Dr. Grayson and Tumulty. The President could see no one; he could not be accosted with any matter the least unsettling in nature. His little entourage decided what papers came to his attention and made numerous decisions without his knowledge or direction. The President's condition was enveloped in absolute secrecy, inevitably encouraging untold outbursts of wild conjecture that he was dead or insane, and that his signature was being forged.

Colonel House was locked out from all access to the President. Two letters which he dispatched to Wilson on November twenty-fourth and twenty-fifth elicited no response whatever, not even a flicker of acknowledgment. Although privately critical of the Regency for propping up the tottered President "at all costs," even to the point of "crucifying his reputation," House resisted the beckoning temptations to venture to Washington and intervene in the situation. When Lansing one night entreated by telephone that House undertake to see Mrs. Wilson and convince her that the Secretary of State should act as President during her husband's illness, House adamantly refused. "It would not be right," he told Lansing, "and I would be open to just criticism." He would go to Washington only upon call of the President. The call never came.

House's abrupt and total ejectment from the arena of power was not long in evoking rumors and stories that the great partnership had finally "broken." In December, the New York World ran an account of six full columns proclaiming that there was a break, with profuse citations of chapter and verse. The sensation which followed was so terrific, because of the World's status as a major Administration paper, that House felt obliged to declare publicly that his "admiration and affection for the President are unchanged." Even in the enforced and beleaguered solitude he was now experiencing, House maintained a steely composure. "Outside of the affection I feel for the President," he mused in his diary on December eleventh, "I view a possible coolness between us with equanimity." And two days later, "I am waiting philosophically, conscious that I have done nothing to warrant a severance of our friendship."

Yet as the weeks and months passed, with no letter, no telephone call, no kindly intermediary making his welcomed appearance at the President's instigation, House could not help but muse over his shattered fortunes. Why had it all happened? What wrong had he done? Perhaps, he wondered at one point, the letters he last dispatched to the President might have offended Mrs. Wilson because they were addressed not to herself, but to her husband. At another point, House admitted "a great feeling that the drive made against me from Washington is engineered by Baruch, Grayson, and Tumulty." Yet, as he quickly acknowledged, he had neither proven fact nor plausible theory by which this feeling could be "justified."

Any explanation of the disintegration of the famous partnership must hark back to the hectic and fevered atmosphere of the Paris conference. In Paris, it is clear, House committed the crime of throwing his weight around. There was every temptation to do so. Long before the conference, he had worked on a basis of intimacy with the European leaders; the President, on the other hand, had known none of these luminaries before coming to Paris. House consequently enjoyed an easy access to his colleagues at the conference which his more austere chief could never secure. The evidence is clear that House did not always use the superiorities of his situation with due deference to the position and sensitivities of the President. One day, for example, Wilson was engaged in discussion with House in the latter's apartment when Clemenceau walked in unexpectedly. Without ceremony, or the pretext of an explanation, House left the President and went with Clemenceau to confer in an adjoining room. There, behind closed doors, "we had," as House put it, "one of our heart to heart talks." Upon its conclusion, after a long interval, they rejoined Wilson, who was cooling his heels in the sitting room. The Colonel's shabby protocol could hardly have gladdened the waiting President.

House's overweening self-importance is also evidenced in the succession of pointed criticisms he privately levied at his chief during the conference. At no other interlude in the long partnership did House register in his diary so many querulous remarks concerning Wilson and his conduct as in the days of Paris. The President, House is concluding on April first, "never was a good negotiator." In the same vein, on May sixth, "the President is the most prejudiced man I ever knew and likes but few people." Or again, the President is "a poor organizer" who deplorably misuses his staff. House's self-image was one of contrasting excellence. "I believe I can do more work in a day," wrote House in self-congratulation, "than he can do in a week." Again on May thirtieth, House was lamenting, ". . . when we meet, it is to settle some pressing problem and not to take inventory of things in general or plan for the future. This is what we used to do." And, in the final days of the conference, occurs this summary evaluation, "He is one of the most difficult and complex characters I have ever known. He is so contradictory that it is hard to pass judgment upon him."

Probably the most festering source of irritation between House, on the one hand, and the President and Mrs. Wilson on the other, was the press. On several occasions in the Paris conference, British and American papers carried articles lyrically delineating House as nothing less than "the brains of the Commission," and insinuating that the only constructive work of the conference had been accomplished while the President was absent in the United States and the admirable Colonel House was in charge. One day Mrs. Wilson, who was greatly perturbed by the press accounts, sternly confronted House with one of the more flagrant articles. The two were alone in the presidential quarters at the time, House having come to see Wilson, who was out but was expected momentarily. Examining the article thus thrust upon him, House cried out in dismay, according to Mrs. Wilson, and fled from the premises, taking the article with him, not waiting to see her husband as he had planned. This was the last private meeting that ever transpired between House and Mrs. Wilson. The instigator of the offensive articles, it was generally believed, was not House but his son-in-law, Gordon Auchincloss.

Such, then, are the strands of human frailty which choked off the thriving partnership of Colonel House and Woodrow Wilson. For the sake of the historical record, it should be added that although House was forever separated from the President, he was by no means banished altogether from the world of Mrs. Wilson. At her direct request, for example, House mediated the award of an honorary degree from Oxford University for her husband subsequent to his retirement from the Presidency, and over the years performed various other personal favors in her behalf. Sometime after Paris, Mrs. Wilson corresponded with Mrs. House. But the association, it must be granted, was concluded solely by the written word.

House bore up well under his banishment from the presidential circle, losing scant time in remorse and inactivity. For the remainder of the Wilson Administration and for many years thereafter, until his death in 1938, luminaries and hopefuls in all walks of political life trekked to House's apartment to partake of his oracular advice. Until the very end, Miss Denton was fully occupied handling correspondence and arranging appointments. Most of House's wartime colleagues, on both sides of the Atlantic, proved to be not tentative associates whose good will was evoked by passing crisis, but interested lifelong friends. For years after the war, House corresponded regularly with Grey, Balfour, Lloyd George and numerous others in his large British circle. Bernstorff was in touch with him, as were his many associates of the other continental powers. Few European statesmen of present or past importance ventured to the United States without making an ample visit to the 53rd Street apartment. When Clemenceau made his grand tour of the United States in 1922, House personally handled the multitudinous details of his appearances and engagements. On a single day in the 'twenties, two distinguished Americans with whom House had been considerably associated in the war, came to his apartment to discuss their respective aspirations for the presidential nomination. They missed each other on the elevator only because House frantically sandwiched in another half-hour appointment between the departure of one distinguished visitor and the arrival of the other. "You know," House observed to a friend one day, while pausing on his oracular treadmill, "I am busier now than I ever was in the war."

Tommy the Cork

——————

THOMAS G. CORCORAN

SOME MONTHS after Pearl Harbor, when the United States was still achieving only indifferent success on the battle fronts of World War II, and the mobilization on the home-front was proceeding in ragged fashion, a plain citizen, a Joe Smith, disturbed by the lamentable showing of his country, wrote a letter to President Franklin D. Roosevelt, diagnosing the several troubles and confidently pointing the way to improvement. In citing chapter and verse on the mistakes of the past, the plain citizen referred at length to the career of Thomas G. Corcoran, which recently had received considerable attention in the press. Once a favorite unofficial assistant to President Roosevelt, Corcoran had ventured from his government employment into private life where, according to stories in the newspapers, he was securing for imposing fees fat war contracts for his many clients. So heavy, indeed, was the demand for his services, Corcoran revealed, in testimony before a Senate committee, that he was turning away clients "by the hundreds." "Isn't there anything that can be done to curb the activities of Mr. Thomas Corcoran?" the troubled plain citizen asked the President of the United States. "There surely must be someone cleverer than he in Washington. You, yourself, must be at least his equal, if not his superior." Having a flair for putting one and one together, the citizen went on to offer a constructive suggestion both for the country's plight and the presumed menace of Corcoran. Put Corcoran back on the job, he pleaded to the President where "at least he would be working for us and not against us." "Such an action, as you know," the recommendation continued, "would further the war effort immeasurably."

The Thomas Gardiner Corcoran of the New Deal and World War II was, indeed, a conjurer of events, a man of large affairs. He was an adventurer who, in his time, has sought to introduce banana-growing on the island-fortress of Taiwan and to establish across the length and breadth of Brazil a chain of restaurants under the auspices of the Union News Company. In reality he belongs not to the twentieth century, but to another age. He is a medieval character who operated in the era of the New Deal with the fervor, bravado and finesse of a top-notch Grand Duke of an Italian principality. He was equally adept at leading his forces across the moat and bursting over

249

the main wall, or achieving his purposes by Jesuitical machination and ma-neuver. Intrigue was his middle name and practical politics his forte. When colleagues in the good fights of the New Deal were bewildered by the opposing forces, Corcoran would commend to their attention the leading philosopher of medieval ducal power—Machiavelli—for realistic and instruc-tive expositions on statecraft and human nature. For every difficult or per-plexing situation arising in the rough march to a policy goal, he had a fitting aphorism handy. "If you hit at a king," he would say in a kind of situation which tended to recur, "you must kill him." His interpretation of the Presi-dency, on the basis of his intimate association with the office, is essentially Machiavellian. The President, Corcoran has said, "must deceive, misrepre-sent, leave false impressions, even, sometimes, lie . . . and trust to charm, loyalty and the result to make up for it. . . . A great man cannot be a good man." For the young and ambitious, Tom Corcoran offered a recipe of success, whose validity was amply demonstrated by his own public career. "The way to get ahead," he would say, "is to fish in troubled waters."

Corcoran's most rewarding troubled waters was the New Deal, in which he had more than his fill of turbulence in pushing through legislation to regulate the stock exchanges, the securities in which they and others deal and public utility holding companies in the aftermath of the crash of 1929. He also exposed the incredible malfeasance in the inner sanctums of high finance where the public had supposed pure virtue held sway. But Corcoran was on hand in seasons of defeat as well as in those of victory. He was a top White House legman in an interval when the New Deal was at the nadir of its prestige and traveling its roughest course; when F.D.R., for all of his political genius, was making his worst political mistakes. Corcoran was the good soldier in the ill-conceived plan to pack the United States Supreme Court; he was chief engineer of the famous and abortive purge of Senators and Congressmen in the elections of 1938; he sought to push a dawdling President into coping with a deepening economic recession which in the late 'thirties imperiled the continuance of the New Deal; he attempted to bring the reluctant F.D.R. to designate a worthy heir to succeed himself in the Presidency, an effort which ended in fiasco and hastened the crumbling of the movement's support.

Corcoran, the New Dealer, was flaming in beliefs, an intense crusader for the little fellow—the unemployed, the consumer, the innocent babe in the stock-market woods, the small businessman. The viper he labored mightily to crush was big economic enterprise and its abuses of oppression, greed and sheer stupidity. His philosophy of action was the natural reflex of a man who has a strong streak of paternalism in his character. Like his medieval forebears, Corcoran was a man of mystery, who provided abundant grist for the mills of legendry. Hurtling about Washington to confer with squads of young and admiring lieutenants posted in departments and agencies all over town, his comings and goings crackled with excitement. "He's on his way here," his awaiting conferees would say. "He's just outside." "Here he is." "That's him." And Corcoran would gallop in, followed by key men and protégés, and deliver a muffled rat-tat-tat of instructions into alert and straining ears. In a moment he was gone. His youthful audience, their energies recharged and their inspiration renewed, would gladly work through the night—as, indeed, they were customarily asked to do—to complete the assignment just conferred.

Corcoran reached the crest of his influence in his public career as a trusted assistant to Franklin D. Roosevelt. His lofty place in F.D.R.'s confidence, from 1936 to 1940, has been attested to by a judicious fellow presidential assistant, Samuel I. Rosenman. Corcoran, Rosenman has written, was "as intimate and important a part of the Administration as any Cabinet officer or Presidential adviser . . . and much more so than most of them." In his season of favor, Corcoran rated high in the President's affection and esteem. "Tommy the Cork," F.D.R. liked to call him, after his manner of address to an older and cherished friend, Henry Morgenthau, otherwise known in presidential parlance as "Henry the Morgue." F.D.R.'s habit of stylized nicknames once provoked the snickering comment of General Hugh Johnson, a former high official of the New Deal, who had become disenchanted with the Administration and turned for release to journalism. Inspired by "Tommy the Cork," Johnson contemplated in his syndicated newspaper column the extension of the nickname formula to the several personalities then gracing the New Deal landscape. Harry Hopkins, Frances Perkins, Daniel Roper, Leon Henderson, Harold Ickes and Senator Alben Barkley, as dubbed in the common style, became Harry the Hop, Fanny the Perk, Danny the Rope, Leon the Hen, Harold the Ick and Alben the Bark. "Try this new White House game," mirthfully proposed Johnson, "on your acquaintances, mah frens."

Tommy the Cork's identification with the New Deal was encouraged, if not foreordained, by family background. The Corcorans of Pawtucket, Rhode Island, into which family he was born on December 29, 1900, were firmly linked with the liberal tradition and the Democratic party. His father, who hailed from New York, whence his father had migrated from Ireland, was a lawyer with do-gooder tendencies, who made occasional sorties into local politics. Until his death, in his eighty-eighth year, Corcoran's father practiced law. The younger Corcoran's two brothers also are lawyers. His mother's family, the O'Keefes, were pre-Revolutionary New Englanders who arrived locally via Canada.

After schooling in Pawtucket, Tom went on to nearby Brown University, where he dazzled professors and fellow students with his rapid and sharp intelligence, fantastic industry and breadth of interest in his studies. Valedictorian of his class, he made Phi Beta Kappa in his junior year and won prizes and scholarships galore. When engaged in an intellectual project of some magnitude, he was addicted to working round the clock. A believer in the ideal of the well-rounded person, Corcoran faithfully applied his philosophy to his college experience. His choice of studies was truly liberal. Majoring in English, he also cast his interests among modern languages and the classics, and the natural and social studies. As to his extracurricular record, "There are few activities he has not had a liberal share in," said his senior yearbook, "and very very few men who do not know him." Captain of the debating team and class vice-president, he was also a radio performer and an enthusiastic stage actor, whose roles ranged from humble parsons to silky counts. He became an accomplished pianist with a large memorized repertoire of classical and popular numbers. Gilbert and Sullivan, it was said, "he knew from A to Z." A rugged, square-built youth, Corcoran was a backfield star of his class football team and champion hiker of the school. His summers he passed hewing trees with a lumber company, as a telephone lineman, an Appalachian Mountain guide and sports director in a boys' camp. With his own hands, he built a cabin on Mount Washington. His devotion to sports and the outdoor life did much to develop the stamina that enabled him to face so well the grueling hours of his subsequent New Deal assignments. Corcoran took his master's degree at Brown, intending to teach English and, having a flair for words, to establish himself as a serious writer. But after further thought, his bent for practicality, which is strong, intervened, and he concluded it would be wiser to study law. As generations of estimable Brown graduates have done, he enrolled in the Harvard Law School.

At Harvard, Corcoran again amazed his professors with his nimble-witted recitations and the superiority of his examinations. He was virtually a member of the faculty himself. To build up income, and as an outlet for a hardy sense of enterprise, in his last years at Harvard he gave lectures—at two dollars a head—on how to pass examinations in the tougher courses. His ability to take a five-pound text or treatise and cover the high spots in a single evening, endeared him to his vexed and anxious clientele. His other major extracurricular activity was that of Note Editor on the *Law Review*, a coveted honor accorded only to highest-ranking students. As Note Editor, Corcoran was borne by the consuming self-confidence which typifies his later career. "I just wrote a Note that will be quoted by the Supreme Court someday," he remarked of one contribution. Upon completing his baccalaureate degree in law in 1925, he put in a year's graduate study at Harvard for his

S.J.D. (Doctor of the Science of Jurisprudence). Again, Corcoran was envisioning a teaching career, this time as a professor of law.

His march into pedagogy was interrupted by his capture of an honor prized by graduating Harvard law students above all else: his scholastic primacy and the intercession of a professor, Felix Frankfurter, who had been impressed with his bountiful talents, won him a secretaryship under the eminent Justice Oliver Wendell Holmes of the United States Supreme Court. Corcoran as secretary did research and writing chores for the Justice and absorbed his abundant wisdom with eager and worshipful attention. Holmes became the first of several mundane gods at whose shrine he worshiped deeply. Holmes was impressed, too. He always proudly averred that Corcoran was the most brilliant of his many gifted clerks, most of whom went on to outstanding careers. While in Holmes's service, Corcoran came to know and revere another high priest and prophet of the legal world, Justice Louis D. Brandeis, and formed a lasting aquaintance with the young Justice Harlan Fiske Stone. If Corcoran had a greater love than law, it was politics. From the quiet sanctuary of the Court on Capitol Hill, he had a window upon the errors of the Coolidge Administration in the gathering storm of economic debacle.

When the clerkship expired, Corcoran entered the employ of Cotton, Franklin, Wright, and Gordon, one of the few important Democratic law firms in Manhattan. The firm's head man, Joseph Cotton—descendant of John Cotton, the Puritan divine; class poet in Harvard College; top man in his Harvard Law School class; assistant to Herbert Hoover in World War I —overnight became a Corcoran god. One of the ablest men of his time, Cotton is still hailed in the trade as "the greatest Wall Street lawyer who ever lived." At Cotton, Franklin, Corcoran specialized in corporate practice, developing an acute familiarity with stock issuances, mergers, consolidations and other intricacies which stood him well later. As was his custom, he amazed his colleagues with his feats of industry. He was given to wearing a green eye shade to protect not his vision—which was perfect—but his concentration against interruption. Corcoran, however, was not all work. Sunday mornings, he would rouse his younger colleagues, hustle them across the Hudson River, load them onto the West Shore railroad and head upstate for a tramp in the woods. At Corcoran's fast pace and sizable mileage, many a younger barrister showed up at work on Monday lame in body but refreshed in mind. When a member of the firm left to locate in Hawaii, Corcoran composed, for a farewell party, a skit written entirely in blank verse. In staging the skit, for which he was also responsible, Corcoran gayly outfitted the male chorus in authentic hula skirts.

In his five years with Cotton, Franklin, Corcoran embarked upon a special line of activity which was to become his hallmark. At the instigation of the then Professor Frankfurter, Cotton agreed to operate what amounted to a placement bureau for Harvard Law graduates in New York City. The stock market had crashed, the depression had set in, lawyers were desperate for jobs. Cotton turned his newly acquired responsibility over to Corcoran, who brought to it the fervor of a missionary and a phenomenal knack at putting the right man in the right job. In his placement activities, Corcoran covered the Stock Exchange, the Livestock Exchange and the banking field generally. He dealt both with recent Harvard graduates and with established men who began looking for a change as the depression worsened. He was not so parochial that he would not help an able job seeker who had made the mistake of attending a law school other than Harvard. The principal gadgetry of his thriving enterprise was a notebook in which was listed the name of every first-class man he came upon and the assignments for which the man was qualified. Scores of able young lawyers helped by Corcoran would soon be following him confidently to Washington.

It was becoming increasingly difficult for Corcoran not to migrate to the capital. His chief, Cotton, who had enlisted as Under Secretary of State, and John Lord O'Brian, the distinguished Buffalo attorney who had become Assistant Attorney General, then the number-two post in the Justice Department, both urged Corcoran to join their respective departments. These invitations he declined. The third request, to which he succumbed, emanated from Eugene Meyer, Governor of the Federal Reserve Board. Meyer had first invited George Franklin, senior partner of Corcoran's law firm, to come down as counsel to the newly established Reconstruction Finance Corporation. In the meantime, however, Cotton had died, following an automobile accident in Baltimore, making Franklin's leaving the firm impossible. Corcoran was dispatched as a substitute. The Democratic Corcoran took up his duties in the Republican Hoover Administration altogether willingly. Herbert Hoover, as perceived by Corcoran, was at most a quasi-Republican possessing sturdy affinities with the Democratic party. The President had served with distinction as a principal official in the Democratic Wilson Administration and in subsequent years had displayed sufficient ambivalence in his party ties that responsible Democratic chieftains had urged his presidential candidacy on their party's ticket. In 1932, as the Hoover Administration was dragging to its close, the oncoming Corcoran viewed sympathetically the President's efforts to unfreeze the general economic situation via RFC loans. Once inside the RFC, Corcoran's heart went out even more to Hoover when he saw the havoc wrought in months past by that impenetrable iceberg of do-nothingness, the man who had been hailed as the foremost Secretary of the Treasury since Alexander Hamilton, Andrew Mellon.

In the midst of his RFC duties of floating loans and rescuing once proud and now imperiled and thoroughly unnerved bankers, Corcoran had resumed his attentions to Justice Holmes. Ill, his strength failing, the Justice had retired from the court. On most évenings, the dedicated Corcoran, who has always had an older man or two to whom he has been devoted, would repair to the Justice's house at eleven o'clock, regale him with pointed anecdote, and read him to sleep. To the Justice, his faithful attendant was "Sonny." "Now Sonny, remember this," Holmes would say, and Corcoran would absorb the forthcoming aphoristic wisdom for quotation in decades to come. When Holmes died in 1935, Corcoran was at his bedside. But the young man had no monopoly of the attentions rendered the fading Justice. In one of his first acts after taking his oath as President on March 4, 1933, Franklin D. Roosevelt visited the bedridden Holmes. It was then that Corcoran first met his future chief and idol.

The young man thus presented to F.D.R. was thirty-two years old, a broad-shouldered six-footer, supercharged with vitality, whose slightly cherubic appearance was dominated by twinkling Irish eyes, a square chin and a shock of black hair streaked with gray. Careful in dress, he was given to blues and grays. His conversation was brisk and fluent, rich in vocabulary and the telling phrase. His manner was totally bereft of the unworldly bookishness ordinarily encountered in the holder of four academic degrees. He was a songster and storyteller in the best Gaelic tradition, who could charm and amuse a sophisticated gathering an entire evening. Entertainment, however, was only his side line. The Corcoran poised at the brink of the New Deal was single-minded in objective with a large habit of success. His way of life was unremittingly Spartan. He didn't smoke and never drank except under pressure of social necessity and then only sparingly. When in need of bracing, he turned not to cocktails but to a can of dextrose, kept handy in a desk drawer, or to a coffee loaded with sugar. His engrossment in his work made him no great favorite among the ladies as a dinner partner. On another count he would never have won a feminine popularity poll. The institution of marriage he tenaciously abhorred as an impossible interference with one's occupational responsibilities. Not until he was thirty-nine and well advanced in his New Deal career did he abandon bachelorhood to marry his secretary, Margaret Dowd, in St. John's Catholic Church at Leesburg, Virginia.

With the advent of Franklin D. Roosevelt's Presidency, a policy and administrative revolution was proceeding in Washington. Jesse Jones, the monumental Texan and big operator, succeeded to the chairmanship of the RFC. Corcoran persisted as counsel at ten thousand dollars a year, serving under Stanley Reed, the General Counsel. At this juncture, Corcoran's distinction as one of the few Democrats in the Administration familiar with the labyrinthian intricacies of Wall Street finance made his services in demand. In the Administration's early weeks, he passed many an evening assisting a small task force recruited by Professor Frankfurter to draft the Securities Act. The venture originated from disclosures by the Senate Banking and Currency Committee and its chief counsel, Ferdinand Pecora, of widely prevalent misrepresentation and fraud in the marketing of securities. The new law, modeled after British legislation, endeavored to assure to the public full and complete disclosure of information by which to judge the securities they purchased, and to provide adequate safeguards against misrepresentation. The Securities Act passed easily, borne by the momentum of crisis and Roosevelt's popularity.

The Securities Act constituted the first major achievement of Corcoran's phenomenal partnership with a member of the Frankfurter task force, Benjamin V. Cohen. So close and staunch would their association soon become that they would be known nationally as "The Gold Dust Twins," "The Whiz Kids," and "The Happy Hot Dogs"—the latter title inspired by their identification with Felix Frankfurter. Tall, high-browed, bespectacled, and slightly stooped, Cohen was thirty-nine years of age. His clothes rumpled and flecked with cigarette ashes from chain-smoking, he had the air of a professor of calculus at M.I.T. Although his seeming timidity, mildness of manner, and quavering voice were sometimes misinterpreted as weakness, Cohen in actuality possessed great toughness of purpose. Son of a prosperous scrap-iron dealer in Muncie, Indiana, Cohen as an undergraduate had studied economics at the University of Chicago under Harold G. Moulton—"the most brilliant student I ever taught." He took his law baccalaureate also at the University of Chicago and went on for postgraduate legal studies at Harvard, quickly becoming a favorite of Frankfurter. Later he served as clerk to Circuit Court Judge Julian W. Mack and, following introductions by Frankfurter and Mack, became a friend and ardent disciple of Justice Louis H. Brandeis. By no means was Cohen a stranger to Corcoran at the outset of the New Deal. Only a year before, they had served on a joint assignment from Professor Frankfurter in Albany, near the close of Roosevelt's Governorship, to assist in the preparation of the New York minimum-wage law.

Corcoran and Cohen brought to their association certain contrasts of temperament and similarities of talent. Corcoran was the extrovert, thriving on human contacts, a ready and expert fighter, and bold to a degree. Cohen, in contrast, was kindly, dreamy, shy, intellectual. Cohen was an outlet for Corcoran's paternalistic instinct and craving to work with someone he admired. To Corcoran, Cohen was "the wiser of us," "the greatest lawyer in the world." The differences of temperament governed the division of work between them. Corcoran was the promoter and contact man dealing with the outside world. With more time for reflection, Cohen became the slightly preponderant intellectual influence. Cohen concentrated more on the tasks of the office, especially on drafting, in which his gifts were exceptional, although Corcoran, too, was highly regarded as a draftsman. In their several legislative projects, both partners in the early stages worked on drafting. When the point of presenting and selling was reached, Corcoran did the front work, testifying before Congressional committees and corralling witnesses, while Cohen listened and took notes, and was ready the next day with a redraft of a bill incorporating any necessary revisions. Corcoran was the trial lawyer, Cohen the briefing attorney.

Midway in the banking crisis which greeted Roosevelt when he came into office, Corcoran temporarily left the RFC to join the Treasury Department with the official title of Assistant to the Secretary. In actuality, Corcoran worked with the Under Secretary, Dean Acheson. The transfer was arranged by Frankfurter who in the earlier Theodore Roosevelt Administration had been pleasantly associated with the father of the current Acting Secretary of the Treasury, Henry Morgenthau, Jr. Corcoran's new work entailed a conjoining of his RFC activities with Treasury banking policies. He determined the eligibility, under the regulations of the two agencies, of banks which had failed or were ordered shut down, and were seeking to reopen with government financial assistance. Things went swimmingly until Corcoran's superior, Acheson, became locked in a fierce policy dispute with Morgenthau over the gold-purchase program. So intense became the battle and the misunderstandings it evoked that Acheson was summarily fired one afternoon at three o'clock. Within two hours, by five o'clock, Corcoran had both resigned from the Treasury and was back securely on the payroll of RFC. Although Corcoran was not himself involved in the Acheson-Morgenthau dispute, he deemed Acheson to be in the right and resigned out of loyalty as an associate. Jesse Jones at the time was also feuding with Morgenthau, which facilitated Corcoran's return to the RFC.

Meanwhile, Corcoran's mentor, Frankfurter, who was often in Washington, was singing his praises to Raymond Moley, the dour, pipe-sucking chief of the famous original Brain Trust, who was acting as F.D.R.'s general assistant. Repeatedly, Frankfurter had been urging Moley, who was struggling hard to keep his head above his rising multifarious duties, to take on Corcoran as an assistant. One day, Corcoran went around to Moley's high-ceilinged office behind latticed saloonlike swinging doors of the State, War and Navy building next to the White House. Moley and his visitor were beginning to confer when Senator Huey Long barged loudly into their presence. The canny orator and dictator of his home state of Louisiana, whose growing national popularity would one day gravely concern F.D.R., took an instantaneous liking to Corcoran. In fact, the Senator had a business proposition. Did Corcoran have a law doctorate degree? The response being in the affirmative, Huey Long proposed, on the spot, to make Corcoran the dean of the University of Louisiana Law School. The flabbergasted New Dealer, who quickly concluded that his future was in Washington, managed to decline gracefully. As for Moley, he too was impressed, but since he was planning to leave Washington shortly for private life, he declined to take on the budding New Dealer in a regular capacity, but in time came to use his talents in spot assignments.

Moley was not the only source from whom assignments were received. From Ferdinand Pecora, the Senate Banking Committee chief counsel and his associate, Max Lowenthal, Ben Cohen picked up the task of developing a companion piece to the Securities Act, a bill to regulate the stock exchanges. Cohen instinctively brought in Corcoran, and the pair, aided by James M. Landis, Telford Taylor and I. N. P. Stokes, produced an intricate bill of fifty pages. Although preceded by a forceful presidential message, the bill, in the opinion of Sam Rayburn, who introduced the measure in the House of Representatives, was opposed by "the most powerful lobby ever organized against any bill which ever came up in Congress." So formidable became the opposition, whose headquarters were situated in a glittering Washington mansion rented by Richard Whitney of the New York Stock Exchange, that Corcoran and Cohen had to recast their bill to win over the more enlightened segments of the industry. Without the concessions made, the bill would never have passed. Corcoran helped with drafting and appeared as a witness in committee hearings. As he testified, the lawmakers showed interest in his precise capacity in working on the bill. "Do you speak for the Reconstruction Finance Corporation?" asked Congressman John G. Cooper, Republican of Ohio.

CORCORAN: "No, sir, absolutely not."
COOPER: "What is that?"
CORCORAN: "The Reconstruction Finance Coproration has nothing to do with this bill."
COOPER: "But you are with the Reconstruction Finance Corporation?"
CORCORAN: "I am with the Reconstruction Finance Corporation."
COOPER: "Did they authorize you to come here?"
CORCORAN: "They know I am here."
COOPER: "Did they authorize you to come here?"
CORCORAN: "The General Counsel said I might come; yes. The chairman of the committee asked me to come down here and I cleared the matter. I am here at the request of the chairman of the committee."
COOPER: "Who authorized you to take part in the drafting of the bill?"
CORCORAN: "That is something extracurricular."

Of the several co-operative working arrangements cultivated by Corcoran and Cohen on Capitol Hill, one of the most rewarding was their association with Senator Burton K. Wheeler, the Montana progressive, superb parliamentary tactician, bloodthirsty investigator and old friend of the Brandeis family. Pooling their efforts on various bills, Wheeler, Corcoran and Cohen achieved their most notable triumph in the Holding Company Act of 1935. The Act was evoked by the gross abuses of the holding company device in the fields of electric and gas utilities: the bringing of competing companies under single management, often with monopolistic results; the blatant lobbying and propoganda activities to ward off government regulation; the unsound financial structures and intricate intercompany dealings which saddled operating companies and ultimately the consumer with exorbitant expenditures.

Wheeler set the Interstate Commerce Committee, of which he was chairman, to work drafting a holding company bill. Soon bills began sprouting elsewhere, in the Treasury and the Interstate Commerce Commission. President Roosevelt, not intending to leave the field to others, established a Power Policy Committee of broad mandate, with Secretary of the Interior Harold Ickes as chairman. Cohen was named committee counsel and charged with preparing a holding company bill. Cohen quickly brought in Corcoran and, working literally night and day, they developed a sixty-page bill, a maze of interdependent and interlocking clauses, but milder in its net effect than the products of their competitors.

The several authors with their bills gathered early one afternoon with the President in the Oval Room of the White House to choose a single bill to bear the Administration's endorsement. Corcoran, who was on hand, had been in F.D.R.'s company several times previously but never before had broached any business to the Chief Executive. The discussion, as it commenced that afternoon, was decidedly unpropitious. Roosevelt leaned to the most drastic of the plans—the Treasury's—which would abolish holding companies altogether. But Corcoran, with Cohen by his side, in an argument of fluent cogency, swung the President around to the Power Policy Committee's approach, emphasizing the regulation and reorganization of holding companies. Harold Ickes, who was present, provided indispensable support. By late afternoon, the President gave his nod to the Corcoran-Cohen bill, on condition that a violent but meaningless preamble and the famous "death sentence" provision be added, aimed at divesting holding companies of their geographic sprawl and excessive pyramiding. Neither the President, nor Corcoran and Cohen, expected the provision to survive in Congress.

Roosevelt deputed Corcoran and Cohen to see to Congressional enactment of their bill. Corcoran drafted a presidential letter of fitting exhortation to accompany the bill and next morning called on Wheeler and Sam Rayburn, chairman of the House Commerce Committee, securing their assent to introduce the Administration measure in their respective houses. Meanwhile the horrendous lobbying juggernaut of the utility companies rolled into action. Their wiliest lawyers and most dextrous contact men invaded Capitol Hill; the Congressional mail room was swamped with protesting letters and telegrams from "constituents" who later were proven by the hundreds to be nonexistent. One Congressman averred that the power lobby had tapped his telephone conversations with the White House, and another startled his colleagues by pointing out the power company lobbyists of his state watching in the gallery. A House committee proposed to subpoena the books and records of the Mayflower Hotel, the power lobby headquarters, to determine "how much was spent for White Rock and propaganda." The enormous lobbying effort was successful, for the Administration bill was stopped dead in the House of Representatives.

Thereupon Corcoran induced Wheeler to commence hearings on the bill in the Senate Commerce Committee. To face the lobbying onslaught, Corcoran and Cohen journeyed to Wheeler's suburban home to coach the Senator nightly on the intricacies of the bill until he knew its multitudinous parts backward and forward. In his daytime hours, Corcoran drilled government witnesses, and for Senators and Congressmen, friendly to the bill, he ghostwrote letters addressed to colleagues and constituents, entreating their support. With Senator Joe Bailey of North Carolina, he worked out advantageous compromises necessitated by twelve eviscerating amendments launched by the bill's foes. At the conference-committee stage, Wheeler took the exceptional step of bringing Cohen into committee sessions as his adviser; and in the debate on the Senate floor, the young counsel was by his side assisting with whispered recommendations. Corcoran, for his part, was frantically lobbying in cloakrooms and hallways, lining up votes. His advocacy became so intense, his critics said, that in an outrageous assault on legislative dignity he "thumbed his nose" at a Congressman pledged to vote against the death sentence. (Corcoran subsequently denied under oath committing this unsocial gesture.)

Corcoran's several activities were conducted with remarkable unobtrusiveness until an explosion of publicity was touched off by Congressman Ralph O. Brewster, former Governor of Maine. On a hot midsummer day, Brewster rose and declared, "During the consideration of the 'death sentence' clause in the Holding Company bill, Thomas G. Corcoran, Esquire . . . came to me in the lobby of the Capitol and stated to me with what he termed 'brutal frankness' that, if I should vote against the death sentence for public utility companies he would find it necessary to stop construction on the Passamaquoddy dam in my district." (The dam was a huge work relief project established primarily to develop public power. Situated across from

Campobello, the Roosevelt family's summer home, "Quoddy" was a pet enterprise of the President, fondly designed to brighten the economic future of a badly depressed area.) Brewster appended to his report several interpretive observations which evoked heavy applause from both sides of the aisle. "Such a suggestion, from such a source," he said of Corcoran's representations, "is repugnant to every instinct of decency in legislation and proper regard for our constitutional oath of office. . . . I share with the President his concern at the concentration of economic power. It seems necessary, however, that the Membership of this House, without regard to party, shall keep the country alert to the dangers implicit in the concentration of political power." An aroused House instructed its Rules Committee to investigate the Corcoran-Brewster encounter.

In addition to the Rules Committee, the beleaguered Corcoran had to face a cryptic request from F.D.R. "Please send me as promptly as possible," wrote the President, "a complete statement of all your dealings on governmental matters with Representative Ralph O. Brewster of Maine." Working through the night, Corcoran composed an eight-page single-space reply on legal-size paper. The President was evidently satisfied and the relieved Corcoran turned to his next ordeal, the Rules Committee hearings. These were something less than genteel. The charges made against him, declared Corcoran, were baseless. "You're a liar!" shouted Brewster. What had really happened, said Corcoran, was that Brewster had first agreed to vote for the death sentence provision and make a strong speech on the House floor in its behalf, only to change his mind at the last minute upon discovering a "delicate political situation in Maine." The harassed Congressman, seeking to mend what Corcoran called "a series of broken promises," had agreed to "go back to my hotel and not be present at all during the voting." There were no threats whatever, said Corcoran. The young New Dealer presented his story in rapid-fire style, and for collaboration trundled in Ernest Gruening, Director of the Division of Territories of the Interior Department, "who was present at the time and can tell the committee all that was said." Brewster was grievously handicapped by having no witness to his side of the story. At Corcoran's side throughout the encounter was Ferdinand Pecora, then a New York Supreme Court Justice, who occasionally patted his young friend on the back, whispered advice, and exuded approval. "It was marvellous," he said afterward. The New York Times, which earlier had editorialized that Corcoran's alleged activity was "in a strict and moral sense . . . a corrupt way of trying to win favor and gain support," now changed its mind. With the Rules Committee investigation completed, the Times dismissed the incident with a shrug, "Hot weather makes hot words."

· The Holding Company bill eventually staggered through to victory, and the usual joyous signing ceremony transpired at the White House, with

F.D.R. presenting the pen employed to Corcoran. A line-up of other pleased officials, including Cohen, were also in attendance, beaming for the press photographers. While the jubilation was subsiding, power companies across the country were rushing into court challenging the constitutionality of the Holding Company Act. Thrashing desperately to stay above the rising tide of cases, the Acting Attorney General, with F.D.R.'s approval, summoned the aid of Corcoran and Cohen. Corcoran, who had been impressed with Robert H. Jackson of the Treasury Department in the early executive maneuvering over the Holding Company bill, induced the President to wire Henry Morgenthau from Warm Springs, requesting Jackson's release from his departmental duties to help in the crisis of impending litigation.

The center of preparations quickly shifted from the Justice Department to the offices of Corcoran and Cohen at the RFC and Interior Department. There with a handful of dedicated young lawyers and stenographers, Corcoran, Cohen and Jackson tackled the immediate task of choosing from a huge pile of potential cases the one on which the government might most advantageously concentrate in testing the constitutionality of the act. The feverish scanning occupied an entire afternoon, until, at five o'clock, an appropriate case was settled upon, involving a gigantic utility holding company enterprise, the Electric Bond and Share Company. From that moment of decision until three thirty A.M., the assembled hands were busy writing and rewriting assigned portions of the government's brief. As sections were completed, they were turned over to the waiting stenographers. Finally, in the late morning hour, a drooping assistant whisked the entire finished document to the airport for the four-o'clock plane to New York where the case was to be tried in lower court. Corcoran, Cohen and Jackson repaired to an all-night restaurant and celebrated sleepily on scrambled eggs as dawn began lighting the eastern skies. The weeks following were passed battling the country's best law offices in the federal courts. In the climactic proceedings of the United States Supreme Court, Cohen, who presented the government's case in a learned and nervous style of quivering hands and voice, prevailed over the suave pleaders of the utility companies.

As for Corcoran, the holding company episode had for the first time brought him into frequent association with the President. On the many evenings when the battle hung in balance, Corcoran would venture to F.D.R. to report the day's progress and discuss next steps. Roosevelt came to know and admire the young man's talents. The President's impressions were buttressed by the happy outcome of the struggle.

Approximately one year prior to the Holding Company Act, Felix Frankfurter had written to F.D.R., pointing out that there were not enough hours in a day or strength in one mortal to see all the people and to deal with the countless situations requiring the President's attention, and that, indeed, a wise Chief Executive would conserve his time and strength for higher business, leaving the abundance of lesser things to a capable, all-round assistant. More specifically, Frankfurter envisioned this general aide as an "intelligent energetic younger man." In fact, said Frankfurter, he knew exactly the "right young man," and would the President see him? The nominee, it turned out, was Corcoran, and by early 1936 he was taking on a large measure of the functions conjectured by Frankfurter.

There were other needs which the newly arrived Corcoran conceivably might satisfy. In 1936 and after, the President craved companionship rather more than usual. His children had grown up and left home, returning to the hearth only for occasional visits. His crony of several decades and original political mentor, the elfin Louis McHenry Howe, had passed on after a long illness, leaving a vacuum of companionship to be filled. But the need was balanced by doubt. His relationship with his original Brain Trust had crashed upon the reefs. The chief Brain Truster, Raymond Moley, F.D.R. was convinced, had gone over to the enemy, the conservative business interests, who were fighting his Administration tooth and nail. After Moley's departure, another original Brain Truster, Rexford G. Tugwell, the Columbia economics professor and Under Secretary of Agriculture, was for a time the President's chief confidant, but he, too, ran into trouble. His condescending manner irritated Congress and he fell into the ill grace of several leading White House inhabitants, including Mrs. Roosevelt. Tugwell was not long in departing.

In other respects, F.D.R. might facilitate or hamper an oncoming assistant such as Corcoran. Vibrant, warm, an unremitting activist, F.D.R. was undogmatic, a man without a theory in a time rich in formulations. Yet he had his blind spots—a consummate faith in his luck and political invincibility. He valued procrastination, viewing time as the great healer in politics. He was prone to keep around him counselors of varying policy outlooks. His cabinet ranged from the progressivism of Harold Ickes to the budget-balancing conservatism of Henry Morgenthau. He could use strong men like Jesse Jones and Cordell Hull more than they used him. Suspicious, mischievous, even malevolent, he played his associates off against each other by awarding them overlapping commissions, keeping them in the dark, and rudely shifting policy. He jealously guarded his freedom of action, by ignoring channels and organization charts when it served his purpose. "The President reigned," observed Rex Tugwell, "in an informal splendor which shed its glow over all Washington."

The most compelling reason for Corcoran's accession to the White House circle was his possession to an eminent degree of the talents which the times and the New Deal unmistakably called for. Affairs were at a juncture where the idea men and philosophers who constituted the original Brain Trust were distinctly less valuable than the administrators and operators who knew how to do the job of transmuting goals and programs from bare ideas and conjectural memoranda into specific action. Legislation had to be passed, court battles won, elections faced. The momentum of crisis, which in the first presidential term had made all things possible and had imparted to Roosevelt the aura of invincibility, was decidedly slowing. Times were better, production was rising, unemployment falling. The relaxation of emergency was displacing the social unity on which the Administration had coasted with the cross-purposes and conflicts which normally occupy the American political scene. Congress was stirring with long-repressed yearnings for self-assertion. The progressives—Borah, Norris, Hiram Johnson, Couzens, and others—were becoming increasingly critical. The city bosses were waiting insinuatingly to be paid off for their support in 1932 and 1934. The hostility of the Supreme Court in striking down New Deal laws was reaching grim proportions. In such a milieu, Corcoran, the legal craftsman, the operator who could get things done, was clearly the kind of man needed around the White House.

Tom Corcoran's accession to the presidential circle represented more than a personal triumph, a major notch in the belt of his own career. Equally important, it gave the close-knit group of Washington attorneys, chiefly of Harvard background, who drew their inspiration from Justice Louis D. Brandeis, their first full-time emissary in the White House. Until Corcoran's entree, the Brandeis group was handicapped by the transient character of its representation. Brandeis's Supreme Court Justiceship and advanced years sharply limited his participation in the business of the Presidency. His first lieutenant, Frankfurter, occupied with his Harvard Law professorship and his envisoned role as a kind of Colonel House, could provide only telephone calls and occasional visits to the White House.

The philosophy and measures of the Brandeis group were rooted in the old progressivism. Big business was deemed an evil, or "curse," in their leader's term, to be regulated or carved into smaller units. Government's essential role was to tell business what it must not do rather than what it could do, and such latter-day expedients as collectivism and central public planning were rejected as unsafe and inefficient. The Brandeis philosophy served to assure that the Roosevelt revolution would be a conservative revolution. Paradoxically, although the Brandeis group abhorred business monopoly, they employed the tactics of monopoly in building their own control of the Executive Branch in Washington. The Second New Deal was not long under way when Henry Wallace was voicing his concern over the group's possession of "pipelines in every department of the government." The well-placed Corcoran would become the instrumentality of the Brandeisians—up to a point.

Corcoran never came on the White House payroll or assumed any one of the several vacant administrative titles that were available about the premises. He pursued his assignments neither by formal commission nor written instructions. A large element of his strength was the lack of information in Washington of the precise scope of his White House mandate. Corcoran, when necessary, could skillfully exaggerate his authority, and those he dealt with found it salutary to accept him as he appeared. It was a subtle game which amused Roosevelt and was encouraged by him. Corcoran scrupulously held on to his RFC position, and depended on its ten-thousand-dollar salary for his daily sustenance. His possessiveness toward his old job stemmed from the unforgettable lesson of his predecessor, Moley. With no other place than the White House to retire to—his State Department capacity was largely nominal—Moley time and again was helplessly exposed to playing the fall guy. For Corcoran, the RFC functioned as a refuge in time of trouble.

In his White House endeavors, Corcoran was no gray eminence counseling mysteriously and confidently on high policy, but a chief engineer, toiling below decks to keep the administrative machinery of the New Deal in efficient running shape. The Cork took over quantities of paper work of the Presidency, the reports and memoranda, especially the more verbose variety, which snowballed into the White House. Corcoran was a time saver, who could reduce the bulkiest document to pithy summation. "Will you let me have a digest of the enclosed in about three sentences?" the President would ask, enclosing a twenty-page memorandum. The Cork drafted sundry letters for the President's signature—to a Congressional committee witness who had delivered himself of sentiments friendly to the Administration, to a private citizen who proposed the creation of a new agency—or dispatched a recently made speech for the President's information.

Corcoran was a channel to the President. Administrators seeking the President's blessing for pet projects would hopefully look to Corcoran to play the friend in court. When David Lilienthal worked out plans for a new agency, the future Electric Home and Farm Authority, which through government credit would help farmers in the TVA region equip their homes with all sorts of electrical gadgetry, he looked to Corcoran for access to the President. Corcoran was similarly valued by his innumerable contacts outside the government in the worlds of business, Wall Street, the universities, the church, the press and radio. Robert W. Johnson, President of Johnson and Johnson, the giant pharmaceutical company, J. David Stern, publisher of the *Philadelphia Record*, Sidney Hillman of the CIO, and Cardinal Mundelein all found it profitable to sound out Corcoran on the lay of the land before taking up matters with the President.

Corcoran was a premier odd jobber around the White House—legman, trouble shooter, and expediter, all rolled into one. If the PWA housing program in New York City is bogged down in an internecine brawl, with several members of the local advisory commission shrieking to the heavens their intention to resign, Corcoran is dispatched to the metropolis to set things right. Within a matter of days, the *status quo ante bellum* has been restored and nobody has resigned. The odd jobs Corcoran came upon had the variety of a grab bag at a church bazaar. Once, in the interests of solidifying United States' relations with the countries of Central America, a project was conceived to bring a company of cadets from the West Point of Guatemala to the White House to pay a courtesy call on the President. Everybody agreed it was a wonderful idea until a problem of forbidding practicality materialized: how would the expedition be financed? Guatemala was not a wealthy country; indeed, not a single centavo was lying around in the local treasury for the venture, however praiseworthy it was. At this point, Corcoran came to the rescue. By dint of adroit negotiating in the right places, he arranged to have the United States government foot the entire bill, commandeered a cruiser to transport the cadets and obtained quarters for their stay in the United States. The project was a huge success, and forged new links between the U.S.A. and the military upper crust of Guatemala.

Corcoran arranged the hiring and firing of major executive personnel. His most accustomed beat was the several independent regulatory commissions, and especially the Securities and Exchange Commission of which he was a prime founder. Office seekers hungering for appointments and legislators with firm ideas on the subject rushed to Corcoran. A New Deal Senator, who abhorred a Maritime Commissioner whose term was about to expire and who could not bear to see the gentleman renominated, candidly conveyed his sentiments to Corcoran. "I spoke to Thomas Gardiner Corcoran about this," the Senator wrote confidently to the President, "and he will talk with you later on." Many a Republican legislator, sensing where the power lay, beat a path to Corcoran to bring a protégé into the vacancies due the G.O.P. on the regulatory commissions. From Corcoran, many were delighted to find, you could get a decision. "A commitment was made to Congressman————" White House Secretary Early inscribed on a memorandum to the President, "through Tommy Corcoran which very definitely promised Congressman—that something would be done for————"

Corcoran was a member of F.D.R.'s speech-writing team, whose colleagues included Judge Samuel I. Rosenman and at various times Harry Hopkins, journalist Stanley High and Ben Cohen. The pattern of the ghost writers' applications varied. Sometimes Corcoran provided the framework of the speech, High the imagery and nippy phrases, and F.D.R. the final revisions which might be extensive. Other times, Corcoran contributed the speeches' general theme, the President a first draft, Corcoran and Rosenman the preliminary revisions, and F.D.R., again, the final touches. As a stylist, Corcoran was at his best in the "indignation" passages. True to the Brandeis school, his favorite whipping boy was "bad" business, and his masterpiece of excoriation was the Madison Square Garden speech of October 31, 1936. "Only desperate men with their backs to the wall," the speech began, "would descend so far below the level of decent citizenship as to foster the current pay-envelope campaign against America's working people. [Boos] Only reckless men, heedless of consequences, would risk the disruption of the hope for a new peace between worker and employer by returning to the tactics of the labor spy." [Boos] In this vein, the speech continued.

By his writing colleagues, Corcoran was regarded as a Bartlett's Quotations in breeches, with phenomenal powers of recollection of the most telling lines of the Bible and the literary masters. He always kept a copy of the Bible handy in his desk drawer. He contributed such memorable phrases as "rendez-vous with destiny" and "an instinct for the jugular" (the latter a favorite of Justice Holmes), and he was always ready with Dante's direst passages. "The immortal Dante," he had F.D.R. say at Philadelphia on June 27, 1936, "tells us that Divine Justice weighs the sins of the cold-blooded and the sins of the warm-hearted in different scales." Like other Roosevelt ghost writers, Corcoran maintained a speech and message file, where data and themes were stored for future oratory. Not only Corcoran, but his friends all over town contributed to the stockpile. Stanley Reed, the Solicitor General, provided data on conditions in the corn belt for a possible agriculture speech and a Commerce Department statistician a chart indicating how long an average industrial laborer had to work in various countries to earn a basket of food. Clippings from the press and magazines, slanted against as well as for the Administration, were collected for the message file. One of the brisker additions was a fussing and fuming editorial of the *Washington News* headed, "Still a Mess."

Corcoran saw F.D.R. at no regular intervals. When portentous affairs were afoot, Corcoran showed up daily at the White House for weeks on end. If the President said "Do this," Corcoran might not return until he could say "It's done," several weeks elapsing between the command and its fulfillment. Like other presidential intimates, Corcoran found the cocktail hour before dinner one of the choicer interludes for bringing up business. On occasion, he with several Administration colleagues stayed on for dinner. If, as sometimes happened, he was a member of a larger and more formal White House dinner party, F.D.R., after the meal was finished, would steer his several guests to a movie in the upstairs hall and proceed to his study where Corcoran would be waiting. When absent from the White House premises, Corcoran kept the secretariat informed of the several places he might be reached during his scheduled round of activities on a given day. Every night when his work was done, no matter the hour, he would make a last call to the White House operator to pick up any assignment which might have suddenly been conferred and whose completion couldn't wait.

Corcoran rendered several inestimable contributions not directly related to his concerns with official business. He was the President's leading and unrivaled entertainer in moments of relaxation at the White House. His gifts of mirth and song were encouraged and sought out by the presidential staff, for F.D.R., because of his disability, did not go out socially. Corcoran's career as White House entertainer in actuality antedates his achievement of status and influence in presidential business. His talents were unveiled one night in 1933 when he attended a small informal party which F.D.R.'s secretary, "Missy" Le Hand, liked to arrange to brighten the life of her boss. Corcoran brought along his accordion—he had learned to play the instrument in off hours after coming to Washington. Before the evening was very far along, Corcoran was called upon for a song. The President was delighted with the ensuing rendition, and called repeatedly for more numbers the rest of the evening. At one little gathering after another, whenever the President liked to relax with five or six favorite people, Corcoran had top billing. Of his various tunes, F.D.R. preferred ballads and old ditties, of which Corcoran had ample store. The President's favorites were "Father O'Flynn," a polysyllabic tongue twister, and "The Yellow Rose of Texas." In his Harvard days, F.D.R. had first come upon "The Yellow Rose" and in a version different from the one current in the nineteen thirties. By some diligent digging, Grace Tully, a presidential secretary, managed to locate the older score which Corcoran thereafter steadfastly featured.

Corcoran excelled in still another social department which counted considerably in the White House. F.D.R. being so largely a prisoner of the edifice, his associates took pains to bring in humorous tidbits from the world outside to brighten his day with laughter. Little jokes and family anecdotes, homely gossip of Washington life and reminiscences of old-fashioned times especially pleased him. For a visitor with a story of some major Washington personality, he would eagerly lay aside his work. Corcoran was one of those most fortunately situated to titillate F.D.R. The young man had an incredible store of anecdotes, and the slight jokes he so skillfully made raised the President's laughter. His far-flung network of alert associates, covering the entire Executive Branch, provided the latest gleanings on the ambitions and maneuvers of striving public figures which Corcoran relayed to his chief with unfailing accuracy and penetrating commentary.

To F.D.R., Corcoran was affectionately known as "Tommy," and to the latter, as to others of the intimate circle, F.D.R. was "the Boss" or "the Skipper." In some respects a highly considerate employer, F.D.R. was always concerned with the state of Corcoran's health especially in periods of prolonged overwork. Time and again, he would "order" the Cork to take a "holiday," usually upon completion of some large hard-fought project, to which Corcoran's energies had been long and unstintingly committed. The President was also solicitous in the several illnesses and injuries the robust Corcoran sustained in his tour of duty in the inner circle. These included a nasal operation, an appendix operation at Johns Hopkins, a sprained ankle and, in 1940, a nasty gash on the crown of his head received when he bumped into the dome light of an official car as he was boarding after a conference with Mayor La Guardia at the World's Fair City Hall in New York. For his part, Corcoran, although he worshiped deeply at the shrine of F.D.R., was never fanatical or uncritical in sizing up the President. He was toughly realistic in appreciating his strengths and foibles. Several reservations in Corcoran's approach to F.D.R. foreordained that his association with his boss could never be as close as Louis Howe's had been or as Harry Hopkins's was later to be. One factor prompting Corcoran's more limited status was the several allegiances he maintained collateral to his affiliation with the President. He paid fealty to Jesse Jones, to the Brandeis group, to the several high-level administrators who were his allies, and to his protégés throughout the Executive Branch. Corcoran considered his plural loyalties an indispensable element of his aspired role as catalyst. As a presidential emissary seeking to unite variant groups and factions, he had to be trusted by those with whom he dealt. Only through demonstrating by convincing deed his interest in their concerns could he generate their trust. But while Corcoran's multiple attachments strengthened his position in the Executive Branch generally and increased his usefulness to the White House, they qualified and circumscribed his status with the President. To any man who aspired to be his intimate associate, F.D.R. displayed a womanly characteristic in demanding nothing less than complete and exclusive devotion. First Louis Howe and later Harry Hopkins passed this exacting test. Equally like a woman, F.D.R. could sense instinctively when, in even the smallest particulars, the devotion he sought was lacking.

Although as presidential assistant, Corcoran dealt in large affairs, he was not given to the minor pretenses that persons coming into power often manifest. His office in the RFC totally lacked the appurtenances of the lofty status-conscious executive, but was a standard-sized room, with sparse and battered furnishings. Papers and books were piled untidily on every conceivable resting place, and the walls, bereft of diplomas or pictures, contributed nothing to the splendor. Mostly, Corcoran didn't work out of his RFC habitat, but from any office that was handy, where in his daily circuit from one end of Washington to another, he might momentarily alight and require a desk or telephone. At the White House, his usual working place was the cabinet room with its elongated table at which the President met with his department secretaries.

Corcoran worked outlandish hours. To him hard work was a virtue. Although he was brilliant to the point of precocity, although he always sounded awfully right, he was never glib or superficial, but well prepared. A jet-propelled operator who refueled in mid-air, he almost literally never slept, working until dawn, for days on end. The delighted F.D.R. would often exploit Corcoran's capacity for insomnious industry in doling out assignments. A draft of a bill or presidential speech would be requested with a deadline that could barely be met by several days and nights of round-the-clock application. To Corcoran, the nighttime work shift, in addition to serving as an outlet for irrepressible energy, had undeniable strategic attractions. It was a handy way to beat the opposition, which ordinarily consisted of gentlemen of sane habits who worked by day and slept by night. But the tireless Corcoran would have the jump the next morning, emerging with a fresh draft of policy while his competitors were breakfasting or shaving.

Corcoran's pace could have been followed only by one of his young years. For his nocturnal marathons, he steeled himself with the old expedients of his law-school days, the cup of strong coffee, loaded with sugar, or the inevitable can of dextrose kept in his desk drawer. Corcoran's mad schedule required that he employ an office force of secretaries and stenographers of at least two shifts. The daytime force was predominately female, the nighttime, male. In rush sessions, a third shift was employed to provide service around the clock. Corcoran's chief secretary, Margaret Dowd, who later became Mrs. Corcoran, was blessed with the energy and devotion to endure uncomplainingly through several shifts until the last word was typed.

Corcoran's industry was one of the few features of his operations which received publicity during his tenure in the inner circle. By friend and foe alike, it was regarded with admiration. Once Bruce Barton, the Republican Congressman and prominent advertising executive, addressing a gathering of young Republicans on the question of how they might revive their dwindling party, suggested that there was no better way to achieve their purpose than to emulate Tom Corcoran. To be sure, Barton conceded, the young New Dealer had brilliance and charm, but "the secret of Tommy's great prestige," he told his audience, "divested of legend and fairy tale, is that he works sixteen hours a day in a town where six hours is nearer the normal work day." And, to bring his observation into proper partisan perspective, Barton added, "It can be said truthfully of him, as was said by a contemporary of Sir Walter Raleigh, 'I know that he can toil terribly.'"

Like F.D.R., Corcoran preferred working on a basis of speedy informality. Organization blueprints and work-flow charts he did not take seriously. He abhorred committees and wasted little time at conference tables. He did business largely by tête-à-tête and rarely with more than several of his fellow mankind simultaneously. The channels so sacred to bureaucratic administrators he would blithely disregard to hasten a wanted decision. He negotiated not by memorandum, but by telephone. Indeed the era of Corcoran's ascendance could properly be labeled "government by telephone." For Corcoran the instrument multiplied the frontiers of his operations, giving the entire continental United States the proximity of the office next door. He did much of his long-distance calling at night, free from the distractions of the day. If the hour was late, as it often was, and his sleepy listeners seemed to resent the interruption, Corcoran would bring them to respectful wide-eyed attention with the words, "I've just come from the White House." The time differential on the West Coast was a great boon to the Cork, for it provided a vast audience to whom the hour of his telephoning could not seem outrageous, as it did to the greater part of his national audience.

Although Corcoran wisely never proclaimed his special status in memoranda or on White House stationery, he did so freely and with great effect by telephone. With it, he communicated at will with the most important people of Washington. "This is Tommy Corcoran talking from the White House," his conversation would begin. Confronted with such a salutation, excited secretaries lost little time in fetching Senators and department heads from meetings of top importance. Corcoran was truly a virtuoso with the telephone. He excelled at using two telephones simultaneously, one on each shoulder, leaving his hands free for other work. (This was before the shoulder-resting attachments of today's telephones had been developed.) His favorite gambit was to put two parties to a negotiation on his respective lines and then act as the middle man, promoting agreement by relaying to one listener what the other party had said and adding his own consensus-building comment. Another memorable feat was his ability to talk simultaneously on both phones and with officials gathered in his office.

In tackling a project of some complexity—drafting a bill or presidential message, or preparing for a court case—Corcoran didn't work alone or just with Ben Cohen, but mobilized the assistance of a task force of bright young lawyers, chiefly of Harvard vintage. When the constitutionality of the Holding Company Act was being tested, for example, nothing less than eighty-five of the country's leading law firms were arrayed against the government. To stand off this high-priced Justinian mob, Corcoran organized a pick-up team of no mean talent recruited from the Bureau of Internal Revenue, the SEC, the Labor Department, and the RFC. He took deserved pride in the fact that his task forces sometimes consisted of men who months or even weeks before they were brought together in common effort had been fighting fiercely with one another. In substituting co-operation and teamwork for administrative fratricide, Corcoran excelled at finding out what the other fellow really wanted, and in building workable compromises. When the government was involved in several major tests of litigation at once—the holding company and the gold-clause cases, for example—Corcoran would have two task forces functioning, each on a basis of specialization customarily found in the larger law offices. The results of this vast investment of effort were highly rewarding. No statute, drafted by Corcoran and Cohen, and defended in the courts under their supervision, was ever declared unconstitutional by the United States Supreme Court. This accomplishment is all the more remarkable when one remembers that it occurred in an era when the Court was declaring New Deal statutes unconstitutional right and left. "Corcoran," it has been truly said, assembled the "number-one law firm in United States history."

Much of Corcoran's New Deal success was owed to his large capacity for single-minded purpose. Nothing was impossible, persistence was the key and costs were never counted—bruised feelings, lasting enmities, jeopardy to his own future career—nothing deterred Corcoran. When the battle was going badly, he was unswerving in optimism, wisecracking his way through the gloom. Pessimists he couldn't abide and any who somehow turned up on his staff were quickly washed out. So single-minded was Corcoran that he weighed his social activities purely in terms of their promise to advance his occupational purposes. To parties and dinners he went unwillingly unless by his presence he could make contacts to further some project he was striving to put across. Once at a tea-dance given by a high official, Corcoran, who by his accustomed standards had doubted the value of coming to the affair at all, carefully came late. After shaking hands with the host and hostess, and nodding to several friends, he whispered in the ear of a colleague, "This doesn't fit into my scheme," and vanished from the premises.

Corcoran worked in tight secrecy, carefully avoiding the limelight, and thus provided a minimum target for the pot shots of his foes. He achieved his incalculable advantage by his own skill and the special nature of his position. His subordinate status at RFC was removed from the current of top officialdom where press conferences are obligatory. He neither wrote articles nor made public speeches. "I never have anything to say," Corcoran once told a reporter who somehow had managed to corner him. "Professionally I am deaf, dumb, and blind." The many young men who gathered around him, Corcoran also expected to remain inconspicuous and took pains to drill them in keeping "their heads down." He had ample experience to draw upon. In 1939, for example, when the press carried stories that a Thomas Corcoran had been conferring with Mayor La Guardia concerning the impending National Democratic Convention, the Cork blandly announced that "it must have been another Thomas Corcoran." To avoid attention on a mission to Warm Springs, he gave the Secret Service man guarding the gate at F.D.R.'s resort his first and middle names, "Thomas Gardiner," and withheld his last name. The maneuver unfortunately backfired. The Secret Service man, who was a trifle obtuse, began phoning noisily about the premises to identify this Mr. Gardiner who was fuming before him. The commotion aroused nearby reporters, who joyfully began turning out copy detailing Corcoran's sudden and mysterious arrival.

To avoid publicity, Corcoran entered into alliances of mutual assistance with the sharpshooting columnists of the day. He could do things for them. He could arrange for a favored writer an interview with the President. His deputies, scattered over the length and breadth of the Executive Branch, provided an endless quantity of "inside" intelligence which constitutes the bread and butter of the gossip columnists. One leading member of the trade hailed Corcoran as "the best single source of information in Washington." As quid pro quo, the columnists maintained unbroken silence on the doings of Corcoran. Sometimes their gratitude was expressed more positively. They might in their daily prose throw a hostile light on those administrators Corcoran currently was fighting with, or light fires behind those of his colleagues who were dragging their feet when he wanted action. He might plant with a friendly reporter a useful question to be raised in the President's or a cabinet secretary's press conference. His contacts with the columnists, Time magazine, and the Hearst Sunday papers were such that he could know their respective editorial positions on current lively issues well before publication deadlines. Of the columnists, Corcoran was closest to Drew Pearson and Jay Franklin, and a degree less removed from Walter Winchell. Upon them he conferred the choicest news tips, and they in turn could be counted on to pull out the stops in "going after" such doughty intramural opponents of Corcoran as Jim Farley and Cordell Hull. In his partnership with the fourth estate, Corcoran even had a hand in the founding of the liberal newspaper, PM. With Cohen, Frankfurter and others, he met with Ralph Ingersoll, publisher of PM, to counsel on the future editorial policy of the new enterprise, and just before *PM* got under way, Corcoran brought Ingersoll to Hyde Park for an interview with F.D.R. The Cork always had a soft spot for *PM*.

Corcoran conducted much of his business with the President through the White House establishment, which in reality consisted of two organizations. One was official, the other unofficial, and both competed for influence and power. The chief members of the official organization or "front office" were the three presidential secretaries, Steve Early, Marvin McIntyre and Colonel Edwin M. "Pa" Watson. Each secretary administered a circumscribed set of affairs: Early, the press; McIntyre, the President's appointments or daily schedule of visitors; and Watson, the paper work. The several secretaries crystallized the conduct of their functions around a set of rules, and followed the line of least resistance of treating everyone alike by applying the rules rigorously. Officials eager to see the President, for example, had to take their turn in line and were allotted a standard quantity of time. The several secretaries were ideally oriented mentally to administer the rules. They had no active political interest and little awareness of the policy revolution in progress. Their devotion was to Roosevelt personally and not to the substance of the New Deal.

The unofficial organization in the White House establishment, being invisible and flexible in functioning, was far more useful to Corcoran. Its dominant member was the President's personal secretary, Marguerite Le Hand, known affectionately to the Roosevelt family and her friends as "Missy." (The Roosevelt children in their younger years had invented the name.) By grace of F.D.R.'s extraordinary confidence in her, Missy could at her discretion set aside important rules of the front office. McIntyre, acting by rote, might arrange for you to see the President in several days; Missy, dispenser of the justifiable exception, could get you in within the hour.

In her late thirties, exceedingly attractive in features and coloring, chic in dress, but delicate in health from rheumatic fever contracted as a child, Missy was utterly loyal to Franklin D. Roosevelt. Associated with him since 1920, his personal secretary as Governor, Missy had shared in epochal moments of her boss's life—at Warm Springs when F.D.R. discarded a brace and walked for the first time, and at Chicago in 1932 when he accepted the Democratic presidential nomination. In the years of the Presidency, until she retired because of illness in '42, Missy occupied the housekeeper's apartment of the White House. Capable, free of possessive jealousy, a liberal strongly sympathetic to the underdog, Missy had a shrewd practicality that Mrs. Roosevelt at first lacked.

Corcoran was a kind of protégé of Missy Le Hand. Mrs. Roosevelt has even suggested that Missy sought to establish Corcoran as a White House intimate in the image of the President's late crony, Louis Howe. Special ties indeed existed between Corcoran and Missy. Both were of the Catholic faith and friends of Cardinal Spellman. Missy was fond of Corcoran's secretary and future wife, Margaret Dowd, and for a time the two ladies worked together in the White House. Above all, the brilliant, witty Corcoran, fanatically devoted to the New Deal, seemed ideally qualified, intellectually and socially. The social aspect weighed heavily with Missy. F.D.R., she was convinced, could survive his oppressive responsibilities only if the strain were periodically relieved. Corcoran, the gifted entertainer, was made to order, and she put his talents to work. When Mrs. Roosevelt was absent from the White House, Missy was given to inviting in for an informal social evening, six or seven people whom she thought the President would enjoy, or, as Mrs. Roosevelt has put it, less kindly, "whom she personally wanted." On occasion, Missy achieved the extraordinary feat of whisking the President from the White House to a new and refreshing locale for a social evening. Late one July afternoon in 1936, for example, Missy guided the President and a small party consisting of Grace Tully, the secretary who took his dictation; the C. R. Larrabees, Alfred T. Hobson, assistant secretary of RFC, and Corcoran to the suburban home of Harold Ickes. On the cool lawn, a festive and relaxing party ensued. A meticulous host, Ickes offered the choicest viands and wines. The feature of the evening, however, was not gastronomical in nature, but Corcoran and his accordion, brought at Missy's request. Tom "played and sang practically the whole evening," Ickes recounted afterward, the President entering the fun "naturally and spontaneously."

As his friend in court, Missy was invaluable to Corcoran. She could quickly and accurately bear messages to and from F.D.R., sparing Corcoran the necessity of seeing her chief. She kept Corcoran informed of how his projects and proposals were faring in the White House. As co-ordinator of the President's multitudinous affairs—a turmoil of telephone calls, personal conferences and scribbled notes—she, better than anyone, knew the current status of developments and commitments. Missy, too, was a source of follow-up, who could prod the President, as Corcoran never could, into doing something he had agreed to do. If, for example, F.D.R. had promised to write to Colonel Joseph M. Patterson, publisher of the New York Daily News, enlisting his editorial support of the Administration candidate for a New York Democratic Congressional nomination, Corcoran looked to Missy to spur the President. "I'm just writing you," stated Corcoran, "in the hope that the note or the telephone call won't be overlooked in the rush of other things; it's very important."

Anyone working through Missy risked incurring the disapprobation of a principal White House figure, Mrs. Roosevelt. One couldn't work through both. In her published memoirs, Mrs. Roosevelt has written unfavorably of the partnership of Corcoran and several other presidential aides with Missy. "I . . . think they exploited Missy's friendship," Mrs. Roosevelt has stated, "believing her more interested in them personally than in what they could contribute to Franklin's work. In that they were mistaken; she was deeply interested in seeing that the best possible results were achieved in whatever work my husband was doing. . . ." Or again, "Missy was young and pretty and loved a good time, and occasionally her social contacts got mixed with her work and made it hard for her and others. To me she was always kind and helpful, and when I had to be away she took up without complaint the additional social responsibilities thrust upon her." Since Mrs. Roosevelt's word and counsel were valued highly by the President, her unfriendliness could be costly. It would prove so for Corcoran.

Corcoran also aroused the unfriendliness of two leading members of the official secretariat, Steve Early and Marvin McIntyre. The latter resented the rearrangements of the appointments schedule which Corcoran effected through Missy. Early was sometimes irritated by Corcoran whom he considered overbrash. "Steve has been pretty jealous of Tom Corcoran for a long time," wrote Harold Ickes, an authority on jealousy, in 1939. That year, F.D.R., in a reorganization of the White House staff, created several new posts, carrying flexible work assignments. The incumbents were to be known as administrative assistants to the President. F.D.R. announced the development in a Hyde Park press conference. Press Secretary Early, who was present, declared, in response to a reporter's question, that under the new order of things "the brain trust was out of the window." In the context of the times, the term "Brain Trust" could mean only Corcoran and Cohen. They therefore would be replaced in their White House roles by the incoming administrative assistants. Though Cohen took the incident philosophically, Corcoran, according to Ickes, was "very much hurt," nor was he satisfied when Early, telephoning from Hyde Park, endeavored to explain and square himself. Early, Corcoran was convinced, had planted the question with a friendly reporter "to take a crack at me."

Corcoran's influence in the White House rested on a firm foundation of power in the executive departments and agencies. He, with Cohen, in fact, presided over a government within a government. "My kids," "my chicks," "a well-integrated group," Corcoran would say of the bright young men whose fealty derived from the unforgettable fact that he had placed them in their jobs. With Frankfurter and the New York law offices supplying the talent, Corcoran commenced his vast personnel operation upon arriving in the capital during the Hoover Administration. His bags were scarcely unpacked when nine other attorneys of Cotton, Franklin followed in his tracks, each becoming in time a departmental counsel or agency commissioner. Before many months of the Roosevelt Administration, a feeling was sweeping the principal New York law firms that the old order was finished, and that it would be better to release their brightest attorneys for duty in Washington than to forfeit the oncoming social revolution to the exclusive management of Cotton, Franklin.

Regardless of the law firms whence they came, the Washington-bound attorneys, particularly those from Harvard, found it wise to go to Corcoran. He was well organized and the results he commanded were impressive. His RFC had been converted into a staging area for receiving, training and dispatching legal talent to the many fronts of the Executive Branch. In a brief period of employment at RFC, incoming lawyers were trained in governmental method, indoctrinated with the New Deal faith, and observed for their strengths and weaknesses. RFC became a mother lode for attorneys richly enough endowed to staff the new agencies and expanded departments of the New Deal. Even after a man had ventured from RFC into another government job, Corcoran kept tabs on his progress. If it developed that the man had been placed in the wrong job, he was transferred to a more suitable spot. The better men were often switched from one agency to another as crises arose and high-order talent was needed.

"Corcoranized" attorneys were denoted by ability and devotion to their leader, who had a knack of inspiring younger workers. Sometimes conflicts of ambition and policy outlook would arise in the ranks in those passionate times, and Corcoran would gallop in to mediate peace and dissuade valuable men from resigning. Indeed, merely keeping the organization in operation became a big job, although its worth was never doubted. Corcoran's bright young men gave him a hand in policy in numerous agencies, even in those whose leadership was unfriendly.

Of the several departments, Corcoran was most comfortably associated with Interior and its presiding doyen, "Honest" Harold Ickes. Corcoran and Cohen first met Ickes in 1933 and an intimate friendship quickly developed. The Secretary's Bull Moose background made him fully acceptable to the Brandeis school. Cohen's several official jobs were located in the official domains of Ickes and to the Secretary Corcoran was always helpful. He was a link to the White House, the provider of nuggets of inside information: who was falling from grace, the current state of a rival administrator's ambitions, whether the moment was propitious to be firm with the President and not be put off with his "pleasant ways." Corcoran and Cohen helped draft the Secretary's speeches with happy results. "Tom Corcoran certainly improved my speech," Ickes declared in typical exultation, "and it went over in good style." Corcoran was a peacemaker between Ickes, who was Public Works Administrator as well as Interior Secretary, and his archrival in the relief domain, Harry L. Hopkins, the Civil Works Administrator. The warfare of the relief czars was brassy and politically costly, and Corcoran gave unstintingly of his ingenuity to quell the din. Time and again, he concocted truces blending the known ambitions of the rival administrators. He would propose, for example, that for the sake of peace, Ickes turn over the remainder of his shrinking public works program to Hopkins if the latter supported Ickes's fondest dream: the expansion of the Interior Department into a Department of Conservation. In his dealings with Ickes, Corcoran was busiest in keeping the Secretary from quitting, a plunge he seemed perpetually on the brink of taking. But Corcoran kept purring like a worn-out record that Ickes was "the last hope of the Progressives in the administration," that "the situation will improve materially," and so on.

Corcoran and Cohen and their far-flung associates constituted a super Department of Justice. Officially, Corcoran held the nonsalaried title of "special assistant to the Attorney General," but his influence was far greater than his modest designation suggests. With Cohen, he chose the test cases of major New Deal laws, fashioned briefs, and on occasion Cohen himself appeared before the Supreme Court to joust with John W. Davis or some other Goliath of the bar. For Homer Cummings, Attorney General from March 4, 1933, to January 2, 1939, Corcoran seems to have drafted some of the more difficult state papers. Shortly after the historic Washington State wage case was settled by the Supreme Court, several newspaper reporters were allowed to see a skillful analysis of the decision prepared by Corcoran. The day after this occasion, the Attorney General issued an analysis of his own which, in its main body, was identical word for word with Corcoran's. Either the Cork had functioned as Cummings's draftsman or was in such mental harmony with the Attorney General as to suggest a telepathic connection.

Corcoran exercised so much power in the Justice Department with so little official responsibility because the top echelons of the department were occupied by men politically indebted to him. Francis Biddle's appointment as Attorney General in 1941 was, by all accounts, due mainly to Corcoran. The Solicitor Generalship, the number-two post of the department, was virtually a Corcoran preserve. His old RFC boss, Stanley Reed, was brought into the departmental post, thanks largely to a campaign masterminded by Corcoran. When Reed was raised to the Supreme Court in 1938 by a tidal wave organized by Corcoran, another protégé, Robert H. Jackson, took over the departmental vacancy. Thurman Arnold, the Assistant Attorney General in charge of antitrust activities, a subject close to Corcoran's heart, enjoyed a similar sponsorship.

Corcoran's own agency, the RFC, experienced a constant accretion of functions. Business loans, loans for rural electrical appliances, first mortgages, the export trade, railroad securities, the public-works program, interest rates, the havoc of flood and hurricane, all were the concerns of RFC and its subsidiaries. RFC grew mightily, thanks partly to Corcoran, but mostly to his boss, Jesse Jones, a sixty-year-old titan with a hard, square face, compressed lips and an erect figure of well over six feet, crowned by a silver-white mane. Jones loved power, thought big and had his way. Even F.D.R. deferred to him.

With Jones, Corcoran was close but not intimate, admiring but not worshipful. "Incredibly effective," Corcoran said of him. Jones, for his part, liked the clever Corcoran, and tolerantly countenanced his departures over long intervals for White House assignments, requiring only a minimum of checking in. If Jones's approval of a projected Corcoran excursion was doubtful, F.D.R. would circumspectly intervene. When the Public Works Architect and a National Parks representative proposed to journey to Puerto Rico in 1934, with Corcoran accompanying them, to develop projects on the island, F.D.R. co-operated by expressing the "hope" that Corcoran would be granted leave from the RFC. Jones, as always, approved. Although Corcoran was devoted to his RFC chief, he was seized with occasional moments of restiveness. A hard dealer, Jones was totally bereft of sympathy for the underdog and impervious to the welfare philosophy of the New Deal. His views, however at odds with the Administration's, were thoroughly reflected in the lending policies of RFC and unanimously supported by the agency's directorship. "When Mr. Jones favored something," a fellow director admitted, "it never occurred to any of us to oppose it." To Corcoran, however, in Roosevelt's first presidential term, Jones's approach was "stingy" and completely unsuited to speed the progress of economic recovery. A vacancy was about to occur on the RFC board, and Corcoran, a man of foresight, perceived the necessity of lining up a candidate of sufficient strength to take on the titanic Jones. After some thought, Corcoran alighted on Gifford Pinchot who, in the days of Theodore Roosevelt, had instituted the national conservation policy against the violent resistance of the most powerful entrenched interests. When Pinchot, in an exploratory meeting at the Hotel Roosevelt in New York City, protested that he knew very little about finance, Corcoran replied in effect that that was beside the point. What was required, he pointed out, was an obstinate man capable of standing up in RFC meetings and opposing the tightfisted Jones. A better policy could then be instituted to restore buying power and bring about recovery, by pouring money into circulation in the greatest possible quantities and at the highest possible speed. The ideal thing, said Corcoran in his vivid and emphatic way, would be for fleets of airplanes to fly over the countryside, discharging money as they went, so that anyone needing cash could pick it up from the ground. "The conversation," Pinchot wrote afterward to F.D.R., "is one which I shall not soon forget."

Where the power of his own organization ended, Corcoran reached out to build coalitions, working agreements, and general good will with executive colleagues whose policy philosophies were not all square with his own. If it served his purpose, he made common cause with law professors of schools other than Harvard, with businessmen and administrators with whom he once had feuded. Executive personalities who were on the rise were watched and courted. William O. Douglas, the Yale Law School professor, who was brought to Washington in 1934 by Joseph P. Kennedy on special assignment for the SEC, had scarcely arrived when Corcoran appeared in his office with a handshake and a cheerful welcome. When Leon Henderson, the burly, sharp-tongued NRA economist, who titillated the capital by wearing khaki trousers and sneakers on the job, began to impress the higher levels with his memoranda of cogent analysis, Corcoran and Cohen were not long in calling on him to discuss the state of the nation and make friends. Corcoran's lively sociability was based on the altogether plausible conviction that by winning friends in the departments, he could more easily influence the President in the White House. Many voices joined in common sentiment were ordinarily more imposing than the expressions of a solitary assistant. Coalitions were also a means to hold off the advocates of competing policy proposals seeking the President's assent. Corcoran's skill at coalition politics was busily applied in the emergence of presidential policy in the economic recession of 1937–38.

The recession was a political and economic body blow which toppled the New Deal to its nadir in popular esteem. In October 1937, stocks dropped alarmingly, unemployment rose and prices fell. Congress grew restive, and the opposition, with telling effect, began blaming the country's plight on the New Deal. Within the Administration, rival groups with conflicting solutions for the Administration's sudden bedevilment began to form. One group, consisting of Corcoran, Cohen, R. H. Jackson, Henderson, Douglas, Isador Lubin, the Commissioner of Labor Statistics, and economists Lauchlin Currie of the White House, Herman Oliphant of the Treasury and Mordecai Ezekiel of the Agriculture Department, among others, blazed away in reports and memoranda for stepped-up relief appropriations as the readiest way out of the crisis, and blamed the country's predicament on monopolies and price maladjustments. The Administration conservatives, led by Henry Morgenthau, a presidential favorite, contended that balancing the budget was the surest avenue to business confidence and an upturn of the economic cycle. Morgenthau expounded his thesis publicly in an address to the New York Academy of Political Science. Corcoran and his friends were filled with consternation when they learned that F.D.R. had read Morgenthau's speech line by line beforehand.

To organize a counter-campaign, Corcoran, Cohen, Oliphant, Henderson and Lubin met in Jackson's princely office at the Justice Department. Their most feasible step, they concluded after anxious searching, was to blame the recession on the monopolies and go after them. As an immediate move, they won Harry Hopkins, then the President's closest intimate, over to the plan. His discreet soundings indicated that the President was reasonably ready for an antimonopoly drive, although how far he would go was not at all clear. Corcoran and his friends, at any rate, felt sufficiently emboldened to launch the antimonopoly crusade without making the President a party to it and thus risking his subsequent repudiation. The one public figure of the group, Jackson, proceeded to make two speeches with antimonopoly allusions. Acting as his own draftsman and being given to mildness of statement, Jackson unfortunately created little public stir. The undaunted group arranged a third Jackson speech, this time with Corcoran and Cohen as draftsmen. Peppered with epithets and delivered by radio at a choice hour negotiated by Corcoran, it excited screaming headlines. As the din pleasantly re-echoed, Corcoran and Cohen called upon Ickes. "We have half an hour on the air for you," said Corcoran. "We want you to follow Bob up." Ickes served up a speech well remembered by its fervent references to "the sixty families." Both Ickes and Jackson presented repeat performances in the same vein.

While Corcoran's friends thundered onward, the President provided no inkling of his reaction. Days passed. Corcoran and his friends waited anxiously, but nothing transpired. Finally, the eagerly awaited sign appeared, when an Administration conservative in an interview with the President roundly denounced Ickes. F.D.R. broke in to speak of his Secretary of the Interior with calm, but unqualified, approbation. The joyous news of that interview was not long in achieving an exalted place on the executive grapevine. Corcoran and his colleagues had gambled and won. The Cork, who never rested, succeeded in inserting into the President's subsequent State of the Union Message the spirit of the Jackson-Ickes speeches and the promise of a separate message on monopoly.

F.D.R.'s endorsement of Ickes by no means constituted a lasting endorsement of the Secretary's policy position. Within a matter of days, F.D.R. seemed to be veering to another proffered solution of the recession, the approach of "planning" which contemplated large-scale business-government co-operation to iron out the business cycle. Donald R. Richberg, a former presidential adviser now in private law practice, was championing joint planning by business and government, a direct antithesis to Corcoran's anti-monopoly position; Myron C. Taylor, chairman of the board of United States Steel, whom F.D.R. respected, talked convincingly of the possibilities of co-operative effort; a business advisory council, led by Averell Harriman, looked for presidential leadership around which the business community could rally. The impact of these several exhortations was registered in F.D.R.'s declaration in mid-January, 1938, that the way to end depressions was for everybody to get together and plan production and consumption. Corcoran and his confreres were distraught with surprise and grief.

Matters continued to deteriorate. Hopkins, the group's friend in court, retreated to Florida to recuperate from an operation for a stomach ulcer. Jackson, the antimonopolists' public orator, failed to secure the prestige-rich Democratic gubernatorial nomination in New York, which the President had bidden Corcoran to arrange. For his part, Corcoran continued to devote his audiences with F.D.R. to urging aggressive antimonopoly action, until word was passed around that the President was beginning to feel nagged. Nervously exhausted from the indecisive debate and maneuver, Corcoran removed himself from the scene by retreating to St. Jovite, Canada, a skiing resort, leaving the field to the budget balancers and planners.

Corcoran's competitors were just beginning to enjoy their new found position when the depression suddenly and seriously worsened. Instead of a spring upturn, unemployment increased, the stock market further deteriorated. Even Morgenthau admitted to desperation, although he persisted in his budgetary philosophy. In private soundings, Harry Hopkins, finding the nation's leading businessmen friendly to government spending, ventured from his Florida retreat up to Warm Springs in March to urge the policy on the President. The encouraged Corcoran flew back to Washington. But the President, for all of the positive signs, still vacillated, and the despairing Corcoran returned to St. Jovite. More voices with more proposals were heard, refueling the President's determination to delay. Finally, however, the speeding economic decline seemed to force his hand. From a luncheon with F.D.R. at Warm Springs, Hopkins learned that a vigorous spending program would commence at once. Corcoran, who had proceeded from Canada into the interior of South Carolina, where he was traveling with his father, rushed back to Washington. Messages to Congress and a fireside chat, proclaiming the new policies, were frantically written. Corcoran contributed vigorous paragraphs to the spending message, and with Cohen and Jackson hammered out the monopoly message. Hopkins helped with verbiage and clearances with the President; Henderson, Lubin and Currie provided indispensable economic facts and figures. Soon after the monopoly message was delivered, the recession had run its course and the sun of economic recovery shone again. The message was almost superfluous.

Corcoran, by F.D.R.'s designation, was manager of the Senate, responsible for pushing Administration-sponsored legislation through to enactment. He was a lobbyist par excellence, whisking through Capitol corridors, trading, purring, cajoling, threatening and cracking down, in flushing out votes. The recalcitrance he encountered was well noted in the White House, and undue offenders were subject to various penalties, of which the most terrible was the falling off of relief projects and government contracts in their states. For some wayward legislators, the most immediate and chilling retribution was Corcoran's practice of not speaking to them, offering only a menacing sulk. The most distressing aspect of this social negation was not its manifestation of Corcoranian disapproval, but the possibility that it accurately reflected the attitude of the President.

As White House liaison to the Senate, Corcoran engaged in many activities less dire in nature. For friendly legislators he drafted bills, letters and even speeches. His bill-drafting talents were greatly in demand, for these were the days before legislators had professional administrative assistants and the Legislative Reference Service had been enlarged. On the White House side of his activities, Corcoran would induce the President to see particular legislators whose help might speed a desired bill. He drafted for F.D.R.'s signature letters of commendation and exhortation to various legislators, recommended bills for signature or veto, and on occasion prepared the rationale or substance of a veto message. Corcoran's function from time to time offended certain legislators. Congressman Samuel B. Pettengill of Indiana, sponsor of a resolution calling for a memorial to Casimir Pulaski, the Polish patriot and American Revolutionary hero, was one who became unfriendly. "I am getting very well fed up with Mr. Thomas Corcoran," Pettengill declared one day on the floor of the House, an expression that was received with applause. Pettengill disclosed that Corcoran had threatened that unless the Congressman changed his attitude on another measure and voted as the White House wanted, the Pulaski resolution wouldn't stand a chance. Corcoran, when tracked down for comment, presented an altogether different version of the situation. Pettengill, he said, was really proposing to make Pulaski's birthday a permanent national holiday, which was objectionable because the step would unleash a flood of similar demands for numerous other heroes of hyphenated national backgrounds.

Corcoran's sundry duties involved him intimately in the major facets of the legislative program of the Second New Deal, but of all the legislation for which he lobbied and fought, the most arduous, the most thankless, and the costliest to his own public career was Roosevelt's famous plan to pack the United States Supreme Court.

In 1937, when the plan was introduced, the Court had become increasingly oppressive to the Administration. In their marble temple, the assertive Justices, often by 5 to 4 vote, were unmaking the laws and flaunting the popular verdict of the polls. In four years of the New Deal, the Court in twelve instances had found provisions of New Deal laws unconstitutional, five of these in 1935. The Court had cut into the heart of the New Deal in invalidating the National Industrial Recovery Act, the first Agricultural Adjustment Act, the wages and hours regulations of the Guffey Soft Coal Act, the original Railway Pension and Farm Mortgage Moratorium Acts. In confronting the problem of judicial hostility, the President had understandably rejected a remedial constitutional amendment as politically impractical, and in seeking an alternative espoused the Court-packing plan, which in its original form constitutes a masterpiece of political misjudgment. The real purposes of the plan were unacknowledged and hidden behind a veil of the flimsiest indirection. The President proposed, in part, that for every Justice who was over seventy years of age, with ten years of service, and who did not resign, an additional justice might be appointed. In 1937, six justices fell within the plan, entitling the President to appoint six "liberals" to the Court and ensuring favorable consideration of New Deal laws in the future. The court plan's original sponsor was Attorney General Homer Cummings who, in its incubation, insisted that Corcoran and Cohen be kept out of the discussions. Although Corcoran, according to the Ickes diary, knew in a general way of the furtive happenings, F.D.R. did not disclose to his assistant what was afoot until the special message to Congress, setting forth the court plan, had been drafted. Corcoran was thoroughly horrified by the message's indirection, sophistic reasoning and implied condemnation of old age. But no matter how Corcoran was repelled by the approach, the time for change was past. Like the good soldier, Corcoran helped put the finishing touches on the message to Congress, although he didn't conceal his wrath toward Cummings for maneuvering the President into an impossible political position and putting the inner circle on a terrible spot. F.D.R., knowing of the rancor between his two associates, resorted to a favorite expedient to minimize its impact on the ensuing court project. The President instructed Sam Rosenman, who was assisting with the drafting, to keep Corcoran out of conferences involving the Attorney General; and the latter, too, if possible, should not know of Corcoran's participation. The candid Rosenman informed Corcoran of the arrangement, but he took no offense. He had, as Rosenman put it, "grown used to this weakness" of the President.

Corcoran plunged into the court fight, pained by its havoc to old loyalties and cherished attachments. The concept of the superannuated Justice, determined by rigid chronological test, was in reality an attack on Brandeis, Corcoran's revered friend and idological mentor; upon the brilliant Cardozo, to whom he was only slightly less devoted, and upon the memory of Holmes, much of whose judicial service would have been discredited under the wooden formulae of Roosevelt's plan. Caught in the conflict between Roosevelt and the Brandeis school, Corcoran unhesitatingly and unqualifiedly chose to support the President. By enlisting in the court fight, Corcoran weakened his ties with another sponsor of long standing, Felix Frankfurter. In his Harvard lair, to which he was confining himself increasingly, Frankfurter was offended by the indirection and the age provisions of the court plan with their implicit attack on the eighty-year-old Brandeis. Frankfurter took no public position on the issue, a tactic which further removed him from the White House circle as the fight exacerbated. Roosevelt's presumed friends, Corcoran was known to say in those days, "were a million miles away." In Congress, Corcoran, brought into conflict with the liberals and progressives with whom he had hitherto been allied, fashioned his most striking achievements.

At the White House, a special task force was assembled for the legislative struggle, with the President in personal command. Its membership consisted of sharply contrasting humanity. Joseph B. Keenan, patronage manager of the Justice Department, on loan to the White House, was short and red-faced, suggesting a type often encountered at race tracks and political clubhouses. Keenan suffered the disadvantages of being a new man and a practical politician, a class his colleagues generally discredited. Charles West, Democratic ex-Congressman from Ohio, tall, gangly, pleasant and shrewd, was an ideal listener to a legislator's troubles. James Roosevelt, amiable and politically ambitious, had lately taken up administrative duties in residence in the White House because of his father's desire to have someone around he could trust completely. The younger Roosevelt was resented as an interloper who displaced to a degree his colleagues' contacts with the President and served as his father's informant. Corcoran and Robert H. Jackson and, on occasion, Steve Early, rounded out the group. As the court fight gained in intensity, the group met in the White House in early morning before the legislators had reached the Hill or in late afternoon when they had ventured home. In such gatherings, or at an occasional staff luncheon, their pooled information provided the latest reading of the legislative barometer. Each member of the task force, including Corcoran, was sparring for position and tended to act with the abandon of Little Jack Horner. Corcoran was easily the most important of the group because of his superior access to the President and his pre-eminence on the firing line on Capitol Hill.

To Corcoran, the court fight was a showdown test of the President's status and power, a challenge to the empire. An irresistible opportunity was at hand to humiliate F.D.R. for legislators who hitherto had small choice but to go along with him. The very future of the New Deal was at stake. The drive for progressive legislation would lose its momentum if the court plan were defeated. But there was another side of the coin. "If the President wins the court fight," Corcoran declared to Harold L. Ickes, "everything will fall into his basket." The prospects quickly grew dismal. In the usually servile House of Representatives, the court bill was hopelessly bottled up in the Judiciary Committee. To break the impasse, Corcoran counseled the application of heavy-muscled pressures, but F.D.R. sided with the Democratic leadership of the House, Speaker Bankhead and Rayburn, who considered such tactics too risky. In the Senate, Corcoran discovered that sentiment against the plan was climbing to dangerously high levels. His report, which was utterly candid, stunned and chagrined the President. Undefeated on any major matter in Congress for the better part of two presidential terms, F.D.R. had come to believe that his unbroken success was based not merely on crisis, but on the affection and regard in which the Congressional membership held him. Placing great store in this conviction, and hopefully incredulous of Corcoran's grievous reports, the President dispatched his son James to the Senate to investigate the validity of the findings, a step which did not especially gladden Corcoran.

While James Roosevelt was double checking, Corcoran launched a high-pressure drive on the Senate Judiciary Committee which was considering the court bill. Members who had received indispensable help in the last elections were pointedly reminded of the fact. The Kelly-Nash machine of Chicago was jogged into pressuring another committee member, Senator William H. Dietrich of Illinois, who was sitting overlong on the fence. Another fence sitter, Senator Marvel M. Logan, learned that his much desired flood-control legislation for his home state of Kentucky was assured if he supported the plan. Over luncheon at the Dodge Hotel, Corcoran offered his old ally, Senator Burton K. Wheeler, in consideration for his support, the privilege of "sitting in" on the naming of the expanded court. The Senator not only declined, but declared that he would fight the court plan. The discussion quickly became acrimonious. "It's going to pass," said Corcoran of the plan. "I tell you it isn't going to pass," Wheeler answered. "And what's more I'm going to fight it with everything I've got." Several days later, Wheeler was visited by Charles Michelson of the Democratic party's national headquarters and Sidney Hillman and John L. Lewis of organized labor, presumably at Corcoran's initiative, but Wheeler wouldn't budge. For a time, Corcoran didn't speak to the Senator, who assumed the leadership of the opposition forces in the upper house.

In the White House phase of his activities, Corcoran was more successful. With Cohen and Jackson, he induced the President to drop the indirection of the plan, which had spurred and magnified the opposition, and to substitute a more appealing approach of candor—that the Court was arbitrarily hamstringing the progress of the New Deal and the expressed will of the people. Corcoran had greater difficulty, although eventual success, in bringing the President to convey this new approach in two addresses to the nation. Of these, Corcoran and Cohen were the principal authors. Meanwhile, Corcoran, assisted by Keenan, was organizing the presentation of the Administration case before the Senate Judiciary Committee, lining up prominent witnesses recruited from the bar and academic life, followed by labor and farm leaders. Such exertions were decidedly necessary, for the American Bar Association and the nation's major law firms were providing distinguished older lawyers and clever younger men to manage the argumentative cannonade of the opposition. In his envisioned timetable of the unfolding events, Corcoran, who was rather impatient of the legislative process, proposed that the hearings of the Senate Judiciary committee be completed within two weeks. Instead they settled down to a crawling pace. The committee chairman, Senator Henry Ashurst of Arizona, a perfect example of the popular stereotype of a Senator—tall, with aquiline features, flowing gray locks; an orator given to flowing periods, but withal vastly cagey —was in no hurry. As the Judiciary Committee hearings dragged on, Ashurst, in Corcoran's harried view, was in reality sanctioning a filibuster. To break the impasse, Corcoran implored F.D.R. to call Ashurst in and make clear to the dawdling Senator that no patronage would be handed out until the court bill was reported favorably out of committee. F.D.R. declined to take the drastic step and Ashurst's hearings lumbered along for an ultimate duration of three months and thirteen days.

Elsewhere, the fight was passing into a stage of climactical maneuvering. Senator Wheeler released a letter from Chief Justice Hughes, a masterpiece of exposition, attacking the President's indirection and exposing the hollowness of his charge that the court was dilatory and overworked. Justice Van Devanter of the Court's conservative wing resigned and Joe Robinson, the Democratic leader in the Senate, after a fiery oration in behalf of the bill, was found the next day dead of a heart attack, sprawled on the floor of his apartment bedroom in his pajamas, his glasses on the bed and a copy of the *Congressional Record* by his hand. Even God seemed to oppose the court plan. The Senate Judiciary Committee voted down the court bill. Corcoran took the drastic step of writing a minority report for the committee and presented his document to chairman Ashurst with instructions that Ashurst prod the committee's pro-Administration Democrats into signing it. Aghast at this invasion of Senatorial prerogative, the wily Ashurst slithered out of reach and Corcoran's draft never saw the light of day.

Faced with the impasse in the Senate, F.D.R. turned to the politically wise John N. Garner, requesting the Vice-President to extract the best compromises possible from the wreckage. By dint of Garner's obscure maneuvers, the Senate rushed through an emasculated bill, making minor reforms and improvements in the federal court system which F.D.R. half-heartedly signed into law. In its final stages, the court fight became entangled in the struggle over the selection of a new Democratic leader in the Senate to succeed the late Joe Robinson. Fierce competition developed between Pat Harrison of Mississippi, who had opposed the court plan and symbolized Senatorial independence against the assaults of Corcoran and his White House colleagues, and Alben Barkley, who had faithfully supported the plan. The Administration pulled out the stops for Barkley. F.D.R. wrote his famous "My Dear Alben" letter, with its public show of friendship, which constituted an unaccustomed interference in the affairs of the Senate. Corcoran and Hopkins were unloosening the most intense pressures on Democratic Senators. Senator Dietrich was revisited by the Kelly-Nash machine, and in a phone call to Kansas City, Corcoran summoned the Pendergast machine to put the heat on Senator Harry Truman. The machine frankly and fully informed the Senator of what it had been bidden to do. Truman became so mad that he voted for Harrison, although theretofore he had been inclined to Barkley. His reversal was just a whisker or two short of being fatal, for Barkley squeaked through to victory by the margin of one vote.

Although F.D.R. lost many a battle in the court fight, he eventually won the war. Even as the court bill was being debated in Congress, the court in its decisions was executing a most gratifying judicial flip-flop. With a rush of approval, it upheld the constitutionality of the National Labor Relations Act, the Tennessee Valley Authority, the Second Agricultural Adjustment Act, the Railway Labor Act, the Social Security Act and other legislation. Under less venturesome management than Corcoran's, the court fight might have collapsed in its early stages, leaving only the wreckage of defeat. Thanks in no little way to his unstinting and little accompanied soldiery in the front trenches—most of F.D.R.'s usual supporters were far from the battle—the Second New Deal achieved a judicial sanctification which the First New Deal never enjoyed.

Promptly after attaining his capacity as favorite presidential legman, Corcoran delved into party politics, finding new release for his zest for maneuver. By the 1936 presidential elections, he was a major member of the White House speech-writing team and contributed copiously to F.D.R.'s campaign oratory. With Cohen, Corcoran prepared a preliminary draft of the Democratic platform which strikingly resembled the final draft. He dragooned many a reluctant Democratic spellbinder into taking to the stump, and was influential in routing F.D.R.'s campaign train into the districts of loyal Congressmen facing difficult campaigns.

Corcoran's 1936 role was but a mild prelude to his dynamic part in the Senatorial and Congressional elections of 1938. This was the year of F.D.R.'s famous, ill-fated purge, a project with which Corcoran became unforgettably identified. The purge originated in F.D.R.'s embitterment over the fate of his court-packing plan and his reverses on subsequent key legislation. F.D.R. fumed most at those who had run with him on a liberal party platform and, after the elections were over, voted against legislation mirroring the very planks and pledges on which they had been elected. To colleagues, F.D.R. repeatedly expressed his scorn at such "shenanigans." For months, purge talk reigned at the White House, with the strongest approbation voiced by Corcoran, Ickes and Hopkins. All were then engaged in large and futile struggles to drive programs through Congress. In its first version, the plan, as developed in F.D.R.'s conversations with his aides, was to get rid of Democratic Senators and Congressmen who had opposed him in the court fight, but it soon was extended to include recalcitrance toward various other major Administration projects in Congress. As technique, the purge was singularly uncomplicated. The President would merely intervene in the Democratic primary where the purgee was seeking his party's nomination and openly support his opponent. In all, a handful of Senators and Congressmen were given the treatment.

Aside from F.D.R., Corcoran was the member of the Administration most identified with the purge. Although Hopkins possessed equal zeal for the project, his headship of WPA tied him down somewhat, while Corcoran's more junior duties at the RFC permitted more freedom of action. There was much to do. Jim Farley, National Democratic Chairman, gave notice that it was not part of his function as national chairman to interfere in local fights. Corcoran and like-minded New Dealers moved into the resulting vacuum. The first public announcement of the purge, was a fireside chat of June 24, 1938, of which Corcoran was a principal draftsman. "Copperheads," an epithet employed in the address and applied to those urging the President to terminate his program of reform and coast out the term, was proposed by Corcoran. Shortly after this speech, F.D.R. embarked on a long vacation trip across the United States, down through the Panama Canal, returning via Florida and Warm Springs to Washington, making speeches along the way. In his prepared addresses—a few were extempore—Corcoran supplied the chief assistance. Rosenman was otherwise occupied and Cohen was in Europe.

Of the several purge campaigns, Corcoran was most directly involved in the warfare upon Congressman John O'Connor of New York City's downtown Manhattan. O'Connor's opponent, James H. Fay, of impeccable Irish antecedents and war record, and thoroughly persona grata at Tammany Hall, had been induced to run by Hopkins and Corcoran. The latter passed a month in New York, directing the campaign at the ward and precinct level. On primary day, O'Connor was defeated, the one and only instance of a successful purge campaign. Corcoran's precise contribution to this singular victory is a matter of dispute. Ed Flynn, the wily Democratic boss of the Bronx, has made a decidedly negative appraisal of Corcoran's part. While Corcoran was discharging his stewardship in lower Manhattan, Flynn was vacationing in California, until one day he received a telephone call from F.D.R. "Apparently," Flynn has written of the conversation, "the President felt that the campaign was not going well. He urged me to come back to New York to see what I could do to nominate Fay." Flynn reluctantly re-turned—he had originally advised F.D.R. against the purge—and talked to Fay. Of one of his first acts after making his soundings, Flynn has written, "I called the President and advised him that if Corcoran or any of his ilk had anything to do with the campaign, I would immediately withdraw." Although Flynn in his memoirs unstintingly praises himself for the defeat of O'Connor, not a few onlookers offer a wholly different explanation of the outcome. O'Connor's most effective enemy, they contend, was not Corcoran or Flynn, but himself. At odds with Democratic Congressional and Assembly leaders and other local party potentates, a considerable store of opponents were eagerly waiting to beset him.

The purge also ended in a fiasco of defeat and embarrassment for the President and was costly to Corcoran and his future public career. He had aroused the unforgiving hostility of powerful Democratic Senators, and lost the anonymity which had for so long shielded his operations from attention and attack. Senators Tydings and George, survivors of the purge, spoke dis-dainfully to the press of "two little Wall Street lawyers who want the power to say who shall or who shall not be Senators." The extent of Corcoran's new publicity is also suggested by an exchange transpiring at the presidential press conference when the purge campaign was in high gear.

"Well, isn't Tommy kind of crowding you off the first page?" a reporter observed.

"What makes you ask that?" the President countered.

"It seems to me that, so far as the newspapers are concerned, Tommy is stealing the show."

"Well, so far as the newspapers are concerned," the President rejoined, "you are not going to hold me responsible for that, are you?"

After the purge, Corcoran turned to another delicate venture, the presidential nomination for the impending elections of 1940. Prior to the outbreak of World War II in 1939, F.D.R., it was assumed, because of his own inclinations and the third-term tradition, would retire to the Hyde Park dream cottage. A new standard-bearer had to be groomed, and Corcoran had no difficulty settling upon his own candidate, his friend and ally, Robert H. Jackson. The plan for Jackson's build-up entailed his running for the New York Governorship. F.D.R. was none too enthusiastic about Corcoran's favorite, feeling that he lacked "political it." To be considered seriously for the gubernatorial nomination, Jackson had somehow to be elevated from his subcabinet status as Solicitor General to a loftier place in the Roosevelt Administration. On January 2, 1939, the desired opportunity seemed to materialize when Homer Cummings resigned as Attorney General. Corcoran lost no time in urging Jackson's appointment to the vacancy, as eminently suited for his talents and political necessities. The difficulty with this altogether logical projection was that another cabinet post, the Secretaryship of Commerce, was also vacant, and on it the eye of Harry Hopkins was possessively trained. Hopkins, too, had presidential ambitions. The common longing of Hopkins and Jackson for cabinet status created a serious if not impossible, problem. Both were New Yorkers. The Empire State already controlled three secretaryships in the cabinet. As Jim Farley and others earnestly remonstrated to F.D.R., the addition of two other New Yorkers in the persons of Jackson and Hopkins would exaggerate the already lopsided geographical profile of the cabinet to unheard-of proportions. One feeble ray of hope shone through the impasse. Hopkins, although a resident of New York, was a native son of Iowa. If he could be "charged" to Iowa instead of New York, then Jackson might with some justification be added to the cabinet. Unfortunately, however, the Iowan Democratic leadership wouldn't accept Hopkins as a charge. Undeterred by the rebuff, Hopkins said he still wanted to become Secretary of Commerce even though his appointment would be drawn against New York. Jackson and his friends had to drop their campaign for his promotion to the cabinet, and soon Frank Murphy of Michigan came in as Attorney General. The misfortune of Jackson, as Harold Ickes put it, left Corcoran "much disturbed."

Meanwhile, Hopkins's maneuvers for the presidential nomination were growing apace. Ickes was noting a "growing feeling" that the President was building up Hopkins as his successor, and Corcoran was convinced that Hopkins was the only New Dealer "who had a chance" for the Presidency. Yet Corcoran was also certain that, in the end, F.D.R. would have to run for a third term. In Hopkins's continued advance upon his goal, Corcoran co-operated up to a point. He supported the aspirant's designation as Secretary of Commerce and helped with an early draft of an intensely political speech which Hopkins delivered at Des Moines, Iowa. Although the Des Moines speech fell terribly flat, Hopkins pressed on. He requested Corcoran to raise funds in behalf of his candidacy. Not one to quail at the price of candor, Corcoran bluntly informed Hopkins that the request was impossible because he simply was not presidential material. Thereafter things were never quite the same between Corcoran and Hopkins.

While coping with the ambitions of his colleagues, Corcoran was increasingly concerned with the New York political scene. His special assignment was to assure that the New York delegation to the impending National Democratic Convention would be of New Deal orientation. Two potent forces, in the eyes of Corcoran and his colleagues, threatened their key objective—Tammany Hall and James A. Farley. Suspected of nurturing strong presidential ambitions of his own, Farley had been growing progressively further away from F.D.R. He and Tammany would have a large hand in the selection of convention delegates. In his New York sojourn, Corcoran challenged the Tammany leadership by building up a Wigwam brave, Congressman James H. Fay of the purge, and by encouraging local district fights. Mayor La Guardia was solicited by Corcoran to join the crusade. Corcoran's fiercest maneuvers, however, were directed at Farley. He dared to challenge the national chairman in the filling of a key patronage appointment in his own state, the post of United States Attorney for the Southern District of New York. The political world was aghast when Corcoran, and not Farley, emerged triumphant. John T. Cahill, Corcoran's candidate triumphed over Farley's first and second choices, Charles T. Murphy and Gregory F. Noonan, the acting United States Attorney. After this success anything seemed possible, and by the summer of 1939, rumors were flying about that Corcoran would soon be ousting Farley as Chairman of the National Committee.

"Mr. President," a reporter asked at a White House press conference, "are you going to have any corroborations or denials, or other comment on reports that Mr. Corcoran is trying to remove Mr. Farley as Chairman of the Democratic National Committee?"

"I do not know what you can call it," replied Roosevelt. "You can call it tommyrot. Isn't that a good idea? [Laughter] That refers to your story, you see, and not to Mr. Corcoran." [Laughter]

The outbreak of war in Europe signalized the necessity and inevitability of F.D.R.'s candidacy for the third term. Hopkins, Corcoran, Rosenman and others became increasingly involved in the multitudinous details preparatory to the convention. The President had to work through his personal assistants rather than through the regular party officialdom, because he could not disclose his intentions prior to the convention and the latter, in any case, would not take kindly to a third term. Corcoran concentrated on lining up friendly state delegations and, as the zero hour of the convention approached, he, with Cohen, Hopkins and others of the White House circle, worked on the platform. Corcoran also discussed with F.D.R. the selection of the vice-presidential nominee, and left with a vague feeling that William O. Douglas had the nod.

In those hectic and final days when the platform and the President's speech accepting the nomination were hammered into final shape, Corcoran and Cohen had little part. A split between the President and Corcoran was developing "and it produced," wrote Rosenman, "a situation that I personally found uncomfortable." The full measure of the difficulty Rosenman discovered when he asked F.D.R. if Corcoran and Cohen should be brought in to help with the final drafting. Although both had been on hand at a small White House dinner party the night before, where both documents had been discussed, the President said no. "Of course I could not tell Tommy this," Rosenman has written, "and I am sure that both he and Ben must have considered it strange that they were not invited to the conferences that were taking place." Only in the final hours of the several drafting enterprises did the President relent and Corcoran and Cohen were resummoned to the inner councils.

Rosenman was not the only member of the presidential circle who noticed Corcoran's altering status. Subsequent to the Chicago convention and as the campaign for the third term was proceeding, Harold Ickes marked that Corcoran was not playing anything like the part which his talent and large experience in prior campaigns warranted. One day the doughty Secretary of the Interior broached the matter in an interview with F.D.R. The President pleasantly and generously agreed how valuable Corcoran was, but Ickes departed with a queasy sense of dissatisfaction. "The President seemed a little vague concerning Corcoran," the Secretary mused.

Corcoran's part in the third-term campaign was played not in Washington, the center of impulse and decision, but in New York City. There he worked with not the official Democratic organization, but with the Citizens Committee for Roosevelt, established with Senator Norris as honorary chairman, Mayor La Guardia as chairman, and Corcoran, vice-chairman. The committee's function was to rally Republicans and independents to F.D.R.'s support. Because his service on the committee was incompatible with the recently enacted Hatch Act, regulating political activity by government employees, Corcoran had to resign from his RFC post and his several other official capacities. The change of status did not pass unnoticed. Harold Ickes was troubled. "I am surprised," he wrote of Corcoran at the time, "that he is willing to operate under a title of no significance at all and I admire him for it." The Republican presidential candidate, Wendell Willkie, was less kind. "That," he said of Corcoran's appointment, in a partisan outburst, "ought to elect me 100 per cent with Tommy on the other side."

Corcoran's shift of assignment was symptomatic of the continuing deterioration of his influence in the White House. His removal to New York, Rosenman has written, emanated from F.D.R. himself, who decided, "Tom should not be permitted to do all the things he had been doing." Since the young New Dealer would be unhappy in Washington with his operations so curtailed, F.D.R. initiated the transfer to New York.

Corcoran's decline has its origins in the political defeats sustained by the President in the purge and the court-packing plan. When the New Deal, as betokened by these ventures, became unpopular in the country, Corcoran became unpopular in the White House. He dated his own slippage in F.D.R.'s grace from that moment in the court fight when he reported the distasteful intelligence that Congress was not supporting the President's program, but was hostile to the point of revolt. In the ancient days of Persia, the soldier who reported to the king the bad news that the royal armies were being routed was customarily beheaded. In Corcoran's case, history in a sense was repeating itself.

His decline was also speeded by hostile voices heard in the White House, with inevitable effect upon the President's attitude. Party leaders, bitter at Corcoran's violent interference in their proper domains in the ill-fated purge, and in his influence over presidential appointments, emerged from everywhere with complaints to F.D.R. Corcoran, they said, had been badly hurting the party. Several leading party figures threatened to quit unless Corcoran was called off and reassigned to other duty. Such inestimable chieftains as Jim Farley and Ed Flynn had been deeply antagonized.

Within the White House circle, Corcoran's strength had been steadily waning. His chief ally, Missy Le Hand, was commencing an interval of broken health, touched off by the intensity of the infighting of the third-term campaign. Mrs. Roosevelt was becoming increasingly unfriendly. The remote and sickly Hopkins, now a resident of the White House, was rising inexorably in the President's esteem. Corcoran alone stood in Hopkins's way to the achievement of status as the unrivaled general favorite in F.D.R.'s trust and affection. The new competition of Hopkins and Corcoran was little cushioned by earlier co-operative association, although both had long been major New Deal personalities. In fact, until the interlude of Corcoran's declining fortunes, his dealings with Hopkins had been limited. Their orbits had touched concerning Ickes. Their partnership in the purge and court fight, although born of common cause, had been limited. Each had jealously preserved his independence. In the spring of 1939, as the European war clouds were gathering, Hopkins and Corcoran differed in their counsel to the President over the desired relationship of government and business in the growing crisis. Hopkins advocated a rapprochement, Corcoran proposed to extend the New Deal and gird for defense, not by bringing Republican businessmen into government, but by keeping them out after the Wilsonian pattern of World War I. On other occasions when their paths crossed, their association was uneasy. Working with equals was not Corcoran's forte, and Hopkins, of course, he regarded as an equal. Yet for all of the Corcoran-Hopkins competition, their association, superficially, was always cordial. When Hopkins journeyed to Mayo Clinic to restore his brittle health, Corcoran wrote the departed rival a substantial letter, extolling his contribution to the common cause. Hopkins, for his part, although not the demonstrative type, was thoughtful enough to dispatch to Corcoran a copy of *The Southern Harmony Song Book* which he had come upon.

The precise part Hopkins played in Corcoran's decline cannot now and perhaps never will be authoritatively established. Corcoran was bound to slip if for no other reason than that Hopkins's steadily burgeoning influence with F.D.R. permitted only a constantly shrinking status for anyone else in the immediate circle. Rexford Tugwell, in *The Democratic Roosevelt*, is convinced that Hopkins acted aggressively to eliminate his rival. Corcoran's continued presence, Tugwell believes, must have seemed intolerable. Sick and driven, Hopkins made a sorry contrast to the robust halfback, Corcoran. Hopkins, Tugwell surmises, must have encouraged and coached the cavalcade of visitors who plied F.D.R. with statements hostile to Corcoran. But associates of the Cork do not accept this theory. Hopkins, they are convinced, engaged in no direct hostilities against their friend. His only sin, if it be one, is that he made no gesture to save the falling Corcoran. Hopkins did not counterbalance the angry politicians with words of praise; he gave Corcoran no comfort in a time when, physically run down and overwrought, he needed it. But the same criticism is also applicable to another figure who enjoyed ready access to F.D.R. and long had shared Corcoran's ordeals and triumphs —Felix Frankfurter. The Justice does not appear to have spoken out when an approving word might have counterweighed the hostile politicians.

Corcoran's relations with Frankfurter, indeed, had been deteriorating. Although Corcoran had looked in filial devotion to Frankfurter for counsel and approval after rising to the White House circle, difficulties of some magnitude arose. Frankfurter, in distant Cambridge, could not discern and weigh the imponderables Corcoran had to cope with on the firing line in Washington. As Corcoran's activities extended, the counsel from Cambridge appeared increasingly less valid and welcome. More serious conflicts erupted over patronage. Frankfurter, who cherished the pre-eminence of the Harvard Law School, rejected Corcoran's sponsorship of William O. Douglas, a professor of the Yale Law School. Corcoran successfully supported Douglas first for appointment as chairman of the SEC and subsequently to an associate justiceship on the United States Supreme Court in the conviction that the necessities of the United States government could not be wholly satisfied by the resources of Harvard Law School. Frankfurter and Corcoran also disagreed over the appointment of the Administrative Officer of the United States Courts, a post created by the legislation ensuing from the court-packing plan.

The elections came and passed, Roosevelt triumphed easily, and Corcoran attended the modest inaugural ceremonies at the White House for the third term. On that day also his first child was born, and intermingled with the accustomed joys such occasions inspire was the sober and haunting reflection that in the interests of the child's future it was high time he secured employment more stable than his White House assignments and endowed with a measure of prestige suitable for his services in the seven years of the New Deal. More specifically, he proposed to become Assistant Secretary of the Navy, a post now vacant, and his various Administration friends fell to campaigning vigorously in his behalf. But the appointment, to his dismay, was conferred upon another candidate. In the summer following the inaugural, another attractive opportunity materialized. The Solicitor Generalship became vacant, a post worthy of his talents, his quest for status, and his progeny's future. Corcoran candidly informed F.D.R. that he wanted the appointment. In a rare exertion of pressure from the Olympian heights of the United States Supreme Court, no less than five justices made known to the President their preferences for Corcoran for the capacity by which he would become the chief pleader of the government's causes before the high bench. Corcoran's heart and ambition were concentrated upon the job. But Franklin Roosevelt never sent the name of his faithful assistant to the Senate.

F.D.R.'s inaction is not to be interpreted as callous ingratitude. Indeed, from all the evidence, the President would gladly have proceeded with the appointment, except for one impossible difficulty. In conversations with knowledgable Senators, he had felt out the likely reactions to Corcoran's nomination if it were received in the upper house. Their almost uniform advice: Corcoran would never get by. The lingering rancor of the court fight and the purge, those unforgivable assaults on the prerogatives and pride of the United States Senate, assured that not a few members of that body would have their axes honed and poised to whack at Corcoran if he dared appear in the form of a presidential nomination for high office. F.D.R. therefore held back Corcoran's name. Only recently, indeed, he had suffered the embarrassment of sending to the upper house, and then withdrawing, in the face of unyielding Senatorial opposition, the designation of Ed Flynn as Ambassador to Australia. The Solicitor Generalship was a far more important office than the ambassadorial post, and Corcoran would raise far more spleen than the affable Flynn.

Corcoran, by all accounts, took F.D.R.'s decision very hard. The President, he felt, was much too timid, had placed too great store on a handful of

Senatorial opinions of dubious validity. Not from sympathy, but from a genuine desire for his services, F.D.R. did the next best thing of inviting Corcoran back in an official White House capacity, which would not require Senatorial approval and would encompass approximately all of his previous duties. Corcoran, acting from several considerations, declined. The proffered post lacked the prestige which his advancing career required, and the going in the White House, it was clear, would be far rougher than in the past. Missy Le Hand, after fighting gallantly to preserve her fading health, had passed away. Her death, more than any other factor, made Corcoran decide not to return. In a sense, the unfriendly Hopkins had become her successor. Now a firmly entrenched White House resident, Hopkins had become the President's favorite companion as Missy once had been. Like Montaigne who, when the politics of his community had become unpromising and unbearable, retired from its affairs and withdrew to his hill home, Corcoran decided to return to private life. Ben Cohen tried desperately to induce his partner to stay on, but to no avail. Cohen, however, followed his own advice, and served first with Ambassador John G. Winant in London, and then with James F. Byrnes, who left the United States Supreme Court to become Director of the Office of War Mobilization. In setting up his organization, Byrnes told F.D.R. that he wanted for his general counsel "the best lawyer in the country." The President replied that the wish was granted. And who was the gentleman in question? "Ben Cohen," replied Byrnes.

Corcoran, having taken to private life, set up a Washington law practice. The new enterprise concentrated not upon the courts and litigation, but upon the government bureaus of wartime Washington. Within a few months, in 1941, he testified to the Truman investigating committee that he received fees totalling one hundred thousand dollars for legal and organization work mostly in connection with government business. His aggressive lobbying incurred the journalistic wrath of the respected columnist, Thomas L. Stokes. Several years later he was again in the news when F.D.R. removed Norman Littell as Assistant Attorney General in charge of the Lands Division, the climax of a running feud between Attorney General Francis Biddle and Littell. In a departing statement of twelve thousand words, Littell said in effect that Corcoran's concern for the interests of wealthy clients had prompted him to pressure Biddle to bring Littell into line. Thomas L. Stokes, who was again aroused, observed, "The susceptibility of Biddle to the influence of his friend and sponsor, Corcoran . . . smacks too much of making government a private matter among friends. . . ."

But Corcoran's activities in World War II were not entirely Washington-centered. He contributed both brains and leg work in outfitting General Claire Chennault's gallant Flying Tigers with planes and pilots. Both were exceedingly scarce after Pearl Harbor, when American effort was concentrated on the European front and the Japanese were bombing the defenseless cities of China at rooftop level. With F.D.R.'s blessing, Corcoran fought his way through the echelons of the Pentagon, entreated with the British Royal Air Force and American aviation companies, and somehow scrounged together a quantity of planes sufficient to put and keep Chennault and his men in the skies against vastly superior Japanese forces.

Although in the passing years, his law practice has continued to flourish, Thomas G. Corcoran is happiest when engaged in public service improving the lot of mankind. He is at his best in interludes of crisis, such as his country knows today, calling for leadership and a supporting officialdom of imagination, energy and drive. It is not impossible that Corcoran will be back again in a White House capacity in the near future. For, with Ben Cohen, he belongs to the little circle of counselors which Senator Lyndon Johnson, a political prodigy of the original New Deal, has recently gathered around him. Should Johnson capture the Democratic presidential nomination in 1960 or after, and traverse victoriously from the Senate to the White House, the familiar faces of Corcoran and Cohen may reappear in their old locale. At least, it is unlikely that they would decline the opportunity. For that remarkable team and their numerous associates, the most exciting, the most rewarding time of their lives was the New Deal of F.D.R., when they drafted, worked and fought through the night, from one project to the next, in a grand unflagging effort, as an exuberant young assistant just out of law school loved to say, "to save the country." But they were doing more than that. They were saving the world.

Lord Root of the Matter

HARRY HOPKINS

"HARRY HOPKINS always went to the root of the matter," Winston Churchill said of his most intimate American friend in the Second World War. When chieftains of the Allied nations struggled in great conferences with momentous and elusive decisions of the war, when discussion slowed and all seemed baffled, Hopkins would throw out the way clearer, his irresistible question, "Surely Mr. President, here is the point we have got to settle. Are we going to face it or not?" Faced it always was, according to Churchill and, being faced, was conquered.

Harry Hopkins was playing his favorite and most expert role, the role which was simultaneously the touchstone of his ethics and his measure of success. To Hopkins, the essence of life was action. His own life is a saga of perpetual motion, and he was always contriving to put others into approximately that state. All through the history of the man, those who knew him admired his rare capacity for action and for bringing others to act. "He thought of himself simply as a catalyzer," said a colleague of his early days in the New York Tuberculosis and Health Association. "He is a man of good will with a sense of responsibility. He created an atmosphere in which other men of good will could work."

All through the war, Hopkins flourished at the White House in this same capacity. Franklin Roosevelt, for all of his reputation and accomplishment as a man of action, had to be watched and prodded and even nagged into decisions that were vital to the war. First and foremost a politician, Roosevelt had the politician's instinctive caution, kept his ear to the ground, and if the signal was "go slow," he was inclined to proceed accordingly. He came to value procrastination as a refuge and shield for the officeholder and his harassments. Hopkins was a gadfly who could sting Roosevelt into dropping his habit when it no longer paid off, and who could keep things hustling at the White House. All down the line in the departments, Hopkins performed the same mission with the consecration and fervor of a zealot. He kept enterprises stirring, badgered proud officials in conference and by telephone, and deftly pulled a complicated set of wires to advance the progress of the war. To obstructionists, the Judases and the Doubting Thomases, he meted out the same deadly and righteous effectiveness that Saint Patrick gave the snakes.

Certainly it took a zealot's fervor to sustain the constant driving activity which Hopkins required of his own frail and fading body. Mr. Churchill and his aides were thus impressed on their first encounter with him on a gray January morning in 1941, when Brendan Bracken, Churchill's representative, climbed into the plane which had brought Hopkins to Poole airfield, south of London. The poor man, sick and shrunken, lay motionless in his seat midway in the plane. His face, or what could be seen of it beneath a battered fedora pulled forward against the light, was cadaverous. His eyes, which opened now and then to reproach his untoward circumstances, were two glazed black beads. The rest of his body was a shortened version of Ichabod Crane, all bones and sockets, loosely gathered in a figure that had the breadth of a match stick. He still wore his safety belt; he was too far gone to unfasten it.

Exactly one hour after this strange introduction, Bracken saw Hopkins turn, without warning or explanation, into a dynamo surging with activity and plans. With the American Charge d'Affaires, Herschel Johnson, he examined Britain's ability to withstand the Nazi invasion, expected in the spring. He conferred with Eden at the Foreign Office; then in his rooms at Claridge's he gathered from Edward R. Murrow of the Columbia Broadcasting System a number of succinct portrayals of British personalities and public morale. Two hours later, he was coaching Lord Halifax, the ambassador-elect to the United States, on the hazards of Washington. Then came the drive through Berkeley and Trafalgar squares to Downing Street for discussions through luncheon and most of the afternoon. Later Hopkins held two conferences with the press, and walked off with Bracken to tour the bombed-out areas of London.

These pursuits, taxing to anyone in sound health, and Hopkins's unflagging execution of them, amazed Churchill and his aides. Here was a man who scarcely held the breath of life, who seemed ready to topple over at the least exertion, suddenly transformed into one who worked at the pace of a demon. How was the miracle to be explained? Churchill has ventured an answer. "His was a soul that flamed out of a frail and fading body," he said of Hopkins. "He was a crumbling lighthouse from which there shone the beams that led great fleets to harbor."

This fortunate combination of body and soul commenced on August 17, 1890, when Harry Lloyd Hopkins was born, the fourth son of five children in Sioux City, Iowa. His father, at the time a harness maker, was a

Jack-of-all-trades, working variously as newspaper carrier, prospector, sales-man and storekeeper. A touch of this versatility the father gave the son. By Midwestern hard work, frugality, and courage, "Dad" Hopkins, as he was known, achieved for Harry the common parental goal, a college education and the prospect of a better living. In 1908, young Hopkins entered Grinnell, a small Iowan college with a high reputation for scholarship. There he is remembered as an average student, a hustling, shrewd campus politician, with a knack for uniting quarreling factions behind his candidates and for staging gaudy campaign parades which in noise and size outstripped the resources of the college community. He was a devotee of Professor Jesse Macy, originator of the first college course in political science in the United States, and an expert at the Socratic method, which Hopkins himself was to use in public life with striking effect. But other elements of future statesman-ship—ideals, youthful faith and worldly impressions—Hopkins did not evi-dence in these years. Though Macy painted in his lectures an alluring vision of the unification of all the democratic nations of the world, his pupil, intently reared upon isolationism, was unimpressed.

Even the idealism which causes the social worker to take up a task that is poorly paid, routine and often sordid did not spark Hopkins's choice of that calling. Here, as at other turning points of his life, his lot came by accident, not by his own design. Upon graduation from Grinnell, he planned to join a failing newspaper in Bozeman, Montana, when a professor found him an apprenticeship at Christadora House, a charitable institution in the New York slums. Hopkins broke into his new work with the clatter and brash initiative which had enlivened his campus politics. At Christadora House, and in other professional posts of his early years, his colleagues marked him as a formidable operator, who combined the energy of forked lightning and the promotional competence of a Talleyrand. He blazed through endless weeks of sixteen-hour workdays, always kept on his staff a rough-talking nonprofessional who knew his way around the precinct club-houses, and coaxed municipal bigwigs into supporting projects of social im-provement that were politically vulnerable. Hopkins's accomplishments covered the welfare gamut. He organized boys' clubs from scrapping neigh-borhood gangs in a tawdry era of Tammany corruption. He made pioneer surveys of unemployment in New York when unemployment was considered an irrefutable sign of moral weakness, and thus unworthy of public attention. He set up a network of bureaus to care for destitute transients after long battles before a City Council which reckoned only in resident votes; and he ventured successfully into untouched domains of heart disease, children's welfare and dental and outpatient clinics. These triumphs carried Hopkins into the top executive posts of leading welfare agencies: the Association for

Improving the Condition of the Poor, the New York City Board of Child Welfare and the New York Tuberculosis Association.

When the Great Crash of the 'thirties forced its challenges upon the welfare profession, Hopkins's versatile labors and professional standing in New York prompted his appointment as deputy to Isador Straus, Chairman of Governor Franklin Roosevelt's Temporary Emergency Relief Administration. After a year, Straus resigned under the pressure of private affairs (he was President of Macy's), and recommended Hopkins as his successor. Roosevelt at once agreed. From quick impressions, he saw and valued Hopkins as a self-starter, who promised to function with minimum trouble to an overburdened Governor. Hopkins lived up to that mark. Uninvolved and pleased, Roosevelt witnessed his new administrator prevail over scores of hidebound county boards and private charities which either blocked relief to thousands of unemployed, or limited their grants to a miserable pittance. The Hopkins success formula was simple. Up and down the state, he convinced local politicians that the Biblical precept—"Thou shalt be thy brother's keeper"—could yield to the devoted a big earthly reward—the support of the unemployed at the polls. In 1932 that lesson of politics was not yet obvious.

When Roosevelt entered the White House, Hopkins, like many another New York luminary bearing the laurels of devoted service, awaited the call to Washington. But the days and weeks passed, until finally, two long months after the inaugural, the word came. Hopkins, though not the President's first choice, was made Federal Emergency Relief Administrator. Overnight, he rose to a novel place in the public legends—the nation's number-one spendthrift. In his first two official hours, he handed out five million dollars and fifteen million thereafter to relieve, by schemes of "boondoggling" and beneficial public projects, millions of unemployed—bank clerks, plumbers, roadmen and salesgirls—all without work by no fault of their own. The final oddity was the valiant Federal Arts Program for writers and artists, which earned for Hopkins and his "wild-eyed radicals" brickbats from patronage-hungry politicians and the conservative press. But the program pushed ahead and Hopkins defended his wards with a defiant, "Hell! They've got to eat just like other people."

As Administrator of FERA and its successor agencies, CWA and WPA, Hopkins grew schooled in the arts of improvisation and action. Relief for five million unemployed was a problem of staggering novelty and immensity in a hitherto prosperous land. Action had to be swift and inventive; the grim possibility posed by Iowa milk strikes, Farmers' Holiday forces and the miserable Hoovervilles was revolution. Hopkins acted with intelligence and frantic speed; the relief program and the other great programs of the New Deal burgeoned, and soon the danger of revolution passed. Five years later came a new and more terrible tragedy, the Second World War. Hopkins, as adviser, confidant and general alter ego of the President, employed these same arts of improvisation and action over the entire world. The new cataclysm, like the old, required action that was bold, imaginative and forthcoming at a tempo which precluded the usual planning and orderly effects of administration in easier times. Thus the endless snap decisions, the brief interviews, the terse scribbled notations for the President, the frenzied telephoning, the sudden flights to London, Moscow, the Crimea, and to places with unheard-of names—Hopkins's workaday implements in the furious enterprise of war.

So thoroughly did Hopkins play his hectic part in the crises of two decades that he thoroughly looked it, like one to whom action is both impulse and fetish. He had the bent and gangly shape and thinning hair of an ill-used Raggedy Andy. His face was sallow, heavy-lined, irregular and intensely mobile, twisting into brief smiles that could change abruptly from pleasant to sardonic. His eyes, close-set and beady, gleamed with suspicion and intent. His mouth had the sharp arrogant curve of a zealot's. To unknowing, somewhat timorous callers, his features conveyed a menacing premonition of certain upheaval, especially when he sat well down on his spine and stared and scowled like a hungry thunderbird over heavy-rimmed spectacles. In deliberation, he slid down to his backbone, and from there the grimaces were even more unnerving. But those who knew him well also saw a figure beset by the numerous pathologies of the modern administrator—nervous ferments and ulcers, chain-smoking, black-coffee drinking, and the undone appearance of the average welfare executive, of dandruff and ashes, and clothes which a night in a hayloft could never harm.

The drive for action tyrannized Hopkins's habits. His talk unwound with unpunctuated rapidity, and he was addicted to every means of mercurial progress, particularly the telephone. Blunt and direct, his favorite weapon in tribulation was a way clearer, the naked insult. Yet the man was also simple and modest, if only because those virtues avoided the slowness of pomposity. He never turned into the insufferable bore many mortals in his position might have become, the big official. Hopkins's little office in the FERA days had faded walls, uncovered water pipes running to the ceiling and an unshining desk, modesty itself. He loathed red tape and therefore tolerated only a minimum staff about him. One hundred and twenty one employees administered the fifty-million-dollar FERA program, a force phenomenally small by Washington standards, each member hand-picked for his messianic faith and stamina. Other honored adjuncts of the administrator, like the "organization chart," Hopkins banished with cavalier edicts. "I don't want anybody around here to waste any time drawing boxes," he barked one day to a subordinate. "You'll always find that the person who drew the chart has his own name in the middle box."

Hopkins's love of action excluded from his long administrative life the conception and statement of a general political and social faith. He was the lavish improviser; he was not the philosopher. Others divined the integral purpose; the most he did, in rare contemplative moments, was to supply a rule of thumb for particular occasions. "I don't see why," he once explained a new venture of public relief, "because a man is lazy, his wife and children shouldn't eat." But beyond events at hand, his homely wisdom seldom turned. He did not ponder the far horizons of his profession—its proper beginning and end, its appropriate effects upon other parts of a complex interlocked society. He was engrossed in fighting the stark havoc of war and unemployment. It is true that he registered as a Socialist in New York City's election of 1916. But he admitted to friends that a desire "to see the United States keep out of war," not some compelling idealism, prompted that step. Indeed, isolationism seems the principle implanted most deeply in his political faith, for it alone extends over the long span from his college days even beyond his entry into the White House circle. "The only interest here, as everywhere," he wrote to his brother, Emory, four weeks after Hitler invaded Poland, "is the war and I believe that we really can keep out of it. Fortunately there is no great sentiment in this country for getting into it, although I think almost everyone wants to see England and France win."

Hopkins's slender doctrinal ties often failed to confine his private behavior to bounds consistent with his professional labors. Poverty was his crusade, yet his favorite diversion, fully reported by the press, was high living. Race tracks, theaters, night clubs, café society and romps with the celebrated, he pursued with the zest of a playboy. He excelled at the most intricate tangos and sambas; he hobnobbed with Winston Guest, the younger Cushings and the Elsa Maxwell crowd. Although he invariably patronized the two-dollar window at the race track, his poker losses for a single night were known to be as high as six hundred dollars. Though many an admirer recoiled from these heresies, and Mrs. Roosevelt thought his interest in the high life a regrettable contradiction of character, all this was logical to a nature which thrived on variety, attacked situations with indiscriminate gusto and regarded life in general as a lark. In his pleasures, Hopkins also discovered and fostered a secret pride. He alone, he delighted to note, of all the chief New Dealers could weekend comfortably with the Long Island aristocracy or play poker at Saratoga with Mrs. Dodge Sloane.

But the hustling pace of work and play exacted its toll. Professional ambitions and pressures sometimes made Hopkins unfeeling toward friends and colleagues and rude to those he loved. His practice, each time he advanced up the professional ladder, was never to carry a subordinate with him, and to previous friends he became remote and inaccessible. Although most men carry several friendships with them through a lifetime, Hopkins maintained not a single one, from Iowa, or even from New York, during his subsequent career. Indeed, in the last of his New York days, Hopkins's failings broke through all restraint and shattered the pillars of his private life. His first marriage ended in divorce (he paid five thousand dollars annually in alimony from his eight-thousand-dollar Washington salary, leaving little margin for his cabinet-level position); he broke with John Kingsbury, the social-welfare executive who had been his booster up the ladder of a New York career, and swept through a series of petty quarrels of which he was soon ashamed. After treatment by an eminent psychiatrist, he took up the new life of national affairs, mended and penitent. But other effects of over-exertion, those upon his body, could never be mended, and broken health became a permanent ordeal. A duodenal ulcer seized Hopkins, and exacted rigid diets, total abstinence, hospitalization at the Mayo Clinic, convalescence in Florida, and heavy schedules of alutropin, amino-acid powder, Haliver oil with vitamin "D" and calcium bloconate. These expedients prolonged his life until January 29, 1946, when he died, a victim of hemochromatosis, a disease of inadequate digestive equipment.

Yet affliction raised Hopkins to a place more fascinating and more powerful than any his lively ambition had ever conceived—that of confidant of Franklin Roosevelt. Victor in his own fight against a dread illness, the President came to take up personally the fight of Hopkins. Though other events first implanted Hopkins in Roosevelt's concern. There was, above all, the steady efficiency of the relief program—a matter of surprise—and Hopkins's victories over its foes, the big howlers, Huey Long and Gene Talmadge, and the shrewd infighters, Martin Davey of Ohio and William Langer of North Dakota. Roosevelt delighted to see the Administration, thanks to Hopkins, stand in virtue resplendent, and the state leaders as cheap subverters of the public good. The President's awakened interest was steadily fanned by Hopkins's friend in court, Mrs. Roosevelt, who admired the ingenious humanity of the relief program more than any other phase of the New Deal. First at Mrs. Roosevelt's behest, and soon the President's, Hopkins was invited to the White House. A steady visitor in 1934, he soon was accredited with being as close to Roosevelt as any of the numerous figures then constituting the presidential circle. Hopkins himself seems to have regarded Henry Morgenthau as "the Number One Man" whom the President used most "to do things and see people," (Hopkins's phrases). At this time, associates noticed definite signs of Hopkins's enduring hero worship of the President—a disposition to evaluate personalities and issues strictly in terms of their potential to do good or ill for his chief.

Hopkins was even closer to Mrs. Roosevelt. When his second wife, Barbara, to whom he was very devoted, died tragically of cancer in 1937, Mrs. Roosevelt was a sympathetic and helpful friend. As nearly as anyone, she served as a mother to little Diana, the offspring of the marriage, and told Hopkins that if it would make his mind any easier, he should put a clause in his will designating her the guardian of the child in the event of his prior death. Hopkins's White House ties also extended to the younger Roosevelts, for all of whom he had great affection. He became the companion of the eldest son James in gambols among the horsy set and saw much of the President's only daughter, Anna. Indeed, many friends expected the widower Hopkins to marry Anna following her divorce from Curtis Dahl.

In 1938, Hopkins was briefly prominent as a possible candidate for the 1940 Presidential election. Hopkins's associates are divided in their interpretations of this curious byplay of his public life. Some claim his ambition drove him to any incongruous extreme to get up the ladder. Others hold that Hopkins sought the office only because Roosevelt wanted him to. Until the war intervened and Roosevelt concluded that he would have to run for a third term himself, Jim Farley felt that Hopkins was Roosevelt's own first choice as a successor. Meanwhile, Hopkins was carefully photographed with his chief at every opportunity and, probably at the latter's suggestion, leased a farm in his native Grinnell, Iowa, with great ado. This step goaded Harold Ickes into the uncharitable comment: "There is hardly anyone I know who is less spontaneously associated with farm life." As part of the build-up, Hopkins was appointed Secretary of Commerce on Christmas Eve, 1938. Most of the next eighteen months, he lost to illness. He spent not more than thirty days, on and off, at his department, and the remainder of his time recuperating at Warm Springs, the Mayo Clinic, at Bernard Baruch's South Carolina plantation, and in an old pre-Revolution house on the Patuxent River in Maryland, among other places.

In May, 1940, Hopkins returned to Washington from treatment during a low ebb at the Mayo Clinic and rest in Florida. The President, anxious to aid the recovery of his friend, invited him to spend ten days at the White House. Hopkins arrived shrunken and faint; he could barely make it from his bedroom to the dining table. The President, in mingled sympathy and challenge, became absorbed in the complicated game of restoring his guest to health. He directed the Navy medical department to diagnose Hopkins's ailments "from A to Z," and personally enforced an intricate series of prescriptions through rigid discipline and homely rewards. "Teacher is glad you have gained two pounds," Roosevelt commended a report of Hopkins's weight, and pinned on it two crisp one-dollar bills. His patient, reputedly the occasion of a popular comedy, *The Man Who Came to Dinner*, settled down in the bedroom of Abraham Lincoln for the longest visit (three and a half years) and the strangest convalescence in the history of the White House.

Hopkins could not have chosen a worse place for recuperation if he tried to. In the torrid Washington summer of 1940, the White House seethed with tensions from Europe's incredible disasters. The French Republic crushed; Poland, Denmark and Norway overrun; Britain, alone and valiant, in her long ordeal of blockbusters and U-boat wolf packs. The succeeding months were even worse. The Balkans toppled. The invincible Nazis smashed into Russia and tracked rapidly to the Volga and the Don, well ahead of Hitler's timetable. Pearl Harbor was not far off.

The central contact of the United States with these events was the White House. Franklin Roosevelt perceived their implications better than anyone in his circle, and his confident talents kept the British afloat, bolstered the Russians and enheartened free men everywhere, notwithstanding limiting neutrality laws and the powerful hard-fighting isolationists. Lend Lease, the Atlantic Charter, destroyers-for-bases, a host of measures "short of war" were Roosevelt inventions which kept munitions, money and encouragement crossing the sea lanes.

After Pearl Harbor, if previous events had not proven so already, the President was content with nothing less than running every important phase of the war himself. The North African invasion was his "baby," as he would say, and he shepherded the Normandy campaign through the assaults of Winston Churchill and various United States generals, who preferred a drive up through the Balkans to block the Russians from occupying too much of central Europe. Roosevelt was his own Secretary of State. The aging, ailing Cordell Hull was conspicuously absent from Casablanca, Cairo and Quebec, and from many a White House conference where the President concluded momentous agreements with allied chieftains. At Yalta, Hull's successor, Edward R. Stettinius, although present, had, by his own account of the conference, an unquestionably minor role.

On the home front, Roosevelt proceeded to elaborate extremes to keep under his own control the job of mobilizing the American industrial colossus. The President's approach would have the greatest consequences on the later operations and fortunes of Harry Hopkins. Roosevelt never yielded to clamors from various quarters that he appoint a single top assistant to run the home front. There would be no "Czar," "Poobah," or "Akhoond of Swat," he carefully informed the press on several occasions, fearing that such a figure would take over a dangerously large part of the presidential power and have sufficient stature to undercut the Chief Executive himself. Thus

Roosevelt's tactic time and again was to appoint boards and committees for the home front, in lieu of a single executive, notwithstanding that since ancient times these many-membered bodies have proven abominably inefficient for large-scale executive operations.

His other favorite tactic was to see that the ranking appointees in a given agency were rivals. "A little rivalry is stimulating, you know," the President explained one day to Secretary of Labor Frances Perkins. "It keeps everybody going to prove he is a better fellow than the next man. It keeps them honest too."

In the din of the unabated Battle of Washington, voices continued to cry out for the appointment of an Assistant President to end the chaos and run the home front. But Roosevelt, for his usual and proper reasons, would have nothing of it. Yet he was the first to admit that he needed help. Countless memos had to be read, committees had to be watched, visitors received and squabbles quieted—suitable tasks for a subordinate the President could trust. It was altogether clear who would *not* fit into this more modest version of presidential assistant. Not the more dedicated breed of New Dealer who would be continuously consulting his ideals to the neglect of the war. Not one of the department heads, a favorite source of Roosevelt's prewar advisers, since they would be prone to grind the axes of departmental interests, whereas in a total war the President's aide must see things in their broadest conceivable reference. Not a big-business man or important politician, or other species of success. For Roosevelt had always preferred as personal advisers individuals who were not too well established, who, after outliving their usefulness, could be easily brushed off with a minimum of incident or embarrassment. Where to find the man? Roosevelt's thoughts promptly turned to the unemployed invalid upstairs in the Lincoln study.

Rallied by medicine and the exhilaration of crisis, Hopkins took up the President's calls for aid. These began modestly, but soon quickened as Roosevelt directed strong currents of papers to Hopkins with the scribbled requests: "Check this Harry," "Give them the spur," "Will U.S. Steel comply?" Hopkins would act swiftly—nearly always by telephone—and his ability to get results in the turmoil tremendously impressed his chief. For Hopkins combined experience with contacts which, with his established talents, enabled him to operate with quick effectiveness in the colossal job of United States mobilization.

As Secretary of Commerce, he had made friends with the potentates in business circles whose co-operation was essential for building America's strength for war: Coonley of the National Association of Manufacturers, Batt of SKF industries, Stettinius of United States Steel, Biggers of Libby-

Owens-Ford, Harriman of Union Pacific, and numerous others. All discovered him to be not, as they feared, a rabid New Dealer, sputtering fire and brimstone at industrial villains, but one who sought to bring the New Deal and the business community to terms for fighting the war. The President valued and used Hopkins's ready approach to these stalwarts—"Hopkins's Tame Millionaires," he liked to call them—in all matters concerning the potential and problems of American industry. And, as Roosevelt and countless others soon discovered, no one in Washington excelled Hopkins at the art of bringing captains of industry to the telephone and entreating them, in the name of victory, or, if necessary, bulldozing them by some lusty language into undertaking production schedules that ordinary prudent men would consider impossible.

The coin of Hopkins's services developed another side. People everywhere, in the government and outside, found him a perfect contact, for their own purposes, for gaining the rarest prize of wartime Washington, Roosevelt's attention. Department secretaries, generals and admirals learned that complex matters which could not be conveniently presented in ordinary-length conferences with the President or in full meetings of the President and his aides, could be efficiently communicated through the good offices of Hopkins. So effective did he become, that "If it's about defense, see Harry," became a byword in the capital and tribute to his talents, which sent long lines of visitors of all levels of importance to the office which he had set up in the Lincoln study. "I make myself available to people who've got something to say about the war," Hopkins proclaimed his discriminating standard, and small-talkers, self-seekers and other infidels who dared approach he cut down brusquely. "The President isn't going to be bothered with anything as nonsensical and unimportant as that if I can help it," he would snap, and send offenders flying with shots of torrid profanity.

But many visitors came with solemn matters. Soon after Paris fell, Dr. Vannevar Bush, then without access to the President, discussed with Hopkins plans to set up a new government agency, bearing the innocuous title, "National Research Council." Hopkins arranged an interview with the President, coached Bush on tactics, and Roosevelt approved the plans. By that simple mediation began the organization which eventually developed the atomic bomb. A few days later, Grenville Clark, New York lawyer and crusader for military preparedness in two World Wars, also came armed with plans for a Selective Service System. Roosevelt, with presidential elections pending, was playing the man-power issue cautiously, and Clark found his appointment switched to Hopkins, who gave encouragements which Roosevelt endorsed, but could not state officially. Hopkins had stepped into a role which rapidly expanded: confidential contact between the President and private individuals and groups on matters of touchy politics.

Hopkins's activities evolved according to no particular plan. They simply unraveled, impelled largely by Roosevelt's penchant as an administrator to entrust a task to the first man he came upon he believed could do it. Since Hopkins was living in the White House and was proving himself daily, he usually was that man. This, however, was by no means the only factor in the Hopkins rise. He was much too enterprising to allow his White House role to develop only when the President and felicitous accident got around to it. He kept his own sharp-eyed vigil for opportunities and never shrank from pouncing on a good one when he saw it. One day near Christmas in 1940, while discussing problems of British armament purchases in the United States with his adviser, Roosevelt remarked, "A lot of this could be settled if Churchill and I could just sit down together for a while."

"What's stopping you?" Hopkins asked, his acquisitive instincts aroused.

"Well—it couldn't be arranged right now. They have no ambassador here—we have none over there."

Hopkins swooped in, his beady eyes dancing with high adventure. "How about me going over, Mr. President?"

Roosevelt turned him down cold. But undaunted, and never letting go of his promising idea, Hopkins enlisted the aid of the important Marguerite Le Hand, the President's personal secretary, and Justice Felix Frankfurter, who, in spite of his elevation to the Supreme Court, was not unconcerned with proceedings at the White House. One week after he had broached his idea, the phone rang in Hopkins's study. It was Steve Early, F.D.R.'s press secretary, to congratulate him on the President's announcement, made ten minutes earlier to the press, that Hopkins was going to London.

By virtue of this and four subsequent trips to Britain, and two each to the European Continent, Africa and Eurasia, Hopkins established himself as Roosevelt's personal liaison with the war overseas, with the political and military chieftains and the fighting fronts. He did the leg work on which Roosevelt based his central political decision of World War II, namely, that the war must be fought in alliance as close as possible with Britain and the Soviet Union. The British regarded Hopkins as "Roosevelt's Personal Foreign Office," for with Winston Churchill he transacted more business than has ever engaged the representatives of two powers. From catgut and zircon bearings to the Atlantic Charter, their negotiations advanced and concluded scores of agreements which bolstered imperiled Britain and sped the ultimate victory. On the day the Germans crashed into Russia, Hopkins, then in London, promptly grabbed the transatlantic telephone and volunteered to his chief to do for Russia what he had done for the British. In long conferences with Stalin over charts and tables, he found out what Russia needed, advised on what America could do, and penetrated the sullen-witted armor of the dictator better than any Anglo-American official ever has. Hard-to-impress Soviet purchasing agents called him "Big Boss, Mr. Hopkins."

Hopkins's overseas endeavors were a big factor in the build-up of his role inside the United States. His incomparable on-the-spot knowledge of the fighting fronts made him the President's ready choice to head up Lend Lease when it became a going concern on March 27, 1941. After Pearl Harbor, Hopkins, practically overnight, became one of the biggest administrative guns in the expanded war machine. He functioned as an interlocking director in behalf of the President in the central organizations concerned with military strategy, munitions allocations, and home-front production. He was the one civilian whose presence Roosevelt regularly insisted on in White House sessions of the Joint Chiefs of Staff on military strategy. He participated similarly in the Combined Chiefs of Staff which Roosevelt and Churchill established in their Washington meeting following Pearl Harbor, to achieve closer Anglo-American military co-operation. Hopkins was in the thick of sessions in Washington and London, thrashing out the decisions and details of the North African and Normandy invasions and the alternative Mediterranean campaigns. Every principal American member of those discussions has acknowledged Hopkins's contribution in the vein of Eisenhower's tribute: "He had a grasp of the broad factors in military problems that was almost phenomenal."

Along with the Combined Chiefs, Roosevelt and Churchill established the Munitions Assignment Board with Hopkins as chairman and headquarters in Washington, and what amounted to a branch in London under Lord Beaverbrook, British Minister of Production. Chairman Hopkins had the ticklish and bewildering job of allocating the supply of material to all of the United States armed services, to all of the Allies, and to all of the theaters of war. Among Hopkins's clientele were such doughty prima donnas as General MacArthur, "Vinegar Joe" Stillwell, Field Marshal Montgomery, ill-mannered Kremlin warriors and General de Gaulle. The MAB function extended Hopkins from his going role of presidential adviser into the more taxing and involving role of deputy presidential administrator. Although there was much strife, Hopkins's genius for decision got the right armaments in the right place at the right time without a single major mishap. Although as Chairman and presidential spokesman Hopkins ran MAB with a firm hand, he was always wary of allowing formal responsibility for its actions to settle on his doorstep. At his insistence, the Board operated simply as a "subcommittee" (his term) to the Combined Chiefs of Staff. Technically, therefore, the Chiefs made, and answered for, all allocations decisions. According to William D. Leahy, the President's personal military deputy, the Combined Chiefs never rejected a single Board "recommendation" in the entire war.

Inevitably, Hopkins became considerably involved in the production problems of the materiel he had to distribute. How could his clamoring clientele be satisfied if the tanks, planes, guns and myriad other commodities were not on hand on schedule? This further aspect of Hopkins's concerns was nicely served by Roosevelt's established preference for committees to run the production sector of the war effort. Hopkins acquired membership on the several committees that counted most. When Roosevelt established the War Production Board with Donald Nelson as chairman, Hopkins, as "Special Assistant to the President supervising the defense aid program" (Lend Lease), was named a member. He was likewise a member of SPAB (Supply Priorities Allocations Board), the superagency created on August 28, 1941, to co-ordinate the allocation of materials between the defense program and competing civilian demands, and of innumerable ad hoc committees. Hopkins's sizable committee work gave him a finger in the center of the big production-program pie. At committee sessions, he learned what was going on in many high places, and as presidential spokesman his word was listened to.

His influence touched everywhere—even the White House menus were manipulated by his fickle constitution. He came to have a big say on appointments, numbering among his nominations General Marshall as Chief of Staff, Donald Nelson as Chairman of the War Production Board, Mrs. Roosevelt to a directorship of the Office of Civilian Defense, Averell Harriman as Ambassador to Russia, E. R. Stettinius as Secretary of State, and Brigadier General William O'Dwyer as Surplus Property Custodian, a job entailing the disposal of billions of dollars' worth of war-built factories, flashlights, bulldozers, walky-talkies, et cetera, shoals on which honest government customarily flounder. With Judge Samuel Rosenman and playwright Robert Sherwood, Hopkins was a full-fledged partner in the President's favorite speech-drafting triumvirate. Although he did little original drafting, Hopkins excelled at tearing drafts apart, exposing weaknesses and dangers, offering fresh ideas and phrases, and running brilliant interference for his colleagues with the President.

Solely because of his tie with Roosevelt, Hopkins was a power in the tenebrous nether world of professional politics in 1940. His most impressive triumph, although one which later backfired badly, lay in swinging Roosevelt into accepting the anxious but unreliable Henry Wallace as his running mate for the third-term presidential election. Chicago, the convention city, beheld the intriguing spectacle of Jim Farley, the national chairman, established in Democratic headquarters at the Stevens Hotel, to whom, as everyone knew, Roosevelt had not confided his third-term intentions, and across the street at the Blackstone was Hopkins with, as everyone also knew, a private telephone line to the White House. Hopkins, having easily quarterbacked Roosevelt's nomination while the forgotten Farley looked on, tore into the big test, Wallace. The delegates hooted and jeered and nearly broke ranks, grumbling that Hopkins was a meddling upstart New Dealer, who was not even a bona fide delegate and got on the floor only because Mayor Kelly had made him a deputy sergeant at arms. But Hopkins sweated and insulted his way victoriously through the back-room bargains and pep talks, and had strength enough left over to tell Wallace off, when the future Vice-President, flying into the face of the obvious, proposed to appear before the convention and accept the nomination.

There was nothing quite like Hopkins and his far-flung capacities any-where else in the war. No executive subordinate in the Allied democracies, or, for that matter, no subpotentate in the Nazi, Fascist and Soviet dictator-ships, touched on the variety of affairs that he did. Since he worked on what-ever was uppermost in Roosevelt's mind, and since, when that lively mecha-nism shifted, he did likewise, his activities assumed the inexhaustible variety and dimension of the Presidency itself. Literally and figuratively, he had the run of the White House. There was little business he could not transact, few presidential secrets he didn't share, and no papers he couldn't see. He was one of the few mortals who had untrammeled access to the most heavily guarded portion of the White House, the Map Room, where military dis-patches were sent and received by the President and where flags and pins in wall maps showed the disposition of American forces all over the world. Never a tidy soul, Hopkins habitually made the military nervous by his casual treatment of important papers. When he moved out of the Executive Mansion late in 1943 to a rented house in Georgetown, White House clerks were forever scurrying out to the suburb to retrieve some top secret paper or message which Hopkins had carried off in his pocket and forgotten about.

As he did of everyone engaged with public duties, Roosevelt insisted that Hopkins come on the public payroll, and put in a line for him in the White House budget as "Special Adviser to the President" at ten thousand dollars a year. Even in this formality, Hopkins was a privileged character. Roosevelt's customary practice was to put his advisers on the payroll of some department, rather than that of the White House, for the practical reason that it facilitated getting rid of those gentlemen when they lost their use-fulness. Hopkins's shift in status, from guest to paid official, in no way re-stricted his affairs. He never worried about legal limitations anyhow, for his capacity was founded not in law, but in the President's favor. There were more substantial perils of which to beware. A galaxy of critics, of assorted motives and methods, who could not conveniently strike at the President, found Hopkins a useful punching bag for getting at Roosevelt indirectly. Probably the severest of these critics tirelessly belabored the theme that Harry Hopkins, by living in the White House, was sponging off the tax-payers. Actually, Hopkins added few dollars to the taxpayers' burden, for the meager caloric intake of his feeble constitution, as well as all other food consumed in the Executive Mansion, was paid for by the President. Although it wasn't his fault, Hopkins was more vulnerable when Bernard Baruch staged a gaudy feast in his honor on December 16, 1943, with eighty guests at forty dollars a plate at the Carlton. There were choice steaks and chops galore, delicacies which Hopkins had discussed in a wholly different context only two weeks before in an article in the American Magazine titled, "You and Your Family Will Be Mobilized." Among other things, Hopkins said in his article: "No family should object to meat rationing when they realize the beef and bacon they don't get is being served to their sons and brothers in the Army." The editorial uproar over the party and the pietistic essay was terrible, but Hopkins rode it out, carefully observing his practice of saying nothing when under public fire.

Being free to fasten onto almost any task that he wanted to, Hopkins sometimes tried to do too much, and off he would go to the Naval Hospital or the Mayo Clinic for weeks at a time.* Although faced with the prospect of an early death, Hopkins not only did not provide for a successor, he didn't even keep his records tidy. His notations of Britain's military requirements on his first transatlantic journey were scribbled on the back of some old United States Treasury requisitions and stuffed in a shoe box. "The people who dislike Hopkins," a coworker once said, "are the people who like order." Sometimes he declined measurably, although never fatally, in the President's favor. Indeed his long unbroken tenure as adviser constitutes his great unsung distinction. He lasted longer and had broader powers than any other major confidant in Roosevelt's four terms of office. F.D.R.'s habit of playing others off against a confidant or of dropping him the moment he was the least liability, had evolved the gloomy statistic that the average staying time of his more prominent advisers, from 1933 until Hopkins's advent in 1940, was something less than a year. This figure is a trifle arbitrary, for being dropped by Roosevelt was a subtle, rather extended experience. It ranged from a

*The periods of Hopkin's major illnesses are as follows:
August 22, 1939, until late spring, 1940, to Mayo Clinic and later back to Naval Hospital, Washington
October 31 to December 3, 1941, at Naval Hospital
January 16–30, 1942, to Naval Hospital following the Arcadia conference
August, 1943, to Naval Hospital for undetermined stay following the Quebec conference
January to May, 1944, to Naval Hospital, Mayo Clinic, Miami, White Sulphur Springs for operation and post-operative treatment; and convalescence until July, 1944
February, 1945, Hopkins present but ill during most of the Yalta conference
Beyond these major periods, Hopkins was under care of doctors even while on duty. It is difficult to establish dates for these briefer interludes of ill health. A colleague reports doing business with Hopkins when it must have been extremely painful for him to see anyone. On one such occasion, while being shot with a syringe big enough to use on a horse, Hopkins never whimpered nor did he appear to lose the trend of the conversation.

failure to consult on certain questions to banishment to some obscure mission to Scandinavia, the Orient, or what for the adviser constituted some other Point of No Return. Hopkins survived, basking as Prince Charming as long as Roosevelt lived. Although numerous other struggling confidants tried as mightily as Hopkins, he alone mastered the hazards of his occupation with an incisiveness, and when necessary a ruthlessness, wholly worthy of one who got at the root of all matters.

In his approach to Roosevelt, Hopkins profited from the instructive examples of two White House predecessors, Colonel Edward M. House and the late Louis McHenry Howe. Just as Roosevelt carefully studied Woodrow Wilson to avoid his mistakes, Hopkins, with equal purpose, pondered the record of his First World War counterpart. The more recent Howe was one of the few long-lasting original Roosevelt favorites. A wizened little gnome, who looked and acted like a character out of Dickens, ex-newspaperman Howe had fastened onto Roosevelt in the early Albany days, helped him conquer the tragedy of poliomyelitis, and guided his star through the New York political haze into the White House. Howe moved in too, and although illness soon cut him down, fatally in 1936, he was on his better days an invaluable factotum. His principal and most unusual capacity was that of Roosevelt's crony. For Franklin Roosevelt, for all of his geniality and dedication to his fellow men, was not given easily to friendships. His friends, in the customary sense of the word, could be counted on one hand, and dated strictly from Harvard and Hyde Park. Ambitious Washington men, who gained access and considerable temporary influence at the White House, tried desperately to establish a permanent foothold of friendship—they played accordions, labored over anecdotes, and were indefatigably genial. But Roosevelt, who used these men-on-the-make and their brilliant talents while he needed them, never counted them as friends, making it easy to drop them later.

Howe's capacity as White House crony-in-residence thus lay vacant between his death in 1936 and Hopkins's succession in 1940. It was Hopkins's luck that history, in a sense, was repeating itself. Both these extraordinary men appeared at the peak of a crisis, Howe in the depression, Hopkins in the war. The President, who is always a lonely figure amid the bustle of office, is even lonelier in a crisis and craves companionship more. Both confidants were desperately ill, which aroused the President's poignant instincts, and both reciprocated in their thoroughgoing dedication to his interests. General Eisenhower, who dealt constantly with Hopkins, described him as "almost fanatically loyal to the President." Marquis Childs, the columnist, observed in 1941, "Hopkins would jump off the Washington Monument if Roosevelt ordered it for the national welfare." By no means should it be judged that Harry Hopkins had lost his ambition and drive upon settling down in the White House. What evidently happened was that illness and its continual threat of death had prompted him to transfer them in all their vigor to a hero who could color his final years with superlative excitement.

If anything, then, the place beside the throne was even more cherished and sought, and of the several possible routes to the indispensability necessary to win and keep that prize, Hopkins followed the rare example of Louis Howe by quickly establishing himself as the President's companion and friend. There is general agreement on Hopkins's exceptional command of the necessary qualifications for this status. "There was a temperamental sympathy between the men," Frances Perkins once explained, "which made their relationship easy as well as faithful and productive." As social animals, the two men were astonishingly alike. Each thrived in human contact and exuded ample charm, Roosevelt more or less perpetually, Hopkins when he wanted to. Neither was a bookman, but found leisure, sought knowledge and tested ideas in conversation. In social hours, Roosevelt preferred company that wouldn't talk business continuously, but could relax as he did, when there was time for it. Yet he also liked to break off a gay interlude suddenly for serious discussion. The flexible Hopkins excelled as critic, small-talker, patient listener, and in every other expected capacity. Roosevelt was a raconteur of risqué and homely stories, which he repeated over and over again—Judge Rosenman has said that he heard some at least five times—but Hopkins, in even the severest tests, was always the amiable listener. The President, who enjoyed opposing wits, found his adviser a perfect foil, who could ride with a joke against himself and then hit smartly back. "I'm a Jester," Hopkins once described his capacity. Both were accomplished mimics. Roosevelt's *pièce de résistance* was a take-off on the hillbilly ways of his World War I boss, Secretary of the Navy Josephus Daniels, and Hopkins's best was a pantomime of Churchill lecturing Anthony Eden on how to speak in the House of Commons, including stance, gaze, inflection and how to wave papers significantly in his listeners' faces.

Roosevelt was especially delighted by Hopkins's wartime parlor specialty of cutting down to size the more arrogant members of the steady parade of displaced royalty who made their way to the White House. The President, who was a stickler for being accorded the amenities that were due him, was occasionally shortchanged by his distinguished visitors. One extremist, for example, was insulting to the point of mixing his drinks in his room and then sitting abstemiously through the predinner cocktail sessions which Roosevelt staged for his guests in the Oval Study. The exalted status of this offender never stopped Hopkins from bringing him crashing down with one well-aimed shaft. In so doing, Hopkins was not stepping out of character simply to please the President. For he had a long record of ingenious assaults on the proprieties, always under justifiable circumstances. According to well-verified report, he punctured the conceit of one high and mighty Washington society matron when, upon arrival at her home for dinner one night, he pulled out an electric razor and began shaving before an entrance-hall mirror. The most solemn occasion never phased him. In 1939, at the reception of the British embassy for the King and Queen, Hopkins sneaked off behind some bushes where an inquisitive old lady, spotting him through the foliage, found him sitting on the ground with his shoes off. "I'm here because my feet hurt," Hopkins explained.

Roosevelt saw more of Hopkins than anyone else during the war, not excepting Mrs. Roosevelt, his secretary, Grace Tully, or his earnest chief Secret Service agent, Mike Reilly. According to established routine, they were together at certain hours of the day. From seven fifteen P.M. sharp until eight P.M., they took predinner cocktails in the President's study, either alone, or with not more than two or three favored guests present. Hopkins once privately remarked that the President's untutored tastes in liquor made these most intimate occasions something of an ordeal, particularly his fad of shaking gin and grapefruit juice into his mixture, but the eager confidant stoically downed his daily potion. Hopkins was also Roosevelt's inveterate companion at lunch or dinner—breakfasts, the President took alone in his bedroom—also small affairs centered in the study, Roosevelt avoiding the gatherings of twenty or more guests that Mrs. Roosevelt liked to hold in the downstairs dining room. Sunday mornings and at late hours, when Roosevelt, tieless and in shirt sleeves, relaxed in conversation or shuffled his stamp collection, did crossword puzzles, played solitaire, or mused over his favorite game—figuring out ways you could disappear with fifty thousand dollars—Hopkins was the favorite stand-by. In fact, there wasn't any time, day or night, that Hopkins couldn't reach the President. "Hopkins," noticed one observer, "is the only man in Washington who can interrupt any White House conference and get the President's signature." Their bedrooms were located in the same corridor, and the pilgrimages the adviser made down the hallway in a tattered old dressing gown to plead pet measures and consult on doubtful items provided his best moments of influence.

In doing business with Roosevelt, Hopkins was uncanny at knowing when to introduce a subject, when to attack frontal and when to go around, when to break away, when to listen and when to play dumb. Hopkins talked the President's language. Each saw issues in terms of people, and people not as a mass or a statistic, but as individual personalities. What Roosevelt probably valued most in Hopkins's missions overseas was his confidant's forte at describing the strengths and foibles of generals and statesmen with a vivid accuracy that was almost as satisfying as if Roosevelt had seen these men himself. Hopkins seldom argued with his chief, and on the few occasions when he is known to have offered constructive suggestions on how to succeed with Roosevelt, he advised others not to do so. He would give his opinions honestly, but knowing that the President could never stomach opposition too well, frequently agreed with him regardless of his own opinion, or tried to persuade him in indirect ways. In this particular, Hopkins did not follow his predecessor, Howe, who sometimes opposed the President. But Howe, in doing so, enjoyed two distinct advantages over Hopkins. He was older than the President, and had "brought up" Roosevelt politically. Hopkins had no comparable accomplishment to trade on.

Some eyewitnesses to Hopkins's rise attribute his success to the fact that he, better than any other White House figure, convinced the President that he could be trusted. Whether it was a mission to Churchill or to the Democratic National Convention, Hopkins could be relied upon to follow orders to the letter and to communicate to others only what Roosevelt wanted. In his studies on Colonel House, Hopkins figured that House's big mistake lay in involving the President in commitments which the adviser had no authority to make. For his part, Hopkins, when abroad on missions, conscientiously kept his chief fully informed by cable and transatlantic telephone of every turn of events promptly as they occurred. In many cases, his cables provide the fullest statements extant of the background and alternatives of the big decisions of the war.

Hopkins was equally successful in beating off the several threats to his position which developed inside the White House. At least one of these threats was major, even to the point of challenging his continued residence in the Executive Mansion, and if there was anything worth fighting for, it was Hopkins's leasehold on the Lincoln study. This priceless privilege was suddenly jeopardized, ironically by the confidant himself, when a romantic project he had been pursuing, materialized in his engagement to Louise Macy. On July 30, 1942, the couple provided the White House with its first wedding in twenty-five years, with Roosevelt as best man. The grave occupational question raised by this third matrimonial venture of Hopkins was: How could he plus his bride and his daughter, Diana, now aged nine, go on living at the White House? It is basic to an understanding of Hopkins's acute possessiveness for his position, to note that he did not abide by Emily Post and wait for his host to issue a suitable invitation. The worried Hopkins proceeded to his chief and put the question directly. Roosevelt unhesitatingly replied that they must positively stay on. But this was only half the battle, the easier half. There was also Mrs. Roosevelt, who by that time was reconsidering her earlier fondness for her protégé, finding him as a house guest "irritable and unreasonable." Since a voluntary invitation from the First Lady was unlikely, Hopkins carried the fight to her. Bluntly, he asked if she would object to his augmented family living in the White House. She replied that she would have to consult her husband, implying as politely as she could that she did object. But the President insisted that, since winning the war was paramount, the Hopkinses absolutely must stay on in the White House. For a year and more after his marriage, until the end of the war was in sight, Hopkins clung to his White House vantage point and induced his bride to face what Mrs. Roosevelt has termed "a difficult situation."

Anyone who sought access to Roosevelt or became in any way close to him, had to run a gantlet of Hopkins's defenses, ranging from ill-concealed suspicion to boorish hostility. Winston Churchill, for all of his affection for the adviser, noticed, with the understatement which characterizes his memoirs whenever they treat of American personalities, that Hopkins was "jealous" of his position and "did not encourage" competitors. Old friendships and past favors meant nothing if they got in the way. Once installed in the White House, Hopkins treated Mrs. Roosevelt, his original benefactor, with such unrelenting rudeness, that she concluded that she had better stay out of his orbit, which was exactly what he wanted. His fellow literary craftsmen, Rosenman and Sherwood, found that whenever their White House stock was rising, Hopkins would chop them down by the unnerving tactic of agreeing with them in conference and then proceeding secretly to the President to represent a different point of view. More than one on-the-scenes authority has claimed that Hopkins, who did not like Bernard Baruch, chanted such poisonous notes into Roosevelt's ear about the venerable adviser to Presidents, that his presence was precluded from several wartime situations where he would surely have proven helpful. To a great degree, Roosevelt saw through Hopkins's game and tried hard to control it, although there is reason to believe that he rather welcomed the plot against Baruch and found Hopkins a useful scapegoat.

Yet for all of his busy palace politics, Hopkins could never have graced the White House scene so long if he hadn't offered the very talents which Roosevelt prized most in any top adviser. Whenever the Administration veered from its number-one objective—winning the war as fast as possible— Roosevelt liked a confidant, more detached than he could ever be from the pressures of office, to nudge him back. Especially in the pre-Pearl Harbor days, Roosevelt would sometimes slow down, or even grind to a halt, in deference to the isolationists or to disgruntled New Dealers who resisted the shutdown on reforms for the duration. Hopkins's job was to rectify such situations and, if possible, prevent them from happening in the first place. When Mrs. Roosevelt, one of those disturbed about the New Deal, came in one day with a comprehensive new health program for low income groups, Hopkins snapped that he and the President were too busy to be bothered. He appalled the left wing by coming out strongly for a national labor draft. He informed the chiefs of two favorite New Deal agencies, the Rural Electrification Administration and the Farm Security Administration, aggrieved when the House cut their budgets to the bone, that they had "no claim on money" while the war was on. The President had his bad days, too. When he did, Hopkins, "the main-prop and animator," as Churchill called this busy capacity, would take over. In the fall of 1940, an especially bad fit of shilly-shallying seized the President. On November twenty-sixth, he guardedly informed the press of a meeting with Lord Lothian, the British ambassador, on the decorous but improbable basis that nothing was discussed about United States aid to Britain, "not one thing—ships or sealing wax or anything else." Hopkins lapsed into a tizzy of private rage and at every opportunity tactfully put the pressures on Roosevelt. In several weeks he had results. In a press conference of December sixteenth, Roosevelt introduced the Promethean idea of Lend Lease with the statement, "there is absolutely no doubt in the mind of a very overwhelming number of Americans that the best immediate defense of the United States is the success of Britain in defending itself."

Hopkins was no pathbreaker, no bold new idea man, nor does it appear that Roosevelt expected him to be. He valued Hopkins primarily as a sounding board for discussions of the best means for achieving goals which the President set himself. In terms of talent, this was the ideal division of labor between the pair. Roosevelt's general historical perspective, breadth of mind and political genius, Hopkins did not have, and the major transitions in the partnership's preoccupations were therefore taken at the President's initiative, with Hopkins following, from loyalty or conviction, and in time both. He started out as an orthodox isolationist until Roosevelt tutored him in the rudiments of the Nazi menace and global strategy. But once the lesson was mastered, the pupil pushed to apply it faster than his more cautious chief. The conversion was in viewpoint only, not in habit of mind. Hopkins remained the "doer," not the "talker"—his categories for people, penetrating to the root of only those matters which appeared starkly before him and venturing upon no general ground that Roosevelt did not chart. Unlike Colonel House, who early in World War I began planning the peace settlement entirely on his own initiative, Hopkins lived in the present only, fighting the war. In actual fact, despite his superior reach of mind, his chief did little more. Except for generalized visions of a United Nations organization following the war and some hopeful notions for the salvation of colonial peoples, Roosevelt was engrossed in his self-styled role of "Dr. Win the

War." Hopkins never questioned that emphasis. "He's got an uncanny intuition about what should be done and what shouldn't," he once said of the President. "And after all, it's his job. Who are we to say he's wrong anyway?"

Beyond the White House, Hopkins's influence penetrated into every nook and cranny of the Executive Branch. His principal endeavor in his far-flung associations was a barbed technique which ranks among his best services to the President and which Admiral Emory Land, the War Shipping Administrator, once aptly described when he called Hopkins "Generalissmo of the Needle Brigade." As Generalissmo, Hopkins sought to rouse in the bureaucracy the dedicated efficiency his own failing body gave to advancing the war. Administrators who were overcautious, cantankerous and self-seeking, who snarled deliveries of tanks and guns, blighted plant construction projects and dallied over office memos, Hopkins badgered, scolded and pep-talked into mended ways. If a suspected general responsible for supply projects in the War Department was en route to the West Coast, Hopkins would bark to the White House switchboard, "Get him wherever he is." The general would be hauled off his plane at Sioux City, Iowa, hustled to the telephone, and slapped with a brusque indictment: "Why are there 280 P-39s waiting at the Bell plant for those Pesco pumps? What the hell is going on here anyway?" If the offense continued, Hopkins's follow-ups advanced by degrees of ruthless severity. He would expose bottlenecks and the names of the guilty to blaring publicity. When masses of planes were grounded in the Nevada desert because they lacked propellors, he rushed the press to the scene to take pictures and lash out in editorials.

As part of his needling operation, Hopkins copied Winston Churchill's practice of compiling elaborate central data on the progress of the war effort. Astonished at Churchill's grasp of facts—on demand he could tell how many heavy tanks were in passage to Egypt and the tonnage launched the month past in the Liverpool yards—Hopkins discovered that the secret genius of this omniscience was Lord Charwell, an Oxford professor of physics and personal statistician to the Prime Minister. Hopkins moved to install a comparable service in the White House to add scores of eyes and ears to the presidential sense of the nation's effort. He brought in Isador Lubin, Commissioner of Labor Statistics, who hailed as a colleague and friend from the 'thirties, and offered acute perceptions of the numerous links and subtleties running between data and policy. Before he knew it, Lubin had a White House office, a Secret Service man by his door, and a book of tables Hopkins had borrowed from Churchill to model the new operation. Then Lubin began his big statistical collections from United States agencies on munitions schedules, man-power supply, ship construction and sinkings, and kept an eagle eye on bottlenecks. He made weekly statements to the President and regularly took over sessions of the Munitions Assignment Board with huge charts and graphs and extensive analytical commentary, which General Somervell, chief of the Army Services of Supply, called "Lubin's floor show."

When he had the President's backing, Hopkins as needler could be exceedingly tough. One War Department official found he could always tell Roosevelt's current attitude toward his department from Hopkins's manner, which was seldom friendly, since Roosevelt did not take kindly to the Army. In his own right, Hopkins could shake an occasional big stick at the department men. He had a kind of "patronage" in his ability to get things for the departments and to nudge the White House into giving assignments to certain people, which enabled him to step up pressures and exact concessions in return. Hopkins was best situated of all with "Hap" Arnold, Commanding General of the Army Air Forces. When the war began, the air forces were the orphans of the War Department. Arnold has written that Hopkins, as much as anyone, sold Roosevelt on the mass-production approach to aircraft and got the air forces a place on the Joint Chiefs of Staff. Such inestimable services enabled Hopkins to confront Arnold with profane bluntness when the production of aircraft control boards sagged or the training of British and Canadian pilots in the United States was slowing down.

In situations where he had little leverage and the President's attitude wasn't clear, Hopkins usually was caution itself, and for the most part, in dealing with department personalities, he operated on the theory that to be of maximum usefulness to the President, he must have access to every part of the Executive Branch. He therefore cultivated contacts and friendships with the men of every major clique and vested interest in official Washington. His closest associations were circumspectly distributed among New Dealers Leon Henderson the OPA Administrator and Robert R. Nathan of WPB; businessmen Donald Nelson and John J. McCloy, the Assistant Secretary of War; the leading professional military; Marshall, King and Arnold, and General Brehon Somervell. Hopkins's favorite tactic was to bring businessmen, New Dealers and the military into ad hoc committees and conferences to work out common policy on matters ranging from the establishment of shopping hours for mothers working in defense plants to the allocation of the limited steel supply among the many essential users. Hopkins's usual demeanor toward these assorted groups was to make sure that everyone having an interest in a matter was consulted, and his constant objective in conference, in his favorite phrase, was "a meeting of minds," a decision which all might accept and which would do credit to the group. When members were disgruntled with the outcome, Hopkins was good, as one conferee put it, at "coming up on the side." If the Navy felt shortchanged on the tankers it was allocated, Hopkins would surprise and please by volunteering an allotment of some less scarce commodity. No matter how tempers flared in these momentous sessions, no matter the occasional intrigue and deceit, Hopkins steadily observed his principle of maintaining the relation with the person at any cost.

The striking upshot of Hopkins's meticulous self-discipline was that he didn't make a single enemy during the war, even though Washington had more than its share of combative spirits and roaring feuds. The closest approximation to an enemy was Harold Ickes, but Ickes was a holdover from the WPA days and Hopkins never reciprocated the honest Secretary's bilious style. The principal occasion on which Hopkins lapsed in his good intentions to department chieftains transpired late in the war, when he launched a brisk conspiracy to take over nothing less than Henry L. Stimson's job as Secretary of War. Apparently, Hopkins coveted the War Department post as a fitting climax to his career, and one which would give added luster and respectability to his eventual place in history, of which he became extremely conscious. Roosevelt, who chafed under the paternal manner of the older Stimson, appears to have encouraged Hopkins's ambition. Coincidental with these stirrings in the White House were the frequent stories in gossip columns and magazines in 1943 that the seventy-six-year-old Stimson was "losing his grip" and growing "senile," and yearned to retire to his Long Island estate. Probably because of the feared reaction in Congress, Hopkins's conspiracy withered on the vine. Stimson, however, knew of it, and Hopkins knew he did, which cast a pall over their extensive and otherwise profitable relations. Yet in the summing up, Stimson took pains to record in his memoirs his heartfelt tribute: "It was a Godsend to have Harry Hopkins in the White House."

Although Hopkins's coup of the War Department failed, his severest critics claim that like Rasputin he was phenomenally successful at installing his own favorites and "yes men" in the big jobs. The most important members of his considerable janissariat were strictly mediocre and, were it not for Roosevelt's statesmanship, the superior productivity of United States industry, and sound generalship on the battlefield, Hopkins's palace mischief might have incalculably harmed the war effort. Not that Hopkins was not patriotic and faithful to Roosevelt. He was, but with the conviction that nobody could serve better than he, and that strong men in certain high posts might jeopardize his own position, Hopkins developed a lively professional interest in mediocrities. He sought them out, built them up, and when it was necessary, systematically sabotaged every competent man who threatened this pattern—or himself.

Exhibit A is Donald Nelson, the jovial Chairman of the War Production Board. Hopkins put Nelson into his job of co-ordinating home-front production, dealing with the Army Services of Supply and its chief, thistle-tongued General Brehon Somervell, and other haughty military, and keeping a handful of squabbling civilian individualists in line. Plainly required were a firm hand, a plenitude of swift decisions, and dexterity at the infighting of bureaucratic jungle warfare. Nelson, by general consensus, was weak on all counts. "He was too nice a guy for the job," an associate explained. To get Nelson, Hopkins blocked the appointment of Supreme Court Justice William O. Douglas, a strong man, as Assistant President. Operating from the White House, Douglas's functions would have included the job assigned to Nelson. Ranging far and wide, the brilliant, aggressive Douglas would soon have turned Hopkins into a surplus war commodity. Apparently the gathering calamity proceeded right into zero hour, because Roosevelt offered the appointment to Douglas and he accepted. But before the ink was dry, Hopkins launched a desperate three-pronged counterattack. First, he broadcast on the high-frequency Washington grapevine, quotations from Winston Churchill and his Minister of Supply, Lord Beaverbrook, the conservative multimillionaire, to the effect that Douglas was a callow "bleeding-heart" liberal, greedy for personal power, unsympathetic to businessmen, and unawakened to the urgencies of the war. Since an Assistant President would have to succeed with the British, this was a neat first strike on the Justice. Next, Hopkins cautioned Roosevelt, who looked upon the appointment as possibly setting up a candidate for the 1944 elections, that Douglas would be just another New Dealer, whereas, say, a businessman would give the ticket more plausible variety. Hereupon Hopkins paraded in his candidate, Nelson, Director of the OPM Division of Purchases, former president of Sears, Roebuck and Co., the country's largest mail-order house, and former munitions procurement chief for the Treasury Department, which had taken on that function early in the war. To the British, the President, and many others who counted, Hopkins showed off Nelson as a knight-errant in the shining armor of Sears Roebuck, who would end the duplication, overlapping and agency conflict which were hamstringing wartime Washington. In his final move, Hopkins addressed a skillful memo to the President reviewing the situation and the candidates, to the effect that Nelson was easy to get along with while Douglas was not.

The rest is history. Nelson, as WPB chairman, staggered through ten months of contretemps. Decisions lagged, agencies quaked with struggles, there were leaks and counterleaks to the press, embarrassments which Roosevelt could never tolerate. Reluctantly, he removed Nelson in the customary manner, by dispatching him to China to undo certain of the many messes of Chiang Kai-shek's Administration. Nelson was never heard from again in the war. Even after the China announcement, when everyone said Nelson was through, the frightened Hopkins, whose own skin might have to be saved all over again, was chattering animatedly that his protégé would soon be back at his old job.

Exhibit B is Edward R. Stettinius, the smiling, handsome, silver-haired ex-chairman of United States Steel, son of a Morgan partner, and friendly host at a vast estate in the horse country of Virginia. Irreverently, but not undiscerningly, observers called him "Junior." From as early as 1939, Stettinius had been building up a consistently undistinguished record as a wartime administrator. First he headed the War Resources Board, established in 1939 to plan for the country's mobilization for war. The Board, which seldom met, made only one major report which, in some unexplained fashion was lost, and exactly what it did in its brief three months' existence constitutes an interesting minor mystery of the war. Next Stettinius was one of seven members of the ill-fated National Advisory Commission, which grappled unsuccessfully with defense problems in 1940. For the purposes of Harry Hopkins, however, this wellborn individual was ideal. To Congress and the public, Stettinius dazzled with the respectability of the upper-crust business world, and his consistently easy nature made him easy to use, which Hopkins proceeded to do on two most important occasions. In September 1941, he set up Stettinius as Director of Lend Lease. At this juncture, the first major appropriations for the program had to be requested from Congress and for such a task a revered businessman was clearly preferable to an ex-WPA boss and mysterious White House favorite. Hopkins next used Stettinius when Cordell Hull resigned as Secretary of State and Roosevelt was veering toward James F. Byrnes as Hull's successor. Byrnes, a strong man, would hardly tolerate Hopkins's intense preoccupation with foreign policy. Complicated maneuvers ensued, Byrnes was sidetracked, and Stettinius moved from Lend Lease into the Department of State.

How could Hopkins swing Roosevelt so easily on the Nelson and Stettinius appointments? The answer, it seems plain, is that Hopkins's self-interest in these matters happened also to coincide with Roosevelt's interest. The President was never friendly to the Assistant President idea, and only after the greatest pressure did he finally set up a limited model of that concept, the Office of War Mobilization, on May 27, 1943. As for the Secretary of State appointment, one can't see how Roosevelt, who made most of his own foreign policy, could have gotten along with the proud, assertive Byrnes. Stettinius, in his fashion, was useful to Roosevelt, too.

Indeed, the record is reasonably clear that in at least one of these appointments—Stettinius as Lend Lease Administrator—Roosevelt and Hopkins worked hand in glove in several sharp maneuvers which simultaneously induced Stettinius to take the job while making clear that Lend Lease would be run strictly from the White House. This impressive joint sleight of hand commenced one bright April morning in 1941 when Hopkins—not Roosevelt

—called Stettinius in and offered him the appointment. "Does the President want to talk it over with me first?" asked Stettinius, incredulous that Roosevelt should not personally confer the seals of an office so vital to the war. "Not unless you have something you particularly want to talk over with him," replied Hopkins. "So far as the President is concerned, you're elected, Ed." Stettinius, baffled at this strange departure from an orthodoxy observed at United States Steel and other reputable enterprises, mumbled his acceptance. Then he rose, still troubled, and left Hopkins. A few days later came the half-suspected which rocked even Stettinius's easy nature. It was a letter from the President. "Harry Hopkins," it blandly read, "is, of course, familiar with the administration of Lend Lease, and I hope you will consult with him and with me where matters of major policy arise." Not one hint of that *modus operandi*, which might reduce Stettinius's part to little more than the decorative function of a cigar-store Indian, had crept into the conversation with Hopkins.

Overseas, Hopkins's equally lively undertakings centered upon two men, Winston Churchill and Joseph Stalin. "Churchill *is* the British War Cabinet, and no one else matters," Hopkins discovered. The appraising eye, hunched shoulders and jowlish determination accented by a large Havana, evidenced a will that was pugnacious, immovable and habitually supreme. How could Hopkins, seeking military agreements and a diplomatic alliance, secure conversational equality with this Jupiter whose grand manner was a lifelong trade-mark?

A fine rolling style, rare in public men, gilded this pretense. Churchill trailed eloquence through his working hours and into his favorite pastime, his inimitable war summaries. These were rendered impromptu for an hour or so to cabinet colleagues seated in full meeting while Churchill, discoursing, strode about them; or to dinner gatherings of silent, reverent notables in the library at Dytchey, his country retreat.

For any man dealing with Churchill to exert any greater force than these decorous dinner guests, seemed to call for something approximating the brash art and aplomb of a super lion tamer. The fact of the matter is that Hopkins was loaded with the relevant talents and, what is more, he already had to his credit the taming of one big item of really ferocious game which at least qualified him to take on Churchill. For Hopkins was known to be the one and only man in American public life who could shave the bristling garrulity of Fiorello H. La Guardia, the Civilian Defense Director and ex-mayor of New York, down to quiet manageable proportions. La Guardia, the man-eater, the slashing little demon who could rip strong men to shreds, whose ranting and raving could make a man of good heart quail, would storm into the White House for meetings with Hopkins and instantly settle down with the docility of a dove.

Of course no one has ever tamed Winston Churchill and no one ever will. But Hopkins, using against Churchill the very same methodology he applied to La Guardia, hammered out the most amazing and the most productive diplomatic triumph of the war, a triumph that surely will stand against the best of any age. Hopkins penetrated, as no Englishman has ever done, straight through the shield and breastworks of the Prime Minister's forbidding manner. For eloquence and ceremony Hopkins substituted a frank, free atmosphere, where ideas fared on their merit, and status was forgotten for the cause. Their first meeting set the ground rules. At the time, the Luftwaffe was pounding away with every bomb and plane available to crush England's resistance. The outcome hung in painful suspense. Anxious to court Hopkins, and through him Roosevelt and the American people, Churchill commenced an after-dinner monologue in his best rolling style, to identify, with the difficulty the ardent Tory would have, the fight of Britain and the New Deal's hero, the Forgotten Man. But Hopkins, ignoring tact and the awesome moment, broke in with a roughness fitting for a saloon in Hell's Kitchen to inform the Prime Minister that the United States wanted one thing and one thing only—the defeat of Hitler. The rest of the evening was passed in simple rewarding talk. "I can see," wrote Churchill to Roosevelt of the meeting, "why you are so taken with Mr. Hopkins."

Hopkins consistently used on Churchill a bluntness that he would never dream of using on Roosevelt, and Churchill, on his part, reciprocated with the same brusque, if more elegant, candor. "The Prime Minister threw the British Constitution at me with some vehemence," Hopkins once reported their affairs. "Winston is his old self and full of battle." And so it continued. Only the affection and liberality of friendship could have made these exchanges and the hectic events which beat upon the two men tolerable. Such a friendship quickly developed. Hopkins, conservative in enthusiasms, found Churchill's drive and zest for improvisation and detail the perfect embodiment of his own most cherished values. To Churchill, Hopkins was the gaunt hero of the cause, whose sardonic humor in grim hours of disaster inveterately jogged up one's spirits and official optimism in rallying the English people. Also, the frail American was master of the exact spoken word, which greatly impressed the classicist, Churchill. During Hopkins's missions to Downing Street, which ordinarily lasted a week or more, Churchill would drop official routines, even with great battles in progress, and go off with his friend on extended inspection tours, conferences and country weekends at Dytchey or at Chequers, the Prime Minister's other estate. Both locations, according to good authority, Hopkins hated more than the devil hates holy water, especially in winter when sheets had to be stuffed in the windows to keep out the snow. At Dytchey, Hopkins spent much of his time seated in a great overcoat in a downstairs bathroom, the only place which had "central heating."

In all other respects, however, Hopkins's stamina more than matched the rugged demands of his strenuous, attentive host. After dinner, which customarily ended at ten P.M., followed by brandy at ten thirty, Churchill would ask, "What is the film for tonight?" Thereupon everyone would climb into overcoats and Churchill into a loud bathrobe printed with defiant dragons and trot to the cinema room which was kept at the temperature of a refrigerator. About thirty assorted guests—soldiers, sailors, maids and butlers—viewed the performance, which ended at twelve thirty, with everyone except Churchill sleepy, cold and hungry. At this point, the Prime Minister, now apparently at the crest of his day, would take over with recitations of poetry and running comment on a host of subjects, frequently interspersed with business, until three A.M., when some faltering spirit—Hopkins was proud he was never the one—suggested bed.

Hopkins's intimacy with Churchill ranged from shoptalk on British personalities and politics to functioning, on several occasions, as one of the Prime Minister's own principal advisers. When the Lend Lease bill was under debate in Congress and the isolationists pinned their hopes for victory on a misstep by the British, Hopkins coached his London friends on what to say and what not to, and for Churchill's contribution to the struggle—a speech to the world with United States public opinion as the special target—Hopkins stepped into a part granted no other mortal. For a number of key passages, he was a "ghost writer," making phrases, checking facts and recasting ideas for Churchill, the proudest of authors. An American adviser had become an intimate part of a British Ministry. When Hopkins returned to the White House, Churchill kept the cables busy admonishing and advising on his friend's precarious health, and when the Prime Minister was in Washington, his rooms in the White House were invariably across from Hopkins. Business and chitchat far into the night were the rule—between the two only, unattended by the President, who liked to retire not later than ten o'clock and complained that Churchill's unorthodox hours thoroughly exhausted him the several times he followed them.

Friendship with Churchill enabled Hopkins to fill the role on which the progress of the Western Powers in the war vitally depended: catalyst between the two titans, Roosevelt and Churchill. The task abounded with snares innocently laid by its lofty independent personalities, for Roosevelt and Churchill, regardless of their great common enterprise, were never friends. At most, a surface intimacy prevailed between them, professional in tone and acutely sensitive to their unique status as leaders and prodigious opportunities to forge an epoch for the world. They also were opposite natures: Roosevelt, infinitely subtle, obscure, artful, cautious of detailed commitment; Churchill stubborn and exact. These were the seeds of a fertile irritation. That they never flowered into fact is mainly due to Hopkins's shrewdness in gauging his place between the leaders. He rejected the easy and obvious role of simply championing Roosevelt's interests or America's interests, whatever they might be, at Downing Street. He shot at a more difficult mark—the representative of Churchill before Roosevelt and of Roosevelt before Churchill, serving two masters, one official, the other not, and uniting both into a partnership which always surmounted friction.

Churchill eagerly welcomed the arrangement, for Hopkins was as necessary to himself as to Roosevelt. In 1941, and after, the sagging British Empire was groping its way in requesting enormous grants of American aid. Churchill then scarcely knew the President, the subtleties of United States politics, how much to demand or pressure for. He needed an informal link such as Hopkins, who could sense his chief's tolerance and possibilities for action, who could inform and plead, and above all avoid the embarrassment of the official "no" to British requests. "If you think well of it," Churchill usually concluded a proposal he put to Hopkins, "perhaps you would ask our great friend for his opinion." Hopkins, after consultation, might decide Roosevelt "did not think well of it," and Churchill could withdraw without awkwardness. If Roosevelt approved, Hopkins would cable, "It is felt here that you should go ahead with your proposal." Hopkins seldom pulled punches in advocating Churchill's ideas and, in meetings of the trio, sometimes sided openly against his chief. "When Hopkins was on the job," observed Churchill, "it was remarkable how definitely my contacts with the President improved and our affairs moved quicker."

In the more than 120 days that Roosevelt and Churchill were in close personal contact in the war, many minor occurrences inevitably transpired that could easily have been magnified into serious embarrassments. Part of Hopkins's usefulness was in preventing these little things from becoming big. One potential *casus belli* arose when Churchill, after exhausting post-Pearl Harbor conferences at the White House, went to Florida for a rest. There he decided that before returning home, he should call on Wendell Willkie, which seemed the courteous thing to do, since the former Republican presidential candidate had visited him in England the year before. Churchill proceeded to telephone Willkie to arrange a meeting. The excited and befuddled local telephone operator, however, put the call through to the White House to Roosevelt instead. Churchill was well into his invitation to Willkie before he realized that he was talking with the President. Upon recovering from the shock and embarrassment, Churchill thought it advisable to check with Hopkins to see if Roosevelt had been offended and if he considered a meeting inappropriate. Hopkins thoroughly reconnoitered the

White House situation, reported to Churchill that all was well, and the meeting with Willkie proceeded.

The biggest profit-maker in these busy transoceanic operations was not Churchill or Roosevelt. It was Harry Hopkins himself. As Churchill's intimate, he acquired a monopoly on communications with Downing Street which made him unexpendable at the White House. In the course of three years of London dealings, Hopkins was party to countless gentlemen's chats and policy undertakings of various stages, which no successor could possibly catch up with. There were also Churchill's own unpredictable tastes. Hopkins pleased him; it would take impossible months to groom a successor who might never do as well. By thus becoming indispensable at Downing Street, Hopkins did what no Roosevelt adviser had ever done: he promoted himself to a plane transcending that on which the presidential confidant has to fight for his survival. As Eliot Janeway happily expressed the Hopkins success formula, "The way to go on living in the White House was to be constantly on the verge of leaving for London. The way to return to Roosevelt was to confer with Churchill." Even in the confusion of the war, the Prime Minister himself accurately detected how Hopkins's London connection figured in his Washington fortunes. At a lunch at Hyde Park on August 11, 1943, Churchill noticed, much to his surprise, that when Hopkins arrived a few minutes late just after the appetizer, the President did not even greet their mutual friend. Later, in answer to the Prime Minister's anxious inquiries, Hopkins explained that he had recently declined in favor, a big blowup in the War Production Board involving Donald Nelson, Hopkins's protégé, having just transpired. "Hopkins," concluded the Prime Minister, "was obviously invited to please me."

During interludes when he was not in London, Hopkins's interests were covered by another friend and protégé, Averell Harriman. Wealthy, New Deal minded, and former board chairman of the Union Pacific Railroad, Harriman, upon learning of Hopkins's projected first trip to London, had phoned while vacationing at Sun Valley, Idaho, offering to go along. Hopkins had to turn him down, but a scant three months later, in April, 1941, Harriman was established as Minister in the United States embassy at Grosvenor Square. Until 1943, when he was appointed ambassador to Russia, Harriman acted in such vital capacities as Expediter of Lend Lease and United States representative on the London branches of the Munitions Assignment Board, the Shipping, Food and other combined Anglo-American boards. Harriman operated independently of the ambassador, his longstanding friend, John Gilbert Winant, dealt personally with Churchill, and reported straight to Hopkins, not via the State Department's, but the Navy's communications. After Hopkins, Harriman counted most with power-conscious Britishers. "I am with the P.M. at least one day a week and usually the weekend as well," Harriman described his situation. "He likes to take me on his trips." Poor Winant sadly beheld his work and his prestige dwindle simultaneously and ignominiously. At last, fed up with it all, he sat down and wrote one of the most pitiful letters in the annals of diplomacy. He wrote not to the President, or to the Secretary of State, but to the unofficial creator of his plight, Harry Hopkins. "I have had no business delegated to me as Ambassador that could not have been done by an efficient Foreign Service officer," said Winant with total frankness. "I have been by-passed continuously. I have had no contacts with the Prime Minister except on two occasions when he invited me to meet with him so that he could bring me up to date on Anglo-American relations." Winant pointed a lightly veiled finger at a further member of the transatlantic conspiracy, another Hopkins protégé, Edward R. Stettinius, then Secretary of State. The benign ex-corporation executive had elaborately curtained his department from the view of the chief of the country's number-one diplomatic mission. "Nine tenths of the information I receive," observed Winant, "comes from British sources."

The ambassador got nowhere.

Generalissimo Joseph Stalin, the final member of the great circle, Hopkins sized up as a kindred spirit, a "doer" in the best sense of his favorite label. "There was no waste of word, gesture, nor mannerism," Hopkins wrote of Stalin and their first meeting in the Kremlin on July 30, 1941, five weeks after the Nazis invaded the Soviet Union. "It was like talking to a perfectly coordinated machine. Joseph Stalin knew what he wanted, knew what Russia wanted. . . . The questions he asked were clear, concise, direct." Apparently the regard was mutual. Averell Harriman, who attended almost every Big Power conference, noticed that Hopkins was the only man for whom Stalin ever walked across the room to shake hands. This is significant when it is remembered that Stalin was extremely economical in physical movement and made short work of the amenities.

Hopkins was so impressed with Stalin and his countrymen that he came out strongly for a policy that was exceptionally bold in 1941—all-out aid to Russia when Nazi tank columns were pounding to the Near East oil fields and Moscow was bombed freely, and most United States military opinion was writing off the Russians as done for within three months. Roosevelt sided with Hopkins and thereby was made one of the key politico-military decisions of World War II. Once Hopkins was asked how he could assert such a distinctly minority point of view simply on the basis of conversations, and extremely guarded ones at that, with only a handful of Russians. Hopkins replied that he reached his conclusion very much like Justice Holmes reached his verdicts. "I had a hunch where I wanted to come out," he said, "and then looked around to find some reasons to justify the hunch."

Hopkins did not stop with this extraordinary first decision. He became chairman of the President's Protocol Committee which administered the aid program to Russia. General John R. Deane, head of the United States military mission at Moscow, has observed that Hopkins ran the committee with "a zeal which approached fanaticism." The basis of this zeal was definitely not ideological. Colleagues from his social worker days through the final stages of the war testify that Hopkins abhorred communism as a doctrine. While Secretary of Commerce, he once informed an associate that he would never employ a known Communist. He was interested in the Russians because, in his favorite phrase, "They're killing Germans."

In this vein, Hopkins pushed for a British-Soviet attack upon Narvik, and pulled wires to send Marshall, King and Arnold to Moscow. After the North African invasion commenced, Hopkins advised Roosevelt to invite Stalin to the next Big Power meeting, which was at Casablanca, but Stalin turned down Roosevelt's invitation, saying that he saw no reason for his presence, and that all the Allies had to do was to live up to their promise to launch a channel invasion. Never giving up, Hopkins finally succeeded at Teheran, the first meeting of the Big Three.

Early in 1944, Hopkins began drum-beating for a second meeting. By then Soviet-Allied fortunes were in firm reverse. Western armies under Bradley and Montgomery had pushed the fading Germans back to the Rhine and the Russians had thrust into the plains of Western Poland. But upon the President fell counsels which opposed a journey halfway round the world to Yalta, the meeting place that Stalin had designated. Roosevelt's health had gone into dreadful decline—"The President seemed placid and frail," Churchill noticed at the conference. "I felt that he had a slender contact with life"—and the extent of the journey, more than thirteen thousand miles by air, seemed an undignified concession by the American Chief Executive to the Soviet dictator. "This argument carried no weight with me," said Hopkins, "the all-important thing was to get the meeting."

There was no better way, in his opinion, to brush out cobwebs of misunderstanding, and Roosevelt was master of the tête-à-tête. The President's own analysis was practically the same. The dictator, in his phrase, was "gettable." "I'm sure we'll hit it off, Stalin and I," Roosevelt told Frances Perkins before his first meeting with the Generalissimo. "A great deal of the misunderstandings and the mistrusts of the past are going to get cleared up."

In their approach to Yalta and the other conferences, Roosevelt and Hopkins employed the mode of statesmanship which had animated the New Deal, brilliantly rescued the country from the depression, and in the war itself had boosted the Allied forces to final victory. It was Improvisation.

Roosevelt and Hopkins, playing by ear, set out to harmonize at Yalta the discordant strings which threatened to jar the aftermath of war in Europe, and second, and equally important, they would seek means for bringing the Pacific war to the speediest possible conclusion. Roosevelt was heavily pressed on this latter objective by the Joint Chiefs of Staff to bring the Soviet into the fight against Japan. The Chiefs, in turn, were swayed by Army intelligence which grossly overestimated the strength of Japanese forces in Manchuria and prompted the conclusion that without Soviet help the war might run until 1947. An accurate estimate of the situation would have found, however, that "Japan's unconditional surrender could have been concluded without Soviet action in Manchuria."*

Beyond the badly informed advice of the Joint Chiefs of Staff, the President and his adviser, in proceeding to Yalta, relied upon their personal resources and little else. "The President," observed James F. Byrnes, a member of the American delegation, "had made little preparation." He had just been inaugurated; he had spent long hours over the budget and over the State of the Union Message to Congress; his engagements the month past were overwhelming. Little indeed was done in Washington. Preparations aboard the destroyer *Quincy*, which bore the delegation over, were lost to a severe cold which confined Roosevelt to his cabin. He relied, as he had all through the war when confronted with novel and difficult issues, upon his chief adviser for study and background.

Hopkins's own health, at this juncture, had also dwindled badly. He was suffering a general relapse, surviving on paregoric, small rations of food and sheer fortitude, and remained in bed as much as possible under watch of Admiral McIntyre, the President's physician. Hopkins's preparations for Yalta hewed familiar lines. Unlike Colonel House, who went to Versailles steeped in the memoranda and surveys of several dozen savants and veteran public men, Hopkins enlisted no expert assistance and made no book studies himself. He embarked upon a short series of interviews with leading figures of Europe to get the hang of the issues and prospects. In November, just after the election, he went around to the Soviet embassy in Washington and canvassed with Ambassador Gromyko the matters which clearly would require Big Three agreement following the collapse of Germany. En route to Yalta, Hopkins briefed himself in stopovers with a few strategic persons, three days in London with Churchill, then to Paris, for quick talks with de Gaulle and Foreign Minister Bidault, and to Rome for a late-morning exchange with Ambassador Kirk and an audience of twenty minutes with the Pope.

In relying upon Hopkins, Roosevelt could and did overlook the sizable

* Ellis M. Zacharias, "The Inside Story of Yalta," *United Nations World*, January 1949, p. 12.

treasure of facts and ideas on postwar affairs which had been painstakingly accumulated in the State Department. Early in 1942, the Department began studies and plans for a possible postwar world organization and for political and territorial settlements. Later a body of leading departmental officers and consultants—Isaiah Bowman, President of Johns Hopkins and former aide to President Wilson and Colonel House; Myron Taylor, former Minister to the Vatican; Ben Cohen, the department's counselor and ex-New Deal Brain Truster; Stanley Hornbeck, the department's economist; and Green Hackworth, the legal adviser—took up the work and, aided by a staff drawn from the universities and from the career service, developed elaborate factual monographs and recommendations along lines which the President laid down in a conversation with Sumner Welles. "What I expect you to do," the President had said, "is to have prepared for me the necessary number of baskets and the necessary number of alternatives for each problem in the baskets, so that when the time comes all I have to do is to reach in a basket and fish out a number of solutions that I am sure are sound and from which I can make my own choice." But the President had played bearish on his own and his chief adviser's considerable self-reliance. Though the papers of the State Department group were loaded aboard the *Quincy*, they were never opened by the President, or Hopkins, or others in their immediate entourage. The one substantial preparation made for Yalta thus was wasted.

At the conference, the State Department was repeatedly brushed aside like the hunchback of Notre Dame, and similar unwanted people, from matters of top importance. Nearly every discussion of major consequence found Foreign Ministers Eden and Molotov or their deputies present; Secretary of State Stettinius was conspicuous by his absences. What has since become the most controversial aspect of the conference (the agreement by which Russia would enter the war against Japan in return for Roosevelt's promised intercession with China to secure vast concessions to Russia in Manchuria—among them Russian control of the Chinese Eastern and South Manchurian railroads and lease of Port Arthur as a naval base) was handled personally and solely by Roosevelt and Hopkins's protégé, Averell Harriman, then Ambassador to Russia, in talks with Stalin and Foreign Minister Molotov. C. E. Bohlen acted as the President's interpreter. Hopkins, although ill in bed, was fully consulted and knew everything that was going on. He disclosed that the talks were in progress to Secretary Stettinius, who dutifully asked if there was anything he or his aides could do. Hopkins said no, that it was a "military" matter and "had better stay at that level," and Stettinius withdrew with shining calm. "These concessions," wrote Sumner Welles in 1946 of the deal with the Russians, "which will make it altogether impossible for a new unified China to exercise full sovereignty within Manchuria, are all the more objectionable in view of China's absence from the conference table where they were decided."

Though he did much to win the war, Hopkins did little to win the peace, not only at Yalta, but at the other big conferences as well, where he consistently pushed aside the State Department. As one of the very few men of the twentieth century privileged with the opportunity to leave a lasting imprint on the world, Hopkins left little or nothing. Warmaking called for the man of action which he was; peacemaking and the new-and-better-world called for the man of ideas, which he was not. There were other influences afoot. Virtually bedridden when the most important agreements were negotiated on the postwar world, Hopkins probably had the sick man's tendency to overemphasize the present, namely, the conduct of the war, and a reluctance to consider the future, especially a future, which because of his health, he had little prospect of ever seeing. Certainly, he always saw the war in an exceedingly limited frame of reference. On the basis of numerous intimate conversations, Winston Churchill concluded that Hopkins's war objective was "the defeat, ruin, and slaughter of Hitler, to the exclusion of all other purposes, loyalties, or aims." Accordingly, Hopkins was deaf to Churchill's proposal that primary consideration be given to the postwar power situations of the Allies and the Russians in the Balkans and in central Europe from the moment the Germans showed signs of caving in. Churchill pleaded insistently, but got nowhere with Hopkins, or, for that matter, with Roosevelt.

It is also true that Hopkins's relation with Roosevelt had been running down. Illness and family responsibilities, the two main limiting factors, were decisively intervening. For seven months in 1944, Hopkins was side-lined by illness, dividing his time between the Naval Hospital, Florida and the Mayo Clinic. Following the Casablanca conference, he and his bride had established their own household in a rented house in Georgetown, thus ending the days of the White House crony-in-residence. No longer was Hopkins on hand at mealtime or in leisure hours, when the latest intelligence came in or the newest mission was assigned. Perhaps it was all for the best. Roosevelt's own declining strength had made him less interested in companionship and generally less accessible.

Although the relationship was running down, it never ran out. Hopkins was always the uncontested number-one assistant to Roosevelt. No rival was waiting in the shadows. In these final days, Hopkins's function apparently consisted of acquiescing with little question to every major premise and policy of his chief in the transition from war to peace—with one exception. With Winston Churchill, Hopkins was the champion of fallen France and apologist for her "problem child," de Gaulle, for whom Roosevelt had extreme and unconcealed distaste. Otherwise, Hopkins steadfastly concurred in

his chief's judgments at a time when Roosevelt might have profited greatly
in having an informed and critical adviser at his elbow. Roosevelt therefore
pursued, and Hopkins unqualifiedly accepted, the shaky premises that Stalin
was a "good fellow" and "we could get along with him," and that the
Politburo had abandoned the policy of Revolution and honestly desired
friendly relations with capitalist governments. An adviser versed in Communist ideology and Soviet political history would have been more guarded.
For Hopkins, however, these were largely terra incognita. Said one career
diplomat in an unkind analysis: "The trouble was that Harry only knew two
things about the Soviet Union. The first was that they had had a bad Czar in
Russia named Ivan the Terrible. The second was that Russia was the first
country to recognize the United States after 1776."

Other examples of Hopkins's limited usefulness in building the bridge
from war to peace are unfortunately available. At Casablanca, Roosevelt,
under the pressure of a press conference disclosed that "unconditional surrender" was the only possible way the Germans could end the war, and
Hopkins promptly expressed his complete satisfaction with the formula.
There is impressive evidence, however, that Roosevelt seized on Grant's
famous phrase without realizing its full implications. Every surrender, including Lee's to Grant, has had conditions, and Nazi Propaganda Minister
Goebbels proceeded to make such capital out of Roosevelt's borrowed and
seemingly harsh terms in bolstering German morale that B. H. Liddell Hart,
the eminent British military authority, concluded that "but for the unconditional surrender policy, they . . . would have yielded sooner. . . ." The
Morgenthau Plan, which called for the destruction of much of German's
industry and her reduction to an impotent agrarian state, was another badly
managed policy, which Hopkins waved idly by when he had the opportunity
to flag it down. With Morgenthau, Stimson and Hull, he served on the
cabinet-level committee which Roosevelt established to plan the German
peace. But it was Hull and Stimson, not Hopkins, who went to the President
and pointed out how the Morgenthau Plan's decimation of Germany would
impoverish all Europe and lay the continent wide open to fascist and Communist depredation.

The proposed permanent organization of the United Nations stirred no
evident idealism in Hopkins. This Sumner Welles has sought to explain in
sizing up the confidant as an incorrigible isolationist from earlier environment and individual preference. The job of writing the communiqué calling
the San Francisco conference to draw up the United Nations Organization,
Hopkins, the President's regular draftsman, tossed to the Secretary of State.
"Hurry it up," said Hopkins, "or the Prime Minister will sit up in bed some
morning and dash it off himself, and it will be hard to change."

Yet whatever its shortcomings, Yalta was immediately and everywhere celebrated as a magnificent success. Roosevelt and Hopkins, applying their own pragmatic test, the test of improvisers, were completely satisfied. Every important question which before Yalta had troubled the Big Three powers was either settled or seemed on the road to settlement. "We really believed in our hearts," wrote Hopkins shortly after the conference, "that this was the dawn of the new day we had all been praying for and talking about for so many years. We were absolutely certain that we had won the first great victory of the peace."

But a touch of remorse, coming like a sudden frost, spoiled these happy reflections, and the journey home. Hopkins, his strength gone to the point that he was carried everywhere by stretcher, decided to return to Washington by air, and thus leave Roosevelt on the Quincy. The President was disappointed and mildly displeased. He had counted on Hopkins's company and help with the report to Congress on Yalta, but Hopkins begged off and left the Quincy at Algiers. Roosevelt gave a not very amiable farewell, a sorry little episode, for the President and his adviser never saw each other again. Doubtless Roosevelt's pique was momentary, and the instinctive charity of judgment which illuminated his political and personal affairs must have soon reclaimed the vision of his good friend upstairs in the Lincoln bedroom, dedicating his frail body with demonic fury to the urgencies of the war—to the endless interviews with Very Important Persons, to the cables for the Prime Minister and the drafts of fireside chats, to the sudden flights on crucial missions and the fagging hours at telephone battle stations. Remembered, too, were the suspicious eyes, the blazing animation, the sour candor and the needling questions which pierced to the root of matters and kept airplane propellers, quartz crystals, tin plate, zircon bearings and myriad other commodities moving through the giant co-ordinated maze of war. Roosevelt, and numerous others caught in the vortex, had inscribed forever in their hearts how the ordeal was eased and victory quickened by "a little touch of Harry in the night."

"O.K., S.A."

SHERMAN ADAMS

LIKE HERBERT HOOVER, Florence Nightingale and Walter F. O'Malley of the Brooklyn-Los Angeles Dodgers, Sherman Adams is in danger of becoming one of the misconstrued figures of history. He, like they, stands to have a single fragment of his career become the basis on which the whole of his life's work is to be judged and remembered. Future generations are apt to behold Adams, the friend of Bernard Goldfine, as the perfect synonym in the national culture for vicuña, a free night's lodging and borrowed rugs. But Sherman Adams possesses far greater significance for posterity than that of Mr. Goldfine's self-admitted "old friend." For the better part of President Eisenhower's two terms, Adams exercised more power than any other presidential assistant in modern times. He made decisions and performed acts which Presidents, since the establishment of the Republic, have been given to doing themselves. Indeed, it is demonstrable that his power and impact upon the national destiny have exceeded that of not a few Presidents of the United States. In fairness to this singular man, and in the interests of the accuracy of the several judgments which inevitably will be entered at the bar of history, Mr. Adams needs to be viewed not in the cramped confines of the Goldfine tragicomedy, but in terms of how well or how badly he handled the full measure of the power which President Eisenhower with such prodigality entrusted him.

The real importance of Sherman Adams has been time and again expressed by qualified authority in various ways. President Eisenhower declared in simple candor, "I need him." When Mikhail Menshikov, the Soviet ambassador, commenced his stewardship in Washington by undertaking a round of amity-building conferences, high on his list was the name of Sherman Adams. Paul M. Butler, National Chairman of the Democratic party, once declared in the heat of a partisan peroration that "The Presidency has been butchered by this assistant to the President." In more studied vein, Sidney Hyman, the scholarly Washington journalist, has called Mr. Adams the "de facto Vice President of the United States." Official Washington, which seldom makes jokes, was once inspired to apt, although macabre,

338

irreverence in the case of Adams. "What if Adams should die," they chortled, "and Eisenhower should become President?"

Such pronouncements all are indicative of the fact that Sherman Adams was the instrument by which Dwight D. Eisenhower accomplished one of the most thoroughgoing withdrawals from the duties of the Presidency in the history of the office. His achievement is a tour de force of administrative ingenuity and invention. In its dimension, Eisenhower's retreat from the highest office constitutes the greatest retreat in the national experience since the first battle of Bull Run. The role and power of Sherman Adams, by which the President made his escape, were conceived not by Adams, but by Eisenhower. Neither were they conceived in the desperation of the several illnesses, when the President of necessity had to conserve his energy and limit his activities. The powers and duties of Sherman Adams, as a matter of fact, were delineated by Mr. Eisenhower in their full proportions many months before he actually took over the presidential office. But the most remarkable aspect of Eisenhower's large withdrawal from duties normally discharged by the President is that it took place in an interlude of international crisis, whose magnitude is only beginning to become apparent. The crisis has encompassed an awesome scientific revolution of missiles, Sputniks and thrusts to the moon; the exposure of the American mainland for the first time to the dread possibility of devastating attack; the shrinkage of the military and productive superiority of the United States over the Soviet Union, and the consequent urgency of a creative re-examination of policies in military, education, health, civil rights, antirecession, and other fields.

Sherman Adams, as "The Assistant to the President," his official title, presided over a far-flung staff system whose watchword was "Don't bother the President." Adams was the censorial watchdog at Eisenhower's door, who freely determined whom the President saw and what he read. If matters did go to the President, he would, before taking action, run his eye over the papers involved for the familiar notation, "O.K., S.A." If it was missing, Eisenhower was sure to ask, "Has Governor Adams approved this?" When a caller or official sprang an idea on the President, the President was prone to say, "Take it up with Sherman."

Eisenhower depended upon Adams as Roosevelt never did upon Hopkins, or Wilson upon House, or Jackson upon the stalwarts of his Kitchen Cabinet. One distinguishing mark of the Eisenhower-Adams association was the extent to which the President delegated to his assistant the responsibility for initiative. Eisenhower seemingly vested in Adams and the executive staff a continuing responsibility for the discovery of problems and the formulation of solutions. If somehow a problem was overlooked, the fault, according to official attitude, lay not with the President, but with the staff. When, for example, a reporter observed one day at a White House press conference that the President had been appointing a number of ambassadors to the major capitals of the world who were ignorant of the local language, Mr. Eisenhower made a ready response to this disturbing and undeniable fact. "Why didn't somebody tell me about this?" he asked with a self-exculpating air.

When Adams and the staff proposed policies, the President tended automatically to accept what was placed before him. If, on occasion, he ventured to formulate policies, the President was given to broad, optimistic, and at times contradictory generalities, leaving to Adams and others the difficult decisions of far-reaching "detail." Eisenhower might declare that he was in favor of balancing the budget and substantially stepping up foreign aid. Upon Adams and others fell the task of reconciling these seemingly conflicting objectives. When Little Rock seethed with racial controversy over the school integration issue, the President declared that citizens should obey the law, and the Supreme Court decisions should be observed, leaving it to Adams and others to wrestle with specific measures. The President's appetite for leisure and recreation and the incidence of the several illnesses have entailed throughout his Administration a heavy schedule of absences from Washington. In the seven years he has so far served, fully 25 per cent of his time has been spent away from the capital. Even during the first two years of his Administration, a period preceding his earliest major illness, the President was absent from the capital 20 per cent of the time. When his chief was out of town, Adams made many on-the-spot decisions which normally would go to the President. During Eisenhower's illnesses, Adams was in all but name the Acting President of the United States. Perhaps the severest of these illnesses was the coronary in 1955, when to further his convalesence, the President remained away from the White House for 115 days. Throughout this sizable period, the tasks which normally fell upon Eisenhower were handled by Adams, with only the most major policy decisions going to the President.

Sherman Adams carried on his monstrous toil in a secrecy that was as zealously guarded as an atomic bomb stockpile. He held no press conferences. In nearly six years of duty, his solitary appearance before the assembled press was to read a statement defending his position in the Goldfine imbroglio. Upon completing his statement, he immediately withdrew, permitting no questions, although many hands were raised and voices heard. Few reporters could see him privately without undergoing disheartening difficulty and delay. He was chary about conveying information to Congressional committees. Despite numerous invitations, he appeared before these committees only once in his White House tenure and then only in response to the earthquake of the Goldfine disclosures. Yet he took considerable pains to identify himself in little ways with the democratic ideal of an interested and informed citizenry. Time and again he was known to break away from meetings in his office for spirited five-minute talks on the obligations of citizenship to student groups touring the White House. "You have the citizen's responsibility," he admonished a graduating class at the University of Maine on June 9, 1957, "to take time enough from the daily duties to know what is going on. . . . A sure death for freedom . . . can result from visionless, ignorant citizenry . . .."

Sherman Adams, or "the Governor," as he was called by colleagues and friends, incorporated in his trim and wiry person of fifty-nine years—his age when he retired from office—a labyrinth of contradictions. Beneath the cool and composed exterior, the steely blue eyes, the modulated baritone and the ample white hair of an egregious Roman Senator was an interior of very low boiling point. "He really explodes," it was said of the most fearsome temper to hold sway in many a year in the White House. But although Adams was high voltage on the inside, his appearance was Arctic. Over the years of his presence in national office, he built up a solid reputation as a glacial personality, an artist in the cold treatment. So widely prevailing was this reputation that Leonard Hall, while Republican National Chairman, once entreated Adams to make a special appearance before the party's national committee to prove that the fact was otherwise. "You know," said Hall, "some of my people think you've got horns that are halfway between a Washington snowslide and a bundle of icicles. The fact is they think that in you where the milk of human kindness ought to be, there is only ice-water." Adams put in his requested appearance, with mixed results. To some he was undeniably wintry; others could detect a happier image shining through. Adams's own staff however, was virtually unanimous in resolutely maintaining that the Governor, when you got to know him, exhibited many warm friendly qualities.

In the public speeches he made now and then, Adams tended to prolixity, expressing the same idea several times over in slightly altered verbalization. In private conversation, however, he was a model of terseness, in the rare tradition of his fellow New Englander, Calvin Coolidge. A secretary just starting to work for Adams found that each day, as the noon hour approached, her phone would ring. It was Adams, calling from his inner office, and his conversation consisted of a monosyllable. "Lunch," he would bark into the receiver, and then hang up. The secretary put in a number of nervous noon hours discovering the several broths and sandwich fillings Adams preferred and those which he abominated. He was rather finicky, as the secretary learned by trial and error. He never provided any comprehensive statement of his preferences, but released this vital information in snatches as each offering was placed on his desk before him. His approvals were conveyed by silence, but his rejections were severe and disquieting. Even when he was off the job, Adams's conversation was tightly rationed. Once at a White House dinner, a lady guest asked Adams about his son, Samuel, who was then attending St. Paul's School in Concord, New Hampshire. Adams offered that the boy was on the hockey team and doing well scholastically. "Oh, tell me about him," the lady encouraged. "I just did," Adams replied.

Sherman Adams, the man of contradictions, was born January 8, 1899, in East Dover, Vermont, a characteristic small New England hamlet centered in rolling farm lands and massive forests of maple and pine. Although not a direct descendant of the famous early Adamses, John and John Quincy, Sherman was a proud member of the historic clan; portraits of his distinguished forebears prominently graced his White House office wall. Young Sherman's father, a hardy enterpriser, traversed from farming to grocery store ownership and today, in his eighty-third year, operates a city parking lot. When the boy was two, the family migrated to Providence, Rhode Island, where Sherman subsequently attended the local schools. His summers he passed laboring on his grandfather's farm in Vermont. The long workday in the rugged fields developed the tough physique which stood him well in his White House career, and a love for the North country which borders on infatuation. From his grandfather, a veteran minister, he derived an unslaking flame of religious conviction, and in the old gentleman's library, began an oft-renewed acquaintance with the works of James Fenimore Cooper. Back in Providence he became a chorister of St. Stephen's Episcopal Church, and at the local Hope High School, his mellifluous voice, sure verbal instinct and sharp logic made him the star of the debating team.

In 1916, Sherman entered Dartmouth, primarily because of its proximity to the White Mountain country. He quickly plunged into the traditional outdoor program of the college as a member and later as president of the famous Outing Club. His hiking feats are among the most imposing in the annals of the organization. Among other things, Adams climbed Mount Washington on three successive midwinter days. On a mere five-dollar bet, he set out with Ellis O. Briggs, later United States ambassador to Brazil in the Eisenhower Administration, to walk the 136 miles between Dartmouth and Springfield, Massachusetts, in sixty-six hours. Undertaken in the heavy thaw season, the marathon ended approximately ninety miles and forty hours later in Northfield, Massachusetts, not because of the mileage but because of the ankle-deep slush. At Dartmouth, Adams was also a stellar performer in the dramatic association and the glee club, and served in the Christian Association cabinet. He was a member of Palaeopitus, a top-rung honorary society, then numbering a dozen Big Men on Campus. In his studies, which were interspersed with brief and uneventful service in the Marine Corps in

World War I, Adams majored in economics and in 1920 graduated in the desirable, but not distinguished, Third Honor Group.

After college, Adams worked in a logging camp of the Black River Lumber Company at Healdville, Vermont. His apprenticeship was exceedingly rough. A flying skid knocked out his front teeth; a horse kicked him between the eyes; and a piece of maple, shooting from a spout, took him behind the ear, leaving him partially deaf on the left side. When the company manager succumbed to protracted illness, Adams took over and proceeded to reduce operating costs so much that in 1923 he was transferred to the parent firm, the Parker-Young Company, with headquarters in Lincoln, New Hampshire. Adams gradually moved up the managerial ladder as woods superintendent, general woods manager and treasurer of the Black River Lumber Company. He set up and managed a furniture-stock factory and became an expert "cruiser" who appraised timber tracts his company considered purchasing. He also became schooled in the manufacture of paper pulp and paper. Although Adams never secured in his business career a living of more than modest respectability, his accomplishments elicited directorships on a railroad and the local Lincoln bank.

From his brief but unforgettable tenure in the woods, Adams acquired several lasting personal traits which are basic to his character. He became an addicted "early bird" whose workday commenced at daybreak. In his White House position, he assiduously followed a routine of rising at five thirty A.M. and appearing on the job by eight o'clock. In his logging days, Adams was also saturated with the jagged address of the lumber camp. His manner of discourse, which has offended and alienated many, was originally acquired by force of necessity. A flyweight among brutish lumberjacks, he had to outpace his hulky associates by straight talk and deeds of courage. Even the most intractable critics of his White House career conceded that his courage was bountiful. As for his discourse, this, since his rise to national prominence bids fair to become legendary. At the slightest provocation, Adams was given to clobbering the amenities. Once, when asked why he didn't say such nice things as "hello" and "good morning" to the White House staff, he retorted, "Why should I say 'hello'? They know I'm here." Although a man of seemingly deep religious conviction, Adams in official life suffered the imperfections of his brothers-in-Christ little. He was trigger-happy in dispensing the barb, the lacerating insult, and the dressing down. These he rendered with the considerable ability of a past master, summoning a short-clipped voice, jabbing eyes and an expression that was bloodless. In the climax of detestation, he snapped his fingers at his victim.

While trudging onward in his business career, Adams married the pretty Rachel Leona White, who as Mrs. Adams has become an accomplished painter and shares her husband's love of music. The Adamses have a son, a recent graduate of Dartmouth, and three older daughters. In the course of providing for his increasing family, Adams was literally swept into a new and in time more lucrative calling—politics—by the hurricane which battered New England in 1938. The great swaths of fallen trees cut by the storm in New Hampshire forests created such formidable fire hazards that Adams and other lumber men were convinced of the urgency of a state-wide salvaging effort. But the state populace had to be aroused and Adams was nominated to do the job in an elaborate speaking tour. So impressed were his friends in Lincoln by the elocutionary gifts he displayed, that they pushed him into running on the Republican ticket for the lower house of the state legislature in 1940.

Running in a safe Republican district, Adams triumphed easily. He wasn't long in the capital when he was installed as chairman of the committee on labor. In 1942, he was elected to a second term, half of which he served as Speaker. His conduct in that position was generally considered rather more arbitrary than necessary. The next stop in his new career was the national political mecca, Washington, for a single term in the House of Representatives. This initial Washington interlude he passed in the traditional obscurity of the freshman Congressman. On domestic legislation his voting record was moderately conservative, but in international affairs his position was devoid of any pattern. He voted for the British loan of 1946, for example, but opposed the extension of the recriprocal trade agreements program. His most significant personal achievement as Congressman lay in securing new feed sources for New England dairy farmers, who were suffering badly due to excessive dependence upon Canada. As his term in the House came to a close, Adams was New Hampshire bound in quest of a higher political notch, the Republican nomination for the Governorship. He lost out in a hard-fought primary contest with the incumbent Governor Charles M. Dale by a mere 157 votes. Adams briefly left the public stage by becoming a representative and, when need be, a lobbyist, for the New England Lumbermen's Association.

In 1948, he spectacularly resumed his political career, by easily winning the Republican nomination and election as Governor of New Hampshire. In 1950, he was re-elected by the handy margin of nearly 27,000 votes. Coming into office in the wake of mounting deficits and scandalous handling of state contracts, Adams invoked an austerity budget and set up a little Hoover Commission to promote efficiency. He backed the Commission's recommendations to consolidate the existing 83 departments into 43, formulated a complete reclassification plan for state employees, and instituted surveys of various state departments by private management engineering firms. To his fellow citizenry, the new Governor set a personal example of hard work and parsimony. He showed up at his desk at the crack of dawn and on the hard New Hampshire winter days, he got about, not in an official limousine, but walked to and from his office on snowshoes. Critics of Adams's Administration hold that he was heavily partial to the utility and telephone companies and big business in general, and that while his regime began with economy as the watchword, it soon became spendthrift. Whereas Adams came in with a surplus of $180,000 in the state treasury, he went out leaving a net debt of $18,000,000. Adams and his defenders say the sizable expenditure represented projects long overdue since the war, that one half of this debt consisted of new self-liquidating highways, and another big chunk was the consequence of inflation.

As Governor, Adams exhibited the obdurate disregard for public relations which is his hallmark. One day a delegation of citizens clamoring for special advantage descended upon the State House to put the heat on the chief executive. The leader of the delegation commenced a threat and promise harangue, culminating in the insinuating observation: "We represent 30,000 votes for Governor." Adams, his infinitesimal patience long exhausted, broke in. "Who the hell wants to be Governor?" he rasped. His audience shuffled out in muttering confusion. When at one juncture in the fiscal cycle, the state revenues fell off unexpectedly, and a dash of optimism was called for to chase the gathering gloom, Governor Adams duly announced to the press his confidence that the yield from a major tax source, the liquor tax, would soon be taking an upturn. Christmas was approaching, and the consumption of liquor, he cheerily pointed out, could be counted on to increase substantially in the holiday season. The Governor's baldness of statement didn't sit especially well with nice old ladies and other prim members of the New Hampshire electorate.

In the twilight of his second gubernatorial term, Adams took his historic plunge to support the candidacy of Dwight D. Eisenhower in the impending presidential election of 1952. By no means was Adams at the forefront of the Eisenhower movement. Senators Saltonstall and Tobey, Governor Herter and the Lodge brothers, Henry Cabot and John Davis, long were charter members before Adams rallied to the standard. While the Governor was making up his mind, the intensely competing pro-Eisenhower and anti-Taft forces agitated for his favor. The Republican rank and file of New Hampshire meanwhile were awaiting word of Adams's eventual choice in a state of terrific tension. "I don't know how many months he spent mulling it over," Mrs. Adams has said, "but it took a long time, and it was a hard decision." Adams seems to have dawdled because of fear that Eisenhower would not be strong enough to win, and because it was not at all clear that Eisenhower was a Republican, or for that matter, even a candidate. The General, who was in Paris at the time, was saying nothing. Adams finally came to grips with the situation by having the Attorney General of New

Hampshire query the County Clerk of Abilene, Kansas, Eisenhower's home town, on the subject of the future President's party affiliation. But the response of the county clerk, Mr. C. F. Moore, unfortunately was inconclusive. Eisenhower, it turned out, had never voted since the primary laws had been put into effect in 1928. "I don't think," wrote Mr. Moore, "he has any politics."

Adams got further in negotiations with Senator Henry Cabot Lodge, the de facto leader of the Eisenhower movement. After numerous conversations which culminated in the exchange of published letters, Adams was assured that the General was upon his own word a Republican, and was "in to the finish." This was sufficient encouragement for Adams to commit himself by declaring dramatically on September 30, 1951, at the Governor's conference at Gatlinburg, Tennessee, that Eisenhower's name would be entered in the New Hampshire primary. As the first of the presidential primaries, New Hampshire constituted an omen-making struggle between the Eisenhower forces and those of their formidable competitor, Senator Robert A. Taft. The battle was full and furious. Taft, knowing that his last opportunity for his craved prize, the Presidency, was at hand, toured the length and breadth of the state. The Eisenhower forces, handicapped by the absence and silence of their leader, struggled manfully under Adams, who served simultaneously as campaign manager and chief stump orator. To accomplish the difficult trick of bringing out the crowds in the dead of winter, when the primary was held, the Eisenhower strategists imported Fred Waring and his band from Broadway; Jinx Falkenberg of the theatrical and tennis world; Tony Lavelli, the Yale basketball star, and a quantity of torch singers and dancers. Miss Falkenberg delighted the crowds by batting tennis balls into their midst, and Mr. Lavelli entertained not with his basketball, but with an accordion. On one occasion, when a sudden snowstorm prevented this traveling vaudeville from arriving at a local rally, Adams, who was on hand as the scheduled speaker of the evening, saved the situation by rendering a little medley in his competent baritone.

The frantic commingled effort of Adams and his friends paid off handsomely. Eisenhower won all fourteen delegates of the state, a feat which imparted a great and lasting impetus to the entire subsequent battle. As for Adams, he, for the first time in his career, was projected into the national limelight. The drastic transformation of status didn't affect his equilibrium in the slightest. "He kept his New England style," observed a close lieutenant at the time.

As the battle of the primaries spilled over into other states, Adams made fighting speeches, rallied local politicos and outmaneuvered the

hard-fighting Taft forces. In his precious few spare moments, he helped prepare memoranda which Eisenhower, who by June of 1952 had returned to
the United States, requested from his key supporters outlining possible
replies to troublous questions raised by his opponents. The staff system
which characterized the later Presidency became firmly rooted in the primaries. Among the Eisenhower following, Adams enjoyed distinction as
the only Governor present in the traveling entourage. The fortunate early
date of the New Hampshire primary had released him for full-time service
in the Eisenhower cause while other Republican governors, anxious to do
their bit, were chained down by the impending primaries and other local
battles of their states. Adams industriously exploited his opportunity with
highly beneficial results to Eisenhower and also to himself.

The pro-Eisenhower delegates gathering at the Republican National
Convention at Chicago in July unanimously chose the New Hampshire
Governor as their floor leader. This tiring honor was due to Adams's imposing
contribution in the several primaries and to his freedom from commitment
to any of the several factions constituting Eisenhower's support. By all
accounts, Adams, as floor manager, spectacularly lived up to expectations. His
skill in the fierce infighting of the convention, commencing with the heated,
crucial contests over the seating of the delegates, was deemed superior all
the way. He excelled at methodical mastery of the back-breaking detail which
befalls floor leaders and his drive was unrelenting. When the Taft-Eisen-
hower struggle passed into its climactic stages, for instance, Adams, to keep
tabs on the situation, sedulously met every hour with his seventeen assistant
floor leaders in a side room off the floor. In the ritual followed, each assistant leader reported the exact delegate count as it currently stood for the
region or group of states for which he was responsible. Adams, who presided,
went down the list, calling upon the leaders for their reports. On one such
occasion, as the reports were made, they began to convey the sensational
intelligence that Eisenhower would win on the first ballot. At this juncture,
an assistant floor leader, overwhelmed by the prospect of success and eager to
give credit to the chief architect of the wonderful moment, rose at Adams's
call. Instead of reporting on the delegate count, the assistant floor leader
commenced a warm heartfelt tribute to Adams. The latter broke in quickly
to squelch the nonsense. "Just say how many votes," he snapped. The
assistant floor leader complied with the dazed air of a child who had been
slapped for saying "Thank you."

Adams's first meeting with Eisenhower transpired near the close of the
convention when the General met with his lieutenants to plan the windup.
All through the long ordeal, Ike had been impressed by Adams's brisk competence at staying on top of the job. The ensuing meeting was by all accounts

a complete success. "They hit it off right away," a bystander said at the time. "They seemed to understand each other at once—it was like a chemical affinity." Adams, nevertheless, left Chicago, not expecting to take part in the impending campaign outside of New Hampshire. Before returning home, he detoured to Wyoming for a rest. He had hardly settled down when Eisenhower, then in a Colorado mountain camp, summoned him to the telephone. Would Adams put everything aside, Ike was asking, and stay on as chief campaign adviser and right-hand man? After some resistance, because of his gubernatorial obligations in New Hampshire, Adams acquiesced. Taking leave without pay as Governor, he showed up at the Eisenhower headquarters in the Brown Palace Hotel at Denver in late July.

In the ensuing months, Adams functioned as Ike's chief of staff. He clearly had more to say about the campaign than its titular head, Arthur E. Summerfield, the national chairman, whose energies centered upon the Senatorial, Congressional and local canvasses. Adams was at Eisenhower's side throughout the forty-thousand miles of campaign travel by rail and air. Subject only to his chief's veto, the Governor decided when Ike would speak and where and supervised the small staff aboard the campaign train which hustled up notes between stops for Ike's off-the-cuff, rear-platform talks. The major speeches were written by C. D. Jackson of *Fortune*, and several associates back at the eastern Eisenhower headquarters at the Hotel Commodore in New York. The finished drafts were piped in by teletype to the campaign train. If a speech was a little more controversial than usual or novel in a major way, Jackson would take his manuscript personally to the train, wherever it was. One of these special junkets involved the famous Detroit speech in which Eisenhower made his spectacular vote-getting pledge to go to Korea. On the train, Jackson expounded his proposal to the candidate and his assembled advisers. Forty-eight hours of intensive hasseling ensued. A battalion of advisers seemed to be overwhelming the whole idea with battering-rams of objections. Adams, however, steadily supported it in the most critical hours, and Eisenhower eventually accepted it. "Adams," Jackson has said in retrospect, "couldn't have been more helpful."

The Governor was similarly influential at other fateful junctures in the campaign. The Nixon crisis, precipitated by disclosures that the Vice-Presidential candidate had been subsidized in his personal expenses by California business friends, threw the Republicans into frenzy. A Babellike confusion of voices rose around Eisenhower. One school of thought proposed that Nixon be ditched; another, that Ike rush to his defense. Adams favored the middle-of-the-road position of sitting tight and waiting, which is what Eisenhower did with happy consequences. When Fred Seaton of the campaign entourage made his historic proposal that Ike stump the South, Adams was in the vanguard of his support. The campaign eventually turned into the Southland, an investment of effort which paid off on election day when Ike carried Texas, Virginia, Tennessee and Florida. The several victories shattered a seemingly impregnable century-old Democratic tradition in the Old South.

As the returns came in on election day, Adams was not among the Eisenhower staff milling about the Commodore, nervously awaiting the results. The Governor slipped off with Mrs. Adams to tour the Bronx Zoo. Promptly after the triumph over Stevenson was a certainty, speculation began to rise concerning Adams's future. He was variously talked of for a post in the cabinet, as the next ambassador to Canada, and as the successor to Senator Charles W. Tobey of New Hampshire, who had died the previous summer. The mystery authoritatively ended when Eisenhower sat down with Adams in New York and said, "I have been thinking this over. You had better come down with me to the White House. You be down there at my right hand." Adams was not long in accepting appointment as "The Assistant to the President" and in busily girding himself for his future duties. When the President-elect and several of his cabinet members designate journeyed down to Washington to confer with their counterparts in the Truman Administration, Adams went along to consult with John R. Steelman, who then bore Adams's future job title, and with Matthew J. Connelly, President Truman's secretary. (Ironically, Connelly would soon be convicted under a prosecution initiated in the Eisenhower Administration of conspiring to defraud the government in an income-tax case.)

Soon after returning from his Washington briefing expedition, Adams chose as his own assistant Maxwell M. Rabb, a Boston attorney and former aide to Senator Lodge, whom the Governor had met in the fiery furnace of the New Hampshire primary. Rabb's official title, which occupied nearly half of his official letter of appointment, was a bureaucratic reductio ad absurdum, "The Assistant to the Assistant to the President." The Governor was also working with a special committee, headed by Nelson Rockefeller, with responsibilities for bringing about a reorganization of the Executive Branch, chiefly on the basis of the recent Hoover Commission proposals. Although Adams exhibited interest in all aspects of the Commission's work, his special province was the general reorganization of the White House staff.

On the day after the inauguration, at three o'clock in the afternoon, Adams appeared at President Eisenhower's office for the swearing in. Several colleagues of the campaign train—Thomas E. Stephens, James C. Hagerty, Wilton B. Persons, Fred A. Seaton, Robert Cutler, Gabriel Hauge and Emmet J. Hughes, who likewise were leaping from the train to the White

House staff, were on hand to take part in the ritual. Each one thrust his left hand upon a Bible, raised his right hand and took the oath to defend the Constitution.

In point of fact, Sherman Adams's new and mighty job had no direct basis either in the Constitution or in statutory law. Technically, his title, "The Assistant to the President," was the heritage of the post created in the Truman Administration by presidential order and occupied by John R. Steelman. Steelman's influence and power, however, were at most a shadow of what Adams's turned out to be. Like Steelman's, Adams's appointment was not referred to the scrutiny of the Senate, nor was it founded upon any formal presidential order. Eisenhower's closest venture toward official investiture transpired soon after the Administration got under way, when he met with his White House associates on several occasions and expounded his philosophy on staff work in general and Adams's position in particular. The President's chariness of formal written order derives from his long-standing preference for flexibility in staff activity and his conviction that no set pattern of organization should supersede common sense in adjusting means to needs.

Adams's post, which originally paid $20,000 and later was raised to $22,500 annually, did not change substantially from the time he first assumed it on January 21, 1953, until the tragic Goldfine revelations in 1958. Throughout the nearly six years involved, the Governor steadfastly exercised responsibilities comparable in their massiveness to those of the President himself. "To have an Eisenhower," it once was said, "you have to have an Adams." Adams did what Eisenhower didn't want to do. He was a converse image of the President's tastes and preferences, and since these were many and fixed, they gave the Governor's job its latitude. Throughout his professional career, for example, Eisenhower has abhorred the seamy side of executive work and has been wonderfully dextrous in avoiding it. He is that rarity among Presidents, a man who has made few enemies. The image he will leave upon history is that of a genial, kindly gentleman who exudes goodness and excels at getting people to work together. The harsher intervals of the executive life—saying "no" to insistent pressure, the back-breaking detail and the strain and strife of policy initiative—the President left to others. General Walter Bedell Smith, Ike's chief of staff in World War II, and General Albert Gruenther, his NATO aide, were men who proved themselves in various executive ordeals freely and gladly delegated by their chief. Adams was in their tradition.

In distributing his energies over the far-flung business of the Presidency, Eisenhower centered upon those things which he knew best before assuming his great office. His personal attention was concentrated on national security and foreign affairs, to which he brought the assurance of professional competence and mature experience. He was much less involved in domestic affairs, where he was much less at home. Adams, in his work pattern, was occupied more with domestic affairs and less with the problems of soldiery and diplomacy. Eisenhower likewise downgraded the business of politics. He did not take gladly to electoral campaigning, abhorred patronage, and had little zest for political maneuver. No politician was among his intimate friends. By Eisenhower's default, Adams took over the political command post of the Administration.

Indeed, Sherman Adams ranged so far and wide that he might properly be styled "The General Manager of the Presidency." This vast, all-encompassing role was actually a mosaic composed of many subroles in which the Governor engaged. The principal of these, to which Adams, a monument of ascetic dedication, repeatedly allotted his twelve to fourteen hour workday, are identifiable as follows:

Chief of Staff. In the military practice which Eisenhower transposed to the necessities of the White House, Adams was the man who kept things running on the operational level at the command post by shouldering the mountainous detail and by making all but the most important decisions himself. The "chief of staff" label was not one overly welcome in the Administration because of its militaristic connotation and because it fell somewhat short of total accuracy, but around the White House it was deemed the best available.

As conceived by Eisenhower, Adams's job adhered to several cardinal principles. The chief of staff, Adams, took orders only from the President, and except in the singular case of John Foster Dulles, cabinet secretaries approached the President through the chief of staff. Policy proposals submitted for the President's decision were made in writing, as the fruit of staff study and recommendation. Adams's task was to see that every expert in the Executive Branch who could contribute to a proposal had his opportunity to do so. The suggestions of the experts were expected to shape up into definite recommendation, which higher authority could accept or reject. This, in the jargon of the trade, is the doctrine of "completed staff work." When a proposal was ready for the President's action, the papers on which it was based were topped with a one-page, double-spaced synopsis prepared by Adams. "If a proposition can't be stated in one page," Eisenhower declared, "it isn't worth saying." In an age when military, scientific and economic phenomena have soared in complexity, this maxim placed a terrible strain at times on Adams's artistry at summation.

Most final decisions were made, however, not by the President, but by Adams. Eisenhower was brought in only if the matter was very important or if the executive experts disagreed. One thing Eisenhower especially admired about Adams was his infinite courage in making decisions. Adams always plunged on, spurred by an uncanny intuitive sense of what Eisenhower wanted and a capacity for judicious balance which his superior valued highly. Of Adams, a White House insider once said, "Ike likes his ability to follow a middle course. The President knows Sherm will never swing too far to the right or too far to the left."

Ringmaster. "He is the ringmaster of the circus," Adams's job was sometimes described. He saw to it that the big questions got on the agenda, that responsible people came together, faced the issues and thrashed out conclusions on time. Adams's duties were least where co-ordinating mechanisms like the Budget Bureau, the National Security Council and the Office of Defense Mobilization operated, although on occasion some of his knottiest problems arose in co-ordinating the co-ordinators. As ringmaster, Adams befriended the underdog harassed by entrenched forces of defeatism and complacency. He uplifted some of the Administration's finest achievements in their wobbliest beginnings, the daring Atoms for Peace Plan, the civil rights program, and the Refugee Relief Act. In dark hours, Adams spurred on the proponents of these measures with stratagems and rallying cries—"Don't quit," "Give it another push."

Like any good ringmaster, Adams avoided unnecessary involvement in death struggles with the lions, although, armed with Eisenhower's broad and liberal mandate, the Governor by no means quailed at forcing issues between the departments. Since Adams judged his own effectiveness in terms of his ability to absorb the presidential work load, and matters normally went to the President only in case of deadlock, the Governor badgered the lower echelons unmercifully to reach agreement. Once several departments were vying over the chairmanship of an interdepartmental committee. After witnessing a few minutes of haggling, Adams issued an ultimatum. "Either make up your minds," he declared, "or else tell me and I will do it."

Buffer. One of the sentences that Adams played and replayed like a worn-out record was, "We must not bother the President with this." Adams considered it his high duty to keep people and their problems from the President, leaving him free for other things, both before and after the several illnesses which sapped his strength. Adams went to drastic lengths to protect the President, thinking nothing of blocking the paths of individuals of position and prestige. On one occasion, for example, he refused to permit Secretary of Defense McElroy to see the President concerning a matter of considerable importance to the Secretary, an increased military pay bill. Traditionally, cabinet members, and above all, a leading official like the Secretary of Defense, can see the President at any time. On this occasion, however, Adams kept the Secretary cooling his heels in the White House until late in the afternoon and then refused to let him in to see the President.

Those officials who succeeded in penetrating the Adams barrier would often enter the President's office for a conference, glowing with the pride of accomplishment, and then in the matter of a moment, upon surveying the scene, would drop into the depths of despair. For seated, waiting with the President, would be Adams. Admiral Arthur Radford, the former Chairman of the Joint Chiefs of Staff, is reported to have advised his successor, General Nathan Twining, not to accept the appointment without a firm guarantee of reasonable access to the President. What especially spurred Admiral Radford into offering this extraordinary advice was the fact that neither he nor his superior, Secretary of Defence Charles E. Wilson, had been able to see the President on business alone without Adams or the national security assistant, Robert Cutler, present for well over a year.

Adams also exercised control over the official reading matter coming to the White House for Mr. Eisenhower's attention. From the mass of documents and papers, the Governor selected those which seemed fit to pass before the eyes of his chief. At times the censorship imposed was tight and absolute. The lengths to which Adams would go was demonstrated in the circumstances surrounding the dismissal of Frederick B. Lee in 1955 as Administrator of the Civil Aeronautics Authority. Mr. Lee, a Republican, clearly was let out because on certain occasions he had chosen to disagree with Administration policies. Sometime before he was dismissed, as the storm clouds of trouble were gathering, Mr. Lee moved to protect his declining fortunes. He wrote to the President, asking for a hearing to clear up any misunderstanding which might unfortunately exist. Within a few days, the uneasy commissioner received reply. To his utter consternation, the President's letter said nothing of a hearing but simply accepted his resignation. Mr. Lee's anguish was compounded when he detected from the wording of the letter that the President had known nothing of any request for a hearing. The President by every indication had never even seen his letter.

Hatchet man. Adams took care of several inescapable nasty chores that needed attention around the White House. Harsh words had to be said on occasion and Adams was the man who said them. President Eisenhower nimbly side-stepped involvement in these rougher acts and delegated them to the willing Governor. For himself, Eisenhower was the imperturbable gentleman of good will who saw no evil and spoke no evil.

As the President's ready hatchet man, Adams chopped with varied strokes, from short rebuke to slashing diatribe. When J. Bracken Lee, Republican Governor of Utah, refused to issue a proclamation commemorating a national holiday, United Nations Day, because he considered the world organization to be a terrible flop, it was Adams, not Eisenhower, who administered a flick on the knuckles in a statement to the press. In 1954, when the country was undergoing a mild economic setback, and the Democrats, in Republican eyes, were making political capital by chattering over-dolefully of the situation, some plain talk was decidedly in order. Adams emerged from his lair to render a full philippic in a public address. The Democrats, said Adams, were conspiring to talk the country into a depression. They were, he continued, warming to his subject, "political sadists," who were conniving to substitute the "Fear Deal" for the "Fair Deal."

On occasion, the country was treated to the interesting spectacle of Eisenhower and Adams addressing themselves, in their contrasting styles, to the identical subject. Eisenhower played Jekyll and Adams was Hyde. The President conveyed the honeyed words and Adams the tartness. What the Governor said was sometimes more revelatory of Eisenhower's thinking than what Eisenhower said. One of the more intriguing of these situations came shortly after the first Russian Sputnik was successfully launched. An earnest reappraisal of United States defense policies ensued, spiced with occasional dashes of partisan maneuver. The debate soon became so important, that on the evening of January 20, 1958, both Eisenhower and Adams emerged from the White House to make speeches dealing with the situation. In Chicago, the President took his accustomed highroad, appealing to everybody—in language of lofty principle—to keep politics out of the defense discussion. Three hundred miles away in Minneapolis, even as the President was speaking, Adams was launching a bold political counteroffensive by clawing the Democrats in a speech of sardonic aggression. Lest the public, surveying America's lag in the Sputnik race, identify military failure with the Republicans, Adams, in his oration, took his audience on a partisan tour of recent history. Upon the opposition, he pinned responsibility for such debacles as Pearl Harbor, "the tragic loss of China," and "the scientific catastrophe of losing our atomic secrets." To top matters off, upon reaching 1957 in his little historical survey, he put the blame for the lag in the missiles race squarely at the door of the Democrats.

Job-giver. Probably Adams's biggest headache was dispensing patronage. He reviewed thousands of job appointments before they were consummated, negotiated the more important ones himself, and was on the receiving end of the inevitable disgruntlement. The last was sometimes lacerating in nature. Typical of the scars he accumulated is one dealt in the early months of the Administration by Walter Reuther, then Vice-President of the CIO. Reuther proposed that John W. Edelman, who was reputed in some quarters to be a former Socialist, be appointed as Assistant Secretary of Labor. To Adams, the alleged socialism augured impossible sledding in the Senate where the appointment would be passed upon. Edelman, he said, wouldn't do. Reuther was outraged. He requested a conference, and put his case with Niagaralike forcefulness, but Adams wouldn't budge. So distraught was

Reuther, who is little accustomed to rebuff, that he released to the press several private letters he had written to Adams on the matter. In his communications, Reuther unflatteringly depicted Adams as a timorous official who shrank before "unsubstantiated gossip and hearsay," and whose sense of justice toward Mr. Edelman was exactly zero. Adams, according to Reuther, thought of nothing but the easy way out.

Bouncer. Eisenhower eschewed the unpleasant business of firing a subordinate, when from time to time the procedure had to be resorted to in the interests of the Administration. As a regular assignment, Adams was bearer of the unhappy tidings. This, by all accounts, he did most efficiently, although not always with heed, it was sometimes complained, to the niceties which traditionally adhere to the protocol of firing. When Clarence Manion, the former Dean of the Notre Dame Law School, was let out from his post as Chairman of the President's Commission on Intergovernmental Relations in 1954, Adams reportedly was most unceremonious. According to Manion's account of the incident, he was simply called in by Adams and told to submit his resignation. In the months just before this disconcerting step was taken, Manion had come into ill grace by applying himself not to his job, but to making speeches all over the country in support of the Bricker amendment, which the Administration strongly opposed. When the former law dean ventured to discuss the merits of the case, Adams snapped that it was all settled.

"You still like Ike?" Manion was asked when the news of his dismissal broke upon the world. "Oh, definitely," replied Manion, "very definitely." It is doubtful that Mr. Manion, and certainly not his friends, were disposed with equal affection toward Governor Adams. One Congressman in Manion's corner, Noah M. Mason, Republican of Illinois, when asked to comment on the development, gestured with a clenched fist and shouted a string of angry words to the effect that the Dean was the victim of the "autocratic dictatorship" of Sherman Adams.

Fall guy. Adams took abuse not only for his own deeds, but for the mistakes of others, especially those of his chief. As few men could, the Governor bore up philosophically under the barrages of poison darts that his capacity naturally attracted. If the press was raging, he would snap, "The Presidency is not run for the press." Once in a meeting of Republican party chieftains, which the Governor attended, a bitter discussion developed over the appointment of a Democrat to a major Administration post. The appointment had just been consummated in the face of insistent pressure for a Republican. Quite valid reasons existed for the choice made, but under the circumstances it was undesirable to reveal them. Another significant but undisclosable fact was that the President himself had made the decision. The assembled party chieftains meanwhile were showering brickbats of indignation upon Adams cornered at the conference table in a mammoth leather chair. Conceivably, Adams could have wriggled out of the situation by saying it was the President's decision, by revealing the several confidential reasons involved, or by getting mad. He did none of these. He took the blame entirely upon himself and made a nice little speech to the effect that "we all make mistakes."

White Housekeeper. Adams directed the White House staff of well nigh four hundred clerks and stenographers plus his several personal aides, and exercised varying degrees of direction over the professional staff. He administered the million-dollar White House budget and decided such imponderables of daily housekeeping as to whether the mansion was to have a new paint job, whether a new car was to be purchased to augment the official fleet, or a new chief of records was to be appointed. If so, Adams chose the man for the post.

The Governor's several roles were deepened and extended by various elements in his own and the President's *modi operandi*. Eisenhower's leadership at best was spotty and episodic, leaving spacious vacuums to be filled in part at least by Adams. In domestic policy, as has been noted, the President was given to indifference, a mood he betrayed in several ways. On the issues of the day, he manifested remarkably few convictions. In public pronouncement and specific action, he blew hot and cold on social security, federal aid to education, public power and other ranking issues. He tended to speak on social questions in general terms, with noticeable addiction to platitudes and balanced statements. Thus, "Modern Republicanism" is a capacity to understand following "the Lincoln dictum of what government is for" (a bow to the common man), "and then to do it within the concept of a competitive economy, sound fiscal arrangements, and a sound dollar" (a bow to privileged conservatism).* The President's billowy vagueness gave Adams lots of elbow room in working out policy.

The President abhorred the controversy which normally befalls leadership. When the going got rough his favorite stance was that of disinterested observer rather than that of fighting champion. His capacity for detachment, of riding serenely above the storm, was truly remarkable. On one occasion, after he had proposed a program of legislation to Congress, a few raindrops of criticism began to fall. Eisenhower took shelter by declaring that the several proposals involved were by no means to be considered as "my program." "While my name is attached to it because I am President," he explained, "these programs are not made up just out of my single fertile brain. They are . . . completely examined by the whole Administration,

* Press conference, March 13, 1957, *The New York Times*, March 14, 1957.

Cabinet, and so on . . ."* If two subordinate officials were fighting publicly over policy, the President didn't choose between them, but backed up the right of each to express his views. The business of settling controversy, and riding herd on recalcitrants fell upon Adams. It was nasty work, but it swelled the Governor's impact on policy.

Adams was amply endowed with work habits which Eisenhower admired and required in a chief of staff. Although recreation-minded in arranging his own pattern of living, the President insisted upon having about him those who commanded a sustained capacity for hard work. Adams's appetite for work was nothing less than gluttonous. Even more, Ike, when organizing his own workday, preferred to begin at eight A.M., or better yet, at breakfast, which was a whole hour earlier. At such impossible hours, ruddy and fresh, he fazed slower-starting colleagues. Adams's woodsmanlike capacity to be on the job early, ready to go at peak efficiency, endeared him to Ike. The President abhorred casualness. One of the nicest things he could say about a man was that "he does his homework." Adams always did. He was a factmonger who never relied on rumor or hearsay, but checked things out. Eisenhower liked to thrash through an abundance of staff work in a single conferral. In intense, fast-moving sessions, Adams's capacity for pithy summation and talking always to the point stood him well. So, too, did his capacity as a listener. Eisenhower, who read little and did his thinking by discussion, used the Governor as a sounding board. Perplexed by a problem or viewpoint, Ike would walk around the room, talking on his feet, with Adams sitting by. What discussion there was was only surface deep, philosophical probings were left to the technical staffs. Nor did Ike particularly seek advice. Milton Eisenhower, another favorite sounding board, seldom offers his brother advice. His main job, he says, is to listen.

Adams's several valued talents were energized and directed by his consuming loyalty to the President. To Adams, Eisenhower was "this great man," and the opportunity to serve him "a privilege." Adams's commitment to his chief was demonstrated, as such a state of mind is apt to be, in countless little ways. Typical of these ways is an incident which occurred well into the second term. Adams at the time was visiting the home of a friend (not in this case, Mr. Bernard Goldfine). Just before dinner, Adams, the friend, and the friend's wife had gathered in the living room for cocktails. No one else was present. The cocktails were duly served and while, according to etiquette, a toast was in order, the informality of the circumstances made the call for anything more than a perfunctory "cheers" quite unlikely. Adams nonetheless raised his glass and declared with sheerest sincerity, "To the President of the United States." The Governor's gesture of simple eloquence was not intended to impress his companions, for they were all old friends

* Press Conference, August 7, 1957, The New York Times, August 8, 1957.

who knew one another intimately. Adams's devotion to the President, however intense, was not of the blind hero-worshiping variety. The Governor
was alert to the President's imperfections, and strove in his toil to minimize
them. Neither was Adams a "yes man." On several occasions, the President
had made clear his aversion to such creatures, and Adams, for his part, made
no bones about disagreeing with his chief, even in open conference with
other officials present.

In the positions he took on policy, Adams championed the aspirations
of the liberal wing of the Republican party. In his nearly six years of
office, the Governor strove for an Administration "warmly responsive to the
urgent social and economic problems of the American people." He was a big
gun in the expansion of social security, with its broadened coverage of unemployment insurance, the greatest since the system was installed in the
F. D. Roosevelt Administration. He endorsed revision of the Taft-Hartley
Act, but only on condition that the right of workers to organize into unions
and to bargain collectively be adequately protected. He supported expansion
of the several housing programs, federal aid for school construction with
due weight to differences in local need, extended coverage of the minimum
wage laws, the elimination of discrimination in employment, and other
measures assuring equality before law regardless of race, creed or color. He
sponsored several of the Administration's stronger measures for the Little
Rock school situation. Against the conservative bloc, led by Secretary of the
Treasury George Humphrey, he successfully battled for high spending levels
in the programs for foreign aid. In domestic and foreign programs alike, he
opposed the apostles of "economy" and "budget-balancing," whose voices
and prestige in the Administration were formidable.

But Adams, it seems clear, did not always use his privileged access and
imposing influence to the best interests of the President, the Administration
and the country. At times, the Governor excessively sheltered the President
from the outer world, from officials and citizens he should have seen and
from problems he should have known about. By blocking citizens and communications from reaching the President, by limiting debate and discussion,
and by arrogating decision into his own hands, Adams kept the President
from securing a knowledge of harsh realities which it was the duty of the
Chief Executive to have. To be sure, Adams's intentions were good; he
wanted to spare the President. The Governor in effect functioned as a kind
of tranquilizer, enabling the ailing, uninterested Eisenhower to luxuriate in
therapeutic but unwarranted calm and optimism. By every indication, the
President was allowed to assume that the recession of 1957–58 was less
serious in its early stages than it really was. In consequence, remedial governmental measures were delayed in forthcoming and the recession was
aggravated and extended at great cost to the Administration politically and

the country economically. The President was not apprised when he should have been of the widening lag between the United States missiles program and the Russian. Trevor Gardner, former Assistant Secretary of the Air Force in charge of the missiles program, has testified that in the three years in which he occupied his important post, he was allowed to brief the White House personally only twice concerning the progress of Air Force missile development, which he considered dangerously laggard because of administrative delays and lack of funds.* While his first briefing session at the White House was of adequate duration for his purpose, his second appearance, some four and a half months later, which is a long time in the space age, was incredibly short. In an appearance before the cabinet, Gardner was allowed "between eight and ten minutes" to explain the Air Force missiles programs. The master-controller of the cabinet's time on that occasion was Sherman Adams.

Politically, the most costly of Adams's roadblocks to protect the President's privacy occurred one August day in 1954 when John Sherman Cooper, Republican Senator of Kentucky, whom Eisenhower highly esteemed, called at the White House to lay before the President his several objections to the controversial Dixon-Yates contract,** then under consideration. Adams refused to grant the Senator an appointment with the President. The purpose of Cooper's visit was to offer objections to the Dixon-Yates contract on a number of grounds. As it turned out, the Senator would have spared the Administration a good deal of embarrassment, had his advice been heard and heeded at the time he put in his request for an audience with the President. Some weeks after Cooper's fruitless appearance at the White House, the Administration, under pressure of heavy criticism, abandoned the contract with a considerable loss of face.

Sometimes Adams even took into his own hands the highest questions of foreign policy. One of these occasions transpired shortly after British and French troops had invaded Egypt as the climax of the long and bitter dispute with Nasser over the Suez. The State Department was going along with the Franco-British action, when Henry Cabot Lodge, seeking to gain favor with the Afro-Asian bloc, chose to buck the Department and vote in favor of an

* *Hearings*, Subcommittee on Availability of Information from Federal Departments and Agencies, House of Representatives, 85th Congress, 1st session, November 18, 1957, p. 3076.
** The Dixon-Yates contract had been initiated by the sharply increasing demands of the Atomic Energy Commission upon the Tennessee Valley Authority for electrical power. In lieu of expanding TVA to stay abreast of demand, the Administration planned to have private utilities feed energy to TVA to replace the power fed by it to AEC. Dixon and Yates represented the several private utilities involved, and in their behalf were negotiating a contract with AEC and the Bureau of the Budget. The contract was to be awarded to the Dixon-Yates group without competitive bidding.

Afro-Asian UN resolution requiring immediate withdrawal of French and British troops from the Suez. In his quest for authorization of his maneuver, Lodge turned not to the President or the State Department—he turned to Adams. The Assistant to the President reportedly declared that the matter wasn't important enough to bother Eisenhower with and authorized Lodge to vote for the resolution despite State Department instructions to the Ambassador to abstain. The decision had shattering consequences on America's relations with its traditional Allies.*

However far and free Adams ranged in the official orbit, he had little entree to the President's private affairs. The Assistant to the President was no frequenter of the Gettysburg farm; he was no playtime companion, nor was he apparently privy to the stream of decisions concerning family, fortune and future. Eisenhower drew a strict line between business and pleasure, between private friends and official associates. (Adams did likewise with his own staff.) In Eisenhower's case, the cleavage derived partly from the President's military background, with its flavor of caste, and partly from a disinclination to use the social weapon as a means of staff manipulation. Various situational factors also operated to circumscribe the Adams-Eisenhower association. The President's recreation schedule took him frequently out of Washington; Adams had small choice but to stay in the capital on the job. Only on several rare occasions did they simultaneously escape Washington to go on fishing trips together. When he was in Washington, Eisenhower had no special urgency for Adams's companionship. Ike was amply stocked with long-established local friendships which he continued to pursue in his Presidency. His official staff contained one such old friend, General Wilton B. Persons, his deputy assistant, and his physician, Major General Howard M. Snyder. By nature Persons and Snyder were more companionable than the work-minded Adams.

To qualify as Eisenhower's companion, one had to excel at bridge or golf, and preferably at both. It was to these games that Ike devoted the major part of his frequent vacations, long weekends and a work-week that was punctuated with pleasurable interludes. Daytime hours were passed at golf, nighttimes at bridge, and by relentless application, the President developed a decided competence at both. Since he took his games seriously and hankered for the zest of challenge, he preferred partners with a competence at least somewhere in the neighborhood of his own. Adams, the truth is,

* The episode was reported by Joseph and Stewart Alsop in the New York Herald Tribune, September 10, 1958, and was later denied by Ambassador Lodge. "To say that Mr. Sherman Adams ever prevented me from talking with the President is fantastically untrue," Mr. Lodge declared. "I have never been stopped by anyone from talking with the President and it is cruelly unfair to Governor Adams and to the devoted men and women of the White House to say that I have."

failed miserably by this stern criterion. He seldom got to the golf links, and when he did, his game was nothing to shout about. With the bridge table, he had barely a nodding acquaintance. It is not strange that he was seldom to be found in Eisenhower's party.

Eisenhower's favorite companions were his brother Milton, soldiers to whom he was long accustomed and wealthy businessmen whose success he admired. His former chiefs of staff, generals Gruenther and Smith, numbered among his military favorites. In the world of wealth, Eisenhower's staunchest comrades were George E. Allen, a puckish corporation director and friend to F.D.R. and Truman; William E. Robinson, President of Coca-Cola; and Clifford J. Roberts, a New York banker and chairman of the Augusta National Golf Club, one of the President's most-visited resorts.

Although now and then he engaged in misjudgment, Sherman Adams was blessed with a variety of qualities ideally suited for his horrendous post. He projected smartness, was bright, acute, reflective. His thinking on official problems was not amorphous but in focus and sensitively co-ordinated with political currents and fluctuations in Eisenhower's thinking. In the main, his judgments were informed and his decisions stuck. For conversations and names his memory was photographic—a priceless talent, given the unending march of humanity through the White House. On presidential problems he was a mine of information. When the controversial federal highway program of 1957 was evolving, he amazed colleagues by rattling off from memory the precise allotment of federal funds to various states under any one of several complicated formulae under consideration at the time.

Adams's job entailed a good deal of negotiation and his style in that fine administrative art was distinct and definable. He was respected for his ability as a conference leader to lay out problems and bring the most fugitive nuances to light, and he was deft at chopping through trivia on which outlandish quantities of time might otherwise be wasted. For all of his impressive contributions, Adams, in conferences and meetings, was anything but a chatterbox. If anything, he was closer akin to the Great Stone Face. He was given to lapsing into long silences, and then, when he was almost a forgotten man among the conferees, he would light up suddenly, like a switchboard, to deliver himself of a few terse clinching observations on the problems at hand. He would cut off with equal suddenness, like lights going out, and lapse into a similar cycle of silence and assertion for the next item on the day's agenda.

One Senator who dealt frequently with Adams valued his capacity for giving answers that were "direct, truthful, and realistic." The Governor, it was generally agreed, was no spreader of false sunshine, and possessed neither the taste or talent of two famous progenitors, Harry Hopkins and Colonel House, for mystery and intrigue. Many an executive was impressed with the enduring integrity of Adams's word—"Once you have it, it sticks," observed an official who knew him well. When he rejected commitment, Adams was not the kind who took the easy way out by laying down little smoke screens of evasion. With the Governor, it was "yes" or "no." "He is a man you can get an answer from," a colleague once said, "a quality that is rather rare in government."

Adams took admitted pride in his considerable artistry in serving up the negative. "I am not used to mincing words," he once informed a gathering of party officials, "nor am I accustomed, as the saying goes, to 'shovel smoke.'" Adams was quick to summon several expedients by which he underscored his rejection of a proposal or a situation. He would speak in short-clipped words and intersperse his remarks with profanity which he used freely in the presence of both sexes. He also excelled in such nonverbal manifestations of displeasure as the icy stare, the pointed silence and popping his eyes. Most important of all, he had a kind of genius in fitting his unfriendly expressions into a form which best suited the situations to which they were addressed. When he arrived at the Fitzsimons Army Hospital in Denver on October 1, 1955, where the President lay ill from his coronary, a cluster of press photographers greeted him with a chorus of well wishes and clicked the historic scene as he bounded up the steps. The most Adams allowed was to cast a cold glance of recognition, never lifting his hand in the slightest suggestion of a wave as he strode inside. The press was noticeably circumspect for the duration of his stay at Fitzsimons, which doubtless was what Adams wanted.

On many an occasion, the Governor displayed finesse in dealing with complainers. One day an official, who belonged to this unhappy category, came in whining over some difficulty. Adams demoralized the man by maintaining a complete and frosty silence for the entire duration of a fifteen-minute interview. The complainer, be it said in his behalf, got the point. Henceforth he repaired the stiffening in his backbone in private and never did he trouble the stern and busy Adams again. For years in his business and public careers, the Governor had been conducting a one-man crusade against fools. One victim, who for various reasons was under consideration for appointment to a high level position in the Treasury Department, proceeded to the Department for an interview which Adams had arranged with the Secretary. When the interview ended, the prospective appointee returned to the White House as he had been instructed to do. Adams asked how he had fared. "I was very much impressed with Secretary Humphrey," the gentleman answered pleasantly. "That," said Adams, leaning forward, his expression suddenly flinty, "was not the purpose of the interview."

Adams's tendency to abruptness was explained by certain of his colleagues as a kind of response to the necessities of his work. The job, they said, was next to impossible in its sprawling dimensions and Adams employed rough manners as a necessary shortcut to get on with the next task. His wintry mien really wasn't quite so bad as it seemed, these colleagues also contended, because it was amply tempered by a sense of humor. It wasn't rollicking humor, the kind that puts you in stitches, nor was Adams a storyteller or cutup. He had a dry subtlety that played upon the situation of the moment. A group of officials, for example, showing up at Adams's office, would converge upon the conference table for a meeting. "George," Adams would say to one of the conferees, "you take the comfortable chair." It happened that the chairs around the table were completely identical, each with a straight back and a hard oak seat.

Adams, in his lighter moments, also utilized the delayed reaction. One Christmas, J. Clyde Hall, President of Hallmark greeting cards, presented to a colleague of Adams a beautifully ornamented Christmas card addressed "to one who has been a mother to me." Sniffing an opportunity for a prank, the colleague proceeded to send the card as his season's greeting to Adams. For days, the Governor gave no flicker of acknowledgement to his colleague, who awaited his reaction in a state of expectant amusement. Finally, some three weeks later, the break came. Adams called the colleague on the telephone, and greeted him, "Hello, this is your mother." Adams also went in a lot for joshing and the jibe; was he serious or was he joking? "Twenty-five percent of the time, he's serious in his jab," said an associate, "and seventy-five percent he's comical. It's important that you don't get the proportions mixed."

For all of his power and influence, Adams was not one who ostentatiously threw his weight around. At meetings of his colleagues and on those special semiceremonial occasions at the White House which now and then brighten the existence of the presidential bureaucracy, he was never greedy for the limelight. His deportment, on the contrary, was unremittingly self-effacing. He never assumed the pose of "You know who I am," or played the high and mighty order-giving commissar. At social gatherings, like the President's famous stag dinners, when dinner was announced and the guests filed in, Adams was among the last to enter. After the meal concluded, and the group proceeded to the East Room to form a semicircle around the President for an evening of discussion, Adams invariably took a chair at the far perimeter. At the swearing-in ceremony of a new cabinet secretary, an event which attracts a goodly representation of choice officialdom, Adams was not to be found among those most to the fore, or even among the seated. On such occasions, he stood squeezed in the crowd which always concentrates in the back of the room near the door.

Sherman Adams was that rarity, a man of culture on the payroll in the presidential circle. Since culture is a rather fragile flower, it doesn't normally luxuriate in such rugged climes, but Adams got by. The Governor's tastes, as a matter of fact, are so well rounded that they suggest something of the image of the eighteenth-century cultured man. Adams is one of our few public men of today who can and does use Latin with authority in his speeches. He is well versed, as his speeches also attest, in history and biography, especially when the subject at hand treats of bygone statesmen of New England vintage. A fellow Dartmouth alumnus, Daniel Webster, is his favorite, with Calvin Coolidge, and the Revolutionary War hero, General John Stark, running close behind.

Adams's most passionate artistic pursuit is music, to which he has been devoted since the age of seven when he began piano lessons. Every morning during his White House tour of duty, his hi-fi set was tuned in at six-thirty to the local good music station. With the soothing encouragement of a classical symphonic background, Adams took breakfast and sped through six newspapers. The news, he said, seemed a little less gruesome and the task ahead less formidable, when you started out to the accompaniment of Berlioz or Copland. The Governor's assiduous study of music has carried him a long way toward qualifying as a musicologist. Several years ago, he was even invited to appear on the local hi-fi station in Washington to discourse on a musical topic. Although busy as usual at the time, Adams, for love of his subject, snatched up the opportunity. On the appointed day, he showed up at the studio and was in the middle of a presentation, imposing in its learning, when he was interrupted by a commercial. So nettled was the Governor by the interruption, of which he had not been forewarned, that after the commercial was over, he acidly expressed his conviction that such crass practices are utterly reprehensible when serious music, or the discussion of such music, is in progress. This was the last time he appeared on the station. Adams was an unremitting supporter of the National Symphony throughout his Washington tenure and even in the face of his onerous official duties, he found time to travel up to Philadelphia to take in the opening of the venerable Academy of Music.

The Governor's other great love among the Muses is poetry, and his favorite versifier, given his deep New England roots, is Robert Frost. Adams was generous in sharing Mr. Frost, an old friend, with his White House colleagues. One afternoon, when Frost was in town, Adams called up various members of the staff. "Be at the White House mess at five thirty," he snapped. (For the benefit of the uninitiated, the "White House mess" is not an abominable political situation, but the staff dining room.) At the appointed hour, most of the staff was on hand, seething with curiosity. Adams shuffled in with Frost, and introduced him to the assemblage, saying that he long had thought it would be fun if Frost appeared and read poetry. So here he was. For at least an hour, the hardy eighty-four-year-old Frost read from his own selections and answered requests from the floor. Adams presided throughout, interspersing Frost's renditions with the best of his own drollery.

In the main, however, Adams was not given to sharing his joys and spending his precious few moments of relaxation with his fellow men at large. It is not inaccurate to classify the Governor as a distinctly unsocial animal. He was no mixer; his natural bent was to avoid social contact due largely to his compulsive shyness. During his Washington tenure, various circumstances external to his personality also contributed to his living in a state of walled-in privacy. In the earlier period of the Administration, the serious and prolonged illness of Mrs. Adams exerted a considerable pressure upon the Governor for withdrawal. Likewise, the rigorous occupational regimen which he followed left scant choice to a man in his fifties but for a private life which was extremely home-centered. After an exhausting eleven-hour workday, he would go back to his hi-fi, a quiet dinner, and by eight o'clock he was in bed. The home to which he so happily retired was a 157-year-old rented stone barn on the edge of Rock Creek Park.

Now and then Adams allowed himself the luxury of an outside excursion and these revolved very much about the church. A man of deep religious conviction, he attended the National Cathedral, where he belonged to the choir in his days as a Congressman. He was also to be found in St. John's Church (Episcopal) across Lafayette Park from the White House. There on occasion, he was called upon to read the lesson at the Sunday service.

In the later years of the Eisenhower Administration, but before the Goldfine revelations, Adams's social activities underwent noticeable increase, a development his White House colleagues, mindful of the old adage concerning "all work and no play," subtly encouraged. Adams entertained more at his home, took in more of the official dinners, and was seen increasingly at other occasions of the social *haut monde.* Upon Queen Elizabeth's visit to the capital in 1957, Adams was one of the most-invited members of all officialdom to the whirl of festivities offered in Her Majesty's honor. So formidable indeed was Adams's emergence, that in 1957 the annual social list of Washington accorded the Assistant to the President the most spectacular jump up in its social rankings granted in that year to any personage in the capital. Adams was skipped over no less than the forty-eight Governors and ninety-six Senators to land securely in the upper upper strata, just beneath the members of the cabinet. The social list, or Green Book, as it is known, is, contrariwise, equally sensitive to the tail spins of official fortunes. Less than one year later, in 1958, when Adams ran afoul of the Goldfine investigations, but before he had resigned from his White House post, his name was dropped completely from the social list. The special board which prepares the list made its decision fully three weeks prior to Adams's resignation.

In his occasional less formal outings, Adams was a devotee of square dancing. Among those in Washington who indulged in this gymnastic, he was deemed one of the best dancers in an Administration which contained conspicuously few members who did even tolerably well at the terpsichorean art. In his lighter moments, Adams also excelled as a Scrabble player; cards have never particularly interested him, but words do. Although not a joiner, he is a venerated, long-standing member of the Masons, holder of the honorary 33rd Degree, the highest awarded by the order. With Secretary of Commerce Sinclair Weeks, he received the degree in 1957 "for outstanding contribution to Freemasonry, civic endeavor or other worthy cause recognized by Freemasonry." Adams's other interests centered on the great out of doors. He was still devoted to hiking, thought nothing of a half-day trek, and was an ardent fly fisherman, whose favorite catch was the Atlantic salmon.

For the rest, what Adams did and thought, what he loved and respected, what sustained him in the grim vortex of duty, derived from a web of loyalties which were consuming and enduring. He was devoted to New England in general and the White Mountain country in particular. "Never live south of Plymouth" (he referred to Plymouth, New Hampshire), he earnestly counseled. He was similarly loyal to old vests, to an auto license plate, "New Hampshire 22," which he took pains to secure for years, and Dartmouth. Of Dartmouth, he was by every standard a model alumnus. No matter how duty pinned him to his desk, he always had time for his alma mater. He did not shrink from dropping everything in Washington and rushing four hundred miles up to Hanover to participate, over a period of days, in the much-publicized "Great Issues" course of the college. For years he served on the board of trustees. In moments snatched from his White House job, he even sat for his portrait, painted by Juilus Katzieff of Boston, and presented by friends and college classmates to the college. The portrait offers Adams as an unsmiling man of distinction attired in informal outing clothes, featuring a jacket with "D.O.C." (Dartmouth Outing Club) inscribed upon the breast.

The office in which Adams toiled his full and hectic day was a spacious affair, featuring a massive desk of glossy walnut emblazoned with the presidential seal, a medium-sized conference table, an enormous globe of the world and a wall crammed with pictures. The desk was a gift of Governors Shivers of Texas and Johnston Murray of Oklahoma, and the pictures included a Dartmouth scene, a recent painting by Mrs. Adams, and a rare but incomplete collection of Currier and Ives prints of the Presidents of the United States. Adams discovered most of the prints himself while poking around one day among the pilings of an old woodshed where they had been discarded.

Adams's office, situated in the West Wing of the White House, was a daily scene of mountainous activity and grim concentration. The tension and motion there expended were fully comparable to Grand Central Station at five o'clock. Adams's desk was ordinarily thoroughly paper-strewn, although he displayed uncanny competence at knowing where everything was. Much of his time was spent on the telephone. According to a careful count once made over several days, his calls, in and out of the office combined, averaged 250 a day. On his desk were two telephones, both multi-line affairs, one with a private connection to the President. It was not uncommon for Adams to use both phones simultaneously, one on each ear. The paper work which incessantly converged upon him was colossal. The letters answered each day by Adams's office nearly equalled in number the phone calls. The Governor, who personally disposed of a heavy percentage of the daily epistolary chores, excelled at galloping through a stack of mail in a few minutes time by mumbling a word or two to a secretary, who then did up the letter.

In his prodigious undertakings, Adams was aided by a staff consisting of three secretaries and two assistants, who inhabited a large adjoining office. To his staff, Adams was a tough taskmaster who abominated slackness of any kind. For the slightest deviation from his lofty standards, he meted out punishment that was swift and, in its severity, medieval. Even when there was no offender to be hauled off to the stocks, he would flick out little pointed warnings to those who conceivably might sometime falter. Perhaps the most elaborate salutations he was known to extend to his coworkers were those implying that the coworkers were performing something less than their full duty. "What did you do for your country today?" Adams would ask smartly. When an assistant came in to confer, Adams would offer, "Where do you buy your suits? I hope you're working for them." With that the Governor would jerk his thumb to the chair, into which the thoroughly unnerved assistant sank, and business began.

Adams was constantly doling out these querulous admonitions because of his impossible expectation that everyone should work as hard as he did. He was toughest on his secretaries, among whom there was noticeable turnover. "You either quit Mr. Adams on the second day," one incumbent has said, "or you go through hell for him." It was not unusual for the office scene to be enlivened by a secretary in tears. Some secretaries found that the only way they could maintain a necessary minimum equanimity in their tumultuous surroundings was to shout back at Adams when he was shouting at them. Of the several species of human failing, those that Adams could least abide derived from his passion for accuracy and punctuality. Secretaries knew him as an impeccable speller and indefatigable grammarian, who insisted upon the established usage of the trickiest subjunctives and pronouns. Now and then, his accuracy was a little off, but his insistence never faltered. Tardiness of any kind riled him. Work which was not done on time he could not bear. When a stenographer had the temerity to appear at her White House job at nine o-five one morning, he informed her flatly that she was putting in only half a day. If a file which had to be brought from a nearby building to the White House was not on hand within several minutes, he became bitter, despite the fact that a sprinter, running at his best, could not have covered the distance involved in twice the time.

Like most hard-bitten personalities, Adams on occasion had moments of effusive sentimentality. His sizable, though seldom used, capacity for demonstrativeness is suggested by the several events surrounding the departure of one of his assistants from his hectic White House career for the serenity of private life. This assistant had just been the victim of a blast of adverse publicity attracted, perhaps unavoidably, in his line of duty. The assistant showed up for his final day on the job, with plans to quit his post and entrain for New York at two o'clock in the afternoon. The morning passed uneventfully—only the usual communiques from Adams's office. By eleven o'clock, the assistant was reconciling himself to the eventuality that he would be walking out, in the phrase orbiting around his subconscious, "without a kiss." But at noon the phone rang, and over the wire came the voice of terse authority. "Get lunch," it snapped. "Meet you downstairs." When Adams and the departing assistant entered the staff dining room, every seat was taken, and even more astonishing, fully half the cabinet and all the senior White House staff were present. The convener of the assemblage, it was plain, was Adams. After the meal was over and the tables cleared, the Governor got up and made a touching speech extolling the worth and character of the departing assistant, presented a similarly gracious letter from the President, a desk set from the White House staff and a mounted blowup of a cartoon depicting the assistant and his beloved but turbulent work assignments which he was now abandoning. Two minutes after concluding his heartfelt tribute, Adams was out of the room and off on some fugitive assignment of his own.

Adams was sometimes accused of demonstrating greater appreciation for an assistant's services after the assistant had left the job than in the more vital interval before. Evidence is by no means lacking in support of such a thesis. A secretary who had performed with inspired efficiency for several years finally gave up under the formidable pressures and trailed off into private life. Adams, who cherishes efficiency, idolized this secretary, although he never conveyed any too well his true sentiment during the course of her employment. That he did not is suggested by the fact that the secretary was given to referring to her boss in private as "That Impossible Beast." Some months after her separation from her White House post, the secretary, who was visiting Washington, couldn't resist dropping by her former haunts to say hello. She had hardly arrived when Adams spotted her in the lobby of the West Wing, impulsively picked her up and swung her around the length of the spacious floor. "If only," said the secretary in remorseful retrospection, "he had acted like that when I was here."

Although Eisenhower delegated duties and authority lavishly, Adams was no delegator. He dealt out lots of tasks, his weary associates can well attest, but kept the reins tightly gathered in his fist, by staying in touch with everything and everyone. This he did by maintaining an attitude of supercilious disrespect for jurisdictions and by regarding organization charts as scraps of paper, fit only to be ignored. His professional assistants wrote few papers that he did not see. He called his assistants constantly on the telephone and gave all concerned to understand that for them his door was always open. One assistant who thought he was seeing an awful lot of his chief decided to clock the quantity of time he spent with Adams. On the day selected for observation, the assistant was amazed to find that he had put in nothing less than three full hours in Adams's office. In a sense, Adams couldn't delegate to his associates because he was in reality the prisoner of the staff system he seemingly dominated. Under the chief of staff plan, as conceived by Eisenhower, the President dealt only with Adams, who therefore had to have all the facts in hand in conferring with his chief. Having to face only the Governor greatly simplified life for Eisenhower, but made it immensely difficult for Adams, who had to patrol all the many fronts.

Adams would have been swallowed up quite early in his mountainous job were it not that he was a remarkably fast actor. "A memo you get to him today will be answered tomorrow at the latest," an assistant said. But Adams was capable of swift and deft response in things more complicated than answering office memoranda. In October 1953, for instance, the directorship of the United States Information Agency, which contained the Voice of America program, was vacant and had to be filled quickly. The "Voice" was a whipping boy that Congress for years has taken homicidal glee in lashing, and its headship is without doubt one of the most difficult incumbencies in the history of the Republic. C. D. Jackson of *Fortune*, a White House assistant working in the information field, believed he had the ideal man for the fearsome post. He was Theodore C. Streibert, and one day in a con-

versation with Adams, Jackson delineated Streibert's considerable qualifications. "Get this guy here," ordered the Governor. Streibert, who was on duty
in Germany at the time, arrived on the next plane. He was half willing to
take the job, but only on fulfillment of six formidable conditions which he
had worked out in writing with careful exactitude. Jackson, who met Streibert
at the airport, ushered him around to Adams's office. Just as the prospective
appointee was about to discuss the all-important conditions, Gerald Morgan,
the President's counsel, rushed in to announce that at that very moment
Congress was debating the Voice of America's appropriation and was gesturing menacingly to liquidate the agency. Without asking Streibert, Adams
barked to Morgan, "Take Streibert to the Hill." Streibert put in a busy
morning saving the life of the agency. A cut of twenty-five million dollars
was successfully restored in committee on the assumption that Streibert
would take the job. "What about my conditions?" Streibert asked wearily
after his ordeal. "Forget about the conditions," admonished Jackson. They
returned to Adams's office where Streibert capitulated without a shot.

Adams's most intimate colleagues, aside from his own office force and
President Eisenhower, were a corps of presidential assistants known collectively as the White House staff. The press secretary, the deputy assistant
to the President, the special counsel, the appointments secretary, the secretary to the cabinet and the staff secretary were the V.I.P.'s of the 412 administrators, subadministrators and clerks of the staff, crammed in the maze
of offices in the rooms, basements and hallways, of the East and West Wings
of the White House and the Executive Office building across the street. A
bond which tied these motley officials and lent harmony to their applications
was their unswerving fealty to Adams. Although competition for power and
position characterizes most organizations, animal and human, Adams had no
rival to contend with among his White House colleagues. His primacy was
accepted by one and all as a fixed and unalterable condition of employment.
   In the White House organization of Adams's time, the forces which
spice organizations with lively competition within the membership were
conspicuously lacking. Several powerful factors worked to produce the resulting state of interpersonal calm. For one thing, the key men of the White
House staff had become thoroughly acclimated to Adams's predominance
as chief of staff well before the Administration commenced. In that capacity
he had reigned, while they subordinated themselves, on the campaign train.
The very nature of Adams's position in the Administration was such that it
allowed for no competitors. He was the one member of the staff who could
speak massively with the President on affairs; his colleagues were specialists
—press, Congress, appointments and the like. He dealt with policy in sweep;

they in chunks. The several members of the staff who, by the wildest thrust of the imagination, could possibly challenge Adams were in their upper sixties, a point in the life cycle when the fires of ambition usually recede. In one way or another, the few younger men of the White House staff fitted into the scheme of things. Strictly junior positions were allotted them, and the several who eventually were promoted were denoted by the modesty of their power appetites. The several Taft men who took posts in the White House organization were consigned to positions a step or two down in the hierarchy of power, and a Dewey man, like James Hagerty, wisely and thoroughly transformed himself into an Adams man. In all the years of Adams's reign, the one individual who did not come to terms with the Governor was summarily fired. The victim, Arthur Vandenberg, Jr., son of the late distinguished Senator, had served on the campaign train and was subsequently appointed to the White House staff. After brief service, Vandenberg, spurred by Adams, suddenly resigned.

The entire White House operation was built around the Governor. The several major positions smoothly interlocked with Adams's undertakings and contributed to the increment of his power. They extended his controls over the communications system running to and from the President; they projected an unremittingly favorable image of his handiwork to the public; they provided him supplementary tools of power and opportunities for their exercise. The appointments secretary, for example, deemed it his duty to keep in constant touch with Adams. In setting up the President's daily list of appointments, he routinely checked with Adams, enabling the Governor to veto prospective visitors or fit others in. On the basis of the information received, the Governor could also arrange his own schedule in order to be on hand, as was often desirable or necessary, when Eisenhower met with visitors. The appointments secretary also had a direct telephone line to the President's private secretary, Anne Whitman, to cover in his own and Adams's behalf any alterations in the appointments list initiated by the President himself. As a regular practice, visitors were required to state beforehand the business they proposed to take up with the Chief Executive, and the Governor had free access to the file cards on which the information was recorded. Adams's lively interest in the ingress of visitors derived from his high duty to enforce the inviolable principles of completed staff work. The most horrible breach of efficiency imaginable was for the President to be confronted with a matter which the various relevant experts of the Executive Branch had not yet had opportunity to research, discuss and convert into recommendations. A constant hazard lurked that some fiendish individual, under the guise of a visitor, might sneak an end run around Adams and the executive staff by calling on the President with a proposition before staff studies and clearances had finished their course. By means of his firm grip on the appointments list, Adams forestalled such rascality from materializing.

With James Hagerty, the press secretary, Adams had a partnership which in its method and robust success is reminiscent of a famous collegiate football combination of the nineteen forties, "Mr. Inside" and "Mr. Outside." While Adams toiled behind steely ramparts of secrecy, Hagerty presented the emerging policies to the public with a high Madison Avenue gloss. As a favorite tactic, Hagerty identified good news with the White House—with the President, Adams and the staff—and the not-so-good news with the remoter executive departments. When the satellite, Explorer II, was about to be launched into orbit, for example, Hagerty was asked by reporters if the White House would announce the outcome, as it had done in the case of Explorer I which had been fired successfully. "If it is in orbit," Hagerty said of Explorer II, "we would have an announcement." Suppose Explorer II did not orbit successfully, he was asked. Would the announcement still come from the White House? "No," said Hagerty. Unfortunately, Explorer II fizzled; the Defense Department, not the White House, disclosed the disappointing news.

When necessary, Hagerty also excelled at diverting Adams's considerable activities from public attention. In President Eisenhower's first and severest illness, the coronary, Hagerty was at his artistic best. In a step never before ventured in the history of the United States, he took the country into the President's sickroom, so to speak, by detailing to the press a mass of minutiae concerning the President's diet, hours of sleep, bowel movements and other essentials of daily existence. This seemingly orgiastic candor of the press secretary was in reality a skillful diversionary movement. The country, enraptured by the trivia, was told little, if anything, of the mighty activities of Adams behind the scenes. While Eisenhower lay ill, the Governor in actuality was operating around the clock, in Denver and in Washington, as nothing less than the Acting President of the United States.

Although Adams scrupulously stayed away from the press, his boss, President Eisenhower, has been more accessible to reporters—far less, however, than his immediate predecessors, Harry S. Truman and Franklin D. Roosevelt. The chief engineer of these encounters with the fourth estate was the well-meshed team of Hagerty and Adams. To them, the press conference was a sort of guessing game. Under the rules of the game, a reporter could ask any question he wished without forewarning the White House. To save the President from being caught unprepared, Hagerty, Adams and their colleagues resorted to several precautions prior to the press conference which normally transpired on Wednesdays at ten thirty A.M. By late Tuesday afternoon, Hagerty, after much thought and consultation, developed a list of questions likely to be asked. These he talked over with Adams, who had pretty definite ideas of what the President would wish to say, and sometimes, too, the Governor had his own views of suitable answers. At eight thirty on Wednesday morning, the White House staff gathered with Adams and Hagerty to discuss the press conference scheduled two hours hence. The anticipated questions were run through—how the President might answer them, what information should be given out, and the like. In the several crises of the Benson farm program and the Salk vaccine imbroglio in 1955, the meeting was large and lively. After it broke up around nine thirty, a smaller group met with the President for the final discussion. In a semicircle before Eisenhower's desk, chairs were set out for Adams, Hagerty, General Persons, Mrs. Whitman and a few other assistants. This meeting concluded at least by ten twenty when the President departed for the conference room in the Executive Office building, west of the White House, to face the press.

In Eisenhower's time, the White House has had to meet the onslaught of record-breaking quantities of paper work spewing from the dictaphones and typewriters of the executive departments. Paradoxically, Sherman Adams kept better tabs on the substance and progress of the mountains of documents involved than any other official engaged in the paper work of the Presidency since the founding of the Republic. Aside from the Governor's own remorseless industry, the chief basis of his imposing accomplishment was the little-known staff secretariat. The secretariat system, which is a major administrative innovation of the Eisenhower Presidency, was installed soon after the first inauguration at the President's behest by Carter Burgess, later president of Trans World Airlines. Mr. Burgess had done the same chore with brilliant success in Eisenhower's days at SHAPE. In the presidential administration, the staff secretary, General Andrew J. Goodpaster, kept records on the routing of hundreds of papers, many highly secret, dealing with national security, and many others, not so secret, dealing with domestic affairs. Through the facilities flawlessly managed by Goodpaster, Adams could track down within minutes the location and status of reports, memoranda and letters which had come into the White House or gone out for clearances into the vast reaches of the Executive Branch. He could tell who had prepared a given document, the concurrences received and objections encountered, who was dragging his feet, and other such vital facts of paperwork life. The presiding genius of the massive bookkeeping operation involved, Goodpaster, was tall, scholarly looking, modest in mien and a man of exceptional breadth. The solitary incumbent of his White House post since its establishment, Goodpaster was a West Point graduate and holder of a doctorate of philosophy in international relations and a master's degree in engineering from Princeton University.

Adams was particularly close to General Wilton B. Persons, the deputy assistant to the President whose specialty was Congressional relations. In the scheme of things, Adams often got into legislative matters when policy and politics led him there. To Adams, General Persons was an unfailing ally who thrived on Congressmen. General George C. Marshall once called Persons "the best public relations man in the world." Totally unlike a general, Persons, who was in his sixties and of an old Montgomery, Alabama, family, was an exemplar of Dixie charm and sporty dress. His career as an aide harked back to a day in 1936 when General Malin Craig, Chief of Staff of the Army, resplendent in a white dress uniform, set out for the funeral of Speaker Joseph W. Burns. For this stately occasion, Craig had "borrowed" Major Persons as an aide. "General," said the young major, "I haven't had much experience in this aiding business. If I do anything wrong, please let me know." "That's all right son," answered General Craig, who tended to directness, "just keep your damn feet off my white shoes and you'll be all right."

As close friend and associate of Eisenhower for twenty-five years—their acquaintance commenced when Ike was senior aide to Chief of Staff General Douglass MacArthur—Persons nevertheless accepted Adams's hegemony and genuinely admired him. "A courageous little devil," he would speak of the Governor. Their offices adjoined one another, and the door between was readily opened. When Eisenhower was out of town, both Persons and Adams stayed on duty at the White House. On those rare occasions when Adams left the capital, he did so only by prearrangement assuring that Persons, as the Deputy Assistant to the President, would spell him on the job.

The President's special counsel, a post first established by Franklin D. Roosevelt, was, in the Eisenhower Administration, a favorite refuge for the presidential staff in times of trouble. The incumbent of that lively spot for the greater part of the Administration, Gerald D. Morgan, time and again gladdened Adams and others of the staff by his coolness and competence when the heat was on. He had served briefly on the legal staff of a giant corporation and then ventured to Capitol Hill as a legislative draftsman. Until 1949, he was a registered Democrat. At the outset of the Eisenhower Administration, he took on as assistant to General Persons, and later, when Bernard Shanley, the incumbent special counsel, became appointments secretary, Morgan moved into the vacancy. His main field, as his experience warranted, was legislative policy. He advised Adams in the Governor's encounters with Congress involving knotty questions of law and legal interpretation. Morgan is widely credited with proposing the plea of "executive privilege" which Adams employed on several occasions in refusing information to Congressional committees panting to explore his executive activities. On the fateful day Adams appeared before a House subcommittee to explain his friendship with Bernard Goldfine, Morgan was the only member of the Administration at the Governor's side.

In addition to the invaluable contributions of loyal colleagues in key posts, Adams maintained his undoubted dominion over the White House staff by several contrivances of his own. Although the staff functioned on the basis of specialization, everybody sticking strictly to his bailiwick, Adams himself pried into everything and was readily accessible to one and all. The staff fast learned the wisdom of the unwritten rule, "check with Adams." The Governor also held staff meetings regularly with the major members and many junior members of the White House organization present. The meetings, which occurred twice a week in the Administration's earlier years, subsequently transpired once a week, usually for exactly forty minutes running time. With an agenda and swift pace, the meetings better enabled the Governor to keep up with the doings of the staff and to delineate to one and all the policies he wished advanced.

Adams more easily held his sway due to the extraordinary stability of the membership of the staff. Although now and then they changed jobs within the White House organization, the tenure of nearly all the major members of the staff dated back to the founding of the Administration. This pleasing spectacle of friendly familiar faces, Adams helped perpetuate with several well-chosen measures of his own. If on occasion vacancies did arise, they were filled not by recruitment from the outside, but from within. When by unusual necessity the outside had to be resorted to, there was noticeable preference for former members of the White House staff, who for one reason or another had retired to private life, to be brought back in. Thomas E. Stephens, for example, one of the more politically sophisticated members of the White House circle, after service as appointments secretary, retreated briefly to his Washington law practice, only to be redrafted to his old job. Robert A. Cutler, finishing a stint as assistant for national security affairs, retired to his Boston banker's trade, but before many a month was hauled back to his former official post. But the usual practice of the White House staff when vacancies arose was for the major personnel already on the job to shift about, and for junior persons—usually Adams's own assistants—to be raised to the lesser of the senior positions left open by the adjusting. Various senior personnel, consequently, put in stints in at least several top-level posts. Bernard Shanley, for example, served successively as special counsel and appointments secretary, and Gerald Morgan as administrative assistant and special counsel. This was how they played the game of musical chairs at the White House, and the big winner was invariably Governor Adams.

In adapting the military staff system to the necessities of the Presidency, Eisenhower viewed his cabinet secretaries essentially as theater commanders. Like field generals, the several secretaries were invested with broad initiative and responsibility for allotted sectors of operations. The President, in contrast, skillfully and consistently minimized his own involvement. In the wake of the unsettling exposures by the McClellan Committee on Improper Activities in the Labor-Management Field, for example, the President was asked whether he considered new legislation necessary to cope with the problems typified by Dave Beck, Jimmy Hoffa, and the Teamsters' Union. Eisenhower's reply was one of characteristic withdrawal. "Well," he said revealingly, "I have merely been told by the Labor Secretary they are watching this very closely and see whether we have any responsibility or anything we could do reasonably."* Yet for all of the seeming freedom of the executive departments to pursue their separate destinies, the Eisenhower Administration has been denoted by a unity, or, to use the idiom of the day, a "teamwork," which contrasts sharply with the skull-breaking interdepartmental donnybrooks of the preceding administrations of Roosevelt and Truman. The man most responsible for maintaining tranquillity in lieu of brassy chaos was Sherman Adams. Wielding a big stick, with flourishes of varying subtlety or lack thereof, Adams made the departments behave.

A survey conducted in 1957 revealed that in an amazing preponderance of instances, department secretaries who followed the rules and saw Adams first, never got to see the President. For most business, Adams was the point of final decision. One department secretary, when asked how often he saw the President, answered candidly, "I deal mostly with Sherman Adams." Members of the Governor's staff, seeking in the interests of public relations to play down Adams's role, were tireless in pointing out that on the desk of every cabinet secretary was an ivory telephone connecting directly with the President's line. But according to the evidence compiled, the special telephones were seldom used. One department secretary said, "I call the President on the phone maybe twice a month; see him privately only occasionally." Another explained, "It may be once a month that we talk on the telephone, unless a crisis comes up." And another, "I see the President at cabinet meetings, have private talks several times a month, talk to him rarely on the telephone."

The solitary exception was the Secretary of State, John Foster Dulles. When he was in Washington, Dulles might telephone the President twenty-five or thirty times a week, drop in at the White House three or four times in addition, and, on weekends, if Eisenhower was in town, stop in on Sunday afternoons. The President revered Dulles as a mentor and accorded him enormous latitude in foreign policy. Dulles, on the other hand, in his unremitting communications, gave the President an account of what often were almost hour-by-hour developments in a situation, thus enabling Eisenhower to approve or disapprove the formative steps as they were taken. Unless the matter became political, Adams stayed on the periphery of these proceedings.

* Press conference of April 17, 1957; *The New York Times*, April 18, 1957.

The Governor, however, was given to interpreting "political" broadly, and when he did, the consequences for Mr. Dulles and the State Department were sometimes shattering. As the scheduled conferences of the heads of state of the North Atlantic alliance approached in 1958, for example, Dulles was especially eager that Adlai Stevenson be made a member of the United States delegation. The presence of the former Democratic presidential candidate would strike a needed blow for bipartisan foreign policy, and would bring to the common task a man of experience and resourcefulness. Stevenson at the time was serving as special State Department consultant, assisting in preparations for the conference. Secretary Dulles proposed that the President extend a fitting invitation to Stevenson to join the delegation and attend the Paris meetings. But the presidential invitation issued only after some delay and, even worse, its tone was decidedly halfhearted. Stevenson, under the circumstances, had small choice but to decline. The disappointed Mr. Dulles and his departmental aides did not blame the coolness toward Stevenson upon the President but upon his several domestic advisers, the chief of whom was Adams. For it was the Governor, who in the course of a speech in Chicago declared—without naming Stevenson—that some advisers the Administration had considered taking to the NATO conference were of dubious quality. Mr. Stevenson was said to have regarded the Governor's remark as being in "bad taste."

Adams was equally successful in throttling another cherished project of Mr. Dulles several years earlier, in 1955. Dulles, at the time, was eager to place Benjamin V. Cohen, the New Dealer, on the American delegation to the United Nations. The two had worked closely in the Truman Administration where Dulles was a kind of roving ambassador and symbol of bipartisan co-operation, while Cohen served on the UN delegation with acknowledged distinction. Several years later, in the Eisenhower Administration, Dulles thought it would be good for the Administration and the country if Cohen repeated the UN assignment. He sounded out the ex-New Dealer, and to the great delight of the Secretary of State, Cohen expressed willingness to take on the job. As rumors of the impending appointment began to circulate, several members of the Republican right wing, outraged at the prospect that an extra-liberal Democrat should represent the United States in the era of a Republican Administration, went to Adams and forcefully made known their dissatisfaction. Dulles at the time was out of the country. Adams, mindful that the appointment would have to run the gantlet of Senatorial consent, took the extraordinary step of calling on Cohen at his Washington apartment to ask him to withdraw his acceptance of the Dulles offer. A lot of trouble was in store on Capitol Hill, said Adams. Would Cohen therefore forget his promise to Dulles, spare the Governor from sending his name to the Senate, and avoid the embarrassment of an inevitable row? After thinking it over, Cohen acquiesced. His withdrawal was a *fait accompli* some days before Dulles returned to the United States.

Adams also shaped the destinies of the departments by his impact on the functioning of the cabinet. In the Eisenhower Administration, the cabinet, which historically is typified by innocuous meandering discussion, has for the first time been put on a businesslike basis. A cabinet secretary, agenda, position papers, records of action taken and other impedimenta of orderly procedure have been installed. The renovation of the cabinet originated with Eisenhower, who considered it sheer folly to send men into meetings without any foreknowledge of what it was they were to talk about. First to serve as cabinet secretary was Maxwell Rabb, a former aide to Senator Henry Cabot Lodge and a valiant battler in the rugged New Hampshire primary of 1952. Chosen for his post jointly by Eisenhower and Adams, Rabb was a man of kinetic vitality and monumental industry, who served as secretary until 1955 when he stepped down to enter private law practice. His successor was the bright and personable Robert Gray of Nebraska. The cabinet secretary worked very closely with Adams. Indeed, both Rabb and Gray put in apprenticeships as assistants to Adams previous to their cabinet assignments. Although the secretary organized the cabinet agenda, Adams often made the big decisions involved. Perched on the apex of the executive structure, he could best spot the issues requiring consideration and was constantly consulted in preliminary stages, when the agenda was being pulled together and just before it was hammered into final form. In his blue-penciling, which was uninhibited, Adams might say that some items had already been taken care of or could be handled in other ways, that others should be added, or still others dropped because they might evoke conflict, which for the present had better be avoided. Adams got into decisions concerning the placing of items on the agenda and the time allotted for their consideration. There were sizable opportunities for tactical maneuvering, and he used them.

Adams attended all meetings of the cabinet, taking his place at the end of the long coffinlike conference table, somewhat removed from the President, who sat in the middle. Never talkative in meetings or conferences, the Governor spoke seldom in the cabinet and then only briefly. Normally, he took the floor only if called upon, or if he wished to cast out observations of some urgency. His chief impact upon the cabinet derived from his role in implementation and follow-up. Although the departments might agree in cabinet meetings on general principles and plans in outline, they were prone to disagree, dawdle and renege, in the acid test of applying decisions taken in cabinet. Sherman Adams excelled as a breaker of impasses, or as one department secretary put it, "Adams is a strong influence to solutions." Among the Governor's more powerful inducements was the "Action Status Report," which, through the cabinet secretary, was exacted from the departments every three months or oftener if necessary. The report disclosed the action taken or not taken, as the case might be, in response to cabinet determinations. The reports were considered in full cabinet meeting, an occasion that was referred to, in semijest, as "operation needling." The embarrassment of exposure as a delinquent before the President, as the Action Status Reports could bring to pass, ordinarily sufficed to spur a department into honoring its obligations. If there wasn't time to wait for the report, Adams worked intensively through a subcabinet of his own—of under secretaries who met weekly, with the Governor presiding. There he got things done because the under secretaries were the real control centers of implementation in the departments. Adams also worked with the "cabinet assistants," a group of assistant secretaries and executive assistants to the Secretaries. This more junior category in the hierarchy of command comprised the younger men, the principal sources of energy and the focus of ideas in the departments. The cabinet assistants met after each cabinet meeting. In their undertakings with Adams, the assistant and under secretaries worked in an atmosphere whose compulsion was "teamwork," and the watchwords pasted securely in everyone's mind were, "Don't waste the President's time."

Adams was a major wirepuller in the hiring and firing of cabinet secretaries and their seconds-in-command, the under secretaries. By every indication, the Governor was prime mover of the sudden departure of Mrs. Oveta Culp Hobby from her post as Secretary of Welfare in 1955. Mrs. Hobby was widely blamed for the failure of federal testing procedures to prevent production of lethal batches of polio vaccine and for the lack of a plan to assure a fair distribution of the newly developed vaccine when supplies again became available after having been shut off for weeks pending retests. Adams picked up the feeling in many places that Mrs. Hobby should go and took initiative in urging the move upon the President. The Governor was similarly influential in 1956 when Douglas McKay suddenly found himself no longer the Secretary of the Interior, but an unsuccessful candidate in Oregon for the United States Senate. As Interior Secretary, Mr. McKay's unflagging devotion to private-power interests and limited forcefulness in his post, embarrassed the Administration politically, prompting Adams to launch his spirited maneuvers.

Some cabinet secretaries resigned not because Adams particularly wanted them to, but because they could no longer stomach his interferences in the affairs of their departments. When Herbert Brownell stepped down with pointed abruptness as Attorney General in 1957, his drastic action was attributed to recurrent differences with Adams. This state of limited hostilities, which quickly became intolerable, commenced with the ill-fated natural gas bill of 1956. Adams had urged Eisenhower to recommend the bill; Brownell opposed it and only after copious argument succeeded in bringing the President to veto the enacted legislation. Even then Brownell prevailed only because the bungling tactics of the natural gas lobby had offended public opinion. Various other clashes with Adams followed until matters came to a head in the first Little Rock school crisis. Brownell was upset at Adams's instigation of the invitation extended to Governor Orval Faubus of Arkansas to meet with Eisenhower at Newport, Rhode Island, where the President was vacationing at the time. Adams's hope was that a face-to-face conference would result in a workable consensus. Faubus came to Newport, but the meeting proved completely abortive. What troubled Brownell was not so much the failure of the meeting, but the issuance of the invitation in the first place. This act, the Attorney General argued, seemed to cloak Faubus with a dignity he didn't deserve.

Although Adams tended to judge the department heads severely, he by no means had a perfect batting average in toppling every luminary who in his opinion was a drag politically upon the Administration. One secretary, who endured like the rock of Gibraltar against the crashing political waves, was the Secretary of Agriculture, Ezra Taft Benson. Sometime before the Congressional elections of 1956, Adams became convinced that Secretary Benson had become an impossible liability because of the anguish the Secretary's program had wrought among farming interests far and wide. Vice-President Nixon and other Administration notables strongly concurred with Adams's analysis. But try as the Governor and his allies might in their importunities to the President to depose Benson, they got nowhere. The President's loyalty to his Secretary of Agriculture was fixed and immovable.

Sherman Adams not only cast out department secretaries; he had a large hand in filling vacancies and, in time, in reshaping the cabinet. The changes involved were substantial. At the close of the President's first term, the cabinet and subcabinet included many men basically out of sympathy with Modern Republicanism. Secretary of Defense Charles E. Wilson, Secretary of the Treasury Humphrey, Under Secretary of State Herbert Hoover, Jr., Under Secretary of Defense Reuben Robertson and others were all conservatively oriented in their social thinking. On questions of public expenditure, foreign aid and social security, their predisposition above all else, was to balance the budget. In the second Eisenhower Administration, the several earlier conservatives were supplanted by men of more liberal persuasion, of whom Robert B. Anderson, Neil H. McElroy, Christian Herter and Donald A. Quarles were typical. Although the new regime did not necessarily make the Administration more liberal, it permitted the development of policy with less of the internal conflict and uncertainty which afflicted Eisenhower's first term.

Meanwhile, President Eisenhower's own sympathies, interestingly enough, gravitated, not to the left, in the manner of his cabinet, but to the right. The President himself said as much in a press conference on May 15, 1957, when he engaged in the following passage of self-analysis. "If anything," he declared, "I think I have grown more conservative. . . . I am absolutely against trifling with our financial integrity, and I believe that all of these [social] programs must be studied very, very carefully to see that we are not taking on more of a load than is good for the whole country." The Eisenhower Administration, accordingly, presents an arresting paradox. As the cabinet grew more liberal, the President grew more conservative. The first cabinet was more a reflection of Eisenhower, the second, in contrast, was more a reflection of Adams. The explanation of this political "believe-it-or-not-by-Ripley" seems to be that the President tended not to originate appointments, but to confirm automatically those selected by others. One of the busiest of the selectors, it is clear, was Sherman Adams. It was not for nothing that the President's older brother, Edgar, startled the nation by baldly declaring one morning that Ike was under the "excessively liberal" influence of "Milton" and "Sherm." Edgar Eisenhower deserves to be accredited as a man of some perception.

"I don't believe," Sherman Adams once said, "there's a different set of rules for working with Congress than for working with other people." This statement deserves to be ranked either as one of the most naïve or one of the most arrogant ever made in the annals of politics. It is also an indicator of incontrovertible accuracy of Adams's approach to Congress. He did, in fact, treat Congressmen no better or no worse than he treated general mankind. The Governor, accordingly, growled and snapped and took healthy bites out of the pride of influential legislators just as he did with citizens of lesser station. Although some legislators, realizing the pressures Adams was under in his big job, were tolerant of his manner, his slights and rebukes prompted scores of Congressmen to turn against him. Of those he singled out for punishment, Adams was roughest on fools and blabbers, and since Congress is truly representative of human frailty, the Governor was busy. Another specie he couldn't abide was the man who mulls things over. Like most politicians, Congressmen are exceedingly prone to do this, and it was they who gave the fast-acting Adams his most terrible moments of apoplectic exasperation.

It can reasonably be contended, however, that Adams's business with Congress, by its very nature, inevitably involved stepping on toes and curdling sensitivities. Adams, for example, handed out job plums. Dozens of constituents, aided and abetted by legislators, might clamor unmercifully for the same job. "Patronage," William Howard Taft sagely observed decades ago, "creates nine enemies and one ingrate." Adams daily learned the awful truth of Mr. Taft's cheerless aphorism.

Adams had other powers of dispensation whose mere exercise created more enemies than friends. He worked out the President's speaking itinerary and other personal appearances in election years and off years. As a normal condition of things, everybody wants the President to speak everywhere all the time. In discharging his responsibility, Adams considered it his sacred trust to protect the President's interests, particularly the demands upon his energy, a duty the Governor regarded with uncompromising purpose after Eisenhower's several illnesses. To Congressmen or Senators embroiled in fights for re-election, the appearance of the President in their constituencies for a stopover or a speech is manna from the heavens. Even the most tactfully delivered negative from Adams was apt to be taken ungraciously by the legislator battling for his political life. Typical of the quandaries Adams had to face was one arising several years ago when the President made a brief trip to New England under circumstances which permitted but one speech to be scheduled. Republican legislators and local party chieftains from the several New England states clamored wildly for the privilege of Eisenhower's presence. Adams duly decided in favor of the annual dairy festival held at Rutland, Vermont. This decision, when it was handed down, didn't exactly ingratiate Adams with the Republican organizations in at least several New England states where the outcome of the impending electoral struggles was exceedingly doubtful.

The President's personal appearances about the country involved several subsidiary decisions of consequence in which Adams's influence was important, if not controlling. It is of great moment to the local candidate whether the President makes a two-minute appearance at the railroad crossing on the far edge of town, or takes part in a ceremony in the central public square. Equally momentous to the local candidate is the place assigned him in the drama to be played by the group on the platform with the President— whether he is to be near to or far from the Chief Executive, whether the President will put his arm around the candidate's shoulders for the photographers, and whether warm or lukewarm references will be made to the candidate in the President's speech. In settling these magnitudinous issues, Adams had room for maneuver which, upon checking the candidate's voting record and campaign promises, he was not averse to using.

The brunt of White House dealings with Congress fell not upon Adams but upon General Persons and his seven assistants, who served as links between Congress and the departments and oversaw the progress of Administration-supported legislation. No neat dividing line existed between Persons's and Adams's jobs. Southern legislators tended to do business with Persons because he hailed from their region, and New Englanders likewise resorted to Adams. Congressmen of both parties who knew Adams during his term in the House of Representatives were apt to work through him in the White House. Legislators were also apt to go to Adams when seeking some personal favor from the President—a letter from the Chief Executive congratulating a local college upon its birthday, or an autographed picture of the President which a deserving constituent was eager to come by.

Adams was much involved in the more formal occasions of Executive-Congressional affairs established by law and practice. He participated in the President's regular Tuesday-morning meetings with the Republican Congressional leaders where goals, measures and stratagems for the Administration's legislative program in the coming week were discussed and formulated. Eisenhower presided at these sessions; General Persons saw to the agenda and acted as secretary. Others regularly in attendance included the several Congressional leaders, the Vice-President, the Director of the Budget and Adams. If business required, department secretaries and the senior Republican members of the relevant House and Senate committees also were on hand. Adams's customary deportment in these sessions was to keep silent unless called upon for comment. When he did take the floor, he scrupulously avoided embroilment with the legislators. The Governor's self-restraint, which admittedly was rather out of character, was in deference to Eisenhower's preference for constructive negotiation in a friendly atmosphere. When he had to get tough with Congressmen, Adams did so on the telephone and in his own office. If a fight was called for, he struck at his legislative foes not in Eisenhower's presence, but on the more favorable terrain of patronage and in the arrangement of presidential speaking appearances.

Adams oversaw the mammoth preparations made in the Executive Branch each year for the impending session of Congress. His efforts were focussed upon three great presidential documents conveyed to Congress in January: the Budget, the State of the Union Message and the Economic Report. To the departments, these documents were crucial, for much of the program planning and policy innovation at the department level takes legislative form—appropriations, appointments, new statutory authority, and the like. In budgeting, Adams constituted the first court of appeal for the departments against the Bureau of the Budget. No one, it should be added, exercised similar power and responsibility in the preceding administrations of Roosevelt and Truman. Adams was terribly busy in his appellate capacity in the long days when the budget-balancing philosophy of George Humphrey held sway. The parsimony of the Secretary of the Treasury bore down especially hard on domestic activities and therefore on such departments as the Department of Health, Education and Welfare, in which social aid programs are largely concentrated. HEW was repeatedly in conflict with the

Budget Bureau, an organization Mr. Humphrey freely dominated as an outlet for his views. But each time its finances were in jeopardy, HEW turned for surcease to Adams, the apostle of modern Republicanism. He never let HEW down.

Adams was in the thick of preparations of the State of the Union Message, which incorporated the departments' proposals and plans in general terms and was followed by special messages of fuller detail and drafts of legislation. Each fall, Adams staged intensive meetings with department officials, who outlined in broad strokes their major projects for the coming legislative session. The Governor exercised sharp scrutiny over the business before him, ruthlessly ripping out the impractical and imparting clarity to the fuzzily conceived. After the purifying ordeal with Adams, the departments refurbished their programs and trotted them out for discussion in special sessions of the cabinet, followed by similar sessions with the legislative leaders. But it was usually in the interchange with Adams that the definitive far-reaching decisions were made.

In legislative, as in executive affairs, the President took on the pleasant missions, while Adams conveyed the harsh word and sprang the fierce maneuver. Eisenhower eschewed conflict to the point that he used the veto power only sparingly, not wishing to impair the atmosphere of good will he was striving to build with the implicit hostility of the device. The President courted Congressional understanding and support by systematically entertaining groups of legislators at breakfasts and luncheons at regular intervals. He applied unstintingly his great personal magnetism to the cultivation of his formidable erstwhile rival, Senator Taft. The lasting peace consummated with Taft was a major achievement of the Administration in legislative relations. It was due partly to Eisenhower's charm, the Senator's own good sense and the diligence of I. Jack Martin, a White House assistant and a former aide to Taft. Adams, it seems, played a minor but constructive part in the great diplomatic venture, although the ferocity of his battle with the Taft forces at the Chicago Convention of 1952 had hardly augured well. Faithful to Eisenhower's wishes, Adams was always nice to Taft. One of the last things the Senator was heard to say at the capitol before his death was, "Adams goes out of his way to seem friendly."

More characteristically, Adams, as the center of political maneuver in the Administration, was in the thick of the roughest legislative fights. As the attacks of Senator McCarthy upon the Administration mounted in 1953, for example, Adams, according to sworn testimony, first suggested that in retaliation the Army draw up a record of its dispute with the Senator, and the resulting compilation provided the basis of the later explosive Army-McCarthy hearings. Adams's proposal was made at an Administration strategy conference held in the Justice Department early in the quarrel, with the Governor playing the dominant role. McCarthy himself averred that the charges subsequently made against him grew out of this meeting.

Adams was one of the few members of Eisenhower's inner circle endowed with substantial political experience, and its only figure who had left high public office—a Governorship—to come to Washington. The President regarded the knowledgeable Adams as something of a political genius, and upon the Governor's shoulders fell large responsibilities for devising political strategy and overseeing the grinding detail of party affairs and political management.

Adams was master of patronage. He approved every job appointment before it was made and supervised the elaborate checking involved. Altogether patronage was his most voluminous duty. In the Administration's first two years, approximately fifty-seven thousand jobs were filled, and oftentimes the figure soared to a prodigious one hundred. Helping Adams to face the manswarm of job-hungry Republicans, was an assistant plus a force of six outrageously overworked secretaries jammed in a room on the second floor of the White House West Wing. The assistantship was one of the more harassed positions in government employment. Of the three assistants who successively served under Adams, one was forced out by the unmerciful cudgeling of newspaper columnists, another cracked up under the terrific tension and the third transferred to other employment in the White House office with noticeable alacrity when the opportunity arose. The incumbent who served first and longest was Charles F. Willis, a business executive with no prior government experience, who had headed up Citizens for Eisenhower in the 1952 campaign. Although Republicans, twenty years out of power, couldn't push to the patronage trough fast enough, Willis was able to superimpose a remarkable amount of order upon the chaos.

He installed a Remington Rand card index system, itemizing the essential facts of the jobs to be filled. When the system really got rolling, the index encompassed jobs to be available up to as much as eight months prior to the date on which the vacancy would arise. Characteristically, names to be considered for a given vacancy poured in from every side—from Senators, Congressmen, the Republican National Committee, state and local party organizations, the executive departments and citizens of various influence. Each name proposed was entered on a file card, on which was also placed the several kinds of information accumulated for every candidate. The National Committee researched the man's political soundness, Willis his ability, and the FBI did the security check. As the file on a serious candidate built up, Willis consulted with Adams, who pointed out aspects meriting further exploration. Adams was also the link to Eisenhower; on many appointments the President had suggestions of his own. Eventually, Willis put together a package of six names and he and Adams took on the sometimes harrowing chore of narrowing it down to a single recommendation to the President. In judging a candidate, Adams's pet criterion was the man's industry. If the assembled reports gave the least scintilla of an impression that "he's lazy," the fellow was done for. Ability and politics took a back seat to application when the Governor was filling jobs. Once a choice had been settled upon, and before any official announcement issued, Adams or Willis sounded out the candidate as to his receptivity, thus sparing the President the possible embarrassment of being turned down.

Various other hazards lurked in the patronage trade. When a candidate was clearly leading the pack for a major vacancy, the danger loomed that the imminence of his appointment might leak out to those most interested in the outcome. In that event, a decidedly less pleasant phase of the game commenced. Legislators and party figures championing other candidates would gang up on the man in the lead with all sorts of objections, born of the ingenuity of desperation. As the tempest spread, Adams and his aides had to struggle hard to keep their perspective, and the chances of not a few front-runners were lost in the deluge of criticism.

In dealing out jobs, Adams and Willis were dealing out heartbreaks. Sherman Adams's worst enemies in the Republican party were those who were incensed over his job decisions. Purveyors of patronage, as Adams and his assistants well knew, are also viewed as devils incarnate in quarters devoted to the protection and advancement of the merit system in the public service. In the Governor's time, the guardians of the merit system were alert and vocal, and commanded wide and ready support. Indeed, Willis, Adams's assistant, was ejected from the Administration by the outcry of one most articulate defender of merit, Jerry Klutzz, whose influential and widely read column on life in the civil service, The Federal Diary, appears in the Washington Post. In a front-page article, accompanied by a screaming headline: "Jobs for Republicans Campaign Headed by Adams' Office," Klutzz reproduced the several forms and a covering memorandum developed by Willis and distributed to high officials in an effort to earmark desirable merit jobs for deserving Republicans. Promptly after Klutzz's exposé, cries of outrage reverberated from such various sources as the Democrats in Congress, the National Civil Service League and Drew Pearson. Adams's chief assistant was not long in resigning his post and heading for the sanctuary of private life.

Adams on occasion was a major party orator. Although he shrouded his administrative activities in absolute secrecy, he loved nothing better than to get on the political stump and swing a verbal shillelagh. There the Governor didn't explain or defend himself and his work; he concentrated on attacking others. Quite possibly his periodic indulgence in such routs was a kind of therapy for the frustrating silence of his pent-up White House position. Certainly the most vituperative attacks upon the Democrats in the Eisenhower Administration issued from the mouth of the Governor. In the uninhibited stridency of his oratory, he clearly ranks with Harry Truman— Adams, too, "gave 'em Hell!" In the Congressional elections of 1954, for example, he wailed that unless a Republican Congress were elected, the nation "could be turned back once more to the spending sprees and political orgies to which the American people called a halt in 1952." In general, the Democrats were mauled pretty badly at the Governor's partisan hands. The party of the opposition was variously depicted as "fused by lust for privileges of public office . . . our befuddled foe, the donkey! . . . a party unbridgeably split . . . a political monstrosity that has two heads, two hearts, and two souls . . . addle-brained donkey . . . split personality all shook up."

Adams's renderings of sledge-hammer statements were not limited to the Democrats. When the situation called for it, he cauld give his own Republican party a thumping good lecture as well. He loved to employ the dire threat. When in Adams's judgment (and probably Eisenhower's too), Congressional Republicans were laggard in supporting the President's program in 1955, the Governor concluded that it was high time to instill a little fear into his party colleagues. This he did by baldly declaring that unless the legislative output improved, which could occur only by the casting of more Republican votes for Administration-sponsored measures, Eisenhower would soon become so discouraged with the situation that he absolutely would not be a candidate for re-election in 1956. Adams hoped and expected that the eagerness of Congressional Republicans to have the President run again would bring them to their voting senses. The Governor also excelled in the straight rebuke. Once, fed up with the incessant feuding in Republican ranks, he declared to a regional conference of the party's leaders at Trenton, New Jersey, on May 24, 1957, "It's time we looked hard at our growing propensity to find motes in our colleague's eyes, to harp about our primly adjusted party haloes, to pass judgments, and to bandy about epithets, as though we ourselves were our own worst enemies—political or otherwise. It is time that we, as a Party, mind an old adage—'What Peter says about Paul tells more about Peter than it tells about Paul.' "

As the President's deputy, Adams dealt with many sectors of the Republican party organization. In peak seasons, he was usually in touch by telephone with the national committee chairman two or three times a day. Both Leonard Hall and Meade Alcorn, the successive chairmen during Adams's tenure in the Eisenhower Administration, dealt far more with Adams than with Eisenhower. (Alcorn, indeed, was a fellow Dartmouth alumnus and old friend of Adams. When Hall stepped down, the Governor put the necessary pressures upon Alcorn to abandon private contentment and success for the ordeal of the party post.) Characteristically, Adams and the chairman explored and settled problems, resorting to the President only when a matter was buttoned up and higher approval was necessary.

All manner of business occupied Adams and the chairman—knotty patronage questions; aid for a Governor or Congressman imperilled in an approaching election; the time, place and substance of the President's speeches. The Governor was also a bridge between the party and the executive departments. In 1957, for example, both organizations were interested in the position to be taken on the "right to work laws," already enacted in a handful of states and augured in more. The laws, in effect, prohibited the union shop by forbidding the requirement of union membership as a condition of employment. Bitterly resisted by organized labor, the right-to-work laws promised to constitute a leading issue in the impending 1958 elections. Meanwhile, the Administration, struggling to determine its position, was sharply divided. Several cabinet secretaries were arguing that legitimate union interests and political reality required that the national government displace the states by prohibiting right-to-work laws altogether. Other cabinet secretaries, whose inclinations were conservative, favored national legislation to encourage and support state laws. The party organization, its eye on the approaching elections of 1958 and the divisions on the question within its ranks, bucked for a middle-of-the-road position, leaving the laws wholly to the states, the Administration taking no position, pro or con. Adams cast his lot with his party friends, and they prevailed.

In the electoral campaigns of 1954 and 1956, the Governor or his deputy met at least several times weekly with the Chairmen of the Republican Congressional and Senatorial campaign committees. With the chairmen, Adams engaged in a constant tug of war, they pulling for more presidential speeches to help the ticket, he pulling for less. In the heyday of his power, Adams was given to intervening behind the scenes in state committee meetings and conventions engaged in selecting delegates to the national convention. The purpose of Adams's manipulations was to see that of several possible delegates, the right one, from the White House's standpoint, was ultimately chosen. In 1957, the Governor also dared to approach the California situation, a caldron bubbling over with trouble. Senator William F. Knowland, whose term was expiring, coveted the impending gubernatorial nomination. The difficulty was that the incumbent Republican Governor, the popular Goodwin J. Knight, proposed to succeed himself in office. For some weeks, the two local Republican mastodons were locked in a behind-the-scenes struggle when Adams headed west as an envoy of peace. He conveniently made a speech in San Francisco, thus reducing the appearance of crisis or presidential intervention. While on California soil, however, he had a long unpublicized conference with Governor Knight. In the meeting, Adams urged that an intraparty fight be avoided at all costs and that, everything considered, it might be well if Knight discussed the situation with the President. Subsequently Knight came on to Washington for the recommended conversation, renounced his interest in the Governorship, leaving the field to Knowland, and became a candidate for the latter's seat in the Senate. Although a large amount of bad feeling persisted between Knowland, Knight, and their followings, Adams's and Eisenhower's mediations avoided a public explosion.

For all of his usefulness, Adams at no time in his White House career would have rated very high in a Republican popularity poll. He was least liked among the Republican right wing, which he irreparably alienated in his battle with the Taft forces in Chicago in 1952. His distribution of patronage was also not to their liking, and even less his plumping for a liberal party course. For the Right Wingers who couldn't afford to attack the popular Eisenhower, Adams was a favorite whipping boy. In moments of displeasure, Senator McCarthy was apt to hit at Adams as head man of a little conspiratorial clique insulating the President from the Republican organization and political reality. In right-wing quarters generally, party tragedies were indiscriminately blamed upon Adams. When the Republicans did poorly in the 1954 Congressional elections, Clarence Buddington Kelland, the author and conservative Republican committeeman of Arizona, instantaneously blamed the debacle on "the dolts who have usurped control of the party." He had Adams and company in mind. When, finally, Adams floundered in the Goldfine swampland, those who most shrilly encouraged him to sink into the depths and out of sight for the good of his party were the Republican conservatives.

Adams's special and most solemn responsibility was to keep the Administration pure and incorruptible. In the 1952 campaign, Eisenhower repeatedly pledged himself to substitute for the moral sloth of deep freezes and mink coats of the Truman era a new presidential administration, whose affairs would, in his powerful vote-getting cliché, be "as clean as a hound's tooth." Again and again, long after the election, the President voiced his dedication to the loftiest standards of official conduct. "I do not believe," he declared on July 7, 1955, "any man can hold public office merely because he is not guilty of any illegal act. . . . His actions [have] to be impeccable both from the standpoint of law and from the standpoint of ethics." On May 4, 1956, "If anyone ever comes to any part of this government claiming some privilege for even to as low as an introduction to an official he wants to meet, on the basis that he is part of my family or my friends, that he has any connection with the White House he is to be thrown out instantly, and I cannot believe that anybody on my staff would ever be guilty of anything indiscreet, but if ever anything came to my attention of that kind, any part of this government, that individual would be gone." (sic)

Adams also was a vocal high priest of moral probity. Eisenhower won in 1952, the Governor declared in his vivid manner, because the people were "sick and tired of reading in the papers about some mischievous rascals trying to steal the gold out of Fort Knox." He pursued his special responsibility of policing the morality of the Administration with the fervor of a Salem witch hunter. For infractors, minor and serious, his justice was stern and swift. Peter Strobel, Commissioner of the Public Buildings Service, is a case in point. It was brought to light that Strobel, in his official capacity, was passing upon contracts awarded by the Public Buildings Service to companies which were customers of a firm Strobel in private life headed in New York City. Although Congressman Emanuel Celler, head of a House committee investigating the matter, concluded that nothing illegal had been done, he did question the "propriety" of Strobel's conduct. Adams quickly moved in on the case and, in his efficient way, saw to it that Strobel's resignation was immediately forthcoming. When the House Subcommittee on Legislative Oversight revealed in March, 1958, that Richard A. Mack, as a member of the Federal Communications Commission had received loans and other financial assistance from a friend interested in the award of a Miami television channel, Adams acted with force and dispatch. On the day of the subcommittee's revelations, he called Mr. Mack on the telephone and declared that while the President was willing to let the commissioner resign instead of dismissing him, a suitable letter would have to be forthcoming at once. Mack pleaded with Adams to wait until "all the evidence is in" before judging the case, but the Governor was adamant. In fact, the commissioner's friends said he was still protesting his innocence when Adams hung up.

But Sherman Adams, the man of contradictions, was far more than a one-man moral posse for the Federal Communications Commission, the Civil Aeronautics Board, the Securities and Exchange Commission, and other such bodies which license television stations, airlines and stock issuances, and choose between private entrepreneurs avidly competing for the privileges bestowed. The Queensbury rules do not apply in the struggle, and it is easy to see why. In handing down a decision assigning, say, a television channel, or authorizing the operation of a station, the commissions are, as a commonplace, doling out potential fortunes worth millions of dollars. Although the commissions are supposedly "independent," they are in fact subject to varying degrees of executive and legislative influence and control in carrying on their monumental business. Adams, for example, met periodically with various commission chairmen to go over policy and personnel. The Governor didn't just engage in chitchat in these sessions; the evidence is indisputable that he intervened rather positively in the affairs of the commissions on at least several occasions.

In 1955, for example, Sinclair Armstrong, Chairman of the Securities and Exchange Commission, testified under oath before the Kefauver committee that Adams had telephoned him on June eleventh of that year, asking that he postpone hearings scheduled for June thirteenth by the Securities and Exchange Commission on the Dixon-Yates power project. On this same day of June thirteenth, the Dixon-Yates project faced a critical test in the House of Representatives. On the day on which the SEC hearings were to take place, the House of Representatives was scheduled to commence debate on a $6,500,000 appropriation for a vital transmission line to the Dixon-Yates site. The SEC hearings, had they proceeded, would have wrecked the project in the House. For the hearings, it is clear from subsequent disclosures, would have revealed that Adolphe Wenzell, a former investment banker whose firm was financial agent without fee for the project, had also served as a principal government consultant to map out its development. Indeed, he, as much as anyone, put the project across in Administration councils. With these several indulgences of Wenzell and Adams brought to light, the Democrats for a time endeavored to build a case against the Governor. But the effort was shortly abandoned, the story proving much too complicated to fire public indignation.

Adams was less fortunate in two situations unearthed by Bernard Schwartz, in his brief and harried tenure as counsel of the House subcommittee on Legislative Oversight. By virtue of assiduous digging, Mr. Schwartz secured and laid upon the record two letters written by Adams in 1953 to Murray Chotiner, acting counsel for the North American Airlines and a former campaign manager for Vice-President Nixon. In one of these letters, marked "personal and confidential," the Governor informed Mr. Chotiner that he had discussed a case involving North American Airlines, at the time a large nonscheduled line, with Herman B. Denny, then acting chairman of the Civil Aeronautics Board. Adams's letter disclosed that he and Denny in their tête-à-tête had considered the moves North American might make to delay the effective date of a CAB ruling, revoking its operating authority as a "nonscheduled" company. The airline operated extensively without regularly assigned routes, which, the CAB said, violated its rules. In his letter, signed "Sherm," Adams reported that Denny promised that the effective date of the order, which would have done nothing less than put the company out of business, would be delayed until an appeal could be carried through the courts. Put another way, North American was being advised by its adversary, the government, to appeal to the United States Circuit Court, a step, as Adams stated to Chotiner, which "might delay the operation of the order in this case for as much as two years." Testifying to the House committee, Schwartz observed, "Delay was what North American wanted, and that was what it got, a few more years in business."

The second case assembled by Mr. Schwartz, and continued after his dismissal by the House subcommittee on Legislative Oversight, was the Bernard Goldfine spectacular. Mr. Goldfine, a far-ranging New England industrialist with a yen for government contacts, whose friendship with Adams harked back to the New Hampshire gubernatorial days, was, at the time Schwartz turned on the spotlight of exposure, in trouble with both the Federal Trade Commission and the SEC. In 1956, the FTC had issued a complaint against Goldfine, his son Horace, and several Goldfine companies, charging that fabrics made by the companies were incorrectly labeled and contained "substantially" less guanaco in the wool-blend fabrics than the labels stated. (Guanaco is a high-grade fiber of the cashmere class obtained from a South American animal.) Over at the SEC Goldfine was also in trouble, not because of his woolens, but because of real estate operations conducted through another of his companies, the East Boston Company. For some years, East Boston had failed to file reports required under SEC regulations. In the House subcommittee hearings, FTC officials testified that Adams, by letter and by telephone, asked for two meetings between Goldfine and the agencies in 1954 and 1955. The case lay dormant until late in 1956, although FTC attorneys had recommended that a civil suit be launched against Goldfine and his companies. For reasons which have never been satisfactorily explained, this advice was ignored. On November 26, 1956, a milder consent order or settlement was submitted by Goldfine's attorneys and on February 7, 1957, the FTC adopted the consent order and issued an appropriate cease-and-desist order against the mills. In the SEC, where Adams in a phone call inquired about the status of the case, the proceedings against Goldfine came to a standstill.

The doldrums into which the Washington summer season customarily lapses were utterly by-passed when Mr. Goldfine ventured down from Boston, accompanied by a caravan of lawyers, bookkeepers, secretaries, public-relations experts and his family, to testify before the House subcommittee on Legislative Oversight. As a personage, Mr. Goldfine commanded as much attention in the capital limelight as the disclosures of his bizarre enterprises. Short, square-built, ruddy cheeked, his big velvety dark eyes heavily lidded and arched with dark curving brows, Goldfine was voluble and gregarious. His prepared statement, which one subcommittee member characterized as "a good example of a professionally written scenario," set a modern endurance record, occupying several committee sessions because of the snaillike tempo of his oral delivery. Meanwhile, committee investigators established that Goldfine had paid $3,096.56 in hotel bills and done other nice things for Adams. While Goldfine faced up to the disclosures in his appearances before the committee, Adams was busy explaining the startling facts in statements to the press. The expressions of the two sources were perfectly co-ordinated. The Governor and his friend acknowledged the hotel bills and sought to justify them on the ground that Adams was the equivalent of a house guest, even though in his several acceptances of hospitality he had stayed in various hotels and in different rooms in the same hotel. The two good friends also acknowledged that Goldfine had paid for a vicuña coat and two suits for Adams and bought a $2,400 oriental rug reposing on the living room floor of Adams's Washington home. The rug, they agreed, was on "loan" and would revert to Goldfine whenever Adams might some day choose to give up his Washington residence.

The nation did not exactly resound with approval of the several statements, whereupon Adams appeared before the subcommittee at its invitation. The Governor ventured into the hearing room jammed with spectators accompanied by Mrs. Adams and Gerald Morgan, the White House special counsel, and the unqualified backing of the President expressed in a statement to the press. "The President also asked me to say," announced Press Secretary Hagerty, "that he knows of no individual in or out of Government that he has more confidence in than Sherman Adams." In his appearance before the House subcommittee, the Governor read a prepared statement and answered difficult questions with impeccable composure. His face and figure, however, showed the attrition of long weeks of gnawing anxiety. His eyes had a harried gleam, and he had lost weight. His suit was slack upon his frame and folds of skin hung loosely on his neck just beneath the chin. Adams insisted that he had done no wrong. What about the gifts? Well, he explained, Mr. Goldfine was an old friend and their families often exchanged gifts. "If there were any mistakes made," declared the Governor, "they were mistakes of judgment and not of intent. If I had the decisions now before me to make, I believe I would have acted a little more prudently." He denied ever trying to influence the SEC in Goldfine's behalf or bringing pressure on the FTC. The inquiries he made of those agencies, he said, were "routine and proper." But the subcommittee's counsel, Robert W. Lishman, successor to Bernard Schwartz, contended that Adams had violated FTC rules, and therefore the law, when he obtained a memorandum from the Commission's chairman identifying a complainant against a Goldfine company, and passed the information along to the industrialist. While admitting to the act, the Governor contended that he did not violate the law knowingly. As the investigation further unfolded, Adams was not helped by the continued deterioration of the public image of his "old friend," Mr. Goldfine. At one point in his testimony, Goldfine acknowledged that he had written off the hotel bills and the gifts to Governor Adams as legitimate business expense in his federal income tax returns. When Goldfine refused to answer questions concerning a tidy $776,000 in uncashed bank checks in his possession, some of which had been gathering dust for years, the House of Representatives voted a contempt citation against the reluctant witness.

President Eisenhower persisted in defending his embattled assistant. Promptly after Adams completed his statement on Capitol Hill, Jim Hagerty announced to the press that "the President has full confidence" in the Governor and that the White House now considered the matter "a closed book." On the day following Adams's appearance before the subcommittee, the President made clear that Adams would stay on the job. He had done no wrong. A gift, the President said, is "not necessarily a bribe. One is evil, the other is a tangible expression of friendship." The President acknowledged that the Governor had been "imprudent," but, he concluded, "I need him." Yet there was no gainsaying the fact, as the London *Daily Express* put it, "the high priest of the cult of clean government has broken his own rules." Clearly, Eisenhower was not applying to Adams the lofty standards of official conduct so uncompromisingly proclaimed in the 1952 campaign and solemnly restated thereafter. Nor was Adams, in turn, subjecting himself to these standards which he, too, professed and administered with merciless severity against his executive colleagues, often for offenses less reprehensible than his own. In effect, when the Governor decided to stay and the President said "I need him," they both were decreeing that there was one law for Adams and another law for everybody else.

The tidings of Adams's retention were glumly received in Republican quarters and in some instances with outspoken protest. Senator John J. Williams, Republican of Delaware, somberly announced that he could not accept Adams's explanation and that his "resignation is in order." Congressman John B. Bennett of Michigan voiced the wide sentiment of his fellow Republicans in the House of Representatives when he declared that Adams's "continued tenure in the high position he holds does not seem justifiable." The 1958 Congressional elections were just around the corner, and there was no gainsaying the fact that the imprudent Adams had killed the goose whose golden eggs of honesty and integrity in government and unremitting honking about cleaning up "the mess in Washington," had paid off handsomely for the G.O.P. in every electoral campaign since 1952. In 1958, when Republican candidates would be terribly handicapped by a recession and the trend represented by a decided voter preference for the Democrats in the last several Congresses, the golden goose would be sorely missed. In its place was the battered, discredited Adams, clinging tenaciously to his official post. Quite understandably, Republican Senators and

Congressmen, facing imminent and unpromising battles for their political lives, continued to mutter that Adams should go.

As passing weeks brought the elections closer, the mutterings grew until Adams's ejection from his office-fortress seemed imminent. Hereupon, to his great good fortune, an international crisis exploded in Lebanon. For weeks while the world wobbled on the brink of general war, Adams and his dwindling career were shunted off the front pages of the press. Then as the Near Eastern discord began to wane, another crisis, of equally awesome proportions, happily for Adams, erupted in the Far East. The Chinese Communists chose to bombard the offshore Quemoy islands, and again the American public was engrossed with the possibility of general war. For more weeks Adams was forgotten. He had clearly reached a point where his best friends, or those who could do most to preserve his job security, were not in Washington, in the White House or on Capitol Hill. They were the sinister figures huddled around the drawing boards of Communist strategy in Moscow and Peiping. By their conspiratorial grace, Sherman Adams was leading a charmed life.

A fall from power is seldom a pleasant spectacle, and Adams's overthrow possessed pathos even for his enemies. Although shielded temporarily by international crisis, his position was undeniably deteriorating. In his daily tasks, he suffered a noticeable decline in self-confidence, and his office lost its accustomed snap and brisk efficiency. When his associates tendered their commiserations, Adams brushed them off gruffly—he wanted no sympathy. There were innumerable embarrassments to suffer. Adams still joined the President in his regular meetings with Republican legislative leaders; at first "the Adams case," as one leader called it, was discussed, and then it was permanently dropped. Its pointed omission, as a kind of political leprosy, doubtless was more painful to the Governor than if it had been candidly explored. There were irritating pinpricks like the proper and well-intentioned inquiry from Tran Van Ky, correspondent for the Viet Nam press in Washington. From his homeland, Van Ky had received many letters asking how the United States could preach so piously against corruption in high places in Asia, while back in Washington, a principal official, Adams, seemingly pursued a double standard. Van Ky, an admirer of the United States, asked the White House for an explanation of this seeming unconsistency to pass along to his Asiatic friends. Adams struggled over a reply clarifying and justifying his stewardship, and closing prayerfully, "I hope the unfortunate publicity will soon subside so that we may get on with the business of the day."

Adams's expression of hope was a whisper lost in a rising din of unpleasant facts. As the Far Eastern crisis subsided and the elections of November 1958 neared, Republican leaders viewed the Governor's continued presence in official life with growing nervousness and resentment. On August twentieth, Vice-President Nixon put before the President a distressing summary of the prevailing ill feeling. Virtually every one of the thirty-six Republican candidates for the Senate and most of those for the House of Representatives, Nixon reported, insisted on Adams's retirement before election day. An equally lugubrious sentiment was discovered by Meade Alcorn in a survey made at meetings of the Republican National Committee and Finance Committee in Chicago on August twenty-sixth and twenty-seventh. In private soundings among the conferees at the Sheraton-Blackstone hotel, Alcorn learned that the well-nigh unanimous judgment of the party's leaders and financial godfathers was that Adams had to go. As Alcorn was conferring, the pressures kept rising. It took all of the party chairman's considerable powers of persuasion to hold down Congressman Richard Simpson of Pennsylvania, chairman of the House Republican campaign committee, from publicly demanding Adams's ouster. Meanwhile, one after another of the party's big contributors were snapping their purses shut and rumbling about keeping them shut until "the Adams mess" was cleaned up. Sidney Weinberg, distinguished New York financier and leading Republican donor, sniffed, "When Adams used the word 'imprudent' regarding his conduct, he was using a word meaning 'stupid.' "

When the dreary conclave in Chicago ended, Alcorn returned to Washington and laid his distressing findings before the President. The Adams cause was now just about hopeless. Against the united pressure of the party politicians, the only voices raised in his behalf were those of his colleagues and friends of the White House staff, Morgan, Persons and Hagerty, and several members of the cabinet. Together they waged a doughty campaign for the Governor's retention, but were finally overwhelmed in the councils of the President by the superior strength of the politicians. With great reluctance and unconcealed emotion, according to one account of these unhappy events,* President Eisenhower acquiesced to the conclusion of Alcorn's report that Adams had become too onerous a liability for the Republicans in an election year when the odds against the party were already overwhelming. Adams, the President agreed in his conference with Alcorn, had to go. Afterwards, Eisenhower termed his fateful acquiescence as "the most hurtful, the hardest, the most heartbreaking decision" in all his years of office. Under the circumstances, he could not personally ask for Adams's resignation. Alcorn, the Governor's old friend and fellow Dartmouth alum-

* John Steele's in *Life* magazine, September 29, 1958. At least several parts of Steele's article were denied and contradicted in subsequent statements by President Eisenhower and Republican Chairman Meade Alcorn.

nus, would have to do it. "You've got to handle it," said Eisenhower. "It's your job, the dirtiest I can give you."

Alcorn did not exactly rush into his mean assignment. Nearly one week after the party chairman's conferral with the President, Adams was evidently still uninformed of what was in store. On September sixth, he and Mrs. Adams, who was mastering the trying circumstances with loyalty and fortitude, loaded their fishing gear into their 1958 pea-green Oldsmobile station wagon and set out for the distant woods of Renous, New Brunswick. Accompanying them in a second car were General and Mrs. Persons. The foursome hoped for privacy and surcease, while pursuing the Governor's favorite pastime—salmon fishing—on the Miramichi River. But the grim mood of Washington clung like barnacles to their thoughts, and even the local environment at Renous conspired against their pleasure. Day after day of unbroken rainfall left the river much too high for good fishing. For all of the distance Adams had put between himself and the clawing world of politics by pitching his camp beyond reach of telephones and roadways, the Governor's sanctuary was penetrated. By a long-distance call, reporters induced a local storekeeper, D. D. Sullivan, to venture through the woods to Adams's remote habitat and confront the Governor with the rumors now widely circulating that he had resigned. Adams declined to comment, and Sullivan, with this report, trudged back to civilization.

Three days after Adams and his party had encamped at Renous, the returns of the Maine elections—a traditional provider of national sentiment—were in. The emerging picture showed a Republican debacle. Senator Payne, the Republican nominee, who had admitted to borrowing from Bernard Goldfine to purchase a home in Washington, and to approaching the SEC concerning Mr. Goldfine's ensnarled affairs, was crushingly defeated. In addition, a Democratic Governor and two Democratic Congressmen were elected in this normally Republican state. Back in Washington, Meade Alcorn had hardly begun to assess the damage when Senator Ed Thye of Minnesota and Arthur Watkins of Utah, whose own seats in the Senate were badly imperiled, were on the telephone insisting that it was high time for Adams to go. Elsewhere, Senator William F. Knowland, Republican leader in the Senate, facing a very difficult electoral fight in California, was declaring publicly that Adams had become a political liability. Congressman Daniel A. Reed, powerful Republican of upstate New York, observed that Adams "should have resigned at the start of the investigation . . . for the good of the Administration and the good of the Republican party." And the Republican senatorial candidate in New York, Kenneth B. Keating, asserted that Adams should leave for the "good of the President and the country." Except for President Eisenhower and Vice-President Nixon, Sherman Adams had no public defenders. In the face of mounting pressures, Alcorn concluded that action could be delayed no longer. Through storekeeper Sullivan, he got a message through to Adams on September tenth, requesting that he return to Washington at once.

At four o'clock in the morning of the following day, the Adamses commenced the long dispiriting trek back to the capital. There is some dispute over the precise details of what followed. According to one informed account,* the Governor conferred with Alcorn early the following morning and learned for the first time of Eisenhower's concurrence that the Governor's resignation was necessary. The Governor, it was said, took the grim news without visible emotion. Alcorn, for his part, however, contended that no one told Adams to resign. "The decision was made by the Governor," the Republican Chairman averred, "on his own information and his own judgment." President Eisenhower too backed up Alcorn's explanation. "I did not instruct anyone to ask for a resignation," the President declared at a press conference. "He [Adams] did resign voluntarily. Now, there is no question that other people advised him very strongly at this time, during these last weeks and months, I guess it is now, but he was never advised by me to resign."

President Eisenhower, nevertheless, had for some time been launching the most powerful inducements to bring about Adams's departure. In the weeks prior to his resignation, the Governor was cut off from participation in all major policy developments. This drastic and hurtful penalty could have been imposed only with the sanction and co-operation of the President. Only a year before the tragic events through which he was passing, Adams had been master strategist in the Little Rock crisis over integration in the public schools. Now, one year later, as his time was running out, Adams had no part in a new crisis boiling at Little Rock, the nation's most pressing domestic problem. It was the Attorney General, William P. Rogers, who in Adams's declining hours flew to Newport (where the President was vacationing) to work out policy with the President. Indeed, in the week of Adams's resignation, Eisenhower conferred with the Governor by telephone but once and then only on routine business. Adams's descent into the pit of neglect came to pass only by the acts and intent of the President.

For several days after his meeting with Alcorn, Adams pondered over the procedure to follow, and drafted and redrafted a public statement of his retirement. When the document was at last completed, he made an unheralded visit on September twenty-second to Eisenhower, who was still at Newport. Arriving by plane at eight A.M., the Governor conferred with the President an hour and a quarter, at which time, Adams himself has said, he tendered his resignation. Upon leaving the President, Adams spent a half

* *Life*, September 29, 1958.

hour with Hagerty and then returned to the President for another conference. At eleven A.M. he enplaned for Washington.

Late that afternoon, he set out from the White House for the local CBS television studio, driving his own station wagon, and accompanied only by a White House policeman riding in the passenger seat. Morgan and Persons followed along in another car. Hagerty, who had come down from Newport to manage the television arrangements, was on hand, overseeing the layout of the standard office-suite background, complete with a leather-covered desk and chair, an American flag unfurled in a standard behind and a small table with books and a telephone. Just before air time, Hagerty discovered to his chagrin that one of the books was boldly titled, *The Happiest Man in the World*. He snatched it away. On the air, Adams was an image of dignity and self-possession, with a sparkle in his eye, and his voice confident and professional in modulation. He informed his radio and television audiences that he was herewith resigning, a decision necessitated by the "campaign of vilification" calculated to destroy him and embarrass the President and the Administration. Rather than suffer such consequences and endanger Republican chances for winning Congress in November, the Governor was yielding his post. "I have done no wrong," he declared. As Adams was speaking, a letter of President Eisenhower addressed, "Dear Sherman," accepting Adams's resignation "with sadness" was made public. "Your performance has been brilliant," the President wrote, "you have had throughout, my complete trust, confidence and respect. . . . You will be sorely missed." (Actually, Adams had written no letter of resignation. This, however, did not forestall the President from writing a letter of acceptance.) When the day was done, one G.O.P. official conveyed the wide reaction of his party colleagues, "They all said the same thing—'Thank God.'"

The resignation of Sherman Adams gained the Republican party little and cost the President much. Neither poll takers or postelection analysts have demonstrated or even suggested that Adams's banishment affected appreciably the magnitude of the Republican defeat in the 1958 elections. The recession, the Democratic party's vast hold upon the public, the voters' distrust of Republican conservatives—these, far more than Adams's imprudences—fashioned the outcome. Indeed, the Democrats, at the time the Governor resigned, considered the issue to be fading and anxiously wondered how to keep it alive. Adams's ejection and televised valedictory fitted beautifully the necessities of Democratic strategy.

As for the President, he lost an invaluable and, as it proved, an irreplaceable assistant. It is a mystery, still to be clarified, why the President forsook his assistant and surrendered to the clamors for his dismissal. Prior to the Adams case, Eisenhower had displayed monumental stamina in standing by colleagues whose heads were called for by imposing political voices. Time and again John Foster Dulles was in jeopardy, but the President always saved him. For years, the resignation of Secretary of Agriculture Ezra Taft Benson had been demanded, at times with terrible stridency, by Senators, Congressmen and the potentates of organized farm groups hurt by the Secretary's conservative policies. But it was always to no avail. Eisenhower stuck by Benson. It is easily demonstrable that Benson's deportment in office cost the Republican party more votes than Adams's traffic with Goldfine.* If the President's conduct in the period of Adams's eclipse is in part mysterious, the further part of it is not altogether flattering. By keeping the Governor on long after his imprudences had been exposed, and then in effect firing him, the President seemed to shilly-shally and lack courage and firmness. If he had dismissed Adams immediately instead of later, the President would have shown that he meant what he had said about misconduct, and turned Adams's errors to the party's best advantage.

Although Adams had surrendered his office, he by no means withdrew altogether from the center of power. He was the only source in the White House Eisenhower consulted in choosing his successor. The Governor proposed but one name, General Wilton B. Persons, to which the President readily acquiesced. But Person's health was frail and his age—sixty-two—advanced for the grueling pace, making imperative the careful selection of his assistants. Here, too, Adams had suggestions. As an ideal nominee, he proposed Fred C. Scribner, Jr., at the time Under Secretary of the Treasury, an able experienced official, imposing personality, hulking figure and fellow Dartmouth alumnus. Eisenhower seems to have acquiesced to Scribner's appointment as Deputy Assistant to the President, and the impending announcement was widely anticipated in the press. Just as the machinery for making it official was about to turn, the anti-Adams forces in Congress learned what was afoot and, with fire in their eyes, rushed to block it. Chairman Richard Simpson of the Republican Congressional Campaign Committee vehemently protested that Scribner's appointment signified that Adams was still running the White House. Other powerful legislative Republicans, including Senator Styles Bridges, chairman of the Policy Committee in the upper house, forcefully re-echoed Simpson. Under the accumulated pressure, Scribner was dropped and the rearrangement of the White House staff proceeded along somewhat different lines. The number-two post went instead to Gerald D. Morgan, Adams's unshakeable ally. The Governor, in effect,

---

* Adams's case is distinguishable on moral grounds, but Eisenhower has not disclosed that he acted on the basis of such a distinction.

had won the victory after beating a minor retreat. In addition, he was remaining indefinitely on the payroll as a minister without portfolio, at $22,500 a year, to assist the transition to the new staff arrangement.

By late October, the "trial run" was satisfactorily completed, and Adams at last could clean out his desk and pack his effects. Friday, October twenty-fourth, was his last day at the White House. At least six of his associates separately proposed to arrange the leave-taking party customarily tendered to departing members of the staff, but the Governor declined, preferring merely to disappear at the close of work. He did, however, call on the President to say good-bye before boarding his station wagon and driving home. The Adamses were giving up their house near Rock Creek Park, and their household possessions were in transit to their permanent home in Lincoln, New Hampshire. None of the multitudinous details of moving was left undone. The famous rug "lent" by Bernard Goldfine was dispatched to a Washington cleaning emporium with instructions that it be processed and shipped to the Boston industrialist.

The Adamses' arrival in Lincoln on October twenty-seventh was something of an occasion. Awaiting them was a special resolution passed by the local three-member Board of Selectmen—all Democrats—hailing the returning couple as "fine and outstanding community-minded citizens." For the Governor, the flattering citation was decidedly in order in at least several respects. During his years with Eisenhower, he had provided direction and energy in an interval when leadership was badly needed. The President was ill, uninterested, aging and absentee as the nation faced the swelling challenge of Soviet power, the incalculable potentialities of the new scientific age, and the urgency of a creative social policy and an economy operating at high productivity. Within the limits of his power, Adams halted drift, faced problems and imparted vigor.

As much as any man, Sherman Adams held the Administration to a predominately liberal course, and away from the reefs of a politically unrealistic conservatism, toward which it naturally tended. It required the summoning of all of Adams's vast power to offset Eisenhower's intrinsic conservatism and its powerful insistent encouragement by influential businessmen around him. Although the President accepted with modifications the social changes of the 'thirties, his thinking was most akin to the budget-balancing, states rights predilections of George Humphrey and Charles E. Wilson, and in some respects the eighteenth century *laissez-faire* economics of Sinclair Weeks. Yet the profile of Administration policies which emerged in the interval of Adams's presence was substantially more liberal than Eisenhower himself. In its economic, social and political posture, the Administration mirrored Adams more than it did the President. The true significance of this fact is to be gleaned from another major paradox of the times in which Adams served. In the Eisenhower era, American voters lost faith in Republican Congresses, rejecting them at every electoral opportunity, but their faith in the Republican Presidency endured. The unfaltering popularity of the Republican Presidency is in no small measure attributable to Adams. While Eisenhower supplied the indispensable magic of his personality, Adams worked and fought for a complex of liberal policies possessing wide voter appeal. Without those policies, or "Modern Republicanism" as they were sometimes termed, Eisenhower's great political personality would have been wasted.

Yet the reach of Adams's achievements was fixed and circumscribed by the limitations of his position and the defects of his own personality. In his anonymous secretive office, he never could give the nation the articulateness and the sense of conviction which problems warranted and only a robust full-time President could provide. Adams's staff operation, however it crackled with efficiency, was no substitute for a Chief Executive committed in mind and emotion to the challenge of his job. Adams was also ill-served by the make-up of his own personality. It was more than brusqueness or a rowdy talent for losing friends. Adams's gravest derelictions in office were his occasional lapses in imagination and judgment. The times called for an assistant to the President endowed with nothing less than the breadth of vision of a Leonardo da Vinci. Through no fault of his own, Adams was no Leonardo. Yet, on occasion, his imagination and judgment fell badly below even the most ordinary standards. At one juncture in the race to develop an American Sputnik, for example, Adams dismissed the project, for which millions of dollars were expended and American scientists were straining their ingenuity, as "a bunch of foolishness." Another time, he cavalierly discounted the Russo-American competition in the orbiting of satellites as being at the level of significance of an "international basketball game." Characteristically, the Governor overlooked or grossly undervalued the enormous psychological or propagandistic aspects of the venture.

Considering the nature of his job, Adams was not particularly inventive in discharging it. He contributed nothing to the Eisenhower Administration that was strikingly new in an era calling for novelty of approach. Adams's forte was organizing, expediting and evoking consensus. Beyond this point, his usefulness seldom penetrated. Adams, accordingly, was no associate the President could dream with of future plans and bold new programs. The Governor was geared to the daily task and the visible problem. But this, after all, was the kind of man the President wanted. In his civilian and military careers, Eisenhower has evidenced little disposition to have visionaries about him. He prefers men of action who button up problems.

Adams diminished his effectiveness by his inaccessibility to the world outside the government. While the President consorted with businessmen, academicians, scientists and foreign citizens through stag dinners, interviews and correspondence, Adams was denoted by the sparseness of his contacts. In bed by eight o'clock, all-business when he was on the job, he had little time for the rest of the world. In an interval of prodigious change, Adams was out of touch with the sources of the community which could make, shape and interpret it. He knew few scientists and professors, and the circle of business-men and politicians among his acquaintances was astonishingly small. Partly, Adams's withdrawal was required by the colossal burdens of his job; partly it was a reflection of his shyness, whose expression his post facilitated. In a sense, his office was a refuge for the introvert.

If Adams related himself imperfectly to the universe outside his White House office, his order of things inside the Executive Branch was faulty, too. Adams suffered from, and eventually succumbed to, the hazards of unre-viewed judgment. Far too often, what he did was in fact subject to no higher authority. Eisenhower, ill and distracted, was no real check; the President's habit was to approve automatically and with limited comprehension what his assistant put before him. By shutting out the press and Congress until the late day of the Goldfine crisis, Adams further deepened and extended his freedom of action. He was enabled to exercise his imposing authority un-harassed by the questions which the public, through their representatives, have in a democracy a right to ask. It is true that Adams worked hard, doing far more in line of duty than his President and his countrymen might legiti-mately expect of him. But the danger of hard work in a high and lonely sta-tion is that the toiling hero loses perspective, develops overweening self-righteousness and becomes uncritical of his acts. This in some degree may account for Sherman Adams's strange astigmatism in the Goldfine, Chotiner and Dixon-Yates cases. But the most disturbing feature of the cases is not the minor immoralities in which Adams was engaging. Their really haunting aspect is that Adams was guilty of misjudgment. On how many other matters, it may be asked, vital to the country's welfare and disposed of in absolute secrecy, did Adams indulge in misjudgment? Since errors in statecraft are sometimes slow in catching up to the visible reality of events, years, if not decades, may elapse before the toll is known.

Although driven from his seat of power, Adams, for his part, has ex-hibited no doubts concerning the ultimate judgments of history on his diffi-cult stewardship. In the heyday of his career, well before the Goldfine tragedy, various journalists and editors, chafing at their lack of access to Adams's tightly walled domain, arranged for a handful of their number to interview the Governor one evening at the home of Philip Graham, publisher of the

Washington Post. It was off the record, and although Adams really didn't say very much, the questions were sometimes pointed. One most direct interrogation invited the Governor to evaluate candidly the massive operation to which he had been giving himself so unstintingly. He answered without hesitation. "I think," he said confidently, "we have done a good job."

DESIGN FOR TOMORROW

THE FUTURE of the American nation may well depend on how much the President utilizes personal favorites and general assistants of the Hopkins, Corcoran, House varieties, and how much he resorts to committees and bureaucratic staffs. At mid-point in the twentieth century, we live in an age of government by committees. While favorites have been toiling in the White House shadows, committees and staffs have steadily been proliferating all over Washington. Most of these bodies, which specialize in agenda, position papers, clearances and other documentary impedimenta, are little known to the general citizen, but their numbers and influence are vast. The years since World War II have seen the rise of the National Security Council, the Operations Coordinating Board, the Council of Economic Advisers, and the Office of Defense Mobilization, while the more traditional Bureau of the Budget and White House staff have markedly expanded. Beyond these several constituent elements of a presidential bureaucracy, a web of ever multiplying interdepartmental committees envelops the Executive Branch. In 1948, the State Department, for example, held membership on nearly forty interdepartmental committees; in 1959, the number was close to seven hundred. Committees and staffs doubtless will continue to expand, for without them the sheer volume and technical complexity of executive business could never be managed.

But committees and bureaucratic staffs pose formidable difficulties in an era of challenge and change like that through which we are passing. In confronting the multiple crises of our times—the survival of mankind, the Soviet challenge, the mastery of outer space and various other slightly less-exacting imponderables—committees and staffs can serve us badly. They are cumbersome and slow moving. They cannot be aroused to swift and decisive action and radical innovation except when disaster is obvious and imminent. They put a premium on inaction and the mechanical continuation of safe routines. They have little stomach for the risks of innovation. All too often, their labored product is an innocuous common denominator of agreement, having the zest and zing of gruel. Initiative is discouraged, conformity rewarded, and individual responsibility lost in the faceless group.

The presidential favorite has thrived most in eras of challenge and change. He is a source of creativity, initiative, variation and flexibility, prime virtues in critical times. The favorite is a means by which a President endowed with greatness can place the stamp of his personality and talent upon the office. He is a means by which the President can escape on occasion

407

from the massive institution over which he presides. If the cabinet is hostile, if committees are doddering with arthritic procedures, if the party leadership won't go along, if the bureaucracy is laggard, a skillful President can often get what he wants by resourcefully deploying his personal assistants.

Future Presidents who choose to employ favorites in the major tasks of their administrations might well consider the disclosures of the past. It is striking that George Washington, a systematic administrator, and Andrew Jackson and Franklin D. Roosevelt in the New Deal, both unsystematic administrators, followed similar patterns in their resort to favorites. All three Presidents applied the principle of competition. They had not merely one favorite, but an inner circle whose several members stood high in the confidence of the President. When decisions of policy were to be made, the favorite and his colleagues of the inner circle were invited and expected to offer recommendations and proposals, and to criticize the handiwork of their fellows. Although an Alexander Hamilton enjoyed the gratifying experience of seeing his product adopted in a large preponderance of instances, he could not, in the greater part of his tenure, bring forward a proposal without anticipating its critical review by his colleagues of the inner circle.

Unassailable advantages exist in the competitive arrangement. Competition keeps favorites on their toes; they put out better and coast less, if subject to challenge by others. No one man can claim to possess all the human wisdom relevant to the complexities of a given problem of statecraft. But competition is not easily maintained. The texts of the past reveal that favorites tend to aggrandize their influence to the point where they can and will eliminate opposition and monopolize the counsel on which decisions are based. In certain seasons, Alexander Hamilton, Harry Hopkins and Sherman Adams were depended upon too exclusively by their respective Presidents. In such intervals, presidential decisions may be based on insufficient information, analysis and deliberation. The mistakes of Yalta are a monumental warning against overreliance on a single favorite.

Our future Presidents might well consider a further principle applied by Washington, Jackson and Franklin Roosevelt. The favorite and his fellow members of the inner circle should be representative of the several sources of information and ideas, in the government and outside, by which the President might profit. The inner circle should contain one or more department secretaries to assure the utilization of the vast store of data and analytic skills of the bureaucracy. It should contain the head man of the White House staff, an officer whose authority should stand somewhere between the excessive reaches of Sherman Adams as the Assistant to the President, and the former office of Secretary to the President, as occupied by William Loeb, Jr., and George B. Cortelyou. The inner circle of the future should include an outsider or two, who hold no government station. Their presence can impart the advantages of a fresh and even critical point of view, and the likely absence of vested interest in existing policy. In its totality, the inner circle should provide access to the many places in society where thought and feelings relevant to presidential policy-making are to be found. The favorite of tomorrow must build rapport not merely with spokesmen for major voting strength and predominant economic power, but with the intellectual community as well on which the nation's survival will come increasingly to depend. The indications of the past are that a favorite can do no better service for his President than to bring in ideas and information from the several worlds outside the White House office. A favorite is valuable less for his own ideas than for his efficiency as a receptacle of the ideas of others. Van Buren, House and Corcoran will not rank among the most original and creative thinkers of their times. Their greater value lay in catching up useful ideas abroad in society.

Our future Presidents may employ favorites with high expectations of success. The record of the past is one of impressive accomplishment with only occasional hours of misjudgment and corruption. Our most successful favorites have served in the administrations of our strongest Presidents. Our least commendable favorites are identified with such weakling presidencies as those of Grant and Harding. The best way to secure good favorites, it would appear, is to elect good Presidents. The world of palace politics, in which favorites toil, is not a place, if the past be a guide, where our most morally upright citizens, or just nice guys, are likely to thrive. Presidential favorites, quite understandably, do not number among the heroes of American history whom we are pleased to commend as examples for our children.

Favorites, on the basis of the past, are not to be feared as a potentially undemocratic practice. They have been reasonably within reach of Congress and our political parties; they cannot easily elude the press. If the President's approval, which is usually a fragile thing, snaps, they are quickly ejected from the inner circle. The parties and Congress toppled such potentates as Hamilton and Sherman Adams into the dust and snuffed out Tom Corcoran's public career. House slipped fatally and Hopkins substantially in the graces of their Presidents. If anything, it is more difficult to keep favorites on the job than to cast them out. Catastrophes are readily blamed on them, and the good they do is either unacknowledged or attributed to their master, the President. When under attack, they have pitifully few means to defend themselves. They have meager incentives to stay in harness. Apart from the momentary exhilaration of sharing personally in the making of history, their rewards are severely little. Neither wealth or high office will likely accrue from their travail. Indeed any man contemplating the unpromising career of presidential favorite, would do well to heed a wise passage from Edmund Burke, which hangs framed in an honored place in the Washington law office of Thomas G. Corcoran:

> Those who would carry on great public schemes must be proof against the worst fatiguing delays; the most mortifying disappointments, the most shocking insults, and what is worst of all, the presumptuous judgment of the ignorant upon their design.

SOURCES CONSULTED

PART ONE

Adams, Henry, *The Life of Albert Gallatin*, Philadelphia, 1879.

The Diary of John Quincy Adams, 1794–1845, A. Nevins ed., New York, 1928.

Allen, George E., *Presidents Who Have Known Me*, New York, 1950.

Barton, Bruce, "The Man Who Asks for Nothing," *Collier's*, May 2, 1925, p. 16. (Frank Stearns)

Brownlow, Louis, *The President and the Presidency*, Chicago, 1949.

Bryson, Lyman, "Notes on a Theory of Advice," *Political Science Quarterly*, September, 1951, p. 321.

Burgess, John W., *The Administration of President Hayes*, New York, 1916.

Chitwood, Oliver P., *John Tyler, Champion of the Old South*, New York, 1939.

Cleveland, Grover, *Presidential Problems*, New York, 1904.

Corwin, E. S., and Koenig, L. W., *The Presidency Today*, New York, 1956.

"The Secretary to the People," *Harpers Weekly*, January 3, 1903, p. 20. (G. B. Cortelyou)

Daniels, Jonathan, *The End of Innocence*, Philadelphia, 1954.

————*Frontier on the Potomac*, New York, 1946.

Farrand, Max, *The Records of the Federal Convention of 1787*, New Haven, 1937.

The Forrestal Diaries, W. Millis, ed., New York, 1951.

Fuess, Claude, M., *The Life of Caleb Cushing*, New York, 1923.

Harrison, Benjamin, *This Country of Ours*, New York, 1897.

Herring, E. P., *Presidential Leadership*, New York, 1940.

Hersey, John, "Mr. President," *The New Yorker*, April 7, 1951, p. 42.

Hillman, William, *Mr. President*, New York, 1952.

Hinsdale, Mary T., *A History of the President's Cabinet*, Ann Arbor, 1911.

Hoover, Herbert, *The Memoirs of Herbert Hoover*, New York, 1952.

Hoover, Irwin H., *Forty-Two Years in the White House*, Boston, 1934.

Hull, Cordell, *The Memoirs of Cordell Hull*, New York, 1948.

Hurd, Charles, *The White House, A Biography*, New York, 1940.

Hyman, Sidney, *The American President*, New York, 1954.

Laski, Harold, *The American Presidency*, New York, 1939.

Learned, Henry B., *The President's Cabinet*, New Haven, 1912.

Macfarland, Henry B. F., "George Bruce Cortelyou, Secretary of Commerce," *Review of Reviews*, Vol. 27 (1903), p. 297.

Correspondence between Thomas Jefferson, and Pierre Samuel Du Pont de Nemours, 1798–1817, Dumas Malone ed., Boston, 1930.

Milton, George F., *The Use of Presidential Power*, Boston, 1944.

Morgenthau, Henry, Jr., "The Morgenthau Diaries," *Collier's*, September 27, 1947.

Nevins, Allan, *Grover Cleveland, A Study in Courage*, New York, 1932.

Nichols, Roy F., *Franklin Pierce, Young Hickory of the Granite Hills*, Philadelphia, 1931.

The Diary of James K. Polk, During his Presidency, M. M. Quaife, ed., Chicago, 1910.

Pringle, Henry F., *Theodore Roosevelt, A Biography*, New York, 1931.

————*The Life and Times of William Howard Taft*, New York, 1939.

Redfield, William C., *With Congress and Cabinet*, Garden City, 1924.

Rosenman, Samuel, *Working with Roosevelt*, New York, 1952.

Roosevelt, Theodore, *An Autobiography*, New York, 1920.

Rossiter, Clinton, *The American Presidency*, New York, 1956.

Stanwood, Edward, *A History of the Presidency*, Boston, 1898.

Stevens, John A., *Albert Gallatin*, Boston, 1899.
Stiles, Lela, *The Man Behind Roosevelt*, Cleveland, 1954.
Small, Norman J., *Some Presidential Interpretations of the Presidency*, Baltimore, 1932.
Taft, William H., *Our Chief Magistrate and His Powers*, New York, 1916.
——*The Presidency, Its Duties, Its Powers, Its Opportunities, Its Limitations*, New York, 1916.
Thach, Charles C., Jr., *The Creation of the Presidency, 1775–1789*, Baltimore, 1922.
Truman, Harry S., *Memoirs*, Garden City, 1955.
Tugwell, Rexford G., "The Preparation of a President," *Western Political Quarterly*, June, 1948, p. 131.
——"The Two Great Roosevelts," *Western Political Quarterly*, March, 1952, p. 84.
Tyler, Lyon G., *The Letters and Times of the Tylers*, Richmond, 1884.
The Diary of Gideon Welles, Boston, 1911.
White, William A., *A Puritan in Babylon, The Story of Calvin Coolidge*, New York, 1938.
White, William L., *Bernard Baruch, Portrait of a Citizen*, New York, 1950.
Wilson, Woodrow, *The President of the United States*, New York, 1916.

PART TWO

HAMILTON

Letters of John Adams, Addressed to his Wife, C. F. Adams, ed., 2 Vols., Boston, 1841.
Ames, S., *Works of Fisher Ames*, 2 Vols., Boston, 1854
Anderson, D. R., *William Branch Giles: A Study in the Politics of Virginia and the Nation from 1790 to 1830*, Menasha, Wisconsin, 1914.
Austin, M. S., *Philip Freneau: Poet of the Revolution*, New York, 1901.
Atherton, G., *The Conqueror*, New York, 1902.
Bemis, S. F., *Jay's Treaty: A Study in Commerce and Diplomacy*, New York, 1923.
——"The London Mission of Thomas Pinckney, 1792–1796," *American Historical Review*, January, 1923.
Bowers, C., *Jefferson and Hamilton, The Struggle for Democracy in America*, Boston, 1925.
Brown, W. G., *The Life of Oliver Ellsworth*, New York, 1905.
Brooks, N., *Henry Knox: A Soldier of the Revolution*, New York, 1900.
Brush, E. H., *Rufus King and His Times*, New York, 1926.
Caldwell, K., *The Administrative Theories of Hamilton and Jefferson*, Chicago, 1944.
Callahan, N., *Henry Knox, General Washington's General*, New York, 1958.
Davis, J., *Travels of Four Years and a Half in the United States of America, 1798–1802*, New York, 1909.
Drake, F. S., *Life and Correspondence of Henry Knox*, Boston, 1873.
Fitzpatrick, J. C., ed. *The Diaries of George Washington*, Boston, 1925.
——*The Writings of George Washington*, Washington, D.C., 1932.
Forman, S. E., *The Political Activities of Philip Freneau*, Baltimore, 1902.
Ford, P. L., *The Works of Thomas Jefferson*, New York, 1904.
Freeman, D. S., *George Washington, a Biography*, 6 Vols., New York, 1948–54.
Memoirs of the Administrations of Washington and John Adams, G. Gibbs, ed., 2 Vols., New York, 1846.
Griswold, R., *The Republican Court: or, American Society in the Days of Washington*, New York, 1867.
Hacker, L., *The Triumph of American Capitalism*, New York, 1940.
Hamilton, Allan M., *The Intimate Life of Alexander Hamilton*, New York, 1911.
Hamilton, John C., *Life of Alexander Hamilton*, New York, 1834.
——*The Works of Alexander Hamilton*, New York, 1841.

Harlow, R. V. *The History of Legislative Methods in the Period before 1825*, New Haven, 1917.

Hazen, C. D., *Contemporary American Opinion of the French Revolution*, Baltimore, 1897.

Hunt, G., *First Forty Years of American Society, Portrayed by the Family Letters of Mrs. Margaret Bayard Smith*, New York, 1906.

Hunt, G., *The Department of State of the United States*, Washington, 1893.

Life and Correspondence of Rufus King, C. King, ed., 6 Vols., New York, 1888.

Krout, J. and Fox, D., *The Completion of Independence, 1790–1830*, New York, 1944.

Kent, W., *Memoirs and Letters of James Kent*, Boston, 1898.

Lippincott, H. M., *Early Philadelphia: Its People, Life, and Progress*, Philadelphia, 1917.

Lodge, H. C., *The Works of Alexander Hamilton*, New York, 1904.

Loth, D., *Alexander Hamilton, Portrait of a Prodigy*, New York, 1939.

Maclay, E. S., *The Journal of William Maclay*, New York, 1890.

McMaster, J. B., *History of the People of the United States*, New York, 1883.

Diary and Letters of Gouverneur Morris, A. Morris, ed., New York, 1888.

Nock, A. J., *Jefferson*, Boston, 1926.

Oliver, F. S., *Alexander Hamilton: An Essay on the American Union*, New York, 1907.

Schachner, N., *Alexander Hamilton*, New York, 1946.

———*The Founding Fathers*, New York, 1954.

The Life and Correspondence of Gouverneur Morris, J. Sparks, ed., Boston, 1832.

———*The Writings of George Washington*, Boston, 1836.

Stephenson, N. W., and Dunn, W. H., *George Washington*, New York, 1940.

Sullivan, W., *Familiar Letters on Public Characters and Public Events*, Boston, 1834.

———*The Public Men of the Revolution*, Philadelphia, 1847.

Swiggett, H., *The Extraordinary Mr. Morris*, New York, 1952.

Twining, T., *Travels in America 100 Years Ago*, New York, 1894.

White, L., *The Federalists, A Study in Administrative History*, New York, 1948.

Woodward, W. E., *George Washington, The Image and the Man*, New York, 1926.

VAN BUREN

I. Manuscripts

A. C. Flagg Papers, New York Public Library.

Andrew Jackson Papers, Library of Congress.

Andrew Jackson-W. B. Lewis Papers, New York Public Library.

Martin Van Buren Papers, Library of Congress.

II. Books and Articles

Alexander, D. S., *A Political History of the State of New York*, New York, 1906.

Alexander, Holmes, *The American Talleyrand*, New York, 1935.

Ambler, Charles H., *Thomas Ritchie, A Study in Virginia Politics*, Richmond, 1913.

American Historical Association, "Calhoun Correspondence," *Annual Report for the Year 1899*, Volume 2, Washington, 1900.

Correspondence of Andrew Jackson, J. S. Bassett, ed., Washington, 1926–1933.

———*Life of Andrew Jackson*, New York, 1928.

Bancroft, George, "Correspondence with Martin Van Buren," *Proceedings of the Massachusetts Historical Society*, Volume XLII, pp. 381–442.

———*Martin Van Buren to the End of His Public Career*, New York, 1889.

Benton, Thomas Hart, *Thirty Years View*, New York, 1857.

Binkley, Willard E., *American Political Parties, Their Natural History*, New York, 1943.

Bowers, Claude G., *The Party Battles of the Jackson Period*, Boston, 1922.

Bryant, William C., *A Discourse on the Life, Character, and Writings of Gulian Crommelin Verplanck*, New York, 1870.
Burke, G. D., *Emily Donelson of Tennessee*, New York, 1941.
Butler, Benjamin, *Butler's Book*, Boston, 1892.
Butler, W. A., *Martin Van Buren; Lawyer, Statesman and Man*, New York, 1862.
Catterall, R. C. H., *Second Bank of the United States*, Chicago, 1903.
Chancellor, W. E., *A Life of Silas Wright*, New York, 1913.
Calhoun, J. C., *Works*, R. K. Cralle, ed., New York, 1851–1856.
The Autobiography of Peggy Eaton, C. F. Deems, ed., New York, 1932.
Dewey, D. R., *The Second United States Bank*, Washington, 1910.
Donovan, H. D. A., *The Barnburners*, New York, 1925.
Dix, John A., *Memoirs*, New York, 1833.
Duane, William J., *Narrative and Correspondence concerning the Removal of the Deposites and the Currencies Connected Therewith*, Philadelphia, 1838.
Ellet, Elizabeth, *The Court Circles of the Republic*, Hartford, 1896.
The Autobiography of Martin Van Buren, J. C. Fitzpatrick, ed., American Historical Association, Annual Report, Washington, 1918.
Foote, Henry S., *Casket of Reminiscences*, Washington, 1874.
Forney, John W., *Anecdotes of Public Men*, New York, 1873.
Fox, Dixon Ryan, *The Decline of Aristocracy in the Politics of New York*, New York, 1918.
Hamilton, James *Reminiscences*, New York, 1869.
Hamilton, Thomas, *Men and Manners in America*, Philadelphia, 1833.
Holland, W. M., *Life and Political Opinions of Martin Van Buren*, Hartford, 1836.
Hammond, Jabez, *The History of Political Parties in the State of New York*, Syracuse, 1852.
James, Marquis, *Andrew Jackson, Portrait of a President*, Indianapolis, 1937.
Jenkins, J. S., *Life of Silas Wright*, Auburn, 1847.
July, Robert W., *The Essential New Yorker: Gulian Crommelin Verplanck*, New York, 1957.
Lawrence, Rachel Jackson, "Andrew Jackson at Home," *McClure's Magazine*, Vol. 9, (July, 1897) pp. 792–794.
Logan, Mrs. John A., *Thirty Years in Washington*, Hartford, 1901.
Lynch, D. T., *An Epoch and a Man, Martin Van Buren and His Times*, New York, 1929.
The Correspondence of Nicholas Biddle, Dealing with National Affairs, 1807–1844, Reginald, McGrane, Boston, 1919.
Martineau, Harriet, *Retrospect of Western Travel*, New York, 1938.
——Society in America, Paris, 1842.
Diary of John Quincy Adams, 1794–1845, Allan Nevins, ed., New York, 1928.
Diary of Philip Hone, 1828–1851, Allan Nevins, ed., New York, 1927.
Parton, James, *Life of Jackson*, New York, 1860.
Schlesinger, Arthur M., Jr., *The Age of Jackson*, Boston, 1946.
Shepard, Edward M., *Martin Van Buren*, Boston, 1888.
Smith, Margaret B., *The First Forty Years of Washington Society*, New York, 1906.
Smith, W. E., *The Francis Preston Blair Family in Politics*, New York, 1933.
Autobiography of Amos Kendall, William Stickney, ed., Boston, 1872.
Swisher, Carl B., *Roger B. Taney*, New York, 1935.
Turner, Frederick J., *The United States, 1830–1850*, New York, 1935.
Van Buren, Martin, *Inquiry into the Origin and Course of Political Parties in the United States*, New York, 1867.
Van Buren, Martin, Letter to his Son, John, in *The Collector, A Magazine for Autograph and Historical Collectors*, Vol. 65, March, 1952.
Williams, Stanley T., *The Life of Washington Irving*, New York, 1935.
Wiltsie, Charles M., *John C. Calhoun*, Indianapolis, 1944.

LOEB

I. Interviews

Cortelyou, George B., Jr., son of George B. Cortelyou, secretary to Presidents McKinley and Theodore Roosevelt.
Loeb, Amelia, sister of William Loeb, secretary to Theodore Roosevelt.
Loeb, Mrs. Katherine, wife of William Loeb.
Loeb, Lillian, sister of William Loeb.
Loeb, William, Jr., son of William Loeb.
Longworth, Alice Roosevelt, daughter of Theodore Roosevelt.
Millard, James, secretary and clerk, New York State legislature, 1890–1944.
Moore, James, American Smelting and Refining Company.
Phillips, William, State Department; last surviving member of the Tennis Cabinet.
Smith, Howard Caswell, Oyster Bay neighbor of Loeb and Theodore Roosevelt.
Roosevelt, Archibald, son of Theodore Roosevelt.
Youngs, Mary F., daughter of William Youngs.

II. Manuscripts

Charles J. Bonaparte Papers, Library of Congress.
James Rudolph Garfield Papers, Library of Congress.
John Hay Papers, Library of Congress.
William Loeb Papers, Theodore Roosevelt Association.
Whitelaw Reed Papers, Library of Congress.
Theodore Roosevelt Papers, Library of Congress.
Oscar S. Straus Papers, Library of Congress.
William Howard Taft Papers, Library of Congress.
William Allen White Papers, Library of Congress.

III. Newspapers

Albany Argus
New York Herald Tribune
The New York Times

IV. Books

Abernathy, John R., Catch 'em Alive Jack, New York, 1936.
———In Camp with Theodore Roosevelt, Oklahoma City, 1933.
Amos, James E., Theodore Roosevelt, Hero to His Valet, New York, 1927.
Bailey, Thomas A., Theodore Roosevelt and the Japanese-American Crises, London, 1934.
Beale, Howard K., Theodore Roosevelt and the Rise of America to World Power, Baltimore, 1956.
Bishop, Joseph B., Theodore Roosevelt and His Time, New York, 1920.
Blum, John M., The Republican Roosevelt, Cambridge, Mass., 1954.
Buskey, L. W., Uncle Joe Cannon, New York, 1927.
Butt, Archibald, The Letters of Archie Butt, Garden City, 1924.
———Taft and Roosevelt, The Intimate Letters of Archie Butt, Garden City, 1930.
Cortissoz, Royal, The Life of Whitelaw Reid, New York, 1921.
Davis, Oscar King, Released for Publication, Boston, 1925.
Depew, Chauncy, My Memories of Eighty Years, New York, 1922.
Douglas, George W., The Many-Sided Roosevelt, New York, 1907.
Eliot, Charles W., Harvard Memories, Cambridge, Mass., 1923.
Foraker, Joseph B., Notes of a Busy Life, Cincinnati, 1916.
Garraty, John A., Henry Cabot Lodge, A Biography, New York, 1953.

Gosnell, Harold B., *Boss Platt, and His New York Machine*, Chicago, 1924.
Hagedorn, Hermann, *Roosevelt in the Bad Lands*, Boston, 1930.
——The *Roosevelt Family of Sagamore Hill*, New York, 1954.
Hale, Wiliam B., *A Week in the White House with Theodore Roosevelt*, New York, 1908.
Hone, Philip, *The Diary of Philip Hone*, New York, 1889.
Hoover, Irwin H., *Forty-two Years in the White House*, Boston, 1934.
Kennan, George, *E. H. Harriman*, New York, 1922.
Kohlsaat, H. H., *From McKinley to Harding*, New York, 1923.
The Autobiography of Thomas Collier Platt, Louis J. Lang, ed., New York, 1910.
Longworth, Alice Roosevelt, *Crowded Hours*, New York, 1933.
Looker, Earle, *The White House Gang*, New York, 1929.
The Letters of Theodore Roosevelt, Elting E. Morison, ed., Cambridge, Mass., 1954.
Phillips, William, *Ventures in Diplomacy*, Boston, 1952.
Pringle, Henry F., *The Life and Times of William Howard Taft*, New York, 1939.
——*Theodore Roosevelt, a Biography*, New York, 1931.
Putnam, Carleton, *Theodore Roosevelt, The Formative Years, 1858–1886*, New York, 1958.
Rhodes, James Ford, *The McKinley and Roosevelt Administration*, New York, 1927.
Roosevelt, Theodore, *Autobiography*, New York, 1920.
Sewall, William, *Bill Sewall's Story of Theodore Roosevelt*, New York, 1919.
Stoddard, Henry L., *As I Knew Them*, New York, 1927.
Straus, Oscar, *Under Four Administrations*, Boston, 1922.
Sullivan, Mark, *Our Times*, New York, 1929, 1930.
Thayer, William R., *Theodore Roosevelt, An Intimate Biography*, Boston, 1919.
Wister, Owen, *Roosevelt, The Story of a Friendship*, New York, 1930.
Wood, Frederick S., *Roosevelt as We Knew Him*, Philadelphia, 1927.

V. Articles

Anonymous, "His House in Order," *Outlook*, December 25, 1909.
French, Willard, "Private Secretaries of the Mighty," *The World of Today*, March, 1907.
Howard, Clifford, "The Spirit of Graft," *Outlook*, October 14, 1905.
Howland, Harold, "The Case of the Seventeen Holes," *Outlook*, May 1, 1909.
Nelson, Henry, "The President at Home and at Work," *Harper's Weekly*, November, 30, 1901.
O'Brien, Robert L., "Last Christmas at the White House," *Ladies' Home Journal*, December, 1903.
Willey, Day, "The Men About the President," *Munsey's Magazine*, July, 1903.

HOUSE

I. Interviews

Coughlin, John, realtor, Manchester, Massachusetts.
Grew, Joseph, member of diplomatic service with assignments to Berlin, Vienna, and Washington.
Phillips, William, Assistant Secretary of State.
Tucker, Mrs. Randolph, daughter of Colonel House.
Seymour, Charles, author and editor of various works pertaining to House.

II. Manuscripts

Edward M. House Papers, Yale University Library.
Sir William Wiseman Papers, Yale University Library.

III. Books

Annin, Robert E., *Woodrow Wilson, A Character Study*, New York, 1924.
Bailey, Thomas A., *Woodrow Wilson and the Great Betrayal*, New York, 1945.
———*Woodrow Wilson and the Lost Peace*, New York, 1944.
Baker, Newton D., *America at War*, New York, 1931.
Baker, R. S., *What Wilson Did at Paris*, New York, 1919.
———*Woodrow Wilson, Life and Letters*, Garden City, 1927–1939.
———*Woodrow Wilson and the World Settlement*, Garden City, 1922.
———*The Versailles Treaty and After*, New York, 1924.
Balfour, Arthur J., *Chapters of an Autobiography*, London, 1930.
Baruch, Bernard M., *Baruch: My Own Story*, New York, 1957.
Bell, H. C. F., *Woodrow Wilson and the People*, New York, 1945
Bernstorff, Count, *My Three Years in America*, New York, 1920.
Blum, John M., *Joe Tumulty and the Wilson Era*, Boston, 1951.
———*Woodrow Wilson and the Politics of Morality*, Boston, 1956.
Bonsal, Stephen, *Unfinished Business*, Garden City, 1944.
The Memoirs of William Jennings Bryan, Mary B. Bryan, ed., Philadelphia, 1925.
Bryan, Wiliam J., *A Tale of Two Conventions*, New York, 1912.
Wilson's Foreign Policy in Perspective, Edward H. Buehrig, ed., Bloomington, 1957.
Buehrig, E. H., *Woodrow Wilson and the Balance of Power*, Indianapolis, 1955.
Clark, Champ, *My Quarter Century of American Politics*, New York, 1920.
Clemenceau, Georges, *In the Evening of My Thought*, Boston, 1929.
Coit, Margaret L., *Mr. Baruch*, Boston, 1957.
Colby, Bainbridge, *The Close of Woodrow Wilson's Administration*, New York, 1930.
Cooper, Kent, *The Right to Know*, New York, 1956.
Daniels, Josephus, *The Wilson Era: Years of Peace, 1910–1917*, Chapel Hill, 1944.
———*The Wilson Era: Years of War and After, 1917–1923*, Chapel Hill, 1946.
Dodd, William E., *Woodrow Wilson and His Work*, Garden City, 1920; rev. ed., 1932.
Elliott, Margaret A., *My Aunt Louisa and Woodrow Wilson*, Chapel Hill, 1944.
Ford, Henry Jones, *Woodrow Wilson, the Man and His Work*, New York, 1916.
George, Alexander L. and Julliette L., *Woodrow Wilson and Colonel House, A Personality Study*, New York, 1956.
Gerard, James W., *My Four Years in Germany*, New York, 1917.
Grey, Edward, *Twenty-Five Years*, New York, 1925.
Hendrick, Burton J., *The Life and Letters of Walter H. Page*, Garden City, 1926.
Hoover, Herbert, *The Ordeal of Woodrow Wilson*, New York, 1958.
House, Edward M., *Philip Dru: Administrator*, New York, 1920.
———*What Really Happened at Paris*, New York, 1921.
Houston, David F., *Eight Years with Wilson's Cabinet*, Garden City, 1926.
Hulbert, Mary A., *The Story of Mrs. Peck*, New York, 1933.
Jaffray, Elizabeth, *Secrets of the White House*, New York, 1927.
Johnson, Willis F., *George Harvey*, Boston, 1929.
Lansing, Robert, *The Peace Negotiations*, Boston, 1921.
Link, Arthur S., *Wilson: The Road to the White House*, Princeton, 1947.
———*Woodrow Wilson and the Progressive Era*, New York, 1954.
Lloyd George, David, *War Memoirs*, Boston, 1933–1937.
———*Memoirs of the Peace Conference*, New Haven, 1939.
Lodge, Henry C., *The Senate and the League of Nations*, New York, 1925.
McAdoo, Eleanor W., *The Woodrow Wilsons*, New York, 1937.
McAdoo, William G., *Crowded Years: The Reminiscences of William Gibbs McAdoo*, Boston, 1931.
McCombs, William F., *Making Woodrow Wilson President*, New York, 1921.

Miller, David H., *The Drafting of the Covenant*, New York, 1928.
Myers, William S., *Woodrow Wilson, Some Princeton Memories*, Princeton, 1946.
The Letters and Journal of Brand Whitlock, Allan Nevins, ed., New York, 1936.
Notter, Harley, *The Origins of the Foreign Policy of Woodrow Wilson*, Baltimore, 1937.
Redfield, William C., *With Congress and Cabinet*, Garden City, 1924.
Reid, Edith G., *Woodrow Wilson, the Caricature, the Myth, and the Man*, New York, 1934.
Riddell, George A. R., *Lord Riddell's Intimate Diary of the Peace Conference and After, 1918–1923*, London, 1933.
Seymour, Charles, *American Diplomacy During the World War*, 1938.
————*The Diplomatic Background of the War*, New Haven, 1916.
————*The Intimate Papers of Colonel House*, Boston, 1926.
————*Woodrow Wilson and the World War*, New Haven, 1921.
Shotwell, James T., *At the Paris Peace Conference*, New York, 1937.
Smith, Arthur Howden, *Mr. House of Texas*, New York, 1940.
Steed, Henry W., *Through Thirty Years*, Garden City, 1934.
Memoirs of Count Bernstorff, Eric Sutton, trans., New York, 1936.
Tirpitz, A., *My Memoirs*, New York, 1919.
Tumulty, Joseph, *Woodrow Wilson as I Know Him*, Garden City, 1921.
United States Department of State, The Lansing Papers, 1914–1920, (Foreign Relations of the United States), 1939.
Viereck, George S., *The Strangest Friendship in History*, New York, 1932.
Viviani, Rene, *As We See It*, New York, 1923.
Watterson, Henry, "*Marse Henry,*" New York, 1919.
White, William A., *Woodrow Wilson*, Boston, 1924.
Whitlock, William A., *Forty Years of It*, New York, 1925.
Wilson, Edith Bolling, *My Memoir*, Indianapolis, 1939.

CORCORAN

I. Interviews

Brownlow, Louis, chairman, President's Committee on Administrative Management.
Burling, Edward B., member, Covington and Burling, Washington.
Cahill, John T., U.S. Attorney for the Southern District of New York, 1939 to 1941; member, Cahill, Gordon, Reindel and Ohl, successors to Cotton, Franklin, Wright, and Gordon.
Catledge, Turner, *The New York Times*.
Cohen, Benjamin V.
Corcoran, Thomas Gardiner
Farley, James A., Chairman, National Democratic Committee; Postmaster General.
Krock, Arthur, *The New York Times*.
Lubin, Isador, Commissioner of Labor Statistics.
Moley, Raymond, head of original Brain Trust; Assistant Secretary of State.
Pecora, Ferdinand, counsel, Senate Banking and Currency Committee, 1933–1934; member, Securities and Exchange Commission, 1934–1935.
Rauh, Joseph, Jr., counsel to various government agencies, 1935–1942.
Roosevelt, Mrs. Franklin D.
Roosevelt, James, administrative assistant to the President.
Rosenman, Samuel I., counsel to the President.
Taylor, Telford, counsel to various government agencies.
Tugwell, Rexford, Assistant and Under Secretary of Agriculture.
Tully, Grace, secretary to the President.
Wheeler, Burton K., U.S. Senator, Montana.

Wolfsohn, Joel D., executive secretary, National Power Policy Committee, 1934–1937.

Youngman, William, chief counsel, power division, Public Works Administration; general counsel, Federal Power Commission, 1940–1941; partner, Corcoran and Youngman, 1941–1949.

II. Correspondence

Herrick, Elinore, executive vice-chairman, National Labor Relations Board, Region II, 1933–1935.

Tugwell, Rexford G.

III. Manuscripts

Harry L. Hopkins Papers, Roosevelt Library, Hyde Park, New York.
Franklin D. Roosevelt Papers, Roosevelt Library.
Franklin D. Roosevelt, Press Conferences, Roosevelt Library.

IV. Newspapers

New York Herald Tribune
The New York Times

V. Books

Allen, Frederick, *Since Yesterday*, New York, 1940.
Alsop, Joseph, and Kintner, Robert, *Men Around the President*, Garden City, 1938.
Alsop, Joseph, and Catledge, Turner, *The 168 Days*, Garden City, 1938.
Burns, James M., *Roosevelt: The Lion and the Fox*, New York, 1956.
Byrnes, James F., *Speaking Frankly*, New York, 1947.
Eccles, Marriner S., *Beckoning Frontiers*, New York, 1951.
Farley, James A., *Behind the Ballots*, New York, 1938.
———*Jim Farley's Story*, New York, 1948.
Flynn, Edward J., *You're the Boss*, New York, 1947.
High, Stanley, *Roosevelt—And Then?*, New York, 1937.
Hull, Cordell, *The Memoirs of Cordell Hull*, New York, 1948.
Ickes, Harold, *The Autobiography of a Curmudgeon*, New York, 1943.
———*The First Thousand Days, 1933–1936*, New York, 1953.
———*The Inside Story, 1936–1939*, New York, 1954.
———*The Lowering Clouds, 1939–1941*, New York, 1954.
Lindley, Ernest K., *The Roosevelt Revolution*, New York, 1934.
Michelson, Charles, *The Ghost Talks*, New York, 1944.
Moley, Raymond, *After Seven Years*, New York, 1939.
———*27 Masters of Politics*, New York, 1949.
Perkins, Frances, *The Roosevelt I Knew*, New York, 1946.
Rauch, Basil, *The History of the New Deal, 1933–1938*, New York, 1944.
Roosevelt, Eleanor, *This I Remember*, New York, 1949.
Roosevelt, Franklin D., *Public Papers and Addresses*, New York, 1938–1950.
Rosenman, Samuel I., *Working with Roosevelt*, New York, 1952.
Schlesinger, Arthur M., *The Age of Roosevelt*, 2 Vols., Boston, 1957–58.
Sherwood, Robert E., *Roosevelt and Hopkins, An Intimate History*, New York, 1948.
Stimson, Henry L., and Bundy, McGeorge, *On Active Service in Peace and War*, New York, 1948.
Stokes, T. L., *Chip off My Shoulder*, Princeton, 1940.
Tugwell, Rexford G., *The Democratic Roosevelt*, Garden City, 1957.
Tully, Grace, *F.D.R., My Boss*, New York, 1949.

VI. Articles

Alsop, Joseph and Kintner, Robert, "We Shall Make America Over," *Saturday Evening Post*, November 12, 1938.
Bolles, Blair, "Cohen and Corcoran: Brain Twins," *American Mercury*, January, 1938.
Johnston, Alva, "The Saga of Tommy the Cork," *Saturday Evening Post*, October, 13, 20, 27, 1945.
Smith, Beverly, "Corcoran and Cohen," *The American Magazine*, August, 1937.

HOPKINS

I. Interviews

Paul Appleby, Under Secretary of Agriculture; assistant director, Bureau of the Budget.
Jacob Baker, a close working associate of Hopkins in the New Deal.
William L. Batt, Vice-Chairman, War Production Board.
Wayne Coy, Special Assistant to the President and liaison officer, Office for Emergency Management; assistant director, Bureau of the Budget.
Arthur Goldschmidt, assistant to Secretary of the Interior Ickes.
Harriman, W. Averell, the President's special representative in Great Britian; U.S. ambassador to the U.S.S.R.
Isador Lubin, Commissioner of Labor Statistics.
McCloy, John, Assistant Secretary of War.
Roosevelt, Eleanor.
Rosenman, Samuel, counsel to the President.

II. Correspondence

Hyman, Sidney, assistant to Hopkins in organizing Hopkin's papers.
Somervell, Brehon, commanding general, Army Services of Supply.

III. Printed Materials

Adamic, L., *Dinner at the White House*, New York, 1946.
Alsop, J., and Kintner, R., *Men Around the President*, New York, 1938.
Busch, N. F., *What Manner of Man?*, New York, 1944.
Butcher, H., *My Three Years with Eisenhower*, New York, 1946.
Byrnes, J., *Speaking Frankly*, New York, 1947.
Churchill, W., *The Second World War*, Boston, 1949–1953.
Watching the World, Mrs. R. Clapper, ed., New York, 1944.
Deane, J. R., *The Strange Alliance*, New York, 1947.
Eisenhower, D., *Crusade in Europe*, Garden City, 1948.
Farley, J., *Jim Farley's Story*, New York, 1948.
Flynn, E. J., *You're the Boss*, New York, 1947.
Flynn, J. T., *The Roosevelt Myth*, New York, 1948.
Forrestal, J., *The Forrestal Diaries*, New York, 1951.
Hull, C., *The Memoirs of Cordell Hull*, New York, 1948.
Janeway, E., *The Struggle for Survival*, New Haven, 1951.
Johnson, G., *American Heroes and Hero-Worship*, New York, 1941.
———*Roosevelt: Dictator or Democrat*, New York, 1941.
Ickes, H., *The Secret Diaries of Harold Ickes*, New York, 1954.
King, E. J., and Whitehall, W. M., *Fleet Admiral King, A Naval Record*, New York, 1952.

Langer, W. L., *Our Vichy Gamble*, New York, 1947.
———and Gleason, S. E., *The Undeclared War, 1940–41*, New York, 1953.
Leahy, W. D., *I Was There*, New York, 1950.
Marshall, K., *Together*, New York, 1946.
Michelson, C., *The Ghost Talks*, New York, 1944.
Morgenthau, H., "Diaries," *Collier's*, Sept. 27 to Nov. 1, 1947.
New Yorker, "Profile of Hopkins," August 7 and 14, 1943.
Nelson, D., *The Arsenal of Democracy*, New York, 1946.
Perkins, F., *The Roosevelt I Knew*, New York, 1946.
Reilly, M. F., *Reilly of the White House*, New York, 1947.
Roosevelt, Eleanor, *This I Remember*, New York, 1949.
Roosevelt, Elliott, *As He Saw It*, New York, 1946.
Sherwood, R., *Roosevelt and Hopkins, An Intimate History*, New York, 1948.
Smith, Merriam, *Thank You Mr. President*, New York, 1946.
Stettinius, E. R., Jr., *Lend Lease, Weapon for Victory*, New York, 1944.
———*Roosevelt and the Russians*, New York, 1949.
Stimson, H., and Bundy, M., *On Active Service in Peace and War*, New York, 1948.
Taylor, R., *Winston Churchill, An Informal Study of Greatness*, New York, 1952.
United States War Production Board, *Industrial Mobilization for War, History of the War Production Board and Predecessor Agencies, 1940–1945*, Washington, 1947.
Welles, S., *Where are We Heading?*, New York, 1946.
Winant, J., *Letter from Grosvenor Square*, Boston, 1947.
Zacharias, E., *Secret Missions, The Story of an Intelligence Officer*, New York, 1946.
———"The Inside Story of Yalta," *United Nations World*, January, 1949.

ADAMS

I. Interviews

Aiken, George D., U.S. Senator, Republican, Vermont.
Alcorn, Meade, chairman, Republican National Committee.
Bridges, Styles, U.S. Senator, Republican, New Hampshire.
Cohen, Benjamin, member U.S. delegation to the United Nations in the Truman Administration.
Donovan, Robert, *New York Herald Tribune*.
Drummond, Roscoe, *New York Herald Tribune*.
Gray, Robert A., Assistant to Adams.
Jackson, C. D., Special assistant to the President.
Lodge, Henry Cabot, U.S. Representative to the United Nations.
Minnich, Arthur L., Assistant to Adams.
Persons, Wilton B., Deputy Assistant to the President.
Purtell, William A., U.S. Senator, Republican, Connecticut.
Rabb, Maxwell, Secretary to the Cabinet.
Reston, James, *The New York Times*.
Rockefeller, Nelson A., Under Secretary of Health, Education, and Welfare; Chairman, President's Advisory Committee on Government Organization.
Saltonstall, Leverett, U.S. Senator, Republican, Massachusetts.
Schwartz, Bernard, Counsel to subcommittee on Legislative Oversight, U.S. House of Representatives.
Shanley, Bernard, Counsel and appointments secretary to the President.
Shoepel, Andrew F., Chairman, Senate Republican Campaign Committee.
Stephens, Thomas E., Appointments Secretary to the President.
Willis, Charles F., Jr., Assistant to Adams.

II. Correspondence

Brandt, Raymond P., *St. Louis Post-Dispatch.*
Brightman, Samuel C., Deputy Chairman for Public Affairs, Democratic National Committee.
Briggs, Ellis O., U.S. Ambassador to Brazil; Dartmouth fellow-student with Adams.
Fowler, William P., Attorney, Boston, Massachusetts; Dartmouth fellow-student with Adams.
Furnas, Cliford C., Chairman, Advisory Panel on Aeronautics, Defense Department.
Moss, John E., Chairman, Government Information Subcommittee, Committee on Government Operations, U.S. House of Representatives.

III. Books

Butcher, Harry, *My Three Years with Eisenhower*, New York, 1946.
Childs, Marquis, *Eisenhower: Captive Hero*, New York, 1958.
Donovan, Robert, *Eisenhower: The Inside Story*, New York, 1956.
Eisenhower, Dwight, *Crusade in Europe*, New York, 1948.
Merson, Martin, *The Private Diary of a Public Servant*, New York, 1955.

IV. Articles

Donovan, Robert, "The Man at Ike's Right Hand," *Collier's.*, October 14, 1955.
Harper, Kenneth, "The Man Eisenhower Calls Boss," *American Magazine*, February, 1953.
Monohan, Robert, "A Woodsman in Washington," *American Forests*, February, 1953.
Murphy, Charles, "Eisenhower's White House," *Fortune*, July, 1953.
Phillips, Cabell, "The Eisenhower 'Inner Circle,' " *New York Times Magazine*, February 3, 1957.
Rovere, Richard, "Boss of the White House Staff," *New York Times Magazine*, January 25, 1953.
Smith, Beverly, "Ike's Yankee Lieutenant," *Saturday Evening Post*, January 24, 1953.

V. Magazines

Newsweek
Time
United States News and World Report

VI. Newspapers

New York Herald Tribune
New York Post
The New York Times
Washington Post and Times Herald

INDEX

Abernathy, Jack, 41, 181
Acheson, Dean, 44, 257
Ackerman, Carl W., 225
Adams, Henry, 7, 9, 180
Adams, John, 17, 50, 84, 143
Adams, John Quincy, 89, 92, 95, 100–101, 133
Adams, Sherman, 16, 34; birth and parentage, 342; bouncer, 355; brusqueness of, 347; buffer, 352; business career, 343; and the cabinet, 378, 380; candor of, 361–62; and Murray Chotiner, 391; chief of staff, 1952 campaign, 348; Presidential chief of staff, 351; approach to Congress, 381; and Congressional and Senatorial campaign committees, 388; U.S. Congressman, 344; contradictions of, 341; his contribution to the Eisenhower Administration, 401; Dartmouth student, 342; and the departments, 376; description of, 341; and Dixon-Yates contract, 391; role in Eisenhower's absences and illnesses, 340, 372; and Eisenhower's Presidential candidacy, 345; first meeting with Eisenhower, 347; Eisenhower invites him into Administration, 349; loyalty to Eisenhower, 357; and Eisenhower's private affairs, 360; visits Eisenhower concerning resignation, 398; fall guy, 355; family of, 343; floor-manager at Chicago Convention, 347; and Bernard Goldfine, 393; Governor, 344; and James Hagerty, 372; hatchet man, 353; hobbies of, 366; White Housekeeper, 356; humor of, 362; industry and speech, 343; in "inner circle," 20; intellectual qualities of, 361; job-giver, 354; leaves Washington, 401; saved by Lebanon and Quemoy islands crises, 395; and legislative leaders, 383; hostility of Republican legislators to, 394; liberal Republican, 358; his limitations, 402–403; Marine Corps service, 342; and messages to Congress, 383; and missiles program, 359; modesty of, 363; and G. D. Morgan, 374; guardian of Administration morality, 389; musical interests of, 364; as negotiator, 361; office of, 366–67; vacations in New Brunswick, 397; and New Hampshire 1952 Presidential primary, 346; overprotects the President, 358;

party orator, 386–87; and patronage, 385–86; and W. B. Persons, 373–74; loves poetry, 364; as pre-convention campaigner, 346; and press, 372; and regulatory commissions, 391; and Republican party organization, 387; resigns White House post, 398; resignation little affects elections, 399; ringmaster, 352; salary and duties, 350; secrecy of, 340; his self-appraisal, 404; social activities, 365; and Washington social list, 365–66; and President's speeches, 382; and his staff, 367–68; state legislator, 344; and choice of his successor, 400; and Suez crisis, 359–60; and R. A. Taft, 384; television address on resignation, 399; his terseness, 341–42; title and powers, 35, 339; consults with Truman Administration, 349; and White House staff, 370, 373, 375; work habits of, 357, 369; workload of, 367
Adams, Mrs. Sherman, 343, 393, 397
Administrative Office of the United States Courts, 296
Advice, as received by the President, 44
Albany Argus, 91
Albany Business College, 137
Albany Medical College, 138
Albany Regency, 91, 93
Alcorn, Meade, 387, 396–97
Aldrich, Nelson, 20
Aldrovandi-Marescotti, Luigi, 239
Algeciras Conference, 148
Alien and Sedition Acts, 108
Allen, Andrew, 73
Allen, George E., 21, 361
Alsop, Joseph, 360
Alsop, Stewart, 360
American Bar Association, 287
American Geographical Society, 237
American Smelting and Refining Company, 187–88
American Sugar Company, 182
American Sugar Trust, 32
American War Mission, 235
Ames, Fisher, 58, 67, 83
Amherst College, 37
"Ananias Club," 172
Anderson, Charles, 172
Anderson, Rasmus B., 166
Anderson, Robert B., 380

423